Xavier Reyes-Ayral is a French author who has worked since the 1990s on Marian apparition sites through books he published in France, Germany and Italy. Having, for a few years, briefly collaborated with world-renowned Msgr. René Laurentin, Xavier Reyes-Ayral has continued to study apparitions of the Blessed Virgin Mary throughout Europe, Canada and Latin-America.

In 2013, Xavier wrote and published in France as well a book entitled *Héroïsme* relating to the extraordinary World War II adventures of his uncle, Jean Ayral; a highly decorated Free-French officer, whose missions during the occupation and liberation of France have been recorded in the annals of the British and French intelligence services.

Xavier Reyes-Ayral is today a fourth degree Knight of Columbus and Grand-Knight of his own council, and since Msgr. Laurentin's passing away in 2017, has decided to write more books on Marian apparitions and on the extraordinary but alarmingly urgent messages they bring to an oblivious human society; unaware of the impending threats that are about to reshape the 21st century…

En dédicasse
à Jeanne et à son Altesse Royale
que nous attendons avec ferveur et profonde foi…

Mont Joie Saint Denis!
Dieu Premier servi!

Xavier Reyes-Ayral

REVELATIONS

The Hidden Secret Messages and
Prophecies of the Blessed Virgin Mary

AUSTIN MACAULEY PUBLISHERS™

LONDON * CAMBRIDGE * NEW YORK * SHARJAH

Ordering Information
Quantity sales: Special discounts are available on quantity purchases by corporations, associations, and others. For details, contact the publisher at the address below.

Publisher's Cataloging-in-Publication data
Reyes-Ayral, Xavier
Revelations

ISBN 9781649790989 (Paperback)
ISBN 9781649790996 (ePub e-book)

Library of Congress Control Number: 2022901020

www.austinmacauley.com/us

First Published 2022
Austin Macauley Publishers LLC
40 Wall Street, 33rd Floor, Suite 3302
New York, NY 10005
USA

mail-usa@austinmacauley.com
+1 (646) 5125767

All my thanks to my wife, Lisa, who was behind the idea of this project, and who helped me in the realization of this book.

Table of Contents

His Holiness Pope Paul VI abolished Canons 1399, § 5 and § 2318 of the old Canon Law Code, which prohibited the publication of books relating to new apparitions, visions, prophecies and miracles, and which excommunicated their authors (14 October 1966 Decree of the Congregation for the Doctrine of the Faith, Acta Apostolicae Sedis, 29 September 1966, page 1186).

Other books written by the same author:

«UN MESSAGE D'AMOUR» (EDITIONS RESIAC)
Éditions RÉSIAC
B.P. 6, F 53150, Montsûrs, France
Tél: (+33/2) 43.01.01.26
Fax: (+33/2) 43.01.04.20
E-Mail: resiac@wanadoo.fr
OR
1416, 4e Avenue
La Pocatière, Québec, G0R 1Z0
CANADA
Tél: (+1/418) 856-6111
Fax: (+1/418) 856-3913
E-Mail: information@librairiescml.ca

German Version:
«EINE LIEBESBOTSCHAFT» (EDITIONS DU PARVIS)
Éditions du PARVIS
CH 1648, Hauteville, Suisse
Tel#: (+41/26) 915.93.93
Fax#: (+41/26) 915.93.99
E-Mail: librairie@parvis.ch

Italian Version:
«UN MESSAGGIO D'AMORE» (SEGNO EDIZIONI)
Edizioni SEGNO
Via Del Vascello, 12-33100 Udine, Italia
Tel#: (+39/432) 52.18.81
Fax#: (+39/432) 60.31.95

«UN APPEL À LA CONVERSION» (EDITIONS RESIAC)
Éditions RÉSIAC
B.P. 6, F 53150, Montsûrs, France
Tel#: (+33/2) 43.01.01.26
Fax#: (+33/2) 43.01.04.20
E-Mail: resiac@wanadoo.fr
OR
1416, 4e Avenue
La Pocatière, Québec, G0R 1Z0
CANADA
Tél: (+1/418) 856-6111
Fax: (+1/418) 856-3913
E-Mail: information@librairiescml.ca

«HÉROÏSME, JEAN AYRAL, COMPAGNON DE LA LIBÉRATION»
(EDITIONS L'HARMATTAN)
5,7, rue de l'École-Polytechnique,
75005, Paris, France
Tél: (+33/1) 40 46 79 20

Prologue

*T*he tree is judged by its fruits, *says the Lord, and it is the only criterion of discernment that comes from Him (Mt 7:20; 12:33). There is, however, an ambiguity we should be well aware of. Apparitions, where faith becomes evident, where the invisible becomes visible, are a superficial and secondary phenomenon in comparison to the Gospel and the holy sacraments. Even where the Church recognizes an apparition (including Lourdes and Fatima, the most solemnly recognized), she does not employ her infallibility or even her authority, since it is not a question of a dogma, necessary for salvation and taught in the name of Christ, but of a discernment, only probable and conjectural.*

She does not say, "You have to believe", but, "There are some good reasons to believe. It is beneficial to believe." The responsible authority itself can even add, "I believe"; but it does not impose this judgment under the penalty of sin. If I would not believe in Lourdes nor in Fatima, I would not have to go to confession if I had reasons to doubt. It was in this spirit and with a completely open mind that I undertook my investigations about Lourdes. Similarly, if authority says, "There are serious reasons not to believe", then it is wrong to believe. Our judgment is called upon to obey the Church, but permits freedom of examination and of discernment."

(Monsignor René Laurentin, 1997)

Since the middle of the 19th century, there have been many cases of Marian apparitions that warned with gravity of the disastrous events that were already beginning in the world. The appearances of the Blessed Virgin Mary in Paris to sister Catherine Labouré, in La Salette to two little shepherds named Maximin Giraud and Mélanie Calvat, in Lourdes to Bernadette Soubirous, and in La Fraudais to Marie-Julie Jahenny, an extraordinary Breton woman who bore all the stigmatas of our Lord Jesus Christ, are but five of the most imposing examples of such Heaven's admonitions in that century. It would be a few years later that Our Lady would appear in Tilly and Fatima to announce and confirm the catastrophic events for the end of an extremely disturbed 20th and 21st century...

Between May and October 1917, while the first world war was on its third year with no end in sight, the Blessed Virgin Mary appeared yet again, this time in a little village in Portugal, to announce a prompt end to the war while warning of yet another... one that would follow this one shortly thereafter under the reign of a new Pope who would be named Pius XI. This Second World War, she added, would be more devastating and costlier in human life than the present one if mankind were to ignore her warning and her call to conversion.

Likewise, the Blessed Virgin Mary forewarned of the dangers of Russia spreading her errors throughout the world. But who heard? Who believed? Indeed, in the later part of 1917, Russia was on its knees and out of breath from an unprepared conflict with Germany, leaving the Russian Empire in disarray and held by a wide remnant of a disorganized parade-army and drunk horse-riding Cossacks… Such a prophetic warning was considered at the time nothing more but the product of children's rubbish, hysteria, or at best utter hallucination… However, as a sign of her presence and of the veracity of her admonitions, the Blessed Virgin Mary announced a sign that was to take place on 13 October 1917 which would be seen by all in the Cova da Iria…and indeed, the extraordinary happened before over 70,000 witnesses: the miracle of the sun!

The reported visions at Fatima gathered thereafter widespread attention, as numerous pilgrims from the four corners of the world began to visit the site in masses, and after 13 years of profound and meticulous research, exhaustive investigations and theological studies of the messages received by Lucia, Jacinta and Francisco, a canonical inquiry, headed by the Bishop of Leiria-Fatima, officially declared in October 1930 the visions of Fatima as *worthy of belief*, permitting the belief of Our Lady of Fatima's messages and encouraging pilgrimages to the little Portuguese village.

Today, in 2022, the message of Fatima and its three secrets take a meaning of the greatest importance, as the admonitions brought forth by the Blessed Virgin Mary have become most relevant; however, for almost 100 years, the Church's apprehension of frightening the masses, inspired inaction. Rome's decision to silence—founded more on fear than on caution—led millions of faithful in the darkness of ignorance and therefore to a lack of necessary prayers and intercession for peace… Sadly, we reflect today, almost in disbelief, on the accuracy of our Lady of Fatima's messages and predictions.

Indeed, a few days after the last apparition of Fatima (13 October 1917), Russia was taken over by a major *coup d'état* ending with the execution of the Tsar and of his family, and seeing the installation in its place of a most barbaric and liberticidal regime. The First World War's armistice and cessation of hostilities that took place over 13 months after the miracle of the sun (November 1918) demonstrated the accomplishment of the Virgin Mary's second prophecy[1]. As for what followed, it is argued that the beginning of the Second World War was indeed accurately foretold by the Blessed Virgin Mary, as it began with the Spanish Civil war under the reign of Pius XI, which saw the first military combats, since 1918, between various Western forces and the newly modernized German Wermacht in Spain. Alas, the warning of Fatima was utterly ignored and World War II did indeed take place, costing in its process over fifty million lives worldwide…

Four years after the end of World War II and the destruction of Hitler's war machine, a Europe coming out from the still smoking ashes of a revengeful German ideology saw itself threatened now by a new Sovietic menace, no less

---

[1] **The first accomplished prophecy of Our Lady of Fatima was the passing away of Jacinta and Francisco Marto.**

dangerous than its German predecessor, detonate its first atomic bomb in Kazakhstan. This new rising power, which originated from the passion and diabolical ploy of a former Russian butler named Lenin, had for almost half a century all the lands and seas of the entire world tremble.

Between 1945 and 1989, the U.S.S.R had indeed propagated *its errors* throughout a zone of influence extending into every continent of the world, and has subdued, often with its air force, army and navy, numerous peoples under the tyranny and the chaos of its red yoke, leaving behind ravages whose consequences the world still witnesses today... If that weren't enough, there still was the next prophesy to take under consideration: the announced conversion of the powerful Communist, atheist and militaristic Russia.

Understandably, such a prophecy seemed as unrealistic in 1917 as it was seventy years later; however, in 1989, the Berlin Wall fell against all expectation; the Warsaw Pact crumbled and, in a period of four years, between 1990 and 1994, all Soviet troops and nuclear arsenals installed in Eastern Europe withdrew eastward, behind the Ural mountains... Shortly thereafter, the Communist system collapsed all but entirely, and the Soviet-Union dismembered to transform itself into 13 sovereign and democratic republics.

The Virgin Mary loving Russian-Orthodox Church returned in full force, causing millions to return in its arms, and democracy was electing Russia's next leaders for the next decades to come. This unimaginable upheaval in Eastern Europe fulfilled indeed the prophesy given by Our Lady of the Rosary more than seventy years prior to its realization, and was symbolized by the countless numbers of coronation of statues of Our Lady of Fatima in Moscow's red Square; however, despite what seems to be but a brief pause since the end of the cold war, there remains, nonetheless new dangers, no less terrifying than any other seen before: a peril which depicts the idea of evil itself surfacing from the core of the Middle East and which translates into an Islamic expansion throughout the lands of the "infidels" by ways of organized massive immigrations, regional wars, terrorism at the heart of Western nations (New York, Paris, London, Cologne, Berlin, Madrid, etc.).

As for Eastern Europe, surely, the cold war with the Soviet Union is over but a new one is brewing with a newly reborn Russia that is strengthening with its Chinese ally all economic and military ties, threatening thus the very existence of an increasingly fragile world peace... The West is not prepared... In Europe, more so than in the United States, paganism raises as well a sword of Damocles, thought to have been buried centuries ago, which corrodes the very foundations of Christian civilization... Despite it all, the final promise of the Virgin Mary still echoes in the hearts of men:

Do not be afraid! At the end, my Immaculate Heart will triumph.

Indisputably, the dilemma of Fatima's third secret remains in this first quarter of the 21st century, more pressing now than it was in 1960, year of its requested revelation to the world... However, the incomprehensible silence of the Vatican on this third secret, and the reasons which have led to that decision are the same as that which led to the Holy See's prior silence about the five prophecies of Lourdes (see page: 480), the admonitions and prophetic warnings of La Salette (see Chapter I) and the revelations of La Fraudais (see Chapter II).

Nevertheless, today one asks oneself: what awaits us in the future? What warnings have we been given about the years to come? Surely enough, the vision of the third secret of Fatima has been released by the Vatican on 26 June 2000 while withholding its accompanying message (see page 283)... Indeed, too many prelates who have read the third Secret of Fatima (beside every Pope from John XXIII to Benedict XVI) have given tangible testimony of the fact that the vision in the third Secret of Fatima was in fact accompanied by a grave message; nonetheless, we have been able to discern, from past and contemporary approved apparition sites, religious, stigmatist, and mystic revelations what some already call today the hidden fourth secret of Fatima.

Yes, clearly, the approved apparitions and most disconcerting secrets of Our Lady of La Salette (1846), La Fraudais (1876), Fatima (1917) and of Akita (1980), along with the extraordinary revelations given to Saint Padre Pio, Rev. Father Louis-Marie Pel, Rev. Father Souffrant, and so many others, unveil that which is still ever so jealously hidden by the highest hierarchy of the Church today...

Prophecies, warnings, admonitions... Yes, these are important parts of the apparitions of the Virgin Mary, but these Heaven's calls are meant to warn and urgently call men to repentance and conversation, a forewarning yet heard before long ago in the depth of the Jordan river by none other than Jesus-Christ's own cousin, John the Baptist:

Repent of your sins and turn to God, for the kingdom of Heaven has come near!

(Matthew 3:2).

The Blessed Virgin Mary has brought forth repeatedly, for the better part of the past 200 years, the same warning, alerting the Church and men of good will, of the father of lies' assault upon man's society through an aggressive and subtle cultural corruption of values, and yet, Pope John XXIII refused to divulge Heaven's message in 1960 as requested by the Blessed Virgin Mary. Why? Was the Pontiff's disobedience reflective of an arrogance that led him, and his successors alike, to believe being wiser than Heaven Itself, judging the third Secret not to be appropriate for immediate disclosure? Would it be that God made an error of judgement by asking His Holy Mother to have Heaven's message divulged to the world in 1960?

The Virgin Mary's numerous messages and prophecies, though echoed by messengers all across the world, were swept away by the Church for an alleged "fear of sensationalism", and yet these messages called men to immediate conversion, to return to the teachings of Jesus-Christ, to live the Gospels, the Ten Commandments, and the Sacraments of the Roman, Catholic and Apostolic Church. What's more, with the pressing call to return to the Holy Sacraments, particularly that of the Holy Mass, these extraordinary revelations from Heaven likewise call men to intercede and pray for the coming of a long announced holy

Pope and for a great French Monarch, mentioned ever so repeatedly in the messages of La Fraudais, of La Salette, of Tilly, and through various saints and mystics.

These two men, we are told, will be called to restitute and rebuild a collapsing Catholic Church to its glory of yesteryears, a Church which has been shattered for decades by reformists and liberals who have for sole aim the forging of a new Church bathed in compromise, self-denigration and culture of integration, sacrificing in the name of popular inclusion and cultural values of the times Catholic Dogma itself[2]... But before the "Resurrection", the "Passion" must first run its course should we yet again ignore Heaven's admonitions however well hidden, disregarded and swept under Rome's dusty carpet of convenient forgetfulness...

The Church and the World, we are told, are to go through an epic purification of the likes have never ever been seen or recorded before... Notwithstanding, the Blessed Virgin Mary tells us that we are not orphans nor left defenseless against the pernicious onslaughts of Satan's legions. In effect, we are given arms to defend our Faith and ourselves. As armor and chain-mail, we are given the Holy Eucharist and the holy sacramentals; as a shield we are given the Sacrament of Confession; as a sword we are given the Holy Rosary and the Holy Gospels; as a lance we are given the opportunity to perform acts of reparation for one's sins and for the sins of others with a willingness to bear one's cross in life with love and resignation.

Finally, that which gives a knight of Mary his colors and his identity is his self-consecration to the Sacred Heart of Jesus-Christ and to the Immaculate Heart of Mary. These are indeed the defenses we are offered to which Satan, the Virgin Mary assures us, will find utterly impregnable.

Our journey in this life is short, but the Blessed Mother offers her companionship. With perseverance and good will, man can reach the stage of sanctification which merits eternal life. In essence, the Blessed Virgin Mary proclaims an urgent call for a spiritual mobilization, a radical change of lifestyle through a conversion spearheaded by the Sacraments, faith, prayer and love.

The Mother of Christ promises the triumph of her Immaculate Heart, but implores her faithful children to remain steadfast despite the ominous occurrences which soon must take place...

The Frenchmen of my generation have only been able to listen, often with admiration, the tales of the past that our fathers, and theirs before them, have echoed, while not always being able to keep their eyes dry, with a deep sense of dignity and profound emotion. Surely enough, the second world war is over, and from London one does not hear anymore from the B.B.C a French General, consumed with a profound sense of honor and duty, calling men to continue the war and promising the deliverance from German tyranny; however, the call which the men of my generation witnessed is not very much different from the one our fathers have heard in the morning of their youth. John Paul II gave us testimony of our times' challenges and of the future grandest promise:

---

[2] See Pope Francis' **Amoris Laetitia**

...In the light of the mystery of Mary's spiritual motherhood, let us seek to understand the extraordinary message, which began May 13, 1917, to resound throughout the world from Fatima, continuing for five months until October 13 of the same year.

The Church has always taught and continues to proclaim that God's revelation was brought to completion in Jesus Christ, who is the fullness of that revelation, and that "no new public revelation is to be expected before the glorious manifestation of our Lord." (Dei Verbum, 4) The Church evaluates and judges private revelations by the criterion of conformity with that single public revelation.

If the Church has accepted the message of Fatima, it is, above all, because that message contains a truth and a call whose basic content is the truth and the call of the Gospel itself.

"Repent, and believe in the Gospel!" (Mk 1:15) These are the first words that the messiah addressed to humanity. The message of Fatima is, in its basic nucleus, a call to conversion and repentance, as in the Gospel. This call was uttered at the beginning of the 20th century and it was thus addressed particularly to this present century. The Lady of the message seems to have read with special insight the "signs of the times", the signs of our time.

The call to repentance is a motherly one. At the same time it is strong and decisive. The love that "rejoices in the truth" (1 Cor. 13) is capable of being clear-cut and firm. The call to repentance is linked, as always, with a call to prayer. In harmony with the tradition of many centuries, the Lady of the message indicates the Rosary, which can rightly be defined as "Mary's prayer", the prayer in which she feels particularly united with us.

She herself prays with us. The Rosary prayer embraces the problems of the Church, of the See of Saint Peter, the problems of the whole world. In it we also remember sinners, that they may be converted and saved, and the souls in purgatory.

The words of the message were addressed to children, ages seven to ten. Children, like Bernadette of Lourdes, are particularly privileged in these apparitions of the Mother of God. Hence, the fact that also her language is simple, within the limits of their understanding. The children of Fatima became partners in dialogue with the Lady of the message and collaborators with her. One of them is still living.

When Jesus on the Cross said: "Woman, behold, your son," (Jn 19:26) in a new way He opened His mother's Heart, the Immaculate Heart, and revealed to it the new dimensions and extent of the love to which she was called in the Holy Spirit by the power of the sacrifice of the Cross...

In the light of a mother's love, we understand the whole message of the Lady of Fatima. The greatest obstacle to man's journey toward God is sin, perseverance in sin and, finally, denial of God. The deliberate blotting out of God from the world of human thought. The detachment from Him of the whole of man's earthly activity. The rejection of God by man.

In reality, the eternal salvation of man is only in God. Man's rejection of God, if it becomes definitive, leads logically to God's rejection of man, to damnation. (Mt. 7:23; 10:33)

24

Can the Mother, who desires everyone's salvation, keep silence on what undermines the very basis of their salvation? No, she cannot.

So, while the message of Our Lady of Fatima is a motherly one, it is also strong and decisive. It sounds severe. It sounds like John the Baptist speaking on the banks of the Jordan. It invites to repentance. It gives a warning. It calls to prayer. It recommends the Rosary.

The message is addressed to every human being. The love of the Savior's Mother reaches every place touched by the work of salvation. Her care extends to every individual of our time and to all the societies, nations and peoples. Societies menaced by apostasy, threatened by moral degradation. The collapse of morality involves the collapse of societies. "

(Taken from the Homily by Pope John Paul II at Fatima, 13 May 1982)

Through the chapters to come, the messages (and prophetic warnings) given through apparition sites formally deemed "worthy of belief" will be revealed 'without restrain or fear to be *politically incorrect'*. Private revelations to visionaries, saints, religious and laity will be exhaustively and objectively covered in the light of this book without the usual reserve and confinement practiced elsewhere. Likewise, we'll review the messages brought forth in Garabandal and in Medjugorje (both still under ecclesiastical investigation), two of the most popular Marian apparition sites in the world today.

Upon careful review of these truly remarkable messages and calls, one can see the same invitation to pray for the Pope, the Cardinals, Bishops, priests and religious, who are on the front line of a spiritual war, and more often than not its principal victims... The Blessed Virgin Mary implores the faithful not to condemn nor judge the Clergy but to intercede for those who fall into error or weakness.

Notwithstanding, we are called to maintain our fidelity to the One True Church of Jesus-Christ and to the Sacraments and Dogma of the Faith which, despite the tempest and storm crashing on the vessel which is the Catholic Church, is and always will remain infallible. As we shall see, these apparition cases bring forward but a same message, a same admonition echoed sometimes with a same wording, intonation and warmth, not merely to a people or to a specific nation but to a world-wide audience in a specific time-era—ours.

Introduction

The revelations entrusted in apparition sites approved by the Roman Catholic Church have all the extraordinary particularity to be all but one and the same; on occasions to be even complementary, but always the same in their nature and in their pre-emptive call to conversion... The purpose of the Blessed Virgin Mary's apparitions, and, on many occasions, of Our Lord Jesus-Christ's (Paray-le-Monial, La Fraudais, Tilly, Crakow, Kibeho) are to call-back mankind to the teachings of the Gospels and to the Church's Dogma of the Faith before it's too late. Heaven tells us that ignoring or rejecting this final urgent call will have the gravest of consequences...

As we shall see in the chapters of this book, the admonitions and warnings mankind is given by Heaven through Heaven's First Emissary are quite critical, quite shocking in their brutality and in their utterly devastating amplitude; however, by no means is the Source of these forewarnings from Heaven to be seen as severe, bitter, unforgiving, uncharitable or unjust God, but on the contrary as a deeply Loving and Merciful One. Indeed, for centuries mankind has slipped down on a slope of violence, hatred, atheism and paganism, particularly in the 19th, 20th, and 21st centuries, where mankind has given itself to a conception of self-adoration, self-assurance, self-satisfaction, egoism, a paganism rooted in the replacement of Christian values and morals by the cultural practice of spiritualism, freemasonry, luciferian idolatry and atheism.

Indeed, the dreadful depths of horror, indifference and inhumanity which man has sunk into these past centuries, decades and years have gone in credescendo despite the many miracles, apparitions and imploring calls of Heaven's loving Mother. Instead of conversion, indecency, crime and vice have become a cultural trend that must be tolerated under the justification of open-mindedness, freedom and democracy, and its acceptance is demanded by Society under the penalty of being branded a fascist or even a neo-Nazi.

And yet, God has opted not to cleanse the earth as He did in times of old...not to destroy a civilization which, in its immense majority, lives in a continuous contempt of God, with heartlessness, cruelty, hatred, self-centeredness, corruption, abortion, bestiality, rape, incest, homosexuality... And yet, instead of sending the punishment the world rightfully deserves, God sends His loving Mother again and again to give Humanity one last chance, one last opportunity to redeem itself of its inconceivable crimes.

The punishing arm of Jesus, the Blessed Virgin Mary tells us, has been held through her continuous imploring supplications and intercessions for a very long time, but the time approaches when God's Mercy must give way to God's Justice; and yet...a new hope arises, a new beginning for Humanity is announced after a "purification" which will annihilate the forces of the fallen angel and thus bring about the Triumph of the Immaculate Heart of Mary.

Let us not be fooled, as his holiness John Paul II stated, we are indeed living in the end of times when an epic battle is taking place between Good and evil, a battle whose outcome has already been decided… The author of this book, in his immense gratitude to Heaven, profoundly hopes and prays that the readers of these revelations will be inspired to respond "present!" to God's urgent invitation to return to His Holy Church and to its Sacraments. In the words of Our Lady:

"Do whatever He tells you."

(John 2:5)

Chapter I
The Message and Secrets of Our Lady of La Salette

Our Lady of La Salette

"I address a pressing call to the Earth! I call the true disciples of the Living God who reigns in Heaven! I call the true imitators of the Christ made man, the Only and True Savior of men! I call men, my true devout ones, those who have given themselves to me so that I may lead them to my Son, those that, in other words, I carry in my arms, those who have lived of my spirit! It is time they come to us and come forth to enlighten the earth!"

(Our Lady of La Salette)

How can the theme of contemporary Marian apparitions' history in France be pursued without addressing the Blessed Virgin Mary's apparition to the two little shepherds of La Salette? Indeed, on Saturday, 19 September 1846, the Blessed Virgin Mary appeared in tears for the first time on the mountain of La Salette in the French Alps, before two awestruck children named Maximin Giraud and Mélanie Calvat. Here is the testimony given by the two young children (copied exactly as it was published and received by the Church, translated from the original French into English):

Mélanie Calvat's written testimony:

On the 18 of September (1846), the eve of the Holy Apparition of the Holy Virgin, I was alone, as usual, watching over my Master's cows. Around eleven o'clock in the morning, I saw a small boy walking towards me. I was frightened at this, for it seemed to me that everyone ought to know that I avoided all kinds of company. This boy came up to me and said:

Little girl, I'm coming with you, I'm from Corps too.

At these words, the natural evil in me soon manifested itself, and taking a few steps back, I told him:

I don't want anybody around. I want to be alone.

But the boy followed me, saying:

Go on, let me stay with you. My Master told me to come and watch over my cows together with yours. I'm from Corps.

I walked away from him, gesturing to him that I didn't want anybody around, and when I was some distance away, I sat down on the grass. There, I used to talk with the little flowers of the Good Lord.

A moment later, I looked behind me, and there I found Maximin sitting close to me. Straightaway he says to me:

Keep me with you. I'll be very good.

But the natural evil in me would not hear reason. I jumped to my feet, and ran a little farther off without saying a word and again I started playing with the little flowers of the Good Lord. In an instant, Maximin was there again, telling me he would be very good, that he wouldn't talk, that he would get bored all by himself, and that his Master had sent him to be with me, etc. This time, I took pity, I gestured to him to sit down, and I kept on playing with the little flowers of the Good Lord.

It wasn't long before Maximin broke the silence by bursting into laughter (I think he was making fun of me). I looked at him and he said to me:

Let's have some fun, let's make up a game.

I said nothing in reply, for I was so ignorant I didn't understand what games with other people were, always having been alone. I played with the flowers, on my own, and Maximin came right up close to me, doing nothing but laughing, telling me the flowers didn't have ears to listen to me and that we should play together instead. But I had no liking for the game he told me to play. I started talking to him, however, and he told me that the ten days he was to spend with his Master would soon be over and then he would go home to his father in Corps, etc.

While he was talking, I heard the bell of La Salette, it was the Angelus. I gestured to Maximin to lift his soul up to God. He took off his hat and was silent for a moment. Then I said:

- **Do you want to have dinner?**
- **Yes**, *he replied,* **let's eat.**

We sat down and I brought out of my bag the provisions my Master had given me. As was my habit, before breaking into my little round loaf, I made a cross with the point of my knife on the bread, and a little hole in the middle, saying:

If the devil's in there, may he leave, and if the Good Lord is in there, may he stay!

And I rapidly covered up the little hole. Maximin burst into laughter and kicked the loaf out of my hands. It rolled down the mountainside and was lost from sight. I had another piece of bread which we shared. Afterwards, we played a game. Then, realizing that Maximin must still be hungry, I pointed out a place on the mountainside covered with all kinds of berries. I urged him to go and eat some and he went straight away. He ate a few berries and brought back his hat full of them. In the evening, we walked back down the mountain together and promised to come back the next day and watch over our cows together.

The next day, the 19 of September, I met Maximin on the way up. We climbed up the mountain side together. I discovered that Maximin was a very good, simple boy, and would willingly talk about what I wanted to talk about. He was also very flexible and had no fixed opinions. He was just a little curious, for, when I walked away from him, as soon as he saw I had stopped, he would run over to me to see what I was doing and hear what I was saying to the flowers of the Good Lord. And if he arrived too late, he would ask me what I had said.

*Maximin told me to teach him a game. It was already late morning. I told him to gather some flowers for the "Paradise" (*a Paradise is a small stone construction*). We set to work together. Soon we had a number of flowers of various colors. I could hear the village Angelus ringing, for the weather was fine and there wasn't a cloud in the sky.*

Having told the Good Lord what we had learned, I said to Maximin that we ought to drive our cows on to a small plateau near the gully, where there would be stones to build the "Paradise". We drove our cows to the selected spot and then had a small meal. Then we started collecting stones to build our little house, which comprised of a so-called ground floor which was where we were to live, and then a story above which was to be, as we called it, "Paradise".

This story was decorated all over with different-colored flowers, with garlands hanging from flower stalks. This "Paradise" was covered by a single large stone which we had strewn with flowers. We had also hung garlands all the way round. When we had finished, we sat and looked at the "Paradise". We began to feel sleepy and having moved a couple of feet away, we went to sleep on the grass.

When I woke up I couldn't see the cows, so I called Maximin and climbed up the little mound. From there I could see our cows grazing peacefully and I was on my way down with Maximin on his way up, when all of a sudden I saw a beautiful light shining more brightly than the sun.

Maximin, do you see what is over there? Oh! My God!

At the same moment, I dropped the stick I was holding. Something inconceivably fantastic passed through me in that moment and I felt myself being drawn. I felt a great respect, full of love, and my heart beat faster.

I kept my eyes firmly fixed on this light, which was static, and as if it had opened up, I caught sight of another, much more brilliant light which was moving, and in this light I saw a most beautiful lady sitting on top of our Paradise, with her head in her hands.

This beautiful Lady stood up; she coolly crossed her arms while watching us, and said to us:

Come forth, my children; do not be afraid. I am here to tell you great news.

If my people does not want to submit, I am forced to let my Son's arm go... It is so Strong and so Heavy that I can no longer sustain it! I have suffered so long for all of you! If I want my Son not to abandon you, I am charged to pray to Him unceasingly for all of you. You are indifferent to it! Despite your prayers and your deeds, you will never be able to compensate the sorrow that I have taken upon myself for all of you...

I have given you six days to work; I reserved for Myself the seventh, and they do not want to grant it to Me. That is what makes my Son's arm Heavier... Likewise, those who drive the carts do not know how to swear

without using my Son's Name. These are two things that make my Son's arm ever so heavy...

If the harvest goes bad, it's only because of you. I showed you last year with the potatoes, but you did not take heed! On the contrary, when you found spoiled potatoes, you swore, you used my Son's Name in the middle of it. The potatoes will continue to be spoiled, and this year at Christmas there won't be anymore...

Until now, the Blessed Virgin Mary spoke in French. She answered a question from Mélanie and finished her message in French-Patois:

You do not understand, my children! I shall tell you in another manner: 'Si la recolta se gasta... If you have wheat, you must not sow it. Everything that you will sow, the beasts will eat it, and what will come will fall into dust when it will be harvested.

A great famine will come. Before the famine comes, little children younger than seven will have a shake (a trembling) and will die in the hands of the people who will hold them... The others will do penance through famine. Nut-shells will be empty and grapes will rot...

At that moment of the Blessed Virgin Mary's apparition, Mélanie saw that the beautiful Lady was saying a few words to Maximin which she couldn't hear... Then it was Maximin who saw the Lady say a few words to Mélanie which he couldn't hear...

Once the secrets were revealed to each child, the Blessed Virgin Mary continued on with "the Message for the people of France" heard by both young shepherds at the same time:

-    **If they convert, stones and rocks will become heaps of wheat, and potatoes will be seeded by the land.**
  Do you do your prayers well, children?
-    *Not so, Madam.*
  Ah! My children, do your prayers well evening and morning, even if it were but a 'Pater' (Our Father) and an 'Ave Maria' (Hail Mary) when you cannot do more. When you'll be able to do better, you must say more prayers.
  In the summer, only a few somewhat older women go to Mass. The others work on Sundays during the whole summer and the whole winter. When they do not know what to do, they only go to Mass to poke fun of religion. During Lent, they go to the butcher-shop like dogs...
  Have you ever seen spoiled wheat, my children?
-    *No, Madam.*
  But you, Maximin, my child, surely you must have seen some, in the corner, with your father.
  The Master of the field asked your father to come see his spoiled wheat. You (both) went (to see it). Your father took three ears of

wheat, crumbled them and they all fell into dust. **Going back, when you were only but half-an hour away from home, your father gave you a piece of bread saying:** 'Take this, my little one. Eat bread this year for I do not know who will eat of it next year if the wheat continues like this…'

- *Ah! Yes, Madam. I remember now! I did not remember earlier.*

Well, my children, you will pass it on (my message) to all my people! Go on, my children, pass it on to all my people!

The secret revealed to Mélanie by the Blessed Virgin Mary was to be revealed no later than 1858, the same year when the Blessed Virgin Mary appeared in Lourdes, thus confirming the complementarity of these two Marian apparitions. Was this a mere coincidence? Only the blind would say so. La Salette and Lourdes are unmistakably connected to one another, as La Fraudais would complement in a major manner these two prior apparitions, later to be confirmed by the messages given in Tilly and by the apotheosis of all apparitions: Fatima and its "Miracle of the Sun". Notwithstanding, the integral text of the secret revealed to Mélanie was more than once contested and hidden by the bishop of Grenoble and by the religious who inhabited the sanctuary of La Salette…

Fortunately, the authentic text was discovered (by accident) over one hundred years later in the secret archives of the Holy See in the Vatican's Library by a French priest, Abbot Cotteville, who received the permission of Cardinal Ratzinger, the then Prefect of the Congregation of the Doctrine of the Faith (and future Pope Benedict XVI) under His Holiness Pope John Paul II to make the proper research on the Secrets revealed in La Salette. These were the secrets that the Blessed Virgin Mary revealed to the children, as they were written in 1851 to His Holiness Pope Pius IX by young Maximin and Mélanie:

The Secret of La Salette

Mélanie, what I shall tell you now will not always be a secret. You will be able to publish it in 1858.

The priests, ministers of my Son, through their bad life, through their irreverence and their impiety in their celebrating the Holy Mysteries, because of their love of money, their love of honor and pleasures, priests have become cloaks of impurity… Yes, priests demand vengeance, and vengeance is suspended above their heads.

Woe to priests and to people consecrated to God who, through their infidelities and their bad life, crucify once again my Son! The sins of the Consecrated people scream towards Heaven and call for vengeance, and here is vengeance at their door for there is no longer anyone to implore mercy and forgiveness for the people; there is no longer any generous soul; there is no longer anyone worthy to offer the Stainless Victim to the Eternal

One in favor of the world... God will strike in a fashion like none other before.

Woe to the inhabitant of the earth! God will exhaust His Anger, and no one will be able to escape from so many ills together. The chiefs, the conductors of the people of God have neglected prayer and penance, and the Devil has darkened their intelligence; they have become these wandering stars that the old Devil will drag with his tail to have them perish. God will permit the old snake to put division amongst the leaders in all societies, in all families. There will be physical and moral sufferings. God will abandon men to themselves, and will send chastisements which will follow one another for more than 35 years... Society is at the eve of most terrible plagues and of great events! One must expect to be governed with an iron rod and to drink a chalice of Divine Wrath.

Let the Vicar of my Son, the sovereign Pontiff Pius IX not leave Rome after the year 1859, but let him be firm and generous. Let him fight with the weapons of Faith and Love! I shall be with him. Let him be aware of Napoléon; his heart is double-sided, and when he will want to be at the same time Pope and Emperor, God will soon thereafter withdraw from him... He (Napoléon) is that eagle who, wanting to rise always higher will fall on the sword which he wanted to use to force the people to raise him...

Italy will be punished in its ambition by wanting to shake the Yoke of the Lord of Lords; it too will be delivered to war. Blood will spill on all sides; churches will be shut down or profaned; priests and religious will be chased away; they will make them die and die of a cruel death. Many will abandon their faith, and the number of priests and religious that will separate from the True Religion will be great. Amongst these people, there will even be bishops! Let the Pope be on his guard against miracle-doers, for the time of the most astonishing prodigies has come and will take place on the earth and in the airs.

In 1864, Lucifer, with a great number of demons, will be detached from hell. They will abolish the Faith little by little in the people consecrated to God; they will blind them in such a way that, unless they receive a particular grace, these people will take on the spirit of these bad angels... Many religious will lose the Faith and will lose many souls. Bad books will be numerous on the earth, and the spirits of darkness will spread everywhere a universal relaxation on everything that involves the service of God; they will have a very great power on nature.

There will be churches to serve these spirits! People will be transported from one place to another through these evil spirits, even priests will be so because they will not be led by the Good Spirit of the Gospel which is a spirit of humility, of charity and of zeal for the Glory of God.

They will make the dead and the just resurrect...

There will be extraordinary prodigies everywhere because the true Faith has been extinguished and because the false light enlightens the world... Woe to the Princes of the Church who will be busy to amass wealth upon wealth, to safeguard their authority and to dominate with pride! My Son's Vicar will have to suffer a great deal, because for a time, the Church will be delivered to a great persecution; it will be the time of darkness. The Church will have a ghastly crisis…

The Holy Faith of God being forgotten, each individual will want to guide himself and to be superior to his fellowman. They will abolish civil and ecclesiastical powers; all order and justice will be trampled on; one will see only homicide, hatred, jealousy, lies and discord without love for country or for family. The Holy Father will suffer a great deal. I shall be with him until the end to receive his sacrifice. The evil ones will try many times to attempt on his life but without succeeding to hinder his days; neither he nor his successor—(brief silence)—will see the Triumph of the Church of God.

Note: In the last sentence of this paragraph, Mélanie noticed a space, a brief silence of sorts… This is but a mere personal speculation, but could it be that the Blessed Virgin Mary refer herself to Pope John Paul II, whose life was attempted on 13 May 1981, and the status of his successor being somewhat unclear as, for the first time in half a millennia, the world has two living Pontiffs in the Vatican… Could that brief space or silence be the reason of that… 'uncertainty'?

In 1865, one will see the abomination in holy places; in convents, the flowers of the Church will be purified, and the devil will become as a king of the hearts… Let the heads of religious communities be on their guard against the people they must receive, because the devil will use all of his malice to insert inside religious orders people who are abandoned to sin, for the disorders and the love of carnal pleasures will be widespread everywhere on earth.

If a man has sexual relations with a man as one does with a woman, both of them have done what is abominable. They are to be put to death; their blood will be on their own heads.

(Leviticus 20:13)

That is why God abandoned them to their shameful desires. Even women turned against the natural way and instead went against nature. And the same was for men, abandoning natural intercourse with women, they burned with lust for each other. Men did shameful things with other men, and as a result of this sin, they suffered within themselves the penalty they deserved.

(Romans 1: 26, 27)

France, Italy, Spain, and England will be at war; blood will be spilled in the streets. Frenchmen will fight against Frenchmen, the Italians against the Italians, then there will be a general war (world war) which will be dreadful... For a time, God will no longer remember France nor Italy because the Gospel of Jesus-Christ is no longer known. The evil ones will use all of their malice; people will kill each other, they will mutually massacre each other even within homes. Upon the first strike of His powerful sword, mountains and all of nature will tremble with fright because the disorders of man's crimes are piercing Heaven's Vault.

Paris will be burnt and Marseille will be sunken... Many great cities will be shaken and engulfed by earthquakes. People will believe that everything is lost. One will see only homicides and will hear the noises of weapons and blasphemes... The just will suffer a great deal; their prayers, their penance and their tears will rise to Heaven, and all the people of God will ask forgiveness and mercy, and will further ask for my aid and intercession. Then, Jesus-Christ, through an act of His Justice and of His Great Mercy for the just, will order His angels to be all put to death.

All of a sudden, the persecutors of Jesus-Christ's Church, and all the men self-given to sin will perish, and the earth will become like a desert; then peace will be made, as will the reconciliation between God and men; Jesus-Christ will be served, adored and glorified. Charity will flourish everywhere. The new kings will be the right arm of the Holy Church which will be strong, humble, pious, poor, zealous, and imitator of Jesus-Christ's virtues. The Gospel will be preached everywhere and men will make great progress in the Faith because there will be unity amongst the laborers of Jesus-Christ, and because men will live in the fear of God.

Note: It appears that this passage of the Secret of La Salette refers to the three days of Darkness, the period of the world's purification that will clearly be described a few years later by the locution of the Holy Spirit, the apparitions of Our Lord Jesus-Christ, the Blessed Virgin Mary and St. Michael the Archangel to Marie-Julie Jahenny, and later yet to Father Pio.

This peace among men will not be very long... Twenty-five years_of abundant harvests will make them forget that the sins of men are the cause of all the troubles that come to the Earth. A harbinger of the Anti-Christ, along with the troops of many nations, will fight against the True Christ, the only Savior of the world. He will spill a great deal of blood and will want to destroy the cult of God to appear himself as a god.

The earth will be struck of all sorts of wounds; there will be wars until the last war which will be waged by the ten kings of the Anti-Christ who will all have the same objective and who alone will govern the world. Before this happens, there will be a false peace in the world; everyone will only think to divert himself. The evil ones will commit all sorts of sins, but the children of the Holy Church, the children of the Faith, my true imitators, will grow in the love of God and in the virtues which are dearest to me. Happy be the humble souls led by the Holy Spirit! I shall fight with them until they reach the fullness of age. Nature demands vengeance for men, and she trembles with fright awaiting what must happen the earth which is soiled with crimes.

Tremble, Earth! And you who make profession of serving Jesus-Christ and who within yourselves adore your selves; tremble will deliver you to His enemy because the holy place are in corruption. Many convents are no longer the houses of God, but rather the pastures of Asmodeus and his family... It will be during this time that the Anti-Christ will be born of a Hebrew nun, a false virgin who will have communion with the old snake, the master of impurity; his father will be a bishop.

As he will be born, he will vomit blasphemes; he will have teeth; in one word he will be the devil incarnate... He will make frightening screams; he will make prodigies; he will nourish himself with impurities. He will have brothers who, although they will not be like he, incarnated demons, they will be children of evil. When they will be 12 years old, they will be noticed by the valiant victories they will win. Soon, each one will be at the head of armies, assisted by the legions of hell.

Seasons will be changed. The earth will only produce bad fruit; the stars will lose their regular movements; the moon will reflect only a weak reddish light; water and fire will give to the earth's globe convulsive movements, and horrible shakes that will engulf mountains and cities.

Rome will lose its faith and will become the Seat of the Anti-Christ. The demons of the air with the Anti-Christ will perform great prodigies on earth and in the airs, and men will pervert themselves more and more. God will take care of His faithful servants and of men of good will. The Gospel will be preached everywhere; all the nations will have knowledge of the Truth!

Note: Here, stating that Rome will lose its faith and will become the Seat of the Anti-Christ is denouncing a Pontiff who would be an Anti-Christ... This message is of the utmost gravity and announces what the Third Secret of Fatima will as well announce seventy-one years later. It is interesting to point-out that both secrets, similar in both La Salette and Fatima, have been sealed and hidden by the Church for decades...

I address a pressing call to the Earth! I call the true disciples of the Living God who reigns in Heaven! I call the true imitators of the Christ made man, the Only and True Savior of men! I call men, my true devout ones, those who have given themselves to me so that I may lead them to my Son, those that, in other words, I carry in my arms, those who have lived of my spirit!

It is time they come out and come forth to enlighten the earth! Go, and show yourselves as my beloved children! I am with you and in you as long as your faith is the light which enlightens you in these days of sorrow. May your zeal make you famished for the Glory and Honor of Jesus-Christ. Fight, children of Light, you the few in numbers who see, for behold the time of times, the end of ends.

The Church will be eclipsed; the world will be in consternation. But behold Enoch and Eli filled with the Spirit of God. They will preach with the strength of God, and men of good will believe in God and many souls will be consoled. They will make great progress by the virtue of the Holy Spirit, and will condemn the diabolical errors of the Anti-Christ.

Woe to the inhabitants of the earth! There will be bloody wars and famines, pestilence and contagious diseases; there will be rains made-up of horrifying hailstones; there will be thunder which will shake cities, earthquakes which will engulf countries. One will hear voices in the air. Men will hit their heads against walls; they will call for death, and, on side death will be their torture: blood will spill on all sides. Who could win if God does not diminish the time (of this difficult moment)?

Through the blood, the tears and the prayers of the just, God will let Himself be moved (and thus ease somewhat the intensity His Anger). Enoch and Eli will be put to death. Pagan Rome will disappear; the fire from Heaven will fall and will consume three cities... The entire universe will be hit with terror, and many will let themselves be seduced because they haven't adored the True Christ living among them.

It is time! The sun is darkening, only the Faith will survive. Here is the time! The abyss opens-up. Here comes the king of kings of darkness; here comes the beast with his subjects calling himself the savior of the world. He will rise with pride in the airs to go to Heaven. He will be mortally-smothered by the breath of Saint Michael the Archangel; he will fall, and the earth which for three days will be in continuous evolutions, will open itself filled with fire; he will be engulfed forever within the eternal depths of hell. Then water and fire will purify the earth and will consume all the works of pride of men... and everything will be renewed. God will be served and glorified.

(Our Lady of La Salette, 18 September 1846)

Mélanie Calvat:

Then, She walked up to the place where I had gone to see our cows. Her feet touched nothing but the tips of the grass and without bending them. Once on the top of the little mound, the beautiful Lady stopped, and I hurried to stand in front of Her to look at Her so... so closely, and try and see which path she was most inclined to take. For it was all over for me. I had forgotten both my cows and the masters I worked for. I had linked myself forever and unconditionally to my Lady. Yes, I wanted never, never to leave Her. I followed Her with no other motive than to be with Her, and I was fully disposed to serve Her for the rest of my life.

In the presence of my Lady, I felt I had forgotten paradise. I thought of nothing more but to serve Her in every way possible; and I felt I could have done everything she could have asked me to do, for it seemed to me that She had a great deal of power. She looked at me with a tender kindness which drew me to

Her. I could have thrown myself into Her arms with my eyes closed. She did not give me the time to do so.

She rose imperceptibly from the ground to a height of around four feet or more; and, hanging thus in the air for a split second, my beautiful Lady looked up to Heaven, then down on the earth to her right and then her left, then She looked at me with Her eyes so soft, so kind and so good that I felt She was drawing me inside Her, and my heart seemed to open up to Hers.

And as my heart melted away, sweetly gladdened, the beautiful face of my good Lady disappeared little by little. It seemed to me that the light in motion was growing stronger, or rather condensing around the Most Holy Virgin, to prevent me from seeing her any longer.

And this light took the place of the parts of her body which were disappearing in front of my eyes; or rather it seemed to me that the body of my Lady was melting into light. Thus, the sphere of light rose gently towards the right. I cannot say whether the volume of light decreased as she rose, or whether the growing distance made me see less and less light as She rose. What I do know, is that I was a long time with my head raised up, staring at the light, even after the light, which kept getting further away and decreasing in volume, had finally disappeared. I took my eyes from the firmament, I look around me.
I see Maximin looking at me, and I said to him:

Maxi, that must have been my father's Good Lord, or the Holy Virgin, or some other great saint.

And Maximin throws his arms into the air and says:

Oh! If only I knew!

The evening of the 19th of September, we went back down a little earlier than usual. When I arrived at my master's farm, I was busy tying up my cows and tidying up in the stable, and had not yet finished when my mistress came up to me in tears and said:

Why, my child, why didn't you come and tell me what happened on the mountain?

Maximin, not having found his masters who were still at work, had come over to mine and recounted everything he had seen and heard. I replied:

I did want to tell you, but I wanted to get my work finished first.

A moment later, I walked over to the house and my mistress said to me:

Tell me what you have seen. De Bruite, the shepherd (that was the nickname of Pierre Selme, Maximin's master), has told me everything.

I began, and towards the middle of the account, my master arrived back from the fields. My mistress, who was in tears at hearing the complaints and threats of our sweet Mother, said:

Ah! You were going to harvest the wheat tomorrow (Sunday). Take great care. Come and hear what happened today to this child and Pierre Selme's shepherd-boy.

And turning to me, she said:

Repeat everything you have said.

I started again, and when I had finished, my master said:

It was the Holy Virgin or else a great saint, who has come on behalf of the Good Lord, but it's as if the Good Lord had come Himself. We must do what this Saint said. How are you going to manage to tell that to all her people?

I replied: **You tell me how I must go about it, and I will do it.**

Then, looking at his mother, wife, and brother, he added:

I'll have to think about that.

Then everyone went back to their business.

After supper, Maximin and his masters came over to see my masters and to recount what Maximin had told them, and decide what was to be done, they said:

It seems to us that it was the Holy Virgin sent by the Good Lord. The words which She spoke convince us of this. And she told them to pass it on to all of Her people. Perhaps these children will have to travel the world over to make it known that everyone must observe the commandments of the Good Lord, lest great misfortunes come upon us.

After a moment's silence, my master said to Maximin and me:

Do you know what you must do, my children? Tomorrow, you must get up early and both of you go and see the priest and tell him everything you have seen and heard. Tell him carefully how it all happened. He will tell you what you have to do.

The 20th of September, the day after the Apparition, I left early in the morning with Maximin. When we reached the presbytery, I knocked at the door. The priest's housekeeper came and opened the door and asked us what we wanted. I said to her (in French, and I, who had never spoken French):

- *We would like to speak to Father Perrin.*
- ***And what have you got to say to him?** she asked.*
  We wish to tell him, Miss, that yesterday we went up to watch over our cows on Baisses Mountain and after dinner, etc... etc.

We recounted a good piece of the Most Holy Virgin's words. Then the church bell rang: it was the final call for Mass. Father Perrin, the parish priest of La Salette, who had heard us, flung open his door; he was in tears and was beating his chest. He said to us:

My children, we are lost, God will punish us. Oh! Good Lord! It was the Holy Virgin who appeared to you!

And he left to say Holy Mass. We looked at each other, Maximin, the housekeeper, and I. Then Maximin said to me:

Me, I'm off home to my father in Corps.

And we parted company.

As my masters had not told me to return to work immediately after speaking to Father Perrin, I saw no harm in going to Mass. And so I was in church. Mass begins and after the first reading from the Gospel, Father Perrin turns to the congregation and tries to recount to his parishioners, the story of the Apparition which had just taken place, the day before, on one of their mountains, and he urges them to stop working on Sundays. His voice was broken with sobs, and all the congregation was greatly moved.

After Holy Mass, I went back to my masters to work. Mr. Peytard, who still today is the mayor of La Salette came to question me on the Apparition, and when he had made sure that I was speaking the truth, he went away convinced.

I stayed on in the service of my masters until All Saint's Day. Then I was boarded with the nuns of Providence, in my hometown of Corps.

The Description of the Blessed Virgin Mary (as per Mélanie Calvat)

"The Most Holy Virgin was tall and well-proportioned. She seemed so light that a mere breath could have stirred her, yet She was motionless and perfectly balanced. Her face was majestic, imposing, but not imposing in the manner of the Lords here below. She compelled a respectful fear. At the same time as her Majesty compelled respect mingled with love, she drew me to her.

Her gaze was soft and penetrating. Her eyes seemed to speak to mine, but the conversation came out of a deep and vivid feeling of love for this ravishing beauty that was liquefying me. The softness of her gaze, her air of incomprehensible goodness made me understand and feel that she was drawing me to her and wanted to give herself. It was an expression of love which cannot be expressed with the tongue, nor with the letters of the alphabet.

The clothing of the Most Holy Virgin was silver white and quite brilliant. It was quite intangible. It was made up of light and glory, sparkling and dazzling. There is neither expression nor comparison to be found on earth.

The Holy Virgin was all beauty and all love; the sight of her overwhelmed me. In her finery as in her person, everything radiated the majesty, the splendor, the magnificence of a Queen beyond compare. She seemed as white, immaculate, crystallized, dazzling, heavenly, fresh and new as a Virgin. The word LOVE seemed to slip from Her pure and silvery lips. She appeared to me like a good Mother, full of kindness, amiability, of love for us, of compassion and mercy.

The crown of roses which she had placed on her head was so beautiful, so brilliant, that it defies imagination. The different colored roses were not of this earth; it was a joining together of flowers which crowned the head of the Most Holy Virgin. But the roses kept changing and replacing each other, and then, from the heart of each rose, there shone a beautiful entrancing light, which gave the roses a shimmering beauty. From the crown of roses there seemed to arise golden branches and a number of little flowers mingled with the shining ones. The whole thing formed a most beautiful diadem, which alone shone brighter than our earth's sun.

The Holy Virgin had a most pretty cross hanging round her neck. This cross seemed golden, (I say golden rather than gold-plated, for I have sometimes seen objects which were golden with varying shades of gold, which had a much more beautiful effect on my eyes than simple gold-plate). On this shining beautiful cross, there was a Christ; it was Our Lord on the Cross. Near both ends of the cross there was a hammer, and at the other end, a pair of tongs.

The Christ was skin-colored, but He shone dazzlingly; and the light shone forth from His holy body seemed like brightly shining darts which pierced my heart with the desire to melt inside Him. At times, the Christ appeared to be dead. His head was bent forward and His body seemed to give way, as if about to fall, had He not been held back by the nails which held him to the Cross.

I felt a deep compassion and would have liked to tell His unknown love to the whole world, and to let seep into mortal souls the most heartfelt love and gratitude towards a God who had no need whatsoever of us to be everything He is, was and always will be. And yet, O love that men cannot understand, He made Himself man, and wanted to die, yes, die, so as to better inscribe in our souls and in our memory, the passionate love He has for us! Oh, how wretched am I to find myself so poor in my expression of the love of our good Savior for us! But, in another way, how happy we are to be able to feel more deeply that which we cannot express!

At other times, the Christ appeared to be alive. His head was erect, His eyes open, and He seemed to be on the cross of His own accord. At times too, He appeared to speak: He seemed to show that He was on the cross for our sake, out of love for us, to draw us to His love, and that He always has more love to give us, that His love in the beginning and in the year 33 is always that of today and will be forever more.

The Holy Virgin was crying nearly the whole time she was speaking to me. Her tears flowed gently, one by one, down to her knees, then, like sparks of light, they disappeared. They were glittering and full of love. I would have liked to comfort her and stop Her tears. But it seemed to me that she needed the tears to show better Her love forgotten by men.

I would have liked to throw myself into her arms and say to her: "**My kind Mother, do not cry! I want to love you for all men on earth.**" but she seemed to be saying to me: "**There are so many who know me not!**"

I was in between life and death, and on one side, I saw so much desire by this Mother to be loved, and on another side, so much cold and indifference... Oh! My Mother, most beautiful and lovable Mother, my love, heart of my heart!

The tears of our sweet Mother, far from lessening her air of majesty, of a Queen and a Mistress, seemed, on the contrary, to embellish her, to make her more beautiful, more powerful, more filled with love, more maternal, more ravishing, and I could have wiped away her tears which made my heart leap with compassion and love. To see a mother cry, and such a Mother, without doing everything possible to comfort her and change her grief to joy, is that possible?

Oh! Mother, who is more than good; you have been formed with all the prerogatives God is able to make; you have married the power of God, so to speak; you are good, and more, you are good with the goodness of God Himself. God has extended Himself by making you His terrestrial and celestial masterpiece.

The Most Holy Virgin had a yellow pinafore. What am I saying, yellow? She had a pinafore more brilliant than several suns put together. It was not a tangible material; it was composed of glory, and this glory was scintillating, and ravishingly beautiful. Everything in the Holy Virgin carried me firmly and made me kind of slide into the adoration and love of my Jesus in every state of His mortal life.

The Most Holy Virgin had two chains, one a little wider than the other. From the narrower one, hung the cross which I mentioned earlier. These chains (since they must be given the name of chains) were like rays of brightly shining glory, sparkling and dazzling. Her shoes (since they must be called shoes) were white, but a silvery brilliant white. There were roses around them. These roses were dazzlingly beautiful, and from the heart of each rose there shone forth a flame of very beautiful and pleasing light. On Her shoes there was a buckle of gold, not the gold of this earth, but rather the gold of paradise.

The sight of the Holy Virgin was itself a perfect paradise. She had everything needed to satisfy, for earth had been forgotten. The Holy Virgin was surrounded by two lights. The first light, the nearer to the Most Holy Virgin, reached as far as us. It shone most beautifully and scintillatingly.

The second light shone out a little around the Beautiful Lady and we found ourselves bathed in it. It was motionless (that is to say it wasn't scintillating) but much more brilliant than our poor sun on earth. All this light did not harm nor tire the eyes in any way.

In addition to all these lights, all this splendor, there shone forth concentrations or beams of light and single rays of light from the body of the Holy Virgin, from her clothes and from all over her.

The voice of the Beautiful Lady was soft. It was enchanting, ravishing, warming to the heart. It satisfied, flattered every obstacle, it soothed and softened. It seemed to me I could never stop eating up her beautiful voice and my heart seemed to dance or want to go towards her and melt inside her.

The eyes of the most Holy Virgin, our Sweet Mother, cannot be described in human language. To speak of them, you would need a seraph, you would need more than that, you would need the language of God Himself, of the God who formed the immaculate Virgin, the masterpiece of His omnipotence. The eyes of the majestic Mary appeared thousands of times more beautiful than the rarest brilliants, diamonds and precious stones. They shone like two suns; they were soft, softness itself, as clear as a mirror. In her eyes, you could see paradise. They drew you to Her, She seemed to want to draw and give herself.

The more I looked, the more I wanted to see; the more I saw, the more I loved her and I loved her with all my might.

The eyes of the beautiful Immaculate One were like the door to God's Kingdom, from which you could see all that can elate the soul. When my eyes met those of the Mother of God, I felt within me a happy revolution of love and wanted to declare that I love her and that I am melting with love. As we looked at each other, our eyes spoke to each other in their fashion, and I loved her so much I could have kissed her in the middle of her eyes, which touched my soul and seemed to draw it towards them, making it melt into hers. Her eyes set up a sweet trembling in all my being; and I was afraid to make the slightest movement which might cause her the smallest displeasure.

Just the sight of the eyes of the purest of Virgins would have been enough to make the Heaven of a blessed creature, enough to fill the soul with the will of the Most High amid the events which occurs in the course of mortal life, enough to make the soul perform continual acts of praise, of thanksgiving, of atonement and expiation. Just this sight focuses the soul on God, and makes it like a living-death, looking upon all the things of this earth, even the things which seem the most serious, as nothing but children's playthings. The soul would want to hear no one speaking unless they spoke of God, and of that which affects His Glory.

Sin is the only evil she sees on earth. She will die of grief unless God sustains her.

Amen.

Signed: MARIA OF THE CROSS, Victim of Jesus, born MÉLANIE CALVAT, Shepherdess of La Salette, Castellamare, 21 November 1878."

Additional words of Mélanie Calvat:

The great chastisement will come, because men will not be converted; yet it is only their conversion that can hinder these scourges. God will begin to strike men by inflicting lighter punishments in order to open their eyes; then He will stop, or may repeat His former warnings to give place for repentance. But sinners will not avail themselves of these opportunities; He will, consequently, send more severe punishments, anxious to move sinners to repentance, but all in *vain. Finally, the obstinacy of sinners shall draw upon their heads the greatest and most terrible calamities.*

We are all guilty! Penance is not done, and sin increases daily. Those who should come forward to do good are retained by fear. Evil is great. A moderate punishment serves only to irritate the spirits, because they view all things with human eyes. God could work a miracle to convert and change the aspect of the earth without chastisement. God will work a miracle; it will be a stroke of His mercy; but after the wicked shall have inebriated themselves with blood, the scourge shall arrive.

What countries shall be preserved from such calamities? Where shall we go for refuge? I, in my turn, shall ask, what is the country that observes the commandments of God? What country is not influenced by human fear where the interest of the Church and the glory of God are at stake? (Ah, indeed! What country, what nation upon earth?) In behalf of my Superior and myself, I have often asked myself where we could go for refuge, had we the means for the journey and for our subsistence, on condition that no person were to know it? But I renounce these useless thoughts.

*We are very guilty! In consequence of this, it is necessary that a very great and terrible scourge should come to revive our faith, and to restore to us our very reason, which we have almost entirely lost. Wicked men are devoured by a thirst for exercising their cruelty; but when they shall have reached the uttermost point of barbarity, God Himself shall extend His hand to stop them, and very soon after, a complete change shall be effected in all surviving persons. Then they will sing the **Te Deum Laudamus** with the most lively gratitude and love.*

The Virgin Mary, our Mother, shall be our liberatrix. Peace shall reign, and the charity of Jesus Christ shall unite all hearts... Let us pray; let us pray. God does not wish to chastise us severely. He speaks to us in so many, so many ways to make us return to Him. How long shall we remain stubborn? Let us pray, let us pray; let us never cease praying and doing penance. Let us pray for our Holy Father the Pope, the only light for the faithful in these times of darkness. O yes, let us by all means prays much. Let us pray to good, sweet, merciful Virgin Mary; for we stand in great need of her powerful hands over our heads."

Likewise, Abbot Cotteville discovered in 1999, in the secret archives of the Vatican, Mélanie Calvat's letter to his Holiness Pope Pius IX. This version of the Secret entrusted by the Blessed Virgin Mary holds no difference of the original text published in 1879 except for its length and for some extremely interesting additional information which will likewise give a greater sense to the reality of what is to be expected today in the 21ˢᵗ century.

<u>Letter of Mélanie Calvat to his Holiness Pope Pius IX</u>

Secret the Holy Virgin gave me on the Mountain of La Salette on September 19, 1846:

"Mélanie, I shall tell you something that you will repeat to no one: The time of God's anger has arrived! If, when you will have told the peoples what I told

you earlier, and after what I shall tell you more, if after this they do not convert (if we do not do penance and if we do not stop working on Sundays, and if we continue to blaspheme the Holy Name of God) in other words if the face of the earth does not change, God will avenge himself against the ungrateful people and slaves of the devil. My Son will let His power go.

Paris, this city soiled by all sorts of crimes, will infallibly perish. Marseille will be destroyed in little time. When these things happen, disorder will be complete on earth. The world will abandon itself to its ungodly passions. The Pope will be persecuted from all sides. They will shoot him. They will want to put him to death, but they will not be able to do anything; the Vicar of God will triumph once again. Priests and religious and the true servants of my Son will be persecuted, and many will die for the Faith of Jesus-Christ.

A famine will reign at the same time. Once all these things will have taken place, many people will recognize the Hand of God upon them. They will convert and will do penance for their sins.

A Great King will rise on the throne and will reign for a few years. Religion will flourish and will spread throughout the world, and fertility will be great. The world, happy not to lack anything, will start again its disorders, abandon God and will abandon itself to its criminal passions.

Among the ministers of God, and the spouses of Jesus-Christ, there are some who will subject themselves to disorder, and that will be what is most terrible. At the end, a hell will reign on earth. This will be when the Anti-Christ will be born from a nun, but woe to her! Many people will believe in him because he will say to come from Heaven; woe to those who believe him! The time is not far off. Twice 50 years will not pass. My child, you will repeat what I just told you. You will say this to no one. If you have to say it one day, you will not say what this is in regards; well, you will not say anything before I tell you to say it!"

I pray our Holy Father the Pope to give me his holy blessing.

Mélanie Mathieu, Shepherdess of La Salette
Grenoble, July 6, 1851

Letter of Maximin Giraud to his Holiness Pope Pius IX

On September 19, 1846, we saw a beautiful lady. We never said that this lady was the Holy Virgin, but we've always said that she was a very beautiful lady. I do not know if it's the Holy Virgin or another person. I for one think today that it's the Holy Virgin.

Here is what this Lady told me:

If my people continue, what I shall tell you will take place sooner; if it changes a little bit, it will happen a little bit later.

France has corrupted the universe. One day she will be punished. Faith will be extinguished in France: **Three parts of France will no longer practice religion, or almost no longer, the other part will practice it, but without**

46

practicing it. Then after that, nations will convert and Faith will be re-enlighten everywhere. A great country in the north, today protestant, will convert. Through the support of that country, all the other countries of the world will convert.

*Before this takes place, great troubles will come in the Church and everywhere; then afterwards, our holy father the Pope will be persecuted. His successor will be a Pontiff that no one expects. Then, after that, a great peace will come, but it will not last long. A monster will come to disturb it. Everything I am telling here will happen in the next century, **or at the latest in the years 2000.***

Maximin Giraud
(She told me to say this sometimes before)
My most Holy Father, your blessing for one of your lambs

Grenoble, July 3, 1851

La Salette's Secret on the Future King of France

This secret has been one of the most hidden subject of controversy that the republicans and other "societies" in France have tried, with a great deal of effort, to "sweep away under the carpet", but as with all things, the more something is hidden away, the more it becomes at one time or another found, in this case no doubt through Divine Providence.

<u>Mélanie Calvat:</u>

*It is Lucifer who governs France…**God will give us a hidden King whom no one will think of, and He will give him to us after the scourges**. God alone will give him (to France).*
   *I have never announced the return of the d'Orléans (family), and I would think it a chastisement of God upon France if they sat on the throne… There will be only one herd. **The Holy Pope with the most Christian King will make one in the Faith**. The grand triumph of the Church will be seen under the angelic Pastor (and) with **the terrestrial angel who will be of the descendance of the Martyr King** (Louis XVI).*

<u>Maximin Giraud:</u>

Maximin Giraud, Shepherd of La Salette received secretly the instructions from the Blessed Virgin Mary to reveal the survival of Louis XVII (son of the Martyr King Louis XVI and of Marie-Antoinette) and of his descendance to the Count of Chambord who was thought, at the time, to be the closest member of the Bourbon family to be direct in line to the French Crown. Hence, Maximin went to meet with the noble and most Christian French Count of Chambord at Frohsdorf (Austria).

The secret of Mélanie Calvat, Sister Marie de la Croix, has been published. Everyone can meditate on this document revealed by the Blessed Virgin, a document that liberalism itself no longer dares to attack today, for a Commission of Cardinals has publicly and after due investigation, declared it irreproachable in substance. This revelation given by the Blessed Virgin Mary concerns especially the misfortunes of France and the Papacy.

Maximin's secret, on the other hand, regards the triumph of the Church and the restoration of the French Monarchy. **The message of the shepherd of La Salette was kept sealed and under deep secret by the Vatican, until 1999.** This said, the remarkable secret was revealed through another avenue: the de Vanssay family[3]. This is yet an extraordinary confirmation of the upcoming restoration of the French Monarchy:

Maximin Giraud, some years before his death, went to Froshdorf, Austria, to fulfil a mission entrusted to him by the Lady in the mountains, and to meet with the Count of Chambord, the then thought direct heir to the French throne... At first, Count Henri de Chambord was somewhat hesitant to receive the visionary of La Salette, but upon reading a letter of recommendation, the audience was granted. De Chambord asked his secretary, the Count Henri de Vanssay, to be present during the meeting.

Once the shepherd was introduced to the good Count Henry, the French seer asked his host to speak with him alone. At once, the Count of Vanssay took his leave, but with an imperious hand Henry of France stopped him while gently taking Maximin's arm, leading him towards a window asking him to speak in a low voice. The Count of Vanssay was observing the two men speaking from afar. The exchange lasted a good 20 minutes.

During that time, the Count of Chambord appeared subject to lively emotions... He appeared extremely surprised, even stupefied, then anguished, soon followed by fearful... The Count of Vanssay saw at the end of the meeting the French prince presenting a golden roll which Maximin refused by saying out loud:

"I came to bring a message. I have accomplished my duty. Money would be out of order."

Henry of France insisted that the Shepherd accept at least the trip expenses to which Maximin finally accepted.

After the meeting was concluded, the Count of Chambord came to walk down the property's park with the Count de Vanssay who was following him from a short distance... As he was walking on the property's garden, the Count of Chambord appeared absorbed with his hands behind his back, exclaiming:

---

[3] The Count of de Vanssay was the personal secretary and friend of the Count Henri de Chambord, who was in the late 19th century the direct heir to the Crown of France in the event of a French Restoration (which did not take place for reasons which will be revealed herein).

"Oh... that's extraordinary!... but no, it's impossible!... It couldn't be! This couldn't happen! What a revelation!"

Shortly after this remarkable encounter, The Count Henri de Chambord had a rich marble alter built in the Basilica of Our Lady of La Salette. But what is even less known is the confidence that the Count of Chambord did his faithful secretary. Indeed, on the day of the meeting between Maximin and the French Prince, the Count of Vanssay, observing the extraordinary scene, wrote his family a letter describing this extraordinary event:

I saw that the Count of Chambord was moved and spoke at length and with a great deal of kindness to the young visionary. When Maximin left the room, profoundly moved, the Prince turned towards me:

Now I have the certitude that my cousin Louis XVII exists; I shall not sit on the Throne of France, but God wants us to keep this secret. It is He alone who reserves Himself (the right) to re-establish La Royauté (French Royalty).

And the Count of Vanssay added a couple more lines for his nephews and grand-nephews:

"Most of all, let them keep the hope that one day God will bring back on the Throne of France the Descendant of the Lys (Fleur de Lys) whose head was cut off, and that our Motherland, eldest daughter of the Church, will find again its greatness and its glory of yesteryears."

Secret on Two Future
Popes in the 20th Century

Rev. Father Malachi Martin revealed that a sentence from the Secret of La Salette has been universally erased as per instructions of a contemporary Vatican authority who, he insisted would remain nameless... This sentence, according to the well-known Jesuit exorcist, stated:

In the course of the next century, there will be two worm-ridden popes...

The Church's formal approval of the apparition of our Lady of La Salette:

Mgr. De Bruillard, Bishop of Grenoble, named two commissions to examine the dossier of the La Salette apparition, and it was at last in September 1851 that Mgr. Bruillard officially recognized this apparition case. Here is an excerpt of the official document issued by the Dioceses of Grenoble on September 19, 1851:

"A most extraordinary event which appeared to be incredible, was announced to us five years ago as having taken place on the mountains of our dioceses. It was nothing less than an apparition of the Holy Virgin who, it was said, showed herself to two shepherds on September 19, 1846. She would have told them of sorrowful events that threatened her people, mostly because of blasphemes and of the profanation of the day of Sunday, and she would have confided to each one of them a particular secret with the prohibition to reveal them to anyone.

Maximin Giraud and Mélanie Calvat in La Salette

Mélanie Calvat (1903)

Drawing of the apparition of Our Lady of La Salette to Maximin Giraud and Mélanie Calvat

Louis XVII   **Count Henri de Chambord**

King Louis XVII   **Marie-Antoinette and the little princes**

Despite the natural candor of the two shepherds, despite the impossibility of a
concert between two ignorant children and who barely knew each other; despite
the constant firmness of their testimony which have never changed, neither

51

before human justice nor before thousands of people who have exhausted every means of seduction to have them fall into contradiction or to obtain the revelation of their secret, we have had to show ourselves difficult to admit as incontestable an event which seemed to us ever so wonderful...

While our Episcopal charge forced us the duty to temporize, to think, to implore with fervor the lights of the Holy Spirit, the number of prodigious facts which were being published from every direction was always growing. They announced extraordinary healings, operated in diverse parts of France and abroad, even in countries far away. They were sick patients, desperate and condemned by doctors to a soon to come death or to perpetual infirmities who, it was said, were returned to perfect health as a result to the invocation of Our Lady of La Salette, and following the usage of a source of water upon which the Queen of Heaven appeared to the two shepherds.

An another fact which appeared to us a prodigy is the affluence, hardly believable but nevertheless above all contestation which has taken place on this mountain in different times, but especially on the anniversary of the apparition; an affluence which is quite surprising in view of the distance and other difficulties that such a pilgrimage represents...

- *(Hence) Considering in the first place the impossibility where we are to explain the fact of La Salette in any other way than through Divine Intervention (...)*
- *Considering in the second place that the following wonderful events from La Salette are the testimony of God Himself, manifesting Himself through miracles, and that this testimony is superior to men's and to their objections.*
- *Considering that these two motives hereinabove taken separately, and for greater reasons together must dominate all the questions while taking away all sorts of value to any pretentions or contrary suppositions which we declare to have perfect knowledge of.*
- *Considering that the docility and submission to the warnings of Heaven may preserve us from new chastisements from which we are threatened, while a prolonged resistance may expose us to plagues without remedies... we declare the following:*

FIRST ACT: *We judge the Apparition of the Holy Virgin to two Shepherds on 19 September 1846 on the mountain of the Alp chain, situated in the parish of La Salette, of the Archiprêtre of Corps, carries in itself all the characteristics of truth which the faithful are founded to believe as indubitable and certain.*

SECOND ACT: *We believe that this fact has acquired a new degree of certitude through the immense and spontaneous participation of the faithful on the places of Apparition, and the multitude of prodigies which have followed said event and which is impossible to revoke without violating the rules of human testimony.*

THIRD ACT: *This is why, to testify to God and to the Glorious Virgin Mary our profound gratefulness, we authorize the cult of Our Lady of La Salette.*

Done in Grenoble, on 19 September 1851 (fifth anniversary of the renowned Apparition)

As a follow-up to this official declaration, Rome favored as well the devotion to Our Lady of La Salette.

1. A writ of 3 September 1852 grants a plenary indulgence, once a year, to all those who visit the Church of Our Lady of La Salette.
2. An indult of 2 December 1852, by which his Holiness Pius IX grants permission to solemnize every year on September 19th, the anniversary of the apparition, or the following Sunday, in all the churches of the Diocese of Grenoble, with a solemn Mass and the song of vespers in honor of the Blessed Virgin.
3. The elevation of the pilgrimage church of La Salette as a minor Basilica and, in 1879, the coronation of the statue of Our Lady of La Salette. This ceremony took place on 21 August 1879.

In 1937, Rome deigned to favor the Reconciliation of sinners, by granting 500 days of indulgences to the recitation of the Recollection, and of '300 days to the invocation':

"Our Lady of La Salette, Reconciler of Sinners, pray without ceasing for us who have recourse to you."

The Church Hides the Secret of La Salette

Shortly after the death of both seers, the secret given by Our Lady of La Salette mysteriously disappeared... It was widely whispered that the local bishop, irritated by the unflattering message given by the Virgin Mary about the French Clergy, did away with the revelation given to the two young shepherds; however, over a century later, on 2 October 1999, a French priest named Fr. Cotteville was doing research work in the depths of the Vatican's underground library, when by sheer accident he discovered an old box containing old folders and carefully tied up papers.

The outside of one of these boxes bore the dates of the pontificate of Leo XIII. But inside were folders from the time of Pius IX. One of them contained the whole dossier of La Salette with all its original documents, including the several manuscripts of the secrets! Finally, the original Secrets of La Salette given to Pope Pius IX in 1851—**buried for more than one century in the Vatican archives**—were at last discovered... by accident!

Fr. Cotteville marveled at the old documents of the newly-opened package. Unfortunately, the bell rang to close the period of consultations. As he returned to his residence with an inexpressible joy, Fr. Cotteville began to study those documents in detail in order to dispel all the doubts that lingered about the matter. The results of that work soon became the cornerstone of the thesis he successfully defended at Rome's celebrated Dominican Order's Faculty of Theology of the Angelicum.

That thesis, with more than one thousand pages, was initially written with the assistance and collaboration of Abbot René Laurentin (see page: 418), world renowned French Mariologian, and published with him a remarkable book entitled: **The Great News of the Shepherds of La Salette**. The book carries the Imprimatur of Mgr. Michel Dubost, Bishop of Evry, and *nihil obstat* from Dom Bernard Billet, of the Abbey of Notre Dame of Tournay.

The French Fayard Publications have published **The Great News of the Shepherds of La Salette** in April 2002, and its content, it was quickly enough argued, was a most taboo subject to the Catholic Church: the elucidation on the question of the authenticity of the Secret of La Salette, known especially in its last version, the one of 1879 which had received the *imprimatur* of Bishop Zola, bishop of Lecce in Italy.

Our Lady of La Fraudais pronounced herself as well over forty years after the apparition to the two little French shepherds on the mountain of La Salette to the stigmatist Marie-Julie Jahenny:

(...) I have truly suffered when holy shepherds-priest wanted the last lines of my secrets, on the mountains of sorrows, to be known by all my people, (while) other shepherds revolted (against that idea)...

I had the painful sorrow to see placed under seal these last pages which should have been delivered to the world... It is because it involves a great deal of shepherds and the priesthood that they have revolted (against my instructions) and that they folded the last pages of this divine secret... How can you expect for the chastisement not to befall earth?

They go as far as enveloping my last words on the holy mountain and to have them disappear! (They go as far) as making suffer those who devoted themselves for this holy cause with the joy to glorify me in this solemn prediction. It's because these last lines are all about the priesthood, and it was because it was I who pronounced them, who revealed them, (that) pride was mortified. I show how they serve my Son in the holy Orders, and how they live in all times in their priesthood. How can you expect Heaven to bless them? I do not speak of all shepherds, of all of priesthood, but the number I am exempting is truly small.

They let all the souls wonder (blindly) in utter emptiness. They take care in a very small manner of their salvation. They like rest, good food and good living... My dear victim priests; the true ones are truly few... They love the Holy Tribunal with indifference. They walk up the Altar because they are forced to accomplish this act, but you will see soon their joy for not having to do so any longer; you will see their happiness to be discharged of souls and of their forgiveness. What vain words! What conversations that are ever so unpleasant to Heaven!

What will they (the priests) **be on the great day? What will they be in those horrible and unforgettable days? I do not repeat the bad part that you know of my secrets given on the holy mountain.**

(The Blessed Virgin Mary to Marie-Julie Jahenny, 4 August 1904)

I prayed, I cried, I suffered. I came down on earth to warn them. I promised them salvation if they did penance.

I announced to the Clergy fatal perditions. I had them receive my warnings if it weakens in the storm and tempest. I cried upon France. I trace thereupon the Way of the Cross I opened fountains to cleanse the sick (i.e., Lourdes). **I consoled my people promising it to keep it save. This hasn't touched the guilty one. He remained in crime. His chastisement is close at hand.**

(The Blessed Virgin Mary to Marie-Julie Jahenny, 29 November 1877)

I still have on my eyes the trace of my tears that I shed on these days when I wanted to bring to my children the good news if they converted, and the sad news if they persisted in their inequities. They paid little heed to what I revealed...

My children, when I recall the day when, on the holy mountain, I brought forth my warnings to earth... when I remember the harshness with which they received my words, not all of them but many of them; and (when I remember) those who should have spread them in the hearts of my children with immense trust and deep discernment, they have not listened (to me). They despised them, and, for the greater part of them, they refused to trust them... Well, I assure you that all these promises, these intimate secrets, will take place. They must visibly take place.

When I see what will happen on earth, I still shed tears...

When the earth will have been purified by the chastisements of its crimes and of all the vices it is dressed with, beautiful days will return with the savior chosen by us and unknown yet by our children until now (i.e., King Henry V of the Cross).

(The Blessed Virgin Mary to Marie-Julie Jahenny, 29 September 1901)

Conclusion

The revelations of the full secrets of La Salette were at last revealed publicly under John Paul II, and the world was told through various publications of the full message of the Blessed Virgin Mary *(it was said that the message of La Salette was the holy Father's favorite nightstand reading)*, but few, ever so few prelates, pastors and priests around the world echoed Heaven's warning to the faithful under the reason that the message was over 150 years old and thus was no longer relevant in the 21st century, or simply that the message is "too sensationalistic" for what is too often considered a child-like audience...

But again, is this restraint truly wise? Do the Pope and his vicars around the world know better than Heaven to remain in such a way silent and almost indifferent to these insistent and repetitive exhortations from Heaven? Since practically none of Our Lord's and our Blessed Mother's admonitions are being actively echoed, the immense majority of the faithful remain in the dark and are barely aware of the messages and warnings brought forth by the apparitions of Our Lord Jesus-Christ and of the Blessed Virgin Mary, even the most contemporary ones such as Akita, or through revelations in the 20th century to mystics and saints such as Padre Pio, Father Pel, Father Constant, etc., all of which, confirm the same omens to come, as that of La Salette, La Fraudais and Fatima.

Yet with ignorance of the facts comes lack of prayers, lack of required penance and lack of conversion! The Church's stubbornness, blindness and misplaced pride refuses to pay heed to an urgent message which was not addressed to Popes, nor to the Church's high Hierarchy alone, but unquestionably and principally to all the peoples and countries in the 19th, 20th, and 21st centuries.

The prophetic revelations of La Salette are truly nothing short of being extraordinary. Indeed, the prophecies of wars to come, and the origins and coming of an antichrist are alone quite chilling and remarkably unsettling; however, the message of hope is not absent in the message of La Salette, for we are told that a man, a son of France predestined by Divine Providence, is to come forth and restore, from the ashes of a corrupted republic, a reborn kingdom of France destined to become the returned prodigal daughter of the Church. This savior, we are told, would be of the Royal House of France and a direct descendent of their Royal Highnesses Louis XVI and Marie-Antoinette. This grand secret was to be revealed, upon the precise instruction of our Lady of La Salette, to the noble Count of Chambord. The French prince, grandson of King Charles X, First in line to the Crown, was offered in 1871 – after the fall of the Second French Empire – the French Throne by a newly reconstituted assembly preoccupied in maintaining, amongst never-ending political divisions, a unified nation under a newly recognized Crown. Henry de Chambord was called to take his place as the new King of France..., but, as he received the secret message from our Lady of La Salette on April of 1865, the good Count realized that he would not, should not, ascend to the throne of France, and thus used the political debate involving the change of the French colors as a false pretext to refuse the Crown:

- *"Now I have the certitude that my cousin Louis XVII exists;*
  I shall not sit on the Throne of France, but God wants us to keep this
  *secret. It is He alone who reserves Himself (*the right*) to re-establish*
  *La Royauté (*French Royalty*)."*

(Count of Chambord, April, 1865)

And the Count of Vanssay, in a private letter to his family, confirmed this extraordinary secret:

"Most of all, let them keep the hope that one day God will bring back on the Throne of France the Descendant of the Lys (Fleur de Lys) whose head was cut off, and that our Motherland, eldest daughter of the Church, will find again its greatness and its glory of yesteryears."

When his Holiness Pope Paul VI stated that "the smoke of Satan has entered the Church...", it is widely rumored that he already knew that outside reformist lobbies, secular, and anti-Marian groups and secret societies had inserted themselves inside the Vatican lobbies, dioceses, convents, monasteries and seminaries around the world with the objective to impose a more globalist, socio-communist and ecumenical approach to Catholicism for the Church to sponsor no longer a sole Faith, a sole Dogma founded on the Gospel brought forth by Our Lord Jesus-Christ, but rather a conglomeration of beliefs and cults from different denominations and creeds.

Was it perhaps the reason why Pope Paul VI abolished Canons 1399, § 5 and § 2318 of the old Canon Law Code which prohibited the publication of books relating to new apparitions, visions, prophecies and miracles (October 14, 1966 Decree of the Congregation for the Doctrine of the Faith, Acta Apostolicae Sedis, September 29, 1966, page 1186? This appears today more and more likely...

Chapter II

The prophecies and messages of La Fraudais

(Notre Dame de la Bonne Garde)
(Our Lady of Good Guard)

"My children, make the Way of the Cross, which, in next to no time, will bring many souls to Heaven… Receive often Holy Communions, and say the rosary."

Unquestionably, one of the most remarkable Marian apparition case in Church History, the case of La Fraudais has been approved, although informally through a signed letter of Nantes' local bishop, Mgr. Fournier on 6 June 1875. The apparitions of the Blessed Virgin Mary to the Breton stigmatist Marie-Julie Jahenny (1850–1941) was unquestionably the most detailed and complete case ever studied in the annals of Marian apparitions' History. Hence, the second chapter of this book will undoubtedly be the most important one along with that of La Salette, Lourdes, Tilly, Fatima and Akita as all six apparition cases perfectly complement one another.

Although the apparitions of La Fraudais have taken place well after that of La Salette and those of Lourdes, it has continuously occurred before, while and after those of Fatima. The astonishing messages of Our Lord Jesus-Christ, of the Blessed Virgin Mary, of St. Michael the Archangel and of multitudes of saints, represent a most capital piece of the overall message and prophetic warnings issued in the period of time beginning in 1873 until 1941.

Indeed, if any doubt remained as to the relevancy of these extraordinary and yet alarming messages for our times, the contemporary Church-approved apparitions of Our Lady of Akita, Japan (1973–1981), which came to an end exactly forty years after Marie-Julie Jahenny's passing away, confirm the severe forewarning to Humanity given in La Salette and Fatima, a prophetic admonition addressed first to the Roman Catholic Church, but above all to all of mankind, a pressing and most startling message which was purposely ignored, feared and, in utter disobedience to Heaven's orders, carefully hidden for decades by a Holy See that thought "knowing better".

However, there were those who, faithful to themselves and to God, accepted being made an instrument of God's Will. Such a man was Monsignor Fournier, Bishop of Nantes, who approved, permitted and encouraged the public revelations of the messages received by Marie-Julie Jahenny near the little town of Blain, France.

Statement from Monsignor Fournier, Bishop of Nantes, about Marie-Julie Jahenny

The reports that I receive daily on Marie-Julie show me more and more the action of God on this soul. He grants her graces of an obvious supernatural order. At the same time she grows in virtue and noble sentiments. The natural and human disappear in her, and she often speaks to people she sees or who are referred to her, giving instructions which are not in keeping with her normal state.

(...) She is sincere. What she manifests is supernatural. I see nothing but good, edifying and in conformity with the principles of spirituality. Therefore it

is God who favors her.

(Mgr. Fournier, Bishop of Nantes, on 6 June 1875)

Marie-Julie Jahenny was born in Coyault on 12 February 1850, in the village of Blain in Brittany, France. Her parents, Charles and Marie Boya, had five children of which she was the oldest. When she was but a toddler, her parents moved into a cottage in a hamlet in the southwestern part of Brittany called La Fraudais, northeast of Blain where she lived until the end of her life in 1941.

For Marie-Julie Jahenny, everything began on 6 January 1873. A few days before her twenty-third birthday, the young Breton woman grew seriously ill and was diagnosed with a scrofulo-cancerous tumor... Soon enough, Marie-Julie's physical health quickly worsened to the brink of death itself... On 15 January Abbot David, Marie-Julie's confessor and Vicar of Blain, was quickly convoked to administer her the last rights; however, her time had not yet come, and on 22 February, Marie-Julie suddenly sat upright on her death-bed and saw the Blessed Virgin Mary assuring her with warmth and love that she would be healed.

As Marie-Julie Jahenny quickly and unexplainably recovered, she dedicated hours of her days before the holy Tabernacle of her village's church. One day, upon an apparition of the Blessed Virgin Mary, Marie-Julie was asked if she would be willing to suffer the Passion of her Son for the conversion and redemption of sinners, and for France. Without hesitation, the young French woman accepted and embraced the mission to become a victim-soul. The agonies she accepted to undergo were foretold in advance and were bestowed gradually with time, allowing the young woman to prepare, and surely enough, on Friday, 21 March 1873, with two hundred people present, her first stigmatization took place!

Our Lord Jesus-Christ appeared to Marie-Julie at 9:00 AM with His Five Wounds dazzling brightly... From each one of them a blinding light would come striking her body. Five times Marie Julie shook, and five times she lost consciousness... Then, after recovering her senses, Jesus addressed her and said:

My dear child, this wound will serve to convince men. They will try to erase it but they will not be able to do so. I shall confuse them. When the wounds will be almost erased, I shall thrust the nails deeper therein, and the nails will leave a sharper mark.

(Our Lord Jesus-Christ to Marie-Julie Jahenny, 21 March 1873)

Marie-Julie received all five wounds on 21 March 1873, the Crown of thorns on 5 October 1873; on 25 November of the same year, she showed the same Wound Our Lord suffered on His left shoulder when He carried His Cross... Remarkably enough, these were not the only sufferings Marie-Julie Jahenny accepted and welcomed. On 6 December 1873, the dreadful Wounds of Our

60

Lord's Scourging could clearly be seen on her back... Likewise, on 12 January 1874, the young French stigmatist received painful marks on her wrists where Our Lord's hands were held bound, along with a somewhat curious wound over her heart.

Two days after that, she received additional scourge marks on her ankles, legs and forearms on the same day an epigraphic stigma appeared over her heart... Two days thereafter, she suffered two particular scourge stripes on her side. Marie-Julie was more and more drawn to the tabernacle and would spend long hours of prayer in church, or find a quiet place to pray and meditate. Her devotion and calling had her enter in the Third Order of St. Francis of Assisi where she was noted by one and all to be a model of piety, modesty, and spiritual perfection. As the months went on, her gradual stigmata and the apparitions of Our Lord and of the Blessed Virgin Mary were becoming more and more numerous.

As such, it began to be widely whispered in the neighboring villages and in the city of Nantes that God had sent His Blessed Mother to visit France yet again, this time through young Marie-Julie Jahenny of La Fraudais! Monsignor Fournier, the local regional Bishop, quickly got word of the rumors that were running about the extraordinary and pious young woman. Consequently, in view of the stigmatas and of the alleged apparitions the young woman had received, Mgr. Fournier ordered an immediate formal investigation on the gradual appearances of Marie-Julie's stigmata and on her "alleged" ecstasies...

Likewise, the French bishop appointed a medical inquiry headed by a renowned and celebrated Professor from the prestigious Faculty of Medicine of Clermont-Ferrand, Doctor Imbert-Gourbeyre.

In September of 1873, Marie-Julie Jahenny's stigmata continued to develop. Her hands began to bleed front and back (as if a nail had pierced them), and she received the stigmata of the Crown of Thorns seven months thereafter... On 5 October and on 5 November 1873, Marie-Julie confided into her newly appointed spiritual director, Abbot David, Vicar of the village of Blain, and told him:

Our Good Lord will come in an apparition. He will ask me if I have renounced to all the pleasures of the world and to all that is loved on earth. On that day, I shall detach myself of everything. I shall be Christ's fiancée. The Blessed Virgin Mary also told me:

You shall see the world through a thick cloud, and on your right hand there will be a ring made-up of your flesh.

The Passion of Our Lord manifested itself on her body by degrees of intensity, but, as she was foretold by the Blessed Virgin Mary, a new wound appeared on the ring finger of her right hand on 20 February 1874. This, she was told, was a wedding ring of blood under the finger's skin, thus showing that she had been chosen by Our Lord as His Spiritual Spouse.

Having witnessed the extraordinary announcement become a reality early the following year, Abbot David, wrote to Dr. Imbert-Gourbeyre:

Praise be to God! Deo gratias! Yesterday we had the most consoling day possible. Everything that was announced last April has occurred... I had organized everything according to Monsignor's orders (Mgr. Fournier's): *14 men as witnesses. Three from Nantes sent by the diocese. At 8:30 am, we saw that the wounds were dry; that the ring finger of the right hand was normal, pale as death and no trace of a ring.*

After 9:00 am, bleeding of all the wounds... Towards 9:15 am, we noticed the finger swelling and reddening under the skin. Towards 9:45 am, blood flowed above and below the finger, and little by little we saw the ring taking shape. It is now well marked for all her life... Monsignor (Fournier) is enthusiastic.

(Letter from Abbot David to Dr. Imbert-Gourbeyre, 20 February 1874)

Abbot David wrote the following description of the young woman's wedding ring appearance:

Made of flesh, similar as a red coral ring entrenched inside the skin. She will say having been blessed directly by the Lord.

As the supernatural events were increasing at La Fraudais, the Bishop of Nantes, Mgr. Fournier, began to take a personal interest in the stigmatist who was becoming the subject of so much talk in the entire region; hence on 18 July 1874, the French bishop visited for the first time the young stigmatist. He quickly became emotionally touched by this first meeting which was to establish his firm conviction in the authenticity of Marie-Julie's experiences.

Indeed, after having witnessed the young woman re-living the Holy Passion in ecstasy, he presented her some relics whose origins Marie-Julie divulged without mistake. One of these relics was a cross made in the famous apparition site of Paray-le-Monial[4]. Marie-Julie put it to her lips without looking at it and said: "*Marguerite-Marie...*" (Margaret-Mary). The good French bishop was utterly astonished as this was the name of Paray-le-Monial's famous visionary and saint... How could she have known?

Bishop Fournier returned to Nantes, leaving for instructions the theological, medical and scientific investigation to pursue its course while recording every single occurrence related to Marie-Julie Jahenny's extraordinary experiences and revelations.

The last and most astounding stigmata Marie-Julie received was on 7 December 1874 seen by many witnesses, a wound that, it appeared, had never manifested itself with other stigmatists of the Church before: a cross and a flower on her chest with the words **O Crux Ave** (Hail to the Cross), perfumed by an extraordinary fragrance emanating from her body.

---

[4] Paray-le-Monial: Apparition site in a small town of the Bourgogne region, in eastern France, where the Sacred Heart of Jesus-Christ appeared to Margaret-Mary Alacoque in the late 17th Century. Apparition calling for the spreading of the devotion to the Sacred Heart.

When Marie-Julie Jahenny was asked of the visions she saw when she received the stigmata, she answered:

When I received the stigmata, Our Lord appeared to me with radiant wounds, it was as if a sun surrounded them. A luminous ray came out of each Wound and struck my hands, feet and side; at the end of each ray there was a drop of red Blood. The ray that left the side of Our Lord was twice as wide as the others and was shaped like a lance. The pain I felt was great, but it lasted barely one second.

The bewildered doctor quickly observed that Marie-Julie's wounds were not of a natural origin nor self-inflicted, and were indeed... *supernatural in origin...* Doctor Imbert-Gourbeyre wrote his findings to Bishop Fournier, stating that:

There is no fraud in La Fraudais. This young woman has embraces suffering. There is in her a (certain) predisposition to which one must add a prophetic spirit.

It was especially in that Marie-Julie Jahenny revealed herself completely. She disrobed her soul, her frankness, her love for God, for her enemies and for her closed ones. Likewise, she displayed her love for suffering, for the Eucharist, her extraordinary devotion to the Blessed Virgin, her respect of priests, her faithfulness to the Church, her generosity to suffer for the conversion of sinners and for the Glory of the Lord. Her ecstasies are the most beautiful proof of her soul's excellence.

Bishop Fournier also agreed with the good doctor's findings as seen by a letter he wrote to him on 6 June 1875:

The reports that I receive daily on Marie-Julie show me more and more the action of God on this soul. He grants graces of an obvious supernatural order. At the same time she grows in virtue and noble sentiments. The natural and human disappear in her, and she often speaks to people she sees or who are referred to her giving instructions which are not in keeping with her normal state (in life). Therefore be confident, dear Doctor, the time will come when Marie-Julie herself will be the proof... She is sincere: what she manifests is supernatural. I see nothing but good, edifying and in conformity with the principles of spirituality. Therefore it is God who favors her, you may be sure it will turn out well.

As such, a new name was given to her, for she humbly stated during an ecstasy dated 14 March 1876 that St. Francis of Assisi appeared to her with a white stone, apparently a great cornerstone for the great and holy work of the Cross that was to begin at La Fraudais. Our Lord blessed the stone, and angels brought a book displaying Marie-Julie's new name in golden letters:

Marie-Julie Jahenny:

I see, my dear Spouse, this place marked where I am going to keep in your presence. This stone is a white carved stone brought from Heaven by my Seraphic Father (St. Francis of Assisi). Our Lord has blessed it, angels surround it. Other angels bring an open book, written in letters of gold and blood. I see signed my name at the top of the book. Tell me what that means; I see my name: **Marie-Julie of the Crucifix**.

Marie-Julie then revealed that the mystic book would not be opened until seven months after her death (October 1941), only then would the work of the Cross that started during her lifetime begin to spread throughout the world.

As if to proclaim Marie-Julie in her mission as a victim-soul and spouse of Christ, the Eternal Father asked her on 1 August 1876 what was her name:

I am Marie-Julie of the Crucifix, virgin of the Cross, the great sign of the sinful; I, Madeleine repentant, contrite, penitent and forgiven, my dear Spouse who promised grace to whom He gave the flower. He made me His spouse. It is I who He will soon reap the harvest of the Cross, of suffering, of the Eucharist. (...)

A few months later, Our Lord would call her by her new given name, as seen in His apparition to her on 22 February 1877:

Marie-Julie of the Crucifix, come and stay in My loving Wound.

In humility, Marie-Julie was afraid to approach the Wound in His Heart due to her human misery, but Our Lord invited her yet again:

Come, My crucified spouse, come to receive these sweet consolations. Our Lord added: **You are My highest elect**.

Our Lord would later reveal to Marie-Julie her mission on 27 October 1887 with St. Margaret-Mary at His side:

(Speaking to St. Margaret-Mary):
Victim of My Sacred Heart...

(Then addressing Marie-Julie):
And you, victim of My Cross. You are not chosen for the same work. Blessed Margaret-Mary was chosen to publish the glory of My Sacred Heart, and you, you are chosen to publish the glory of My Cross. She is the victim of My Sacred Heart, you are the victim of My Cross. The Work of My Cross is beautiful and grand, it will quickly follow the Work of the Sacred Heart.

(Our Lord Jesus-Christ, 27 October 1887)

Twelve years before, Our Lord promised the Breton seer:

I will not be long in making known to you My secrets. Soon the secret will be discovered and the whole world will witness My love and My Power.

(Our Lord Jesus-Christ, 25 June 1875)

Our Lord further promised:

I will operate greater miracles for you than for your sister Margaret-Mary.

(Our Lord Jesus-Christ, 28 June 1875)

In her living-years, Marie-Julie always received the support and assistance of Monsignor Fournier, and years later of one of his successor, Monsignor Le Fer de la Motte—doctor in theology and in philosophy at the Academy Saint-Thomas d'Aquin, bachelor in Canonic Law, Laureate of various international religious science competitions—who became bishop of Nantes in 1914. Both French bishops visited and talked to the French visionary and stigmatist often at La Fraudais, always returning to Nantes moved to the core.

Mgr. Fournier, after stating on 6 June 1875, that Marie-Julie Jahenny's case was supernatural and from God, even went to Rome to present her cause. The medical investigation on Marie-Julie Jahenny continued for years onwards with Doctor Imbert-Gourbeyre's continued well recorded observations.

Marie-Julie's stigmata bled every Friday, then later, only on Good Fridays, but the pain of the various wounds continued to increase systematically, particularly on Fridays... All the stigmatas displayed were always announced beforehand. On All Saints Day 1884, Our Lord declared He would envelope Marie-Julie with a coat of light, a prophecy which was fulfilled that December on the Feast Day of the Immaculate Conception. Her family witnessed indeed a stream of light, about the size of a pea, radiate from the wounds in her hands for what appeared to last an eternity: five minutes.

And yet, Marie-Julie was willing to suffer further for the salvation of sinners and for France, thus she was inflicted with utterly unexplainable sickness and physical agonies... One such instance began in June 1880: she particularly suffered extreme pains during her ecstasies on Mondays, Tuesdays and Thursdays of each week, predicting each time what manner of suffering she would undergo. Naturally, Doctor Imbert-Gourbeyre was never far, and was always recording and writing all the occurrences, always in utter astonishment... We have one of his texts dated September 1880 describing one such period of atonement:

During the Way of the Cross, the preceding Friday (September 24, 1880), Our Lord appeared and addressed Marie-Julie who repeated His words during her ecstasy. The message was recorded by a secretary:

On Monday, to expiate the culpable offences that I shall receive and that I have already received this month, I will oppress you in a different way. All your limbs will shrink, I will reduce you to being so small that you will have no freedom in any limb; your head will be fixed to your bones, and you will be like the worm that I destroy. In this pain your sufferings will be very violent, all your joints will suffer. With this pain you will have a burning fever. Your tongue will be swollen, very large. There will be a visible swelling at all the joints of your bones and this will show how strong the pain is.

(Our Lord Jesus-Christ, 24 September 1880)

All this prophetic program was to take place before my eyes. This took place on Monday September 27, 1880... A few days after having assisted at these extraordinary sufferings, I heard Marie-Julie announce in front of me in profound ecstasy that she would soon have a new and long illness. In the preceding six months, she had often said that God had asked her for the complete sacrifice of her ears, eyes, speech and movement. She accepted everything...

(Doctor Imbert-Gourbeyre's medical journal, September 1880)

The complete offering of her senses began later that year, which she foretold again on 19 December. Each sense, however, was affected gradually. On the Tuesday after her prediction, Marie-Julie lost her speech and her hearing. Three days afterwards, she became blind. The suffering also included a strange transformation of her tongue, which became immovable, hard as a rock, and completely pushed backwards with the tip bent under, completely blocking her throat... Her mouth then closed shut, her lips remained motionless. However, she was released from this oddity shortly thereafter. On 10 February 1881 she announced the next stages of her excruciating martyrdom. Our Lord asked her if she was willing to suffer again, and she accepted. He then replied:

Well, from next Monday, you will no longer be able to stay on your stake, (i.e., possibly a reference to the mystical 'gibbet' on which she had suffered up to then) **... all your limbs will become disjointed, but without changing position. All the limbs on your left side, from the sole of your feet to the top of your head, will no longer move. (...) You will stay in your armchair, there; new crucifixions of sufferings will come to keep you company, one by one.**

This agony lasted for many years; what's more, a series of other phenomena, that were physically unexplainable, took place at the same time. On one occasion, her family members wanted to move her so as to make her somewhat more comfortable, and, in the process of doing so, found she was heavier than a stone and thus were unable to lift her from her chair[5]... Seeing her family's

---

[5] **Similar occurrences took place years later in the little Spanish village of Garabandal, Spain, to the children/visionaries in the 1960s (see Chapter VII).**

anxiety, Marie-Julie would give her kinsmen a time at which they could move her, but until then she remained unmovable.

When the appointed time came, she mysteriously became light as a feather… Likewise, despite her deafness, she could hear and understand the priest present when he would speak or pray in Latin, a remarkable marvel as she was uneducated and not knowledgeable in foreign languages, let alone Latin… Notwithstanding, Our Lord informed her she would be able to speak during her ecstasies, and her tongue was indeed softened as promised; however, once the ecstasies were over, her tongue resumed unexplainably its hardened condition…

Despite what appears as a severe harshness upon the devoted Breton woman, Heaven granted her brief periods of mobility every Friday at 9:00 in the morning, allowing the linens and her clothes to be changed. Marie-Julie was allowed as well full function of her person for her customary "Way of the Cross" at 1:00 in the afternoon, wherein she literally relived, while in ecstasy, the Passion of Jesus-Christ in Jerusalem. Immediately upon the conclusion of the last Station of the Cross, Marie-Julie's paralysis returned and each mystical ailment progressively resumed… This period of martyrdom lasted for four continuous years, according to Doctor Imbert-Gourbeyre who further reported:

First the hemiplegia disappeared, then in succession the dumbness, the deafness, and the blindness.

All the circumstances of this symptom (of contracture) prove that it is was not of a hysterical nature. Besides, who has ever seen … a contracture that ceases regularly every Friday for several hours, to allow the subject to talk and walk in ecstasy? The observation of the Breton virgin dispels all the observations of known hysteria. It is enough to be a doctor to understand.

Before proceeding in the further descriptions of Marie-Julie's experiences, it is important to underline that, despite what seems to be a cruel and pitiless treatment, Marie-Julie Jahenny was willing and most happy to share in the Passion of Our Lord Jesus-Christ out of an indescribable love for Him. For Marie-Julie, this "finite" suffering was a means of union with He Who has given His Life for humanity and for its redemption.

Although for many, such willing suffering is difficult to understand, this *Cyrene devotion* (in reference to Simon of Cyrene) can only be understood if one understands the profound will of the Breton stigmatist to be one with Christ in the redemption of sinners and of the country of her fathers which fell a century before her time, and which was yet to have its greatest collapse within the next one to come…

Similar to other well-renowned mystics, Marie-Julie Jahenny experienced complete and total periods of fasting wherein she took neither drink nor food while living on the Eucharist alone. The first occasion of such occurrences took place on 12 April 1874 and lasted for 94 days. Marie-Julie then announced the next period of unceasing fasting to begin on 28 December 1875 'for the next five years, one month and 22 days!'

The good Doctor Imbert-Gourbeyre, who was first taken by sheer panic, later recorded with raw consternation that **during the whole of this period there were** *no liquid or solid excretions*; in other words, the impossible... The good doctor was confronted to a volley of miracles all of which simply and utterly defied all known laws of medical science, and yet, others continued to add to what was already an extraordinary series of supernatural marvels... Indeed, Marie-Julie regularly received miraculous Holy Communions that simply appeared out of sheer nothingness.

As these events were foretold and brought to the attention of the dioceses of Nantes, Mgr. Fournier sent immediately witnesses with Doctor Imbert-Gourbeyre to investigate this most remarkable occurrence. The first miraculous Communion took place on 4 June 1874, and again on three separate occasions that year... The next period of miraculous Communions occurred from May 1876 to 29 January 1877, where apparently thirteen holy and miraculous Communions were received during said period time, all of which during her Fridays' ecstasies. These events were formally observed by over 200 witnesses![6]

With the thirteenth Miraculous Communion given on 27 January 1877, came the announcement of a 14th holy reception which was due to take place decades later, on the eve of Marie-Julie's passing-away... Three months later, Marie-Julie witnessed another apparition of Our Lord Jesus-Christ:

- *I look forward to receive You in my fourteenth Communion. My death will deliver Monsignor and my father of their distress...*
- **Do you have trust in your fourteenth Communion?**
- *Yes Lord, yes, yes! It is You who have instituted the Divine Eucharist. Yes, I believe in everything the Holy Church proposes me to believe. It does not make mistakes. Yes I believe in the Eucharist in my fourteenth Communion. I feel great joy thinking about it.*
- **Do you believe in all the revelations I gave you for your death?**
- *Yes I believe in them all, in accordance with my father's judgment, for I am very ignorant.*
- **Do you believe in the triumph of the Church?**
- *Yes, Lord, for You have revealed it to Marguerite-Marie; as for me, I wouldn't trust in my own self alone.*
- **Do you believe in the infallibility of the Church?**
- *Yes, yes, my dear Spouse. The Church is infallible. Our Lord said so to Saint Peter. Yes I believe in the triumph of the Church.*
  (Exchange between Our Lord Jesus-Christ and Marie-Julie Jahenny, 24 April 1877)

Other miracles included bleeding pictures and crucifixes in the visionary's house. One day, Marie-Julie asked Abbot David, if he would bring her a picture of the Crucifixion (see page 434). As he did, Marie-Julie stayed mesmerized in contemplation before it for days.

---

[6] Similar Miraculous Communions were given years later in the little Spanish village of Garabandal, Spain, to visionary Conchita Gonzalez (see Chapter VII).

On 21 January 1877, Our Lord appeared to her during an ecstasy and said:

Oh, you who love Me! See how I suffer ... I pour out My Divine Blood to pay for the sins of France... The picture where I am crucified before which you meditate, will remind you of My suffering. The Divine Blood of My Five Wounds which has just flowed on My cross, will flow on the five wounds of this picture... Tell your Father to collect It... and now come back to earth: You will find My five Wounds bathed in Blood.

(Our Lord Jesus-Christ, 21 January 1877)

Three years later, Fr. Lequeux, the Pastor from Blain witnessed and recorded the miracle involving Our Lord's Sacred Blood. This occurred on the Feast of Corpus Christi, 27 May 1880:

On Thursday I was at La Fraudais at about eleven-thirty. While I was addressing a few words to Marie-Julie on the love of Jesus in the Blessed Sacrament, she went into ecstasy, then all of a sudden she exclaimed:

The Crucifix at the end of my bed is bleeding.

I turned at once and saw on the picture a gush of blood of about two centimeters. I called Angèle, (Marie-Julie's sister) who like me saw the prodigy. While I was occupied looking at the picture I noticed that Marie-Julie had her lips glued to her crucifix and seemed to be drinking. I approached her and clearly saw red blood on the Crucifix and on the lips of our dear victim who said to me as she stretched out her hand:

- **Father, give me quickly my other Crucified Love, your Crucifix.**

I gave it to her and she at once drank in the same fashion. After a few moments, she added:

- **My Jesus tells you to purify the two crucifixes with your consecrated fingers.**

With a blessed cloth I then purified the two crucifixes that were all red with blood. Then Marie-Julie said to me:

- **My Jesus wants you to purify my lips reddened with His Adorable Blood.**

I then took the cloth by each end and pressed it on the lips of the seer.

(Fr. Lequeux, 27 May 1880)

This event could easily shock a reader; it did the author but then, upon pondering in a cold retrospective, I asked myself: *Do we not drink Our Lord's Blood at Mass when the Chalice is offered to us during Holy Communion?* Then, a certain passage of the Gospel came to mind:

I am the living bread that came down from Heaven. If anyone eats of this bread, he will live forever. And the bread that I will give for the life of the world is my flesh.

The Jews then disputed among themselves, saying, 'How can this man give us his flesh to eat?' So Jesus said to them, 'Truly, truly, I say to you, unless you eat the flesh of the Son of Man and drink his blood, you have no life in you. Whoever feeds on my flesh and drinks my blood has eternal life, and I will raise him up on the last day. For my flesh is true food, and my blood is true drink. Whoever feeds on my flesh and drinks my blood abides in me, and I in him. As the living Father sent me, and I live because of the Father, so whoever feeds on me, he also will live because of me. This is the bread that came down from Heaven, not like the bread the fathers ate, and died. Whoever feeds on this bread will live forever.'

(John 6:51–58)

For my flesh is true food, and my blood is true drink. Whoever feeds on my flesh and drinks my blood abides in me, and I in him. Isn't the answer to any concerned soul given in the Gospel of St. John? In addition to this exceptional phenomenon, Marie-Julie Jahenny received countless apparitions of a battalion of saints and angels who gave her great consolation and spiritual advice. Naturally, Our Lord and Our Lady were constant companions, but she also saw the Eternal Father, and the Holy Spirit Who would come in the form of a dove or as a flaming tongue of fire. Likewise, saints often appeared to Marie-Julie giving her great details of their lives on earth, unknown until then by historians and theologians.

Furthermore, some of these saints openly corrected some elements that biographers and chroniclers had mistakenly recorded through the years. Unknown saints also visited her and gave her as well thorough details of their lives. On one occasion, Marie-Julie having grown quite close to St. Joseph, grew perhaps somewhat too familiar with him, teasing him during one ecstasy on 1 April 1880 insisting on having certain petitions granted, until... Our Lord Himself had to intervene and say "Enough!", rescuing thus His foster father from the persistent but profoundly penitent and embarrassed Marie-Julie...

From the texts that have been released to the public, principally by the Marquis de la Franquerie and later by his granddaughter, Mrs. Isabelle Sczcebura, we have the following list of saints and angels who have appeared to the Breton stigmatist:

- St. Joseph
- St. Ann, Mother of Our Lady
- St. Michael the Archangel

70

- St. John the Evangelist
- St. Francis of Assisi
- St. Louis IX, King of France (King St. Louis)
- St. Charlemagne, King of France and first Holy Roman Emperor
- St. Germaine
- St. Alphonsus Liguori
- St. Margaret Mary
- St. Aloysius Gonzaga
- St. Bonaventure
- St. Catherine of Sienna
- St. Thomas Aquinas
- St. Titus
- St. Francis de Sales
- St. John of the Cross
- St. Vincent Ferrier
- St. Paul, Apostle
- St. John Francis Regis
- St. Gregory the Great, Pope
- St. Benedict * St. Lucien (of Antioch?)
- St. Nestor, Bishop and Martyr
- St. Abraham, Hermit
- St. Marcellinus, Martyr
- St. Lambert, Bishop and Martyr
- St. John, Pope and Martyr
- St. Felix, Bishop
- St. Pamphilus, Martyr
- St. Vincent, Martyr
- St. Pantaleon, Martyr
- St. Marisse (Marius), Martyr
- St. Didier (Desiderius), Bishop and Martyr
- St. Primus, Martyr
- St. Dieudonné (Adedodatus I, also Deusdedit), Pope
- St. Vitus, Martyr
- St. Distérique, Bishop (unknown saint?)
- St. Paulinus, Bishop and Martyr
- St. Grelut, apparently, a previously unknown martyr
- St. Victorian, Bishop and Martyr
- St. Hermenegilde, Prince and Martyr
- St. Cassian, Martyr
- St. Jules (Julius), Martyr
- St. Celeste (Celestine?), Martyr
- St. Vitalis of Milan, Martyr
- St. Sergius, Martyr

In certain texts, Marie-Julie said she would see visions in 'the sun'. Was it that she was permitted to see her apparitions through a mystic 'window' shaped like a sun? Likewise, during her ecstasies, Marie-Julie experienced frequent bouts of Xenoglossia[7] and could recite prayers or sing hymns in different languages. Moreover, she was observed immediately coming out of an ecstasy if given the order from her spiritual director or from a religious with canonical authority, even when she was spoken in Latin.

As with all true mystics, she was always obedient to her spiritual superiors and immediately returned from an ecstasy when she was ordered mentally, vocally, or simply in writing. This was witnessed by his Excellency Bishop Fournier on 17 July 1874 in company of the Jesuits Superior and of the Superior's secretary. The Bishop declared the knowledge she received was well beyond her normal state in life. Doctor Imbert-Gourbeyre wrote:

The ecstatic discourses have two principal characteristics: infused science and the prophetic spirit. We have assisted several times Marie-Julie's ecstasies. What a surprise, to hear this simple peasant woman without any instruction, speaking of divine things like an accomplished theologian. She spoke admirably on God, Jesus Christ, the Eucharist, giving mystical instruction, disserting the Cross and the Priesthood, telling the life story of a great number of saints she could not have known, quoting Latin texts from Holy Scripture, reproducing entire passages from the Holy Fathers, making numerous revelations and sometimes rising to an incomparable literary style.

Information about the texts of Marie-Julie's ecstasies

Judging from Abbot Gouron's account, dated 6 November 1878, some specially trusted people would come to La Fraudais and give up their time to come and transcribe the dialogues between Marie-Julie Jahenny and her heavenly visitors as they took place. Abbot Gouron names the scribe, on this day, Monsieur Charbonnier, former notary of Nantes, writing down the messages given to Marie-Julie as quickly as his fingers would allow him; however, the Abbot declared *visitors were forbidden to take notes* (although he did write down an account of his visit which was preserved).

We can assume that by ensuring no visitors penned notes, the Bishop was thus securing the integrity of the messages to be later preserved. Likewise, this was ordered in order to prevent the spread of spurious texts with unofficial additions. Two other scribes were particularly noted for offering ever so often their time to take down the texts of Marie-Julie's ecstasies: Monsieur and Madame Cluzeau.

Attacks from the devil and the years of persecution

Marie-Julie also had to suffer the devil's wiles—or Kéké, as she called him—from the time she first received the stigmata. Indeed, Our Lady warned several times Marie-Julie Jahenny of these assaults to come... One final warning came on 26 April 1874, with the solemn promise that Our Lady would never

---

[7] Xenoglossia: Understanding and speaking languages never learned before.

abandon her in the midst of these new trials. Fifteen minutes after this warning, the devil tried to do his worst... He would beat Marie-Julie and cover her with bruises and cuts, which never grew infected and which would quickly and miraculously heal with holy water. He would destroy her sacramentals, break her rosaries, knock her holy pictures off the walls, throw her crucifix to the floor, plus knock blessed objects to the ground, or, if he didn't destroy them, he would try to inflict some type of damage on said objects.

Sometimes, if witnesses were present, he would try to push them over as well... Likewise, he would try to frighten to death the poor old Breton woman by appearing as a frightening beast, as an animal, or as his usual hideous appearance, threatening by promising that he would eventually succeed in damning her soul, thus trying to force her to abandon her mission to save souls... When terror tactics failed, he immediately changed strategy and would come as a tempting beautiful young man promising her everything from wealth to cures for her illnesses, but again without success.

On other occasions, he would try to fool her during her ecstasies by appearing as angels or saints, but Marie-Julie was extremely cautious about every apparition, testing them all to ensure they were from Heaven and thereby exposing the Hellish imposter with prudence when he did appear in this guileful manner. If a mystical visitor complied and made an Act of Love to the Sacred Heart, she knew the apparition was true. When it was Satan, he would suddenly fly off when she demanded this request.

Sometimes she could easily see through the disguise: if the demon appeared as a saint the halo would be lacking its glorious rays of light, or the symbol of the cross would not be depicted correctly on his clothes or vestments, appearing bent or twisted. These attacks were not without fruits, for they were additional means of sacrifice she could offer to save souls. On other occasions, Marie-Julie could get rid of him by simply sprinkling holy water.

If the devil's attacks were not enough, the time of earthly persecution began as well only a few short years after the stigmata appeared, when Bishop Fournier passed away in June 1877... Indeed, the good French Bishop of Nantes had been the greatest supporter of Marie-Julie Jahenny's cause, declaring everything about her, from the stigmata to her ecstasies and revelations to be from God, and now, he was being replaced by a bishop who adopted an entirely different stand on the stigmatist's case, a stand that quickly translated into Marie-July persecution by the newly elected French bishop...

A little less than a month after Bishop Fournier passed away, the Chapter of Curates gave the order for Marie-Julie to be deprived of the Holy Sacraments, including Holy Communion, an appalling decision upheld by the new bishop of Nantes, Bishop Lecoq, for eleven years and a half... However, despite of the new Bishop's unjust decision, Heaven ensured that Marie-Julie was not deprived of the Holy Sacrament of Communion, for the minute the order came from the Chapter of Curates, the miraculous Communions resumed again and appeared, given by Our Lord Jesus-Christ Himself, every Sunday of every week, and on certain feast days.

An ecclesiastic, present with other fellow-priests during these extraordinary miraculous Communions, described the remarkable events to one of the present scribes in the following manner:

We are all grateful to this attention which we never had before... I am about 50 centimeters from Marie-Julie's face, which is enlightened by the window's light, and I see her two hands joined together upon her chest. All of a sudden, she opens her mouth and presents her tongue. There is nothing there... I bow closer towards her and I can see without difficulty her mouth's rooftop. She closes her mouth. She opens it again and presents once again her tongue. There is still nothing there... Her lips tighten, then she presents her tongue again, but there is still nothing there...

It's unquestionable! There is the proof (that there is nothing to the rumors we've heard)... But a prodigy! Marie-Julie opens again her mouth with humility, when a Host, whiter and brighter than snow, appears there, visible to our eyes! A scream of utter admiration comes out from all our hearts! Marie-Julie closes again her mouth and, on two occasions, opens it for us to look, still showing the Holy Host! Doubt and illusion are no longer possible... At last, her lips close up, only to open one last time showing her tongue empty...

To describe properly to you our emotion is quite impossible! This is (for us) an indescribable feeling. But it is now that Marie-Julie offers us the most delicious of spectacles! Her face lightens-up with a soft splendor; her eyes are slightly closed; a tear is slowly rolling down her cheek. This is a smile from Heaven; and her beauty glows. What joy! This is a bit of Heaven (for us) and this lasted for fifteen minutes!

Doctor Imbert-Gourbeyre further reported that on some occasions during holy Communions, Marie-Julie was observed levitating, suspended in the air about 30 centimeters (11 13/16 inches) above her bed! Doctor Imbert-Gourbeyre continued his observations and daily reports of the French stigmatist to bishop Lecoq, and remained her faithful and valiant defender, going relentlessly to the diocese of Nantes and explaining to the hostile bishop that his predecessor had ruled everything pertaining to Marie-Julie as being of a supernatural and heavenly origin. Notwithstanding, the new bishop remained deaf and utterly indifferent to Doctor Imbert-Gourbeyre's truly heroic testimonies, explanations, and reports:

Letter of Doctor Imbert-Gourbeyre to Bishop Lecoq:

The stigmatist of La Fraudais has received a good many miraculous Communions. The first One was on 4 June 1874, followed by three more during the same year. From the beginning of May 1876 to 29 January 1877, there were thirteen communions during the Friday ecstasy which were seen by over two hundred people. Marie-Julie knew beforehand by revelation the day the miraculous communion of Fridays was to take place... On that day, the witnesses, having been warned in advance, were admitted in the cottage; there were usually fifteen... These admissions had been authorized by Monseigneur Fournier, bishop of Nantes.

The little Stigmatist continued to receive many Miraculous Communions as she was never abandoned by her Spouse from Heaven.

On 12 June 1879, Our Lord appeared again to Marie-Julie, judging very harshly those priests who refused her the Holy Sacrament of the Altar, and most particularly Mgr. Lecoq who ordered it so:

- **Despite the refusal, you will have nevertheless the merit. You will have what the hardness and the insensibility of hearts have refused you. I did what they had to do! I lowered Myself to be the mere minister of the earth... I fulfilled the duty of those who are Mine, who do not fear, who do not tremble at the idea of making Me suffer twice; hence, before you leave from here, before I separate you from the earth, I shall tell them: 'I did what you had to do! I lowered Myself to relieve and save souls! You did not do your duty towards Me...'**
  Be consoled, My victim. It is they who have refused the Justice and who will bear the responsibility, and, a little later, when you will be with Me, and when he who has deprived you of so many Communions will be in the judgment, you will come and ask him to give you the Communions he has deprived you.
- *Oh, my Jesus! I shall not come (*to Bishop Lecoq's judgment*). I shall go to a little corner when You judge him, and I shall pray for him so that You may cover him with Your Love.*
  (Exchange between Our Lord Jesus-Christ and Marie-Julie Jahenny, 12 June 1879)

A year before, on 28 February 1878, Our Lord asked Marie-Julie:

- **Why don't you say out loud and everywhere: 'The Authority holds me in iron chains, depriving me of Communion?**
- *My Good Lord, they are the authority...*
  (Exchange between Our Lord Jesus-Christ and Marie-Julie Jahenny, 12 June 1879)

Our Lord Jesus-Christ knew very well the answer that was coming, and the state of mind of His beloved "little victim". The purpose of this exchange was for it to be relayed, for it to be heard... for it to be read... The message is this: Believe in this messenger, for not only is she truly Christ's faithful and obedient Servant, but she is a faithful and obedient subject of Our Lord's Holy Church, even when it is unjust however temporarily so... Indeed, the Roman Catholic Church is the only Christian Church founded by Jesus-Christ upon Peter, His Disciple, His first Vicar, His first Pontiff.

And I tell you that you are Peter, and on this rock I shall build my church, and the gates of Hades will not overcome it.

(Matthew 16:18)

From that moment on, each Sunday and on certain feast days, between 6:00 and 7:00 in the morning, the stigmatist had a miraculous communion which had no other witness than her own family. This lasted for eleven and a half years, until the holy sacraments were given back to her by order of the Holy See as a result of an inquest that his holiness Pope Leo XIII had made through the very Reverend Father Vanutelli, Dominican, cousin of the Cardinal of the same name. This period of persecution ended at last in 1888 when Rev. Fr. Vanutelli officially ruled that:

Marie-Julie had been unjustly deprived of the Holy Sacraments.

Hence, **by Order of his Holiness Pope Leo XIII**, the ban issued by the Chapter of Curates was finally lifted and Marie-Julie was permitted to receive normally Holy Communion from her parish priest.

Despite the heartless and pitiful persecutions Marie-Julie Jahenny had suffered, she never complained or murmured a word against bishop Lecoq or against the local Church, but remained always obedient to the successive bishops of Nantes, recognizing with humble obedience the authority given to them by God. The lesson one can thus deduce from this anecdote—which was witnessed and thus reported as per Heaven's designs – is that in spite of the errors and injustice committed by the Church, the faithful must not condemn but leave it in the hands of God, for Judgement is His and His alone...

Her ecstasies

Her ecstasies occurred on a regular basis, and as with other authentic Marian apparition cases, they showed as well the following phenomena: while in ecstasy, the natural reactions of her senses ceased, and she remained insensible to the point of not reacting when pricked with pins and needles, or while being burned, or when bright lights were being flashed in her eyes...

Sometimes, as we have seen earlier, her body would miraculously levitate almost 12 inches above the ground or above her bed for unspecified amounts of time. Furthermore, she displayed acute abilities of Hierognosis, distinguishing the difference between blessed and unblessed objects. If she discerned a sacramental placed before her that had been blessed, she would venerate it by kissing it with fervor. If it were unblessed, however, she would simply remain unresponsive.

On 18 October 1877, while in ecstasy, reliving the Passion of Our Lord, Marie-Julie stopped her mystical enactment of the Via Crucis and asked for a picture of St. Francis. A visiting priest had one in his breviary and handed it over to her, but she remained motionless and didn't venerate it... Fr. David then knew the picture wasn't blessed and thus, rushing towards it, he blessed it at once.

Upon receiving it again, Marie-Julie revered it profoundly, covering it with kisses.

During the same ecstasy, visitors held a rosary before her, but she refused to kiss the sacramental as was her usual custom... The visitor then recalled they had lost the original crucifix to the rosary and had replaced it with another, but didn't think to have the replacement blessed. The blessing was done immediately and Marie-Julie grew happy, kissing the crucifix and the beads repeatedly before resuming her suffering of the Passion.

On other occasions, she would give surprising information about a holy relic presented to her during an ecstasy that no one had previously known before. One astounding example: without saying a word to her beforehand, a relic was held before her and she immediately confirmed what the owner had only suspected up to then—the relic had a fragment of the lance that opened Our Lord's side, and furthermore, still contained a piece of Our Lord's Heart!

Apparently, the relic belonged to the Marquis de la Franquerie, whose family still possesses this astonishing relic to this very day. Besides being hiergnostic, Marie-Julie had likewise the grace—almost uniquely reserved to stigmatists—of having several auxiliary angels as well as her own guardian one. She enjoyed this privilege during the time she was deaf, dumb, blind and paralyzed.

On Christmas night of 1879, Marie-Julie received a most extraordinary Christmas gift from Heaven: that of being given the grace of holding the Child Jesus in her arms:

I felt in my soul a great heat of love which set me ablaze ; I felt my soul leaving and going in the midst of a multitude of angels who were going to the divine crib, and when I was at the Holy Child's crib, I felt this same burning as I had never felt before ; and at once the Holy Child said to His dear Mother:

'My dear Mother give Me the beautiful robe that we have prepared, you and P. (no further name was given**)'**

And Our Lady gave me a white dress, and the small Child Jesus placed a white cloak over my shoulders. He said to me:

'I want to rest on your heart, in your arms.'

I was about to run away so as not to take Him because I am not worthy when He said to me:

'Stay there, I want you to carry Me.'

I began to cry. He dried my tears with His small hand and there in a crib of fire I received the Holy Infant Jesus. I held Him in my hands, His adorable little head on my heart, while I held Him, He stroked my cheeks with His delicate hands. He gave me a small kiss... there in the middle of my forehead and afterwards, He had in His right hand a golden nail and placed it like this... straight on my heart saying:

77

'One day this same golden nail will remain engraved where I have placed it! From the place of his nail will exude a scent which will be the same when you come out of the tomb before the Resurrection.'

I do not know what this means and I did not ask Him.—The marvels of the scent He said to me, **'... will be the same during your life as after your death!'**

In fact, from that time on, there often came incomparable scents from Marie-Julie's chest which were smelled by numerous visitors and witnesses.

In an ecstasy which took place on August 1939, a week before Hitler invaded Poland, Our Lord and Our Lady gave the following warning: 'a great war' was about to break out; Our Lord further adding:

My little servant must take to his home all documents concerning Marie-Julie in order to avoid a seizure by the Germans...

(24 August 1939)

Indeed, World War II started a few days later, on 3 September 1939 when France declared war on Germany after the spearhead of the infamous Wermacht invaded Poland. The instructions of this message, given on 24 August, was addressed to André le Sage, Marquis de La Franquerie de la Tourre, the 'little servant' who was present at Our Lord's recommendation to ensure the documents would not fall into Germans' hands.

The Marquis de La Franquerie de La Tourre became in 1939 Chamberlain to Pope Pius XII, who, having heard of the French stigmatist, visited Marie-Julie in France before being elected Pope.

A French monarchist and a staunch defender of the Roman Catholic Church, the Marquis de La Franquerie wrote many books after the war, one of which dealt in depth with his experiences with Marie-Julie Jahenny, and which has been translated in English: **The Breton Stigmatist** (1977).

In fact, it is one of the ever so few biographies of Marie-Julie Jahenny that has ever been translated into English. The Marquis de la Franquerie was as well for a time the editor of the **International Journal of Secret Societies**, and was well known to be a staunch 'Foe of Freemasons, attacking their luciferian sects and exposing their conspiracies to infiltrate the Church and the political and industrial circles in France.

The Marquis de la Franquerie was first introduced to Marie-Julie by Monsignor Jouin,[8] a famous French essayist in the 19th century. No doubt, Marie-Julie's prophecies spurred him, for St. Michael the Archangel, in no

---

[8] **Monsignor Ernest Jouin (21 December 1844–27 June 1932) was a** French Catholic **priest and essayist, known for his promotion of the** Judeo-Masonic conspiracy theory**. He also published the first French edition of** The Protocols of the Elders of Zion.

uncertain terms, revealed through the old Breton stigmatist, the Freemasons being the cause of the greater havoc in France, in the Church and in the world, promising that he (St. Michael the Archangel) would one day smite the Freemason lodges and drive them out of France (29 September 1878, Feast Day of St. Michael the Archangel).

The Marquis of la Franquerie had a grand-daughter, Isabelle, who became Mrs. Szczebura, and who created the **Sanctuary de Marie-Julie Jahenny** in La Fraudais, preserving to this day the texts and the house of the Breton visionary for the numerous pilgrims who still come today from the four corners of the world to see the home where the God-sent stigmatist has received all her extraordinary revelations and messages.

Isabelle Szczebura has, with her husband Richard, created a website with numerous reproduced pictures, biographies, prayers, messages and prophecies received by Marie-Julie. Said website is: (**www.marie-julie-jahenny.fr**) and constitutes today the foremost original source of Marie-Julie Jahenny's received messages to the world.

Marie-Julie Jahenny's recorded texts and numerous prophecies were given in a timeline ranging from 1871 to 1941, and all within a complete chronological disorder... This was done in a very purposeful manner, and likewise were mixed with countless private messages, exchanges and conversations often stealthy in nature (written in over 120,000 pages), the reason of which is herein below clearly explained by Our Lord Jesus-Christ:

All this writing-work (recordings of the messages received by Marie-Julie Jahenny), **I want it to remain entirely closed to all creatures until the moment when it will become permitted to possess them throughout all the parts of the world. My Will is that if these words were to be gathered now (and) read by eyes, they be not understood...**

The light that comes out of them would not be found nor recognized as being true. I want that this be observed exactly (as stated).

There are (however) some that must be propagated without further delay and without worry. I shall be the Divine Conductor of those things that are to be known and to be passed before others. For these things, I shall have My orders which will be quite clear and there will be no trace of any cloud (in man's understanding).

Stop upon the words that will be written as they are being pronounced, without trusting that which is sent without the notes under one's eyes. My people will understand Me well.

(Our Lord Jesus-Christ, 2 August 1881)

On 23 February 1880, Marie-Julie Jahenny announced a book concerning the great doctrine, that of the Cross, which was revealed to the Breton stigmatist, a book which obviously cannot be written until all the ecstasies have been studied by a theologian capable of extracting and exposing with the right authority and with all its transcendent fullness the doctrine of the Cross.

In the messages echoed by Marie-Julie, Our Lord is very clear. The time for the understanding of these messages is in His Designs and in His Designs alone. This said, it is most evident, as we can see in Our Lord's message given hereinabove that Our Lord Jesus-Christ maintains and wishes the authority of the Church He himself instituted through St. Peter, respected when He stated: **I want it to remain entirely closed to all creatures until the moment when it will become permitted to possess them throughout all the parts of the world(...),** for let us remember that the public spreading of such messages, admonitions, apparitions, visions, prophetic messages and miracles, according to Canons 1399, § 5 and § 2318 of the old Canon Law Code were utterly prohibited without first acquiring formal approval from the Catholic Church.

However, on 14 October 1966, his Holiness Pope Paul VI abolished said Canons which excommunicated their authors *(Decree of the Congregation for the Doctrine of the Faith, Acta Apostolicae Sedis, 29 September 1966, page 1186).* This formal papal act legally allowed henceforth the spreading and publication of approved and non-approved apparition sites' messages throughout the world.

If nothing else, these passages clearly establish once again Marie-Julie-Jahenny's interlocutor's insistence on unconditional obedience to the Magisterium of the Roman Catholic Church.

In July 1882, while in an ecstasy, Marie-Julie Jahenny exclaimed:

Alone with Jesus, I look with the eyes of my soul the higher part of his sheet of paper where something was written. His Adorable Voice tells me:

Upon the decided day for My writings to be sent to all my servants and to my victims to indicate to them My Hour and the hour of the miracle, against this call nothing will stand.

I shall protect and shall keep those who will be forced to wait a short time to find refuge under the divine tree of the Cross.

The hour will be sent to all the family of the Cross whose destiny is to be protected. This hour will come before the paths of the earth are closed, before the enemy is engaged within the vast spaces of all of France to conquer it and to have it perish.

As one reads the conversations between Marie-Julie and her different heavenly interlocutors in the course of her life, one feels often embarrassed or "intruding" into what is often very intimate and private exchanges... A great deal of said conversations with Our Lord Jesus-Christ, with the Blessed Virgin Mary or with Saints deal with most personal matters... On one occasion, Marie-Julie received a message of prudence from Our Lord concerning the messages she received:

My children, when I shall speak, or when My Holy Mother will come to visit you, if there are a large number of people present we shall be very reserved, and we shall veil our grave words or even hold them for another

time... Many judge the words that we say within a meaning which is not the correct one... I warn you, do not be neither surprised nor worried. Later on, all will be revealed. I know hearts who judge without understanding... This displeases Me and may have grave consequences.

(Our Lord Jesus-Christ, 1 February 1880)

Note: The message hereinabove is wisdom itself, not merely for the messages of La Fraudais but for every message brought forth from apparition sites and from mystics' and/or Saints' private revelations. Notwithstanding, as the author of this book, and in response to these introductory messages of Our Lord Jesus-Christ, it is good to know that this book has been offered through the Merits of Our Lord's Holy Passion, and through the merits of the Sorrowful Heart of the Blessed Virgin Mary at the Feet of Our Lord's Holy Cross.

Marie-Julie Jahenny's Prophecies

The prophecies are, in world-renowned Mariologian Msgr. René Laurentin's own words, always the most controversial part of an apparition site's case; however, the biblical story of Nineveh demonstrates clearly how a prophecy can indeed be averted if man converts and changes his ways in time. The Book of Jonah depicts indeed Nineveh as a wicked city worthy of destruction. God sent Jonah to preach to the Ninevites while warning them of their upcoming destruction if they did not convert. The citizens of the wicked city believed, repented, prayed and fasted (*making their beasts fast as well*). As a result, God spared their forewarned city, showing mercy for its population which became contrite and repentant.

In the modern approved apparition sites discussed in this book, men, we are told, have espoused the depraved libertarian ideology that has become comparable of the pagan times of old under the false titles of *enlightenment of reason* and the *libertinism of thought and deed*... Hence, considering Heaven's warnings through the Breton stigmatist and consequently, the "chilling" prophecies yet to come, we have as a marker of credibility prophecies Marie-Julie Jahenny revealed which actually already took place exactly as she foretold. To name but a few:

-   On 15 September 1879, she predicted Bismarck's 'Kulturkampf' which was to initiate a fierce struggle between the German imperial government and the Roman Catholic Church. Marie-Julie Jahenny prophesied that this conflict would take place in 1881, predominantly over the control of educational and ecclesiastical appointments, and over the place and role of religion in modern politics, usually in connection with secularization campaigns. Two years later to the day (15 September 1881), Bismarck's 'Kulturkampf' became a reality throughout Prussia and today's modern Germany.

- Likewise, Marie-Julie predicted with utmost accuracy the massive and catastrophic eruption of Mount Pelé on the island of Martinique in the French Caribbean, and described the horrific events as they occurred despite the fact she was half a world away.

- Marie-Julie Jahenny predicted without error the date and the place of the Count de Chambord's death. Indeed, Henry de Chambord was a direct descendant of the Bourbon Royal House of France, and passed away on 24 August 1883, in Lanzenkirchen (Austria) ... *because alas, France refused salvation...* This prophesy was proven yet again correct.

- Just before the successor of Pope Leo XIII was elected, Marie-Julie Jahenny declared, a few days before the closing of the gathered conclave, that*... **the 'Adriatic Cardinal' is chosen by God. His reign will be that of Christ. He will not last long and will be called Pius.*** Marie-Julie was correct in that the next Pope chose the name of Pius X. This new Pontiff fulfilled indeed the prophecy as being the 'Adriatic Cardinal' for he was the former cardinal of Venice and was pope for a mere 11 years, while his predecessor Pius IX reigned for over 31 years.

- In 1881, she was shown as well the Transvaal War in South Africa, thus announcing it would take place at the death of Queen Victoria, which happened as predicted in 1901.

- On 2 August 1881, she prophesized the beginning of World War I in 1914, and thus the desolation of the people of France and a number of deaths that cannot be counted...

- On 15 September 1881, Marie-Julie Jahenny foretold that Mélanie Calvat's *(the visionary of La Salette)* would pass away on 15 December 1904, in Altamura, Italy, which took place exactly on the date and place she foretold it would.

- Marie-Julie announced that the first World War would begin in 1914;

- Likewise, she prophesied France taking back the regions of Alsace and Lorraine from Germany as a result of France's victory in World War I.

- She discussed as well the Spanish civil war in the 1930s with the intervention of foreign forces (over forty years before it happened).

- Three years after the apparitions of the Blessed Virgin Mary in Fatima, in November 1920, Marie-Julie foretold details of the Second World War. Speaking of the Germans, the Blessed Virgin Mary said: ***These cruel and barbaric souls are trying, through a tremendous injustice, to pay their horrific debt. They will come back and they will cause a great deal of harm, but I shall keep my kingdom. My Divine Power will stop their rage. I shall push them back.***

- She discussed as well the Spanish civil war in the 1930s with the intervention of foreign forces (over forty years before it happened).

- The announcement of boreal lights in the sky above Europe in January 1938 which would announce the beginning of World War II. (prophecy made by Marie-Julie before Lucia of Fatima in 1917).

- Marie-Julie correctly announced beforehand that France would lose its colony of Algeria to the Arabs, and added that the French priests of that country would suffer horrible trials. This, in effect, took place to the letter, in 1962 and again 34 years later, in 1996…

- Marie-Julie added that the French armies will lose their wars in the lands of the Arabs…

Marie-Julie Jahenny's predictions continued up until her death in 1941, her death being the strangest prediction of all, considering it did not fall on the promised day… Our Lord promised on 1 December 1876, she would die on a Friday, but she died in fact on a Tuesday… If she revealed so many other events correctly, how could she have made a mistake of this caliber? There may be in fact no mistake at all, for this promise of dying on a Friday may have been fulfilled in an unlikely manner.

In one ecstasy (date unknown), Marie-Julie was shown a mystic Chalice placed above her head. She made an unusual request asking to take the Chalice with "her in the earth" (i.e., when she was buried). Our Lord answered:

I shall hide My Heart beneath this veil, and It will live in your heart. Your heart will beat as before. Your love will never slow down, you will not forget My Name beneath the coffin's plank; the breath of life from My Heart will be transplanted inside the tomb.

How could this enigmatic message be interpreted? God may have granted her wish. Considering her last recorded words are dated February 1941, it is not impossible she slipped into a death-like coma on 4 March, or that her last ecstasy on earth before her death was so deep it was mistaken as actual death on that date, which has happened before to a number of mystics recorded in the annals of the Church. Her last penance may have been to remain alive in the coffin and, in that manner, die on a Friday as promised, the true day of her death completely unknown and hidden from the eyes of her friends and family…

Of course, this theory cannot be proven now, yet accurate prophecies were echoed again and again by the brave Breton stigmatist. Marie-Julie further predicted in 1878, eight months after Pius IX's death, that he… *will be elevated one day to a very high level of sanctity, and his sanctity will save Rome from terrible calamities at that time.* Pius IX is already well on the way to official canonization as Pope John Paul II proclaimed him Venerable on 6 July 1985, only to beatify him later on 3 September 2000.

Further prophecies:

In one of Marie-Julie's most famous received messages, St. Michael warned the faithful not to put their trust in one French political ruler (without naming him), for he will not bring about the promised restoration of France. He will be a 'pillar of mud' (29 September 1878) a text that was cryptic until now, but it is argued in our time that this message may well refer to French President Emmanuel Macron… She further predicted Emperor Charlemagne's informal and disputed canonization, an event which we have not yet seen take place. Marie-Julie Jahenny likewise added that Louis XVI would be raised to the altars during the reign of the promised Great Monarch, Henry V of France also known as Henry V of the Cross.

One other astounding prophecy made on 2 January 1885, a year before her sister Angèle died, involved Our Lord promising that Angèle would be one day exhumed and found to be incorrupt, consequently displaying a first of many miraculous events in La Fraudais. Our Lord further declared on 4 May 1877 that **To show that you are all of Me, I will protect your body even in the breast of the earth,** words unquestionably suggesting that Marie-Julie will be likewise exhumed and found incorrupt as her sister would before she.

Furthermore, Our Lord's prophecies concerning Marie-Julie's heart may be a double revelation, first, for her 'hidden' death as mentioned above, and later, when she will be exhumed, **her heart, we are told, will be found still beating!**[9]

He who writes today these lines, can hope that sooner rather than later the extraordinary life of Marie-Julie will be brought to the Dycasterium of the Doctrine of the Faith, and that the official process for her beatification and canonization may commence without further delay…

The warning and prophecies about the Roman Catholic and Apostolic Church

When reading the prophecies of Marie-Julie Jahenny, Our Lady predicts the spread of Freemasonry, the annihilation of children's innocence, world wars, famine, disease, mass destruction, the rise of abominable laws and, moreover, multiple attacks upon the Roman Catholic Church through first the taking away of crosses in hospitals, in schools and in administration buildings, then the closing of monasteries, convents and churches, and the replacement of Christianity by Islam and atheism… It might very well be argued that the numerous apparitions to Marie-Julie in La Fraudais form the frame of all the messages the Blessed Mother has given in the 17th century in Quito (Our Lady of Good Success), in La Salette, in Fatima and, years later in Akita, for Marie-Julie provided a staggering number of messages which involve the Catholic Church, its priests and clergy…

The Breton woman revealed that there will be a great loss of faith throughout France, the introduction of a 'New Celebration' and an abominable 'New Mass' within the Catholic Church. Heaven further stated to her that there would be likewise a general lack of morality that would reverse the understanding of man, having him believe that what is good is evil and evil good… One of the most sorrowful messages of Our Lady engrosses the loss of children's innocence before their attaining the age of reason, all of which, the Blessed Virgin Mary adds, is to bring about the degradation of the human race and, consequently, God's chastisements on a sinful and unrepentful world…

Reading the numerous messages received by Marie-Julie Jahenny requires a very careful and methodical study, for some of the messages seem to be repeated in a time-line that is everything but linear, making it quite difficult to discern

---

[9] **As that of St. Joan of Arc's, after both attempts by the English to consume it with boiling oil.**

when many of these described events are to take place; however, on the positive side, the prophesies of La Fraudais bring about the appearance of a great hope, a "great French Monarch" and of a "holy Pontiff" who would restore together France, the Church and the Catholic Faith throughout the surviving world. One may be tempted to think that the messages echoed by Marie-Julie concern France alone; however, this is not so.

The revelations point out that France will be the first nation to collapse and the first nation to rise again. The Blessed Virgin Mary explained that France is guiltier than other countries for it was the Church's eldest daughter, and as such was bestowed certain vocations, among which that of being the protector of the Church and the propagator of the Faith. Because of its betrayal and its riddance of its "Heaven-blessed monarchy" – through murder, persecution and utter barbarism – and because of it replacing the French monarchy by a freemason inspired republic, France would be punished first.

The Sin of Blasphemy

Our Lady cried out to Marie-Julie on 9 August 1881 when warning her about the horrific days about to be unleashed on earth, mostly for punishment due to the sin of blasphemy, and to the utter disrespect for the things of God:

My children, it is blasphemy that brings hell on earth. I am in sorrow for the clergy. I see that in a great amount, and more so of priests, the mind (or spirit) weakens every day.

Heaven recommends we help make reparation whenever we see or hear the sin of blasphemy committed by saying a **'Glory Be'** (see page: 543):

When you hear a blasphemy, say a 'Glory Be'. It is a consolation for Heaven.

(Unknown date)

Another message given to the Breton stigmatist involved the Three Crisis which contain the full content of the prophetic warnings involving the Church, France and the World:

The First Crisis:

Marie-Julie stated: *In the sun, the voice says:*

Some time ago, the Lord has issued three months of fatal and terrible chastisements. He will shorten this time a great deal...
The next beginning of the Mortal Revolutionary Crisis... *The voice speaks likes that...* **this beginning will last four weeks, not a day more and not a day less, but the extent of it will be immense! The number of those called Murderers of the People will be of an inconceivable immensity... In**

the midst of this terrible hour, the foreigners, whose desire is filled with a violence without measure, will be masters in France. As soon as the news of the fatal event will be known, their ears will not be deaf.

During this first conflict throughout all of France, there will be freedom for everything. There will no longer be prisoners detained for crimes; this liberty will be everywhere (in France)... A very short pause will follow this great entrance of evil (which) will be complete, especially in the Center (Paris) **and in its surroundings** (The Parisian suburbs, today mostly occupied by French Arabs and illegal immigrants).

The Second Crisis:

Marie-Julie continued:

The voice says:

The second and violent Crisis will begin. France will be invaded all the way to the dioceses where Brittany begins... *The voice adds:* **Yours!**

The Second Crisis will put a close to all things, and from the people, only the ones who find an obscure refuge will escape.

In this second epoch, the men of power, after having delivered the kingdom to blood, will assemble in a peaceful place and will form definitive and decisive projects. They will look for a savior to place him on the throne. Many of these great commanders of the kingdom will withdraw in a parcel of that stolen land of France: Alsace and Lorraine! Once there, in secret, they will assign their king, he who is against Providence's designs. They will thus decide, and nothing will deviate their will from having the guilty one sit on a throne which will never belong to him.

The second epoch will go beyond 1 month. It will go on, with neither rest nor pause until the 37th or 45th day. This second epoch will achieve everything. The only saved ones will only be the ones that God promised to protect in the described places through His Word, and kept through His gratuitous kindness.

As Persecution will spread in France, it will receive a great deal of help from neighboring powers (Arab nations?), *from all those who resemble those who, in France, deliver everything mercilessly to blood and fire.* (Arabs/Muslims).

The Third Crisis:

For the length of the third epoch is not in this passage of the sun... (?)

(9 May 1882)

The third Crisis, in fact, involves the liberation of France and of the Pope in Rome by the true King chosen by God, King Henry V of the Cross. This re-conquest of France is to last seven months, while all three crisis should last three years...

Friends of the Sacred Heart, I stay with you; your company is that of Jesus. You are generous and brave soldiers. The Lord desires me to tell you these words: 'Get ready, brave servants of God, as the Divine Master will soon come, first in His Mercy, secondly in His righteous anger and vengeance. He wants me to show this sword to His present friends and (then) I (shall) have done my duty.

(St. Michael the Archangel, 29 September 1881)

St. Michael then shows Marie-Julie Jahenny a sword with which he will help the faithful Christians in the prophetic times; then St. Michael adds:

This is the sword that I delegate to the friends of God; this (one) is mine. (He shows Marie-Julie Jahenny his own sword next to the first one). **They are similar; they both bear the seal of the Lord. It is the Name of Jesus written on the blade, well engraved.**
Dear friends of the Lord, we are here on the threshold of Mercy and the threshold of the justice of God.

The message here is clear. A period of Mercy is to be granted for humanity to repent, convert and return to God before it's too late... Then, will the period of God's Justice will follow... However, Our Blessed Lady told Marie-Julie that Satan will use every means in his possession to take advantage of the time of God's mercy granted to man to accentuate his carefully planned designs, especially by concentrating his efforts against children's innocence.

My beloved children, all is engaged in an irreparable loss, I mean the salvation of souls of children. The nourishment of these poor little souls should be for them the bread of love of their Immaculate Queen, the Queen of Heaven. I suffer to see these souls as pastures delivered to the enemy of the salvation of souls; it is the goodness of my Divine Son that Satan takes to himself. To appropriate it, he has his supporters in every corner on the Earth. I despair, yes, I despair of saving those souls who are in an immense danger (...)
Most of these children have entered the path of corruption, and these souls have not received a drop of my perfume of virtues and purity; it is with an immeasurable pain that I reveal this to you, because if you saw the number (of young victims), you would be frightened and even struck as if by a mortal blow.
(...) My dear children, those carefree mothers who no longer have the faith, those guilty fathers thrown into circles (of bad company) where they do nothing but offend my Divine Son. In Heaven, what a responsibility they will have and how many counts they will have to render! They do not think

about that… What terrible misfortune!

(The Blessed Virgin Mary, 9 February 1904)

I see a multitude of souls that are lost, especially children, even those who do not have the age of reason… Those who are responsible (for the loss of children's souls) **if they knew what awaits them at the dreaded trial! Children are educated now as adults. What shameful words ringing in their ears and echo in their mouths! It is awful and terrible. It makes one tremble to see the youth turn to this point, and they** (the children's parents) **are not watchful, they do not take care, they do not occupy themselves with what they do. Parents laugh hearing what their children say, and they leave them entirely at liberty to their actions**.

(Our Lord Jesus-Christ, 2 October 1903)

It is quite remarkable to note that as I wrote these lines for the first time in this book, a new Movie Trailer appeared in the media and in U.S. theaters advertising a new but most horrid film (2019). These revolting excerpts displayed young children in the fifth–sixth grade acting in an appalling pre-sexual fashion, pronouncing in the course of said film all sorts of sordid obscenities aiming at attracting the viewers' laughter.

Being the father of two young children, I cannot help but to wonder about the state of mind of these children's parents… How indeed, could these fathers and mothers tolerate, for whatever sums of money they were promised, such moral pollution exhibited publicly by their children, surely inducing other young children of the same age (or younger) to follow their example.

As a father, I am at a loss of words before such parental irresponsibility, and find no justification whichsoever to prostitute one's children's moral stands through a means that further endangers the moral well-being of other innocent youngsters. This is a disgrace, and, I regret to say, an example of the 2 October 1903 fulfilled prophetic message of Our Lord to Marie-Julie Jahenny.

In the Gospel of St. Matthew (28:18), we read Christ's declaration—**All power is given to me in Heaven and on earth**—instructing His disciples to make disciples of all nations and baptize them in the name of the Father, the Son and Holy Spirit, after which He was taken up to Heaven and enthroned at the right hand of the Father (St. Mark, 16:19). Four years before his Holiness Pope Leo XIII's witnessed an exchange between Our Lord Jesus-Christ and Satan (see page: 435), Marie-Julie was shown a detailed mystical vision of Our Lord's Ascension on 30 August 1880.

In said vision, Marie-Julie was permitted to witness Satan appearing before Jesus-Christ immediately after His Ascension into Heaven, demanding a portion of the earth for his own hellish kingdom. The devil, Marie-Julie Jahenny explained, was deeply enraged that Our Lord had taken back the world, redeeming it with His Sacrifice on the Cross, and was thus consumed with jealousy due to Christ having been granted supreme power by the Father over the earth:

Marie-Julie:

"I see in the sun the moment when the Lord ascended into Heaven, and took possession of His Eternal Kingdom. At that moment, hell became the kingdom of the enemy. The Lord took possession of His earthly kingdom and said:

- **I am established as the Eternal King.**

Marie-Julie continued:

"Satan is furious and searches for a few rounds about ways to maliciously extend his power...

The Lord says to him:

- **Thou wilt be under submission, you will not do but what is permitted you by My eternal law.**

Satan asks to bear the name of 'prince' and that the finger of the Lord engraves this name under the eyes of us all.
Our Lord answered:

- **Yes, you have all the names. The name of prince: prince of darkness, prince of the abyss.**

But this is not enough for the devil:

- *Do not put limits to Your power. Let me free to extend as largely as You must extend until the end of time.*

Our Lord responds:

- **I will remain as King over all that you do, all that you possess. I will be over (it all), and I shall command.** (i.e., Satan will not be completely free to do as he wishes).

Satan rebelled. Yet he had his portion, but the Lord also took enjoyment of His possessions.

The Lord said to him:

- **Prostrate yourself at My feet and adore My wishes.**
- *"I bow my knee, but on one condition. Leave me liberty,"* Satan said with authority, *"to use, like You and at my pleasure, the power over death, to be its master."*
- **I leave you the power to tempt all men, to make them suffer to a certain measure, but I shall be present.**

Satan also demands the power of working miracles. The Lord does not leave this to him entirely, but He gave him something so that, we might merit more.

- **In the beginning,** *said the Lord,* **you will not do a lot of wonders; they will be a small number. They will serve you to do evil.**

Satan protests that this portion is not fair.

- **A time will come, far off,** *the Lord replied,* **where you will possess in the world a multitude so great that your portion will exceed Mine. You will become a great conqueror for a space of time that will be too long and which, however, will be very short. While you will make the conquest of multitudes, I will operate bright wonders and earthquakes, when the world is ready to perish, when thou will triumph with a victory without measure when almost all parts of the world, the whole of Europe will rise against (itself). In the darkness, there will be many conversions, many of the lost will return to Me in repentance.**

When they were about to separate, to return each to his own kingdom, Satan asked for the authority to take on all forms, to go anywhere.

- **I leave you permission to tempt My people,** says the Lord, **but I do not permit you ever to take the form of divine nor of true figures.**

Satan then dares to use familiar terms with the Lord, But Satan is rebuffed.
Our Lord:

- **Respect Me, on behalf of My Eternal power!**
- *"Yes,"* Satan replies, *"One day, far away from where we are today, you will seem to say to me that I am a mighty conqueror. You put no limits to the ravages of which, already, the desire consumes me."*

Marie-Julie asked the Flame of the Holy Spirit if the timeline is fixed where Satan must reign as such a great master. The Flame responded that it is set in the designs of God, and the devil hastened the time, without knowing (it) exactly…

It is this age in which you are now, children of God, said the Flame…

Satan continues:

- *"In the beginning of that time,"* he says, *"I will use all profanities and all unjust things to the destruction of Your Kingdom. I will transform all into a working tool against You. First I dig this place where the greatest number live."*
- **Do not ignore what he is,** *said the Flame* (Holy Spirit). **I dig this place on which you will fall like lightning. You will destroy first, and, I**

after you, I will finish everything, I will make ruins as there has never been before.

"The Holy Spirit," said Marie-Julie, *"warns that we must not forget that Satan is still a powerful angel, although fallen. The Holy Spirit will cause Satan to fall like lightening once more. Satan will destroy first, but then God will send His powerful chastisements."*

- **I will cover My own with a tender protection,** *says the Lord.*

(Here, Our Lord promises to protect his own children, those who remain faithful to Christ, to His teachings and to His Church).

- *"I will throw in a revolt between yours and mine,"* responds Satan, *"I will move all the kings, I will put in a division that will lead to a civil war in the universe."*
- **For My part,** *the Lord continues,* **I will send My Justice: punishment, miracles, death, plagues, pests, unknown diseases.**
- *"I will overthrow the temple of your prayers!"* Satan claims, *"I will establish the idols we worship. All that is, in times of peace, that resides in Your temples will be broken, dragged out, reduced to dust by mine."*
- **I will show,** *says the Lord,* **that I am the Eternal King. I will crush under the lightning of Heaven, all that will be given to you and to hell. I will restore My people; I will preserve (Mine) from the plagues, I will raise up the ruins. I will cast thee into the abyss, but only after you have used the powers I leave you for now.**

The Flame (Holy Spirit) said that the pain is about to enter the hearts, and hell is ready to sing the great song of its victory."

(End of Marie-Julie Jahenny's vision, 30 August 1880)

In another vision dated 25 October 1881, Satan railed against St. Michael:

"I will attack the Church, I will overthrow the Church, I will rule the people, I will dispose, in their hearts, of a major weakening of the Faith. There will be a great betrayal. I will become, for a time, the master of all things, I will have all under my empire!"

On the same day, Saint Michael warned us of the danger and assured us of Heaven's help:

"There has never been an epoch like this. We must be attentive and prepare so as not to be surprised... All the demons will reassemble, many in the form of man."

Abbot Robert Dell, a well-known Catholic priest and historian of the time, shared, upon a brief visit at La Fraudais, a particular exchange he witnessed between Marie-Julie Jahenny and St. Michael the Archangel:

Marie-Julie interviewed the Archangel on the occupations existing in Heaven:

Marie-Julie Jahenny:

- *"Does one pray the chaplet in Heaven?"*
- **"Yes,"** answers St. Michael.
- *"And does one read books as well?"*
- **"Yes, books as well.**"
- *"And those who read them, learn from them? Who teaches school in Heaven?"*
- **"The Good Jesus, angels, saints…**"
- *"Are the letters in these books handwritten or printed?"*
- **"They are glorious letters that have nothing in common with those of earth…**"

Abbot Robert Dell:

Marie-Julie only read printed letters, like most people of her time. This notwithstanding, St. Michael, as we can imagine, did not appear for such foolish talk:

- **'My friends!'** *said he, addressing those who were present that day.* **'I am coming down to you. The Lord has charged me the task to give you the following Word:**

Be ready, valiant servants of God. Satan has told the Lord:

- *My chains will fall. You will give me freedom and I shall enter as a conqueror, first in a threatened France which will perish!*

The Lord replied:

"Many will perish, but many will be saved. They will have a shelter beneath My Cross and in My Heart."

To these words, Satan blasphemed and swore his hatred, more infernal than ever before, and said:

'I shall attack the Church! I shall stumble the Cross! I shall divide the people! I shall deposit in the hearts of men a great weakening in the Faith. There will be a great renouncement! I shall become for some time supreme master of

everything! I shall have everything under my empire, even Your Temple and all of yours!'

Abbot Robert Dell continued:

St. Michael warned that for a period of time...

"... Satan will have permission to all. He will reign fully upon everything that is of good. Faith, Religion, everything will fall in the tomb of a deep mourning... Satan and his followers will triumph joyfully... but after Satan's triumph, the Lord will take His own, and will take away from the tomb the buried Church, the destroyed Cross, prayer which – in appearance only – seemed non-longer existent, (and) all the people in awe under the empire of massacres. It is impossible, further adds the Archangel, that without a bright Miracle from Heaven, the people of France could be saved, for it will have fallen deep in the furthest limits of shame and evil...

I hold my sword for the hour of combat is about to ring! I shall be on the side of the just!"

(Written testimony of Abbot Robert Dell—No date)

In a text dated 28 June 1880, we read:

"In those years," says Satan, *"I will make many revelations.* (False revelations through apparitions that are actually demonic.) *It will be impossible to expose my language. I will imitate all too well the words of Christ and His revelations. By loading these souls, I want a lot of pious priests to be lost, to mislead them deeply into all these things. I also want to lose many souls who are not (*priest or religious*). If I cannot lose these souls, I will (*make them*) lose their reputation at least, I will make them (be subject to) charges of heavy slander, I will make them denounce (their faith) up to the point of counsels of human laws."*

A possible interpretation of this text: In the years when Satan creates great confusion in the Church, he will cause many false apparitions to occur to mislead even the zealous and faithful with high sounding mysteries. Indeed, today, a number of alleged apparition sites have been already formally condemned by the Catholic Church... Some of those Church-condemned apparition cases are Peña Blanca (Chile), Bayside (New York) and many others around the world which have been declared by the Church as not from Heavenly origin... When I met with Father René Laurentin (foremost expert in Marian apparition sites) in Evry (outside Paris) in 1995, he showed me at the time his office whose four walls were covered from roof to floor with shelves filled with dossiers and folders:

"These are the apparition cases I am presently working on." He told me in his slow and well thought-out speech. *"There are about three hundred right now, but you know the great majority of these cases are not authentic. You see, most of*

*these are the fruit of either hysterical or wishful individuals. Others are from...
(quietly smiling) well... let us say NOT from God."*

It will be difficult to tell the difference between a false message from the true ones as Satan will mimic how Our Lord and our Lady speak. The demon will try to mislead the faithful in several ways; however, according to Fr. René Laurentin, the guidelines to distinguish a true from a false apparition or mystically delivered messages repose on the following aspects: a heavenly apparition will never fear holy water but will welcome it.

A divine truth will always sponsor and encourage the faithful to live the seven sacraments of the Holy Roman Catholic and Apostolic Church (Baptism, Eucharist, Confirmation, Confession, anointing of the Sick, Marriage and the Holy Orders), particularly the receiving of **Holy Communion** (being the true Body and Blood, Soul and Divinity of Our Lord Jesus-Christ), going to **Confession**, receiving **Baptism** and doing one's **Confirmation**.

Likewise, a true Heavenly message will always call the faithful to follow and live the **Teachings of the Holy Gospels** which are the foundation of the Church's Dogma of the Faith. What's more, Fr. Laurentin added with this smile that characterized him so well, the Blessed Virgin Mary's primary message to man will always be the same she gave in Cana 2000 years ago: "**Do whatever He tells you.**"

Apparently, the Church's teachings and Sacraments, being the armor, the shield and sword given to Christians, it is only logical that those who administer them constitute primary targets. Consequently, Marie-Julie warned us of Heaven's caution against an 'attack' aimed at the contemporary Pope of her time, Pope Leo XIII, (pontificate 1878–1903) who witnessed, very much like she did, a most remarkable exchange between God and the Devil.

On 13 October 1884, Pope Leo XIII, just after celebrating Mass, turned suddenly pale and, before witnesses, collapsed as though dead. Those standing nearby rushed to his aid only to find him staring into emptiness with a dreadful look of sheer fright. After coming to, he recounted having a vision of Satan approaching the throne of God, boasting that he could destroy the Church. According to his Holiness, the Lord reminded the devil that his Church was imperishable. Satan then replied:

- *Grant me one century and more power to those who will serve me, and I will destroy it.*

Our Lord, continued Pope Leo XIII, granted him 100 years. The Lord then revealed the events of the 20th century to the good Pontiff showing him the wars, the immorality, the genocide and the apostasy to come. Immediately following this disturbing vision, the overwhelmed Pope went to his office, sat down and wrote **the prayer to St. Michael the Archangel** (see page: 542). For decades this invocation was used as an exorcist prayer and always at the end of every Mass, that is... until the Second Vatican Council (Vatican II)...

Some have speculated that the century of testing the Catholic Church began in 1914. Regardless of when the time of testing officially began, it is important to note that in 1917 (the same year the Communist Revolution in Russia was unleashed), Pope Benedict XV wrote an encyclical entitled **On Preaching the Word**. This remarkable work would prove to be quite prophetic as it addressed an issue of the greatest and most momentous concern:

If on the other hand we examine the state of public and private morals, the constitutions and laws of nations, we shall find that there is a general disregard and forgetfulness of the supernatural, a gradual falling away from the strict standard of Christian virtue, and that men are slipping back more and more into the shameful practices of paganism.

(Excerpt from **On Preaching the Word**, Pope Benedict XV)

Pope Leo XIII likewise made a prophecy of valid concern for the faithful:

The Church will be deprived of its Leader who governs now (Leo XIII). The remains of this present holy Pontiff have to disappear. The imprint of his feet at the Holy Altar will be reduced to ashes by the flames of hell. The head of the Church will be despicably outraged!

(His Holiness, Pope Leo XIII, 7 July 1880).

Could *the imprint of his feet at the Holy Altar* be the **Leonine Prayers** he instituted at the end of each Mass? (The final form of the Leonine Prayers consisted of three Hail Mary's, 1 Hail Holy Queen followed by a vesicle and response, a prayer for the conversion of sinners, the liberty and exaltation of the Catholic Church, and the prayer to Saint Michael the Archangel.)

Prophecies on the Church:

Considering that the Leonine Prayers to be said at the foot of the altar for the protection of the Church and the conversion of sinners have been removed from the New Mass liturgy, this prediction has come to pass with the coming of the "Novus Ordo" Mass brought out by the Second Vatican Council... And yet Leo XIII was not the only one to echo this distressing prophecy. Indeed, Marie-Julie Jahenny received a similar prediction, and one more yet to follow, even more morbid than the first one:

"The Church will suffer the cruelest persecutions which hell has ever yet invented.
Soon, in large parts of this land of the dead, there will be no sanctuaries... The apostles will have fled. The holy souls weep over the ruins and abandonment; see how much they insult Me and how much they offend Me... There will be a relentless hellish (attack) against the devotion to the Sacred Heart."
"There will be a book of the 'second celebration' by the infamous spirits who have crucified Me anew and who await the reign of a new Messiah to

make them happy. Many holy priests will refuse this book sealed with the words of the abyss, but unfortunately there are those who will accept it, and it will be used."

"The Bishops betray. They will give their strength and their life to the fatal government."

"The religion that I have established, the Gospel that I preached, all this, they will tear apart under an appalling form, to make (the Church?) tremble, and they will throw all these infamous things on My shoulders and all over My Adorable Body. They will change My sufferings and My Passion, in writings that will shake the heart of the righteous, and their peaks will crack (...) as the mountain on the day of My Crucifixion.

Before the year which bears a figure of consolation to My French people, before that epoch is sounded, the holy sacrifices of the altars will have taken an infernal form."

"In the streets, in cities, in the countryside and in all villages, the infectious poison of those cursed books will spread greatly and with a rapidity that is hotter than the sun's path, from sunrise to sunset."

(From certain text fragments, all dated 21 July 1881)

Our Lord Jesus-Christ further warned:

The suppression of the ringing of bells and of religious funerals will be demanded... They will erase all memory of the first religion and they will instruct in an impious religion.

(Our Lord Jesus-Christ, 6 September 1880)

According to the book **The Breton Stigmatist**, p. 39, Our Lord revealed on 3 June 1880 other 'innovations' Satan will invent:

He (Satan) will address priests: *'You will dress in a large red cloak... We (devils) will give you a piece of bread and a few drops of water. You can do everything that you did when you belonged to Christ...'* **'But,'** says Our Lord, **'they do not add, Consecration and Communion.'** and Hell added: *'We will permit you to say it in all houses and even under the firmament.'*

(Our Lord Jesus-Christ, 3 June 1880)

On 9 June 1881, Our Lord stated to Marie-Julie:

I see them embrace the religion with a merry heart, without thinking about Me, nor of the Church, nor of their baptism nor of all that is good for the Christian soul... By manifesting these signs to My people, I want to bring back My people before the punishment, because I love them. I see appearing eagerly this guilty, sacrilegious, infamous and similar (religion) to that of Mahomet. There I see Bishops entering.

I see these Bishops, many, so many of them, and, in their following, all their flock, and without hesitation they are rushing into damnation and Hell... My Heart is wounded to death, as at the time of My Passion... I am going to become an object of horror for the most part of My people. All youth will be spoiled and soon will fall in putrefaction, the smell of which will be unbearable.

(Our Lord Jesus-Christ, 9 June 1881)

The Blessed Virgin Mary stated in May 1904:

They will not stop at this hateful and sacrilegious road. They will go further to compromise all at once and in one go: the Holy Church, the clergy and the faith of my children...

(The Blessed Virgin Mary, 10 May 1904)

She further announced the **dispersion of the pastors** (bishops) by the Church itself, real pastors who will be replaced by others formed by hell, initiated in all vices, in all iniquities, perfidious (men), who will cover souls with filth (sadly enough, this can already be seen in China)... New preachers of new sacraments, new temples, new baptisms, new confraternities... Our Lord Jesus-Christ warned us:

I give you a warning even today. The disciples who are not of My Holy Gospel are now involved in a great work of the mind in order to form a second Mass, a copy of sorts, when they will make to their idea and under the influence of the enemy of souls a Mass that contains words odious in My sight. When the fatal hour arrives, when they will put to the test the Faith of My eternal priesthood, it is these sheets that they will give to celebrate in this last period.

The first period, it is that of My priesthood which exists since Me. The second, is the period of persecution when the enemies of the Faith and of Holy Religion have formulated—and they are strongly enforced—these sheets as the book of the second celebration, these infamous spirits are those who crucified Me and who are waiting for the reign of the new Messiah to make them happy.

Many of My holy priests will refuse this book sealed with the words of the abyss. Unfortunately, (they) will be the exception to the rule, for this book will be used.

(Our Lord Jesus-Christ, 27 November 1901 or 1902, or 10 May 1904. Date unclear)

Everywhere in almost all of France the country will rise against the Church. They will spread, without rest, abominable articles on the Faith and on the Church, which the world, without hell, would never have been able to invent on its own: the disgraceful enemies of the Savior-God who assemble in the Lodges (Freemasons?) and fill them. The moment approaches. They will rise full of hope to throw mud and scandal upon the apostles of God and upon His Church. It's through them that the youth forgets its Creator and Redemptor. This time makes one shudder when one thinks of those Christians whose faith will be unshakable.

(The Holy Spirit, 12 February 1875)

Our Lord Jesus-Christ:

Woe to the priest who does not reflect on the enormous responsibility which he will have to give account back to Me. And the pastors of the Church (the bishops) what will they do for the faith? The great number is ready to give (up) their faith to save their bodies... The suffering they cause will never be repaired.

In a short time the pastors of the Church will have spread great scandals everywhere and will have given the last sword thrust to the Church.

(1881) (From the "Breton Stigmatist")

This, sadly enough, is but already an ongoing fulfilled prophecy... Indeed, Clergy scandals have spread, these past decades, throughout the world, not merely with countless cases of corruption, money laundering, illegal financial activities but of pedophilia and homosexual abuses, and with the Church's "highest positions" too often ignoring these dreadful crimes, or attempting to cover them up and concealing them through multi-billion financial settlements.

Too many cardinals, bishops and priests have caused some of the most morbid scandals in the History of the Church, destroying on many occasions the credibility of the Faith Itself. This is yet another undeniable example of the utter relevance of Marie-Julie Jahenny's prophetic messages for our time... Notwithstanding, Marie-Julie begged Our Lord not to send punishments upon the Church nor upon the world, but He replied to her on 20 October 1903:

"My daughter, sinners are too numerous and too guilty. They have abused My graces, especially those who have My Adorable Body at their disposal because of their status, and because of their profaning it. No, I can no longer forgive... Justice has to be done. Soon you will need all your faith."

(Our Lord Jesus-Christ, 20 October 1903)

Message of the Blessed Virgin Mary, August 1881:

My children, in this unfortunate time, days of abstinence are no longer kept. My children work on Sundays! (Transgression against the day of rest)... Soon they will see no more than a few Christians attend services! The confessionals will be empty... My children, it is blasphemy that brings hell

98

on earth. I am in sorrow for the clergy. I see that, in a great amount, and more of priests, the mind (or spirit) weakens every day. Many pastors are no longer, as were many of our priests, determined to die in honor of their sacred ministry.

(The Blessed Virgin Mary, 9 August 1881)

Our Lord in conversation with St. Joseph:

- **My Father, My zealous apostles, My priests will have a share of consolation; however, they will suffer since they are the pillars of the Church. But woe to him who will step-up the altar with a conscience veiled! Woe to him whose heart will be one fiber to the right and the other to the left!**
- I argued about their apostasy and my Son said:
- **That's what gives Me the most pain! To see those in the priesthood apostatize, (those) who were dedicated to My service!**
  My father, when all these infamies will have spread across the world, the earth will be in the biggest scandal.

(Conversation of Our Lord Jesus-Christ with St. Joseph, 19 March 1878)

The Blessed Virgin Mary:

More than ever before the number of priests, known as the true ministers of God, is very small... It is ever so small... If I named their (full) extent, you would shudder of sadness... I can tell you that there are many priests in France, and outside of France, who (will) have no shame to violate—in the days of terror—the secrets of the confessional, spoiling the Faith, defiling the Church. I will reveal that a priest can do a thousand times more evil than a man in the world... In this moment, there are those working under the veil waiting until they leave their priestly garments to better throw out horror and abomination among the people.

(The Blessed Virgin Mary, 19 September 1881)

For a period of time, all the works approved by the infallible Church will cease to exist as they are today. In this sorrowful annihilation, brilliant signs will be manifested on earth. If because of the wickedness of men Holy Church will be in darkness, the Lord will also send darkness that will stop the wicked in their search of wickedness...

(The Blessed Virgin Mary to Marie-Julie Jahenny, 1 June 1880)

Despite these concerning messages about the Clergy, Our Lord warned us that we are not to judge priests:

Respect priests, it is I who judge!

(Date unknown...)

Our Lady emphasized the high dignity of the priesthood, which people will no longer respect because the priests themselves will forget the greatness of their office and their exalted mission to serve God and save souls, and all this under the auspices of new ecclesiastical reforms.

The Blessed Virgin Mary:

-   **My children, in these sad times the days of abstinence are no longer observed.**
    My children, Sunday labor is progressing every day.
    My children, it is blasphemes that brings hell onto earth.
    My children, my last grievance, the one that places the sword about hearts: I make grievance about the Clergy! My victims, my servants, I have such sorrow for the Clergy... This is for me the greatest of sorrows, because for them forgiveness is most difficult to obtain... The life of a priest is so elevated in graces! The gifts they possess are so powerful that if they were known, everyone who lie at their feet and would speak to them with the same respect as if they spoke to my Son!

Marie-Julie Jahenny:

-   *It is true, good Mother, but the dignity of the priest is no longer respected.*
-   **But my daughter, many do not know how to respect themselves; words that tear apart the heart of the sovereign priest!**
    My children, I see that the mind weakens every day. The thinking of the present time makes the choice for them difficult as to the side they will prefer to choose following.
    (...) The true royalty of our fathers' souls is not known... With the larger numbers, the mind, the (overall) opinion goes in direction of those who govern this poor country...
    What a disgrace (there will be) before soon upon the priestly family! What great dishonor (due to) the collapse of the Faith and the attachment to the laws issued by these sad men from the Center (Paris) that do so much harm and that want to transform the home of my Saints (into) a theater, a place of hell and abomination. My children, it's not just our priests; the greatest number is on that (evil) side... There are ever so few on the other... If I were to name them, it would take me but one second to name them all...
-   *Oh, good Mother, it hurts so when one thinks about it!*

-   Oh my children, I am aware who I speak before. Oh, if my words were heard outside, they would weaken a great deal of people because of the Clergy's weakness.

    My children, do you believe... could you believe that in the Center, in the South and in the East (of France) bishops will abandon the Church without regret, thinking only of saving themselves in the times we live?

    My children, in all the new bishops, there is not a complete generation of faith. There is above all in their faith a weakness against my Son... They will never be forgiven for it... They do not deny His Powers, but they do not admit that my Son uses the earth to do good, to assure the salvation and protection of souls. Oh! They will be punished for their unbelief, and punishment is in the Hands of my Son... The Clergy is quite weak... The French Clergy will turn, in its greater number, towards the perishable side. The French Clergy will be punished for its lightness of heart... Measureless punishments shine in my Son's Hands...

    My children, the French Clergy is the most responsible because it is the most instructed. Religion, (in France), is more widely spread than in any other country. Catholicism has existed in France when it was so obscure in others; for this reason, they will be punished more severely. But the Clergy is bad everywhere... everywhere, my children!

(The Blessed Virgin Mary with Marie-Julie Jahenny, 9 August 1881)

Our Lady kept reminding Marie-Julie Jahenny of the great need to pray for priests and for sinners. Believing in her Son is not enough to earn one's salvation... Indeed, priests, she explains, do believe in Jesus-Christ and in His teachings, but again so does the Devil and no one is more condemned than he is... It is not enough to believe in God and in His Divine Son; men, and priests alike, must live their faith, combat one's evil tendencies and live the Faith with deeds and acts of conversion.

To that effect, the Blessed Virgin Mary asks for Confession, for frequent Communions, for many prayers of the rosary, and for many Ways of the Cross:

Pray much for the Church, for the priests and for sinners, for those who are going to rise up in disorder and (who will) re-crucify my Son. My children, make the Way of the Cross, which, in next to no time, will bring many souls to Heaven... Receive often Holy Communions, and say the rosary.

(The Blessed Virgin Mary, 2 February 1881)

In Rome the storm will be the blackest. The storm of Rome will be even worse than the storm in France. All the wrath of the ungodly is in Rome. All the anger of the wicked is focused on the Holy See; **however, the chastisements will begin with Paris**.

(Marie-Julie Jahenny, 8 December 1874)

In another message, we are warned there will be signs in the sky before the 'storm' breaks over Paris and France:

Twenty-four hours before the burst of this storm (which will be) ever so black, Our Lord will give signs in the firmament. Ah! Without the Sacred Heart, we would all perish. All priests who are not good will be punished.

(Marie-Julie Jahenny, 18 December 1874)

All (Church) authorities will have to undergo this Passion in their paternal seats. They will have to flee to escape the pursuit, the fierce prosecutions. The Church must see its Head (Pope) under vengeful hatred. The temple of God is to be deserted. In the beginning, the Lord's ministers may, despite the threats, obey the laws of their sacred ministry. It will be by force that they will be dragged out of the Temple. Then the order will come out to flee quickly. The vengeance of hell will rise to the altars of the most infamous of all men (those possessed). They will take the place of the true servants of the Lord.

Everything will be against the Faith and against the holy laws in their sacred ceremonies. The law will oblige parents to leave them to pervert their children. These sacrileges will last 44 days. Many Christians will suffer martyrdom. These crimes will be followed closely, (by) the vengeance of the Lord.

(Marie-Julie Jahenny, 10 August 1880)

In a particular apparition of Pope Gregory the Great, Marie-Julie was told:

Pray for the Church that is threatened by a conspiracy hatched by a horrible jealousy of perverted minds banded together to overthrow it. The storm is terrible, but the Church will remain infallible and its walls shall not be shaken. But there will be martyrs... Pray for the Church and ask God for the return of a lost family, a people corrupted, a degraded society. All are our brothers in the Lord. They are souls redeemed at the price of His Blood.

(Message of Pope Gregory the Great to Marie-Julie Jahenny, 19 August 1878)

In a text dated 19 March 1878: St. Joseph also forewarned of a great apostasy that would happen during the times of the desecrations of the Church... St. Joseph pleaded with his Son and prayed for the restoration of the Church without bloodshed, but Our Lord answered him:

- **The Holy Father will suffer torments that are beyond his powers. He will be discarded and thrust aside, pushed and shoved, like the sea when it braces.**

St. Joseph then said:

- *The Triumph will only come through victims and much bloodshed (martyrdoms). Many of these martyrs will be cloistered religious, there will be evil ones setting traps in the Church and will seek to destroy these religious.*

At this time, St. Joseph revealed that plagues will appear and spread, and the promised signs and warnings will occur. The faithful of France should flee to Brittany which will be protected.

You are about to see those who govern the Church giving their lives and their strength to those who will establish a fatal government... They will close the sanctuaries... and surrender to the disorders of Hell...

(St. Michael the Archangel, 25 October 1881)

A particular message given to Marie-Julie stated with gravity that the Church will be several months without a Pontiff:

The Church will have its seat vacant for long months... (...) <u>There will be two successive antipopes that will reign all this time over the Holy See</u>...

(29 September 1882)

However, a third Pope's arrival is announced as successor of the "two antipopes..."

The third Pope will be the most holy, but will not reign but three years before God calls him for his reward.

(16 May 1882)

As a holy Pontiff is indeed announced in Rome, another ruler of Italy is likewise foretold, a man who will be a persecutor of Christians...

The enemy of God will pass through Persia (Iran) and the other kingdoms, and will rise for one year upon the unfortunate seat of one who will cut off the head of the apostles and who will make a martyr of he who supports the Church and the Faith.

This announced enemy of God coming from Iran will be, Marie-Julie tells us, a man of German-Turkish descendance, and his name, as we shall find later through another of Marie-Julie Jahenny's revelations, will be **Archel de la Torre** (see page: 131) and he will take the head of the Italian government after the fall of a prior tyrant; however, his one year rule will be even more bloody than that of his predecessor's as he will persecute and butcher countless religious throughout Italy, but most particularly in the city of Naples...

The reformed Church:

In **The Breton Stigmatist**, we find the following text dated October 1882, a revelation given to Marie-Julie stating that bishops disobedient to the Holy Father will bring about the infamous and blasphemous 'new' religion:

The heart of the diocese of (Space left blank... place not revealed in the original texts' copies) **will revolt and will not be pacified. Its cries, and menacing words will make the strong tremble... In the days when the gloom of the great vengeance will surround the people with struggles and conflicts, this pastor** (The Bishop of...), **like the others will not submit to the orders of the Roman Pontiff.**

When the power of mortal men—soiled, corrupt men who are threatened with a terrible death—when this power will order a frightful religion in the whole Kingdom, I see only a small number enter this religion that will make the whole world tremble... From the height of My glory, I see Bishops joining, with alacrity, this guilty, infamous, sacrilegious religion... At the sight of these many, many Bishops, ah! My Heart is wounded to death, and the whole flock following them, all of it without hesitation, hastening to damnation and hell; My Heart (becomes) wounded to death as at the time of My Passion!

Others will follow these French Bishops... If I tell you that upon founding this infamous and accursed religion, the Bishops and priests will not leave (this false religion upon hearing) the second call. You may be sure, my children, that (these) bishops and priests will not be in favor of the one I have destined to raise up your country. There will be very, very few in favor of him... They will be against the King... (King Henry V of the Cross).

(Our Lord Jesus-Christ, October 1882)

In another message dated November 1882, there is a warning that underlines another great strike upon the Church before the chastisements. This new attack will begin when bishops will demand to separate themselves from the Pope and thus create a new schism:

Marie-Julie Jahenny:

*The crowd roars around the Vicar of Jesus Christ. A meeting of the Fathers of the Church will form councils against the Father of the universe. It will be presented (*a written declaration*), at the hands of the governor, the Holy Father,* *a piece of paper written and worked on by hands that, many times, will hit the Body of Christ. This written piece of document will include three demands:*

- 1) That the Pope leaves more liberty to the greater part of those over whom he rules with his authority of Pontiff. (They will demand that their obligation of obedience to him be relaxed.)
- 2) They will state: "We have met (or we have all united) and we are of the opinion that if the mortal head of the Church makes an appeal to his Roman clergy to reform the Faith to an even stronger degree, at the same time when they want to force us to declare in the face of the powers of the earth that there must be obedience and submission to them, we declare (that) we want to keep our freedom. We consider ourselves as free to do nothing more in the eyes of the people, than that what we are now doing, and further state that it is we who will do all."

Bitter and agonizing pain awaits the Pope before such insubordination and disobedience to answer the call of his heart. It will not be in person by which he will make the call, but in writing. The voice of the Flame says that the third thing written will thrill the little people of the earth. It will come from the clergy that aspires to a broader freedom: the clergy of France, Italy, Belgium and many other nations that God reveals. This schism will get worse before the people can be assured of the sign of God's wrath...
The next call will throw consternation into the hearts where the Faith still reigns. (These bishops) want to break the unity between the Holy Father and the priests of the universe, to separate them from the Head of the Church, so that everyone is free to himself, and without any supervision... A poster will be (publicly) posted and will only mention this disunion and this separation of the apostles of God with the Pope. The people will be invited to lend support and agreement to the ever so guilty authority (rebellious and treacherous bishops) of that time.

(Marie-Julie Jahenny, November 1882)

Despite the announced two Anti-Popes, despite the scandals manufactured by the Shepherds of the Church, the breaking-up of Clergy from the Pontifical Supreme Authority, the Church, St Joseph assures us, will remain steadfast... Once again, as these lines are being written (2019), one can read and watch in the news the German schism being prepared in Germany under the direction of Cardinal Reinhard Marx (President of the Commission of the Bishops' Conference of the European Community, President of the German Bishops' Conference, Coordinator of the Council for the Vatican's economy).

Under the leadership of this renegade Cardinal, the German Bishop's Conference is organizing a national synod, that is to last two years, to forge the foundations of a declaration of independence from the Magisterium of the Church in Rome (see page: 513). Such a course of action would not be in Communion with the Magisterium of Rome... Marie-Julie Jahenny's message is not subject to any interpretation: separating oneself from the Roman Catholic and Apostolic Church is to separate oneself from Christ Himself.

The corruption of children, society and the Church:

The corruption of the Church and of the most innocent, children, are indeed two of the enemy's primary targets, with a third and most subtle objective: the destruction of the Roman Catholic Church from within... The Sacred Heart warns of a time which is to be understood as a marker of sorts, a point of reference that would be the introduction of events that are to follow and bring about the prophetic "Justice of God".

This cornerstone in time, we are told, would be defined when Christians would have no peace amongst themselves and would confront each other with a division that would split the Church into two hard-set groups entrenched into their respective convictions. Might this be a prophecy of the division between the reformists and the conservatives which already is plaguing the Roman Catholic Church today, most particularly since the election of Pope Francis?

Clearly, a division has, de facto, been established throughout the world amongst Catholic dioceses and faithful. This line in the sand, as it were, is marked today not merely by what some view as Pope Francis' laxed attitude towards the LGBT, remarried couples, women's role in the Church, priests' celibacy, ecumenical stands and the Pope's distinct penchant for the Protestant liturgy (particularly that of Lutherans'), but, most alarmingly, what many within the Church consider Pope Francis' anemic response to the overwhelming and ongoing sexual scandals that have hit so many dioceses around the world, including the Vatican itself...

We know from Marie-Julie Jahenny's prophecies that the Clergy, the Hierarchy and the Vatican will have to go through two major crisis which will lead to its fall before it rises again... This grave prediction was confirmed repeatedly and through various means. Indeed, very few people ever knew that, in addition to the Holy stigmatas Marie-Julie Jahenny bore on her feet, hands, wrists, back, legs, arms, side and crown, the Breton Stigmatist likewise had on her chest the following stigmata:

Deliverance of the Holy Father, Triumph of the Holy Church

The most abominable sins will be committed without shame or regrets... The greatest number of priests will turn towards the side of evil...

(Our Lord Jesus-Christ, 25 October 1881)

Satan is joyous... He travels the earth in the fences of his houses where his disciples live of his doctrine, where he reveals them his Satanic secrets to lose souls... He gives his advises, and his supporters drink deeply his doctrines made of sacrileges and spells...

(The Blessed Virgin Mary, 5 January 1904)

106

Four months later, The Blessed Virgin Mary added:

On this odious sacrilegious path, they will not stop. They will arrive upon others which will, on one stroke, compromise everything at the same time: the Holy Church, the Clergy and the faith of my children.

(The Blessed Virgin Mary, 10 May 1904)

As we have seen before, the Blessed Mother announced "the dispersion of the shepherds" through the Church Itself, true shepherds who will be replaced by others who will be initiated to all vices, to all perfidious inequities which will cover souls with utter filth... There will be new preachers, new sacraments, new temples, new baptisms, new confraternities...

Innumerable were the apparitions to Marie-Julie Jahenny concerning the horrible crisis which is to disfigure the Catholic Church. Indeed, over and over again we are being warned with great insistence that our faith will need to be strengthened in order for the faithful to be enlightened and fortified in the course of an uncertain time of utter confusion; hence, I shall inscribe herein below some tactically chosen messages of importance originally recorded by Dr. Imbert-Gourbeyre, designated as one of Marie-Julie's formal recorder and historian:

Scandals will go before your eyes. Only pray, and invoke the Divine Mercy. You must be prepared for everything. The heart of the Church is nothing more but an open wound... It only claims the conversion of poor sinners. Today the crime is being brought forth to the feet of altars... The Lord is offended by those who should serve Him.

(St. Michael the Archangel, 29 September 1879)

The suppression of the ringing of the bells (for Masses) and for burials will be demanded... They will erase all memory of primary religion and they will teach an impious one.

(Our Lord Jesus-Christ, 6 September 1880)

These Church's reforms will consequently not be inspired by the Holy Spirit... On 21 September 1881, Marie-Julie Jahenny explained to Doctor Imbert-Gourbeyre:

Being with Our Lord, who was letting escape bitter grievances against His people, particularly against His Apostles who do not respect Him anymore, who outrage Him and who make the Holy Church suffer, He let me see a deep wound within His Sacred Heart and He told me:

The Holy Church is likewise wounded by a great number of them who should console her but instead afflict her. If you didn't want to accept for them your immense suffering, I would have let go of my arm burdened with

chastisements... Your charity has supported it, but when the time comes, the chastisements will be no lighter; they force Me to strike them! They lose their respect even in confessionals! They come out of the boundaries the Church imposes on them, and they are cause of a great part of the offenses made to her.

Woe to the priests who do not think of the immense responsibility they will have to render count to Me! They are the cause of an immeasurable harm! They are opposed against the good I operate to awaken the Faith, to inspire souls to serve Me more faithfully. Soon, they will be terribly punished!

Marie-Julie Jahenny:

- *I was making an effort to implore mercy, but He told me:*

I am listening to you, but (only) for a little time... And the Shepherds of the Church, what will they be in their faith? Their greater number is ready to deliver their faith to save their bodies. The Church is crying; the sorrows that they cause her will never be healed. In very little time from now, the Shepherds of the Church will have spread everywhere scandals, and they will have given the last blow with the lance to the Holy Church... Let all this be known so that the Church may know how much I suffer in the persons of My priests, and so that they may have compassion of My sorrows. They place Me in their hearts during these great and terrible faults.

On October 1881, Our Lord told Marie-Julie:

I announce a terrible chastisement for those whom I dressed with a sacred character and filled with graces. It is closed. I shall wait for them. They persecute My Church. They are quite guilty; not all, but many. The greater part is not on the Royal side (*side of King Henry V of the Cross*).

Marie-Julie Jahenny:

My Jesus, they do not do it on purpose. They think they are doing well.

Our Lord Jesus-Christ:

I know well their designs. I know their thoughts. I see weakness taking over My priest to such a frightful extent. I see them go on the side of those who will plant on this poor country the standard whose color is that of blood, that of terror (red flag – Communist flag?)... You will be, some months thereafter, scandalized by many books. Religion will be targeted, attacked, and at the place of this beautiful religion there will be infamous writings. It will be the Schism entered in France. Everything will be (affected) thereby,

and its foul odor and abominations will be spread everywhere...

(Exchange with Our Lord Jesus-Christ and Marie-Julie, 25 October 1881)

Announcement of an upcoming apparition site of the Blessed Virgin Mary in France:

In the land of Amiens (France), the Mother of God is about to set-up her visit with the Child Jesus in her maternal arms, and warn the people, mixed as everywhere else. There will be a sign in the sky... The voice of a little child will announce with Divine Permission, the terrible sorrows that await the country; he will announce them a very short time before these projects occur... This child will speak for about 27 minutes, with tears in his voice which will affect even the leaves of the grass. This announcement, terrible for France, will be universal.

(16 November 1882)

Prophecies of catastrophic natural disasters, curious spots in the sun and signs in the sky:

In October 1929, Our Lady appeared to Marie-Julie Jahenny:

You will receive the warning precisely by the appearance of spots in the sun... I said before... You will see the firmament streaked with bands. There will be a white band that will contain the protection of our right ones (faithful). There will be a red one to envelop the chastisement of the wretched (ones) who insult their Creator. There will be a black one where they will struggle under Satan in his army. (The latter) will be wider, because Satan has more souls to serve him than my Divine Son does to comfort His Heart and dry His tears.

(The Blessed Virgin Mary, 4 October 1929)

Marie-Julie was likewise shown 'grotesque rains'. In one vision she saw a pestilential red 'blood' rain that coagulated followed by a 'burning' phenomenon that would last for weeks. In another vision Marie-Julie saw a 'black and blue' rainbow shedding a 'rain of blood' followed by a miraculous sign of the cross (in the sky?).

"My children, out of this cloud will come a rain so extraordinary, that the world has never yet seen one alike, and will never see another until the end of time. It will be a red rain that will remain coagulated on the earth for seven weeks... The land itself will be coagulated by this rain that will give off a poisonous breath, a smell that no one can bear. My people will remain locked up for seven weeks. It will be difficult to leave, as the world will be in fear.

Thus the first storm is announced and will come truly soon. Following this storm, I will make emerge from the earth a horrible scorch… Christians will neither stand the smell nor the heat. My children, do not open your doors, nor your windows."

(9 March 1878)

I see in my sun, a black and blue rainbow. It rains from this rainbow when the murder-attempts and crimes are being committed; it rains a red rain. On the roofs of houses, it (the rain) remains stuck as paint; when on the ground, it cannot be drunk. It falls with a frightening speed. In this rain, there will be produced a sign of fear: a cross formed in the rain that bears the imprint of Christ. It produces signs of terror that will not be erased. The cries of the righteous are frightening. In this rain will perish all who are open to impiety, they will be struck with terror. After three days, the rain from the rainbow will visibly stretch through all the universe.

(Marie-Julie Jahenny, 8 April 1880)

In another vision about the Days of Darkness, the Holy Spirit warned of another filthy rain. These rains may indeed be related. It is difficult to tell from the original texts:

The earth will shake from this place until sunrise for a period of six days. A day of rest and (on) the eighth day, the trembling will begin again. France and England will respond with their cries of despair. The land will shake so hard that the people will be thrown-out up to 300 steps… The thunder will sound more violently than in the months that will lead up to the end of the world, with a strange noise.

(Message of the Holy Spirit to Marie-Julie Jahenny, 8 March 1881)

Our Lord revealed to Marie-Julie Jahenny that revelations were given to St. Catherine Labouré (*visionary of the 1830 apparitions of the Blessed Virgin Mary in the Chapel of the Sisters of Charity Convent, rue du Bac, Paris—the Miraculous Medal*) about these warning-signs. These prophecies, however, were hidden away for future times but will be discovered in a monastery:

This day (of warning) **is noted in five rolls tightly closed (by) the sister of Saint Pierre Tours. This roll remains (hidden) in secret, until the day when a person of God brings his predestined hand on what the world has ignored to the inhabitants of that monastery…**

(Unknown Date…)

On several occasions, Our Lord Jesus-Christ and the Blessed Virgin Mary appeared to Marie-Julie, accusing the local bishops and priests of La Salette to

110

have hidden Heaven's message given on the mountain of the French Alps when no one knew yet of the scandalous deed. News of this apparition was not spread as much as it should have been. Our Lord Jesus-Christ and the Blessed Virgin Mary reproached the French clergy as being the culprit for its willing omission to echo Heaven's admonition to the people of France, and through them to the people of the world. The faithful were not properly warned about the punishments coming to the earth, or the evils that would soon befall humanity if men did not convert and repent.

In August 1904, the Blessed Virgin Mary reminded Marie-Julie Jahenny of her message given years before at La Salette:

(...) Finally, I have truly suffered when holy Shepherds-priest wanted the last lines of my secrets, on the mountains of sorrows, to be known by all my people, (but) other shepherds revolted (against that idea)...

I had the painful sorrow to see placed under seal these last pages which should have been delivered to the world... It's because it involves a great deal of shepherds and the priesthood that they have revolted (against my instructions), and that they folded the last pages of this divine secret... How can you expect for the chastisement not to befall earth?

They go as far as enveloping my last words on the holy mountain and to have them disappear! (They go as far) as making suffer those who devoted themselves for this holy cause with the joy to glorify me in this solemn prediction. It's because these last lines are all about the priesthood, and it was because it was I who pronounced them, who revealed them, that pride was mortified.

I show how they serve my Son in the holy Orders, and how they live in all times in their priesthood. How can you expect Heaven to bless them? I do not speak of all shepherds, of all of priesthood, but the number I am exempting is truly small.

They let all the souls wonder (blindly) in utter emptiness. They take care in a very small manner of their salvation. They like rest, good food and good living... My dear victim priests; the true ones are truly few...

They (the corrupted ones) love the Holy Tribunal with indifference. They walk up the Altar because they are forced to accomplish this act, but you will see soon their joy for not having to do so any longer; you will see their happiness to be discharged of souls and of their forgiveness. What vain words! What conversations that are ever so unpleasant to Heaven!

What will they (the priests) be on the great day? What will they be in those horrible and unforgettable days! I do not repeat the bad part that you know of my secrets given on the holy mountain.

(The Blessed Virgin Mary, 4 August 1904)

I prayed, I cried, I suffered. I came down on earth to warn them. I promised them salvation if they did penance.

I announced to the Clergy fatal perditions. I had them receive my warnings if it weakens in the storm and tempest. I cried upon France. I trace thereupon the Way of the Cross I opened fountains to cleanse the sick (Lourdes). I consoled my people promising it to keep it save. This hasn't touched the guilty one. He remained in crime. His chastisement is close at hand.

(The Blessed Virgin Mary, 29 November 1877)

I still have on my eyes the trace of my tears that I shed on these days when I wanted to bring to my children the good news if they converted, and the sad news if they persisted in their inequities. They paid little heed to what I revealed...

My children, when I recall the day when, on the holy mountain, I brought forth my warnings to earth... when I remember the harshness with which they received my words, not all of them but many of them; and (when I remember) those who should have spread them in the hearts of my children with immense trust and deep discernment, they have not listened (to me). They despised them, and, for the greater part of them, they refused to trust them... Well, I assure you that all these promises, these intimate secrets, will take place. They must visibly take place.

When I see what will happen on earth, I still shed tears... When the earth will have been purified by the chastisements of its crimes and of all the vices it is dressed with, beautiful days will return with the savior chosen by us and unknown yet by our children until now.

(The Blessed Virgin Mary, 29 September 1901)

Notwithstanding, Marie-Julie was told that Our Lady will appear yet again in the vicinity of this old apparition site (La Salette-Fallavaux) to warn the people of France a second time, as before, the greater punishments befall France.

The Mother of God, moved by the love of her heart, will come down to earth, appearing to her people in a way that is immeasurable. She will renew her descent from Heaven to earth in the surrounding mountains of La Salette. She will appear, suspended on a white cloud, surrounded by a garland of roses, to say:

The earth will be a tomb, from Alsace-Lorraine which is not counted, to the edge of Brittany (see page 469).

Marie-Julie was likewise told that Our Lady will appear in northern France, to deliver yet another warning to 'a dozen visionaries':

In the north of France, she will come with signs of mourning, and will give only three words that will be heard by a dozen souls:

112

- All the earth (or, land), except for Brittany, will be only a lifeless tomb.
- The Church will suffer such persecutions that hell itself never before had invented more cruel ones.
- The Center (Paris) will become a land soaked in blood. The last who will sink will be the one amongst men that Heaven has cursed because of his crimes.

In September of 1901, Our Lady appeared again during the anniversary of her apparition at La Salette and on the 29th of the same month and stated, in both messages (not to confuse one apparition and message with the other), almost word for word with profound sadness that the warnings she gave on her holy mountain were not heeded, and the evils foretold then were now about to take place:

My eyes still have a trace today of the tears that I shed on that day when I wanted to bring my children the Good News if they converted, but sad news if they continued with their inequities. They take little notice of what I revealed... Now is the time that these great promises will be accomplished (and) that the Church authorities have despised... They did not want the light!

I have suffered a great deal for all of this. Pain oppresses my heart at this moment... The most painful sword right now is to see the preparations that have been made and that are in the making... (How painful) it is to see the pastors detaching themselves from the Sacred Bond that directs and governs Holy Church... My children, I remember the day I brought my warnings to the Holy Mountain (La Salette), to the threatened world.

I remember the harsh reception of my words, not by all, but by many; and those who should have made them known to the souls, hearts and spirits of children with great confidence, deep penetration: they took no notice! They despised them and most of them refused them their trust...

My Divine Son, Who sees everything in the depths of consciences, Who saw the contempt for my promises, made arrangements in Heaven for a measure of severity for all those who refused to make known my word to my children as a bright light, true and just. When I see what awaits the earth, my tears flow again... False apostles under the appearance of honeyed words and false promises and tell lies soliciting my dear children to save their lives from the storm and the peril of blood... I assure you, flee from the very shadow of these men who are none other but the enemies of my Divine Son!

I once again refer to this immense sorrow: I see some pastors at the head of Holy Church... (brief pause as the Blessed Virgin Mary is trembling...)... when I see this irreparable outrage, the deadly example of which will be a disaster for my dear people; when I see this bond breaking... my sorrow is immense, and Heaven is greatly irritated... Pray for those pastors whose weakness will cause the loss of multitude of souls (last sentence repeated three times).

When I see the enemies presenting their promises... to many of those who are priests of my Divine Son; when I see those souls allowing themselves to descend to the bottom of the abyss, I tell you this: I am surprised, as the Mother of God Almighty, that my Son does not immediately open the Heavens to pour out the blows of His anger on His enemies who insult and outrage Him...

(The Blessed Virgin Mary, 19 September 1901)

France and Europe Before a War to Come, and World Chastisements

France is at the eve of its sorrows and of its joy: the sorrows for sinners, and the joy for the just. (...) Before peace flourishes again upon the earth, a great penance must bend Divine Anger. It is the Lord Himself who exercises His Anger. It is only up to Him whether or not to chastise, but while chastising, He will purify the earth and His people. He will not spare anything. He will cultivate the earth for a new harvest.

(St. Michael the Archangel, 25 May 1877)

Marie-Julie Jahenny explained:

On a background of confusion and disorder, (various) epochs (eras) will be established which will be like 'degrees of progression'... It will be, first, like a thundering storm which will increase in great density, finishing with a great strike which will bring peace.

- The first epoch will be the extend of evil on the eldest daughter of the Church: France.
- The second epoch will be the Church being invaded and the beginning of a terrible struggle in the Eternal City (Rome). This struggle in the Eternal City will last for 5 months until sad and grave consequences of death take finally place.

(Our Lord, 4 May 1882)

Marie-Julie revealed that in these times, preceding a war in Europe, the Lord reserved three months of "fatal and terrible" chastisements for France... However, He will shorten said period of time a great deal (due to His Faithful's responses, prayers, penance and fasting).

"The next crisis," Marie-Julie Jahenny added, "will begin with the revolutionary beginning in France which will last four weeks, but the extent within the country will be immense... Indeed, the number of those called 'Murderers of the People' will be... of an inconceivable immensity."

114

During this hour, the foreigners, who are possessed by a feeling of violence that can no longer be contained, will be masters in France. (...) During this first struggle, within the entire surface area of the country of France, there will be no longer criminals held in prison...

(9 May 1882)

When the time to purify the Earth will be close, when minds (will) revolt one against the other, when there will be neither peace nor justice among My Christians—not in the world *but among My Christians*—the hour of My justice will be close. I shall purify the earth of all those impure and unjust souls that insult and outrage Me. I shall strike down their bodies with a feature of My Justice that will be so sudden, so swift, that it will be as fast as lightning... (...) Never has any punishment happened like this, a punishment which is now close, very close.

Never has the world been as corrupt, deceitful, deceptive, greedy, ambitious and wicked (as it is now). (...) I do not want you to open the depth of these infamous crimes. If you only knew the infamous correspondences that are under the influence of Satan... They sell My Holy Church; they sell in secret the head of the priest; they sell in secret the poor earth that they subject to a horrible punishment.

It has not seen, it has not understood, and today it makes a hellish trade the likes of which the world has never seen before... All is delivered up, everything is sold, and plots are being hatched every day. The hunger to devour human flesh, the thirst for human blood makes all their bodies seethe with unrest, and (consumed with) a desire to reach their goal as quickly as possible. All this is happening in the room of hell (Chamber of Deputies, Paris France), under the chairmanship of souls sold to the spirit of evil.

(Our Lord Jesus-Christ, 12 November 1924)

St. Michael:

> The hour of God is not far. This profound terror will (bring about) the triumph of New France. But this triumph cannot come before (if) Justice is not (pressed down) on this rotten land.
>
> Do not expect anything of him who reigns as king and who, today, sits in the same chair as the others – a chair that bears no mark of a special power or much grander (the President of the French Republic). His mind is in accordance with the thoughts of others, his word to their word, his will to their will. His power and authority are not more than he who is the last.
>
> Do not expect anything from this side: he does not deserve any more respect than all the rest. In the storm, his voice will cry as loud as the others, against all that God has established. There is no strength in him; they lead him, they have directed him. This is the portrait of

115

this man; he is a pillar of mud (President of the French Republic)... **Grieve about it, but do not give it much thought.**

Marie-Julie:

- *I will not think about it, good Saint Michael.*

St. Michael:

- **To reinstate the chosen and destined by God King, it is necessary that all those who are present be swept away...**

(St. Michael appeared to Marie-Julie on 29 September 1879)

My people, the laws will achieve their design, and France, before 2 years (two years after the adoption of said laws?) (...), **France will become almost entirely 'Mahometan' and without religion** (...). **It's during this troubled period of time that disgraceful laws will be promulgated aiming, among other things, to establish a control of power upon religion, subjecting the Clergy to the revolutionary power, persecuting thus all opposition, cutting off all hierarchical ties with Rome.**

Some revolutionaries will install a totalitarian power center with an expeditive justice regime aimed at dealing with opposition militants, involving surveillance, (and) denunciation...

Insufficient crops and (natural) calamities such as torrential rains, will lead to great delays in agriculture, and these will be forewarning signs of this revolution to come...

(Our Lord Jesus-Christ, 13 April 1882)

The strong (political) party will be the one of evil's victory... The small number will fall under the thunder of these voices who call for the blood and the flesh of bodies, to 'stretch their instruments', as they say...

The Christian judges will be replaced. In every part of France; the people will have to submit to surveillers or suffer being sent into prison and finish one's life under cutting weapons (axe? Guillotine?).

In many a place, Satan will be publicly invoked... The traditional guardians of the peace (name of the French Police's) **will no longer be able to circulate in cities... It will be the signal for pillage (and) of a terrible civil war... Many people who are jobless are but waiting for the signal. The Church will be deprived of its Head, and bells will no longer ring...** (...) **It will no longer be possible to return these foreigners away for they will mix the dust of their kingdoms to the land of France. They will have the proud ambition to tear-away the remainders of the treasures, honor and dignity of France!**

(24 January 1882)

116

(...) On the 8th, the ungodly, the profaners, the remorseless consciences (will plan) one of the darkest plots that France could ever imagine without the breath of the infernal soul... From this infernal project all the wickets will be set and will light-up the spirit of revolt, and will attract the terrible chastisements. It's been a long time that the usurpers have hidden a violet fire, small fore under the walls of the great city of Paris. As soon as the little breath of air comes upon these violet sparkles, they will become fiery braziers which will devour homes and will kill many inhabitants (of the city). Know that these men without faith, who only desire disorder and death, use the powder from the coal taken from hell...

(Jesus-Christ, 1 June 1877)

When (the French) government will see these upheavals and the revolt taking place, it will do like a bird and fly away, and France will see itself free to pursue its revolution. The first rise to civil revolt will take place in Paris, and this throne of bad kinds (the Elysée Palace?) will collapse like the city itself, and its victims will perish within its walls. Often enough, flames and fire have shown themselves in this criminal city, but this time... it will be a sulfured-hail that will suffocate all the guilty ones...

There, they will violate Tabernacles. There the priest of churches will be pursued with great rage. Many will never leave. I shall receive the blood of martyrs to help the true Frenchmen to obtain victory. It is there that the flames will devour churches, and that statues of the Blessed Virgin Mary will be split and thrown into fire...

France will receive no support. She will be alone, and why? Because she has no King.

(27 April 1877)

Here, naturally, the scenario depicted in the messages hereinabove underline the fact that France will be subjugated by the "Mahometans" and leftists, and will be taken over by revolts throughout the country that will quickly transform into civil war. The presidential palace (the Elysée) in Paris will be burnt to the ground and everyone inside will be killed. The French government will flee and seek refuge abroad. The Catholic Church will be persecuted. Churches in Paris will be sacked, burnt and ravaged. Priests will be forced out, beaten and/or killed. New horrid laws will be passed by a newly imposed government (Socio-Communist?).

The France of yesteryears will become unrecognizable... France will receive no support from her allies simply because France will have no longer any legitimate government... This opens the door to another possible conclusion. Indeed, although a war in Europe, as we shall see in the upcoming pages, is clearly announced following a civil war in France, it does not mean that this announced military conflict will be a world war. It certainly might have the potential to turn into one, but the revelations received by Marie-Julie Jahenny do not state with clarity that it will be so...

Visionary Conchita Gonzalez—from the Marian-apparition case of Garabandal—Spanish apparition case still under investigation by the local Bishop Santander (supported and confirmed by Saint Padre Pio – see Chapter VII) – explained that, in 1962, when a third world war was being feared in France and in western Europe (due to the explosive Cuban crisis), the Blessed Virgin Mary informed Conchita that there will not be a third world war.

May it as it be, was this statement meant for the crisis of the time or did the Blessed Virgin Mary state that there would never be a Third World War? The civil war in Yugoslavia in the 1990s, the military conflicts in Georgia, the tensions between China, Taiwan and the U.S. in the pacific, the civil war in Ukraine, the maintaining of the Crimean peninsula under Russian possession, the victory of the Taliban in Afghanistan, and the continuous military tensions and "incidents" between Russia and Turkey in Syria have proven that a Third World conflict is still quite possible.

However, one thing remains absolutely certain: no matter all the efforts invested in trying to decipher prophecies or discover the secrets of the future, tomorrow's destiny is and will remain in God's Hands, and in God's Judgment alone.

Marie Julie:

The (French) military will be sent away from France in Eastern and Arab countries, and the police forces will be reduced to critical numbers in France. It's during these trouble periods of time that infamous laws will be established which will have for aim, among other things, to control religion, and to have the Church submit to the revolutionary power while persecuting any and all opposition and cutting off every hierarchical tie with Rome (the Vatican).

Revolutionaries will establish an authoritarian power with an expeditionary system of justice against its opposition, enforcing a tight surveillance, a system of denunciation, etc.

In mid-late 2020, we were able to see the French army, navy and air force present in Mali, Syria, Iraq, Jordan, United Arab Emirates, Lebanon, Afghanistan, in the Persian Gulf, and in central African countries such as Gabon, Ivory Coast, Cameroon, Chad, Central African Republic, Senegal and Niger. In each country, France has begun a large scale mission involving the eradication of a very efficient and yet elusive ISIS force that has become international in its action and armed forces, but which, to date, has been reduced to commando-gorilla operations due to lack of a major country's logistic and military support.

Marie-Julie Jahenny stated that France would be more and more involved in foreign land conflicts, Leaving France's homeland unprepared for an internal civil unrest which with time would become… uncontrollable… The arrival of a particular government would see the French Capital being the first victim of a slow and subtle takeover of Catholic assets for the "alleged" national good of the country.

Could this mean that a French party of the far right be elected (the Rassemblement National headed by Marine Le Pen or Eric Zemmour), and consequently lead to an islamo-Communist protesting forces in the country?, for only such a scenario in France would lead the far left wing to start in France such civil unrest against National institutions and against the Catholic Church in France.

Marie-Julie further added, the 'Temple' dedicated to the Sacred Heart in Paris will be requisitioned by an evil government made-up of conspirators (prediction concerning the Sacré Coeur Basilica in Paris). The Holy Spirit further warned Marie-Julie Jahenny that:

(…) the people of the Centre (Paris) hastened to devote itself to the Sacred Heart elevated above this land! This temple, which heard so many prayers will be transformed into a boardroom, (or, council room). This is where the enemies, in part, will decide, at last, to launch the announcement of terror and death throughout the whole of this kingdom.

(Unknown date…)

Our Lord Jesus-Christ further stated:

My Sanctuary of Montmartre (i.e., the Sacré Coeur Basilica) is already destined to serve as a theatre for the impious and all those involved with human laws.
It would not be long before the place of prayer of Saint Geneviève would become a theatre for dances and for the most infernal crimes…

(Unknown date…)

I remember a few years ago—after the Franco-Spanish socialist politician, Anne Hidalgo, was elected Mayor of Paris—how the Sacré Coeur on Montmartre was discussed into a city-project which consisted in eradicating the Basilica and rebuilding on said terrain a new building for a common popular project that would exude solidarity amongst the different communities of Paris. Here is an article of the magazine **France-Ouest**:

An inhabitant of the 18th, arrondissement of the Capital suggested on the website of the participative budget of the City of Paris to demolish the Basilica of the Sacred Heart (Sacré Coeur) which *"insults the memory of the Paris Commune"*. It is one of the most photographed Parisian monuments. The Sacré Coeur has been covering the Montmartre Hill since the 19th century. While many tourists visit the Basilica every year, the building does not seem to please everyone.
A Parisian from the 18th arrondissement showed his deep disgust for the monument considered *"awful and disproportionate"* and simply proposed to *"shave it off"*. This fanciful proposal was formulated last February 11 (2017) on the participative budget platform of the City of Paris. The Municipality offers the inhabitants of the Capital the opportunity to propose and elect a project that is important to them. The Parisians had until February 21 to

share their ideas. The one that will receive the most votes in September can be financed up to a total of 100,000,000.00 Euros.

"Versailles' wart"

Under the pseudonym Nathalie Lemel, named after a feminist figure of the "Paris Commune", the Parisian explains that the Sacré Coeur is *"a wart from Versailles that insults the memory of the Paris Commune"*. *"The project involves the total demolition of the basilica for (the benefit of) a popular party"* he imagines. *"It is a provocation to recall what the Sacré Coeur is in the memory of the Paris Commune."* Says the man behind the project interviews by France Info (Radio show).

As a reminder, the basilica was erected at the precise place where the communal insurrection began March 18, 1971 in response to the decision of Adolphe Thiers, head of the Provisional Government of the Republic, to withdraw from Parisians their weapons and guns.

Many partisans of the communards have seen in the decision to build the building a will of the Third Republic, (of) conservative and royalist inspiration, to punish the crimes of the Commune and to put in good place the Catholic religion. "Not admissible"

His idea has attracted many internet users. "Remember that Zola stood against this *obscurantist construction* said one of them. *"What a wonderful project!"* enthuses another... The wacky project records 186 "likes" on the website of the participative budget of the City of Paris. In the 18th arrondissement, he is a favorite.

The disappearance of the Sacré Coeur of the Parisian landscape is nevertheless not for tomorrow. The Deputy Mayor of Paris, Pauline Veron, says that this project is *"not admissible and will not be part of the projects for which Parisians will be able to vote in September"*.

The criteria for selecting the projects submitted to the vote are listed on the participatory budget website. It includes, among others, taking into account the general interest, projects that come under the jurisdiction of the City of Paris, and the absence of operating expenses.

"The Sacré Coeur does not belong to the City of Paris and it is a historical monument," argues Pauline Veron. *"... and then we try to build things rather than destroy them."*

(Article of OUEST-France: Published on 23 February 2017)

Although the project of "shaving off" the Sacré Coeur has been rejected on this first vote in 2017 (over one hundred years after the prophetic message received by Marie-Julie Jahenny), one can say that this plan will be replaced by another for a later time, but according to the warnings from Heaven, this project will indeed be brought back to a vote which will win the motion of transforming the Basilica in a "Council-room/Boardroom"... **where the enemies, in part, will decide, at last, to launch the announcement of terror and death throughout the whole of this kingdom...**

Notwithstanding, as a Frenchman, the impression of this passionate plea to eradicate one of France's greatest monument of Catholic Faith was, at the very least… odd… as it appeared to the Deputy Mayor of Paris, Pauline Veron, and surely to many more Parisians who refused to participate in this strange impassioned project…

Paris, it appears, will not be the only major French city where the Faith will find itself under assault:

In the South, in Lyon, there will be infamous performances of the Mass, profanations. In Lyon and other places there will be Satanic apparitions, there will be worship of infamous goddesses, false miracles that will deceive many. The bishoprics, monasteries will be looted. The crosses will be broken. Tabernacles desecrated. Religious burials / funerals will be forbidden. The religious sacraments are parodied. Sacrilegious baptisms will be established. There will be many souls that will be possessed and make a loud noise and will make prophecies of happiness… the enemies will trample on the cross.

(There will be) Profanations at Lourdes. They will be furious against the devotion to the Sacred Heart. The cloister of Paray le Monial will be burned… In Paris, the Sanctuary of Montmartre will become the boardroom of drama for the rebels. But the Blessed Virgin will protect Our Lady of Victories (i.e., famous Marian shrine in Paris)**… All the miraculous statues of Our Lady (will) resume an almighty mission on the places that she protects and conserves.**

(Recorded ecstasy, Unknown date…)

All the workers whose employment furnished everyday an occupation, were never exposed to doing evil deeds. The designs of those who rule France planned of taking away all work and every employment… My children, there will no longer be any rest. Night and day, the 'runners' do evil deeds, cause fire, and horrible assassinations… They will use the most violent of powders that pulverize the strongest buildings on earth.

(Recorded ecstasy, Unknown date…)

Here, clearly this message addresses what appears to describe to perfection the multiple acts of terrorism that have taken place, and continue to take place in France since 2012, and which have caused the death of over 240 French Police, military and civilian victims at the hands of Jihadist terrorists (between 2012 and 2022)… And yet this prophecy announced something somewhat more extreme.

The Flame of the Holy Spirits said:

Many 'runners' call the workers to revolt because of the lack of work which is their daily bread. The little cities, as the larger ones, will be lost by

group of workers who have neither asylum nor refuge. They will spread everywhere, especially when the hour for them to find relief will soon ring...

Who hasn't heard of the French "Yellow-Jackets" who, since December 2018, have organized—because of the drastic raise of French taxes—non-stop weekly protests throughout the largest cities of France, beginning with Paris, soon to be joined-up one year later (November 2019) by France's overall working-force which has continuously caused major national strikes, violence, car-burnings, shop destructions, etc., due to Emmanuel Macron's strangling retirement pensions, pushing the legal retirement age to a few years more. This describes to perfection the beginning effect of the prophecy hereinabove (in red): They will spread everywhere, especially when the hour for them to find relief will soon ring...

The screams of despair will rise to Heaven. The months of the Sacred Heart (June) and of My Blood (July) will be the signal of the chastisements: Civil War.

(Our Lord Jesus-Christ, 23 November 1882)

This raises a problem which has indeed the potential to ignite to an already quite explosive scene: immigration... Indeed, with France receiving every year over 250,000 legal immigrants, the country's population issued of Northern Africans and Middle-Easterns is quickly shifting into a population volume that can no longer be ignored. As Catholic Churches and chapel are every year sold or destroyed, mosques are continuously being built in the Land of King St. Louis.

In 2022, over 2,200 Muslim prayer centers and mosques are frequented by a population of approximately 9,000,000 to 11,000,000 practicing Muslims, a large portion of which is composed of intolerant and militant Salafists. Today, according to the latest French polls, over twenty-eight percent (28%) of said practicing French Muslim nationals declared wishing leading their lives according to the rules of the Islam's Sharia rather than to the laws of the French Republic[10]... Furthermore, the bitterness felt by the younger generations of Arab and sub-Saharan living in France today, reflect a profound animosity towards a country which, they feel, has subjugated through past French colonies in Africa their countries of origin; but more and more, this resentment is becoming mutually felt.

Further to attest of the unrest and uneasy feeling presently existing in France, some of the latest polls in France show the bitterness felt by French locals in regards to the lack of foreign efforts to integrate themselves into French society and culture:

---

[10] **28% of 9,000,000 Muslims represents 2,520,000 fundamentalist Muslims.**

LES FRANÇAIS SUR L'IMMIGRATION :
Source : IPSOS/LE MONDE

LES IMMIGRÉS NE FONT PAS D'EFFORTS POUR S'INTÉGRER EN FRANCE — **66**%

LES IMMIGRÉS FONT DES EFFORTS POUR S'INTÉGRER EN FRANCE — **34**%

IMMIGRATION : MACRON SE SAISIT DU DOSSIER

LCI

French polls from LCI TV (September 2019)
66% of Frenchmen feel immigrants make no efforts to integrate into French society...

Today, the testimony of the Frenchman who authors this book and writes these lines is this: France today is a multi-cultural society fractioned into three sections: A French secular social elite headed by a predominantly lukewarm Christian, Jewish, or atheist population which has architected and/or tolerated for decades the arrival of millions of immigrants for a multi-purpose design: the lowering of the masses' salaries in national industrial plants, the replacement of a Catholic Faith, a political and social influence by a consortium of non-Catholic, non-Christian communities, and, it is hoped, the entering into a new chapter in History which would see the Globalization of French Society and the

LES FRANÇAIS SUR L'IMMIGRATION :
Source : IPSOS / LE MONDE

ON NE SE SENT PLUS CHEZ SOI COMME AVANT — **64**%

ON SE SENT AUTANT CHEZ SOI AUJOURD'HUI QU'AVANT — **36**%

IMMIGRATION : MACRON SE SAISIT DU DOSSIER

LCI

French polls from LCI TV (September 2019)
64% of Frenchmen do not feel in their own country as they did before...

decomposition of the French National Identity into a multi-cultural population cohabitating into a same land, soon to become but a mere region of a Super Federal United States of Europe.

The second fraction of the French population is composed principally of millions of un-integrated first, second and third generation French citizens of Northern and Sub-Saharan African origin, mostly of Muslim religion, living principally in suburban communities outside but also within the principal cities of France. Some of these suburbs are ruled by Islamic communities who rule with their own patrolling internal police, and commerce with their own internal economy (including drug and weapon trafficking).

These territories—where neither the French police, hospital ambulances nor fire fighters trucks ever dare going into—are called "*Les territoires perdus de la Républiques*" (the lost territories of the Republic). In some of these "lost territories" the French public services do not dare to send vehicles of any sort out of fear to be immediately assaulted with rocks, projectiles and often with heavy fire by assaulting groups of men armed with Kalashnikovs... Paris, Saint Denis, Lille, Strasbourg, Mulhouse, Marseille, Nice, Lyon, and Calais are but a few of the principal cities that are victims today of such... "hostile takeovers", but the French government keeps this fact as quiet as possible to avoid having the principal opposition and first political party in France, "Le Rassemblement National", headed by Mrs. Marine le Pen, stop gaining an alarmingly increasing popularity—credited in 2021 between 35%—46% of the voting population—and to avoid a cultural spark that could ignite a fully blown civil war...

Finally, the third fraction of the French population consist principally, but not exclusively of deep-rooted Frenchmen, patriotic, overwhelmingly Christian, if not Catholic, mostly living in the rural areas of France, but often in withdrawn cities, towns or villages. These are mostly the Frenchmen who live in a country they no longer recognize as their own, in a country where they discover in shock the French National hymn openly being booed in French soccer matches against Algerian or African teams, or cities' street and public pools being more and more filled with Muslim women in hijabs, burkas, or burkinis.

Furthermore, today France sees every year over 1,000 Roman Catholic churches and Cathedrals, and hundreds of Christians and Jewish cemeteries being vandalized by Muslim perpetrators. But most of all, France has been victim of scores of Islamic terrorist massacres in its homeland since 2012 which have claimed hundreds of French lives...

Marie-Julie Jahenny announced that there will be a great cry of despair reaching Heaven during a certain month of June and of July. This would be the sign of a Civil War that is to start in France. Such event is to take such an incontrollable measure that the French legal government will be forced to leave Paris in sheer panic... These political instigators will leave the citizens of France into the hands of terror-mongers and to the tyranny of what is familiarly known today as the "paper Frenchmen" minority:

When the government will see these changes, it will be like a bird; it will fly to another country, and France will be free in its revolution. It is at that moment when it will flee Paris.

(12 April 1877)

The Holy Spirit told Marie-Julie Jahenny:

Dear friends of God, as soon as they (the evil conspirators) **start the spark which will produce such a sprawling fire upon the land of the kingdom that must be subjected to this terror, they** (the evil conspirators) **will retreat to**

124

shelter from the storm and will leave all the doors of France open; all will be able to penetrate (in France) without a defense (*to stop them*).France is going to be delivered at the mercy of all peoples, of all those who will want to take the power of the French land.

(The Holy Spirit, 20 September 1881)

Our Lord Jesus-Christ revealed to St. Margaret-Mary the terror of future days, but His words were not disclosed in her time... He revealed these prophecies again to Marie-Julie Jahenny, saying France will only return to Him amidst the blood and tears of a civil war:

Soon, on the appointed time, there will not remain standing in France any religious house, not a monastery to escape the tyrants of the epoch... There will be a mindset for massacres from the Centre (Paris) to Lyon, from Lyon to the south and to the shores. Brittany is still Catholic, but not as before. The generation of the Faith is everywhere. These massacres will take place in the cold months (of the year).

The earth will become a deluge of blood, as in Noah's time (when) it became a deluge of water. All those who are not in the arch of My Heart will die, as in the time of the flood. (...) Myself, I shall choose; I shall name the true consoler of My people and the Church: (A Great Monarch) one that will rebuild My temples burnt in the violence of a great civil war, although it (the war) will not be long. I cannot, call it anything other than civil war, the war in which France will be delivered.

(Our Lord Jesus-Christ, 15 June 1882)

Here, the message's last line: (...) **I cannot, call it anything other than civil war, the war in which France will be delivered**—says a great deal. Indeed, the emphasis is placed on the fact that the upcoming civil war in France will indeed be a civil war since it will consist of Frenchmen (of long-deep French origins) against newly naturalized "paper-Frenchmen" of Muslim and/or sub-Saharan origins. This topic is today one of France's current subject of political debate: the definition of a true Frenchman...

The First Enemy of France:

The Virgin Mary, on one instance, showed Marie-Julie Jahenny two of France enemies to come:

Marie-Julie Jahenny:

This enemy of France is tall and very thin. His face is long, his hair is gray. His eyes are big and show ferocity and trickery. He appears utterly happy. He takes the heart of France, places it under his right foot and says:

- *I worked for you a long time; I still work and you resist. I have been the friend of the throne who has left you and, since then, I have taken the government of men. I have a few months ago lost a very dear friend of mine and I am still in sorrow… My fellow-mates rejoice. I want to bring religion on its knees. Well, France! I shall bring you to your knees if you do not abjure religion!*

France responds with a bitter voice:

- *I respect God; I respect His temple; I respect French Christians.*

This man says while addressing his friends:

Well, let us all together join and sign a new treaty!

Marie-Julie Jahenny becomes frightened at seeing the evil determination of this man and his friends whom the Blessed Virgin Mary is showing her:

- *Ah good Mother, take me away from here! I cannot stay here any longer; I cannot look at that man who scares me…*

The Blessed Virgin Mary:

My child, listen and repeat everything. Obey!

Marie-Julie Jahenny:

- *I see a part of the enemies of France gather around that man whom it would be difficult to say good things… There are now two groups. This ugly man says to those gathered around him:*
- **You are of my (political) party! Let's look everywhere for reinforcements. I have held the reins of mine; I have not lost any. Others are joining my (political) party. The friend that I have lost would have been my second hand. I do not know why he passed away so early (in life).**

France replies:

- *Yes, I enrolled in this secret society (Freemasonry?); I can no longer get out of it, but there are still faithful Christians who are offering me their hands in my sorrow… I do not want to lose the good ones. I abjure with all my heart, in the Presence of God and of the Virgin Mary! I renounce this sordid society which has dragged me into the abyss…*

The man has still his foot on the heart of France. She gets up nevertheless with difficulty but helped by an invisible force, and rises above this ugly mask.

The Second Enemy of France:

I see the link that ties the heart of France becoming red. It is another man that grasps the link. This man is heavy, short, somewhat fat, his forehead a bit bald and his hair is not grey like the first man. He has a reddish face and a pointy beard. The face of this man is ferocious. His roving eyes are so big that they seem to come out of their orbits when he looks at French Catholics. This horrid looking man says to France:

For a very long time, I have wanted to mold you as I wished, and you always escaped me. Here is the moment when I shall hold you well. I do not want a king in France; neither my committee nor I want one! I am of the strongest (political) party, and I gather those who are mine who are numerous already. I wrote quite a bit. I am looking to destroy everywhere the root of religion! Let's stand true, sincere friends! We have already obtained many results. Let us use all of our power to propagate everywhere perturbation and fright.

Marie-Julie Jahenny:

Then, turning towards 10 o'clock in the morning, towards the point where the sun finds itself at that particular time of the day (Looking from Paris south-eastward, that point would be Rome…), *he adds:*

- **And you, who wait in prison the help of the French! You are sadly mistaken if you think that you will return to your own goods!**

Marie-Julie Jahenny:

I think that he is looking towards Rome, and that his threats are directed towards it…

The reddish-faced evil Frenchman:

- **Oh, if it were permitted to me to enter in that city with my following, I would shut the eyes of he who is the head of this religion** (he would kill the Pope)**; I would put him under my feet and we would dance around** (his burial-ground) **as if in a great party!**

Marie-Julie Jahenny:

- *My good Mother, let me out of here! These men who are so evil scare me!*

The Blessed Virgin Mary:

- **Listen, my child, know that it is very necessary that these things be known, not for you but for my two servants** (King Henry of the Cross and the future Holy Pope?), **in this way, they will be able, under oath, to retrace my true words.**

(The Blessed Virgin Mary, 3 December 1877)

Our Lord stated three years before:

But before she has this king, France will undergo a crisis and a violent storm. The blood of Christians will mingle with the blood of the impious. The just will fall in small numbers, but some, because the blood of the good will help the wicked. But this time will pass quickly. There will be pools of blood. It will last a short time, but to you it will seem long.

(Our Lord Jesus-Christ, 21 June 1874)

But France will not be the only country in the world to be affected by violent crisis and Geo-political upheaval. Indeed, the Blessed Virgin Mary revealed to Marie-Julie Jahenny:

My children, it is with a most sadden heart, filled with anguish, that I recommend to you to pray a great deal for the land of Jerusalem (Israel)**... A bloody struggle will be declared thereupon, with on one side the King of the Persians** (Iran)**, who will want possession in these lands of poor value, that is to say a clear path for those to walk on that land.**

My children, before the first crisis of the eldest daughter of the Church begins (France)**, there will be painful news from England, Persia (Iran) and Jerusalem. They will all suffer first major harm...**

My children, I predict that at the end of this troubling moment, there will be a new reign in the English land, and a choice will be made when suddenly death will strike those who hold the wheel of that kingdom. For that country, a great harm will come, and it will become divided into four parts (England, Wales, Scotland and Norther Ireland?) **for their (respective) will shall not be in agreement with the others. The choice of the Catholics will be rejected.**

(The Blessed Virgin Mary, 25 August 1882)

Here again, we must understand the context and the time this message was given. Indeed, in 1882, Israel was a province that belonged to the Ottoman Empire; hence, for "Persia" (Iran) to enter into a struggle with Jerusalem (which was but a city under the control of the Turkish Ottoman Empire) in order to acquire lands to Palestine was utterly ridiculous and unrealistic... at the time... but most apropos in our present 21st Century Geo-political scene. Truly, this was yet another extraordinary prophecy!

Moreover, Marie-Julie Jahenny added that England will return to Catholicism but after the chastisement. This said, the message of the Blessed Mother to Marie-Julie reveals that before the first crisis takes place in France, There would be disconcerting news from England, Iran and Israel... Sadly enough, tensions have been since 2019 at their highest between Teheran, Jerusalem and London in Syria, Iraq, Lebanon, the strait of Gibraltar and in the Persian Gulf. All three countries have inextricably escalated diplomatic tensions... England having special-forces present in both Iraq and Syria, at the side of their American and French allies, combating Iranian backed Hezbollah forces—whose extent goes from the Western Iranian borders to the land of Palestine—does nothing to ease such diplomatic ills between the United Kingdom Iran and Israel.

England

Marie-Julie announces a new reign in England. Today such an event would not be surprising considering that Elizabeth II is a nonagenarian monarch... Hence, if the Prince of Wales is to sit on the English throne while in his 70s, another matter comes to light. Marie-Julie further announced that "... **there will be a new reign in the English land, and a choice will be made, when suddenly death will strike those who hold the wheel of that kingdom."**

Since the message echoed hereinabove described a sudden death to "**... those who hold the wheel of that kingdom"** as opposed to he or she who holds the wheel of that Kingdom, the interpretation of this prophecy is somewhat elusive as the various scenarios that come to mind are all but too dark to contemplate (plague/contagion, war, terrorist action or simply an accident).

Now, the following partition of the message is clearer to interpret as the division of the United Kingdom into four independent and sovereign states can today be attributed through England's withdrawal from the European Union (Brexit) which took place on 31 January 2020, thus forcing Scotland, Wales and Northern Ireland to secede from the U.K. in order to remain full members of the European Union and thus maintain their economic ties therewith, but again, this is but mere speculation...

Spain

Marie-Julie mentioned as well the Kingdom of Spain which, according to her will be attacked by the new masters of Italy who will wish to make of the Mediterranean countries their domain (Islamic Caliphate). They will assault Valencia but will be pushed back after 40 days of combat.

Oh, once again! Pray for this Roman land that will be cruelly persecuted; (pray) for Spain whose territory will be divided in two through an unjust theft and through countless betrayals. Spain will suffer such cruel events that none of its past revolutions would have seen the likes of this one.

My children, pray for Spain and for this Roman land (Morocco? Morocco was part of the Roman Empire). **The governors of the latter, with all their power and (well planned) designs will want, at all cost, to take away from Spain the point (of land) that's facing their land** (Andalusia?).

The Romans, pushed by their prince and governor, will march on the land of Spain with a powerful army. They will enter (Spain) through its border with barbarism and cruelty, (and will have) a measured rest of 30 to 40 days. This Prince, who will be supported by others from the Roman land, will feel strong and will be animated by violence against the land of Spain which will refuse to seek an agreement (peace terms) with them.

(25 August 1882)

Upon Spain, Heaven has its designs as well. It is the King of this Kingdom who, after two years have passed, will not fear to call the brother of the Royal Crown whose both flags and hopes are similar (Philip VI of Spain and Henry V of France). (Notwithstanding,) at the beginning of this epoch, this (Spanish) Catholic King will be forced to abandon his Kingdom for a few months, and to withdraw to safety from enemy's pursuit, but the time will not be long before he will be able to return (to Spain). His return will be a true triumph which will reanimate Faith and hope.

(16 May 1882)

The Roman land mentioned in this revelation is thought to be a Northern African nation (part of the old Roman Empire), while keeping in mind that Italy will likewise be, before or at the same time, overtaken by invading armies from across the Mediterranean Sea… As for the Iberic peninsula, everything leads to believe that the Spanish King mentioned in Marie-Julie's prophecy will indeed be King Felipe VI as his youth and the fact that he has no son but two daughters indicates that indeed he will be the Spanish Catholic King who, from Spain, will join King Henri V of France. King Philip, it appears, will likewise join the French King—after pushing back to the sea the Islamic invaders from Spain— and join his military force to his to go to the rescue of the Holy Father who will be in great danger in Rome (very likely held prisoner in an occupied Rome).

Italy

Marie-Julie stated about Italy:

Anarchy will triumph over the local government. **The invasions from the exterior which will be almost a consequent thereof will bring to power for almost three years antichristian forces which will harm greatly the Church and the Pope of that time**; *the Pope himself will become a martyr of these antichristian forces.*

Regarding the invasions of Italy, we are told that following the first Italian tyranny that will ensue from a Italian civil war, another tyranny will follow, and will come from a person named **Archel de la Torre** who will not be Italian but of Turkish and German origin. He will come across Iraq and Iran as a result of an invitation from an Italian party which will mean to rule the country. He will enter Italy towards the second half of the second year of the war.

A year after his taking power, Italy will suffer a most cruel and difficult year at the hands of this blood-thirsty tyrant, but, Marie-Julie assures us, that de la Torre will fall, and King Henry of the Cross will free the holy Father and bring at last peace and freedom to the Italian Peninsula... The Voice (Holy Spirit) says:

He lives in the farthest limits of the Kingdom of Persia (Archel de la Torre), **in its outermost borderline, in the deepest depth of this land. Sometime ago, this noble family was Catholic; (However,) in the past few years, it has entered into heresy and has stepped over the Faith...**

He will cross Persia and the other kingdoms, and will sit during one year upon the sorrowful seat of he who will order the heading of the apostles (Cardinals, bishops and priests?), **and who will make a martyr of he who supports the Church and the Faith** (The Pope).

His family will be of nobility in the last parses of the land of Persia. His father is Turkish, and his mother comes from a kingdom I already spoke about: she came out of Germany.

There are two sons. The one who is chosen by Rome is 16 years old, and the other is two years older. The first son will not be Catholic when Turkey will be involved in the European war, for all of Europe will be subject to struggles and revolutions. It will be the great revolution announced before the end of centuries (the end of times); however, one will be able to count many years before the eternal end. The first son (de la Torre) **who will take Turkey will not last many days: he will be thrown to the sea with his head half shattered...**

The king who will cross the kingdoms to respond to the calls of his friends (in Italy) **will reign only 1 year. Under his reign there will be no calm... Until the very last day, the tearing (of the country) will be heard (everywhere). One year will conclude his murdering glory. His successor will escape to Naples to run away from the fury of his hunters.**

The Church will be empty during long months. The third Pope will be holier but will reign only three years before God calls him back for his reward. In Naples, persecution will last over 19 months.

(16 May 1882)

*A massacre will take place during three days in the land of Naples. The 'Flame' forms in large, well-shaped letters, this name which I can read without difficulty. I see it outside the sun. It is **ARCHEL DE LA TORRE**. It is repeated: 'ARCHEL DE LA TORRE'. This is the name of the prince who will have* *carried out the great massacre against religious, priests and nuns of this region.*

(Marie-Julie Jahenny, 6 June 1882)

Paris Destroyed...

Our Lord revealed the following prophecy:

The larger part of the punishments will be directed towards Paris where there are the most treacherous conspiracies. This is the time when the days become dark. It has been a long time since I made you (part of) this confidence, I will have you recall this as the absolute and necessary secret. This is where the ministers are the most persecuted. There will be three days of devastation; there will not be any more Sacrifice, any more Masses... We can call it the Holy Quarantine; it will be three days of hell. Satan will travel the Earth to turn over the shrines, but he will be rejected, broken and defeated.

I shall reveal these confidences (secrets?). I want to warn My people so that it is not surprised, and so that its confidence in Me increases. In these three days, the lights of the heavens will be extinguished and the angels will be dismayed.

(Our Lord Jesus-Christ, 27 October 1876)

There will be great collapses, especially in the Center (Paris). All these rich palaces where all the profits of the nation are produced the Lord will destroy them through a terrible chastisement under the form of the land collapsing (sinking)... All these tall buildings that are part of the bread of France will collapse. God will surprise those who work without thinking of Him nor of His Might which gives everything on earth.

(The Blessed Virgin Mary, 16 November 1882)

You, Christian families, who still wear the Cross (and) the remembrance of My good deeds in your hearts, leave this ingrate city (Paris) which will perish by My Justice!

(6 April 1877)

My children, Nineveh was promised a punishment, and today a grave punishment, a terrible punishment is promised to the new Nineveh (Paris) which I loved ever so much and which is of My Kingdom.

(12 May 1881)

If the Center (Paris) **does not convert, it will be burnt... The stones that protect homes will protect them no longer, for the fire of vengeance will prevent them to be raised again.**

(28 November 1881)

My children, everything is at its saturation point. This is the time when my vengeance will be unleashed. Place your right hand on the wound of my Heart and you will be saved.

(Our Lord Jesus-Christ, 9 January 1878)

Happy are those who will know when to abandon these walls (Paris'), **and who will seek refuge far away for that pitiful place where victims will amass themselves in countless numbers, (and) where the plazas will be stained with blood as in rain falling down during a thunderstorm...**

(Saint Michael the Archangel, 9 January 1878)

Marie-Julie Jahenny addressing Mr. Charbonnier (note-taker/recorder):

Brother, O August Charbonnier, the Lord has stated to me:

'My daughter, now I shall have my true people know before the great days without rest the principal facts to be published in France in these places where can be found both the good and the bad. I do not want to bring forth these announcements to the light of day (for) it would be too late to warn My people...'

*The Blessed Virgin let me see, while shedding a few tears, the incendiary flames which rose in the "Center" along with the fire lit in the midst of terrible combats, especially around the Hell-room (*French parliament*). There will hardly be any wood left in homes as they will take their victory and initiate this fire ever so vast, and ever so widely extended that its measure will not be able to be measured... Three churches that are not far from the Center will not escape these flames of vengeance.*
My brother, the flames of the earth's fire will rise in incomprehensible heights (Atomic explosion?)! The blessed Virgin told me, while sighting:

'My daughter, men light this fire and Satan blows upon it.'

There were only the blackened walls of this temple upon which the blessed Virgin cried upon. She had me see all the tabernacles, all reduced to ashes... The flames, however, did not appear to lessen in intensity after all this destruction.

(Marie-Julie Jahenny, 18 October 1882)

The fire from Heaven will fall on Sodom, and particularly on this Hell-Room where evil laws are made; it will be swallowed-up and in its place there will be such an immensely deep crater, that no one, until the end of the world, will be able to approach it without feeling a gush of horror.

In this Sodom, there will be such shattered places that there will not be one pavement in its proper place. The fire of Heaven will mix with the fire of hell. Water there will be similar to fire. This place will collapse and will have an immense distance around... There will only be left a crater so deep that none will be able to distinguish its depth, nor measure the immensity of its hollow!

(1903)

The last two messages hereinabove underline with great gravity the destruction of Paris coming from high above (Heaven's fire) and from man's fire rising to incomprehensible heights... Might this refer to a nuclear blast destroying, leveling and consuming Paris? The famous French mystic, the Reverend Father Pel, definitely thought so:

Paris will be destroyed by the revolution, and burnt by atomic fire from Russians in Orleans and in the region of Provins... (see page: 468)

(Reverend Father Pel, 1947)

Never forget my words. From age to age, it will be repeated. Never will it possible to build around (Paris).... Never, will these visible marks of God be forgotten on a land where there have been so many beautiful sanctuaries dedicated to the Blessed Virgin Mary.

(The Holy Spirit to Marie-Julie Jahenny, 5 October 1882)

My children, when crime will be at its highest degree, when the subjects of the ruthless enemy will take back their place in the Center (Paris), the Terror and the Hand of my Son will already touch the walls of this ever so guilty city, although they are good souls therein, but they will be victims for the (many) crimes and inequities.

My children, do you know the number of those who will escape this infernal war? This number, I dare not mention it...

My children, all the Christians who will not run away to hide in secret places, those who will prefer to damp the ground with their blood rather than go to a country where there is peace... the number of those who will be protected is written in the Eternal Throne; when I look at that number, I do not console myself and my heart gets broken into pieces with a thousand swords...

My children, 100 will not escape from this city... No, not 100 in the midst of the immense guilty city... Count 12 less from that number and

you'll have the exact number thereof... Never a sorrow has been greater for me...

(The Blessed Virgin Mary, 9 August 1881)

Marie-Julie Jahenny further explained the messages involving the future of Paris:

The entire city will not be destroyed. The suburbs will likewise be much hit (by these catastrophes). The Virgin Mary and St. Genevieve (Saint Patron of Paris) will not abandon the just ones. There will be miracles of protection, particularly at Our Lady of Victories (Paris). I was told that... **"Angels will come to take the Hosts that are threatened to be profaned".** *This said, the principal message is this:*

Leave Paris! The evasive departure of the (French) government will be the ultimate sign (that it is time to leave Paris).

Providence will warn in time. We must pray and be attentive to the Divine Will. Jesus warns long before to avoid the mortal effects caused by panic. Until the very last moment, He will listen to the supplications of His lightning rods, of his victim souls, of Christian families, of fervent communities. I was told:

"These things will take place unless, through a miracle of God, This city converts."

Torrential rains will be catastrophic and will cause disastrous delays in the agricultural industry and will constitute forewarning signs of this revolution.

I shall forewarn My friends with signs of nature. I shall warn them (in advance). Civil war and disease will cause a great many victims especially in the big cities. (...) The enemies will fight amongst themselves. (...) This infamous law will come with many others. No one will be able to disobey them unless condemned to death, or to prison. This law will step over that which is most sacred.

(20 April 1882)

France and the world at war; the coming of the French king:

Marie-Julie Jahenny often, with great distress, talked about a war on European soil and an invasion of France by forces coming from Eastern Europe and from the Mediterranean Sea.

As Persecution will spread in France, it will receive a great help from neighboring powers (Algeria, Tunisia, Morocco, Qatar?) from those who resemble those in France who put everything to fire and bloodshed without any mercy.

(9 May 1882)

The nuance that is underlined in this message does not leave much room for interpretation. Clearly, the last section of this sentence states that the neighboring powers of France *who resemble those in France who put everything to fire and bloodshed without mercy* will offer great assistance to the persecutors of that country. The clue is clear. If one were to ask a Frenchman, any Frenchman today, the origin of the overwhelming majority of those groups that burn and destroy streets, shops, cars, public property, churches, cemeteries, cathedrals, and those who are responsible for the overwhelming majority of assaults, murders and terrorist acts in France, one would get the same answer: "Muslims".

Hence, this passage of the Blessed Virgin Mary's message forces one to conclude that the powers that are to offer assistance to French Muslim groups are not France's immediate neighbors (Spain, Italy, Switzerland, Germany, Luxembourg Belgium nor England) but rather France's neighbors across the Mediterranean Sea: Algeria, Morocco, Tunisia, Libya, Syria, Qatar and other Saharan and Sub-Saharan countries.

LA FRAUDAIS
Marie-Julie Jahenny in her home (La Fraudais)

Une attitude de Marie-Julie
pendant une extase

Marie-Julie Jahenny in her home's garden Marie-Julie Jahenny in ecstasy
during an apparition

Marie-Julie Jahenny between two friends and witnesses

Marie-Julie Jahenny's house in La Fraudais

Marie Julie's room today in her home

Marie-Julie Jahenny's house today (La Fraudais)
(Photo taken in 2011 by Paul J. Dickson)

Cemetery in La Fraudais (Marie-Julie Jahenny's tomb)

Le marquis de la Franquerie en tenue de Camérier vers 1945

Marquis de La Franquerie (1945)

His Excl. Mgr. Fournier, Bishop of Nantes

Our Lord Jesus-Christ:

A very short pause will follow-up this great evil which will come forth, especially in the Center (Paris) **and in the neighboring area** (Muslim suburbs). **On May 24, a major event will take place amongst those men who call themselves victors and higher-up in science, which will shake up this great city** (Paris) **where blood has stained so many times the pavement, and this shaking will not cease... You know that the number 14 has been chosen by Me.**

(Unknown date...)

The second and violent crisis will (then) begin, and will last for 45 days. France will (then) be invaded until the dioceses that begins (the region of) Brittany. He (the invaders' leader) **wants to send the foreign armies through the doors of the stolen lands: Alsace and Lorraine** (Russian & possibly Eastern European military units). **The strongest army will walk upon Orleans and invade spaces of land which I cannot limit. In one single move, they will (quickly) reach the outskirts of the great City** (Paris). **They will enter it only upon the second half of the second crisis** (sometime between the 27th and the 45th day after the beginning of the invasion of France).

Friends of the Cross, when this army penetrates through the door of the stolen land (Alsace and Lorraine), **it will receive a reinforcement which will assist that king (who is) very much like a tiger against the French. The most remarkable elements of this army will be coming from that 'band' that comes from the door of Alsace. They will strike fast towards the Center** (Paris) **(leaving behind) a horrible ravage. They will (at last) set their camp in that place** (Paris) **thus completing the ruin of poor France... They will (then) enter (the region of) Vendée performing abominable vengeance, but the Vendéens will unite their forces to others' (in resistance).**

Many will die, but not all. (The foreign armies) will then move towards Normandy; notwithstanding, I live in this land that I have blessed and where I have consoled so many souls. Only my temple will be protected (Mont Saint Michel?) **and will escape the flames... The fire will not be able to ignite despite a thousand tries attempted by the foreign armies and by the 'mixed ones' who inhabit the Kingdom of Mary** (Frenchmen of Arabic origins and/or Franco-Africans).

(St. Michael the Archangel, 28 September 1882)

In the north, they will go to the limits of (the region of) Vendée and in Normandy. Brittany will not be invaded, but it will not be exempted of chastisement, especially in its un-Christianized northern region. The enemy will abandon themselves to pillage and vengeance... They will come from the East (Russians) **and from the Mediterranean Sea** (Algerians, Northern Africans and Middle-Eastern)**, and many troubled situations will be announced as well in Italy and Spain due to forces that will come thereto from the Orient** (Middle-East).

140

In Southern France, Marseille, Valence... What a butchery! (...) The Regions of Northern, Eastern and Southern France, and Paris itself will be very much affected... The national territory of France will be cut in two. There will be pretenders for the restoration of a power that will appear in one of these two parts (of France). It's in the course of these terrible months' half-time that will appear the Savior-King, but there will be a long reconquest-campaign that will last many months thereafter to push (out of France) the invaders. The King will not establish his throne in Paris for the city will have been destroyed...

France, listen to My Words! You will have to suffer 14 days of terrible combats. During these 14 days of war there will be chastisements... Ah! If My people only knew that it is at the eve of such a magnificent triumph, it would not be able to contain its joy! It would pray every day, and through its prayers, it would receive many consolations; it would even be before Victory a sign of gratefulness...

France, in these days of battle, you will not sadden yourself, you will not lose courage.

When the invaders will come upon France, it will be through a revealed prayer that they will be dispersed and pushed back. He, (the enemy) will come upon France like a furious lion in all its rage, with all its weapons of impiety, to break and scourge the people of France... My Invisible hand will crush them and will cause their fall.

France, without My Mother, you would never have gotten up from your evil-doing. If triumph is being granted to you ever so quickly, it is because of Mary, of her supplications and tears.

France, you will have a terrible fight for King Henry who must bring peace and concordance in his country. You'll have less difficulty in defending the Holy Church. Remember that the deliverance of the Holy Father will be terrible, but less terrible than the fight for the King. France will need of a powerful arm. The first day, the battle will take place through Heaven; the second day it will take place through men.

(Our Lord, 1 October 1875)

(...) These numerous troops, after taking a part of Vendée and a large number of Frenchmen under their guard (prisoners) to have them die, will pass through the middle of the Dioceses of Nantes from the borderline of Vendée to the center of the other borderline which touches the heart of the city.

My children, the enemies will not penetrate the heart of the Diocese. They will be stopped by the Army of the soldiers of the Cross and of Faith. They will come from the Cross (located) on the borderline of the land of Brittany. They (the enemy forces) will not pass... It is there that the Lord waits for them... It is a little bit below (the location) of that Cross that they will pass, but they will be very few... They will try to see if it's possible to attempt incursion, but they will reach only half of the half (quarter) of the distance to the center of the Dioceses. They will be thrown back by the

Bretons who will come out with very few unwounded troops. (This said), never will these foreign lands see their soldiers again...

(Unknown date...)

My children, my maternal heart is more and more shattered... My kingdom of France becomes the center of all depths of evil, and to save it, how many victims! How much bloodshed!

My kingdom, soon, will be divided. The children of France will become (subjects) of another kingdom despite their pretention to remain French.

(The Blessed Virgin Mary, 25 March 1895)

The Blessed Virgin Mary's description of the invasion of France by Eastern European armies and by Muslims powers from the south opens an entire battery of other ensuing questions. First, we know that this invasion campaign of France was not a description of neither the battle plans of the German armies in World War I nor of World War II, for the German offensive of 1914 came from a North-Southern Arc from invaded Belgium and Germany, and was quickly stopped by the French army. Never was Paris taken and never did the German army even get close to Vendee, Normandy, or Brittany:

It could be neither a description of the German 1940 invasion plans of France as the spearhead of the German invasion force was not Orléans nor Paris, but Lille and Dunkirk through, this time, a South-Northern Arc, and no invasion force came from Alsace-Lorraine nor any reinforcements through the Mediterranean sea.

This new invasion of France described by Marie-Julie Jahenny shows a new battlefield plan which is unrecognizable in any chapter in History (see pages 143, and 172).

This said, if this upcoming (partial) invasion of France is indeed to take place, the next question coming to mind is what event would encourage such a radical and risky geo-political move on the part of Russia and its allies? Under this prophecy, the United States does not send armed forced to the rescue of France, either due to a political decision taken in Washington, or because the United States will be impeded from sending reinforcements to Europe, but for what reason?

The first reason could be due to a civil war taking place in France (and in other European nations), and a French contending party calling Russia and/or other Muslim nations to assistance? Another scenario would be the United States having fallen victim to either a major natural or man-made catastrophe, or both.

Finally, another possibility would entail the United States being overwhelmingly engaged in the Pacific and/or elsewhere... Consequently, if the Russians were to initiate an invasion of Europe and reach the Rhine river through conventional armed forces, it would imply that all the NATO forced between Belorussia and France would have to be quickly and completely overrun.

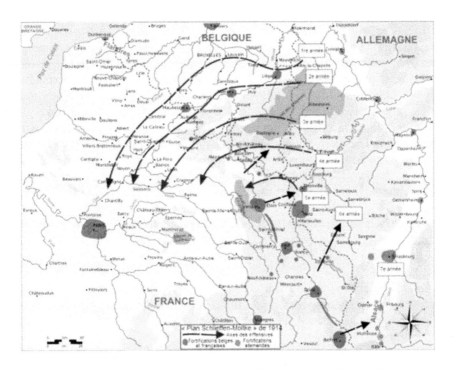

German offensive in France (1914–5) - Wikepedia

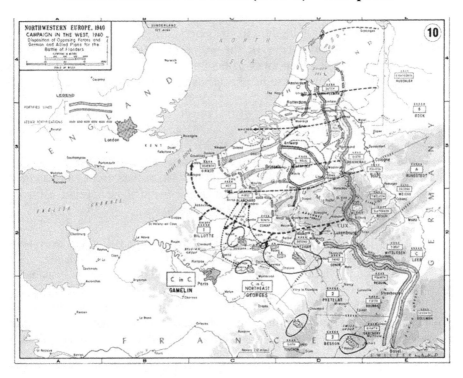

German offensive in France (1940) - Wikepedia

143

Likewise, such a mechanical move so far west from the Russian borders would entail the Russian northern flank being secured before or at the same time through a modern Blitzkrieg throughout Scandinavia (Finland, Norway, Sweden and Denmark), the Baltic states, Poland, central Europe, Germany, Holland and Belgium before reaching the French border. Likewise, it is most likely that a preliminary Russian attack on Scotland and Eastern England would take place before possible American reinforcement arrive. Such large scale attack would have to use all arms of Russia's arsenals and Russian reserves (Air-to-Ground attack and support, Airborne troops, Commando insertions, amphibious units, armored divisions, air-support, naval and tactical-missile attacks), and unconventional weaponry other than Nuclear, such as massive Electro-Magnetic Pulse attacks (E.M.P.), causing satellite and inter-communication interruptions. This said, the risk of nuclear retaliation from France and/or England[11] would be important enough for Russia not to have recourse to WMDs (Weapons of Mass Destruction) upon NATO forces.

France has, since 1962, established its military defense on its Nuclear dissuasion capability; however, in a country whose government would appear to have fled due to a massive national civil unrest, and whose armed forces would appear to be engaged in Arab lands (Syria, Iraq, Mali, etc.) without a proper head-command structure in France.

Naturally, let the reader note that the scenarios described herein are nothing more than the author's speculations based on the prophetic messages received by visionary Marie-Julie Jahenny.

They will divide the Kingdom in two parts. Those who have just entered will reside in the Center (Paris); the other part (Brittany and the French Western shores) **will be given away as beginning of the conquest to he whose name will soon come to light to be proclaimed King of the French.**

(Our Lord Jesus-Christ, 28 September 1882)

This prophecy hereinabove shows that Paris will still stand and be temporarily occupied by the invading force, while Western France will remain under French military control with a front-line established from Normandy to Western Gascony. Hence, one concludes that Paris will be leveled upon the Russian's withdrawal, or sometimes shortly thereafter...

(...) It will be during this land-division that France will enter within the guilty designs of its enemies through the apostasy of complete violence.

France will be invaded all the way to the dioceses which introduces Brittany (...)

The second crisis will put all things at their worst, and from the people (of France), will escape only he who finds an obscure refuge. (...) The men in power, after having placed the kingdom in blood, will assemble in a

---

[11] France and England being, with the United States, the only nuclear powers in Europe.

peaceful place, and will form definitive and decisive projects. They will look for a savior to place him on the throne of France...

(...) Retired in secrecy, they will choose their king, the one who is against the designs of Providence. They will thus decide, and nothing will be able to change their direction and to place the guilty one on a throne that will never belong to him.

(The Archangel Michael, 28 September 1882)

... In the first place it will appear that France takes its savior, but he will not be the true savior. The one who is chosen and sent by God will be of the Fleur de Lys.

(19 May 1898)

This message of May 19, 1898, with the one of October 1, 1875 (see hereinabove) are quite revealing. One might have thought that perhaps all the references of a future King of France would have been referring to the Count of Chambord Henri de Bourbon, but since the good Count passed away on August of 1883, messages clearly mention yet another French King of the '*Fleur de Lys*' (May, 1898), and a war in France that would eventually see Paris destroyed and parts of France invaded (October 1, 1875). Likewise, the message of July 7, 1881 (see pages 148) discusses a 'young soul' who will be assigned the task, 'when Marie-Julie will be no more', to bring the lights to "his Majesty" on the Will of God during a time of war in France; hence, this leaves no room for interpretation: a French King is indeed expected to return to France. The Blessed Virgin Mary:

One word of greeting, my children, to all of you, whether close or far.

I am leading here St. Michael the Archangel, Prince of the Celestial Armies and of mortal armies. I only have one word, my children, to put in your hearts...

I shall leave my tears quite apparent, every day when I shall come amongst the Friends of the Cross. My forehead will be veiled down right above my eyes; my clothes will be black as those of a mother who is in mourning for her poor people... I cry for France who will enter into the most horrible of collapses and apostasies... I see the abominable sacrilege place itself on the altar.

... My children, I stop... I did all that was possible to save France. She will not perish entirely, but a great part thereof. My heart is broken... Pray, my children, for my Son will touch those He spared until now.

(The Blessed Virgin Mary, unknown date...)

In a particular ecstasy, Marie-Julie Jahenny witnessed an exchange between Saint Michael the Archangel and our Lord.

St. Michael the Archangel:

- *Lord, how much longer will You let me groan in Heaven before letting me come down upon the earth?*

The Lord answers:

- **Holy Archangel, you, the Prince of the Friends of the Cross, wait that the others sign the great condemnation of France, the signature that will lead them to peril and to the reign of the last impiety.**

Note: It is theorized that the document to be signed discussed in this message will perhaps be a treaty between the remnants of French political leaders and the Arabo-Russian occupying forces, sealing some kind of collaboration accord with a yet to be formed puppet French government that will raise a head of state whose aim will be to unite the surviving French populations: a king from a treacherous branch of the Bourbon family (the family d'Orléans)—recognized by the Franco-Muslim populace.

St. Michael the Archangel responds:

- *Lord, you shouldn't go very far before acting, for in the present state of things, the earth has only but a few steps left.*

Our Lord:

- **Archangel, they will divide the kingdom in two parts. Those who have just entered therein will reside in the Center (Paris); the other part will be given as a beginning of re-conquest to he whose name will soon come forth to be proclaimed King of the French.**

St. Michael says (addressing now the friends of the Cross):

- *Friends of the Cross, it will be after the return of these great guilty ones in the place where Heaven does not want to punish them. He (Our Lord) awaits them elsewhere to make the horrible chastisement in plain sight. (…)*
  The army which the Lord has chosen for the glorious entrance of peace and of Henry V, this army will be invincible when the entire earth will gather to encounter it. The French army will go through, breaking through these masses as dust. This invincible army is not wished by mortal men; it is written (made) by Heaven's Hand, established and wished by the Eternal Empire within the extend of Its Glorious Power.
  Brothers and sisters, we are decided! We shall have the heads of the superb ones! We shall reduce their tongues to dust! We shall knock them down on this land of malediction where they camp to commit evil

deeds against the exiled one and against the French soldiers...

(St. Michael the Archangel, 28 September 1882)

To dispel all fears and fright, you must touch to your forehead an image or the sweet medal of Mary Immaculate (i.e., the Miraculous Medal). Your minds will remain calm. Your minds will not fear the approach of the terror of men. They will not resist the effects of My great Justice.

(Our Lord Jesus-Christ. Date unknown)

It has been found in Marie-Julie Jahenny's private documents that the unsacred, king who will illicitly and secretly step on the throne of France (for a very brief period of time) will be a descendant of King Louis-Philippe (Jean d'Orléans?), and will be chosen by traitorous French leaders in a secret place in Alsace, France.

These extraordinary messages hereinabove given by our Lord Jesus-Christ, by the Blessed Virgin Mary and by St. Michael the Archangel are four of the ever so few that give great detail on the events to come. Indeed, through these astonishing prophecies, we learn where the invading armies will come from, what will be their first tactical objectives, and where the first military confrontation with the remaining French forces will take place... Hence, as the Russian rapidly advance through the European plains, reach northern Italy aiming to capture Rome, the Russian western spearhead will enter through the Eastern French regions of Alsace and Lorraine from invaded Germany and probably from Southern Belgium and northern Switzerland.

Their main thrust will be directed, with the strongest part of their armed forces, towards Orléans and will spread throughout central and Southwestern France, leaving behind huge spaces of territories in utter destruction, wreck and havoc... The French military port of Toulon (on the French Riviera) will likewise be a tactical objective. The second main attack, although with a somewhat weaker force, will be directed towards Paris, Picardy and Normandy which soon thereafter will fall and will see an occupation force enter therein.

In the meantime, once Orléans is taken, the main push of the Russian-Eastern European army will receive reinforcements from Paris and will pursue its march west and enter Vendée where a first major battle will take place ending up in a French victory in Nantes, and forcing a shaken Russian army to turn north–north-east towards Normandy. However, in the course of this invasion, the Russian will launch assault after assault in Normandy, failing to reach its objectives.

These attacks will be concentrated most particularly on the renown Catholic Mont Saint Michel which, Marie-Julie Jahenny told us, will resist successfully, leaving the Russians and the Muslims no recourse but to initiate a new attack with heavy battery units and missile launchers; however, their numerous attacks and bombings will fail miserably as Michael stated:

(...) **Only my temple will be protected** (Mont Saint Michel) **and will escape the flames... The fire will not be able to ignite despite a thousand** tries attempted by the foreign armies and by the 'mixed ones' who inhabit the Kingdom of Mary...

(St. Michael the Archangel)

The message is clear, and will prove to be most probably the second miracle of this war... Notwithstanding, we see yet a reference of the "Mixed ones", most likely referring to the French nationals of Arabic and African origins joining-up with the Russian armies (the mixed ones). Indeed, we are moreover revealed by Our Lord that in the South of France, as the Russian armies cross the Rhine river into France, a massive Northern African force will disembark and lend assistance and reinforcements to its northern Russian ally in Central and Western France. We further learn that as this massive invasion from the east and the south of France takes place, Spain and Italy will likewise suffer initial invasions from foreign Arabic troops on their southern shores.

In a later segment of this work, we shall see that a Russian force will come as well from Northern Italy and take over Rome where they will fly their flag above the Dome of the Basilica of St. Peter.

Back to France, we are told by Marie-Julie Jahenny that the invasion of France will at last be stopped by a French army on a front-line that lies between Caen and Lourdes (see map on page 469). The <u>invasion of Eastern France will last 45 days,</u> but will stop as suddenly as it began, giving both parties a breathing-period... This particular prophecy was not unlike that of Abbot Souffrant's who stated that the further limits of the enemy's invasion will be set on a line drawn between the cities of le Havre (Normandy) and Bordeaux (Gascony) (see page 469). It must be noted that, as we shall see in chapter IX, Father Pel likewise predict a line that will separate France in two, and which will lie between the cities of Lille (Picardy) and Bordeaux (Gascony) (see page 468).

Everything, he stated, to the east of said line will be ravaged and burnt, while the western side of France will be spared... Three lines but one common general idea as to the extent of a foreign invasion and of the devastation that will consequently ensue as a result thereof... The invasion of France, although incomplete, will stop, leaving Brittany, part of Vendee and the French western coastal borders still under French control, while Paris and the rest of France will remain under a very brief Russian and Arabic occupation...

The Call by God's young messenger to the French King — the war and liberation.

The Flame of the Holy Spirit:

- **Do you remember the young soul who, under the rays of a privileged call, must leave from the depths of Brittany to bring to his Majesty the word from up high?**

Marie-Julie Jahenny:

- *Yes I remember.*
- **Do you remember something that remained that was not said?**
- *Perhaps… but our brothers will remember better than I.*
- **This young soul will be assigned the task, when you will be no more, to bring the lights to his Majesty on the Will of the God of Armies.**

  Here is a secret that will be entrusted by the blessed child: The home where Heaven's Light will have shone upon will become, under the reign of one called by God, a place of graces and prayers. In this Center which will be renewed and rebuilt as another Jerusalem, this home will become the House of God.

  By order of his Majesty, three Crosses will be planted thereupon. They will call this home the Sanctuary of Martyrs, for many priests and friends of theirs will have taken their flight therefrom… Many bishops who will be recognized despite of their being undressed of the vestments they wear today, will suffer the cruel martyrdom.

  Under the reign of peace, a solemn benediction will be made there; it will be performed by the representatives of God who will have come back. Many of our friends and of our brothers will fly there happily. His Majesty will be generous in gifts for that place claimed by the Lord.

(The Holy Spirit to Marie-Julie Jahenny, 7 July 1881)

(…)**This flower is the lily (Fleur de Lys), O King, miracle child, do not prepare to come from exile under a thick dust stirred up by the fury of the murderers of your country. You will prepare to come on the edge of this land that was foreign to you. From the north of the borders, your noble person will pass through the legions that only wait for you to rise up a vengeance. But, as the day of darkness, their eyes will be veiled, the exiled one will be returned (to France) and My Justice will be accomplished. You will pass to reclaim the scepter of glory.**

(Our Lord Jesus-Christ, 22 March 1881)

Our Lord Jesus-Christ addressing Marie-Julie Jahenny:

(…)**To have a king like the one I am reserving for you, new walls will be necessary. This king, when he will arrive in France, will build a new fortress of a fortified religion and of old violated laws that will be renewed yet again. To shelter this great man, this man of faith who wears upon his heart the decoration of his honor and of his faith, a new cover will be necessary in the royal palace…**

This one will spread further the devotion to My Sacred Heart and of My Sacred Cross. He will be one of My illustrious propagators of My Works, that is to say he will consecrate all of France to My Sacred Heart! He will be as a new Louis XVI, with his Crucifix in his hand when he was directing that hand towards Heaven consecrating, from his prison, France to the Sacred Heart!

149

Addressing now King Henry of France:

> **O good king, how often your heart has beaten close to Mine! Good servant, your heart is about to beat upon Mine! Poor exiled child! You are about to see again your Motherland and greet it with your tears! Faith is engraved in your heart, and the Consecration of France to My Heart will strengthen it yet! O Henry, My servant! Don't you see the sail of My Love that navigates towards your far-away regions? This sail is forming as a standard! You will walk under that sail, you and your dear companions and the soldiers of your cause. Henry, entering France, you have the mission to defend the Holy Father (the Pope). Henry, My servant, these arms are enclosed into a gold ring!**

Now addressing Marie-Julie Jahenny:

> **My victim! There are the designs of My servant! Returning to France, he wants to wear a great Scapular representing the Sacred Heart and France imploring Heaven's aid! This man will not redden his face because of his faith! He will not redden his faith for being a Christian! When Henry will enter France, the battles will be terrible... The Center-Right and the Center-Left will come down on the Prince with utter irritation and dark anger! (But) the mere sight of his Scapular will be enough to have them utterly collapse, and Henry will pass through with his Court... My victim, I have great designs for the King and for France. I have in My Domain great preparations which will be revealed as France progresses. Poor France! Without Me, you will never have risen again...The Blessed Virgin Mary asks for France the Salve Regina four to five times prayed a day as an act of contrition, bowing on the ground.**

(Jesus-Christ, 1 June 1877)

... (Henry of the Cross) awaits in solitude and with resignation the call of his brothers to give glorious days to France whose holy kings have in the past governed. But be certain that he whose exile possesses solitude will not be the first (to appear) when the decision will be called upon... There is still the remains of a family who claim the right to the Scepter and the Crown; but this race is not included in God's designs, because its malice (its guilt) has been the cause of an innocent victim: he who has given his blood to keep safe his Faith: Louis XVI.

The descendent of a father who was a murderer pretends to have a right to the Throne. This family has a very bad nature (the family d'Orléans)[12]...

(St. Michael the Archangel, 29 September 1879)

It will be in the third crisis that salvation will come. There will come from the center of His Sacred Heart the salvation, or rather he who is destined to bring peace. With his Crowning (King Henry V's)**, all the sorrows will cease. My children, he comes from the Branch of (King) St. Louis, but this guilty Sodom (France) does not possess him...**

(Our Lord Jesus-Christ, 15 August 1905)

To whom He has chosen (King Henry V of the Cross) **God will give all the graces and lights which will be necessary to know the means by which he will do everything possible for the regeneration of mankind, as God wills it.**

(9 February 1914)

These messages, along with other papers found in the possession of the family of the Marquis de la Franquerie, clearly show that the future King of France, the one chosen by God, King Henry V of the Cross, will indeed be a descendent not merely of King St. Louis of France, but likewise of King Louis XVI and of Marie-Antoinette... This extraordinary revelation opens a series of questions involving the escape from the "Temple" prison of the young ten-year-old Prince (Dauphin), Louis XVII, an escape that has been suspected, discussed and debated with profound passion in France for the past 230 years.

The future King of France, we read, although born in France, French in soul and in blood, will live in exile with his family abroad waiting for the time Divine Providence calls him to assume his destiny. Regardless, the faithful are instructed not to try to find him, for it belongs to God alone to know of his whereabouts, for otherwise, would his location and identity be revealed before the appointed time, his enemies could attempt to his life...

Marquis de la Franquerie:

*Marie-Julie has always assured me that Our Lord and **Our Lady had often told her that the d'Orleans would never reign**; right and justice being opposed to he – who (by his deciding vote) has assassinated (King Louis XVI) – inheriting would not be permitted to Philippe d'Orléans' descendants. She never ceased from telling me that he (the true King of France) would be a descendant*

---

[12] **Louis Philippe Joseph d'Orléans, a/k/a Philippe Égalité, was the traitorous cousin of King Louis XVI who casted the one vote that ruled in favor of the King's execution by guillotine. Today, the pretender to the Crown of France from this family's Branch is Jean d'Orléans.**

of the King and Queen Martyrs, therefore of Louis XVI and of Marie-Antoinette. Heaven has always spoken to her of the hidden king, because God does not want us to know who he is so that the Freemasons, the Republicans or certain pretenders may not attempt to assassinate him. Let us leave to God the care of indicating His Chosen One to us.

(Marquis de la Franquerie, Marie-Julie Jahenny, **The Breton Stigmatist**)

This ball which serves as a throne to my feet, is the one where, in the midst of the Lord's Words of Glory, will sit he who men will fight against in combat, he who will be despised, and he who, in his faith, will come at the feet of the mother of the Mother of God (St. Anne) to renew his faith and his prayer (City of Sainte Anne d'Auray, Brittany?).

(St. Michael the Archangel, 23 November 1882)

Marie-Julie Jahenny:

Here are the words which the mortal savior (His Royal Highness Henry V of the Cross) will address St. Anne in the land of Brittany:

'You know, Saint Anne, the ambition my heart has to reign in the midst of my brothers. This ambition is not for my own interest; it is for that of my brothers and that of my people who I would like to make happy after so many years of sorrow.'

The Blessed Virgin Mary entrusted a most important confidence to Marie-Julie Jahenny concerning the Great Monarch's identity by eliminating contemporary pretenders. This extraordinary revelation took place on 28 March 1874, Feast-Day of Saint Gontran, first canonized King of France.

Why are you not praying more? Why are you not asking more for the salvation of France, your motherland? I shall give her a pious king. He will show a good example to France. He will have faith re-flourished, and religion will be triumphant. The King is a Lys (Fleur de Lys). He is a hero; the world does not know him. He will reign until the end of times in all his beauty and glory, His name is only known by Heaven.

He will come out the Adorable Heart of Jesus a few weeks before the Great peace of France. This peace will take place in times of full trouble, in times of full revolt. He is neither a descendant of Louis-Philippe, nor a Naundorff, nor a Napoléon. He is not amongst the Bourbon pretenders. He is a hidden king who will have the virtues and most of all the beautiful faith of a King Saint Louis...

(The Blessed Virgin Mary, 28 March 1874)

Marie-Julie Jahenny then revealed a special prayer to be said to King St. Louis in his honor and for the coming of the Great Catholic Monarch:

- **Great Saint Louis, King of France**, hero of France, pray for France.
- Great Saint Louis, King of France, beautiful lily of purity, friend of the Sacred Heart of Jesus, pray for France.
- **Great Saint Louis, King of France**, who preserved your purity and your beautiful innocence and who never sullied this crown on the throne that Jesus and Mary gave you, grant peace, pray that France humbles itself at the feet of Jesus and Mary and before you.
- **Great Saint Louis, King of France**, who comes to reconcile Heaven with Earth and to whom Jesus, the God of France, gives His graces, bring peace to France, grant that the Faith will flourish there, pray for France, the Holy Pontiff and the Church.
- **Great Saint Louis**, you, the friend of the Sacred Heart of Jesus, you, the fervent servant of Mary whom you loved so much and for whom you desired to die on a Saturday, a day that was consecrated to her, pray for us, unhappy children of France.
- **Great Saint Louis, King of France**, you whom Jesus and Mary have received in their arms and who they then gave a most beautiful crown, pray for France.
- Great Saint Louis, King of France, France calls you and requests that you bring that beautiful crown that you have never sullied, give it to her like a second crown, pray for France.
- **Great Saint Louis**, who prays with the Immaculate Mary for the Sovereign Pontiff in the midst of his sufferings, the calumnies, the persecutions, deliver the Sovereign Pontiff.
- **Great Saint Louis, King of France**, come today with Immaculate Mary, reconcile France and Heaven. We are all present, we pray together. He will come to our aid, to make truthfulness and innocence flourish in the midst of faded France, as Mary has given him the power, pray for France.
- **Great Saint Louis, King of France**, Jesus and Mary have permitted that you take by the hand the King that will govern and you will give him his crown that you never tarnished. Mary permits you to place this King on the throne, he who will bring peace. Pray for the Sovereign Pontiff who calls upon you for France. We see in you a beautiful hope, we see your blessed hand! Mary will refuse you nothing, you who have loved her so much. Come to our assistance. Come, You also, O Sacred Heart of Jesus, You open it completely that we may hide in It never to come out.
- All for You, O Sacred Heart, all for You Jesus and Mary, and all for you O good Saint Louis, King of France. Amen.

"Never, poor France, will you ever be governed by someone other than the King of My choice. I Myself will come at the moment when there will be the least appearance of hope. I will place Myself in the middle of France; I will call all My children around My Sacred Heart, and I will give the conqueror of France the banner on which is engraved My Sacred Heart.

After this ordeal, I shall shorten the time for punishment because of My victims, because of My Sacred Heart, and finally to give in a faster manner the King chosen and elected by My Divine Heart.

I populate the land of France with flowers, that is to say with pure hearts, generous, repentant (ones) who love the Holy Church, the Holy Father and the King. I will bless the land and My people (who will have) escaped. I will give France a new generation. They grow in My Grace; they will follow during the reign of a very pious King who, by his virtues, will become the ornament of France. I would prefer that you forget other revelations but this one."

(Our Lord Jesus-Christ to Marie-Julie, 1 December 1876)

He will come the one desired by the people of France. He will enter this land with human armies surrounded by angelical armies. In his armies will be found great Christians, great men whose honor will be kept during the whole lasting of this world.

(Marie-Julie Jahenny, unknown date)

The foreigner will enter France with all of his army. He will cross a distance measured by Me. I shall stop them, and in this stop, I shall motivate the savior from the rest of My children. He will come from the East while seeming to come from the depth of the North. I shall lead him to the South (of France), and from there I shall direct him not towards today's throne, for there will be no more throne (there), not even a base to build another one (Paris destroyed)...

(18 September 1902)

On 15 June 1875, Marie-Julie had an extraordinary vision. It was the King again brought by Our Lady, who loves him as her Son because of his innocence. He appeared as Sovereign, crowned in grandeur in the shade of the folds of his flag. After a while the scene changed and was completed, France followed her Legitimate Head. Her small crown changed into a diadem of victory. The Sacred Heart joined the Blessed Virgin Mary to assure her of His Love and to announce once again that He would conquer His enemies with unequalled triumph. *"France is saved! France is saved!"* Marie-Julie kept repeating. The good friends of the Sacred Heart were grouped in large crowds behind France, preceded by all the Saints who protect the Eldest Daughter of the Church.

Marie-Julie had yet another vision which gave details of the time the salvation of France would take place:

When everything seems lost... then will be the time of victory. It will be the time when all the crimes and impieties fall back on those who committed them.

Our Lord addressing Himself to France:

- **I will send Saint Michael, Prince of Victory, to carry the Lily to adorn your head.**

And the Blessed Virgin Mary added:

- **My Divine Son and I have reserved the Lily. My faithful children, keep the simplicity of your opinions.**

All the angels were there at the foot of the Heavenly Throne with the Blessed Virgin Mary who offered a beautiful white flag adorned with Lilies to her Divine Son:

"The time is near when, for a few weeks' time, the oracle will not stop from warning, with a strong and imposing voice, the people who inhabit the region of Marmoutier where St. Martin lived[13], (of) the events, the confrontations and revolutions in the Touraine region. The number of evil people (there) is immense, (while) the number of good souls is reduced to a small number...
After a lady will have spoken for the people of Tours, her voice will change... a sharp cry will come out of her. She will see from that place the first battle begin in the center-region of the Kingdom (the following short passage is not clear...?) **until the hour when the one called by God, the Rejected One, the abandoned One by the greatest number of men will arrive... It is at the time when God's Voice will call him** (Henry V of the Cross) **that the kingdom will be finished with terror."**

(25 August 1882/Feast Day of King St. Louis of France)

On a particular apparition of Saint Michael the Archangel, Marie-Julie was revealed yet further information on the origins of the long awaited future King of France:

I have carried them (the two lilies, Fleurs de Lys) **to the Heart of Jesus, and from the Heart of Jesus to the heart of a new King through the heart of a king who gave his blood, and who the Church will beatify** (Louis XVI, the martyr king).

(St. Michael the Archangel)

And the Blessed Virgin Mary:

You may be sure, my children, that this holy King (Louis XVI) **is already with the saints, and that Heaven will celebrate a feast raising him to the**

---

[13] **Abbey located 3 km away from the city of Tours founded by St. Martin in the IV century.**

honors of the Altars.

Marie-Julie explained:

The triumph of the living will be great when Holy Church, which is today surrounded by thorns, will be surrounded by a crown of golden Fleur de Lys (lilies): the Holy Pope, the Great Monarch and the other Princes of the Lilies who will reign over the world and ensure the triumph of God and the Church.

The defenders of the Faith will be protected from Heaven. The race of the Kings of France, being that of David, therefore the same one as Our Lord's and the Immaculate Virgin, divine in one of its Members, it is natural that it should be this race to be called to reign over the world at the time of the great triumph of the Church.

In 1874, Marie-Julie Jahenny stated publicly:

*The Virgin Mary has spoken to me a great deal of France. She asked me **three prayers for France to recite every day: One Magnificat, One Ave Maris Stella and One Sabat Mater. What's more, one must kneel and pray fervently while looking towards Heaven.** The Blessed Virgin Mary will deliver her (France) through a king who will save her and govern her a long time. She told me that she is not being asked enough for that king and that we do not pray her fervently enough for her to grant him to us. **She names him Henry V, and recommends us to pray a great deal as well St. Michael the Archangel. As for the Sacred Heart, He complained as well on many occasions that Frenchmen do not ask Him for the King...***

*I think that it would be good for me to put emphasis to you upon the fact, as I told you before, that **this king will certainly NOT be a descendant of the Orléans family** since they (its members) do not descend from the male branch of the kings of France which it alone is wanted by God who has instituted this requirement. It's been clearly stated that **this great Monarch will be a descendant from the King and Queen martyrs: Louis XVI and Marie-Antoinette.***

(Marie-Julie Jahenny, 25 March 1874)

When France will be on its knees, battered and beaten, the message of hope echoed by Marie-Julie Jahenny will be remembered by a country that will lose faith but completely... and yet, this message begins with a message given by one of France's greatest Kings, King St. Louis (Louis IX), announcing the arrival of France savior, a King sent and prepared by God, a Capet and a Bourbon of true royal blood, a descendant of King St. Louis and of King Louis XVI and of Queen Marie-Antoinette:

(...) How many blasphemies, how many perjuries on this earthly throne. I come back to reconcile Heaven and earth. You will reconcile France with the

Heart of Jesus. I want France to abjure her errors. Mary Immaculate gives me power and grace. Through my prayers I will give France a new baptism and then I will re-establish her throne. I will bring her this beautiful palm to the center of this throne and my brother in Jesus Christ (Henry V) who will govern her will preserve his innocence and purity, and Jesus and Mary will bless him, will bless his charity and his great heroic faith!

Friends of the Lord, tomorrow I shall pray a great deal for he who must render this land happy, and return to it this same flower (the Royal Fleur de Lys) I wore when I governed it (France).This torch I have in my hand is the symbol of the savior who, full of life and of youth, will crush the (enemy's) troops. Poor France... Very soon, it will be taken to its tomb... The fatal strike, which she deserved, will crush her without her being able to defend herself. But a Defender is chosen (for her) by the True Eternal King.

...These poor souls! In one darkest night, the Center (Paris) will be bombarded, and the victims will not survive... (However,) My friends will no longer be there; they will all have left it before (the catastrophe takes place). I shall pray for this most miserable kingdom where the King of Glory has suffered so many outrages...

(King St. Louis of France, 25 August 1882)

Note: Here, King St. Louis' message received by Marie-Julie announces the long awaited arrival of the King, prepared by God for France; however, what is announced at the same time is most grave, for it announces Paris being "bombarded" during a night in such a severe manner that no inhabitant will survive (or almost none: 88). As we have seen previously, Reverend Father Pel, a French mystic and visionary announced as well that Paris will be bombed through two synchronized nuclear attacks launched by the Russians from outside the cities of Orléans and Reims... But, despite the epic destruction of the French capital, Paris will not be entirely destroyed, Marie-Julie tells us, although the greatest part of the city will be burnt and sunken into a bottomless depth...

Since we know that the Russian invaders will enter Paris shortly after their crossing the French border and thrusting their armed forces towards the Capital, we can only assume that Paris will be destroyed upon their withdrawal...

Take good notice, that in your last struggle (Third Crisis) **when the populace will be more relentless than ever, you will see all the chastisements begin: war, butchery, horrible plagues... Afterwards, it will be... The Call to the King!**

(Our Lord Jesus-Christ to the country of France, 12 February 1876)

Do you hear My voice, O My beloved son? You who for so long has walked upon a foreign land! Don't you see the road through which I shall send to your encounter the princes of the Celestial armies in order for this triumph be beautiful like that of a King of Predilection? My beloved son, dry you tears. The Lily (Fleur de Lys) will be your brother, and My Beloved Mother will be your Mother. Your crown will wear the emblem of the Fleur

de Lys, and the Fleur de Lys will always bloom upon your forehead. From your forehead, it will bloom upon your throne, from your throne upon France, your reserved kingdom, and from there beyond the French borders up to the Eternal City (Rome).

(Our Lord Jesus-Christ, 9 January 1878)

Herein below is an extraordinary exchange between Marie-Julie Jahenny and the Blessed Mother of Christ that gives more light yet on the expected future king of France:

- **My children, the King will come in the Cross, that is to say in the sorrows, because the kingdom will not yet be entirely calm… It is only after having suffered sorrows, crossing the kingdom that he will receive his crown. Once he will manage doing so, calm will be reestablished, but still there will be (many) sorrows… His Faith will make him victorious of all difficulties. The King will have a gift that no other king ever had. St. Louis, King of France, did his duty, but this new king will be even more wonderful in his reign! You will see in this man what no one has ever seen in any other.**
- *Holy Mother, I do not know him, but I love him!*
- **And so do I, my dear child… My Heart beats for you O my king, O my son. It beats still.**
- *Why is he also your king?*
- **Because I love him; because he will be my children's king. I do not speak for you** (for all this will take place after Marie-Julie's death); **because he will fulfill their hopes despite great difficulties.**
  If you do not see the path of my king's coming, do not worry. This path will be miraculous, very much like the rest of his life. Nothing is impossible to God.
- *Yes Holy Mother. Credo! Credo[14]!*
- **Ah! Poor vain hope of blind men! They believe that the King will never be theirs… They are mistaken. You will be truly astonished one day to see my king. Know this: it will not be France who will call him. Know that he will come for his friends. The small amount of those who desire him will be well rewarded. The others, the great number… will be justly punished…**

(22 January 1878)

In this remarkable conversation with Marie-Julie, the Blessed Virgin Mary describes the King of France as "Her king" because she loves him; when she states that he is "Her king" she means a King of hers. Naturally, the Blessed Virgin Mary's King, the One whom she loves as her Sovereign and son, her Lord

---

[14] Credo! Credo!: "I believe, I believe!" (Latin)

and God, the One who "fulfills her hopes" is God manifested through her Son Jesus-Christ.

My Adorable Voice gathers My illustrious and generous combatants. As before in different circumstances, It has chosen true and generous warriors.

This man of faith who has suffered and hoped from the depth of exile will, before many years, rise like a luminous flash. He will wait on French grounds for the arrival of the enemy's army which will be astonished by the dark firmament...

In my designs, the savior sleeps in exile embedded in the Fleur de Lys which his spirit has so much dreamt of. Under a scattered sky filled with stars, he will bring triumph to My Temple, and will rest upon My Heart.

(...) The enemy will oppose himself to the illustrious victor's triumph. Its armies will thirsty for the blood of those who My Glory calls, but Heaven will blind them and thunder will strike them without care.

(Excerpt of Our Lord Jesus-Christ's message to Marie-Julie, 17 January 1882)

"God will help the King so powerfully that men will not understand the speed with which war and peace are made. It is after this that the King will be brought to France by his supporters. He will receive a communication from the Holy Father that he is called by God and that the Holy Church needs his help. The bishops also will invite him, and an invitation from them will be like the invitation of the Sacred Heart. But there will be a very small number (who will invite him)."

(18 February 1876)

The man of faith who has suffered and hoped from the depth of exile, will, before many years, rise like a luminous flash. He will wait on French grounds for the arrival of the enemy's army which will be astonished by the dark firmament...

In My designs, the savior sleeps in exile embedded in the Fleur de Lys which his spirit has so much dreamt of. Under a scattered sky filled with stars, he will bring triumph to My Temple, and will rest upon My Heart.

(...) The enemy will oppose himself to the illustrious victor's triumph. His armies will be thirsty for the blood of those who My Glory calls; but Heaven will blind (the enemy). Thunder will strike them without care.

It's a long distance away from the siege soiled by the guilty man, and soiled again by even guiltier men through which I shall conduct, under a cloud of triumph, My elected on this French land where the enemies have sworn to give death to the savior of the kingdom, Henry of the Cross. His name is inscribed in the golden book.

(Our Lord Jesus-Christ, 17 January 1882)

Here is yet another astonishing conversation between Marie-Julie and St. Michael the Archangel found in Marie-Julie Jahenny's many apparition recordings:

- **The king's enemies' corpses will be stepped upon by all the great ones who will accompany him to the throne (of France) wherefrom he must establish peace, and have goodness re-flourish everywhere; however, there will still remain enemies standing, for the King must come at the most raging moment of the storm. He will be kept safe, as the Mother of God keeps him as her own son, and reserves him as the (rightful) heir to a well-deserved crown that has been stolen from him.**
  The days of exile will have cost this faithful and Catholic King dearly... He will be nevertheless proportionally rewarded.
  Let men say and affirm that he will never come, then ask them if they are prophets?
- *We, shall say nothing, Good Saint Michael!*
- **No... not you.** *(*Since Marie-Julie will not live in these times.*)* **When the reign of this King will come, France will be terribly weaken, terribly depopulated... but God will reward her with wonderful prodigies! Peace will reign everywhere with happiness everywhere. All the other nations will likewise have their own justice after this horrible sorrow reserved to France, for there will be a Renewal of the entire Universe. There will be everywhere chastisements coming from the Divine Justice. There are nations, which I will not name, who will have to suffer... for many years...**
  I think that the friends of the Cross have understood that their future is assured, and that they will have a (special) thought of thanksgiving for their beloved Mother.
- *Yes, in all these days, we shall present them to her...*
- **Not you...**
- *I was not thinking... They will present them a bouquet of lilies, and then they will offer it to the king.*

(29 September 1878)

Here, once again, St. Michael the Archangel confirmed that the King of France will come to save France years after Marie-Julie's death.

In the Presence of the Divine Majesty, I found myself profoundly rested. On the other hand, never has a sorrow afflicted my entire being as the sight that the Lord has made me see of the Earth.

You will wait a little bit, but not long before revealing all that I have deposited in your soul.

(...) I have seen the siege of a land terribly shattered. I have seen Satan and his men make themselves victorious and kings despite God's orders. I have seen

160

*the triumphant armies in the Center (*Paris*). The armies of these guilty victors will want to oppose themselves to the passage of the true servants of God who will come from all over the world with the Faith which we still have today and with a hope that nothing will be able to shatter. The servants of God will confront these armies who will oppose themselves to their passage in a mortal defense. The Great crowned one will raise his voice to say:*

'Take arms! Strike this entire army which, by my authority, I curse'.

I have seen the sword fall upon the head of the (enemy) crowned victor, and above the sword appeared the following words:

'I have declared that there is but one single man destined to the French Empire!
I stand up with Anger and Justice; I shall exterminate the pride of that king made by men and whom My Will has rejected.' (from the House of the d'Orléans family)

And all these walls were destroyed, these walls that have served for the protection of those who have reigned under that roof. But all this is nothing in comparison to what is still coming...

(7 November 1882)

My children, I am the Flame of the Divine Words of Eternal Life.

My children, on behalf of the Infinite Power, I reveal to you out loud that, soon, in (the region of) Savoy (France)**, an old man, mortal son of Adam, will stand as a torch of salvation for these regions. This old man will be poor, living in the countryside, retired from a daily labor, holy and venerable by his Faith and by his piety. He will do a great deal of good to the exiled one** (King Henry V of the Cross) **and to high ranking men. On the opposing side, horrific cries will be raised against the exiled one. The last word will be:**

'He will not pass upon the land of France without bullets whistling around his armies and, especially, around his own ears!'

My children, it will be at the beginning of the great Crisis. Good will be achieved by this old man called by God for a short lasting but beautiful mission. The people will still have the time to read the lines dictated by Heaven under the pen of this old man.

(12 October 1882)

It's towards the end of this last period that they will bring him who holds no hope, who is neither agreeable nor consoling. His name will pass in the Sun, quickly like a flash (the false king from the d'Orléans family)**, so that the people may know that he is NOT the true king who must sit upon the throne. It's then that his friends** (army/commandos) **will march to encounter the true King** (Henry of the Cross)**, before peace is totally rung in France...**

Some friends (of Henry of the Cross) **will come to enlarge the small number of French friends** (that composes the army) **of the true king. They will accompany him until the very border of the kingdom, but they will not leave their land to walk upon that of France...**

The friends of the (false) king that God wants to fall will have as well his own friends. They will march against the new Savior to shatter him upon his entry (in France) **and to stop him from reaching the throne which is destined for him.**

He will come from the East (Belgium, Luxembourg, Germany, Switzerland Northern Italy?).

At about 9 kilometers from the Center (Paris) **will be found the** (enemy) **armies of today's governors. It is there, in a big city that God awaits for them to give them His great marks and blind these barbarians who will oppose the future savior. Others will go further to await for him upon his entering** (France)...

The (true) **King will already have travelled about 50 km inside France, in direction of the throne** (Paris? Reims?). **It is there that God awaits for His true friends to have them rejoice of His Grand Sign. The white standard will be raised in this place whose name will be said** (The name of this city/town has never been found in M-J's archives...). **He** (Henry of the Cross) **will pass despite the rampart** (defenses) **which will be raised against him, and his true combatants will fear nothing, for about them will float 'the Protection'. He** (Henry V) **will step over his enemies whose blindness will have shattered them... Henry will come forth all the way to the throne before the battle is finished.**

He who was actually chosen (by the guilty mixed-people of France: Jean d'Orléans?) **will step down from the throne, ashamed, before the future Great Protector of France** (Henry of the Cross), **at the great confusion of those who have placed him there in the first place.**

The battle will last only a few hours under the eyes of the savior of Peace (Henry V), **but before stepping upon his throne, he will see many weeks pass due to the difficulties to find someone to consecrate him...**

The apostles of the Church (the revolution in France will not be finished yet) will still be dispersed... The one who must have this honor is not forgotten, (but) **he is not the one of the Center** (Archbishop of Paris) **nor the one who is on the side where the sun rises** (Archbishop of Reims), **nor any of those who reside in the surroundings of the Hell-room** (National Assembly/French Parliament)...

(Blessed Virgin Mary, 9 May 1882)

The Reverend Father Vanutelli, Pastor of Blain, accompanied Marie-Julie Jahenny in her spiritual life, but the Church did not intervene officially on the political messages brought forth, for, as we can see, Marie-Julie's revelations were very anti-republican. Marie Julie spoke all the time of the future Great Monarch the TRUE King of France whom she called Henri (Henry V). She affirmed that the French Monarch, Henry V of the Cross, would be sacred in the ruins of Notre Dame amongst the ruins of Paris[15].

One question comes to mind, what proof will Henry V give to substantiate his linage to Louis XVI and to Marie-Antoinette, and who will be the traitorous unsacred king of France who will send forces to intercept him? The only evidence that would be accepted in our time and age is indeed a DNA test. The results of this test will be done and will clearly be known by one and all.

Regarding the Blessed Mother's message of 9 May 1882, it would appear that the collaborating Franco-muslin government—knowing of Henry of the Cross' having crossed the French border from a country bordering France, being on his way to what I presume to be Reims,—would send armed troops and reconnaissance commandos to intercept Henry and his small force. A peace agreement between the traitorous Franco-Muslim government and the Arabo-Russian coalition will not yet be sealed when Henry will have crossed the border.

The first battle will take place and will, in a matter of hours, turn in favor of Henry's small army allowing the future and rightful Prince of France to take and hold the city of Reims. As weeks pass by, Henry will join forces with the French army of the west, beat and push back the Russian forces all the way to Paris. Forced to withdraw, the Russian head-command will decide to pursue its usual scorched-earth policy as the Russian army retreats eastward, launching a nuclear attack on the abandoned French capital... Paris, Marie-Julie Jahenny tells us, will be pulverized, but the Island on the Seine River in the Center of Paris which hosts the Cathedral of Notre-Dame (called l'île de la Cité *'the City's Island'*) will be spared.

As Henry reached the shores of the Seine River and lands on "l'île de la Cité", Henry will wait there for a few weeks as no bishop will be present to place the Crown of France and the blessed Oil on his head... Against all hope, Henry will receive at last a young bishop, not a Frenchman but a German, the Bishop of Achen, who will come to crown Henry of the Cross King of France.

It is not a pastor of the Centre (i.e., a bishop of Paris) **who will have the honor of crowning in glory the King, the heir who has deserved to govern his country. The pastor will be young: (his) 45 years will not have yet sounded. He will come from the diocese of Aix. The pastors who govern the dioceses today are no longer in their Episcopal see. The glorious and worthy child of God who will crown the true King on the ruins of the Centre,** (Cathedral of Notre Dame) **when the earth will be much deserted, will come from far away.**

(The Blessed Virgin Mary, 26 May 1882)

---

[15] **Every King in France since King Clovis' baptism on Christmas 496 (with the exception of Louis XVIII, Charles X and Louis-Philippe) has been anointed and crowned in the Cathedral of Notre Dame in Paris and/or in the Cathedral of Reims.**

From Heaven, you will see the triumph of the Church hovering over the forehead of My true servant Henry of the Cross; (The Great Monarch) **will comfort the destitute, renew the devastated priesthood, weakened and fallen like a branch under the saw of the worker. His charity will renew the priesthood; he will raise the statues of My Mother; he will remount the crosses** (that were) **insulted and cut into pieces.**

(Our Lord to Marie-Julie, 14 February 1882)

Back in Paris, as the news of Henry's triumph and crowning in Notre-Dame spread, the illegitimate king of France (Jean d'Orléans?), at the immense surprise of his Russian and Muslim allies, will officially step down and renounce to the throne... After the crowning, knighting and anointing of now King "Henri V de la Croix", and despite the immense sorrow caused by the tragic destruction of Paris, the French army will resume its victorious campaign of liberation against the Russian and Muslims armies:

*(...) After having contemplated them (*the soldiers of the enemy's army*) on the river-edge of the great torrent, the Immortal Queen from Heaven has vanquished thousands of these perfidious living (men), these blaspheming foreign troops. She said: **They will not be victorious.** The Blessed Virgin Mary turned twice towards the Lord's children, and their battalions (and) walked forward; they all passed without the enemy being able to harm one single soldier of the Cross.*

(Marie-Julie Jahenny, 16 May 1882)

<u>Note</u>: There is a description written by Monsieur Adolph Charbonnier describing other battles before the crowning in Paris: the battle of Orléans, on the heights of Blois, in the region of Sens and even on the river of Vienne, clearly unfolding King Henry V of the Cross' army's victorious path towards Paris; however, it is too difficult to decipher Mr. Charbonnier's tired handwriting and thus recount properly the details of such events (5 September 1882)....

The most resplendent moment was the one when the Christians ministers, who were all dispersed under the teeth of the tigers, came back through horrible paths for the solemn moment. Among the Lord's ministers, friends of the King, I only saw but four bishops... ***<u>The Blessed Virgin Mary has given again the name of he who will have the honor to bless him and to consecrate him in the middle of the land of the Center</u>*** [16].

---

[16] (...) *in the middle of the land of the Center:* In France, it is said that every road, every avenue, and every street in Paris is drawn from the center of the Capital which is the island in the middle of the Seine River (l'île de la Cité) which hosts the Cathedral of Notre-Dame. This implies that, despite Paris being destroyed and sunken, the island on the Seine River will be spared, and the remnants of the

In regards to the Cathedral of Notre Dame de Paris, its fire of April 2019—although it was widely whispered and strongly suspected to be the result of a terrorist act—did not make the Cathedral collapse… miraculously enough… leaving the main altar with its main golden Cross and its two surrounding statues (that of Louis the XVI and of Marie-Antoinette) intact. Marie-Julie affirms that the remnant of this majestic Cathedral is meant to preside the crowning of Henry V of the Cross by a young 44-year-old German Archbishop of Aix la Chapelle (Aachen, Germany). Notwithstanding, King Henry V is to be crowned as well in Reims as his fathers were before him, and theirs before them.

You will see from Heaven the triumph of the Church looming over the forehead of my real servant Henri de la Croix (Henry of the Cross). **His name is written in the golden Book. After this triumph the faithful Pastor will place his consecrated hand on the head of the one Heaven will have led and brought in a miraculous manner.**

My design is that after he has received the holy blessing, he goes with my noble defendants carrying the white banner to the place where the messages of salvation came from (the cottage of Marie-Julie in La Fraudais? Tully?).

(Our Lord Jesus-Christ, 4 February 1882).

The Return of the Holy Dove:

From the beginning, the French Monarchy was specially blessed and chosen by Heaven. Marie-Julie revealed that she was told that the French kings were descendants from the House of David, Christ's royal house, yet, the first French king Clovis I (AD 466–511) was a pagan. He was married to St. Clotilde who was Roman and Catholic, but at the time, the Arian heresy denounced Christ's divinity. This did not stop the doctrine of the Holy Trinity to gain ground in the realm.

Apparently, Clovis was open to conversion but was confused about the true nature of Christian faith, for he remained hesitant to embrace the religion of Jesus-Christ despite his wife's holy example and teachings. It was not until he was on the verge of losing his kingdom to the invading Alemanni tribes that he made a vow promising that, if victorious against his enemies, he would become a Catholic subject loyal to Rome.

Shortly after a most spectacular and crushing victory against the Alemannis, King Clovis fulfilled his oath before God and before his wife and became baptized in the Cathedral of Reims. As a sign of predestiny, Heaven would manifest Its design for France by showing a sign which centuries thereafter would not be able to wipe out from man's memory. Indeed, as Clovis entered the Cathedral's main altar for his baptism, massive crowds entered the Cathedral of Reims. Franks from the four corners of Gaul came to witness the coronation of

---

Cathedral of Notre Dame will remain standing and will be used for King Henry's coronation.

France's very first King. So many people came in fact that the clerks could not get through the Central Isle to bring the blessed oils for the royal anointments.

It was then that Archbishop Rémi, alarmed by such a fiasco, raised his eyes to Heaven and, in the secret of his heart, fervently prayed for divine help... God's Mercy indeed did not take long to manifest itself, as a dove, said to be *whiter than snow*, suddenly flew inside this Cathedral with a mysterious flask and a lily in its beck, which were deposited ever so gently in the hands of the deeply astonished archbishop. After delivering the precious crystal, the heavenly creature gently disappeared into nothingness while still in the hands of a moved and grateful churchman...

According to tradition, Archbishop Rémi, who officiated the King's baptism, preserved the precious vial called "La Sainte Ampoule", the oil from which would be later used for the coronation of every French king in the next twelve hundred years without its level ever lowering! Disgracefully, the sacred relic was later smashed to pieces by the republican revolutionaries in 1793; however, the fragments were all gathered and kept to this day in the Palace of Tau (Reims).

The Sacred Heart foretold to Marie-Julie on 17 July 1874 that when the Royal House of France will be restored, France will once again see the Holy Spirit descend, in the form of a Dove, bringing to the Great King a large banner with an image of the Sacred Heart.

Our Lord further told Marie-Julie Jahenny that from La Fraudais, the King will then go to the city of Sainte Anne d'Auray to thank St. Anne, the Blessed Virgin Mary's mother on earth.

Here, this message reveals yet again a remarkable prophecy. First that, as an act of thanksgiving, Henry V will undoubtedly make a pilgrimage to La Fraudais after his coronation at Notre Dame, and plant thereafter in La Fraudais his Royal white and golden standard as an act of loving devotion... Then, once his pilgrimage to La Fraudais and to Sainte-Anne d'Auray will be accomplished, his holy campaign will resume its course...

Friends of the Cross, it's in a voice that the invincible soldiers will go look for success and Victory. When they will have crossed a city close to the Center (Paris), touching closely the land of Orléans, in between these two lands and the city of Blois, there will be found a luminous torch. This torch will be an immortal soul sent by Him who does all prodigies.

It's by passing through these lands that the vibrating voice of this living soul, pushed by Divine Force, will tell you again where you must walk to, along this great river which is a separation of France and the other land that is not French (the Rhine River) until the very border, friends of Victory, but do not go forward on the other side, for it is on the French side that you must wait, but not for long... The rejoicing sounds of the trumpet will make themselves heard in the distance. This music of consolation and happiness will reach you at the border of the river.

Here we note that the victorious French army will directed towards the Rhine river in Alsace where it will stop momentarily awaiting for further instructions before crossing. Then, upon receiving order to cross, they will enter Germany.

Note: Once again, the description of the ensuing battles written in Mr. Charbonnier's tired handwriting is too difficult to decipher…

(…) The anger and the justice of God will have shattered them when the army of God's apostles (will strike?)… but the enemies will not be all dead.

(26 September 1882)

(…) When the elected King and Savior of France (will) have seen the triumph of France, he will write everywhere "in hoc signo vinces"; by this sign you will conquer! France will be under the banner of the Sacred Heart, the Cross and Mary.

(11 May 1877)

France will save itself. The other nations will refuse her their assistance… *The beginning of their fury will be through the profanation of My Temple. All the big fortunes will collapse. There will be nothing left. Everything will be destroyed through chastisement and by men.*

(Notes taken by Doctor Imbert Goubert of M.J. Jahenny prophetic statements)

The Blessed Virgin Mary:

-   **The army of the just, the soldiers of the Cross, mixed with other brave (people), will cross over through most of France, under the fire of the signs of God. It will come out of Brittany to go back just up to the river (the Rhine) where the Savior of the earth must arrive with his own army. They will join together, under the star of victory. My daughter, mark well this word: it will be under the signs of Heaven, similar to the blood of Christians. Amid these bloody and frightening signs, there will be a white light that will surpass the beauty of the dawn. This whiteness will split the grooves of blood, and it will go before you, on the edge of the river. This whiteness has crossed the blood (on) the day of the memories of the Passion of my Son.**

Marie-Julie:

-   *Yes, good Mother, a Friday.*

The Blessed Virgin Mary:

-   **My children, so that you do not doubt, I described to you the sign that My Son will reveal to you at nightfall, a true proof: a white sign to the West of France, surrounded by a curtain of diamond fringes, enormous, the space of three quarters of an hour. Your homes will be lit up as if by the sun. The streets will be as clear as on an** ordinary day. After half an hour, a red bar will be formed, to the west, in the form of branches; and drops of blood will escape from it. This red bar will surround the whiteness of the sign and will invade the brightness of its light. My children, from the west, this sign will rise up a little, and then the red bar will dissipate, as by the victory of the whiteness (triumph of the King). It will be a Saturday, between five and six O'clock...

After these words, the Blessed Virgin fell to her knees at the feet of the Eternal Father, who replied:

- **Very worthy Mother of God, My Eternal Son wishes to manifest the sign of the mortal Savior** (Henry of the Cross) **and turn His Power on (against) the side of the foreigner. All eyes, in France will be able to contemplate this favor in its regard.**

The Blessed Virgin Mary:

- **It will (appear), as an ornament in the sky, in the form of a square star, bearing in its middle a scepter and a crown that will be well distinguished (by) all the peoples of the earth. And, since my Son cannot convince His people of that happy day that will surprise them in the midst of their bad and guilty ideas, He will commence by placing under the firmament the announcement of the predictions made in past centuries and to this present century.**

(21 November 1882):

This is how we march on the borders of France, bearing the banner and the sword. I hold under my feet all the enemies of God and all (that are of) Freemasonry. I shall exterminate them and the Justice of God will complete (this task), and will crush them under the weight of His Anger. Walking upon France we shall accomplish our duties. When peace will be reestablished there, and the Kingdom of God begun, we shall walk towards Rome, since France must dedicate itself to the defense of the Holy See. The new and holy Pontiff will be a great deal more threatened than the one that God picked-up while carrying His Holy Temple on His Shoulders.

They will attempt to put his days in danger, and if he does not become a martyr at the hands of the barbarians, it will be because God would have performed a brilliant miracle for him. Never... never was a storm so violent against any other Pontiff before. He is already a martyr before having suffered his martyrdom... He suffers before the hour has come, but he offers his person and the blood of his veins for his executioners and for those who have attempted to take his life. Such exiles to suffer!

(Michael the Archangel, 29 September 1879)

168

Henry V of the Cross will not establish his throne in Paris because the city will be destroyed...

(Notes taken by Doctor Imbert Goubert, 18 February 1876)

Once France is liberated, the test will begin for Rome... Five months after peace is reestablished in France by King Henry V of the Cross, a revolution like no other will start in Rome... The horrible war in Italy will be long; it will last for more than two years... The Church will have its Seat (Pope's Seat) vacant for long months... In France human loss will be very important.

There will be many admonitions from Heaven during these difficult moments to open the eyes of those (whose hearts) are harder. But it is only after these preliminary events that the great three days Universal Chastisement will put to an end all hostilities... due to the lack of combatants! Then, King Henry V of the Cross will reign for a long period of time, and the Church will re-flourish under the pontificate of a holy Pope.

(St. Michael the Archangel, 29 September 1882)

The last minutes will be terrible for the land of the Eternal City (Rome).
The scourge will befall upon the Russians there, (and) after only two days (thereafter) terrible trials will be (reserved) for the people.

(16 November 1822)

My France, plunged into crime, (but) will be resurrected into glory. The reign of peace will be extended always to 25 or 30 years, under the direction of a soul that the Divine Heart reserves for Its faithful, saved by His grace and loving kindness.

My little children, the rising of this Prince who will become King of my new France, a France that will be purified, ennobled and beautiful in my eyes... The reign of the Divine Heart, Divine Royalty of the Divine Heart of my Son: it will be of great blessings my little children, and you will have your large share of blessings reserved for that epoch not far away... not far away...

(The Blessed Virgin Mary, 23 July 1925):

Once France has paid its debt, it will be rewarded with such an abundance of graces that in a short time, it will have forgotten everything. To the powers that have fought with such bravery and courage (for the King), they will receive from France the greatest reward: that of taking their place within the Catholic Church, coming out of this baptism of blood rejuvenated and renewed. I will break all the obstacles and reverse all the projects of those that prevent the light to be. France will be saved by means out of all human knowledge.

God has reserved the secret for them until the last moment. I make light of the projects of men, preparing My right wonders. My Heart will be glorified throughout the earth. I appeal to confound the pride of the wicked. And the more the world will be hostile to the supernatural, the more marvelous will the events be that will confuse this negation of the supernatural.

(Our Lord Jesus-Christ, February 1941)

Our Lord Jesus-Christ addressing Marie-Julie Jahenny:

One day My servant Henry of the Cross will ask My Church to place you (picture) on the altars at the same time as his ancestor Louis XVI.
Henry V is your king. It is you who has deserved him and who has obtained him for France.

(Our Lord Jesus-Christ, Unknown date…)

The Warning

As it will be for France, the liberation of Western Germany, Northern Italy, and Rome finally will take place as well. This said a "Warning" will follow-up which will precede the announced "World Chastisement"… This world punishment will at last end the military conflict in Europe and abroad…

The "Warning" announced to Marie-Julie Jahenny, which is to announce the great "Chastisement" about a year thereafter will be confirmed in another apparition site almost a century later, through a same revelation of the Blessed Virgin Mary to four little girls in a small village in northern Spain called Garabandal (see page: 361, Chapter VII). According to Marie-Julie Jahenny, the Blessed Virgin Mary stated:

Wait for that which must arrive: an inner distress will be felt by all, a preview of the Justice of God.
The army of the just, the soldiers of the Cross, mixed with other brave (people), will cross over through most of France, under the fire of the signs of God. It will come out of Brittany to go back just up to the river (the Rhine) where the Savior of the earth must arrive with his own army. They will join together, under the star of victory.

(21 November 1882)

Our Lord Jesus-Christ added:

My children, sometime before these sinister signs are sent onto the Earth, they will already feel in their hearts the effect of My justice; it will be that the heart will say the time is not far away. But a grace of peace is reserved

for faithful Christians, those who have not disregarded the warnings of Heaven and who will conform their lives (to them).

(The Blessed Virgin Mary and Our Lord Jesus-Christ, 27 August 1878)

The Chastisement

Souls are being put into notice so as to choose their camps, that is why one of the objectives we must pursue is to explain the 'why' of the events to come; the dates and the places are the domain of Providence: 'It is not up to you to know neither the day nor the hour', and this Divine Providence has never abandoned anyone...

(Our Lord Jesus-Christ, 18 January 1881)

Four Hours of Darkness over Brittany

My people, My people, My people, your eyes will see the beginning of the terrible hour, when the wheat is not on its third node of growth. At the moment when My people will only have Faith and Hope to arm itself, still in the hard season, lasting for four hours—from 12:00 to 16:00 in France—in those hard days still, the sun will be like a veil of mourning; it will be darkened, without light. Never could anyone on earth believe in the (ever so deep) obscurity of this darkness. The earth will not experience anything else (other than this brief period of deep darkness). The eye will be veiled, without it being able to see any object.

My people, this will be the beginning of the chastisement of My Righteousness. The sun will announce these sorrows: the sky will cry, unable to be comforted, because it will be the beginning of the time when souls will be lost, the entrance, in a word of the terrible misfortune. My people, this darkness will cover Brittany (France) for four hours, but there will be no harm... just a little fright...

(Our Lord Jesus-Christ, 5 October 1882)

The sun shall be darkened before, forewarning the real darkness that will arrive 37 days after the signs of the darkening of the sun, and of signs of the earth and of the announced storm.

(28 November 1928):

Our Lord Jesus-Christ gave more details:

The Invasion of France According to Marie-Julie Jahenny

Invasion limit of France according to Marie-Julie Jahenny
(Line/front between Caen (Normandy) and Lourdes)

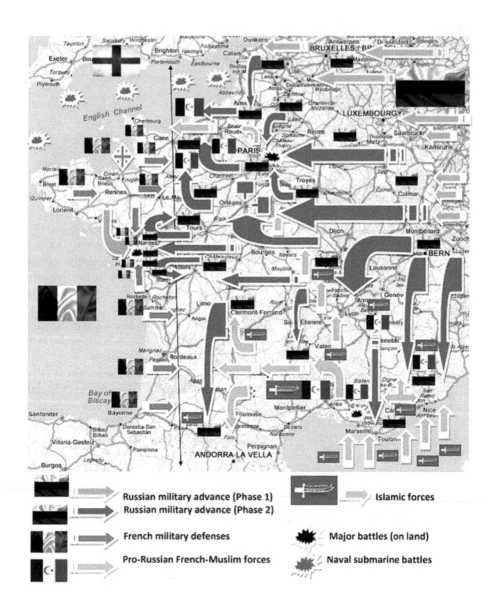

Russian military advance (Phase 1)		Islamic forces
Russian military advance (Phase 2)		
French military defenses		Major battles (on land)
Pro-Russian French-Muslim forces		Naval submarine battles

The Liberation of France by King Henry V of the Cross According to Marie-Julie Jahenny

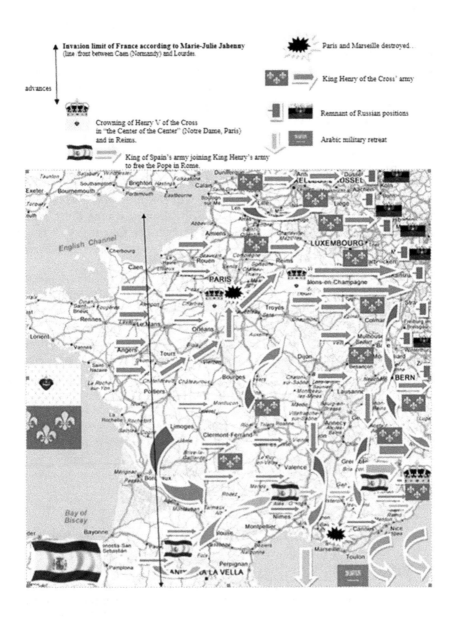

I warn My people of that which follows the number of evils in France. The first (following events) are not far off, and will be followed by many others. I warn you that one day it will be found—and it is marked (written)—that there will be little sun, no stars and no light to make one able to step out of houses, the refuges of My people. The day commences to grow; it will not be at the height of summer or in the longest days, still short. It will not be at the end of a year, but in the first months (of the year) that I will give clearly My warnings...

The day of darkness and lightning, it will be the first that I will send to convert the wicked, and to see whether many will return to Me before the big storm that will follow closely. That day, my children, will not reach all of France, but part of Brittany (that) will be tested. The side where the land of the Mother of My Immaculate Mother (city of St. Anne d'Auray) will not be obscured by the darkness to come, only to you and, beyond that, on the (side of) the sunrise (East).

Everything else will be in the most terrible fright. After the night (dawn) to just until night, a whole day, the thunder will continue to scold; the fire of lightning will do much harm, even in private homes where there will be sin... My children, that first day does not detract (or take away) from the other three marked and described (we must still expect the Three Days of Darkness).

(Our Lord Jesus-Christ, 15 June 1882)

Marie-Julie Jahenny added:

*Our Lord also said more revelations to St. Catherine Labouré (*sister of Charity—visionary of the Chapel of the rue du Bac, Paris, who was instructed to spread the "Miraculous Medal"*) about these warning-signs. **They were hidden away for future times and will be discovered in a monastery.** This day (of warning) is noted in five rolls tightly closed (of or by) the sister de Saint Pierre Tours. These rolls remain (hidden) in secret, until the day when a person of God will bring his predestined hand on what the world has ignored to the inhabitants of that monastery...*

Two Days of Darkness:

Before the dreaded catastrophic Three Days, a warning for the faithful will be sent through another two days of utter darkness...

In September of 1880, the Holy Spirit revealed to Marie-Julie Jahenny:

There will be two days of horrible darkness, distinct from those advertised (different from the three days of universal darkness). **The sky will be purple and red, (and it will be) so low that the clump of tall trees will appear to be as lost. These two days will warn you, as an authentic proof of His goodness, as proof of (the) descent of the wrath of God on earth. You will not be free from the darkness. So far, no soul has mentioned it, because they are not many of those who were made aware of it. To resist all these signs,**

holy water is a strength and consolation, and the candle, but a candle made of bees' wax. *(The Blessed Virgin Mary asked for 100% pure bees' wax candles to be used).* **All those** (candles) **that are not made of this paste will not help.**

During these two days, the trees will be burnt and will not produce any fruit the following year because the sap will be burnt and stopped. The rain that will fall from the sky below will have a foul odor, and wherever it will fall, it will be as a big hailstone of fire that pierces that which is most solid, and it will leave a visible mark of burning. Your homes will be preserved. Only that which is covered lightly will suffer (of weak construction).

The water that will be poured on the earth will be black, a frightening black, and most of the land will bear it equally everywhere, but it will not hurt that which serves as food to the Christians.

In Brittany, during these two days of darkness, under the lowering sky, it will seem light, but no one will be able to see, because they cannot put out their face by day when opening a door; there will be an envoy of God, in the form of a hot flash, which will obscure the human eye. The Lord is urging me to pass on His words and His wishes. The day of these darknesses will still be bearable, despite the obscurity... But if the day is calm, the night will be violent, and during the two nights, cries will come out where they know not; they will hear nothing, nor walk on earth, covered with Justice.

At night, the blessed candle, the candle should not be put out. During the day, they will be able to go without it, a grace that comes from the farthest part of the Heart of God. *(Only during the TWO DAYS during the daytime can we put out the blessed candles, but NOT during the THREE DAYS when the blessed candles MUST remain lit at all times!)*

(The Holy Spirit, 20 September 1880)

The Three Days of Darkness:

I give you for a calm and assured home: My Divine Adorable Heart with this great love of My Blessed Sacrament which they want to destroy in destroying Me, trying every means to obliterate My sweet Heaven on Earth, My tent, My holy place, the faith of My elect... It will be missing on earth, this Bread of Eternal Life the Bread that sustains My little suffering souls, the banquet which strengthens them, but not for long... I will leave to the wicked one hour of power and strength.

They will increase their numbers (with) all the outcasts of the abyss, the eternal abyss, all the damned who are on earth in human forms to destroy everything, to annihilate everything... I will leave them this painful and difficult hour. It will be followed by a profound darkness... The whole sky will be cloudy.

Your blessed lights (the 100% pure bees' wax candles) will serve in the day, and My blessings will be abundant. My peace will be with you in this dark night, I will launch all the features of My Justice. I will blast the losers of souls. I will sift the false consciences. I will annihilate the wicked. I will reduce them like a... *(text missing)*.

This time is not far off when, I assure you, you will not fear. My cross and My Divine Heart will be your shelter, your refuge; stay, do not run away elsewhere. My Justice will pass. The whole earth will continue in My Justice. It is the time that I will rise up, I shall stop all the evil to enter in the beautiful reign of My Sacred Heart.

(Our Lord Jesus-Christ, 13 November 1924)

The three days of darkness "Will be on a Thursday, Friday, and a Saturday". Days of the Most Holy Sacrament, of the Cross and of Our Lady, three days less one night."

(**The Breton Stigmatist** by the Marquis de la Franquerie)

My children, mind my words... In these days of mourning, there will be another earthquake as strong as many others, (and yet) less strong than in many other places. It will be easy to notice: everything will shake except the piece of furniture on which will burn the (bee's) wax candle. You will all group around, with the crucifix and my blessed image. This is what shall take fear away from you, as these days will cause many deaths.

Here is a proof of my goodness, those who serve me well, invoke me, and keep in their homes my blessed image, I will keep safely all that belongs to them. During these three days, I will protect their cattle from starvation. I will keep them because there must not be a single door ajar. The hungry animals shall be satisfied by me, without any food.

During this darkness the devils and the wicked will take on the most hideous shapes... Red clouds like blood will move across the sky. The crash of thunder will shake the earth and sinister lightning will streak the heavens out of season, the earth will be shaken to its foundations, the sea will rise, its roaring waves will spread over the Continent...

(The Blessed Virgin Mary, 24 March 1881)

The Earth will be covered in darkness, and Hell will be loosed on Earth. The thunder and lightning will cause those who have no faith or trust in my Power, to die of fear... During these three days of terrifying darkness, no windows must be opened, because no one will be able to see the earth and the terrible color it will have in those days of punishment without dying at once... The sky will be on fire, the earth will split... During these three days of darkness let the blessed candle be lit everywhere; no other light will shine...

(The Blessed Virgin Mary, 20 September 1882)

To Marie-Julie Jahenny:

No one, outside a shelter, will survive. The earth will shake as the judgment and fear will be great. Yes, we shall listen to the prayers of your

176

friends; not one will perish. We will need them to publish the glory of the cross.

(8 December 1882)

Our Lord Jesus-Christ was describing to Marie Julie Jahenny the course of more events yet to come, a description which had the Breton stigmatist cry for mercy:

- **There will be three days of physical darkness. For three days less one night, there will be a continual night. The blessed wax candles will be the only ones that give light in this terrible darkness: only one will suffice for three days, but in the homes of the wicked, they will not give any light. During these three days and two nights, the demons will appear under the most hideous forms. You will hear in the air the most horrible blasphemies. The lightning will enter your homes, but will not extinguish the candles; neither wind, nor the storm can put them out.**
  Red clouds like blood will ride across the sky. The crash of thunder will shake the earth. Sinister lightning will cut across the dense clouds, in a season when they never occur. The earth will be shaken down to the foundations. The sea will raise thundering waves that will spread across the continent (Tidal wave). **Blood will flow in such abundance that the earth will become a vast cemetery. The corpses of the wicked and the righteous ones will litter the ground. The famine will be great. Everything will be in turmoil and three-quarters of men will perish...**
  The crisis will break out suddenly. The chastisements will be common in the world. It will swell up and will succeed one another incessantly. When My people fall into indifference, I began to threaten it. Today, it deserves My Justice. I came on earth; they want Me out, taking away My Holy Tabernacle, reversing My Cross and ignoring My Power.

- *"O Lord..."* said Marie-Julie, *"have mercy!"*

- **Yes, I will pity the good people, but the others, I shall (have them) swallowed (down). The earth will open and they will disappear forever...**

(Exchange between Our Lord Jesus-Christ and Marie Julie, 4 January 1884)

My children, you will see fall on the world deadly diseases that will leave no one any time to be prepared to appear before my Son. The lightning of Heaven will succeed with a rapid violence. Fire from Heaven will travel the earth to an appalling width: the vengeful lightning will burn any point that produces fruit. Cultivated lands will be devastated by the power of this fire;

grasslands will be burnt and reduced to a land completely stripped. Fruits will not appear. All the trees' branches will be dried to the trunk...

Children of Brittany, you will use, to keep your crops, that which the goodness of my Son has revealed to you (*see page 204*): it is the only way to save your food. My children, for three days the sky will be on fire, furrowed by fear of divine wrath. What saddens me, is that this anger will not stop the forces of hell. They are neither afraid of my Son nor of hell. These times must pass. The danger of France is written in Heaven by the Eternal Power. I cannot intercede (anymore), I am nothing more than a mother without power...

For many years the earth will produce nothing. France will be unhappy, even after its triumph... For two or three years, she will feel ruin and deep misery. The misery will be great, although my people is clear (of it?). Prayer will bring the blessing. My son and I will have mercy on this long penance.

(The Blessed Virgin Mary, 30 November 1880)

Heaven will let pass on earth the signs of Its Justice. The foreign land will not reap any food. A rain of fire will reduce to dust the food of these people who are mixed, non-Catholic Christians and Mohammedans.

The land of France will also be subject to God's righteousness. For three years, the potatoes will rot at the time of the seed, the corn will not grow or stop halfway. Fruits will blacken: a worm will eat the inside, before they reach the size of a finger.

The Center (Paris) and its residences will be crushed by the violence of the thunder of God. The tremors and earthquakes will increase, day and night without ceasing for forty-three days. The sea will be agitated and never in all ages, has its waves and its floods taken a similar form. Everyone at that time will perish forever.

The Chastisement will not limit itself to the Days of Darkness, but to famine, pestilence, and destruction... The days from the time the war in Europe openly begins until three years after the end of the Three Days of Darkness will be a struggle for life, but Humanity will survive and strive within a new revived Church and under the reign of a great Monarch who will lead its people, and other nations across the world to a new civilization and era of Peace, but, before the "Resurrection" comes, the "Crucifixion" must first take place:

I have sent My Mother and they have not believed in her words. I had My Voice heard through, choosing victims through whom I have managed wonders; they despised and persecuted them. I shall now let My Anger go. I shall call (summon) all my lightning-rods.

(Our Lord Jesus-Christ, 1884)

When the rage of the 'unfaithful' will temporarily pause (in France), a great disease will appear almost suddenly... This chastisement will leave victims as if they were lifeless; they will continue to breathe without being able to speak, with skinless wounds as if severely burnt. **This disease will be very contagious and no one will be able to stop it... This will be a punishment of the Lord to bring back many** (back to the Faith).

(The Blessed Virgin Mary, 20 September 1880)

There will be epidemics in the south of France, in Valence, Lyon, Bordeaux, and every distance of land between that and the Center (Paris). Very few people will be able to escape from them. The corpses will spread a horrid odor which causes death...

I shall know how to protect all those who are mine. I have had a ladder placed between the earth and my Heart which is a prepared path for the days of sorrows. The time (of these occurrences) **will not be long, but they will be terrible in all three different sequences...**

(The Blessed Virgin Mary, 5 October 1881)

The earth will shake from this place (La Fraudais?) to where the sun rises (East) for a period of six days. There will be a resting day, and on the 8th day the earthquake will start again. France and England will answer to each other with cries of utter despair. The earth will shake so violently that the people will be thrown 300 steps away... Thunder will rumble more fiercely than in the months that will precede the end of the world with a strange (accompanying) noise...

(The Blessed Virgin Mary, 8 March 1881)

My children, from that cloud, an extraordinary rain will be released which the world has never seen before, and which it will never see again until the consumption of centuries. It will be a red rain which will remain coagulated on the ground for seven weeks. The earth itself will be coagulated by this rain which will give off a poisoned breath, a smell that no one will be able to stand... My people will remain enclosed for 7 weeks. It will be difficult to leave for the grounds will inspire fear. That is the first storm that is announced and that will take place soon.

After this storm, I shall make come out of the earth a horrible 'burning'. The Christian will not be able to stand this foul stench nor the heat (coming out of it). **My children, you will open neither your windows nor your doors. The reign of sin must finish! Never was the earth nor the world in such a state. This must be finished or every soul will be lost.**

(Our Lord Jesus-Christ, 9 March 1878)

Marie-Julie explained on a conversation with the Marquis de la Franquerie:

These rains will come during the General Chastisement that is in relation with the three days of Darkness. This red cloud of blood is the punishment of crimes, homicides, abortions, unjust wars... The darkness is the image of the

179

gloom of the sins of the soul who refuses the Divine Light, who despises love; this despised and outraged light comes back under the form of mighty lightning. Jesus came to put light into darkness, but darkness has not received Him... I remember what Our Lord asked me to repeat:

It will be very dark during these cool days of rain, or mourning, of agony and of death.

There will be a horrible storm. The trees that are deeply rooted will be torn out...

My children, I am the Way, the Truth and the Life.

On the close of these three days, you will only find corpses...

(Our Lord Jesus-Christ, unknown date...)

Reference to the apparitions of Fatima, and warning of the Three Days of Darkness

The text that follows is of the utmost importance and constitutes a message from Our Lord to the Faithful to instruct them how to pass through the announced Three Days of Darkness. The following message received by Marie-Julie Jahenny was found without a signature or a date:

Men have not listened to the words pronounced by My most holy Mother in Fatima. Woe to those who do not listen now to My Words! Men have not understood the language of war. Many men live in sin, very often in the sin of impurity. Woe to those who seduce the innocent!

You must not be upset with those who do not want to believe, for they know not what they do... But woe to those who laugh, or who allow themselves to judge before informing themselves.

The frequent apparitions of My good Mother are the results of My Mercy. I send her with the strength of the Holy Spirit to forewarn men, and to save that which must be saved... I must let happen (that which must) on the whole world so that many souls be saved which otherwise would have been lost. For all the crosses, for all the sufferings and for all that is still to come that will be worse yet, you must not curse My Father from Heaven, but thank Him. It is the work of My Love. You'll understand it later on... I must come in My Justice because men have not recognized the time of My Grace. The measure of sin is at its fullest, but to My faithful no harm will come.

I shall come to the sinful world in a terrible rumble of thunder on a cold winter night. A very hot wind from the south will precede this storm, and a heavy grail will hit the earth.

From massive red-fire clouds, devastating lightening will zigzag, enflaming and reducing everything to ashes... The air will be filled with toxic gases and mortal vapors which, within cyclones, will rip apart the works of daring (pride?), of madness and of the City of Night's will of power (Paris). Humankind will have to recognize that above it, is a Will that will make its audacious plans collapse like a castle of cards. The Angel Destroyer

will destroy forever the lives of those who will have devastated My Kingdom...

You, souls who profane the Name of the Lord, guard yourselves from mocking Me! Guard yourselves from the sin against the Spirit! When the Angel of Death will mow the bad weed with the cutting sword of My Justice, hell will then project itself with anger and tumult against the just and, above all, against the consecrated souls in order to try to destroy them through a frightful terror...

I want to protect you, My faithful ones, and give you the signs which will indicate the beginning of the judgment: When by a cold winter night thunder will rumble so hard as to make mountains shake, then close very quickly all doors and windows (of your house). Your eyes must not profane the terrible events with curious looks... Gather around the Crucifix. Place yourselves under the protection of My most holy Mother.

Do not let any doubt take over you involving your safety. The more trusting you will be, the more impenetrable will the rampart be. I want to surround you with (...). Burn blessed candles and recite the chaplet. Persevere for three days and two nights. The following night, the terror will calm down... After the horror of this long obscurity, with the upcoming rising day, the sun will appear in all its brightness and warmth.

There will be a great devastation... I, your God, shall have purified everything. The survivors must thank the Holy Trinity for Its protection. Magnificent will My Kingdom of Peace be, and My Name will be invoked and blessed from sunrise until sunset.

Pray! Pray! Pray! Convert and do penance! Do not fall asleep as My disciples did in the Garden of Olives, for I am very close. The Anger of the Father against Humankind is very great. If the prayer of the Rosary and the Gift of the Precious Blood weren't so pleasing to the Father, there would already be a misery on earth that has no name... But My Mother intercedes to the Father, to Me and to the Holy Spirit. This is why God lets Himself be moved. Thank then My Mother for the fact that Humankind still lives... Honor her with the respect of a child—I gave you the example—for she is the Mother of Mercy.

Never forget to renew continuously the Gift of the Precious Blood. My Mother begs me unceasingly, and with her, many penitent and expiatory souls. I cannot refuse her anything; it is therefore because of My Mother and because of My elected that these days have been shortened.

Be consoled, you who honor My Precious Blood. Nothing will happen to you.

I shall inspire My Representative to place continuously in honor the Sacrifice of My Precious Blood, and the veneration of My Mother...

Would some of My priests like to be more Pope-like than the Pope himself? They will crucify Me, for they will delay the works of My Mother. Pray a great deal for the favorites of My Heart, the priests. The time will come when My priests will understand all this (...)

(Message of Our Lord Jesus-Christ to Marie-Julie between 1917 and 1938)

Today the miracles of Heaven are blasphemed, rejected, insulted. You, dear friends of God, you are destined to live to see accomplished great miracles, great prodigies among the plagues, great justices, great calamities that the Lord has promised. You will be well protected, but observe well all that the Eternal Voices have commanded.

(St. Michael the Archangel, 29 September 1880)

My little children, I assure you that this time is not far, but do not be frightened. You have for your shelter the Divine Heart, you have for your protection the Adorable Cross, you have for your tent my maternal heart, my white mantle will serve you as a tent, a shelter and strength where you will have no fear because the earth will split, a terrible earthquake will shake the earth, by making it shake up to terrible heights. The sinners will fall into the abyss and will be buried in that tomb, which will close. There will be in other places a plague of one minute. It can destroy thousands of bodies, but my little children, you have your little flowers of hawthorn, you have your blessed crosses, you have your medals, where all our graces fall like heavy rain, in addition you have your promises of truth and peace (see pages: 193-211).

(The Blessed Virgin Mary, 23 July 1924)

On September 1904, Marie-Julie revealed the following message she received from the Blessed Virgin Mary:

...Half the population of France will be destroyed. After the punishments, there will be villages left without a soul. Four towns of France will disappear... I have no more power, I can no longer hold back My Son's arm... My children, the decision of My Divine Son is to let everything carry on until the end. There is only prayer left. If my Divine Son and I were to work miracles greater than all the ones in Judea, than all the miracles of the past, all these marvels would be scorned; they would further insult My Divine Son and His Holy Mother...

(Message of the Blessed Virgin Mary, 16 September 1904)

Victory and the Rebirth of France, the Church, and the World

Our Lord Jesus-Christ promised, through Marie-Julie, that the times of penance would come to an end, for through France, the Reign of the Sacred Heart would commence under the rule of the Great King of France, Henry V of the Cross, a holy Monarch, who would be the direct descendent of King Louis XVI and of Marie-Antoinette; a King guided by God to lead His people in union with an 'Angelic' Pontiff. Monarchies, Marie-Julie assured us, will be restored after the war. The Roman Catholic and Apostolic Church will regain her holy rights. France would triumph and the Holy Catholic Faith would spread throughout the entire world.

Our Lord Jesus-Christ:

I (shall) populate the land of France with flowers, that is to say with pure hearts, generous, repentant ones who love the Holy Church, the Holy Father and King. I shall bless this land and My people (who have) escaped (the terrors). I shall give France a new generation. They grow in My grace; they will follow during the reign of a very pious king who by his virtues, will become the ornament of France.

(Our Lord Jesus-Christ, 1 December 1876)

Our Lord Jesus-Christ further stated to Marie-Julie Jahenny that in reward for its devotion to His Sacred Heart, France would never lose the faith and would further rule until the end of time:

By this promise and love of this devotion, more common in France than elsewhere, I give in return the salvation of France and the triumph of the Church. The Holy Church will shine through her faith and love, and will reign. France will always keep the faith. It will rule, after its triumph to the end of time.

(Our Lord Jesus-Christ, 27 October 1875)

When will the promised King come? Heaven reveals on many separate occasions that spectacular signs and miracles will pronounce the coming of this great King who will bring about the great renewal of the Faith and rebirth of a new world.

O France, my daughter! I will wake her up from her painful sleep and slowly, I shall resurrect her with the prayers, suffering, faith and confidence of My dear children. Before the big event, she will seem forever dead to all... There, will be the fight of Heaven and of earth. It will be short, but terrible and mournful, and after, my good people will wake up, and the hidden Savior will leave here the Sacred Heart with His flower of the lily and his noble heart of Saint Louis. At the same time, I shall lift all my dear children elected for the salvation and triumph of France.
Pray, pray, pray my children, do not be discouraged. Amidst the wrath, there will be beautiful wonders.

(The Blessed Virgin Mary, 3 January 1900)

This is My eldest daughter. This France that abandoned Me. I hold her nevertheless on My Heart. I shall press her more and it will be the day when

she will see the Dove of Heaven (The Holy Spirit) **which will come to bring this banner with the Sacred Heart.**

Our Lord Jesus-Christ added that Henry of the Cross will save the Pope (the Angelic Pontiff) and concluded saying:

Blessed are those who love My Heart, they will be safe!

(Our Lord Jesus-Christ, 17 July 1874)

The Future Glory of La Fraudais

Marie-Julie likewise foretold that after her passing-away, her home at La Fraudais would become a great center of pilgrimage after the chastisements, and the hosting place of the Great Monarch, Henry V of the Cross, for her cottage is destined to become the site of a great and holy sanctuary dedicated to the Holy Cross and to the Immaculate Heart of Mary. This site, we are told, will be known worldwide as a triumphant acknowledgement of the **Work of the Cross** that first commenced with Marie-Julie's mission as a victim-soul and with the disclosure of her revelations and prophecies.

O My spouse, when you are no longer (on earth)**, I will leave great graces in La Fraudais. This place is a blessed land. So far, I have granted graces, (but) this is nothing. It will be especially in the last days that My Grace will be visible and that they will be able to say that it was I who have led you.**

(Our Lord Jesus-Christ, 29 July 1875)

A basilica and a miraculous spring at la Fraudais

Marie-Julie Jahenny was given an incredible number of details concerning the massive construction project to come at La Fraudais, and was shown what the basilica that has been foretold would look like: an immense classic gothic building able to hold about 1,400 people. Our Lord Jesus-Christ Himself declared He would be its architect... Marie-Julie was told how many pillars there would be, and further described the altars.

At first, there would be disputes over the land as the people there will not want to give up their property for the great project, but they will be justly compensated by an exchange in land, and the bitter disputes will be short-lived. No worker will die from accidents during the heavy building work. The wealthy will generously donate costly gifts and presents for its construction and adornment. Wonders were likewise announced: a miraculous spring will bubble forth on the site of her cottage, the waters of which will heal both body and spirit of the pilgrims who come to the sanctuary. The water will eventually be piped through and collected in a special fountain constructed beside the main altar.

Angels would be sent to help with the sanctuary's construction. Workers will leave for their period of rest only to discover upon their return that the walls will have been raised higher! In this manner, the work will rapidly continue to its completion. The builders will also be graced to hear the heavenly choirs and saints singing three times a day to refresh them. A heavenly perfume will permeate the air. Our Lord promised that He Himself would also come to sing and give them refreshment.

Heaven revealed that the Great Monarch and his entourage would come and plant the holy standard at the promised sanctuary in thanksgiving for his great victory and for the prophecies that announced his reign. The surrounding lands will house great convents, cloisters and charitable orphanages. Great conversions will take place; it will become a new 'City of God'.

The Blessed Virgin Mary further stated:

My children, so many pains, so many crosses, so many tears will be highly rewarded. Heaven has you covered. This place (La Fraudais) **will become great (and of) an immense magnitude. Souls will come, driven by an extraordinary grace. My children, a mountain has been raised here … From (the time of) Calvary to this date, I have never seen as many graces, nor as many that have been reserved for this place where I am talking to you now.**

(The Blessed Virgin Mary, La Fraudais, 16 March 1880)

A sanctuary of the Cross and of Immaculate Mary will be raised here. This place will be venerated by all. I shall heal here body and soul through a living water.

(Our Lord Jesus-Christ, 14 August 1875)

Here is the greatness of My Sanctuary! I shall be its Architect. Go My Angels and Seraphims! Cut the stones to begin!

That is how the secret plans will come slowly to term after long having been veiled.

I ask to be, while in Heaven, My friend's little commissioners before God.

(Our Lord Jesus-Christ, 4 March 1884)

Safe Haven: Brittany

Marie-Julie Jahenny revealed being told that in all the universe, there would never be a safer place from God's Divine Justice than in the land of Mary, the land of Brittany (France).

In Brittany I have raised a shelter. Come to this land, friends of the Cross!

(The Blessed Virgin Mary, 22 January 1878)

The Blessed Virgin Mary:

Yes, my children, my most special protection is reserved to you. Look without fear everything approach. I have come to this land of Brittany because I found therein generous hearts.

Marie-Julie Jahenny:

- *It's true mother.*
- My refuge will be as well that of my children whom I love and who do not inhabit that land. It will be a refuge of peace in the middle of the scourges, a very strong and very powerful shelter that nothing will be able to destroy. The birds who will fly away from the storm will take refuge in Brittany. The land of Brittany is in my power.
My Son told me: 'Mother, I give you all power on that Brittany.'
He has given me the power to take away storms from that Brittany ever so dear to my Heart. He gave me the power to come down to Brittany, the power to safeguard sinners, to bless them and also to strike them, but my child, you know my kindness.
- *Oh yes, my good Mother. You will not strike.*
- This refuge belongs to me, and also to my good mother, St. Ann. What a privilege for my Breton children!
- *Why such a great privilege, good Mother?*
- Brittany will one day become powerful, my children. The means thereof I shall let you know at a later time. This will be a land of grace and privileges. My power here is greater than in any other part of France or in the universe.

(Exchange between the Blessed Virgin Mary and Marie-Julie, 25 March 1878)

(...) Brittany, you are marked with three secrets that I have communicated to My Immaculate Mother. Prepare yourself to receive them.

You will rise on your own as a powerful army as soon as the ungodly one's soiled feet come to profane your faith. You will be strong enough not to let them cross your first borders.

(...) Brittany, you have never known the secret of the Alliance I have contracted with you since you wear the name of Brittany. It is you who will show courage when the King's call will be heard. You will march like a victorious army to meet he whom I have miraculously given to save she who is dying of shame (France)...

(Our Lord Jesus-Christ, 22 February 1878)

My dear Brittany, I have for you, in my Heart three beautiful secrets that are on the edge of my lips. I await but one word from the Holy Trinity to entrust them to you in their power and sweetness. They will be for you, Breton children, a true balm. When you'll receive them, your hearts will rejoice and you will fear nothing ever again; neither noises, nor assaults nor

the ungodly voices will ever be heard again in the country of Brittany.

(The Blessed Virgin Mary, 22 January 1878)

Four years after Marie-Julie Jahenny's passing away (1941), a French priest, a mystic called by Saint Padre Pio, a "French saint", Father Constant Louis-Marie Pel, had a well renowned epic revelation that corroborated Marie-Julie's prophecies (see page 464):

(...) with the sins of the world increasing in horror as this age carries on, great punishments from God will come down on the world and no continent will be spared by the Wrath of God. France, being guilty of apostasy and denying its vocation, will be severely chastised. East of a line stretching from Bordeaux in the south-west to Lille in the north-east, everything will be laid to waste and set on fire by peoples invading from the east, and also by great flaming meteorites falling in a rain of fire upon all the earth and upon these regions especially.

Revolution, war, epidemics, plagues, chemical poison gases, violent earthquakes and the re-awakening of France's extinct volcanoes will destroy everything...
France to the west of that line will be less affected... because of the faith rooted in the Vendée and in Brittany... but none of God's worst enemies seeking refuge there from the worldwide cataclysm will be able to find any; wherever they hide, they will be put to death by devils, because the Wrath of the Lord is just and holy. Thick darkness caused by the war, gigantic fires and fragments of burning stars falling for three days and nights will cause the sun to disappear, and only candles blessed on Candle Mass (February 2) will give light in the hands of believers, but the godless will not see this miraculous light because they have darkness in their souls.
In this way, ¾ of mankind will be destroyed, and in some parts of France survivors will have to go 100 km (c. 60 miles) to find another (living) human being. It will reach the point where people have to eat human flesh to survive...
(...) The Mediterranean Sea will disappear totally; the oceans will cast enormous jets of burning steam up to the skies and will deluge the continents in a frightful tidal wave that will annihilate everything in its path. New mountains will erupt out of the earth and the oceans, while the Alps and the Rhine Valley to the north will collapse as they are inundated by the sea in this way, the map of the world will be totally changed; the earth will undergo great shocks (i.e., shakings) that will prevent it from turning normally on its axis.
The seasons will cease to exist for three years, after which the earth will once again produce it plants and vegetation. There will be great famine in the entire world. Paris will be destroyed by the revolution and burned by atomic fire from Russians in Orleans and the region of Provins... In the meantime, Marseille and the French Riviera will collapse and will be immersed under water...

Prophecies of Marie-Julie Jahenny (Satellite picture of Britanny)

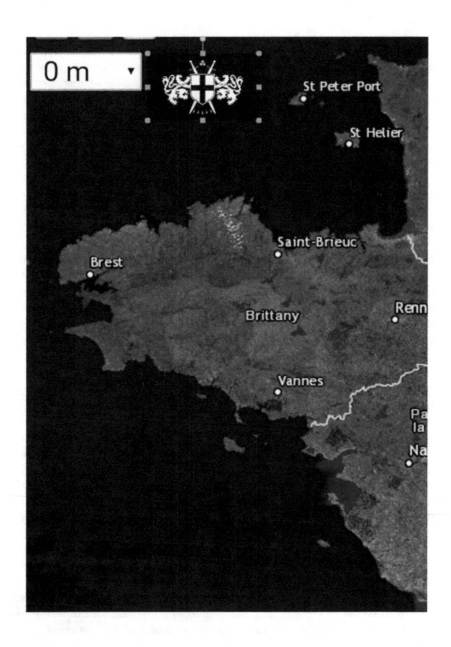

Simulation of Brittany under 35–40 meters of water

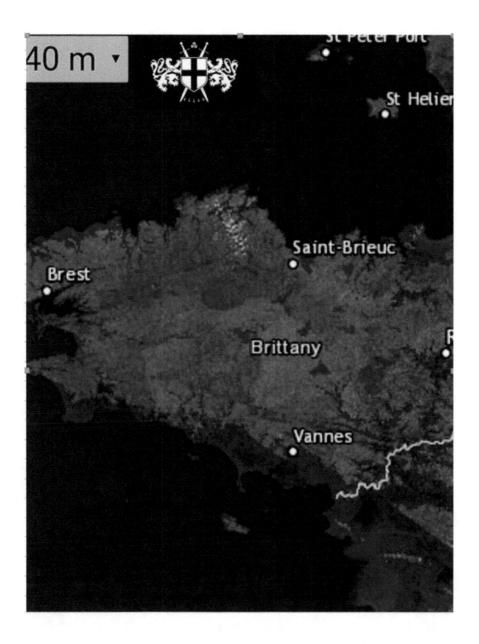

In the future, when you see that this frightful time is near, take leave to Brittany (on the western coast of France) but go to the center, far from the coasts—because they will collapse. This global scourge will begin on a cold winter's night and with a terrifying roar of divine thunder—an unnatural sound filled with demonic screaming—that will be heard by the entire world. It will be the voice of sin that terrified men will hear on that night.

(Rev. Fr. Constant Louis-Marie Pel, 1945)

Means of Protection During the Period of Chastisement

Due to the devotion and faithfulness of the Breton people to Our Lady, she and St. Joseph told Marie-Julie that Brittany, in the North-West of France, will be a 'shelter'; it will be spared much of the Russian invasion (but not from enemy's small incursions), and will be partly sheltered from the plagues and natural disasters (the northern part will know the plague).

Heaven warns the faithful to stay out of Paris and move to Brittany, which will become a refuge for many, including for those from abroad who will come as *"birds flying from far away to take refuge in a great tree"*, but in as much as possible in the central area of Brittany, as the seas will rise 25 to 35 meters above normal sea-level, thus submerging many coastal areas...

Holy Communion:

Marie-Julie Jahenny put, in the course of her entire life, a fundamental importance on the Holy Sacrament of the Altar, the Holy Eucharist, the Bread and Wine of Life through which she lived exclusively for many years of her life with no other sort of food or drink. The Holy Eucharist was indeed food for her soul, for her body, for her life, for her works and mission.

O my dear soul, do not forget that in Holy Communion is Mercy and Love Who give themselves to misery.

(Date unknown...)

My dear soul whom I love, remember that there is (only) a Holy God who is worthy to receive a God.

(Our Lord Jesus-Christ, 28 March 1931)

Our Lady gave beautiful spiritual advice to Marie-Julie on how to prepare our hearts to receive Him in Holy Communion:

My little children, moments before Holy Communion, let me take your heart of flesh with all that is in it and I will purify your lips up to your heart so that there will not be anything left (impurities / imperfections). The perfume will be the lily of my purity, mixing the scent of holy humility and beautiful charity, beautiful charity that has so often her beautiful white robe torn... My little children, ask me, ask St. Joseph who will place the holy scent of his holy death, and afterwards let me purify in the sight of all of Heaven the place of your heart; I will put it in mine with all its holiness, with all its beauty.

It will be the Eucharistic Altar where Jesus will rest, it will be His Heaven in my Heart where the angels will love Him, and I will crown this throne of lilies, violets and roses. I will be the guardian of this Divine Treasure. The angels will guard it and nothing will tarnish the beauty of the tabernacle. It is my Immaculate Heart.

And then, my little children, tell the Beloved that you no longer have a heart yourselves, tell Him to grind it under the wheels of Divine Mercy and tell Him to let the Divine Mercy bring these ashes to the ends of the world with these words: Love, Pity, Mercy, Recognition and Peace to the Earth and thanksgiving to the Adorable Heart that made our miseries marvels of Mercy and sweet charity for the guilty souls.

(Date unknown…)

Homes' Safeguard: O Sacred Heart of Jesus, I trust in You!

Marie-Julie Jahenny mentioned to her recorders of a safeguard that Our Lord Jesus-Christ had recommended long ago to St. Margaret-Mary:

This Divine Heart is a fortress and a sanctuary assured to those who would like to take refuge there to escape Divine Justice.

(St. Margaret-Mary)

Marie-Julie Jahenny added:

Let us wear this picture on us; let us put it on our houses; let us stick the Sacred Heart Safeguards on the doors and on the windows of our homes. After that, can we not hope that the inscription "Stop! (or Cease!) The Heart of Jesus is here!" (or the heart of Jesus is with me!), together with our own profound prayers, will preserve us from our enemies inside and out? (**see larger version on page: 564**)

Remedies Against Upcoming Illness and Diseases

Various diseases and epidemics will spread throughout France, throughout Europe and throughout the world, but one disease in particular was foretold to Marie-Julie: a *burning* disease that will spread ever so rapidly, killing quickly and in masses...

There will pass, in France, countless deaths that the world has never seen (before) and diseases that are unknown... Above all from the Centre (Paris) will this deadly mortality launch its plague. It will strike down just over the parish which is yours (Blain, La Fraudais?), but My children, fear not, for My Heart will be a shelter to protect you.

(Our Lord Jesus-Christ, 15 June 1882)

From the time when the rage of the impious will stop for a short respite, there will come a great disease, almost suddenly. This chastisement will leave its victims as those without life, they will still breathe with the ability to speak, the flesh raw like after a deep burn. This illness will be very contagious and nothing will stop it. It is a punishment from God to bring many (souls) back.

(Marie-Julie Jahenny, 20 September 1880)

1. <u>**Remedy Against the Unknown Mortal Burning Desease**</u>:

There will be serious diseases that human art cannot alleviate. This malady will attack the heart first, then the mind, and at the same time, the tongue. It will be horrible. The heat that will accompany it will be a consuming fire, so strong that the affected parts of the body will be of an unbearable redness, (red blotched / patches). **After seven days, this illness, like the seed sown in a field, will rise rapidly and make immense progress.**

My children, this is the only remedy that can save you: Do you know Hawthorn leaves that grow in most hedges and have long and sharp tops? My children, the leaves of this thorn will stop the progress of the disease. You must pick the leaves, not the wood. Even dry, they will retain their effectiveness. Put them in boiling water and leave them for 14 minutes, covering the container (with a lid) so that the steam remains.

When the malady first attacks, you must use this remedy three times a day. My children, this disease will be very serious in Brittany. The thought of God there will be less great.

Symptoms:

The disease will produce a continual uprising of the heart (blood pressure, increased heart rate?)**, vomiting. If the remedy is taken too late, the affected parts will become black, and in this black, there will be yellowish pale streaks.**

(The Blessed Virgin Mary, 5 August 1880)

Please note: This remedy is given for the time of the chastisements. If you are currently on medications or have heart conditions, seek advice from your doctor. Hawthorn acts powerfully on the heart like a natural form of digitalis. **(To order Hawthorn, see page: 565.)**

White hawthorn shrub
Image by Eugene Zelenko, 2005. CC BY-SA 3.0

Close-up of hawthorn leaves and thorns.
Image by 'Rasbak', July 2006. CC

My children, this sickness will mark the beginning of the period when there will be a foul smell emanating from all the crimes. Everything will suffer greatly, Christians and animals alike. After you have used the leaf for yourselves, it could be applied to infected animals by putting it in whatever food they are eating, or by boiling it in water.

There will be great loss of animals on account of the 'Black' disease. The skin, around the outside of their eyes will blacken. The area affected will be as wide as a finger and a half. The animals will refuse all food; a lot of water will flow from their eyes. This leaf could also be used for this ailment.

I feel compassion for everything. That is what I wanted to share with you, my children, with all the goodness and tenderness of my Heart.

(The Blessed Virgin Mary, 16 August 1880)

 2. Remedy for Cholera

My little lovely souls, the Hawthorn infusion can be used as well as a remedy for this terrible disease: Cholera.

(21 June 1923)

Plagues

According to a text dated 5 October 1881, epidemics will hit France, and from France, very likely, everywhere else in the world. The diseases may become airborne; the stench of the corpses, we do know, will cause the spreading of the diseases.

"There will be epidemics in the South, Valence, Lyon, Bordeaux, everything after this land coming to the Centre (Paris). **Very few people (will be able to) escape. The corpses will spread a stench that kills."**

 3. **Prayer that will preserve against future plagues**

Souls will be protected and preserved who will write down these words, and repeat them during the time when this violent plague will break out, causing great damage. These words written on one piece of paper can suffice for an entire family:

O Very pure Virgin, You who have always carried and who still carries the good and chaste odor of Purity, take away from us this disgusting smell; send it back to that place where we shall never be able to smell it again, by the chaste smell of your Holy Purity, Amen.

(13 September 1880)

 4. **Chest and headache ailments**

You will take the infusion of St. Johnswort—Glechoma Hederacea—especially during crisis, sufferings of the chest and violent headaches.

(21 June 1923)

Ground ivy/Glechoma Hederacea

"Lierre terrestre" in French is 'ground ivy', also known as "Glechoma Hederacea" or "Creeping Charlie", it is the herb for crises, sufferings of the chest, and violent headaches.

In 1923, Marie-Julie Jahenny received yet another revelation from the Holy Spirit:

The Sun says again that this plague of calamities is to spread up to this region (Brittany)*; however, not quite in the same way; it will affect the vines and young crops which will not be tended by Christians.*

*To help save the Christians, there is a plant which exists: whoever will have collected some (Grass of St. John or St. Johnswort) he will be preserved from all this scourge. This plant appears in the Sun to the eye of the soul (*Marie-Julie's at that moment*); I see it perfectly. Its name is written in the light; it is the plant or grass of St. John (St. Johnswort). The leaf is not very large; it has little ribs everywhere. The Sun says that the Christians may drink some drops of it—made up as a herbal tea—without fear, and the scourge will not affect him.*

I see this plant in the Sun; it has little blue flowers; it has what looks like tubes out of which there are flowers; it has a bearable smell.

Our Lord interrupts the Voice in the Sun... to say the following:

I bless this plant, My children. Collect it while it is still available; a lot of people will search for it and will not find it.

My little loving souls, always keep this little plant, because this name is so precious. This name is to Me a name of love. It is the name of the great Apostle who adopted My Mother as his mother, and My Mother adopted him as her son.

(19 April 1923)

 5. **For unknown fevers, the humble violet**

Fevers can be soothed with violet infusion, the perfume of virtue and humility.

Violets

6. __Remedy for violent mental troubles, chest pains, and violent headaches__

The yellow St. John's wort is recommend by Marie-Julie for the times of crisis, depression will be rampant; also recommended for sufferings of violent headaches. The yellow St. John's wort is also mentioned in the texts as a remedy for violent head mental troubles and chest pains.

Herb of St. John/St. John's Wort

The yellow St. John's wort is very powerful; again, please seek medical advice from a health or herbal expert before using these remedies.

In French, the 'herb of St. John' is the yellow St. John's Wort in English—St. John's wort is known to help alleviate depression (mental troubles) and has the following properties which would also help relieve chest pains—marked with †:

Antioxidant (prevents free radicals from causing damage to cells)
Antiviral (effective against disease-carrying viruses)
Anti-inflammatory (reduces inflammation)†
Anti-microbial (disarms microbes)
Analgesic (pain relief)†
Antispasmodic (relaxes muscular contractions)†
Aromatic (digestive)

Astringent (tones and heals)†
Expectorant (provokes the release of mucus)†
Nervine (frees and calms the nervous system)†
Hepatic (favorably influences the liver and gall bladder)

Prayers to recite to the Blessed Virgin Mary before using the plants as remedies

Marie-Julie-Jahenny addressing the Blessed Virgin Mary:

"Good holy Mother, as for the plants that Divine Providence has sown on the earth, we ask you to give them a very special benediction (blessing), particularly on the Hawthorn and on the St. Johnswort—Glechoma Hederacea."

The Blessed Virgin Mary:

- **Oh, my beloved little children, when you use those little flowers and those little plants, pray to me:**

*"O Holy Queen of Heaven,
Health of the sick, prodigy of power,
Extend your benedictions on this infusion, all powerful Mother.
Show us that you are our Mother by relieving our miseries."*

My little children, when you take this little flower, invoke me:

*"O Immaculate Mary! O our Mother! O our Mother!
Look down on us and let your benediction be revealed in our suffering."*

And for those tending the sick?

My dear Child, there is no need to say lengthy prayers. Simply say:

*"O Good Mother!
Look at my little work for someone ill or afflicted.
Please bless it."*

My little children, if it were only up to me, I would heal all bodies, I would heal all souls, but first of all, the Holy Will of the Divine Creator before mine... He is King. He is the Father and He is endlessly good. My little children, faith and trust are the most beautiful prayers which obtain the most and more again.

Please, do not use these remedies to replace seeing a doctor. This is for the times when the faithful will no longer have any immediate medical help.

7. For unknown diseases

Our Lord told Marie-Julie:

A medal with My Divine Heart, a medal where there is drawn the Adorable Cross. You will place in a glass of water these two images, either pasteboard, or metal (Miraculous Medal). **You will drink this water twice blessed, twice purified. One single drop in your food, one tiny drop, will suffice not to move away the affliction, but the afflictions of My Justice.**

Our Lord further said:

You will give a drop of this water to the poor souls reached by the affliction of the unknown diseases that will attack the mind heart and the mouth / tongue.

Another separate source of relief during these sufferings:

My little loving and beloved souls, against the great calamities you will put the medal of My Sacred Heart in a glass of water or a spoonful, as you wish, you will invoke my Adorable Heart, I will relieve you of all attacks, I will console you in your pains and sorrows.

(This pratice will only bring relief and will not be a cure against the 'burning plague' affecting the face; **only the hawthorn will cure if taken in time**.)

 ### 8. Remedy to protect yourself from deadly plagues

Marie-Julie Jahenny one day revealed a most curious recipe for a remedy from deadly plagues:

We are to swallow a very small piece of paper on which the following words are to be written:

'O Jesus, Vanquisher of death, save us! O Crux Ave, Spes Unica!'

(Do not forget to use non-toxic ink! This is for the chastisements. **Please, see page: 565 to purchase rice-paper with said prayer in non-toxic ink**.)

<u>Note</u>: All sacramentals such as medals, rosaries, pictures, etc. must be blessed by a priest.

Additional Sacramentals of Protection for the Period of Chastisement

The Purple Scapular

On 23 August 1878, **The Breton Stigmatist** stated about a particular new Sacramental recommended by the Blessed Virgin Mary:

Here is what the Holy Virgin made me see on her Immaculate Heart, it is a large scapular, larger than ordinary scapulars, it is a little larger than the palm of a hand. It is a beautiful purple, almost the color of violet. Here is what is on it: in the middle, there are the three nails that crucified Our Savior on the Cross; some are crossed on the others, not exactly in the form of a cross, and at the point of each nail, there is a drop of red blood. Above the three nails, there is a type of large sponge that has raised ears, like those of balled oats.

*The three drops of blood will go to join together and fall into a small chalice painted in red, and the chalice is surrounded with a crown of thorns, and there are three little crosses engraved on the front of the chalice. This is the side of the scapular that is on the mantle of the Holy Virgin. I notice that this scapular hangs by two violet straps that pass over each shoulder, and there are **three knots on the left shoulder,** and **two on the right.***

The other side of the scapular represents the Holy Virgin Mary sitting, holding her Adorable Son in her arms, the mouth and the Head of Our Lord rests on the heart of the Holy Virgin. At the lower end of the scapular, at the feet of Our Lord, is an Angel dressed in white, with curly hair, he has a white crown on his head; his belt is red. He has in his hands a white linen with which he wipes the feet of Our Lord. On the side of the Angel, to the right of the scapular, there is engraved a ladder.

Behind Our Lord, to the left, the reed of the Passion painted in red, but without a sponge. The tears of the Holy Virgin fall on her breast, to the right, and they stop at the feet of the Angel. The scapular is edged with a red line and the straps are woolen.

<u>Note:</u> the symbols of the passion are worn on the chest, the image of Our Lord and Our Lady are worn on the back.

She said to me:

Let me now, my dear child, explain to you the meaning of this scapular. I tell you, my victim and my servant. My servants of the Cross, that for a long time my Son and I have had the desire to make known this scapular of benediction. This scapular, my children, is supposed to be made on my heart, because my heart is the emblem of simplicity and humility, hence the color violet.

The nails that have pierced the feet and the hands of my Son have been little venerated and are venerable, hence my Son, in His Divine Wisdom, has

made that these three nails be painted on the front of the scapular. These three drops of blood and the chalice represent the generous hearts gathering the Blood of my Divine Son. The red sponge will represent my Divine Son drinking, in a manner of speaking, the sins of His children but His Adorable Mouth refuses.

I desire that the end of the scapular be of violet (the dark background?), but I desire that the nails, the chalice, the sponge and the crown be on a piece of dark red flannel. This first apparition of this scapular will be a new protection for the times of the chastisements, of the calamities and the famines. All those who are clothed (with it) shall pass under the storms, the tempests and the darkness, they will have light as if it were plain day. Here is the power of this unknown scapular.

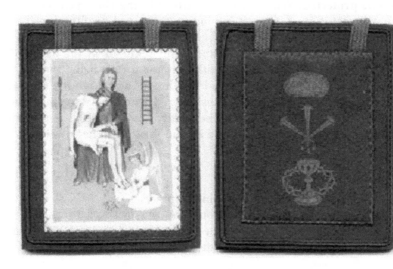

The Holy Virgin Mary presents the scapular to Our Lord, who says in His turn:

I address you, My victim, and also My victims and My servant. My children of the Cross, I see and I come to give you an idea and profound thought: during My descent from the Cross they handed Me to My mother. This descent, this thought, this devotion is little known. I would like by this reproduction on this scapular, that it passes into the hearts of the children of the Cross, and that they salute Me by these three salutations:

- I salute You, Jesus, crucified to grant me life,
- I salute You with all the joy of the Angels and the Saints on Your descent from the Cross.
- I salute You with the sadness of Your Mother when you reposed on her Immaculate Heart and on her Immaculate lap.

My children, very few souls think of wiping the Adorable Wounds of My Feet when the Blood ran and I would like this representation to be known. They also think so little of the tears shed by My Mother during My Passion; these tears are found at the feet of the Angel that wipes My Sacred Feet. By

201

this scapular, I would like you to think on the ladder, the reed and the nails of My Passion.

<u>Other great promises given with the scapular:</u>

My children, all souls, all people who possess this scapular, will see their family protected, their home will also be protected, first of all from fires, which will never enter there. This scapular will strike down the ungrateful which blaspheme My Name in the home where it will be displayed.

If an impious person enters (that home), he will be so completely struck that his conversion will be close. All those who will wear it will be preserved from thunder, from sudden death and from accidents. During chastisements they will be protected. Whoever will deposit it in the Holy Temple (i.e., in a church)**, will cast it away from it impious persons and profanation** (i.e., that church will be protected)**.**

By reminding an obstinate soul about this scapular at the hours of His demise (death)**, he will awaken the Faith in it and a firm belief that all those who will have it and think upon it and love it, will be spared the troubles of souls. Those who will wear it will be sheltered from any danger as though they already possessed Heaven. This scapular, finally, will be as a lightning rod under which the blows of Just and Divine Wrath will not dwell.**

Our Lord further added:

Every priest will be able to bless this scapular.

By wearing this scapular they should say five or seven times the "Crux Ave" (see pages: 206) **and meditate one-three minutes on My Holy Passion. I shall grant great graces to those who desire to be clothed in this Holy Habit.**

(Our Lord Jesus-Christ 23 August 1878)

Blessed water and blessed candles (for days of darkness):

We must have blessed bees' wax candles on hand for the Days of Darkness, and they MUST BE MADE 100% OF PURE BEES' WAX. No other mixture will light... We must be devoted to Our Lady; help to make her be known and loved; have her image in our houses, and be devoted to the Cross and the Sacred Heart. We must trust in Our Lord and Our Lady. Let us not forget the Precious Blood, or Our Lord's Holy Wounds.

(To remain strong when faced with all these signs, Holy Water will be a strength and a consolation as well as blessed candles—but blessed candles made 100% of Bees' wax—all those made of another material will not be of use...)

We must gather around our crucifixes. WE MUST NOT LOOK OUTSIDE DURING THESE DAYS, we shall be struck dead if we do… They will be terrible days, but we must trust Our Lady, faith in her protection will stave off the terror. The Virgin Mary told me:

My little children, I assure you that among the blows of Justice there will be for you, my little children, great signs (said three times) of graces, protections and wonders, all divine.

My little beloved children I want to calm you, I want to reassure you. Always keep close your objects of protection, your blessed candles, your medals and other objects from which flow all the blessings of Heaven, blessings of protection, blessings of all heavenly favors, blessings that keep far (from you) the cries of Satan running through the air and the earth, blessings that will calm the storm unleashed by the Luciferian voices.

The Crucifix and the Blessed image (or statuette) of the Holy Family

My children, mind my words… In these days of mourning, there will be another earthquake as strong as many others, (and yet) less strong than in many other places. It will be easy to notice: everything will shake except the piece of furniture on which will burn the (bee's) wax candle. You will all group around, with the crucifix and my blessed image. This is what shall take fear away from you, as these days will cause many deaths.

Here is a proof of my goodness, those who serve me well, invoke me, and keep in their homes my blessed image, I will keep safely all that belongs to them. During these three days, I will protect their cattle from starvation. I will keep them because there must not be a single door ajar. The hungry animals shall be satisfied by me, without any food.

(24 March 1881)

203

The Saint Benedict Medal

"Our Lady" says the Breton visionary, *"will know how to save their fields during the famine."*

Since the only advice I've seen attributed to Marie-Julie on **how to save crops during the plagues and against the appearance of "black ears" in the wheat is to plant St. Benedict medals in the ground in the form of a cross,** we can assume this must be the remedy. Likewise, Marie-Julie Jahenny stated:

"Put a medal of St. Benedict around the animals' necks. It is this great saint who has been designated by Our Lord to help in these 2 distressing calamities (agriculture and animal/cattle raising)."

(24 May 1880)

"Our Lady" says the Breton visionary, *"will know how to save their fields during the famine."*

Since the only advice I've seen attributed to Marie-Julie on how to save crops during the plagues and against the appearance of "black ears" in the wheat is to plant St. Benedict medals in the ground in the form of a cross, we can assume this must be the remedy. Likewise, Marie-Julie Jahenny stated:

*Put a medal of St. Benedict around the animals' necks. It is this great saint who has been designated by Our Lord to help in these two distressing calamities (*agriculture and animal/cattle raising*).*

(24 May 1880)

<u>Blessing ritual for the Medal of St. Benedict</u>

The St. Benedict's exorcism medal must be blessed with the special prayer of protection composed for it. Any priest may say the blessing of protection, not just a Benedictine priest. If a priest has the Latin form of the rite, so much the better, however, the blessing is still valid in English if blessed by a validly ordained priest. The formula is as follows (the priest must make the sign of the cross at each of the crosses (†) in the prayers herein below):

Priest: **Our help is in the name of the Lord.**

Response: Who made Heaven and Earth.

P: **In the name of God the † Father Almighty, who made heaven and earth, the seas and all that is in them, I exorcise these medals against the power and attacks of the evil one. May all who use these medals devoutly be blessed with health of soul and body. In the name of the Father † Almighty, of the Son † Jesus Christ Our Lord, and of the Holy † Spirit the Paraclete, and in the love of the same Lord Jesus Christ who will come on the Last Day to judge the living and the dead, and the world by fire.**
R. Amen.
P: **Let us pray. Almighty God, the boundless source of all good things, we humbly ask that, through the intercession of Saint Benedict, you pour out your blessings † upon these medals. May those who use them devoutly and earnestly strive to perform good works be blessed by You with health of soul and body, the grace of a holy life, and remission from temporal punishment due to sin. May they also with the help of Your merciful love, resist the temptation of the evil one and strive to exercise true charity and justice towards all, so that one day they may appear sinless and holy in Your sight. This we ask through Christ Our Lord.**
R: Amen. (The medals must be then sprinkled with holy water.)

St. Benedict Medal

Prayers to the Cross:

Marie-Julie was taught two particular manners to pray, saluting the Cross:

The "Crux Ave" Prayer, Number 1:

> **I salute You, I adore You, I embrace You,**
> **O Adorable Cross of my Savior!**
> **Protect us, guard us, save us!**
> **Jesus loved You so much,**
> **Following His Example, I love You.**
> **Your Holy Image calms my fears,**
> **I feel only peace and confidence.**

The "Crux Ave" Prayer, Number 2:

> **O Crux, ave, spes unica!**
> **Et Verbum caro factum est.**
> **O Jesus Vanquisher of Death, save us!**
>
> **Translation:**
> **'O Cross, hail! Our only hope!**
> **And the Word was made flesh.'**

The Crucifix:

My loving and dearly beloved, little souls, when assailed by fears, I say to you: do not be afraid because I shall be with you. You will put My Adorable Divine Cross in a glass of water with this invocation: " O Crux Ave!". You will give a little drop of it to poor souls who are affected by the scourge of hitherto unknown diseases and who will suffer terribly from horrifying bouts of pain. All their pain will be interior while their exterior appearance will be frightening on account of how pale and emaciated they will have become...

My loving little souls, you will be able to save some of these people because the Love of the Redemption on the Adorable Cross will work miracles in their souls—but not in their bodies... They will not be resuscitated, but their souls will be given life for a few hours, and I shall then be merciful to them and Purgatory will be their joy until the end of time.

(Our Lord Jesus-Christ, 21 June 1923)

The Cross of Pardon/ Cross of Salvation/ Cross of Holy Protection/ Cross that calms plagues

I wish that My male and female servants, and even small children can clothe themselves with a Cross. This Cross will be small and will bear in its middle the appearance of a small white flame. This flame will indicate that they are sons and daughters of the Light.

Cross of Pardon / Cross of Salvation / Cross of Holy Protection /
Cross that calms plagues

My little beloved friends, it is to give you an idea of what I endure at the thought of so many souls deprived of endless happiness. My little beloved friends, these past days have left so much evil, but those that are yet to come will be even more terrible because evil will take a terrible intensity, (and will) extend soon with greater measurements. My little beloved friends, you will carry upon yourselves My Adorable Cross which will preserve you from every sort and kind of evils, big or small, and later I shall bless them.

Firstly, it (this special Cross) will wear the name of 'Cross of Pardon'; secondly, it will wear the name 'Cross of Salvation'; thirdly, it will wear the name of 'Cross of Holy Protection'; fourthly, it will wear the name 'Cross that Calms Plagues'; fifthly, it will wear the prayer:

O God,
Crucified Savior,
set me ablaze with love,

207

faith and courage
for the salvation of my
brothers.

(Our Lord Jesus-Christ, 20 July 1882)

The Promises of the Cross of Pardon:

My little children, for all souls who are suffering, riddled with the scourge, all those who will kiss it will have My forgiveness, all those who will touch it will have My forgiveness. I have warned you beforehand, My little beloved friends, so that you are not surprised, so that you have all the time to inform your loved ones and families.

(Our Lord Jesus-Christ, 15 November 1921)

(Please note, the promise of forgiveness attached to this cross does not replace the Holy Sacrament of Confession. This is meant for ordinary and extraordinary times, particularly when churches will be closed and we will not have a priest, especially when the plagues hit and those afflicted will not be able to find a priest or have one sent to them in time.)

The Miraculous Medal (of the rue du Bac):

On another occasion, the Blessed Virgin Mary told Marie-Julie Jahenny:

My children, at the moment when the patch of the abyss is opening forth, I would like you to wear the prodigious medal of grace on which is written:

"O Mary, conceived without sins…

… pray for us who have recourse to thee."

My Son also wants all of His children, young and old, to wear on their hearts His Adorable Cross, even if it should be very small. It is His Cross He has chosen for the epoch in order to conquer those Christians devouring tigers, and also as a means to help keep the Faith of His loyal children.

(11 November 1880)

My little spouses, I assure you that by touching your forehead with an image or sweet medal of My Immaculate Mother, all your apprehensions and fears will vanish. Your spirit will remain calm, your intelligence will not feel the terrible effects of My Great Justice. Either a picture of the Immaculate Virgin, or a medal of "Mary Conceived without Sin" (the Miraculous Medal of the rue du Bac)—this beautiful invocation which delights all of Heaven and makes My Holy Mother smile.

(Our Lord Jesus-Christ, 19 April 1923)

The scapular of Mount Carmel medal aka the medal of the sacred heart

Whosoever dies wearing this Scapular shall not suffer eternal fire!

(Our Lady of Mount Carmel to Saint Simon Stock, 16 June 1251)

The scapular medal aka the medal of the sacred heart

"My loving and dearly beloved little souls, when there are great calamities, you must put a medal of My Sacred Heart into a glass or spoonful of water, whichever you prefer. You must invoke My Adorable Heart—I shall give you relief from anything you are suffering from. I shall console you in your sorrows and in your pains."

(Our Lord Jesus-Christ, 21 June 1923)

What's more, the Scapular Medal was created only for those who suffer grave inconvenience in wearing the cloth, and the indulgence of 500 days does NOT apply to the Medal. To obtain the graces and promises of the Scapular, it must be worn constantly. It should be worn day and night, in sickness and in health.

The Sabbatine Privilege consists of Our Lady's promise to release from Purgatory through her special intercession, on the first Saturday after death, those who meet these three requirements:

1. You must wear the Scapular.
2. You must observe chastity according to your state of life.
3. You must recite daily the Little Office of Our Blessed Mother (the Rosary or some other pious work may be submitted for the Office). All confessors were given faculty to make this substitution by Pope Leo XIII in June of 1901.

The Medal of Our Lady of "Bonne Garde" – Remedy for this Time of Impurity:

"**My children,**" repeated the Holy Virgin, "**I say again to the fathers and mothers that it would be good to have their children wear, small and big** (children or young adults**), a medal, which does not exist yet, but which they could make, big or large, as they like. This medal should bear these words:**

Oh you, Holy Virgin, who crushed the head of the serpent, guard our Faith and the innocence of our little children.

†

O Crux Ave.

The Blessed Virgin Mary wore the medal on her heart, it was round and white. It is not necessary, she said, for it to be expensive, (i.e., of valuable metal like gold or silver), *its efficacy will be the same. It will be to guard innocence in the difficult times when corruption will spread everywhere. Every Christian can take it to arm himself, as a defense and a weapon of faith. Our Lady added:*

Before having come the first time to speak here, I was invoked under the name of 'Notre-Dame de la Garde' (Our Lady of Guard), but I wanted to assert 'Bonne' Garde (Good Guard), because I had in mind (certain)

protections that are so bright that (it is only just that) the word 'Good' belongs to me for it is more honorable.

(26 August 1880)

Medal of Our Lady of la Bonne Garde

This is a particular devotion revealed to Marie-Julie regarding a miraculous statue. The closest title we have in English using the more literal translation from the French: "Good Watch", "Good Protection", "Good Guard", or "Good Care".

<u>Messages of the Blessed Virgin Mary about protection</u>:

The Blessed Virgin Mary:

-    **My little children, I am afraid of the horrible catastrophe (to come). My Divine Son awaits still the return of souls with such admirable patience! How much pure blood and how much guilty blood! All these strikes have not touched all the hardened hearts; they have not brought back the beautiful Faith of the past; all these strikes have not brought back closer the souls to His Love nor to His Grace... My little children, the Earth is quite guilty. It will pay its debt which is quite large and deep... My little children all the earth will not be destroyed. We shall protect our children; we shall keep them to re-populate the world, to bring the Faith back to its feet, to preach the sublime doctrine of charity, union and fraternity.**
     My little children, I assure you that among the great strikes of Justice, there will be for you, my little children great prodigies! (said three times) of graces, of protection, of marvels, all divine.
     My beloved little children, I want to keep you at peace; I want to reassure you. Always keep close your objects of protection, your blessed candles, your medals and objects where all the blessings of Heaven come through: the blessings of protection, the blessing of celestial favors, the blessing which push-back Satan's screams which

run through the airs and the earth, blessings which will calm down the furious and unchained storm made-up of luciferian voices.

Marie-Julie Jahenny:

- *I do not understand these words… I am always afraid to make a mistake and to lead others into error…*
- **No. Worry not. My little children who are present understand my language well which is a language of a mother of protection and of salvation. My little children, there will not only be in this storm screams from hell; there will be (as well) all the lost souls of earth, all these souls who give themselves to Satan by offending my Divine Son, all these souls who live from sacrileges to sacrileges. I am the Mother of the Light. My little children understand me very clearly. (…)**

(Exchange of the Blessed Virgin Mary and Marie-Julie, 17 August 1920)

(…)There will be in other places a plague of one minute. It can destroy thousands of bodies, but my little children, you have your little flowers of hawthorn, you have your blessed crosses, you have your medals, where all our graces fall like heavy rain, in addition you have your promises of truth and peace.

(The Blessed Virgin Mary, 23 July 1924)

The story of Our Lady of "Bonne Garde":

A medieval statue was donated to Marie-Julie by her 'adoptive' mother, Madame Le Camus, a widow who was very pious and had no children. She dedicated her life to care for Marie-Julie and her visitors, spreading the messages given to Marie-Julie about devotion to the Holy Work of the Cross at La Fraudais. Madame Le Camus was in possession of the statue that had been rediscovered at that time, having miraculously escaped the iconoclastic ravages of the French Revolution, and, according to later discovered documents, many extraordinary miracles had taken place through the praying to the Blessed Virgin Mary before it.

One day, Madame Le Camus heard an interior voice asking her to donate it to Marie-Julie, and she complied. Her generous sacrifice was praised by the Mother of God who said to Marie-Julie on 28 November 1878:

Oh, if you knew how my Divine Son and I, we are happy with this gift! I reward this generous soul, your adopted mother.

In other ecstasies, Our Lady would call Madame Le Camus **My Rose**, a most loving acknowledgement of the pious lady's devotion to her and her victim soul Marie-Julie by addressing her through the name of her patron saint, St. Rose of Lima:

My beloved child, Rose, if you knew how I love you, how more pleasing you are to me, because my Rose, you do everything to please me and console me.

My dear child, I tasted so many charms under your blessed roof, establishing me as Mistress, Governess and Director of the work of the Cross.

(Unknown Date…)

Indeed, Our Lady recognized the love given to her when Madame Camus possessed the statue in her home; furthermore, the Blessed Virgin Mary acknowledged the sacrifice of the statue, and the fact that Rose le Camus had helped establish the devotion to Our Lady of "la Bonne Garde" as Mistress, Governess, Director of the work of the Cross through Marie-Julie. Our Lady promised Marie-Julie many graces would flow through her veneration under the title of "Our Lady of la Bonne Garde".

My dear child, you shall bring to my Rose, your dear mother, my words. (…) My name will spread everywhere, my heart will open as an inexhaustible source for all the pilgrims of the Cross. My daughter, I will be greatly honored by all visitors of the work, starting my devotion… The people will venerate me, beg me, giving me votive offerings of gratitude.

(The Blessed Virgin Mary, 15 September 1883)

Marie-Julie then said:

With these words, my Good Mother rose (up) radiantly on a beneficial cloud, so wonderfully that Our Lady of Bonne Garde was as lost in the songs of thanksgiving and gratitude (sung by) the poor humans…

She (Our Lady) said:

I see at my feet, the whole of France with its sovereigns. My daughter, this devotion will start with the favor of the last days of your life on Earth.

Marie-Julie continued to pass on Our Lady's message:

My daughter, I will be gloriously crowned more than I am today; crowned, my daughter, by the Holy Church immortal and infallible in its lights. My First Victim and my Rose will be at my feet on this solemn day when the Church will make me a crown of prayers and hymns (…)

Marie-Julie speaking to Madame Camus:

When I am no longer with you on Earth, my dear mother, she (Our Lady) will give you a comforting sign of her sweet love by the lifting of her right hand, as if to bless you with the workers of the labor.

Our Lady of Bonne Garde revealed to Marie-Julie on 1 October 1935 that she wished to be honored with the following prayers:

During this beautiful month (October), recite to me three 'Hail Marys' in the morning, midday and evening. To obtain my assistance during your life and death, you will say:

- **I salute you, beloved Daughter of the Father,**
- **Lily of Purity, pray for us. (Hail Mary, etc.)**
- **I salute you, Spouse of the Holy Spirit, Violet of**
  - **Humility, pray for us. (Hail Mary...)**
- **I salute you, O Mother of the Word Incarnate,**
- **Rose of Charity, pray for us, (Hail Mary...)**

Important Note: All medals, scapular, candles and Crosses that have been mentioned in this book must be blessed by a Roman Catholic priest after purchasing them. These are being spread and propagated today throughout the world through France and the United States. To place orders for such Sacramentals and healing flowers and plants in the Pacific, in the Northern and Southern American continents, Europe and Africa**, kindly see page 565.**

The "Crux Ave" prayer to be said during the time of evils and great fears:

**I salute You, I adore You, I embrace You,
O Adorable Cross of my Savior!
Protect us, guard us, save us!
Jesus loved You so much,
Following His Example, I love You.
Your Holy Image calms my fears,
I feel only peace and confidence.**

Promise with the "Crux Ave":

"You will feel so many graces, so much strength and love that this big flood will pass by you as something unobserved. It is a grace of My tenderness."

Although the days of wrath and the aftermath will be dreadful indeed, we are told through Marie-Julie that those who live to see them and, later the Great Renewal will be blessed. Those predilected ones will be a predestined generation.

"My Justice will pass. The whole earth will continue in My Justice. It is the time that I will rise up, I will stop all the evil from entering in the beautiful reign of My Sacred Heart. There will be great signs in this reign; there will be resurrections; there will be wonders of protection for My souls that I want to guard, to raise up, to flourish once again. I will re-populate (the earth) with holy souls, with righteous souls, souls full of faith. The peace

will cause (all) to forget past troubles. My Grace will dry tears; My Wonders will delight every heart."

(Our Lord Jesus-Christ, 13 November 1924):

<u>Prayers and new devotions and special graces revealed:</u>

Marie-Julie's heavenly visitors would often share with her new devotions they wished to impart, or, to reveal new promises to already existing devotions, mercifully enriching them with more graces to encourage the faithful to practice them. There are also numerous little prayers, spiritual reminders and aspirations throughout the texts (see pages 535 - 562).

<u>Litany of the Passion: a prayer of reparation before the blessed sacrament:</u>

- **Oh my very dear Jesus, what brought You to suffer for us a mortal agony in the Garden of Olives: It is Love.**
- **Oh My Adorable Jesus, what brought You to separate Yourself from Your Apostles during this Agony: It is Love.**
- **Oh My Jesus, what brought You to let the executioners and the Jews torture and bind You: It is Love.**
- **Oh My Jesus, what brought You to appear before Pilate's tribunal: It is Love.**
- **Oh My Jesus, what brought You to descend into Herod's obscure prison: It is Love.**
- **Oh Holy Victim, what brought You to allow the executioners to scourge You without a complaint from You: It is Love.**
- **Oh Holy Victim, what brought You to separate Yourself from Your Holy Mother in order to suffer insults: It is Love.**
- **Oh Holy Victim, what brought You to cast a glance at St. Peter when leaving the Praetorium: It is Love.**
- **Oh Holy Victim, what brought You to fall before Your enemies under the weight: It is Love.**
- **Oh Holy Victim, what brought You to die for us on a Cross: It is Love.**
- **Oh Holy Victim, what brought You to give Yourself to our souls in the Most Holy Sacrament: It is Love.**
- **Oh Holy Victim, what brought You to reside for us in all the Shrines and Tabernacles in the entire world: It is Love.**
- **Oh Holy Victim, what brought You to tell us: 'Dear Children, do not fear, come close, I sleep, but My Heart watches': It is Love.**
- **Adorable Sacred Victim, what brought You to let us approach Your Holy Tabernacles, to possess You and dissolve into these delights: It is Love. It is Love.**
- **Oh Most Holy Victim, what brought You to love us with a Love so Ardent and full of Goodness: It is Love. It is Love.**

Our Lord requested this prayer to be said to console Him on Thursday mornings at 9 AM before the Blessed Sacrament, and on Fridays in the afternoon. He promised to those who would recite this prayer as a great mark of their love for Him, He would grant them a solemn happiness:

"They will say (this litany) passing over in their heart all that I have done for them for love. As a reward, at their death, I will almost immediately attract them in the eternal sojourn." (The souls will be immediately attracted to Him, and will draw upon themselves all the necessary graces for salvation at that critical moment.)

Our Lord Jesus-Christ said to Marie-Julie-Jahenny:

Burn with love for Me; I will let escape from My Heart the last stream that will set you ablaze. My Love comes to search for your prayers to soften the pain caused by all the offenses.

Our Lord further promised:

I will bless those who say this prayer at least once a day, I will give them a solemn benediction.

When Marie-Julie passed on the litany Our Lord Jesus-Christ taught her, she asked:

- *Lord, will You be willing to remain with us until the end of time?*

He answered:

This is Love.

Prayer to save 1,000 sinners during Holy Mass:

Our Lord gave Marie-Julie on 3 September 1925 a very simple way to save 1,000 sinners every time we receive Holy Communion:

Tell them to rest five minutes on My Heart throbbing with love. Think only of Me by this simple word: *"Thank you, my Beloved, You live in me and I live in You."* You see the sweetness you will taste and how you will give Me consolation. Ask of Me, in the fifth minute the conversion of a thousand sinners. It will be a great joy for My Divine Father; for Heaven, I ask you the same favor. I will be there, inside you, infinite goodness, the splendor of all beauties. Only five minutes thinking about Me and asking Me at the fifth minute the salvation of souls. My Divine Heart is overflowing with joy at this request of graces and I will also grant it.

Promises to the Devotion to the Wound on Our Lord's left Shoulder:

During various ecstasies, Our Lord disclosed to Marie-Julie that the devotion to His Shoulder's Wound was a great consolation for Him, and thus granted great promises to those who would practice this devotion (see page 562).

Our Lord showed to Marie-Julie this open Wound and revealed to her its depth:

The Pain is incomprehensible in the hearts of My children. How this devotion pleases and consoles Me, how often have the prayers of these Wounds rose to My Heart and have torn (open) the (way of) salvation for souls entrusted to Hell.

(17 May 1878)

1. **"I will bless all the souls who propagate this devotion: I grant them abundant graces."** (29 March 1878)
2. **"O souls who love Me, who propagate this devotion, I take you under My protection, I keep you under the mantle of My affection."** (29 March 1878)
3. **"I will dispel the darkness that will come to their heart."** (28 December 1877)
4. **"I will console them in their pains." "I will come in the midst of their greatest afflictions, to enlighten, to comfort them."** (8 February 1878, 28 December 1877, 8 February, and 12 April 1878)
5. **"I will come to bless them in their undertakings."** (29 March 1878)
6. **"I will give them a tender love for the Cross. I will come to assist them at the time of death with this cross and I will introduce them into My Heavenly Kingdom."** (12 April 1878)
7. **"I will sweeten their agony."** (28 December 1877). **"I will come at the hour of death. I will console them in their passage."** (8 February 1878). **"Especially at the hour of death, I will come to give them a sweet moment of calm and tranquility. I will tell them: 'O good holy soul, who has spread this devotion (knowing) that I had so much at heart that it be made known, come to receive the reward of your labors, the fruit of blessing.'."** (29 March 1878)
8. **"I will shelter them, I will assist them, I will console all the souls that seek to propagate this Sacred Wound. At the time of death, I will console the souls that have compensated Me by their devotion and compassion to the Wound so deep and painful. I will come to strengthen them in their final fears. I will come and prepare their passage: Thank you, you who have compensated Me for My pains."** (17 May 1878)
9. **"See,"** *Jesus said, pointing to His Sacred Wound with extreme tenderness*, **"all My children who have recognized this Wound, who have venerated it, who have prayed to it, will have on the Last Day a great and generous reward. I do not simply show it, I pronounce it. My Word is Divine."** (17 May 1878)

Devotion to the Precious Blood, His Holy Wounds:

Our Lord asked us to remain devoted to His Precious Blood and not to forget the pious practice of offering all our prayers and works in union with the Divine merits and graces of His most Precious Blood.

Never forget to renew persistently the offering of Precious Blood. You will be consoled, all you who honor My Precious Blood, nothing will happen to you.

(Unknown date…)

Marie-Julie Jahenny added:

Those devoted to Our Lord's Wounds will also be shielded from punishments like a 'lightning rod'. The devotion to the Holy Wounds will be a lightning rod for the Christians who will have kept it.

On distractions during prayer:

Marie-Julie complained on 21 October 1924 that people seemed so distracted in prayer, often saying an 'Our Father' with the lips, but with little thought and not from the heart and often without respect. She asked Our Lady to teach her poor children how to pray better and Our Lady replied:

My little children, the Divine Father does not always stop distraction and little reflection. He knows this poor humanity (or the poverty of humanity). **A good will suffices for Him to give many graces and obtain His divine friendship, His holy friendship.**

Don't forget your guardian angel!

It was revealed to Marie-Julie during an apparition that she had more than one guardian angel. One of them was a little upset with her one day, for she was forgetting to think of him and not asking for his intercession as often as she should; hence, he reprimanded her for it:

You pray without invoking me! You are so powerful then to be able to pray all by yourself! I am here and you do not invoke me!

The angels purify our prayers before God. Marie Julie Jahenny learned her lesson well, and recited the following prayer:

O our Guardian Angels, when we forget the Divine Presence of the Beloved, pray for us, adore Him for us, to the point that there is not a minute without a thought of the Beloved.

<u>Our Lady of the Lilies:</u>

On 23 June 1936, a young girl from Blain brought Marie-Julie a lily that was offered before the Blessed Sacrament on Corpus Christi at the parish church. The lily was then placed in the arms of the statue of Our Lady of Lourdes, which was near Marie-Julie's bed. During the apparition of the day, replying to a total offering done in Marie-Julie Jahenny's name and in the name of all her friends, Our Lady said:

As a reward, I have in my arms this beautiful white flower which recalls the most beautiful of my virtues (virginal purity)... Scatter this spotless flower... Everyone take a small bit home, it is I myself you will carry away, the Queen of Lilies, the Queen of Peace, the Queen of Prodigies, the Queen of Miracles.

Then at the end of the ecstasy, at the last blessings, Our Lady said to Marie-Julie:

Give a small piece (of lily) to all my small children; it is the flower of my Jesus, with a delicious scent blessed on earth... There must be many lilies for Jesus.

The people who were present during this apparition stated that the lily placed in the arms of Our Lady of Lourdes assumed the same freshness during the ecstasy and looked as if it had just been cut.

On Tuesday, 2 February 1937, feast day of Our Lady's Purification, Marie-Julie thanked her for all the graces of protection in accidents, of preservation in accidents and cures granted to all the faithful who had recourse to the fragments of the lily. Our Lady then confirmed her words of the preceding 23 of June, when Our Lord interrupted her saying:

"Remember My Mother, that I had given My blessings before thine."
(Jesus blessed the Lily first - it was placed before Him in the Blessed Sacrament.)

Our Lady continued:

- **I blessed this lily after my Divine Son; it will do many marvels...**

And she asked Marie-Julie to have her invoked under the title of **Our Lady of the Lilies.**

Two days later, on 4 February, the Blessed Virgin Mary said the following words:

- **Little friends, give me this title: Mother of Purity, Lily of Purity without stain. Spread my love on earth by this Lily which has adored Jesus in the Holy Tabernacle, by this beautiful Lily where**

Jesus has placed His purest graces, the most glowing love, I will give many graces, I will even work prodigies, I will give health back to the sick when they are touched by this beautiful Lily of purity.".... "Oh, little children of the earth, come to my heart, invoke me as Our Lady of the Lilies, Mother of Power, Mother of Prodigies...

Then Marie-Julie said:

- *It does not surprise me, good Heavenly Mother, that a shower of graces overflowed from thy heart to fall on this Lily which thou hast watered with thy favors. This Lily, the white corollas of which thou distribute to encourage us to have recourse to thee, predisposing us (to trust) that this Lily will take us to Heaven, as it took the Most Holy Virgin with her beautiful virtues to the Kingdom of her Divine Son, to love and adore Him eternally.*
Jesus has said many times:

Mother, give thy graces to thy small children on earth, I give Mine. I mingle them with thine, thine with Mine, is it not the same thing, so that it is two great blessings that flow on them from this blessed Lily; their eyes do not see them but the eyes of the souls, their souls are not unaware...

Blessings and promises were renewed on different occasions. On 8 April 1937, Our Lady blessed them:

Oh, my little children, I bless you will all my heart, I bless you with the heart of Our Lady of Lilies.

On 10 June 1937, Our Lord gave His blessing:

Little friends, I give your Lilies the same blessing that I gave those which protected you and which made you find the name so dear to My Gentle Mother of 'Our Lady of the Lilies'. Distribute them... I will work miracles, I will do extraordinary prodigies for My chosen ones on earth...

And again, on 18 July 1939, Our Lord stated again:

I bless the Lilies and give them my powers to relive poor suffering.

Marie-Julie Jahenny's last received message before her death:

Marie-Julie Jahenny died on 4 March 1941, but before the French mystic passed away, she received a last message from Our Lord:

The war (will have) been an act of mercy, and it will be recognized as so later on, and those who will have suffered will be in the joy (of knowing) that they have contributed in making a new France in which God will take

His rightful Place. Once France will have paid its debt, it will be rewarded with such an abundance of graces that, in a little time span, she will have forgotten everything (all its past sorrows).

For all the powers that will have fought with such intrepidity and courage, they will receive from France the greatest of rewards: that of taking their place in the bosom of the Catholic Church, which itself will come out of this baptism of blood rejuvenated and renewed.

I shall overthrow all the obstacles, and overthrow all the projects of those who prevent the Light to glow. France will be saved through means that are unknown by Human knowledge... God reserves for Himself its secret until the very last moment.

I look with indifference at men's projects. My Right Side prepares wonders. My Heart will be glorified throughout the earth. I shall find satisfaction in confusing the pride of the ungodly, and the more the world will be hostile to the supernatural, the more wonderful will be the deeds that will confuse this negation of the supernatural.

Instead of the Beast, two thrones will rise: those of the Sacred Heart and the one of the Sacred Heart of Mary.

It will be acknowledged that it wasn't the strength of men that put an end to the war, which will come to an end only once expiation is completed.

Impatient to see impiety and inequity come to an end, and to see France as I desire it, I shall shorten the time span with intensity... Take courage, for this expiation is soon finished, and be assured that France, once victorious, I shall not abandon to the power of the ungodly.

Marie-Julie added immediately after:

The Kingdom of God is close at hand. It will open with a deed that will be as bright as unexpected.

(February 1941 †††)

Conclusion

The prophetic aspect of any alleged Marian apparition case, let alone one that involves the entire Celestial Court within a timeframe of almost seventy years, is unquestionably a very delicate one to consider... Indeed, if, on one hand, the theological message proves to be in perfect harmony and thus in communion with the Catholic Dogma of the Faith, and if the physical particularities of the seer(s) are considered scientifically to be unexplainable and unquestionably "supernatural" (such as stigmata, levitation, Xenoglossia, Hierognosis, gift of prediction and prophecy, reception of Miraculous Communions, living exclusively on the Holy Eucharist specimens for exceeding long period of time), there are other factors as well that must be taken under consideration as well such as the announcement of Marie-Julie Jahenny's sister's body, and her own after their death, which, according to Marie-Julie Jahenny are to be exhumed and to be found incorrupt.

Such prophetic statement, if proven true, would indicate further proof of the Heavenly nature of Marie-Julie Jahenny's Heavenly mission on earth. Naturally, the ultimate seal of authenticity would have to be provided through the local bishop's formal recognition of her case "being worthy of belief", a recognition which, as we have seen earlier in this chapter, has been granted informally on June 6, 1875 by Monsignor Fournier, Bishop of Nantes, after carefully mounting an investigation witnessed by various prelates and by the most reputable Doctor Imbert-Gourbeyre, renowned Professor at the Faculty of Medicine at Clermont-Ferrand.

Evidently, all the revelations received by Marie-Julie Jahenny were meant to be read and understood, but not merely by the formal authorities of the Church, but by "*the*" Church which consists principally of the Hierarchy and of the faithful and laity. Naturally, these admonitions, messages and prophecies are often… too often… hard to accept, and considerably more so at the time they were delivered, but considering the overwhelming volume of historical evidence, prophecies already come to past the 120,000 pages of evidence and recordings written at the time of these revelations, one can moreover find comfort in relying on the position and approval of Marie-Julie Jahenny's local bishop, Monseigneur Fournier, and actions and statements of Popes Leo XIII and Pius XII who showed and expressed their favorable opinion in the extraordinary French stigmatist.

Upon the decided day for My writings to be sent to all my servants and to my victims to indicate to them My Hour and the hour of the miracle, against this call, nothing will stand. I shall protect and shall keep those who will be forced to wait a short time to find refuge under the divine tree of the Cross.

The hour will be sent to all the family of the Cross whose destiny is to be protected. This hour will come before the paths of the earth are closed, before the enemy is engaged within the vast spaces of all of France to conquer it and to have it perish.

(Our Lord Jesus-Christ, July 1882)

These apparitions of our Lord Jesus-Christ and of the Blessed Virgin Mary, although openly delivering a mortal warning, invite men, not only Frenchmen but men from all nations, to repentance, conversion and atonement, and above all to remain everlastingly faithful to the Roman Catholic Church which, despite of today's and tomorrow's weakness and errors, is promised a new "renaissance" under the leadership of a holy and angelic Pope yet to come. This true Vicar of Christ will heal the numerous self-afflicted wounds suffered since the Mid-20th century to our day.

The main core of the messages received by Marie-Julie Jahenny orbits around France, as she announced that France would be the first country to be chastised and to collapse on its knees, soon thereafter to be followed by the other countries of the world; but it is to be the first country to rise again. At the time when this book is being written (2019–2022), France is in deep internal political turmoil. Acts of Islamic terrorism, daily violent protests take place throughout the country even in the midst of the Covid-19 epidemic.

Aggression of individuals, rape and assaults are counted in the thousands in a daily basis throughout the country. Catholic churches and cathedrals are massively being disfigured every year by Muslim agitators (Sources taken from "Le Figaro" "C-News France" and From "Newsweek" – 24 Aug, 2021 – USA). The Catholic Church is divided amidst countless reforms and a German schism in the making, and a first epic international pandemic (Covid-19/Corona Virus) is spreading and killing victims in over 160 countries around the world by the tens of thousands.

On the international scene, the eight hottest geopolitical spots in 2020 are:

1. **The Persian Gulf** whose antagonist parties are: Iran (Persia), Iraq, England, Israel, the United States, France, Saudi Arabia/United Arab Emirates/Qatar.
    (Indirect antagonists: Syria, Russia, and China)
2. **Syria** whose antagonist parties are: Syria, Isis, Kurds, Western supported Syrian rebels, Russia, the United States, France, England, Turkey.
    (Indirect antagonists: Israel, Saudi Arabia, Qatar, China)
3. **Ukraine** whose antagonist parties are: Ukraine, Russia, the United States, and the European Union.
4. **Kashmir** whose antagonist parties are: India and Pakistan
    (Indirect antagonists: China, the United States, the European Union, Russia)
5. **The China Sea** whose antagonist parties are: China, the United States, Japan, the European Union, Vietnam, Australia, the Philippines, Taiwan.
6. **The Strait of Taiwan** whose antagonist parties are: China, Taiwan.
    (Indirect antagonists: The United States, Russia, the European Union, Japan)
7. **The Korean Peninsula** whose antagonist parties are: North Korea, South Korea, the United States.
    (Indirect antagonists: China, Japan, Russia)
8. **Northern Africa** whose antagonist parties are: France, ISIS groups, Mali, Niger, Nigeria, Cameroon, Burkina Faso, Mauritania, Algeria, the European Union, and the United States.

In matter of prophecies' timing, Our Lord Jesus-Christ mentioned in a 1882 message to Marie-Julie Jahenny some years of reference, the only time a calendar reference has ever been made to the French stigmatist: Year 80, 81, 82 and 83…

The storm will break over France where I wanted to show the prodigies of My Divine Heart and unveil its secrets. My children, France will be the first to be wounded, torn, persecuted. When I showed this Divine Sun to Blessed Margaret-Mary, I let my lips utter these words: 'The land which

saw your birth and which will see your death, will be in dire danger, especially from **80 to 83.'**

I let My humble servant understand that the third one will be full of sorrows. There will 'be nothing but apostasies and violations in the Orders of the persons who are consecrated to Me, whether in the priesthood or the religious life.

(Our Lord Jesus-Christ to Marie-Julie Jahenny, June 1882)

What point of reference would these dates (80 to 83) be based on? One thing is certain. These "dates" were neither for the 19th nor 20th centuries… Hence, could it possibly be that the central reference-point for these mentioned "years" would be Marie-Julie Jahenny's death's date (1941)? If this were to be indeed the case, it would imply that most of the announced events to come would occur in between 2021 and 2024 (1941+80=**2021** / 1941+83=**2024**)… But again there is no foundation to this hypothesis.

Furthermore, God, in His almighty wisdom may very well decide to postpone His Judgment as stated earlier by Maximin Giraud in La Salette (see page 47). The timing of these prophecies is not of Human domain or knowledge, but of God's and God's alone.

Today, considering in an objective and neutral fashion that between 1873 and 1941 the prophetic messages received by Marie-Julie Jahenny were, at the time, considered sheer and unrealistic gibberish, today, 79 years after Marie-Julie Jahenny's passing away, her received revelations inspire a freezing-cold chill down one's spine as they describe an utterly accurate description of today's society, world's geopolitical state of affairs, and church struggles and splitting divisions… Indeed, the consequences of man's folly and stubbornness, the French Stigmatist would later add, can no longer be averted but at best… diminished.

Chapter III

The message and prophecies of Our Lady of Tilly

"My child, I desire that you tell all the priests that they make my presence here be known to my people."

(The Blessed Virgin Mary, 2 February 1903)

The messages and prophecies of our Lady of Tilly to Marie Martel—approved officially by Pope Pius X and the Roman Catholic Church in 1910—by their truly astonishing similarity with those of La Fraudais, faithfully echo and complement the extraordinary heavenly revelations given to the French stigmatist, Marie-Julie Jahenny, whose revelations began before those of Tilly, and proceeded long after Marie Martel's passing away (Tilly's seer).

Marie Martel was born in 1872 in Calvados, Normandy. It would be at the early age of nine that the little Normand girl would experience her very first heavenly vision and, later on, her invisible stigmata, both experiences which would accompany her until the end of her life.

On 18 March 1896, in the little provincial town of Tilly-Sur-Seulles (south east of Bayeux in Normandy, France) three nuns of the order of the Sacred Heart, sixty very young students and some adults present in a Catholic school saw what appeared to be, from 1,200 meters away, a bright appearance of the Blessed Virgin Mary in a little field called "Lepetit". Our Lady appeared as the familiar invocation of the "Immaculate Conception". The witnesses, in sheer awe of the vision, were able to say the Rosary for long periods of time on their knees without feeling any fatigue or pain, even young children between six and seven years old were able to remain in the same position without fatigue, discomfort, pain, or boredom…

Marie Martel heard about the extraordinary apparitions of the Blessed Mother, and after finishing her work, rushed to see the apparition for herself on the little field of "Lepetit". Once arrived, she saw at once the Holy Virgin Mary near an elm tree. The young Marie Martel described her vision:

She was of a heavenly beauty, dressed in white with a blue belt, golden roses placed on her bare feet, and wore a white banner, with the words: **"I am the Immaculate"**.

Between March and July 1896, the newspaper **L'Écho de Tilly**, counted up to 26 appearances in the field of "Lepetit" overlooking the Seuilles. The unfortunate tree where the Virgin Mary had appeared upon was soon however turned into shreds, as all the visitors rushed to take a little bit of bark, a few leaves, or a branch as relics…

While many witnessed the first apparition of the Blessed Virgin Mary in the distant little field outside the Normand town of Tilly, messages and revelations were entrusted, since 1896 well into the beginning of the 20th century, only to Marie Martel.

The messages:

Marie Martel stated:

In the month of July 1896, feast-day of Our Lady of Mount Carmel, I heard for the first time the voice of the Blessed Virgin, who told me:

Penance! My child, Penance!

The Blessed Virgin further said to me:

- **My child, do you want to be happy in this life or in the other?**
- *Right away, I said.*
  O my good Mother, I want to go with you right now, if you want to.
  The Blessed Virgin told me:
- **My child, you will have to suffer much here, if you are faithful to the mission that you have to fulfil. I promise you will be happy in the other life.**

And the last word of the Blessed Virgin was this:

- **My dear children, I beg you to pray well and to do penance. It is through prayer and penance that you will appease the vengeance of Heaven.**

In the month of August 1896, a remarkable phenomenon was observed: In the reflection of Marie Martel's eyes during her ecstasies, countless witnesses saw the bright image of the Blessed Virgin Mary dressed in a white robe tied at the waist with a celestial blue belt, and wrapped in a light veil with rays escaping from her hands, a phenomenon which re-occurred repeatedly again and again.

On Thursday, 14 January 1897, Marie Martel had an ecstasy that lasted ten full minutes, during which she saw the Child Jesus in a cloud beside the Blessed Virgin Mary. A few days later, the Mother of Christ explained to young Marie Martel that the martyrdom she would suffer would consist of very great trials.

A second vision followed sometime thereafter where the Blessed Virgin Mary forewarned her again:

Penance! Remember the trials ahead!

Prophecy of January 1897

1.   <u>Schism in the church, the destruction of Paris, England's demise...</u>

*The first day, I heard the voice of the Blessed Virgin, telling me **Penance!**, I asked her for the strength to suffer with love. The Blessed Virgin further said to me:*

My children, pray, because great evils will strike you. The war will soon be declared on all sides against the Church. A schism is being made.

The Blessed Virgin begged, her eyes turned towards the sky, and then, turned towards me, saying:

Oh! Paris, Paris did not respect the laws of my Divine Son... It will be punished and destroyed by fire... There will be few people who will remain... Those who remain will not recognize themselves... Paris will be destroyed by fire if it refuses to convert... This is the punishment that is reserved for it!

The Blessed Virgin Mary also announced that the wealthy would become very poor leading one to understand an economic catastrophe... Likewise, I was told that England will be punished. I saw ships sinking upon which **'England'** *was written.*

2.   Prophecy of Mt. Pelée volcanic eruption

On Wednesday, 27 January 1897, despite the horrible weather, Marie Martel went to the Field of "Lepetit", where a hundred people were waiting. Immediately, Marie Martel fell into an ecstasy which lasted about 20 minutes:
Marie Martel:

The Blessed Virgin said to me:

My child, you must pray well, especially for Martinique, because it will be chastised, and it will be by a rain of fire from the sky that will not be able to be extinguished. Many will perish... Those who stay, if they refuse to convert, a second stroke will be carried, and the plague will prevail.

The Blessed Virgin showed me the catastrophe; I saw the fire on the sea, which reached the ships. The fire consumed these ships... it was a shower of fire.

Mount Pelée blew up indeed on 8 May 1902, utterly destroying the town of St. Pierre in the French Caribbean island of Martinique. Twenty-eight thousand people died within a few minutes! A second eruption then followed on 20 May 1902, which killed an additional two thousand rescue workers and survivors! It was a mega-volcanic catastrophe that shocked France and the world, and is considered by far the worst volcanic disaster of the 20th century.
The apparition of the Blessed Virgin Mary of 2 February 1897 was accompanied by a luminous banner on which this inscription appeared:

Queen of the Most Holy Rosary, pray for us all who hope in you.

Prophecy: Saint Joan of Arc will Appear and Save France Again

On Tuesday, 18 May 1897, Marie Martel had a longer than usual ecstasy (about 45 minutes). Marie Martel saw for the first time Joan of Arc appear before her (Joan of Arc had not yet been canonized):

Marie Martel:

Oh! Beautiful!… She is Venerable!

Then Marie fell on her knees, and remained in that position for about 20 minutes. She then got up and recited the "Memorare".

Marie's description of Joan of Arc:

Joan of Arc was dressed in an armor, which covers her chest and arms. she had barbs sharp points on her elbows. She had a purple-blue skirt, dotted with golden fleur de lys. Her face is very beautiful. She is bareheaded: her rounded hair on her collar is quite short. She holds in her right hand a sword, and in the left a white standard on which are written in golden letter these words: "**Jésus, Marie**". *A dove is perched at the end of the flagstaff.*

Marie Martel also wrote about the vision in her notes:

*In May 1897, I saw Joan of Arc. The Blessed Virgin told me that she (Joan of Arc) would reappear at the moment of great danger, and again she will come to save France. She will reappear where she had passed. The last word was **Poor Rouen! Woe to Rouen!***

Saturday, 22 May 1897

Marie Martel arrived at "Lepetit" at 4 o'clock. After a few Aves, she fell in ecstasy:

"Oh! The standard!… Venerable Joan of Arc!…"

Then she fell on her knees, and walked the space a few feet. Marie Martel then asked for several graces, and exclaimed:

"Oh! Do not hit them! I beg you, my good Mother!"

She rose again, still in ecstasy, and approached the high barrier behind the Chapel. Her look became very bright.

"Oh! How beautiful," she exclaimed. *"How beautiful! We can never build anything so beautiful!"*

At that moment, one could clearly see in her eyes the image of a basilica. The vision stopped a few moments later. It lasted 42 minutes…

In other ecstasies Marie Martel described a future majestic basilica to be built in Tilly, and thus drew a picture of it. This drawing confirmed what the little children of the school had admired in the apparitions they themselves had witnessed:

Marie Martel added:

I asked our good Mother for the adoration of the Most Blessed Sacrament; where to establish it? I asked. The voice answered, "Here it is.", and at that moment, I found myself transported, and suddenly I saw very clearly the Most Blessed Sacrament, carried by an Angel. Several Angels were in front, in two ranks, and walked in accompaniment; others walked from behind, also in two ranks. The Most Blessed Sacrament left in its path a very luminous trail. Oh! It was beautiful to see! The angels held lighted candles in their hands. All were dressed in white.

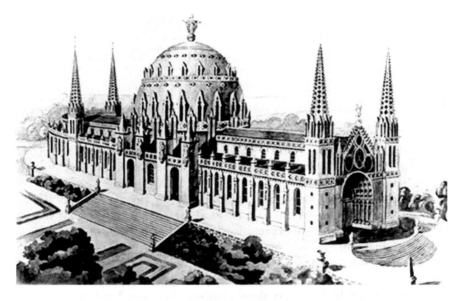

Future Basilica of Tilly as per Marie Martel's vision

Thursday, 27 May 1897, Feast of the Ascension:

On the Feast Day of the Ascension (1897), a large crowd was at the Field of "Lepetit" when Marie Martel arrived (about 6:00 AM). The young woman had two successive ecstasies. A pious pilgrim testifies:

Marie saw the little victims, the children of the Charity Bazaar)[17], crowned. Marie Martel first saw three nuns of Saint Vincent de Paul crowned: on the first day, they only went through the flames of Purgatory.

---

[17] The Charity Bazaar was an annual charity event organized by the French Catholic aristocracy in Paris from 1885 onwards. The 'victims' of the Bazaar is referring to the victims of a tragic fire at the 1897 bazaar which claimed on May fourth of that year 126 lives, many of them aristocratic women, the most eminent of whom was the

Marie Martel then was told that St. Joan of Arc must reappear in Orléans, Domremy, Compiègne, Rouen. St. Joan of Arc said: **Woe to you, Rouen!**

Marie Martel wrote in her notes: *Many times I heard these words:* **"Penance!"** *The Blessed Virgin asked for candles to be blessed.*
That day (27 May 1897), *the Blessed Virgin told me that I would have much to suffer, and that I would have many trials, even from the clergy. Our good Mother asked me if I wanted to suffer for the conversion of sinners. I answered:*

"Yes, for your love, and for all that has been done to your Divine Son."

I was given a relic of the true cross: I venerated it with great respect.

Paris hit, the Montmartre and Fontainebleau spared, Versailles destroyed...

In May of the same year, Marie Martel received the following revelations: The Blessed Virgin Mary:

-   **My child, for you the world will be cruel. There are some who will try to crush you, to trample you; they will spit in your face. Above all, be calm and say nothing. You will be well humiliated. What I have told you is the truth.**
    If God has not yet struck, it is because, in His goodness as Father, He has waited for the return of sinners; and today what has He received from this expectation? What blasphemies... And yet my Divine Son, in his goodness, has made known to them all the misfortunes that threaten them with warnings He sends them.
    Now God will strike if you refuse to pray, to do penance and to convert. Oh! Pray, my dear children, for soon I will no longer be able to stop this divine anger which will be sent from the Divine Master.
    The first blow will be on Paris: theatres will blow up; victims will burn; the blood will flow.

"I saw Montmartre spared, Versailles destroyed, Fontainebleau preserved."

-   **You must pray well. You are in dangerous days, and there will be some preserved. A disaster will pass in a festival that will be given;**

Duchess of Alençon, née Duchess Sophie in Bavaria, sister of the famous Empress Sisi and one-time fiancée of King Ludwig II of Bavaria.
The tragedy was a major shock to the people of France and Europe. A chapel of atonement, Notre-Dame de Consolation, was built on the location of the Bazaar. This chapel is dedicated to victims of fire and serves the Italian Catholic community in Paris.

and the other is nothing next to it [18]. Many will see me rise above danger, and the angels will be with me. The catastrophe is going to be ever so terrible so that the world prays better... I see them coming by God in a more distant time.

Oh! How many weeping mothers! They will shriek to the sky when they see their children writhing in the flames! Oh! It is there that these mothers will forget the feasts of Baal and all their pleasures; and during these days of mourning, the world will pray better. Many will come to prostrate themselves before the divine tabernacles, and ask God's forgiveness... Ah! What repentance! But unfortunately it will be too late!... Since the world does not want to pray, that's how God will strike!

Marie Martel:

And then the word **Penance!** *was repeated.*

- **A great miracle is going to take place, and many more will follow. Do not be discouraged. You must pray, pray well.**
- *Have mercy on Paris! Hold the arm of your divine Son!... After it has passed, they will not think about it!... Forgive us!... Forgive us all!*

(Exchange between the Blessed Virgin Mary and Marie Martel, May 1897)

Marie, who felt no fatigue, then took her rosary. Then Our Lady recommended blessed candles in anticipation of the time of darkness.

Prophecy: Tilly will one day be greater than Lourdes

In August 1899, while in a pilgrimage before the Grotto of Massabielle, in Lourdes, Marie Martel heard the Blessed Virgin Mary's voice:

You see that the world comes here (Lourdes) in great numbers to pray (...) it is not much in comparison with those who will come to Tilly. A day will come when Lourdes will become a little Tilly.

(Lourdes, the Blessed Virgin Mary to Marie Martel, 17 August 1899)

Marie Martel's relic of the true cross:

Marie Martel:

One day the Blessed Virgin said to me:

---

[18] This is a possible reference to the Charity Bazaar disaster of Paris that happened that same year which shocked all of France...

'My child, lend the relic that you wear which is that of the true Cross. Take it to little Bétou: she will heal. From this day, to all those who ask you, do not refuse it... My child,' *she added,* **'by the virtue of this Cross, you will obtain many healings and conversions.'**

Little Bétou was cured shortly thereafter of meningitis...

Likewise, whenever the relic was asked for the conversion of a sinner, the person the grace was asked for was immediately converted...

<u>The Medal blessed at Tilly</u> (Medal not specified, perhaps a Miraculous Medal was blessed by Our Lady at Tilly)

A young girl, member of a pilgrimage group to Tilly, approached one day Marie Martel and asked for a medal blessed in the Field of "Lepetit" by the Blessed Virgin, for a very sick ungodly person on the brink of death. That person was then asked to put the medal on this old hardened sinner. In the meantime, the family of said lost soul introduced a priest to him. As it could be expected, nothing resulted from said encounter but an outpouring of insults and profanities addressed to the poor baffled priest, shocking in the process everyone present.

The roughed-up priest was forced to withdraw, and was unable to do anything more. When the priest left, the grieved family said, *"Well! the Tilly medal did not serve us much!"*; however, the person who was supposed to put the medal on the obscene hardened soul revealed that he actually had not actually used the medal blessed at "Lepetit"... He hastened immediately thereafter to put it on him. The patient then asked his mother:

- *Will the parish priest come back to see me?*
- *"**After all that you have told him, it is impossible for him to even think of setting foot in our house again,**"* his mother replied.
- *Ah, I want him back! Let's go get him! I ask... I need him...*

The priest came back and cried with happiness, for the patient had confessed. The new convert lived another four days, received the last Sacraments with the greatest piety, and died contrite and confessed.

In July 1899, Marie Martel went to her own family and obtained the conversion of her own father who had also been a harsh unbeliever.

<u>Jesus' request one hour of reparation on Fridays</u>

Marie Martel:

In June 1901, the Sacred Heart of Jesus said to me:

My child, from this day, I take you to be, near my people, my intermediary, to ask each of my children to come, every Friday of the year, spend an hour with the Divine tabernacles: that is to say, an hour of worship, (adoration) to repair all the outrages, of which My Heart is showered every day, from My own children.

On Sundays, most of them profane My Holy Day, which I have reserved for Myself, and others blaspheme Me, and even come to sit at My holy table, to receive My Sacred Flesh and My Precious Blood, (in the state of mortal sin): They come to make Me undergo a new agony. It is necessary to pray for these unfortunate ones, so that they become converted. My Holy Mother must be implored for them.

Marie-Martel:

The good Jesus also told me that I had to start with the poor, to ask to do the hour of adoration.

And above all, my child, do not fail to fulfil the mission that I have just given you, and sometimes you will find many troubles and trials: you will even laugh at yourself, you will find yourself in trouble.

My child, place slander underfoot; because for all that comes from Heaven there are more difficulties than for things that come from the earth. Child, be brave! Take courage! Answer My call!

Say to those who apologize for not being able to come every week, to come on the first Friday of each month, and especially that it is necessary to be well prepared, to come to receive Me, to repair all the outrages of which I am showered, as well as My Father, who is ready to strike the whole of France.

She (France) is the most guilty! It is she who has received the most graces and blessings, and I have received only ingratitude! The world will be chastised if it refuses to pray and do penance.

France will be chastised... The trials will come at the moment when the law on the Congregations will pass, forcing religious to leave! The schism against the Church is being made...

(Our Lord Jesus-Christ, June 1901)

Miracle seen in the sun

In July 1901, a crowd of pilgrims saw a phenomena in the sun, and an impressive rain of luminous globes at Tilly.

The Three Days of Darkness

On Sunday, 7 July 1901, on the Three Days of Darkness:

All the balls started from the sun, as if they had come out from behind it. When they started from the bottom of the sun, they were a little elongated like lemons, then they grew bigger; but they diminished as they came towards us, until they became very small.

They swayed then; one meter of earth (...) Everyone was covered: they (the luminous balls) were in countless quantities.

There were some green ones, some rose, some dark blue, some black (of a black of lead mine), some yellow, color of flame, fire... some came in large numbers to us, others went to all sides.

I saw a lot of the sun, and falling on the Church especially, it hurt me a lot. My heart was tight... I also saw several times, below the sun, (something) like a mourning curtain, there was no cloud at all and the sky was all pink. This black was only below the sun; it disappeared quickly and reappeared again... that's when I heard a voice telling me that the black I saw, that's how the darkness will be! And the balls that look like flames, it's the fire for Paris and for different other places! This is how the fire of Heaven will fall.

We will do penance. We refuse now, but we will do penance... We must pray... but a lot, to stop the arm of Divine Justice. The voice was that of the Sacred Heart. With all the other balls that I saw fall, the Voice also said to me:

Here are all the punishments of all kinds, and then also great misfortunes that threaten you. The good ones will also pay for the bad ones.

The voice was very severe, I would have preferred not to hear it. How sad it was!

From February to March 1906, Marie Martel was assailed with slanders. The Blessed Virgin had told her:

My child, you will be well humiliated. It will come a moment that you will be flouted. You will see a lot of trouble around you.

The children, they make them blaspheme. The holy name of God is no longer respected in most families, but the good Master will chastise them.

My children, redouble prayers for the healing of the sick, and especially for the conversion of sinners.

On another occasion, the Blessed Virgin Mary said to Marie Martel:

My child, my child, be brave!... You will always be persecuted by the world and the devil... When you are discouraged, go back, in the memory whenever I showed myself to you. Do not be afraid! I will always be near you... There will be many times that you will find yourself discouraged, even that your faith will be ready to leave you... Reassure yourself, invoke my name... It will be enough to revive you... It is God who allows it to test you. Child, be generous!

The Chastisements

In August 1901, the Blessed Virgin said:

My children, all the balls (of fire) you see are nothing compared to the misfortunes and punishments of all kinds, which have been announced, and which they mock so much... It will be necessary to repair the outrages

committed on all sides. Most of them, on Sundays, do not go to Mass: that is what insults my Divine Son! The others blaspheme: that is what insults my Divine Son! Many others already outrage the Holy Tabernacle.

Pray, pray, my children... You will all be about to be tested: the good ones will pay for the culprits, I will protect many, especially those who have always trusted me.

All the animals that you saw, that's how it will come in many places! They will devour whatever they find in their path. Many people will be devoured.

(The Blessed Virgin Mary to Mary Martel, 15 August 1901)

Marie Martel:

I saw a lot of ships gobbled up. This is how everyone will do penance! The fire on Paris was announced again, and that's when I saw a big banner, on which was written:

War, plague, famine, plagues of all kinds.

I saw a cross surrounded by little angels. Oh! How beautiful they were!

*Afterwards, I saw St. Radegund It was the first time I saw her. She rested her feet on a banner, held by two little angels, and on which was written "**Sainte Radegonde**". How beautiful she was! She was all dressed in white: a beautiful white coat, with a gold border. She was crowned.*

Afterwards, I saw the Sacred Heart. Oh! How much I was seized, seeing the Heart of Jesus bleeding! The Sacred Heart said to me:

You must ask for adorers for every Friday, and you must begin with the poor.

At that moment, the blood flowed, I could not behold it any more, it hurt to see! And always the Voice complained:

Here, and in many other places, you do not hasten to make Me adored. At all costs, it is necessary before the punishments, to appease the arm of the Divine Justice, I will bless all those who will make adoration to Me. Come tomorrow morning recite the rosary!

*During the recitation of the rosary, I heard the word "**Penance!**" several times.*

When I asked the Sacred Heart for Tilly's triumph, the Sacred Heart replied:

It will be at the moment of the great shock, which will pass. They must not despair; you must pray a great deal.

2 October 1901 – The Feast Day of Holy Guardian Angels:

Marie-Martel:

I went to the Field, as the Voice had asked me, about 7:15 pm. Entering the Field, I saw many people, who were grouped in the place where I had the great favor to see the Blessed Virgin Mary. I started my rosary, and it was at the second decade of the first rosary, that I saw the angels who accompanied the Blessed Virgin, and they prayed well, with their beautiful little white rosaries! Suddenly I was surprised by the voice of our good Mother, whom I recognized immediately. The voice told me:

There will be many disasters and misfortunes, even in places very close to this place where I showed myself.

They did not believe in me; many showed me their indifference, and yet, deep down, they were touched, but they wanted to show themselves as those who do not believe... Others have been fervent. Ah! I will bless them, I reserve them many graces.

Marie-Martel:

And then, the voice was silent for a moment. I then offered many thanks to our good Mother of Heaven, for all our dear patients and their healing, and especially many conversions. Many were promised to me, I also asked the Blessed Virgin to bless us, and at that moment, all the Angels I saw made the sign of the cross, which showed me that our good Mother of Heaven blessed us. I also asked for Tilly's triumph. The voice answered me:

It will pass! It will not be long in coming.

At that moment, I saw a very bright light, I could hardly look at it, when all of a sudden, in the middle of this great light, I saw the Sacred Heart, but in bust only the rest was lost in a beautiful cloud white all dotted with bright spots from the rays of this great light. The good Jesus had His arms extended; His face was very severe:

Here, I asked for an hour every Friday, but an hour of adoration. They do not go... and yet you must! I will give so many graces and lights, when you have accomplished what I have just asked!

Marie Martel:

I also asked a lot for the Exposition of the Blessed Sacrament, for the first Fridays of each month. The Sacred Heart answered me:

You'll have it, but not yet. (at the apparition site)

I asked the good Jesus again for the religious congregations, the Sacred Heart answered me:

They (should) not have asked for anything yet, and especially not to run away.

The context of our Lord's answer is here unknown...

Marie Martel:

I saw, at that moment, large drops of blood flow from His Holy Heart, His eyes were full of tears, but I did not see them fall, and the Voice went on:

They are not valiant! They are not valiant! (the clergy)

The Sacred Heart has also announced great misfortunes, of which we are much threatened:

Our Lord Jesus-Christ:

In many different places, little children will be slaughtered, even in the arms of their mothers. Many people will be destroyed by water, others by fire from the sky. (...) All these punishments are terrible... So many priests, who will flee will be massacred!... The blood will flow freely... You must also pray a lot for the Holy Father, the Pope, and for all the clergy... It is not valiant! When all these punishments will pass, they will all be in great terror! That's why we must pray!

I see a lot of everything giving up. They (the clergy) will forget all the commitments they made. They will suffer, and they will forget even their Father from Heaven... All those who will remain peaceful, and who patiently wait for all these misfortunes will be the blessed ones of My Father. This is the last time that I warn you of all that will happen: War, plague, famine, plagues of all kinds. Everyone will have to suffer, plus one less. Your souls must wake up. It's time! It's the test!

Marie Martel:

And then the voice of the good Jesus also told me that it was the last time He asked for the hour of adoration; (then) I heard these words again:

Our Lord Jesus-Christ:

France is guilty; she will be punished and punished. It takes blood to repair the outrages with which My Heart is showered. France is making a huge wound to My heart. She does not content herself; she enlarges it every day. Pray, my children! Come near My tabernacle.

Come to adore this Heart, which suffers horribly because of your ingratitude! Oh! Come comfort My Heart! It is the channel, through which

all the graces of love spread in souls, (and) overflows. It is also the road which leads to the way to Heaven.

Marie Martel:

I asked a lot to quell the divine wrath. I prayed the good Jesus to soften all these punishments; I was very scared... Good Jesus looked to the right and to the left, and blessed us, as if to say to us: Goodbye! His face became radiant and beautiful, and then, a great light has enveloped everything: the vision was lifted. I did not see anything anymore...

When I found myself in the middle of all this world, it seemed very sad to me, and yet, on the other hand, I was happy, because everyone was praying well; I thought that was why the good Jesus had looked right and left: He was probably listening to the prayer of all His children...

2 December 1901:

Marie Martel:

*I went to the Field, as the voice had asked me (...) I got on my knees, and I began the rosary. It was during the Sorrowful Mysteries that I saw before me a very bright light, and at that moment I perceived all the angels that surrounded our good Mother, when she showed herself in this blessed place. I also saw many lilies, and stars falling on the angels, and also falling on us. At that moment, **I heard the voice of our good Mother, who told me that we had to pray a great deal for the Holy Father, and then for the clergy**. The voice of our good Mother was very sad! It seemed to me that her heart was filled with sorrow, for the voice was sobbing:*

The Blessed Virgin Mary:

You must pray for everything that happens in a large part of the clergy. O my children! These things are appalling! When I see the enemies of my Son who lead my children to death; when I see these enemies present their deceitful promises to many who carry the priesthood of my Divine Son, I see them, these souls, (the wayward priests) descend into the hollow of abysses, and I also see the Divine wrath that will strike! All the words that I brought to the earth, most rejected them, and even trampled them.

My words have been blasphemed! They refuse to believe them!

A moment will come when all that I have brought to earth will be preached by the beloved of my Divine Son, and all those who have blasphemed them will be struck. (...) The Heart of my Divine Son is so outraged, that sometimes He Forgets His Blessed Mother! He is ready to split Heaven, to sift them all in the sieve of His holiness.

All the misfortunes which I have come to announce on the mount of La Salette, will arrive. The clergy trod on my words at their feet; they laughed; they did not want to do anything; they did not want to hear me! And today their hearts are going to be tortured, for lack of faith in my words. Here,

they turned a deaf ear to my call! But Divine Justice will wake them up... Their hearts are harder than stone! Only the punishments that will strike them will make them see their cowardice against me!

(The Blessed Virgin Mary, 2 December 1901)

More Prophecies:

On 6 June 1902, in front of 600 people present, Marie Martel's gaze rose and fell, then rose again and finally settled. Her hands stretched forward, her eyes rose, and suddenly she made a brisk movement and exclaimed:

Sacred Heart of Jesus, have mercy on us!

The young Normand woman still on her knees, began walking (on her knees) for a few meters, then she cried again, in a supplicating voice:

Jesus, son of the living God, have mercy on us!
My Jesus, mercy!...
Jesus, son of David, heal our sick!...
(short pause...)
Oh! Stop these misfortunes!...
Protect France!...
Ah! Forgive us, I beg you!...
(short pause...)
Stop! Stop!...
Defend them against your enemies!

(Apparition to Marie Martel, 6 June 1902)

Now here is how Marie Martel wrote in her notes what she had seen and heard:

One of the angels stood up and turned towards us. At that moment, I heard the voice of our good Mother, who said to me:

We must pray well, because of the misfortunes and punishments that will happen.
In France, two volcanoes will blow-up, and mountains will collapse. The misfortunes of Martinique are nothing compared to all that will happen. I see a great destruction of my people: I see many perish in flames, others by water, another by famine, plague and war.

(The Blessed Virgin Mary, 6 June 1902)

Civil war:

Marie Martel:

241

I prayed the good Jesus for all the misfortunes which we are all threatened, and He said to me:

Here you came in large numbers. Many came for prayer, and others to make fun of it. In France, two volcanoes will jump, mountains will collapse, and English ships will sink. The misfortunes that have come are nothing to anything that will happen. Outside France, many earthquakes; Volcanoes will also jump, mountains will collapse.

Marie Martel:

While the Sacred Heart was describing me all the punishments, I also heard the voice of our good Mother who said:

If they prayed! If they wanted to convert! These misfortunes would they not be mitigated?

Marie Martel:

And then the good Jesus disappeared a moment, and He reappeared less severe. He has blessed us.

31 January 1903 – The Call of the King

The Blessed Virgin Mary:

Oh, my children, pray, pray, indulge in penance. I can no longer retain divine justice.
Pray for the King who is coming… In these days you live under a regime of crime… but France will go to the Sacred Heart.
You must come to this place (Tilly-Sur-Seulles) and pray for the King to come. This is the monarchy which will ensure the recovery of France in a new era because the royalty of France is traditionally a Christian regime.

(The Blessed Virgin Mary, 31 January 1903)

3 May 1903 – Pray for the King and the holy Pontiff to come:

Marie Martel echoed the message of her vision of 3 May 1903:

The Blessed Virgin Mary:

… The triumph will come, it will not be long (in coming)… I pray, I beg my Divine Son, with the heart of the tenderest of mothers, so that He removes the plagues… O my children, pray, pray very much!… It will be necessary to pray a great deal during the months of August and September… It is necessary to pray for the future King and for the

Sovereign Pontiff. The Republic, will fall: it is the reign of Satan!... Another world and another reign will come...

(The Blessed Virgin Mary, 3 May 1903)

(**Note:** This prophecy unquestionably confirms Marie-Julie Jahenny's prophecies involving the great Monarch, Henry V of the Cross, and the holy Pontiff awaited by the faithful.)

Marie Martel then reported having seen the massacre of priests in Paris. (This is obviously the Civil War in France that will break out first in Paris which she, the children of La Salette and Marie-Julie Jahenny foretold.)

Prophecies on Pope Leo XIII

Marie Martel:

On July 8, 1903 I heard the voice of Our Lord who said to me:

My children, at this moment the Holy Father thinks of you all: he blesses you.

Marie Martel:

These words were repeated twice.
When I went to recite my rosary, I offered it for the restoration of the Holy Father. After praying for a moment, the voice of our good Mother of Heaven said to me:

My child, the Holy Father (Pope Leo XIII) will soon be with me; he will soon leave you... His hour is very near, I bless him... My child, tell your spiritual father that I will gather his last breath (the Holy Father's); I will appear to him at the moment of his death, and those who surround him will perceive something, and they will not speak of it; they will keep it for themselves, but I, my child, will reveal it to holy souls who will publish it... My child, if you pray well, he will appear to you after his death.

(The Blessed Virgin Mary, 8 July 1903)

On July 13, I prayed for the Holy Father; I heard the voice of our good Mother of Heaven who said to me:

He will soon be happy, because his end is near, and he blesses you instantly. He deserved his crown, because he has always been zealous for his Church. He had much to suffer because of France and the high clergy, but God will deliver him, and give him the beautiful place He has prepared for

him up there. I see him coming to receive his crown...

(The Blessed Virgin Mary, 13 July 1903)

On July 15, the Blessed Virgin told me:

Soon, my child, the Holy Father will be very happy, I shall go get him: I will be accompanied by my Angels... If all my children were like he, how many tears they would spare me!... O my children, you can pray to him: he is a saint! A day will come when they will recognize him (as a saint)...

Marie Martel:

For the feast day of our good Mother of Heaven, I brought her a bouquet of roses. At the same moment, as I put the bouquet at the feet of the Blessed Virgin, I heard these words:

My child, offer me these flowers in honor of the holiness of the Holy Father. My child, when you see the rose from the middle of the bouquet fade, it will be at the moment of the death of the Holy Father.

Marie Martel:

In the morning, at 4 o'clock, the very day of the death of the Holy Father (20 July), I heard a voice from my room telling me that the Holy Father was going to die at 4 o'clock in the evening.

20 July 1903 – The Resurrection of the French Monarchy

Marie Martel:

The Blessed Virgin told me:

Take courage, my children, I assure you: I shall do here (at Tilly) what I have never done in the whole world... The King of France in the Great Glorious Kingdom of Christ King Master of the Nations.

A monastery was there once. It is dead. Another of a new kind will resurrect...

The French Royalty, incarnated by Saint Louis and Joan of Arc, was decapitated in Louis XVI and buried with Charles X... it will be resurrected by Tilly.

(The Blessed Virgin Mary, 20 July 1903)

In her personal journal, Marie wrote on 3 May 1909 the following sentence:

*The Blessed Virgin blessed us, and she recommended us to pray for the clergy '... **because it is not what it should be'.***

Our good Mother told me that I would have to suffer very much from men:

The Blessed Virgin Mary:

Here below (on earth), **my child, you will only have suffering, be courageous, calm and patient. I will comfort you in suffering.**

What you asked me on a day that you suffered much, you will be granted, but for that, it is necessary to ask every day, with simplicity. You will find days when the suffering will be very great, even when your adoptive parents will be discouraged, seeing you suffer. But it must not be; on the contrary, it is you, in suffering, who will console them. Tell them: do not be discouraged. You will suffer for all those who do not want God, especially those who blaspheme and outrage...

O child, be generous! Answer my call and that of my divine Son!

In 1902, Marie Martel became tertiary of St. Francis. She died in France on 24 October 1913. She was always regarded as pure and pious, and was loved by multitude of Frenchmen and faithful across the world for the next decades to come. Her intercession, like that of Marie-Julie Jahenny, Catherine Labouret, Bernadette Soubirous, and the children of La Salette, is sought to this day.

Approval — Controversy — Final Church Approval at Last Confirmed

In May 1905, Bishop Amette formally forbade the clergy to go to Tilly-sur-Seuilles, but then, one year later, on May 1906, his holiness Pope Pius X granted a special blessing to Tilly's dean and also to Marie Martel. Rome had then declared itself 'favorable' of the apparitions of Tilly-sur-Seuilles in 1907 and of Marie Martel's visions and revelations.

In 1908, aware of local bishop Amette's public opposition to the apparitions in the little field of "Lepetit", Pope Pius X ordered an account for the opposition, but then Bishop Amette inexplicably changed his position, and begged Pius X for forgiveness, assuring he no longer doubted that the events at Tilly are genuine. In March of the following year (1909), Bishop Amette did penance for speaking out against Tilly and recognized it publicly.

However, controversy broke out again when his successor refused to authorize pilgrimages to Tilly... Still and all, in 1910 Pope Pius X and the Vatican behind him declared themselves once again as being "favorable of the apparitions of Tilly". The statement was formal and official. This rebellion against Tilly was simply a reflection of disobedience aimed against the Holy See and the Pope's Cardinals, but quickly eradicated by the formal position adopted by the Holy See.

The visions of Tilly to this day are formally approved by the Church and pilgrimages are permitted therein.

Marie Martel (in ecstasy)

Vision of the Holy Family by Marie Martel, 25 April 1899

Chapter IV

The Message and the Three Secrets of Our Lady of Fatima

(*Our Lady of La Fatima*)

In the plans of the Divine Providence, when God is going to chastise the world He always first exhausts all other remedies. When He sees that the world pays no attention whatsoever, then, as we say in our imperfect way of talking, He presents us the last means of salvation: His Blessed Mother. If we despise and reject this last means, Heaven will no longer pardon us, because we will have committed a sin that the Gospel calls a sin against the Holy Spirit. This sin consists in openly rejecting—with full knowledge and will—the salvation that is put in our hands.

(*Sister Lucia Dos Santos, 26 December 1957*)

The beginning of the 20th century marked indeed not merely the beginning of a new revived rivalry, contentions and eventually violence between nations in Europe, but likewise the pursuit of Heaven's untiring call through Its principal Emissary to lead man away from a carefully conceived plan whose aim is to bring about a new "Novus Ordo Seclorum" (New Secular World Order) under the all-seeing eye of... the great architect...

Many church historians believe the earliest apparition of the Blessed Virgin Mary in the 20th century was that of Fatima in Portugal, but that was not the case... As we have seen in the prior two chapters, the Blessed Virgin Mary had appeared quite exceptionally and with an uncommon frequency in France at the end of the 19th century and at the very beginning of the 20th century (La Fraudais and Tilly), for France, we were told is to be the lightning-rod of God's intervention on earth. The beginning of the 20th century began as well with an unknown and yet quite astounding intervention of the Blessed Virgin Mary during the first World War, in the course of the battle of the Marne.

In January 1915, the First World War was raging. Two main European alliances were mortally unleashing their respective arsenal of death and human waves against one another. On one side was the "triple Entente" made-up of France, England and Russia, with Belgium and Serbia adding their forces to the Western Alliance. On the other side was the central alliance which quickly formed with the massive armed forces of Germany, the Austro-Hungarian and Ottoman Empires.

As the war began, Germany all but conquered Belgium and part of Eastern France... As the first units of the British Expeditionary Force disembarked in Northern France, the French first Army Corps formed a solid front-line, amassing its troops against the German invaders. The famous Battle of the Marne was about to be engaged, and as it did... a miracle occurred...

Our Lady of the Marne

An article in the **Le Courrier** periodical of the city of Saint-Lô issued on 8 January 1917:

On January 3, 1915, a German priest, wounded and made prisoner during the battle of the Marne, died in a French ambulance carrying some French nuns as well. The German priest told them before passing-away:

As a soldier, I should maintain silence; as a priest, I think I must say what I saw... During the battle, we were surprised to be pushed back for we were legions compared to the French, and we were counting on reaching Paris! But... we saw the Holy Virgin, all dressed in white with a blue sache; she was inclined towards Paris... She was turning her back to us and with her right hand she seemed to be pushing us back!

Two German officers, wounded and made prisoners, gave testimony as did the dying German priest on January 3, 1915. One of them gave the following testimony:

If I were on the front, I would be shot, for prohibition has been made to us to tell, under penalty of death, what I am about to tell you: You were surprised of our withdrawal ever so sudden when we arrived to the doors of Paris. We were not able to go any further... A Virgin Mary was standing before us, with her arms outstretched, pushing us back every time we were ordered to advance. For many days, we did not know if that was one of your national saints, Genevieve or Joan of Arc.

Afterwards, we understood that it was the Holy Virgin Mary who was forcing us on to be still. On 8 September, she pushed us back with so much force, that, like a single man, we ran away! What I am telling you, you will hear it undoubtedly again for we were 100,000 men to have seen her.

Here is another testimony coming of two German officers who were wounded: A benevolent nurse was accompanying them in a French ambulance of the Red Cross all the way to the French hospital where they were going to be treated. Once they've entered the French hospital, both officers stopped, appearing to be shocked before a statue of the Virgin Mary. One of them exclaimed while pointing at the statue: '*Die Frau Von Der Marne!*' (*The lady from the Marne!*) His companion signed him to be quiet while pointing at the French nurse for she was listening to them. She tried, while treating them to have them talk... but in vain...

This testimony only adds to others. The following one has been written by a nun who was taking care of the wounded in Issy-les-Moulineaux.

It was after the battle of the Marne. Among the wounded taken care in the ambulance of Issy, was a very badly injured German judged soon to be lost. Notwithstanding, thanks to the care which was given to him, he survived more than a month. He was Catholic and showed great signs of faith, the hospital-helpers were all priests. The German soldier received a great deal of religious support and did not know how to show his gratitude. He often used to say: *I would like to do something to thank you.*

Finally, the day he received his last rights, he told the hospital-helpers:

You have taken care of me with a great deal of charity. I want to do something for you by telling you what is not to our advantage but which will please you... I shall pay in this way a little bit my debt. If I were on the front, I would be shot for we have been forbidden to speak about this.

He spoke thereafter of the Virgin's visit which terrorized the German soldiers and caused their running-away in panic.

In another ambulance, a similar testimony was noted. A German soldier was dying. He had been struck by the perfect devotion of the French nun who was taking care of him. He therefore said:

- *Sister, it's over... Soon I shall be dead. I would like to thank you to have taken care of me so well, me an enemy... Hence, I shall tell you something that will please you greatly. In this moment, we are advancing a great deal in France, but despite it all, it's your country that will win.*
- How do you know?
- *At the Battle of the Marne, we saw the Holy Virgin push us back. She protects you against us. The officers have forbidden us, under penalty of death, to speak of this vision. But now, I am finished... When I shall be dead, you will be able to repeat this as long as you do not name me... For many days, our entire division saw ahead of it, in the sky, a Lady dressed in white with a blue sache and a white veil. She was turning her back on us and scared us a great deal... On September 5, 1914, we received the order to advance and we tried to do so, but the Lady was so dazzling... and she pushed us with her two hands in such a terrifying manner that we all ran away.*

In Liège (Belgium), just after the armistice, a soldier confided to his hostess who noted his testimony:

Oh, as soon as the war started, I knew that at the end we would be beaten... I can tell you this because I know you will not repeat this to our officers.

The prohibition was still in effect

He added: *On the first battle of the Marne, we had ahead of us, in the sky, a Lady dressed in white who was turning back was turned towards us, and she was pushing us with both her hands. Despite us, we were in sheer panic. We couldn't advance anymore. At least three of our divisions saw this apparition. It was surely the Holy Virgin! There was a moment she frightened us so, that we all ran away, officers like the others...*

The only thing was that the next morning, they forbade us to speak of it under penalty of death. If the whole army knew what happened, it would have been demoralized... As far as we were concerned, we did not have the heart anymore to fight since God was against us. It was certain that we were going to straight to death for nothing, but we had to march nonetheless. We couldn't do otherwise. War is hard!

(**Le Courrier,** 8 January 1917)

Already, the First World War brought a most necessary intervention of the Blessed Virgin Mary soon to be followed by yet another over one thousand kilometers away from the battle lines, in the little country of Portugal, one that would, at the end, promise, before all who were present, such a monumental supernatural occurrence that even the Catholic Church would not be able to hide it-away from public attention.

The Angel's First Apparition

In 1916, the three little shepherds of Fatima, Lucia Dos Santos (9 years old), Jacinta (six years old), and Francisco Marto (eight years old) went off, like every morning, tend their sheep in the emerald-green hills and plains off the village of Fatima. When, upon the first drops of a drenching rain began to fall, the three children decided to seek a shelter within a small cave on the hillside. After the rain stopped and the sun came out once again, Lucia, Jacinta and Francisco decided to stay a little longer to eat their lunch, say the rosary and play a game of jacks.

They had played but for a short time when an odd wind suddenly blew and a white light suddenly enveloped them… In the middle of that light appeared a cloud in the form of a young man. Lucia described this first experience:

This angel had the appearance of a young man of fourteen or fifteen years old, whiter than snow, which the sun rendered transparent as if it were of crystal, and of great beauty. We were surprised and half absorbed. We did not say a word.

While coming closer to us, the Angel said:

Do not fear! I am the Angel of Peace. Pray with me.

And kneeling on the earth, he bent his forehead to the ground. Prompted by a supernatural movement, we imitated him and repeated the words which we heard him pronounce:

My God, I believe in Thee, I adore Thee, I hope in Thee and I love Thee. I ask pardon for all those who do not believe in Thee, do not adore Thee, do not hope in Thee and do not love Thee.

Having repeated that prayer three times, he got up again and said to us:

Pray in this way. The Hearts of Jesus and Mary are attentive to the voice of your supplications.

And he disappeared.

One must note, that Francisco was witnessing the exchange between the Angel and Lucia, and although he could see perfectly well the apparition of the magnificent being of light, he couldn't hear him speak…

The Angel's Second Apparition

The second apparition of the Angel took place during the summer of 1916. While the children were playing near the well of Lucia's house, the Angel suddenly appeared and said:

"What are you doing?" he asked. "Pray, pray a great deal! The Holy Hearts of Jesus and Mary have designs of mercy on you. Offer unceasingly prayers, and sacrifice yourselves to the Most High."

Lucia asked the Angel how they were to make sacrifices. The Angel replied,

Make of everything you can a sacrifice, and offer it to God as an act of reparation for the sins by which He is offended, and in supplication for the conversion of sinners. In this way, you will draw peace upon your country. I am its Guardian Angel, the Angel of Portugal. Above all, accept and bear with submission the sufferings which the Lord will send you.

Lucia commented:

Those words of the Angel engraved themselves in our spirit, as a light which made us understand Who God is, how much He loves us and wants to be loved by us, the value of sacrifice and how pleasing it is to Him, and that out of respect for it, God converts sinners. The dominant theme in this second apparition of the Angel was the importance of making offerings to God through every possible action and sacrifice, even the smallest ones, and of making offerings with special intentions, especially for the conversion of sinners.

The Angel's Third Apparition

The angel's third apparition took place in autumn at Cabeço. When the children took their sheep to the same place the angel's first appeared to them (Cabeço), the children began to recite the prayer the angel had taught them. Shortly thereafter, an unknown light appeared above them.

Lucia:

We got up again to see what was happening, and we saw the Angel again, who had in his left hand a Chalice which he left suspended in the air with a Host right above from which some drops of Blood fell into the Chalice...
The Angel prostrated himself down to the earth near the children and repeated the following prayer three times:

Most Holy Trinity-Father, Son, and Holy Spirt-I adore thee profoundly. I offer thee the most precious Body, Blood, Soul and Divinity of Jesus Christ, present in all the tabernacles in the world, in reparation for all the outrages, sacrileges and indifferences whereby he is offended. And through the infinite merits of His Most Sacred Heart and the Immaculate Heart of Mary, I beg of Thee the conversion of poor sinners.

Then, getting up, the Angel took the Chalice and the Host. He gave Lucia the Sacred Host on the tongue. Then while giving the Precious Blood from the Chalice to Francisco and Jacinta, he said:

Eat and drink the Body and Blood of Jesus Christ, horribly outraged by ungrateful men. Make reparation for their crimes and console your God.

Then, prostrating himself on the ground, he repeated with the children three times the same prayer: Most Holy Trinity, etc., and disappeared...

The Apparitions of the Blessed Virgin Mary in Fatima

(13 May 1917) – First Apparition of Our Lady of the Rosary

On 13 May 1917, Lucia, Jacinta, and Francisco took their flock of sheep to a natural hollow in the ground known as the Cova da Iria to graze, about a mile from their homes. Then suddenly a bright shaft of light pierced the air. The little shepherds started to gather the sheep thinking a storm was brewing in the distance although the day was pleasant and showed no sign of bad weather, when suddenly, a second flash caused them alarm. Panicked and fearful, they took a few steps and looked towards the right. There, standing over the foliage of a small holmoak, stood a Lady of dazzling light.

Lucia Dos Santos:

A lady dressed all in white, more brilliant than the sun, shedding rays of light, clear and stronger than a crystal glass filled with the most sparkling water, pierced by the burning rays of the sun.

The lady spoke to them and said:

- **Fear not! I will not harm you.**
- *Where are you from?* Lucia asked.

Francisco was noticing the exchange between the Blessed Virgin Mary and Lucia, but, as with the Angel of Portugal, he couldn't hear anything... Jacinta was mesmerized by the sight of the Lady in white and unlike her brother, could hear her perfectly well...

- **I am from Heaven** the beautiful lady replied, gently raising her hand towards the distant horizon.
- *What do you want of me?* Lucia asked.
- **I came to ask you to come here for six consecutive months, on the thirteenth day, at this same hour. I will tell you later who I am and what I wish. And I shall return here again a seventh time.**
- Lucia said: *Do you come from Heaven... and will I go to Heaven?*
- **Yes, you will go.**
- *And Jacinta?*
- **As well.**

- *And Francisco?*
- **He as well, but he will have to say many rosaries.**

In the end Our Lady asked:

- **Do you wish to offer yourselves to God, to endure all the suffering that He may send you, as an act of reparation for the sins by which He is offended, and to ask for the conversion of sinners?**
- *Yes, we do*, said Lucia and Jacinta.
- **You will have to suffer a great deal, but the grace of God will be your comfort.**

Then the Blessed Virgin Mary opened her hands with a loving gesture of a mother who offers her heart. From it an intense light departed that seemed to go through them. The children, driven by inspiration, prayed inwardly:

- *O Most Holy Trinity, I adore Thee! My God, my God, I love Thee in the Most Blessed Sacraments.*

The vision of the Blessed Virgin Mary then rose towards the east, and as she was disappearing into the distance, she told them:

- **Recite the rosary every day to obtain the peace for the world and the end of the war.**

Lucia echoed the message to Francisco who, remarkably, was not bitter at his inability to hear the beautiful Lady in White. Lucia, however, warned her two cousins to say nothing of what they had seen out of fear of disbelief, but little Jacinta was too excited, and predictably, as any little girl would, told her parents about the apparition of the lady dressed in white. Naturally, the general reaction was one of disbelief... Lucia's mother was convinced that her child was lying and punished her quite severely when she refused to deny her story. Other children laughed and spat at them. Their sufferings began...

(13 June 1917) – Second Apparition of Our Lady of the Rosary

On 13 June 1917, accompanied by about 50 people to Cova da Iria, the three little shepherds were reciting the rosary, when lightning was suddenly seen and immediately thereafter, the Lady on the holmoak appeared like the previous month.

- *What do you want from me?* asked Lucy.
- **I wish you to come here the 13[th]of next month; that you say the Rosary every day, and that you learn how to read. In succeeding months I shall tell you what else I want.**

- *I would like to ask you to bring us to Heaven*, said Lucy.
- **Yes… I shall take Jacinta and Francisco soon, but you will remain here for some time yet. Jesus wishes to use you in order to make me known and loved. He wishes to establish the devotion to my Immaculate Heart in the world. I promise salvation to those who embrace it; and these souls will be beloved by God like flowers arranged by me to adorn His throne.**
- Lucy asked: *Will I stay here alone?*
- **Don't be discouraged. I shall never abandon you. My Immaculate Heart will be your refuge and, through it, will conduct you to God.**

Then the Blessed Virgin Mary opened her hands and emanated her light on the children. Jacinta and Francisco seemed to be in the part of the light that went up towards the sky while Lucy in the light that spread on the earth. In front of the palm of the right hand of Our Lady was a heart surrounded by thorns that impaled it. They understood that it was the Immaculate Heart of Mary wounded by the sins of men. The Blessed Virgin Mary then asked for reparation.

When this vision ceased, the Mother of God, still surrounded by light, rose from the little tree and glided toward the east until she disappeared completely… Several persons who were closer to the actual apparition site noticed that the buds at the top of the holmoak where the Blessed Virgin Mary stood upon were bent in the same direction, as if they had been drawn by the Lady's clothes. They returned to their usual position only some hours later.

(13 July 1917) – Third Apparition of Our Lady of the Rosary

On the appointed day, an evidently growing crowd was assembled at Cova da Iria, and as the little visionaries arrived to pray the rosary, Mr. Marto, Jacinta's and Francisco's father, noticed that when the apparition began, a small grayish cloud hovered over the holmoak; the sunlight diminished, and a cool breeze blew over the mountain range, despite it being the height of summer. Mr. Marto likewise heard something curious, like flies inside an empty jug. The seers saw the customary glare, and then the Blessed Virgin Mary appeared in her customary fashion over the holmoak. Lucy addressed her:

- *What do you want from me?*

The Blessed Virgin Mary answered:

- **That you come on the 13th of next month; that you continue to recite the Rosary every day to our Lady of the Rosary in order to obtain peace in the world, and the end of the war, because only She will be able to aid you.**
- Lucy said: *I want to ask you to tell us who you are, and to make a miracle for the crowd to believe that you appear.*

- Continue to come here. In October I will tell you who I am, that which I want, and I shall do a miracle that all can see and believe.

Lucia then made a number of requests for conversions, cures, and other graces. Our Lady recommended the constant recitation of the rosary; thus they would obtain those graces during the year. The Blessed Virgin Mary carried on:

- Sacrifice yourselves for sinners, and say often this prayer, especially during any sacrifice:

"O my Jesus, I offer this for love of Thee, for the conversion of poor sinners, and in reparation for all the sins committed against the Immaculate Heart of Mary."

As she spoke these words, our lady stretched out her hands, and bright rays came forth which seemed to penetrate into the earth. All at once the ground vanished, and the three children saw Hell! Frightened, they lifted their eyes to the Blessed Virgin Mary who told them:

- You have seen hell where souls of poor sinners go. To save them, God wishes to establish in the world devotion to my Immaculate Heart. If what I say to you is done, many souls will be saved and there will be peace.
  The war is going to end; but if people do not cease in offending God, a worse one will break out during the pontificate of Pius XI. When you see a night illuminated by an unknown light, know that this is the great sign given you by God that He is about to punish the world for its crimes, by means of war, famine, and persecutions of the Church and of the Holy Father.
  I shall come to ask for the consecration of Russia to my Immaculate Heart, and the Communion of Reparation on the First Saturdays. (Brief pause…)
  If my requests are granted, Russia will be converted and there will be peace. If not, she will scatter her errors throughout the world, provoking wars and persecution of the Church. The good will be martyred, the Holy Father will have much to suffer, and various nations will be destroyed… But in the end, my Immaculate Heart will triumph. The Holy Father will consecrate Russia to me, Russia will be converted, and a certain period of peace will be granted to the world.
  (Brief pause…)
  Do you want to learn a prayer?
- "Yes we do!" the children responded.
- When you recite the Rosary, say at the end of each decade:
"O My Jesus, forgive us our sins, save us from the fires of hell, and lead all souls to Heaven, especially those in most need of Your Mercy."

Then, the Blessed Virgin Mary showed the children the vision of the third Secret, followed by an explanation and final prophecy (see page: 283)...

Lucia wrote:

Our Lady showed us a great sea of fire which seemed to be under the earth. Plunged in this fire were demons and souls in human form, like transparent burning embers, all blackened or burnished bronze, floating about in the conflagration, now raised into the air by the flames that crossed-through from within themselves together with great clouds of smoke, now falling back on every side like sparks in a huge fire, without weight or equilibrium, and amid shrieks and groans of pain and despair which horrified us and made us tremble with fear.

The demons could be distinguished by their terrifying and repulsive likeness to frightful and unknown animals, all black and transparent. This vision lasted but an instant. How can we ever be grateful enough to our kind heavenly Mother, who had already prepared us by promising, in the first Apparition, to take us to Heaven. Otherwise, I think we would have died of fear and terror.

(19 August 1917) – Fourth Apparition of Our Lady of the Rosary

On 13 August, the children had been abducted by the mayor of Vila Nova de Ourém, who attempted to force from them the secret revealed in the apparition of 13 July; hence, the three little shepherds were forcefully prevented by the civil authorities to go to the meeting of 13 August where now had gathered an immense crowd that was waiting for the next apparition of the Blessed Virgin Mary.

At Cova da Iria, thunder, followed by lightning, was heard at the usual time. The spectators, not knowing anything of the little visionaries being kidnapped, noticed a small white cloud that hovered over the holmoak for a few minutes... Phenomena of coloration were observed on the people's faces, their clothing, the trees, and the ground. Our Lady had certainly come, but she had not found her little messengers...

Lucia, Jacinta and Francisco were confined for two days, and threatened with many torments to make them deny their lady, but they did not falter; they were ready to offer their lives not to betray the promises made to the Lady dressed in white. When, at last, they had been released on August 19th, at about four o'clock in the afternoon, Lucia was with Francisco and another cousin at Valinhos, a property belonging to one of her uncles, when the atmospheric changes that preceded the apparitions of Our Lady at Cova da Iria began to occur.

Feeling that something supernatural was approaching and enveloping them, Lucia sent for Jacinta, who arrived in time to see Our Lady appear—heralded as before by a bright light—over a holmoak slightly larger than the one at Cova da Iria:

- *What do you want from me?* Lucy asked.
- **I want you to continue to go to the Cova da Iria on the 13th; that you continue to say the Rosary every day. I, in the last month will make the miracle so that all will believe.**

Then with a sadder appearance, our Lady of Fatima told them:

- **If they had not taken you to Ourém, the miracle would have been even greater.**
- *What does Your Grace want done with the money that the people leave at Cova da Iria?*
- **Have two portable stands made. You and Jacinta with two other girls dressed in white carry one of them, and let Francisco carry the other one with three other boys. The portable stands are for the feast of Our Lady of the Rosary. The money that is left over should be contributed to the chapel that they will build.**
- *I would like to ask you for the healing of some sick persons.*
- **Yes, I will cure some during the year.**

Becoming sadder, she recommended anew the practice of mortification, saying lastly:

- **Pray, pray a lot and offer sacrifices for sinners. You know that many souls go the hell because there is none who pray for them.**

At the end of her apparition, the Blessed Virgin Mary began to rise toward the east. The three little visionaries cut boughs off the tree over which Our Lady had appeared to them, and took them home. The boughs gave off a uniquely sweet fragrance.

(13 September 1917) – Fifth Apparition of Our Lady of the Rosary

A crowd estimated to 30,000 people accompanied Lucia, Jacinta and Francisco to the Cova da Iria to recite the Rosary. Once arrived, thousands observed atmospheric phenomena similar to those of the previous apparitions: the sudden cooling of the air, a dimming of the sun to the point where the stars could be seen, and a rain resembling iridescent petals or snowflakes that disappeared before touching the ground. This time, a luminous globe was noticed which moved slowly and majestically through the sky from east to west and, at the end of the apparition, in the opposite direction. The little visionaries saw a light, and, immediately thereafter, they saw Our Lady over the holmoak:

- **I want you to come here on October 13, and you to continue to recite the Rosary to obtain the end of the war. In October, the Lord, the** sorrowful Lady, the Lady of Mt. Carmel, and St. Joseph with the child Jesus will also come to bless the world.

- **God is glad of your sacrifices, He does not want you to sleep with the chord to the sides. Use it only during the day.** (The children were wearing ropes around their waists as a sacrifice for sinners.)
- *They have requested me to ask you for many things, for the cure of some sick persons, of a deaf-mute.*
- **Yes, I will cure some, others not. In October, I will perform a miracle for all to believe.**

And rising towards the east, she disappeared in the same manner as before...

(13 October 1917) – Sixth Apparition of Our Lady of the Rosary

On 13 October 1917, the three little shepherds of Fatima came with their parents surrounded by a crowd of 70.000 persons under a torrential rain. As the children made their way to the apparition site with their parents, the crowd was beginning to lose its temper as the weather was turning dreadfully and the mud-creating rain was becoming more and more overwhelming. The children knelt and began to pray... Shortly thereafter, the Blessed Virgin Mary appeared.

Lucy asked:

- *What do you want from me?*
- **I wish to tell you that I want a chapel built here in my honor. I am the Lady of the Rosary. Continue to pray the rosary every day. The war is going to end, and the soldiers will soon return to their homes.**
- *May I ask you for cures and conversions? Will you grant them?*
- **Some yes, others no. It is necessary that they ask pardon for their sins, that they don't offend God our Lord. He is already too much offended.**

  Do you want anything else from me?
- *I do not want anything more.*

Then Our Lady of the Rosary opened her hands and dispatched a ray of light in the direction of the sun as Lucy shouted to look at the sun while pointing at it! At that moment, the promised sign took place: the rain stopped suddenly, and there appeared an exceptionally bright sun; however, people were able to stare directly at it without effort or without harming their eyes. Then... the impossible occurred!

The sun began to turn on itself as if projecting in each direction bands of light of each color that lit the surrounding clouds, the sky, the trees, and the crowd itself. Faces turned blue, red, green, yellow... It was extraordinary! Then, the unthinkable: The sun suddenly grew in size, in heat and in luminosity, and seemed for a moment to plunge towards the earth! At this apocalyptic sight, men and women began to run in every direction screaming in sheer terror! Others knelt crying and beating their chest while others, on their knees continued to pray asking for mercy. The plunging sun then stopped, stayed still for a moment and then ever so slowly went back to its normal position.

Meanwhile, once Our Lady had disappeared in the expanse of the firmament, three scenes followed one another in succession before Lucia, Jacinta and Francisco, portraying first the joyful mysteries of the rosary, then to Lucia alone, the sorrowful mysteries, and, finally, the glorious mysteries. Francisco and Jacinta witnessed only the joyful mysteries.

The First scene: Saint Joseph appeared beside the sun with the Child Jesus and Our Lady of the Rosary. It was the Holy Family. The Blessed Virgin Mary was dressed in white with a blue mantle. Saint Joseph was also dressed in white, and the Child Jesus in light red. Saint Joseph blessed the crowd, making the Sign of the Cross three times. The Child Jesus did the same.

The Second scene: A vision of Our Lady of Sorrows, without the sword in her breast, and of Our Lord overwhelmed with sorrow on the way to Calvary. Our Lord made the Sign of the Cross to bless the people. Lucia could only see the upper part of Our Lord's body.

The Third Scene: Finally, Our Lady of Mount Carmel, crowned queen of Heaven and earth, appeared in a glorious vision holding the Child Jesus near her heart.

In the meantime, after the sun returned to its normal position, the 70,000 people present then became aware that their clothes that were drenched a few minutes earlier had now become completely dry, and the ground that was terribly muddy showed now no evidence of humidity; what's more, many blind, sick and handicapped present at the apparition site became miraculously and instantaneously cured...

Days passed and already the entire country of Portugal was relating the extraordinary miracle of Fatima. All the newspapers of the country, mostly Socialist and profoundly anti-Catholic, were spreading the news of what they familiarly referred to as: "The Miracle of the Sun". One of the principal anti-clerical publications of the day, **O Dia**, a major Lisbon newspaper published on 17 October 1917 the following article:

English translation:

At one o'clock in the afternoon, midday by the sun, the rain stopped. The sky, pearly gray in color, illuminated the vast arid landscape with a strange light. The sun had a transparent gauzy veil so that eyes could easily be fixed upon it. The gray mother-of-pearl tone turned into a sheet of silver which broke up as the clouds were torn apart and the silver sun, enveloped in the same gauzy gray light, was seen to whirl and turn in the circle of broken clouds.

A cry went up from every mouth and people fell on their knees on the muddy ground. The light turned a beautiful blue as if it had come through the stained-glass windows of a cathedral and spread itself over the people who knelt with outstretched hands. The blue faded slowly and then the light seemed to pass through yellow glass. Yellow stains fell against white handkerchiefs, against the dark skirts of women. They were reported on the trees, on the stones and on the serra. People wept and prayed with uncovered heads in the presence of the miracle they had awaited.

(**O Dia**'s front cover article, 17 October 1917)

Multitude of pictures were published throughout the country along with the open admission of the media which, up to now had always been aggressively anti-Catholic. Then, very quickly, from Portugal, the foreign press took the relay of the news, pictures and events that have taken place in Fatima since May of the same year... The Catholic Church had no recourse but to set a formal investigation; however, from 1917 to 1920 the Church's position regarding the Fatima apparitions was one of prudent reserve and silence.

As is the practice of the Church in similar circumstances, she refrained from passing judgment on the event until a thorough investigation was conducted. At the time of the apparitions, the Portuguese clergy was reluctant to encourage belief in the apparitions of the Blessed Virgin Mary in Fatima. It acted as such in a large measure because of the recent persecutions suffered by priests and religious in Portugal at the hands of the anti-Catholic Socio-Masonic government.

Hence, in such hostile environment, the Portuguese clergy did not want to take any steps that would provoke a retaliation... Although President Sidonio Pais had struck down many of the country's anti-Catholic laws by 1918, which in turn led to his murder organized by Masonic lodges in late 1918, the Portuguese clergy was fearful to take actions that would incite their return to power.

The apparitions of Our Lady at Fatima indeed provoked strong opposition from many sides: from the local government, as illustrated by the August 1917 kidnapping of the three children by the village Administrator, and, years later, by the Freemasons destroying the Capelinha (in Cova da Iria) that took place in March 1922[19]. Even from the press, which was controlled by the Freemasons and which scorned the apparitions until witnessing the October 1917 Miracle of the Sun, turned once again against the apparitions and the young seers.

Thus, from every quarter that fostered disdain and hatred towards God and His Church, strong opposition was exhibited and enforced. Nevertheless, in spite of silence and discouragement on the part of the Catholic Church, and the patent scorn and open enmity of the secular realms, the Portuguese people maintained their belief and their support of the Fatima apparitions. Even after the cycle of apparitions ended, while awaiting official ecclesiastical approval, the Portuguese

---

[19] (On 6 March 1922, freemason terrorists put five powerful bombs inside the inbuilt Fátima chapel at Cova da Iria which blew up the hole in the ground thereby enlarging it. In December 1922, reconstruction of the chapel was restarted.)

faithful, joined more and more by a growing number of foreign pilgrims from across the world, continued to visit the sacred place where Our Lady of the Rosary had appeared and delivered her message and her call.

The Virgin Mary's First Prophecy Fulfilled:

Francisco died on 4 April 1919 and little Jacinta died on 20 February 1920. Before she died, the little girl revealed a little-known but quite remarkable revelation made by Our Lady:

More souls go to hell because of sins of the flesh than for any other reason. Certain fashions will be introduced that will very much offend Our Lord. Many marriages are not good; they do not please Our Lord and are not of God. Priests must be pure, very pure. They should not busy themselves with anything except what concerns the Church and souls. The disobedience of priests to their superiors and to the Holy Father is very displeasing to Our Lord. The Blessed Mother can no longer restrain the hand of her Divine Son from striking the world with a just punishment for its many crimes.
(Brief pause...)
Tell everybody that God gives graces through the Immaculate Heart of Mary. Tell them to ask graces from her, and that the Heart of Jesus wishes to be venerated together with the Immaculate Heart of Mary.

The devotion and practice of the first Saturday of five consecutive months:

Lucia moved to Porto in 1921, and was admitted at the age of 14 as a boarder in the school of the Sisters of St. Dorothy in Vilar, on the city's outskirts. On 24 October 1925, she entered the Institute of the Sisters of St. Dorothy as a postulant in the convent in Tui, Pontevedra, Spain, just across the northern Portuguese border. Less than two months later, on 10 December 1925, sister Lucia received an apparition of the Child Jesus and of the Blessed Virgin Mary in her convent cell. The Blessed Mother was holding her child on one hand, and showed her a Heart surrounded by thorns on the other while saying to her:

Have compassion on the Heart of your Most Holy Mother, covered with thorns, with which ungrateful men pierce at every moment, and for which there is no one to make an act of Reparation so as to remove them.
See, My daughter, My heart surrounded by thorns which ungrateful men pierce at every moment by their blasphemies and ingratitude... You at least try to console me.
Say to all in my name that those who:

- **for five months, on the first Saturday, confess**
- **receive Holy Communion**
- **recite the Rosary**
- **and keep Me company for 15 minutes while meditating on the fifteen mysteries of the Rosary, in a spirit of reparation**

I promise to assist at the hour of death with all the graces necessary for the salvation of their souls.

(10 December 1925)

In a letter to her godmother, Sister Lucia explained in greater detail this devotion:

I don't know if you already know about the reparatory devotion of the five Saturdays to the Immaculate Heart of Mary. As it is still recent, I would like to inspire you to practice it, because it is requested by our dear Heavenly Mother; and Jesus has manifested a desire that it be practiced. Likewise, it seems to me that you would be fortunate, dear godmother, not only to know it and to give Jesus the consolation of practicing it, but also to make it known and embraced by many other people.

It consists of this: **During five months on the first Saturday, to receive Jesus in Communion, recite a Rosary, keep Our Lady company for fifteen minutes while meditating on the mysteries of the Rosary, and make a confession. The confession can be made a few days earlier, and if in this previous confession you have forgotten the (required) intention the following intention can be offered, provided that on the first Saturday one receives Holy Communion in a state of grace, with the intention of repairing for offenses against the Most Holy Virgin and which afflict Her Immaculate Heart.**

It seems to me, my dear godmother, that we are fortunate to be able to give Our dear Heavenly Mother this proof of love, for we know that she desires it to be offered to her. As for myself, I avow that I am never as happy as when first Saturday arrives. Isn't it true that our greatest happiness is to belong entirely to Jesus and Mary and to love Them and Them alone, without reserve? We see this so clearly in the lives of the saints.

They were happy because they loved, and we, my dear godmother, we must seek to love as they did, not only to enjoy Jesus, which is the least important—because if we do not enjoy Him here below, we will enjoy Him up above—but to give Jesus and Mary the consolation for being loved... and that in exchange for this love they might be able to save many souls.

(Letter Lucia Dos Santos to her Godmother, Doña Maria de Miranda, 1 November 1927)

Lucia Dos Santos' Memoirs:

Pontevedra, Spain: On the 15 (of February 1926), I was very busy at my work, and was not thinking of the devotion at all. I went to throw out a pan full of rubbish beyond the vegetable garden, in the same place where, some months earlier, I had met a child. I had asked him if he knew the Hail Mary, and he said he did, whereupon I requested him to say it so that I could hear him. But, as he made no attempt to say it by himself, I said it with him three times over, at the end of which I asked him to say it alone.

But as he remained silent and was unable to say the Hail Mary alone, I asked him if he knew where the Church of Santa Maria was, to which he replied that he did. I told him to go there every day and to say this prayer: **O, my heavenly Mother, give me your Child Jesus!** *I taught him this, and then left him... Going there as usual, I found a child who seemed to me to be the same one whom I had previously met, so I questioned him:*

- *Did you ask our heavenly Mother for the Child Jesus?*

The child turned to me and said:

- **And have you spread through the world what our heavenly Mother requested of you?**

With that, He was transformed into a resplendent Child. Knowing then that it was Jesus, I said:

- *My Jesus, you know very well what my confessor said to me in the letter I read to You. He told me that it was necessary for this vision to be repeated, for further happening to prove its credibility, and he added that Mother Superior, on her own, could do nothing to propagate this devotion.*
- **It is true your Superior alone can do nothing, but with My Grace she can do all. It is enough that your confessor gives you permission and that your Superior speaks of it, for it to be believed, even without people knowing to whom it has been revealed.**

Jesus further shared:

- **It is true, my daughter, that many souls begin the First Saturdays, but few finish them, and those who do complete them do so in order to receive the graces that are promised thereby. It would please me more if they did five with fervor and wish the intention of making reparation to the Heart of your heavenly Mother, than if they did fifteen in a tepid and indifferent manner.**

(15 February 1926, page: 197. Lucia's Memoirs)

Fr. Apostoli shares in his book **The Gift of God** the humor of Jesus:

Young Sister Lucia did not recognize the Christ Child when she first saw him. Furthermore, when she tried to get Him to say the Hail Mary on His own, He would not do it because the Son of God does not pray to His mother; His mother prays to Him...

Lucia professed her first vows on 3 October 1928, and her perpetual vows six years later on 3 October 1934, receiving the name "Sister María das Dores"

(Mary of the Sorrows). She returned to Portugal in 1946 (where she visited Fatima incognito).

Apparition to Lucia Dos Santos on 13 June 1929

On the third apparition of the Blessed Virgin Mary, on 13 July 1917, the Lady in white told her three little messengers: **"I shall come to ask for the consecration of Russia"**. She repeated her request on 13 June 1929, when She appeared to Lucia in the Chapel of Dorotheas, in the town of Tuy. Lucia remembering this apparition, later wrote:

I had sought and obtained permission from my superiors and confessor to make a Holy Hour from eleven o'clock until midnight, every Thursday to Friday night. Being alone one night, I knelt near the altar rails in the middle of the chapel and, prostrated, I prayed the prayers of the Angel. Feeling tired, I then stood up and continued to say the prayers with my arms in the form of a cross. The only light was that of the sanctuary lamp.

Suddenly, the whole chapel was illuminated by a supernatural light, and above the altar appeared a cross of light, reaching to the ceiling. In a brighter light on the upper part of the cross, could be seen the face of a man and his body as far as the waist; upon his breast was a dove of light; nailed to the cross was the body of another man. A little below the waist, I could see a chalice and a large host suspended in the air, on to which drops of blood were falling from the face of Jesus Crucified and from the wound in His side.

*These drops ran down on to the host and fell into the chalice. Beneath the right arm of the cross was Our Lady and in her hand was her Immaculate Heart. (it was Our Lady of Fatima, with her Immaculate Heart in her left hand, without sword or roses, but with a crown of thorns and flames). Under the left arm of the cross, large letters,—as if of crystal-clear water which ran down upon the altar, formed these words: "**Grace and Mercy**". I understood that it was the Mystery of the Most Holy Trinity which was shown to me, and I received lights about this mystery which I am not permitted to reveal. Our Lady then said to me:*

The moment has come in which God asks the Holy Father, in union with all the Bishops of the world, to make the consecration of Russia to my Immaculate Heart, promising to save it by this means. There are so many souls whom the justice of God condemns for sins committed against me, that I have come to ask reparation: sacrifice yourself for this intention and pray.

On 29 May 1930, when she was in Tuy, Our Lord revealed to Sister Lucia the reason for His requesting the Devotion of the first 5 Saturdays of the month:

The reason for the five Saturdays of the month is simple, it is because there are five types of offenses and blasphemies against the Immaculate Heart of Mary:

1. **Blasphemies against Her Immaculate Conception**
2. **Blasphemies against Her Perpetual Virginity**
3. **Blasphemies against Her Divine Maternity, in refusing at the same time to recognize Her as the Mother of men**
4. **The blasphemies of those who publicly seek to sow in the hearts of children indifference or scorn, or even hatred of this Immaculate Mother**
5. **The offenses of those who outrage Her directly in Her holy images**

(Our Lord Jesus-Christ to Sister Lucia, 29 May 1930, Tuy)

The Church Finally Approves the Apparitions of Our Lady of Fatima

As the Catholic Church mounted a well-advised investigation on the visionaries, their lives, their families, their ritual, the countless testimonies of the "Miracle of the Sun, the messages of Fatima and their theological assertion with Church's Dogma, another aspect was put under most careful scrutiny... The three secrets the Blessed Mother had entrusted the three little shepherds...

In October of 1930 the Bishop of Leiria-Fatima finally announced, after 13 years of careful and methodical review, the results of the official canonical inquiry in a pastoral letter which stated:

In virtue of considerations made known, and others which for reason of brevity we omit; humbly invoking the Divine Spirit and placing ourselves under the protection of the most Holy Virgin, and after hearing the opinions of our Rev. Advisors in this diocese, we hereby:

> *1. Declare worthy of belief, the visions of the shepherd children in the Cova da Iria, parish of Fatima, in this diocese, from May 13, to October 13, 1917.*
> *2. Officially permit the cult of Our Lady of Fatima.*

On 13 May 1931, all of the Portuguese bishops consecrated Portugal to the Immaculate Heart of Mary, a consecration that they again renewed on 13 May 1938. As a consequence thereof, one of Sister Lucia's prophecies for Portugal would be fulfilled to the letter: "*No Portuguese soldier will take part in the hostilities, and no foreign army will ever occupy Portugal.*" While the whole of Europe will be subjected to a horrendous war that will last five atrocious years...

Two months later, in August 1931, Our Lord Jesus-Christ appeared to Lucia, and very softly told her:

You console Me a great deal by asking Me for the conversion of those poor nations (Russia, Spain and Portugal)... Make it known to My ministers, that if they are to follow the example of the King of France in delaying the execution of My request (reference here to King Louis XIV), **they will follow him into misfortune. Like the King of France, they will repent and will do as I have requested, but it will be very late: Russia will already have spread her errors throughout the world, causing wars and persecutions against the Church. The Holy Father will have much to suffer! But it will never be too late to have recourse to Jesus and Mary."**

(Our Lord Jesus-Christ to Sister Lucia, August 1931, Rianjo)

In May 1936, Sister Lucia, during another apparition of Our Lord, asked Him why did He not want to convert Russia without the Holy Father making the consecration? Our Lord Jesus-Christ replied:

Because I want my whole Church to acknowledge the Consecration as a triumph of the Immaculate Heart of Mary, so that it may extend its cult later, and put the Devotion to My Mother's Immaculate Heart beside the Devotion to My Sacred Heart.

Sister Lucia exclaimed:

- *But the Holy Father will never believe me, Lord, unless You, Yourself move him with a special inspiration!*
- **The Holy Father... Pray very much for the Holy Father. He will do the Consecration, but it will be very late! Nevertheless, the Immaculate Heart of Mary will save Russia which has been entrusted to her.**

(May 1936)

On 6 February 1939, Sister Lucia wrote a letter to Monsignor José da Silva asking him to convey to the Holy Father the following message; these are the principal lines of this letter:

In an intimate communication, Our Lord has informed me that the moment of grace He spoke to me about, in May 1938, was about to end. The war, with all the horrors it accompanies, will soon begin (...) The nations that will suffer the most are the ones which will attempt the end of the reign of God (...) He promises a special protection to Portugal due to the consecration the bishops made to the Immaculate of Mary. This country will suffer a little bit from the war which will end when the Justice of God will be appeased.

(Sister Lucia dos Santos, 6 February 1939)

In March of 1939, six months before the German invasion of Poland, Our Lord Jesus-Christ appeared once again to Lucia:

Ask that the devotion of the first Saturdays of the month in honor of the Immaculate Heart of Mary be recommended. The time is near when the rigor of My justice will punish the crime of many nations.

(Our Lord Jesus-Christ, March 1939, Tuy)

On 15 July 1940, Lucia wrote a letter to the newly elected Pontiff, Pius XII, learning that Father Gonçalves was able to communicate to the new Pope Heaven's request of consecrating Russia:

As to the consecration of Russia, it hasn't taken place in the month of May as his Reverence hoped it would. It must be done, but not right away. God has permitted it thus so as to punish the world of its crimes. We deserve it. Then, He will listen to our poor prayers. Notwithstanding, I have an immense sorrow that it hadn't been done... During that time so many souls will be lost! It is God nevertheless Who permits all this, but at the same time He shows such a great sorrow for not being listened to (...)

(Excerpt of Lucia dos Santos' letter to his Holiness Pius XII, 15 July 1940)

Similarly, Our Lord told Sister Lucia on 22 October 1940:

Pray for the Holy Father; sacrifice yourself so that his heart will not succumb to the bitterness that oppresses him. The persecutions will increase; I will punish the nations with wars and famine: the persecution against My church will weigh heavily upon my Vicar on Earth. His holiness will be able to shorten these times of tribulation if he fulfills My desire of consecrating the whole world, with a special mention of Russia, to the Immaculate Heart of Mary.

(Our Lord Jesus-Christ, 22 October 1940)

Pope Pius XII, on 31 October 1942, consecrated the world to the Immaculate Heart of Mary, but without mentioning Russia in particular, as Our Lord had requested. Sister Lucia commented:

Our Lord has accepted the consecration of the world of October 1942 to the Immaculate Heart of Mary, and promises to put a rapid end to the war. Furthermore, as the consecration was not done fully as He requested, the conversion of Russia will not take place for now...

In May 1943, Our Lord once again appeared to Lucia in Tuy, and told her:

I desire most ardently the propagation of the cult of the devotion to the Immaculate Heart of Mary, because the love of this Heart attracts souls to Me; it is the center from which the rays of My light and My love go through all the earth, and the unquenchable fountain from which the living water of My mercy flows into the earth.

(Our Lord Jesus-Christ, May 1943, Tuy)

Note: Pope Pius XII did not make the consecration which Our Lady had asked Lucia to make known. Pius XII did not consecrate Russia in the form required by Our Lady of Fatima, but consecrated the whole world to the Immaculate Heart of Mary. Pope Pius XII did something similar in 1942, and later consecrated the Russian people in 1952.

Sister Lucy was living at that time in the convent of the Dorothean Sisters of Tuy, in Spain. In June 1943, she suddenly fell gravely ill... Her condition was so alarming that Bishop da Silva, the Bishop of Leiria, became worried and feared that she would die before having revealed the Third Secret of Our Lady, and sensed that it would be the loss of an exceptional grace for the Church. Canon Galamba, the friend and advisor of the Bishop, suggested to him an extremely judicious idea: asking Sister Lucia to write down the text of the Third Secret, place it in an envelope sealed with wax, to be kept in the dioceses for safekeeping.

On 15 September 1943, Bishop da Silva went, therefore, to Tuy and asked Sister Lucia to write down the Secret "if she really wanted to." But Lucia became concerned and was not feeling comfortable with such a vague order... Hence, she requested from her Bishop a formal written order. In mid-October 1943, Bishop da Silva made up his mind and wrote to Sister Lucy, giving her the express order that she had besought of him.

However, new difficulties would arise. Sister Lucy experienced for almost three months, a mysterious and terrible anguish... She has related that each time she sat down at her work-table and took her pen in order to write down the Secret, she found herself obstructed from doing so... Finally, on 2 January 1944, the Blessed Virgin Mary herself appeared again to Lucia, and confirmed to her that it was truly God's Will for her to write the third Secret as requested by bishop da Silva. As such, the Blessed Virgin Mary gave Lucia the permission and the strength to accomplish the task she had been commanded.

The extreme care that Sister Lucy took to transmit the third Secret to its recipient, Bishop da Silva, was a new proof of the exceptional importance which she attributed to these documents, for indeed there were two letters, each placed in a different envelope. She did not wish to entrust them to anyone but only to a Bishop. It was Bishop Ferreira, Archbishop of Gurza, who received from the hands of Sister Lucy, the two envelopes which were sealed with a wax seal containing the precious letters. Bishop Ferreira, in turn, delivered them the same evening to Bishop da Silva.

The "Third Secret" was written by "order of His Excellency the Bishop of Leiria and the Most Holy Mother..." on 3 January 1944.

One envelope was the vision (*revealed in June 2000 by the Catholic Church*), and in the second one was inserted the accompanying message of the Blessed Virgin Mary.

Combined with the fact that this newly released text concerning the apparition of the Blessed Virgin to Sr. Lucia was published by the Carmel of Coimbra itself, there can be no doubt as to the authenticity of this vision. And there can similarly be no doubt that the content of this vision is directly related to the Third Secret itself. As such, it should be worth inspecting this newly published private revelation given to Sr. Lucia in some closer detail:

Towards 16:00 hours on 3 January 1944, in the convent's chapel, before the Tabernacle, Lucia asked Jesus to let her know His will:

I then feel that a friendly hand, affectionate and maternal, touches my shoulder. It was the Mother of Heaven who said:

Be at peace and write what they command you, but not that which you were given to understand about its meaning.

Right after, I felt my spirit flooded by a light-filled mystery which is God, and in Him I saw and heard: the point of the flame-like lance which detaches, touches the axis of the earth and it (the earth) shakes: mountains, cities, towns and villages with their inhabitants are buried. The sea, rivers and clouds leave their bounds, they overflow, flood and drag with them into a whirlpool, houses and people in a number unable to be counted; it is the purification of the world from the sin it is immersed in. Hatred, ambition cause destructive wars. Afterward I felt in the increased beating of my heart and in my spirit a quiet voice which said:

In time, one faith, one baptism, one Church, Holy, Catholic, Apostolic. Heaven in eternity!*' This word, 'Heaven,' filled my heart with peace and happiness, so much so that, almost without realizing it, I continued to repeat for some time: Heaven, Heaven!*

(Sister Lucia, 3 January 1944)

Meanwhile, the war in Europe ended in May 1945, but Japan was still fighting on… On August of 1945, a newsflash flooded all the radio wavelengths and newspapers alike across the world. Indeed, on 6 August 1945 an American B-29 bomber baptized "Enola Gay" dropped the first atomic bomb on the Japanese city of Hiroshima at 8:15am—half a mile from the Jesuit Church of Our Lady's Assumption where eight members of a Jesuit community prayed the rosary daily.

After the cataclysmic pulverization of the Japanese city, it was later known that neither Fr. Hubert Schiffer, the head of the religious community, nor the other Jesuit priests from the Church of Our Lady's Assumption suffered any radiation or ill-effects from the atomic bombing! On a follow-up interview, the good Jesuits stated:

We believe that we survived because we were living the message of Fatima.

Likewise, a few days later, the Franciscan Friary of Nagasaki, established by St. Maximillian Kolbe, was also unharmed after the atomic bombing of that second Japanese city which they attributed to special protection from the Blessed Mother, as the brothers, too, prayed the daily rosary. Like their brother-Jesuits in Hiroshima, they suffered no ill effects from the bomb's massive explosion nor from any radiation thereafter…

In March 1948, after receiving special papal permission to be relieved of her perpetual vows, Lucia entered the Carmelite convent of Santa Teresa in Coimbramade where she made her profession as a Discalced Carmelite on 31 May 1949, taking the religious name of: "Sister Maria Lucia of Jesus and the Immaculate Heart". Sr. Lucia entered the Carmelite convent of St. Teresa in Coimbra, having received special papal permission to leave the Dorothean Sisters, and become a Carmelite which she was for more than 50 years.

In 1950, Sister Lucia confirmed that the scapular is one of the conditions of the Fatima message. During the 13 October 1917 apparition, Our Lady appeared as Our Lady of Mt. Carmel. Sr. Lucia explained that….

… Our Lady wants us to wear the brown scapular as a sign of our consecration to the Immaculate Heart of Mary.

When Our Lady gave the brown scapular to St. Simon Stock in 1251, she told the good Englishman:

Receive my beloved son, this habit of thy order. This shall be to thee and to all Carmelites a privilege, that whosoever dies clothed in this shall never suffer eternal fire.

Pope Pius XII wrote:

For the holy scapular, which may be called the habit or garment of Mary, is a sign and pledge of the protection of the Mother of God. It is as if Mary is saying, "If you wear my habit, faithfully, I will see to it that you never see the fires of hell."

In May 1952, the Blessed Virgin Mary appeared to Sister Lucia and told her:

Make it known to the Holy Father that I continue to wait for the consecration of Russia to my Immaculate Heart. Without this consecration, Russia will not convert and the world will not enjoy peace.

(The Blessed Virgin Mary, May 1952)

This message was forwarded to Pope Pius XII one month later, and the holy Father issued and published in July 1952 the Apostolic Letter: **Sacro Vergente Anno**, consecrating Russia to the Immaculate Heart of Mary; however, this consecration did not meet with the Blessed Virgin Mary's prerequisites since the holy Pontiff did not make any allusion to the Devotion of the first five Saturdays of the month which was as well supposed to contribute to the conversion of Russia, but most of all Pius XII did not ask all the bishop of the world to unite themselves to him in a public act of reparation and consecration...

1957 – Father Fuentes' Interview

On 22 June 1959 the account of the 1957 interview between Father Augustin Fuentes and Sister Lucy—the last interview in which Sister Lucy was permitted to speak freely regarding the Third Secret—was published in the Portuguese daily newspaper **A Voz**.

This interview was published with the Imprimatur of the Bishop of Fatima. It was read widely and its authenticity has never been put into question:

Speaking to the sisters of Motherhouse of the Missionaries of the Sacred Heart in Mexico on 22 May 1958, Fr. Fuentes said:

I want to tell you the last conversation I had with her (Sister Lucy), which was on December 26 of last year. It was in the convent, where I found her very sad, pale and drawn.

He then proceeded to read Sister's Lucy's words to him at the 26 December 1957, interview:

Sister Lucia:

Padre, the Madonna is very displeased because they haven't paid any heed to her message of 1917. Neither the good nor the evil ones have paid heed to it. The good continue on forth with their path without worrying, and do not follow the Celestial norms; the evil ones go through the large path of perdition, not paying heed to the announced chastisements. Believe me, Father, the Lord God will very soon chastise the world. The chastisement will be material, and you can imagine, Padre, how many souls will fall into hell if we don't pray and do not do penance.

Padre, how much time before 1960 arrives? This is the cause of the Madonna's sadness. Father, tell this to everyone: the Madonna has told me so many times that a great deal of nations will disappear from the surface of the earth. Godless nations will be the scourge chosen by God to chastise humanity if we, through the means of prayer and the Holy Sacraments, do not obtain the grace of their conversion. I cannot give more details, because it is still a secret.

This is the part of the Message of Our Lady which will remain a secret until 1960. By the will of the Blessed Virgin, only the Holy Father and the Bishop of Fatima can know the secret. Both have chosen, however, not to open it in order not to be influenced by it. Tell them, Padre, that the devil is attacking through a decisive assault the Madonna, for what afflicts the Immaculate Heart of Mary and of Jesus, is the fall of religious and priestly souls... It will be very sad for everyone, Not one person will rejoice at all if beforehand... if the world does not pray and does not do penance.

Tell them, Padre, that the Blessed Virgin said repeatedly to my cousins Francisco and Jacinta, and to me as well that many nations will disappear from the face of the earth. She said that Russia will be the instrument of chastisement chosen by Heaven to punish the whole world if the conversion of that poor Nation is not obtained beforehand... Padre, that is why my mission is not to indicate to the world the material punishments which are certain to come if the world does not pray and do penance beforehand. No! my mission is to indicate to everyone the imminent danger we are in of losing our souls for all eternity if we remain obstinate in sin.

Padre, the Devil is fighting a decisive battle against the Virgin and, as you know. The devil knows what it is that most offends God and which in a short pace of time will gain for him the greatest number of souls; thus the devil does everything to overcome souls consecrated to God because in this way, the devil will succeed in leaving souls of the faithful abandoned by their leaders, thereby it will become easier for him to seize them. The devil knows that the religious and the priests, despising their high vocation, lead many souls to hell.

We can barely still retain Heaven's chastisement... We have at our disposal two means that are very efficient: prayer and sacrifice. The devil does everything to distract us and to take away from us the taste of prayer. We shall either save ourselves or damn ourselves. But, Padre it must be told to people that they must not remain hoping a recall to prayer and penance from the sovereign Pontiff nor from bishops nor from (parish) pastors nor from general superiors. It is high time for everyone, of his own personal initiative, to accomplish holy deeds (works) and reform his life according to the calls of the Blessed Virgin Mary.

The devil wants to grasp consecrated souls; he works to corrupt them to induce others to final impenitence; he uses all the tricks, suggesting lastly to adjourn religious life! It results therefrom the abandonment of interior life and coldness in the secular subjects in renouncing pleasures and of total self-giving to God. That which afflicts the Immaculate Heart of Mary and the Heart of Jesus is the fall of religious and priestly souls!

The devil knows that religious and priests who fall away from their beautiful vocation drag numerous souls to hell. The devil wishes to take possession of consecrated souls. He tries to corrupt them in order to lull to sleep the souls of lay people and thereby lead them to final impenitence.

Likewise, Padre, tell them that my cousins Francisco and Jacinta made sacrifices because they always saw the Blessed Virgin very sad in all her apparitions. She never smiled at us. This anguish that we saw in her, caused by offenses to God and the chastisements that threaten sinners, penetrated our souls. And being children, we did not know what measures to devise except to pray and make sacrifices...

Remind everyone, Padre, that two facts contributed to sanctify Jacinta and Francisco: the affliction of the Blessed Virgin Mary and the vision of hell. The Madonna finds herself in between two swords: on one hand she sees humanity obstinate and indifferent to the announced chastisements; and on the other she sees us trample the Holy Sacraments and despise the chastisement that approaches while remaining unbelieving, sensual and materialistic.

The Blessed Virgin Mary has expressly told us: "We are approaching the last days." She told me this three times. She affirmed that the devil has engaged the decisive struggle, that is to say the final (battle), where one of them will come out victor or vanquished. We are either with God or with the devil. The second time, she repeated to me that the last remedies given to the world are the holy Rosary and the Devotion to the Immaculate Heart of Mary.

The third time, she told me that the other means, being despised by men, she offered us with fear the last ancre of salvation: the Blessed Virgin in person, her numerous apparitions, her tears, the messages of the visionaries around every part of the world, and the Madonna tells us still that if we do not listen to her and continue to offend Heaven, we shall no longer be forgiven... This is urgent, Padre, that (people) realize this terrible reality. This must not frighten souls, but this is urgent because since the most holy Virgin has given a great efficiency to the holy Rosary, there is no material or spiritual, national or international problem that cannot be resolved with the holy Rosary and our sacrifices. Recited with love and devotion, it will console Mary, wiping away so many tears away from her Immaculate Heart.

In the plans of the Divine Providence, when God is going to chastise the world He always first exhausts all other remedies. When He sees that the world pays no attention whatsoever, then, as we say in our imperfect way of talking, with a certain fear He presents us the last means of salvation: His Blessed Mother.

If we despise and reject this last means, Heaven will no longer pardon us, because we will have committed a sin that the Gospel calls a sin against the Holy

Spirit. This sin consists in openly rejecting—with full knowledge and will—the salvation that is put in our hands.

Also, since Our Lord is a very good Son, He will not permit that we offend and despise His Blessed Mother. We have as obvious testimony the history of different centuries where Our Lord has shown us with terrible examples how He has always defended the honor of His Blessed Mother.

Padre, we should not wait for an appeal to the world from Rome on the part of the Holy Father to do penance. Nor should we wait for a call for penance to come from the Bishops in our Dioceses, nor from our Religious Congregations. No, Our Lord has often used these means, and the world has not paid heed. So, now each one of us must begin to reform himself spiritually. Each one has to save not only his own soul, but also all the souls that God has placed on his pathway. The devil does all in his power to distract us and to take away from us the love for prayer; we shall be saved together or we shall be damned together...

Finally, there is a devotion to the Immaculate Heart of Mary, our Most Holy Mother, holding her as the seat of mercy, goodness and pardon and the sure door to enter Heaven. This is the first part of the Message referring to Our Lady of Fatima, and the second part, which is briefer but no less important, refers to the Holy Father.

(26 December 1957)

Only after the death of Pope Pius XII on 9 October 1958 would the first objections be openly and publicly raised against the unrestricted interview of Sister Lucia.

On 2 July 1959, an *anonymous* report was published by the chancery office of Coimbra. It read as follows:

Father Augustin Fuentes, postulator of the cause of beatification for the seers of Fatima, Francisco and Jacinta, visited Sister Lucy at the Carmel of Coimbra and spoke to her exclusively about things concerning the process in question. But after returning to Mexico, his country—if we can believe an article in "A Voz" of last June 22, and a translation by M.C. Bragança published on July 1 by the same journal—this priest allowed himself to make sensational declarations of an apocalyptic, eschatological and prophetic character, which he declares that he heard from Sister Lucy's very lips.

Given the gravity of such statements, the chancery of Coimbra believed it its duty to order a rigorous investigation on the authenticity of such news whose persons, too avid for the extraordinary, have spread in Mexico, in the Unites States, in Spain, and finally in Portugal.

Mexico's Archbishop Manuel Pio Lopez defended Father Fuentes, arguing *"that he had preached nothing that would contradict the message of Fatima, nor had he attributed frightening prophecies to Sister Lucy."* The Archbishop of Guadalajara, Cardinal José Garibi y Rivera, also came to Fr. Fuentes' defense. Nevertheless, Fr. Fuentes was subsequently relieved of his position as postulator for Francisco and Jacinta's beatification causes...

In 1976, Father Alonso, the official Fatima archivist, would also defend Fr. Fuentes. After his appointment, Father Alonso had adopted the views contained in the Chancery's notice, and he had expressed them publicly. By 1976, however, after ten years of studying the Fatima archives and meeting with Sister Lucy, Father Alonso changed his position! In his 1976 work, **The Secret of Fatima: Fact and Legend**, he clearly attempted to rehabilitate Father Fuentes, stating that the texts of the famous interview...

... say nothing that Sister Lucy has not said in her numerous published writings.

He continued:

The genuine text... does not, in my opinion, contain anything that could give rise to the condemnatory notice issued from Coimbra. On the contrary, it contains a teaching most suited to edify the piety of Christians.

Considering the writings of Sister Lucia in the convent confirming the revelations she and her two little cousins received in 1917, and the interview done by Fr. Fuentes, the covered subjects co-relate perfectly; what's more, many have argued that the chancery office of Coimbra, receiving its instructions from the Vatican can hardly dispute any credibility on the subject matter due to the fact that the Holy See's ignoring the Blessed Virgin Mary's instructions to divulge publicly her third secret to the world no later than in 1960, is hardly in a position to point fingers at anyone trying to fulfill the request of the Blessed Virgin Mary...

The Third Secret of Fatima is sealed and Sister Lucy is ordered to silence...

Despite the fact that Our Lady specifically requested that the Third Secret of Fatima be revealed no later than 1960, the Vatican disappointed an expectant world by announcing on February 8, 1960 via a communiqué of the Portuguese news agency A.N.I. (at Rome), that the Third Secret would not be released and would most likely *remain, forever, under absolute seal*.

The first paragraph of the announcement read:

It has just been stated, in very reliable Vatican circles, to the representatives of United Press International, that it is most likely that the letter will never be opened, in which Sister Lucy wrote down the words which Our Lady confided as a secret to the three little shepherds in the Cova da Iria.

The Church's flagrant "disobedience" to the Blessed Virgin Mary's specific instructions, as Father Alonso observed, "*... made people feel a profound disenchantment and disappointment which did great harm to Our Lady of Fatima, both inside and outside Portugal.*"

In addition to the Vatican's refusal to reveal the Third Secret as requested by Our Lady, the year of 1960 also marked the formal Order to Silence of the last

Visionaries Lucia Dos Santos, Francisco, and Jacinta Marto (Fatima)

Lucia Dos Santos, Francisco and Jacinta Marto

70,000 witnesses of the dancing Sun of Fatima   The three little seers at Cova
Di Iria

Bishop da Silva asked in 1943 Sister Lucia to write down the third Secret of Fatima

Vision on the Third Secret of Fatima (Envelope #1)

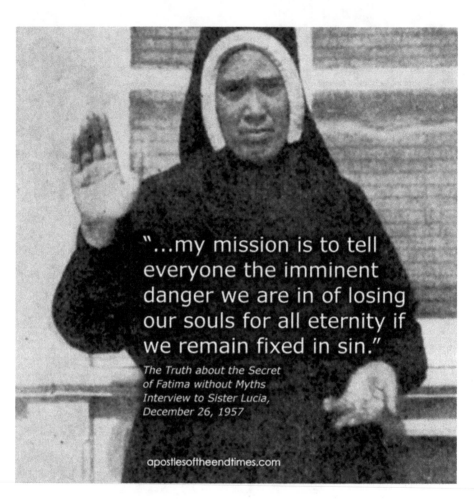

Picture of Sister Lucia dos Santo (1957)

surviving seer of Fatima... Indeed, as per instructions of the Holy See, it became increasingly difficult to see Sister Lucia, and for many years thereafter, none of her writings were published... She was forbidden not only to reveal the Secret but also to speak about the Third Secret at all. She could not receive, from 1960 on forward, any visitors except close relatives.

Even her confessor of many years, Father Aparicio, who had been in Brazil for over twenty years, was not permitted to see or speak to her when he visited Portugal... To that effect, Father Aparicio stated in a plaintive tone:

I have not been able to speak with Sister Lucy because the Archbishop could not give the permission to meet her. The conditions of isolation in which she finds herself have been imposed by the Holy See. Consequently, no one may speak with her without a license from Rome.

More than forty years later, Sister Lucy remained under the chains of silence. Only the Pope or the Dycasterium of the Doctrine of the Faith were able to grant the necessary permission for her to speak openly, or to be visited by any third party... Why such precautions to keep the Third Secret of Fatima underground and thus rebel against Heaven's mandates? If anything, many saw in these dejected attempts of secrecy a suspicious motive... Did the Third Secret of Fatima pointed out a schism within the Catholic Church? Were the religious, the Clergy and the Hierarchy put in cause as in the Blessed Virgin Mary's apparitions of La Salette, La Fraudais and Tilly?

As we have seen earlier, in 1966, his Holiness Pope Paul VI revised the Code of Canon Law, striking down canons 1399 and 2318 which prohibited and penalized the publication of any material concerning any apparitions without beforehand obtaining a bishop's imprimatur. After Pope Paul VI's revision, therefore, anyone in the Church was legally permitted to publish freely any message and/or prophetic warning coming from either an approved or still under investigation Marian apparition site. Yet the paradox lies in that Sister Lucy was forbidden to reveal the Third Secret of Fatima.

The Three Secrets of Fatima
The First Secret of Fatima

The First Secret of Fatima involves the physical reality of hell:

Our Lady showed us a great sea of fire which seemed to be under the earth. Plunged in this fire were demons and souls in human form, like transparent burning embers, all blackened or burnished bronze, floating about in the conflagration, now raised into the air by the flames that issued from within themselves together with great clouds of smoke, now falling back on every side like sparks in a huge fire, without weight or equilibrium, and amid shrieks and groans of pain and despair, which horrified us and made us tremble with fear. The demons could be distinguished by their terrifying and repulsive likeness to frightful and unknown animals, all black and transparent.

This vision lasted but an instant. How can we ever be grateful enough to our kind heavenly Mother, who had already prepared us by promising, in the first Apparition, to take us to Heaven. Otherwise, I think we would have died of fear and terror.

The Second Secret of Fatima

As devastating as it was for the three little shepherds to see the vision of hell, they now had absolutely no doubt about its reality. This certainty and every horrifying detail they witnessed would help them greatly with their devotion in their prayers for sinners. After seeing the vision, the little shepherds did not want anyone to have to go to hell! In fact, little Jacinta would often cry out:

Oh, hell! Hell! How sorry I am for the souls who go to hell! And the people down there, burning alive, like wood in the fire!

The children remained kneeling with profound terror and sadness now looking at the Blessed Virgin Mary after having seen the vision of hell; the Lady then said to them:

You have seen hell where souls of poor sinners go. To save them, God wishes to establish in the world devotion to my Immaculate Heart. If what I say to you is done, many souls will be saved and there will be peace.

The war is going to end; but if people do not cease in offending God, a worse one will break out during the pontificate of Pius XI. When you see a night illuminated by an unknown light, know that this is the great sign given you by God that He is about to punish the world for its crimes, by means of war, famine, and persecutions of the Church and of the Holy Father.

I shall come to ask for the consecration of Russia to my Immaculate Heart, and the Communion of Reparation on the First Saturdays. If my requests are heeded, Russia will be converted, and there will be peace; if not, she will spread errors throughout the world, causing wars and persecutions of the Church. The good will be martyred, the Holy Father will have much to suffer, various nations will be annihilated.

In the end, my Immaculate Heart will triumph. The Holy Father will consecrate Russia to me, and she will be converted, and a period of peace will be granted to the world.

The Blessed Mother of God taught the young visionaries a new prayer to pray at the end of each decade of the Rosary. It is known as the Fatima Decade Prayer:

When you pray the Rosary, say after each mystery:

'O my Jesus, forgive us; save us from the fire of hell.
Lead all souls to heaven, especially those in most need.
Amen.'

The "Complete" Third Secret of Fatima

This Third Secret is and has been a controversy ever since 1960, and only the vision described by Lucia Dos Santos has been revealed publicly on 26 June 2000 by Rome, but as evidence will show, the Vatican has not revealed the accompanying message the Blessed Virgin Mary gave the children of Fatima; however, we have been able to acquire the text through testimonies of prelates who had the privilege of reading in full the Third Secret:

a.) **First sealed Envelope:** The "Vision" in the Third Secret of Fatima.

I write in obedience to you, my God, who command me to do so through his Excellency the Bishop of Leiria and through your Most Holy Mother and mine.

At the left of Our Lady and a little above, we saw an Angel with a flaming sword in his left hand; flashing, it gave out flames that looked as though they would set the world on fire; but they died out in contact with the splendor that Our Lady radiated towards him from her right hand: pointing to the earth with his right hand, the Angel cried out in a loud voice: "Penance, Penance, Penance!" And we saw in an immense light that is God: "something similar to how people appear in a mirror when they pass in front of it" a Bishop dressed in White "we had the impression that it was the Holy Father".

Other Bishops, Priests, men and women Religious going up a steep mountain, at the top of which there was a big Cross of rough-hewn trunks as of a cork-tree with the bark; before reaching there the Holy Father passed through a big city half in ruins and half trembling with halting step, afflicted with pain and sorrow, he prayed for the souls of the corpses he met on his way; having reached the top of the mountain, on his knees at the foot of the big Cross he was killed by a group of soldiers who fired bullets and arrows at him, and in the same way there died one after another the other Bishops, Priests, men and women Religious, and various lay people of different ranks and positions. Beneath the two arms of the Cross there were two Angels each with a crystal aspersorium in his hand, in which they gathered up the blood of the Martyrs and with it sprinkled the souls that were making their way to God.

Tuy-3-1-1944

(Sister Lucia, 3 January 1944)

b.) **Second sealed Envelope:** The "hidden" Message in the 3rd Secret

The accompanying message of the Third Secret of Fatima (as revealed by Rev. Father Villa and by Cardinal Ottaviani):

In Portugal, the dogma of the Faith will always be preserved. A great chastisement will fall on the entire human race, not today as yet, not tomorrow, but in the second half of the 20th Century. No longer does order reign anywhere, and Satan will reign over the highest places directing the

courses of event. He (Satan) will succeed infiltrating the top of the Church. Also for the Church, a time of her greatest trials will come. Cardinals will oppose Cardinals, bishops will oppose bishops and Satan will march himself amidst their ranks, and in Rome, there will be changes. What is rotten will fall, and what will fall will never rise again.

The Church will be darkened and the world deranged by terror. A great War will break-out within the second half of the 20th Century. Fire and smoke will fall from the sky. The waters of the oceans will be turned to steam, hurling their foam towards the sky; sinking everything... Millions and millions of men will lose their lives from one hour to the next, and those who remain living will envy those who are dead. Death will reign everywhere for the errors committed by the foolish and by the partisans of Satan who, then and only then, will reign over the world.

At last, those who will survive all of these events will once more proclaim God and His Glory and will serve Him as before when the world had not yet become corrupted. Go, My child and proclaim this! I shall always remain by your side to help you.

At last, the Third Secret of Fatima is revealed, thanks to the merit and courage of Father Fuentes, Cardinal Ottaviani and of Reverend Father Villa (see herein below "Controversies on the Third Secret of Fatima" and of other Churchmen, as we shall see in this chapter. But now a few questions come immediately to mind... A great war in the second half of the 20th century did not take place (World War III?).

Such a detail should not however cause doubt nor anxiety, for all the messages and warnings brought forth by the Blessed Virgin Mary to the three little shepherds of Fatima were always subject to man's response, prayers and conversion as clearly demonstrated by Our Lord Jesus-Christ's apparition to Mary-Julie Jahenny:

People are disappointed in that what I have ordered to be announced, for men to convert, has not yet taken place... They will think to be able to affront the elected souls who, because of their actions, I shall have delayed somewhat the terrible events that are yet to come. If in My Kindness and because of the expiation which have been offered to Me I delay the disaster, I do not eliminate it! This does not depend on the judgment of ignorant men! Must I Myself give accounts to those who do not want to know anything?

(Message of Our Lord Jesus-Christ to Marie-Julie Jahenny, date unknown...)

Another question comes to mind, perhaps the most important one of all: Why did John XXIII refuse to publish this Third Secret of Fatima upon opening the two envelopes? The reasons, we are told, reside in that it was feared that this message would perhaps inspire the USSR to initiate, sooner than expected, prepared plans of invasion of a European continent that was only then beginning to recover from a devastating second world war.

Another reason, it was rumored, was the revelation in the Third Secret that stated:

"(…) **Satan will succeed infiltrating the top of the Church. Also for the Church, a time of her greatest trials will come. Cardinals will oppose Cardinals, bishops will oppose bishops and Satan will march himself amidst their ranks, and in Rome, there will be changes. (…)"**.

This part of the message is extremely grave, for it depicts an infiltration of the Church and major changes within, resulting possibly from said infiltrations? And the Blessed Virgin Mary to add that this message was to be opened and revealed publicly at the latest by 1960, for it would be then understood… In 1960, the Second Vatican Council—"*architected*" by Pope John XXIII—was indeed in its preparation stage, and the time-table given by the Blessed Virgin Mary could not possibly be a coincidence… It was indeed widely rumored that the Third Secret was clearly judged to have a most realistic potential to destroy the "Vatican II" reform-plan…

Forty years later, Cardinals Bertone, Sodano and Ratzinger publicly declared that the entire third Secret of Fatima revealed by the Vatican in June 2000 from the envelope provided by Sister Lucia contained no further revelations… How could this be true, considering that this statement utterly contradicts Cardinal Ottaviani's revelation and Lucia Dos Santos' assertion to Rev. Father Fuentes in her famous 1957 interview:

Father, tell this to everyone: the Madonna has told me so many times that a great deal of nations will disappear from the surface of the earth. Godless nations will be the scourge chosen by God to chastise humanity if we, through the means of prayer and the Holy Sacraments, do not obtain the grace of their conversion. I cannot give more details, because it is still a secret. This is the part of the Message of Our Lady which will remain a secret until 1960.

Tell them, Padre, that the Blessed Virgin said repeatedly to my cousins Francisco and Jacinta, and to me as well that many nations will disappear from the face of the earth. She said that Russia will be the instrument of chastisement chosen by Heaven to punish the whole world if the conversion of that poor Nation is not obtained beforehand… Padre, that is why my mission is not to indicate to the world the material punishments which are certain to come if the world does not pray and do penance beforehand. No! my mission is to indicate to everyone the imminent danger we are in of losing our souls for all eternity if we remain obstinate in sin.

Controversies on the Third Secret of Fatima

Article by Franco Adessa (author of the **Third Secret of Fatima, The Apostolate of Our Lady of Good Success**):

In the autumn of 1996, shortly before presenting my book **UN Massacre Game**? in Brescia, I asked Fr. Luigi Villa what I should answer if someone asked questions about the "Third Secret" of Fatima. Father Villa, then, showed me the text of "The Secret of Fatima" which was published, in 1963, by the German magazine **Neues Europa** in Stuttgart (see herein below), and told me:

- *If you take the text of the "Third Secret" of Fatima, written by Lucia, and added or removed one comma, you would have created a 'fake.' Now, this text, published by **Neues Europa**, is almost three times longer than the original text of the "Third Secret," and it can definitely be called a 'fake', but a patently 'false' text may contain individual sentences that belong to the original text.*

At that point, before my eyes, he opened the pages of that document and pointed out, one by one, the sentences that were contained in the original text of the "Third Secret," written by Lucia (The parts in red are the sentences underlined by Fr. Villa in the 1963 **Neues Europa**'s article herein below):

Don't worry, dear child. I am the Mother of God speaking to you and begging you to proclaim in My name the following message to the entire world. In doing this, you will meet great hostility. But be steadfast in the Faith and you will overcome this hostility. Listen, and note well what I say to you: Men must become better. They must implore the remission of the sins which they have committed, and will continue to commit. You ask Me for a miraculous sign so that all may understand the words in which, through you, I address mankind. This miracle which you have just seen was the great miracle of the sun! Everyone has seen it—believers and unbelievers, country and city dwellers, scholars and journalists, laymen and priests. And now, announce this in My name:

A great chastisement will fall on the entire human race, not today as yet, not tomorrow, but in the second half of the 20ᵗʰ Century. What I have already made known at La Salette through the children Mélanie and Maximin, I repeat today before you. Mankind has not developed as God expected. Mankind has gone astray and has trampled underfoot the gifts which were given it. No longer does order reign anywhere. And Satan will reign over the highest places directing the courses of event. He (Satan) will succeed infiltrating to the top of the Church. He will succeed in sowing confusion in the minds of the great scientists who invent arms, with which half of humanity can be destroyed in a few minutes.

If mankind does not refrain from wrongdoing and be converted, I shall be forced to let fall My Son's arm. If those at the top, in the world and in the Church, do not oppose these ways, it is I who shall do so, and I shall pray God My Father to visit His justice on mankind. Then you will see that God will punish man still more harsh than He did by means of the Flood. It will come the time of the times, and the end of all the ends. If mankind will not convert, and if everything remains as before, or worse, it will become worse... The Great and the powerful will perish together, the small and the weak.

Also for the Church, a time of her greatest trials will come. Cardinals will oppose Cardinals, bishops will oppose bishops and Satan will march himself amidst their ranks, and in Rome, there will be changes. What is

rotten will fall, and what will fall will never rise again. The Church will be darkened and the world deranged by terror.

Time will come that neither King nor Emperor, nor Cardinal nor Bishop will wait for whom who will come anyway (???), but to punish in accordance with my Father's plan.

A great War will break-out within the second half of the 20th Century. Fire and smoke will fall from the sky. The waters of the oceans will be turned to steam, hurling their foam towards the sky; sinking everything... Millions and millions of men will lose their lives from one hour to the next, and those who remain living will envy those who are dead. As far as the eye can see there will be anguish, misery, ruin.

There will be tribulation as far as the eye can see, and misery in every country. The time is continually approaching, the abyss is growing wider, without hope. The good will die with the wicked, the big with the small, the princes of the Church with their faithful and the ruling sovereigns with their people. Death will reign everywhere for the errors committed by the foolish and by the partisans of Satan who, then and only then, will reign over the world.

At last, those who will survive all of these events will once more proclaim God and His Glory and will serve Him as before when the world had not yet become corrupted.

Go, My child and proclaim this! I shall always remain by your side to help you.

Important note: When the **Neues Europa** published this article on 15 October 1963, neither Pope John XXIII nor Pope Paul VI had the Vatican authorities confirm nor deny the content of the article which spread worldwide thereafter... What's more, the eminent Cardinal Ottaviani gave the endorsement of the article in the German publication Neues Europa which revealed ever so long discussed the full message of the Blessed Virgin Mary to the three visionaries of Fatima. Likewise, Father Coelho, Cardinal Ottaviani formally stated that the **Neues Europa** published Our Lady of Fatima's Third Secret in its most fundamental bases... *It corresponds to the truth,* he added...

Cardinal Ottaviani reportedly exclaimed about the text printed by the **Neues Europa**:

Publish 10,000 copies! Publish 20,000 copies! Publish 30,000 copies!

(Personal testimony of Mgr. Corrado Balducci)

After a few years, I returned to this topic, asking Father Villa:

- *How did **Neues Europa** happen to have this text on the "Third Secret" of Fatima?*

Father didn't answer my question directly, but said:

- *Cardinal Ottaviani wrote that diplomatic document. He was later contacted by those of the **Neues Europa** to find out if they could publish the text. Card. Ottaviani replied in the affirmative.*

On 13 May 2000, being in Fatima for the Beatification of the two little shepherds, Francisco and Jacinta Marto, John Paul II announced the imminent publication of the "Third Secret" of Fatima. On June 26, 2000, the Vatican published a four page text written by Lucia on the "Third Secret" of Fatima, accompanied by a presentation signed by Archbishop Tarcisio Bertone, Secretary of the Congregation for the Doctrine of the Faith, and an interpretation of the "Secret".

This interpretation included a letter from John Paul II to Sister Lucia, the report of the interview Card. Bertone had with Sister Lucia, the speech given at Fatima by Cardinal Angelo Sodano on 27 April 2000, and a theological commentary by Cardinal Ratzinger, Prefect of the Congregation for the Doctrine of the Faith. Two days later, at a press conference on the Third Secret, Mgr. Bertone made an amazing statement that ended with these words:

... the secret has nothing to do with the apostasy tied to the Council, the Novus Ordo (the Mass) and the Conciliar Popes that has been asserted by the fundamentalists (Traditionalists) for decades. For this fact alone, it was worth the trouble to reveal the Secret.

The revealed "Third Secret" consisted of the "Vision" of the three shepherds focused on the "Bishop dressed in White, who climbed to the top of the mountain, and knelt at the foot of a big Cross and was killed by a group of soldiers..." These painful attempts of John Paul II, of Secretary of State, Card. Angelo Sodano and of Cardinal Tarcisio Bertone to relate the "Third Secret" with the assassination attempt of Pope John Paul II at St. Peter's, on 13 May 1981 were also endorsed by Card. Ratzinger, who, in an interview on 19 May 2000, to Orazio La Rocca of **La Repubblica**, stated at the end of the interview:

The connection between the assassination attempt and the "Third Secret" is evident, it exists in the facts!

In the face of this manifest fraud, the press exploded: **Il Messaggero, La Repubblica, La Stampa**, and on 17 May 2000, **Le Figaro** published the indignation of a certain Elichar Alesne clearly expressing the general feeling:

One must really be completely in the ignorance of the history of Fatima to believe the version of the "Third Secret" His Holiness, Pope John Paul II gave us on May 13...

The same John Paul II, however, in Fulda, Germany, in November 1980, spoke differently to those who asked about the "Third Secret" of Fatima. He said:

... as on other occasions, the Church was reborn in blood, it will not be different this time (...)

Then, on the contents of the "Third Secret", the Pope added:

It should be sufficient for all Christians to know this: "when you read that the oceans will flood entire continents, that from one moment to the next millions of people will suddenly perish," if you know this, it is not truly needed to ask for the publication of this "Secret".

And where are these words in the document presented by the Vatican, on 26 June 2000? The words of John Paul II, in Fulda, were recorded by the magazine **Vox Fidei**, Article #10 published in 1981:

"When Pope John-Paul II was in Fula during his trip to Germany (15 November to 19 November 1980), before a limited group, some questions were asked of him, notably on the Secret of Fatima.

What is the Secret of Fatima that was supposed to be revealed in 1960?

Response of the Holy Father:

By its impressive content, and in order not to have the world power of Communism initiate certain measures, my predecessors have preferred a 'diplomatic attitude' (in regards to the Secret); Nonetheless, it should suffice to each Christian to know the following: we read (in the Secret) that oceans will flood entire continents, that men will die suddenly from one minute to the other by the millions...; when we know this, then it is not urgent to publish this secret.
Many want to know only out of curiosity and sensationalism, but they forget that "knowledge" calls upon responsibility... They only want to satisfy their curiosity. This is dangerous when, in these times, people's nonchalance makes them pretend that this serves no purpose!

The Pope, still on the subject, took the rosary saying:

Here is the remedy against this evil! Pray, pray!, and in the future do not ask any more questions. Recommend yourselves for all the rest to the Madonna!

(Translated from its French version)

In 2006, there was an outburst with the case of the "Fourth Secret of Fatima", which culminated with the publication of the book: **The Third Secret of Fatima Published by the Vatican is a Fake, Here's the Evidence**... by Laurent Morlier, and the book by Antonio Socci, **The Fourth Secret of Fatima**. Roused by the statements made by Archbishop Capovilla on the existence of this "Fourth Secret," i.e., the confirmation of the existence of a small sheet on which Lucy wrote the "Third Secret" of Fatima. At that time, I (Franco Adessa) asked

Father Villa if he could shed some light on this issue, but he just told me that it was only a private revelation and, therefore, it was not matters of Faith. I did not insist.

In 2009, when I was collaborating in the preparation of the English edition of the book, **Paul VI beatified?**, we worked on the texts in Appendix 4 that reported on the Apparitions of Our Lady of Good Success in Quito, of Our Lady of La Salette and Our Lady of Fatima. The last text to be defined was the one related to the "Third Secret" of Fatima. Then, I took the document published by **Neues Europa**, transcribed the sentences that Father Villa had indicated as the sentences appearing in the original document of Lucia, printed it out and handed it to Father for his approval:

A great chastisement will fall on the entire human race, not today as yet, not tomorrow, but in the second half of the 20ᵗʰ century. No longer does order reign anywhere, and Satan will reign over the highest places directing the courses of event. He (Satan) will succeed infiltrating to the top of the Church. Also for the Church, a time of her greatest trials will come. Cardinals will oppose Cardinals, bishops will oppose bishops and Satan will march himself amidst their ranks, and in Rome, there will be changes. What is rotten will fall, and what will fall will never rise again. The Church will be darkened and the world deranged by terror.

A great War will break-out within the second half of the 20ᵗʰ century. Fire and smoke will fall from the sky. The waters of the oceans will be turned to steam, hurling their foam towards the sky; sinking everything... Millions and millions of men will lose their lives from one hour to the next, and those who remain living will envy those who are dead. Death will reign everywhere for the errors committed by the foolish and by the partisans of Satan who, then and only then, will reign over the world.

At last, those who will survive all of these events will once more proclaim God and His Glory and will serve Him as before when the world had not yet become corrupted. Go, My child and proclaim this! I shall always remain by your side to help you.

A few days later, Father gave back the paper to me, saying: "*It's okay!*" The English edition of the book **Paul VI beatified**? went to press. On the pages 352 and 353, all the sentences that Father Villa had indicated to me as present in the "Third Secret" of Fatima, written by Lucia on a single sheet of paper, were shown.

In May 2010, during the flight to Fatima, Pope Benedict XVI responded to a question about the "Third Secret" of Fatima, blatantly contradicting the official version of the Vatican in June 2000 (which stated that the consecration of Russia had already been done and that the prophecy of the Third Secret had ended with the assassination attempt on John Paul II, in 1981). The key words of Benedict XVI were:

We would be mistaken to think that Fatima's prophetic message has been completely realized.

(11 May 2010)

Furthermore, his Holiness Pope Benedict XVI expressed the hope the centenary of the Apparitions of 1917, may hasten the fulfillment of the…

… prophecy of the triumph of the Immaculate Heart of Mary, for the glory of the Blessed Trinity.

This sentence was a clear indication that the Consecration of Russia to the Immaculate Heart of Mary had not yet been made, as the "triumph of the Immaculate Heart", the "conversion of Russia" and the "period of peace" had not yet occurred, despite the Vatican statement in 2000 which claimed that the Consecration had already been made by John Paul II on 25 March 1984. This statement of Benedict XVI confirmed the general belief of the Catholic Traditionalists of a fraud perpetrated on the world by the Vatican, in the year 2000.

On 11 May 2010, Benedict XVI also spoke of the **need for the passion of the Church which naturally is reflected in the person of the Pope**, and therefore, he announced sufferings for the Church, specifying that such suffering would have originated not from external enemies, but from within the same Church. Benedict XVI, with his own words pronounced in 2010, brought the issue of the "Third Secret" of Fatima into the limelight, upsetting the previous official position of the Vatican… Why did Benedict XVI make this sudden "U-turn" concerning the "Third Secret" of Fatima?

In 2011, in the presence of a witness friend, I stood before Father Villa, and speaking slowly, I put this question to him:

- *Father, do you remember when, on the document of the magazine "Neues Europa", you indicated to me the sentences that appear in the "Third Secret" of Fatima? Do you remember that these sentences have already been published in the appendix of the English edition of the book "Paul VI beatified?"*

He replied, "*Yes, I remember.*"

And I asked: "*Do you confirm to me that in the text: "The Third Secret of Fatima" published by **Neues Europa** in 1963, the sentences that you showed me are actually contained in the original text of the "Third Secret" of Fatima, written by Lucia?*"

Without hesitation and with emphasis, he replied: "*Yes, I confirm.*"

Shortly before Father Villa died, I went back again to this subject, and asked him: "*Father, what would you think if, one day, I made a testimony about what you told me and what we have already published on the contents of the "Third Secret" of Fatima?"*

Calmly, he replied: *"You can do it. Please, do it."*

(Article by Franco Adessa)

Fr. Luigi Villa

Padre Pio first met Fr. Villa, whom he entreated to devote his entire life to fight Ecclesiastical Freemasonry. Padre Pio told Fr. Villa that Our Lord has designs upon him and had chosen him to be educated and trained to fight Freemasonry within the Church. The Saint spelled out this task in three meetings with Fr. Villa, which took place in the last fifteen years of Padre Pio's life. At the close of the second meeting (1963), Padre Pio embraced Father Villa three times, saying to him:

"Be brave, now… for the Church has already been invaded by Freemasonry!" and then he stated: ***"Freemasonry has already made it into the loafers (shoes) of the Pope!"*** *(*At the time, the reigning Pope was Paul VI.)

The mission entrusted to Fr. Villa by Padre Pio to fight Freemasonry within the Catholic Church was approved by Pope Pius XII who gave a Papal Mandate for his work. Pope Pius XII's Secretary of State, Cardinal Tardini, gave Fr. Villa three Cardinals to work with him and to act as his own 'Guardian angels': Cardinal Ottaviani, Cardinal Parente and Cardinal Palazzini. Father Villa worked with these three cardinals until their passing away.

In order to fight this battle, in 1971, Fr. Villa founded his magazine **Chiesa Viva** (Living Church) with correspondents and collaborators in every continent, and as his works became more and more important, Fr. Villa became victim of various assassination attempts on his life… One of these attempts led him to Paris, where he received a major blow square in his face with an iron fist which displayed his jaw and shattered all his teeth, and since then, Fr. Villa did not have a single tooth left in his mouth… Despite other assassination attempts considerably graver, Fr. Villa survived them all, and wrote a series of books on Fatima and the Faith, and continued writing in his magazine **Chiesa Viva**.

Distortion on the Consecration of Russia

On 21 March 1982, Mgr. Sante Portalupi, the Papal Nuncio to Portugal, Bishop Alberto Cosme do Amaral of Leiria-Fatima and Dr. Francisco Lacerda were sent by Pope John Paul II to meet with Sister Lucy, to learn from her the requirements necessary to fulfill the Consecration of Russia as requested by Our Lady of Fatima. She answered:

… the Pope, together with all the Catholic bishops of the world on the same day, is to consecrate Russia to the Immaculate Heart of Mary.

However, the Nuncio did not transmit Sister Lucy's full message to the Pope... Bishop do Amaral told Bishop Portalupi not to mention to the Holy Father the requirement that the world's bishops must participate in the Consecration...

On 13 May 1982, Pope John Paul II consecrated the world, but not Russia, as Pius XII did before he. The bishops of the world did not participate in the act. However, in July/August of that year, the Blue Army's **Soul Magazine** published an alleged interview with Sister Lucy in which she supposedly claimed that the May ceremony had accomplished the Consecration of Russia. Fathers Caillon and Gruner later exposed this interview as being false! (See *The Fatima Crusader*, Issue 20 June–July 1986 and *The Fatima Crusader*, Issue 22 April–May 1987, for additional information.)

After the 1984 consecration of the world by Pope John Paul II, Sister Lucy's statements in multiple interviews confirmed that the Consecration of Russia had still not been done. Yet in 1989, notes and letters supposedly signed by Sister Lucy suddenly appeared, flatly contradicting all prior statements she had made for more than fifty years about the Consecration...

In October of 1990, in a written report, a highly regarded forensic expert established that Sister Lucy's purported signature on a November 1989 computer-generated letter was a forgery... Excerpts from this letter, published in an Italian Catholic magazine in March 1990, were being circulated widely and cited as "proof" that the Consecration had been done. Several news wire services also carried the magazine's story, thereby helping to spread the fraudulent claim worldwide.

The 1989 Instruction

In July of 1989, Father Messias Coelho, in the presence of three witnesses revealed that Sister Lucy had just received an "instruction" from unidentified Vatican officials, stating that she and her fellow religious were thenceforward to say that the Consecration of Russia was accomplished by the 1984 consecration of the world ceremony, in which the world's bishops did not take part and no mention of Russia was made.

After this development, various persons began repudiating their prior statements that the Consecration of Russia had not been done. These persons had previously clearly maintained, until 1989, that Russia had not yet been consecrated as requested by Our Lady of Fatima because Russia was not specifically named and the world's bishops did not participate.

On 11 October 1992, through an extraordinary circumstance, his Eminence Cardinal Anthony Padiyara of Ernaculam, India, and his Excellency the bishop Francis Michaelappa of Mysore, India, were able to meet with sister Lucia for a brief visit. The following is the exact transcript of this conversation translated from Portuguese to English:

Cardinal Padivara (addressing himself to Sister Lucia Dos Santos):

In our days, people speak only of Paradise and not of Hell. They say that God is All Merciful and that He forgives, hence He will not permit His children to be condemned.

Mgr. Carlos Evasristo (Historian, journalist, and interpreter then present):

I have even heard priests preach that Hell is only imagination, and that the devil is a monster invented by the grown-ups for them to behave. Even at the pilgrimage site (in Fatima) where Our Lady has shown you and your cousins Hell, my wife and I have heard a priest say so.

Sister Lucia Dos Santos (Maria Lucia de Jesus e do Coração Imaculado):

Hell is a reality. It is a supernatural fire and not a physical fire, and it cannot be compared to the fire which burns wood or coal, or to those fires which burn the forests.
Please, continue to preach on the reality of Hell because Our Lord Himself has spoken of Hell, and this can be found in the Holy Scriptures. God does not condemn anyone to Hell. People condemn themselves to Hell. God has given man the freedom to choose, and He respects this human liberty.

(11 October 1992)

<u>Article by Maike Hickson, 15 May 2016</u>

(Dr. Maike Hickson, born and raised in Germany, studied History and French Literature at the University of Hannover and lived for several years in Switzerland where she wrote her doctoral dissertation. She is married to Dr. Robert Hickson, and they have been blessed with two beautiful children. She is a happy housewife who likes to write articles when her time permits. Her articles have appeared in American and European journals such as **Catholicism.org, LifeSiteNews, The Wanderer, Culture Wars, Catholic Family News, Christian Order, Apropos,** and **Zeit-Fragen.**)

Cardinal Ratzinger: We Have Not Published
the Whole Third Secret of Fatima

The Vatican has responded to this story with a direct denial attributed to Pope Emeritus Benedict XVI himself. You may read their statement on the internet at: https://onepeterfive.com/on-fatima-story-pope-emeritus-benedict-xvi-breaks-silence/.

Today, on the Feast of Pentecost, I called Fr. Ingo Dollinger, a German priest and former professor of theology in Brazil, who is now quite elderly and physically weak. He has been a personal friend of Pope Emeritus Benedict XVI for many years. Father Dollinger unexpectedly confirmed over the phone the following facts:

Not long after the June 2000 publication of the Third Secret of Fatima by the Congregation for the Doctrine of the Faith, Cardinal Joseph Ratzinger told Fr. Dollinger during an in-person conversation that there is still a part of the Third Secret that they have not published! *"There is more than what we published,"* Ratzinger said. He also told Dollinger that the published part of the Secret is authentic and that the unpublished part of the Secret speaks about *"a bad council and a bad Mass"* that was to come in the near future.

Father Dollinger gave me permission to publish these facts on this High Feast of the Holy Ghost and he gave me his blessing.

Father Dollinger was ordained a priest in 1954 and served as secretary of the well-respected bishop of Augsburg, Josef Stimpfle. In God's providence, I met this bishop once when I was not yet a Catholic, and I was deeply touched by his humility, warmth and welcome. He invited me to visit him once in Augsburg. When I was in the process of conversion, I did reach out to him, but then, to my chagrin, I discovered that Bishop Stimpfle had already passed away. (He is greatly missed.)

Father Dollinger was himself also involved with the German Bishops' Conference's discussions concerning freemasonry in the 1970s at the end of which came the statement that freemasonry is not compatible with the Catholic Faith.

He later taught moral theology at the seminary of the Order of Canons Regular of the Holy Cross which belongs to the Opus Angelorum. Bishop Athanasius Schneider, auxiliary bishop of Astana, Kazakhstan, is member of that same Order of Canons Regular of the Holy Cross. Most importantly, Father Dollinger had Padre Pio (d. 1968) as his confessor for many years and became very close to him. Dollinger is also personally known to one of my beloved family members.

This sensitive information pertaining to the Third Secret, which has been circulating among certain Catholic groups for a few years now, has now been personally confirmed to me by Fr. Dollinger himself, at a time in history where the Church seems to have fallen into a pit of confusion. It might help explain, at least in part, why we are where we are now.

Importantly, it shows the loving mercy of the Mother of God to warn us and to prepare her children for this battle that the Church now finds herself in. In spite of the decision of those in responsible places within the Church, She has made sure the fuller truth would still be revealed and spread.

This information also might explain why Pope Benedict XVI, once he had become pope, tried to undo some of the injustices that are directly related with this Dollinger revelation, namely: he freed the Traditional Mass from its suppression; he removed the excommunication of the bishops of the Society of St. Pius X (SSPX); and lastly, he publicly declared in 2010 in Fatima: *"We would be mistaken to think that Fatima's prophetic mission is complete."* He also added these words in an interview during his airplane flight to Fatima:

As for the new things which we can find in this message today, there is also the fact that attacks on the Pope and the Church come not only from without, but the sufferings of the Church come precisely from within the Church, from the sin existing within the Church. This too is something that we have always known, but today we are seeing it in a really terrifying way: that the greatest persecution of the Church comes not from her enemies without, but arises from sin within the Church, and that the Church thus has a deep need to re-learn penance, to accept purification, to learn forgiveness on the one hand, but also the need for justice.

With this statement, Benedict XVI effectively contradicted his own earlier words of June, 2000, where he had stated:

First of all we must affirm with Cardinal Sodano: '... the events to which the third part of the 'secret' of Fatima refers now seem part of the past'. Insofar as individual events are described, they belong to the past. Those who expected exciting apocalyptic revelations about the end of the world or the future course of history are bound to be disappointed.

All these actions of Pope Benedict XVI show that he must have known, in his conscience, that he somehow had to correct certain injustices and confusing ambiguities of the recent past. He defended the traditional Mass, he gave back dignity to the SSPX, and he re-inserted the importance of the Fatima message. Additionally, he also tried to deal with the mystery of Vatican II, although, it seems, in too vague of a manner.

In this context, it might be worth mentioning that my husband and I were both together told by a priest who had met privately with Pope Benedict XVI that Pope Benedict himself considers Archbishop Marcel Lefebvre *"to be the greatest theologian of the 20th century"*. My husband and I both vouch for having heard these exact words directly from this priest—words which were allegedly spoken by Pope Benedict in the context of the pope's proposal to re-introduce Marcel Lefebvre's teaching more widely into the Catholic Church.

While we contemplate the gravity of the cumulative omissions and delays concerning the actual release of the full Third Secret, and when Heaven had asked us to do it—namely, not later than 1960—we are grateful to the Holy Ghost that He has seemingly made possible now this affirmative telephone conversation today on the Feast of Pentecost. May the true message of Fatima— together with the recent revelations of Fr. Brian Harrison and Dr. Alice von Hildebrand about what it also contains—spread far and wide and thereby help free all faithful Catholics from any bondage to half-truths and deficient loyalties. May we all freely and fully adhere to the full Truth of the Message of Mary's Mercy—which will surely, under grace, help to set us free!

(Dr. Maike Hickson, 21 May 2016)

Fr. Malachi Martin

Rev. Father Malachi Brendan Martin (Irish: *Maolsheachlainn Breandán Ó Máirtín*) was born on 23 July 1921 and died under most suspicious circumstances on 27 July 1999 from falling a flight of stairs...

Occasionally writing under the pseudonym Michael Serafian, Fr. Malachi Martin was an Irish Catholic priest and writer on the Catholic Church. Originally ordained as a Jesuit priest, he became a renown exorcist and Professor of Paleography at the Vatican's Pontifical Biblical Institute. From 1958, he served as secretary to Cardinal Augustin Bea during preparations for the Second Vatican Council and later adviser to their holiness Paul VI and John Paul II.

Disillusioned by Vatican II, he asked to be released from certain aspects of his Jesuit vows in 1964 and moved to New York City where he later became an American citizen.

His 17 novels and non-fiction books were frequently critical of the Vatican hierarchy, which he believed had failed to act on the Third Secret revealed by the Virgin Mary at Fátima, a secret he was permitted to read in its integrality. Among his most significant works were **The Scribal Character of the Dead Sea Scrolls** (1958) and **Hostage to the Devil** (1976), which dealt with Satanism, demonic possession, and exorcism. **The Final Conclave** (1978) was a warning against Soviet espionage in the Holy See via Soviet spies in the Vatican.

Original Interview by Art Bell of Fr. Malachi Martin, 13 July 1998 (on Coast-to-Coast Radio)

ART BELL: *It is my understanding that you have taken a vow of silence or secrecy. You have read the Third Secret. It was shared with you. Is that correct?*

FR. MARTIN: *Yes, it was given to me to read one morning, early, in February 1960. And of course, before I got it I had to a simple oath you always take of maintaining the secret. So the details of it I cannot communicate—I mean, the actual verbiage and expressions.*

ART BELL: *If this Third Secret of Fatima were made public, could it be the shock that the public, that the Church, needs?*

FR. MARTIN: *It could be. And that is one reason why it is not published; why it sunk into a limbo; out of which it is not going to come easily. It would be a shock. There's no doubt about that. It would affect people in different ways though, Art.*
Some people would, on being told this is authentically the Third Secret of Fatima, they would get extremely angry.

ART BELL: Oh I understand. *Believe me, I understand, father.*
All right. I in no way warrant the following as being authentic. I have no way of knowing. All I can tell you is, it feels real. It is alleged to be the Third Secret of Fatima. You decide for yourself. Here we go:

A great plague will befall mankind. Nowhere in the world will there be order. Satan will rule the highest places determining the way of things. He will succeed in seducing the spirits of the great scientists who invent arms, with which it will be possible to destroy a large part of humanity in a few minutes. Satan will have his power. The powerful who command the people will incite them to produce enormous quantities of arms. God will punish man more thoroughly than with the Flood.

There will come the times of all times and the end of all ends. The great and powerful will perish together with the small and weak. Even for the Church, it will be the time of its greatest trial. Cardinals will oppose cardinals. Bishops will oppose bishops. Satan will walk among them. And in Rome, there will be changes. The Church will be darkened and the world will be shaking with terror. One Great War will erupt in the second half of the twentieth century. Fire and smoke will fall from the sky.

The waters of the oceans will change into steam, and the steam will rise and overflow everything. The waters of the ocean will become mist. Millions and millions of people will die from hour to hour. Whoever remains alive will envy the dead. Everywhere one turns his glance there is going to be anguish and misery, ruins in every country. The time draws nearer.

The abyss widens without hope. The good to perish with the bad. The great with the small. The princes of the Church with the faithful. The rulers with their people. There will be death everywhere because of the errors committed by non-believers and crazy followers of Satan, which will then, and only then, take control over the world. At the last, those who survive, will at every chance, newly proclaim God and His glory, and will serve Him as when the world was not so perverted.

That's it.

(Pause)... Fr. Martin?

FR. MARTIN: *Yes, Art?*

ART BELL: *Any comments on that?*

FR. MARTIN: *I've listened to that, and I suppose the measured response I should give to it is this, in two parts, really, two statements. It is not the text, which was given to me to read in 1960. There are elements in it, which belong in the text.*

ART BELL: *So, in other words... I'm trying to step as carefully as I can... in other words, you're suggesting that this is not precisely what you had but there are elements of what you just heard...?*

FR. MARTIN: *Yes, there are elements, which do belong, in the Third Secret. That's about the most measured response I could give to it.*

ART BELL: *Okay, that's fine, and I won't ask you to say more but bearing in mind what I just read, would you consider the Third Secret to be as traumatic as is suggested in what I read or more so?*

FR. MARTIN: *More so.*

ART BELL: *More so?*

FR. MARTIN: *More so, yeah. Much more so. The... without... again... you know Art, stepping very carefully, the central element in the Third Secret, is awful. And it's not in that text.*

ART BELL: *It's not in the text?*

FR. MARTIN: *No it's not, thank God.*

ART BELL: *Now, I guess I would ask this. I understand you have taken an oath, but have you considered that the shock that is required to turn things around, may be this very serious, it may be that... it should be revealed.*

FR. MARTIN: *To your last sentence, I fully assent. It should be revealed, but here is my difficulty, Art. I'm one small little man. I have no public authority to do that. I do not know if that will be the will of God. And since it would have such dire effects on much more than Christians, and many others, I can't make that decision. Do you understand what I am trying to say?*

ART BELL: *Father, in what manner were you shown the Third Secret?*

FR. MARTIN: *The cardinal who showed it to me had been present at a meeting held by Pope John XXIII in that year, 1960, to outline, to a certain number of cardinals and prelates what he thought should be done with the Secret. But John XXIII, Pope John XXIII, the pope in 1960, did not think that he should publish the Secret. It would ruin his, at that time, ongoing negotiations with Nikita Kruschev, the boss of all the Russians.*
And he also had a different outlook on life, which, in two years later, opening the Vatican council, he echoed very succinctly and almost contemptuously in the middle of his speech on October 11, 1962 in St. Peter's to the assembled bishops who had come to the Vatican council, and the visitors. The place was crowded, huge basilica, he derided, contemptuously, that He was against the people he called "prophets of doom." And there was no doubt in any of our minds he was talking about the three prophets of Fatima.

ART BELL: *There are those within the Church who minimize what is contained in the Third Secret.*

FR. MARTIN: *Absolutely.*

ART BELL: *And then there are others who don't minimize it at all.*

FR. MARTIN: *They exaggerate.*

ART BELL: *They exaggerate. So without minimizing or without exaggerating, you're telling me what's in the Third Secret is more horrible than what I just read.*

FR. MARTIN: *Oh yes, Art, it is. Because, what you have just read, essentially, it is the onslaught of natural powers ... sure, Satan is walking, etc., like that amongst man... but essentially it is as if nature revolted against the human race. That's essentially, through all these terrible catastrophes a chastisement, and that's not the essence of the Third Secret, not the frightening one.*

ART BELL: *Wufff!*

FR. MARTIN: *Yes. It does stagger the imagination.*

ART BELL: *Father, how much weight do you give to the entire Fatima revelations?*

FR. MARTIN: *I consider it to be the key event in the climbing fortune of the Roman Catholic organization, and the defining event for the near future of the Church in the next millennium, the third millennium. It's the defining event. And that is why strong men, strong men but I mean... you see, Art, when we speak about strong men, the amazing thing about this state craft, people, people who practice the craft of state, like Casaroli who just died, or Pope John Paul II, it's what people always remark about great figure in history, like Napoleon, like Hitler, like Stalin.*

They had a will of indestructible power! And they could oppose the united wills of millions and make their point of view stick, to a certain degree anyway, until they fell, till they became a cropper, as we say in England. And similarly, in Rome there are men with strong wills. They're in state craft all their lives. They are engaged in macro-government. Not merely a religion, but in fate. They're up there amongst the greats. And THEY will not touch this with a large pole.

ART BELL: *In what way does the Church have role in what many see coming as a one world government, a one world control point?*

FR. MARTIN: *Two responses to that, Art, very brief responses. One is, the response already chosen by the leaders, by the managers, by the prelates, by the papacy, at the end of this millennium, and then there is what one sometimes thinks will be God's response. The response of the present moment is this: Beginning with John XXIII, and then with Paul VI, and now with John Paul II, the response is: Let us cooperate. It has joined, as Paul VI said in his famous speech in December 1965: "Let's cooperate with man to build his habitat." And John Paul II is an ardent supporter of, the tendency to one world government for geopolitical reasons. He wants to bring in his brand of Christianity, of course, and Catholicism, but he certainly is in favor of it [one world government]. When he addressed the United Nations, in his last big letter to them, he salute was this: "I, John, bishop of Rome, and a member of humanity." Now this was no longer, let's say, Pius IX or Pius X. Pius X would have said at the beginning of this century: "I am the vicar of Jesus Christ. If you do not listen to my voice, then you are going to be damned forever. We will* *not participate in any government behavior, in any government plans that do not recognize the kingship of Christ." That is completely absent. There now is the policy of cooperation with the formation of the European Union, cooperation with the United Nations, and the Vatican and the Church has entered the list in the struggle amongst the general assembly of the United Nations, and in the non-governmental organizations.*

ART BELL: *So it is well under way?*

FR. MARTIN: *Well under way! That is the response, and remember, the Vatican has, on Vatican hill, it has about, what, the figure varies, over one hundred and forty ambassadors from the nations. It is an integral part, and has built itself into it over the centuries of our international life. And it has ambassadors and representatives in over ninety countries, including Russia, including Israel, and it has its representative in Beijing, not quite diplomatic status yet, but they will get to that.*

ART BELL: *Again, Fr. Martin, referring to what I read, which you said had a partial relevance? Would you imagine that the person who wrote this had been privy in some way to the original text?*

FR. MARTIN: *Yes, yes, yes, certainly, at least by word of mouth, not by reading.*

ART BELL: *I understand.*

(later in the program)

ART BELL: *All right, here we go. Just a couple of things I want to quickly read, one from a friend in Australia, Father who says,* **"I had a Jesuit priest tell me more of the Third Secret of Fatima years ago, in Perth. He said among other things, the last pope would be under control of Satan. Pope John fainted, thinking it might be him. We were interrupted before I could hear the rest."** *Any comment on that?*

FR. MARTIN: *... Yes... (brief pause)... It sounds as if... (brief pause)... they were reading or being told the text of the Third Secret...*

ART BELL: *Oh my...*

Interview of His Eminence, Cardinal Carlo Caffarra of Bologna

Rorate Caeli has released a translation of a remarkable interview, originally published in 2008, with Cardinal Carlo Caffarra of Bologna. In it, he references correspondence he had with Sister Lucia:

Q. There is a prophecy by Sister Lucia dos Santos, of Fatima, which concerns 'the final battle between the Lord and the kingdom of Satan'. The battlefield is the family. Life and the family. We know that you were given charge by John Paul II to plan and establish the Pontifical Institute for the Studies on Marriage and the Family.

A. Yes, I was. At the start of this work entrusted to me by the Servant of God John Paul II, I wrote to Sister Lucia of Fatima through her Bishop as I couldn't do so directly. Unexplainably however, since I didn't expect an answer, seeing that I had only asked for prayers, I received a very long letter with her signature—now in the Institute's archives. In it we find written:

... the final battle between the Lord and the reign of Satan will be about marriage and the family. Don't be afraid, *she added*, because anyone who operates for the sanctity of marriage and the family will always be contended and opposed in every way, because this is the decisive issue. *And then she concluded*: however, Our Lady has already crushed its head.

Q. Talking also to John Paul II, you felt too that this was the crux, as it touches the very pillar of creation, the truth of the relationship between man and woman among the generations. If the founding pillar is touched the entire building collapses and we see this now, because we are at this point and we know it. And I'm moved when I read the best biographies of Padre Pio, on how this man was so attentive to the sanctity of marriage and the sanctity of the spouses, even with justifiable rigor on occasion.

A. Does this come as any surprise to those watching the events currently unfolding in the Church? We have referenced various apparitions in the past that are related to this, beginning with Our Lady of Good Success, in the 17th century:

Thus I make it known to you that from the end of the 19th century and shortly after the middle of the 20th century... the passions will erupt and there will be a total corruption of morals... As for the Sacrament of Matrimony, which symbolizes the union of Christ with His Church, it will be attacked and deeply profaned. Freemasonry, which will then be in power, will enact iniquitous laws with the aim of doing away with this Sacrament, making it easy for everyone to live in sin and encouraging procreation of illegitimate children born without the blessing of the Church... In this supreme moment of need for the Church, the one who should speak will fall silent.

When we reflect on the division among prelates at the Synod, Our Lady of Akita comes to mind:

The work of the devil will infiltrate even into the Church in such a way that one will see cardinals opposing cardinals, bishops against bishops. The priests who venerate me will be scorned and opposed by their confreres...

churches and altars sacked; the Church will be full of those who accept compromises and the demon will press many priests and consecrated souls to leave the service of the Lord.

Q. *Catholics are not required to believe in even the most approved and venerated private revelations, but many of us choose to do so. Does this battle relate to the famous discourse Pope Leo XIII was alleged to have heard in a vision between Christ and Satan, which led him to compose the prayer to St. Michael? How long will the final battle last, and what will come after?*

A. *It is impossible to know. But the notion that there is at this very moment a battle taking place for the heart of the Church and the souls of the faithful is no longer in dispute.*

Pope John Paul II beatified Francisco and Jacinta Marto on 13 May 2000 in a celebration attended by more than 700,000 people. Their cause for canonization is currently under consideration. Sometime before, Sister Lucia wrote two books, one entitled **Memories** and another entitled **Calls of the Message of Fatima**; both works will be used extensively for said process.

Discrepancies of the Vatican's Third Secret Release

The vision of a Pope being killed by soldiers does not necessarily reflect the "dangers threatening the faith", nor does it necessarily correspond to the "last times". Furthermore, one can search "other Marian apparitions" in vain to find any reference to prophecy of a pope being shot by a group of soldiers. Nor is there any reference to such an event in Scripture. This is but a mere discrepancy.

Indeed, in 1984, just before retiring at a venerable age, the Reverend Bishop of Niigata, Japan, Bishop John Shojiro Ito, in consultation with the Holy See, wrote a pastoral letter in which he recognized the most extraordinary series of events that had taken place from 1973 to 1981 in a little lay-convent within his diocese, at Akita, Japan as being an authentic manifestation of the Mother of God. Cardinal Ratzinger (future Pope Benedict XVI), in June 1988, approved as well the Akita miraculous events and apparitions of the Blessed Virgin Mary as *"reliable and worthy of belief"*.

Years later, the Philippine ambassador to the Vatican, in 1998 spoke to Cardinal Ratzinger about the Marian apparitions and revelations in Akita, and the German Cardinal made to him the following comment:

These two messages of Fatima and Akita are essentially the same.

On 13 October 1973, the 56th anniversary of the Miracle of the Sun at Fatima, the Blessed Virgin Mary appeared in Akita, Japan (see next page: 304) to warn of a double chastisement: that would involve both the Church and the whole world...

Cardinal Ratzinger has described the Message of Akita as "essentially the same" as that of Fatima. The parallel between the Message of Akita and the Message of Fatima, could not be more alike: both Messages predict a crisis in the Church and the destruction of a great part of humanity if the apostasy of many priests and bishops and lay people against God continues. We have already noted the massive defection of consecrated souls from the priesthood, the religious orders, and the convents since the Second Vatican Council. Hence, in Akita we are dealing with a Church approved intervention of the Blessed Virgin Mary which complements that of Fatima.

And yet... the third message of the Blessed Virgin Mary in Akita (*on the exact 56th anniversary of the Blessed Virgin Mary's last apparition in Fatima*) brings forth specific and most serious warning of a worldwide chastisement, the likes of which appears nowhere in the Vatican's released Secrets of Fatima:

As I told you, if men do not repent and better themselves, the Father will inflict a terrible punishment on all humanity. It will be a punishment greater than the deluge, such as one will never have seen before. Fire will fall from the sky and will wipe out a great part of humanity, the good as well as the bad, sparing neither priests nor faithful. The survivors will find themselves so desolate that they will envy the dead. The only arms which will remain for you will be the Rosary and the Sign left by my Son. Each day, recite the prayers of the Rosary.

With the Rosary, pray for the Pope, the bishops, and the priests. The work of the devil will infiltrate even into the Church in such a way that one will see cardinals opposing cardinals, and bishops against other bishops. The priests who venerate me will be scorned and opposed by their Confreres. The Church and altars will be vandalized. The Church will be full of those who accept compromises and the demon will press many priests and consecrated souls to leave the service of the Lord.

The demon will rage especially against souls consecrated to God. The thought of the loss of so many souls is the cause of my sadness. If sins increase in number and gravity, there will no longer be pardon for them.

(The Blessed Virgin Mary's Third Message in Akita, 13 October 1973)

The chastisement forewarned by the Blessed Virgin Mary in Akita is far worse than the description of Sister Lucia's third Secret-vision released by Cardinals Sodano, Ratzinger and Bertone in June 2000... despite this fact, Cardinal Ratzinger stated that:

"These two messages of Fatima and Akita are essentially the same."

This statement from Cardinal Ratzinger, and the Church's approval of the Akita Marian apparition case are nothing less than a self-incriminating Vatican's contradiction... But chastisement doesn't seem to have been the only part that is still being hidden by the Vatican, but an alleged apostasy within the Church as well.

We have, for introducing evidence, the testimonies of five prelates who read the full Third Secret of Fatima, four of which we have already covered: Rev. Father Fuentes, Cardinal Ottaviani's, Rev. Father Villa's and Rev. Father Malachi Martin's; the fourth being his Eminence Cardinal Ciappi, personal theologian of their holiness Pope John XXIII, Pope Paul VI, Pope John Paul I and John Paul II, who stated:

In the third Secret, it is foretold, among other things, that the great apostasy in the Church begins at the top...

His Eminence, Cardinal Silvio Angelo Pio Oddi was an Italian prelate of the Catholic Church who worked in the diplomatic service of the Holy See and in the Roman Curia. He became a Cardinal in 1969 and headed the Congregation and Dycasterium for Religious Lives from 1979 to 1986. The good prelate died in 2001, and was one of the most outspoken conservative Churchman of his time. He also occupied a special place in the history of the debate on the message of Fatima, inasmuch as he insistently tried to get Pope John XXIII to publish the Third Secret revealed to the three little Portuguese shepherds.

In an unguarded interview with the British Newspaper **The Telegraph**, published in 1990, Cardinal Oddi spoke of his relationship with Pope John XXIII. In the early 1960s when he worked as his Secretary, he told the Italian Pope:

-    *Most Holy Father, there is one thing for which I cannot forgive you.*

The Pope, surprised, asked what it was. Oddi replied:

-    *I cannot forgive you for not having revealed the Third Secret of Fatima, conveyed to three Portuguese children by the Virgin Mary in 1917, which had been scheduled for release in 1960.*

"Let's not talk about it!" replied the Pope.

In Sister Lucia's fourth memoirs, written in October–December 1941, the last surviving seer of Our Lady of Fatima copied the first two secrets from the text of her prior book, but, remarkably enough, she added a sentence that she did not write before: *In Portugal, the dogma of the Faith will always be preserved, etc.*, which stands as a promise that the true Faith will be preserved in that country, although in its vagueness it implies that this might not be so for the rest of the world... The Portuguese prelate Messias de Coelho concluded that:

... this allusion, so positive about what will happen among us, suggests to us that it will be different around us...

Rev. Father Alonso, the official Fatima archivist, had this to say on the Third Secret:

'In Portugal, the dogma of the Faith will always be preserved.' The phrase most clearly implies a critical state of Faith, which other nations will suffer, that is to say, a crisis of Faith; whereas Portugal will preserve its Faith.

In the period preceding the great triumph of the Immaculate Heart of Mary, terrible things are to happen. These form the content of the third part of the Secret. What are they? If 'in Portugal the dogma of the Faith will always be preserved,'... it can be clearly deduced from this that in other parts of the Church these dogmas are going to become obscure or even lost altogether.

Thus, it is quite possible that in this intermediate period which is in question (after 1960 and before the triumph of the Immaculate Heart of Mary), the text makes concrete references to the crisis of the Faith of the Church and to the negligence of the pastors themselves; (hence,) one conclusion does indeed seem to be beyond question: the content of the unpublished part of the Secret does not refer to new wars or political upheavals, but to happenings of a religious and intra-Church character, which of their nature are still more grave...

In 1984, the Bishop of Fatima said:

... the loss of Faith of a continent is worse than the annihilation of a nation; and it is true that Faith is continuously diminishing in Europe...

And in his 1984 interview with Vittorio Messori, Cardinal Ratzinger confirmed Father Alonso's conclusion when he stated that:

... the final part of the Secret speaks of dangers threatening the faith and life of Christians, and therefore the world.

In cold retrospective, we may assume that the fulfillment of the prophecy of the Third Secret began in 1960, for when Sister Lucy was asked why the Third Secret was to be revealed no later than 1960, she responded: *"Because it will be clearer then."*

Padre Pio Knew the Third Secret of Fatima

Chief Exorcist Father Amorth: Padre Pio Knew the Third Secret.
(Article by Maike Hickson)

In a recent article on the Secret of Fatima, Steve Skojec, the founder and editor of **OnePeterFive**, published, to my knowledge, for the first time in the English language words from Rome's chief exorcist, Father Gabriele Amorth (d. 2016), about Padre Pio and his knowledge of the Third Secret of Fatima. They come from a newly published book written by José María Zavala, entitled **The Best Kept Secret of Fatima *(El Sécreto Mejor Guardado de Fátima)*.**

OnePeterFive's contributor, Mr. Andrew Guernsey, was very helpful in finding these quotes. Since Mr. Skojec's own article is somewhat lengthy, many readers may not have realized the importance of this interview with Father Amorth, which was only to be published after the priest's death. In the following, I shall quote extensively from Steve's own post which first speaks about Father

Amorth's own conviction that the specific Consecration of Russia has not yet taken place, and then enters into the larger discussion about Fatima.

It came [a piece of the Fatima puzzle] in the form of an interview with the very famous (and now deceased) Roman exorcist, Fr. Gabriel Amorth, also conducted by José María Zavala. Fr. Amorth personally knew Saint (Padre) Pio for 26 years, and it is from this towering figure of 20th century Catholic sanctity that he claims to have learned the contents of the Third Secret of Fatima.

Fr. Amorth was interviewed by Zavala in 2011, who kept the interview secret until after the exorcist's death, publishing it for the first time in his book about Fatima. In the interview, Fr. Amorth relates—as he has done elsewhere—that he does not believe the consecration of the world by Pope John Paul II in 1984 was sufficient to satisfy the requirements set forth by Our Lady.

"There was no such consecration then," he [Father Amorth] says. "I witnessed the act. I was in St. Peter's Square that Sunday afternoon, very close to the Pope; so close, I could almost touch him."

Pressed by Zavala as to why he so forcefully believes that the consecration was not done, Fr. Amorth replied: "Very simple: John Paul II wanted to mention Russia expressly, but in the end he did not."

Zavala pressed the issue with Fr. Amorth, saying that Sister Lucia herself (as mentioned above) had said that Heaven had accepted the consecration. He describes an incredulous reaction from Fr. Amorth.

- *"Lucia said that...?"* he asked. Zavala continues:
- *"Well, Cardinal Tarcisio Bertone said it, in the year 2000, hiding behind a letter [escudándose en una carta] from Lucia dated November 1989, in which she stated that Heaven had admitted consecration in spite of one of the most important conditions."*
- *"Have you seen that letter?"* he asks, as if conducting a police interrogation in search of evidence.
- *"Never,"* I said flatly.
- *"I do not think you'll ever see it, because I'm convinced that Lucia did not write it."*
- *"How are you so sure of that?"*
- *"Why didn't Bertone show it when he should have, when he announced the Third Secret of Fatima? A simple photocopy of the manuscript, included in the official dossier of the Vatican, would have been sufficient to dispel any doubt. If the Vatican has always been scrupulous in providing the documentary proof that authenticated the information by Lucia on minor matters, what reason would they have to skimp on the only documentary evidence that, according to Bertone, validated a fact that without doubt was of as much importance as the consecration performed by John Paul II?"*
- *"Yes, it's weird,"* I admitted.
- *"You really think Lucia took five years to write that the consecration had been truly accepted? And that Bertone waited no less than sixteen years to announce the validity of something as crucial as the consecration of Russia to the Immaculate Heart of Mary?"* Father Amorth's voice sounds like dry leaves.

- "*It's all very strange, in truth.*" Zavala nods again.
- *"Moreover,"* he adds, *"if the consecration of the world to the Immaculate Heart of Mary made by Pius XII in 1942 was only partially accepted [because he did not specifically mention Russia—ed], for Jesus said that in view of it the war would only be shortened rather than finished immediately, why would He now change his mind with John Paul II, if Russia was not mentioned on this occasion?"*
- "*It would be an incongruity, yes.*"
- "*Rather.*"
- "*So...?*"
- *"I have no doubt that the consecration did not occur on the terms required by the Virgin. But we must not lose sight of what she herself wanted to tell us through Lucia:*
  'In the end My Immaculate Heart will triumph. The Holy Father will consecrate Russia to me and it will become [come to be], [thereby] granting itself to the world a time of peace'..."

The interview digresses here from the topic of Fatima, but Zavala returns to it again later:

- "*Forgive me for insisting on the Third Secret of Fatima: Did Padre Pio relate it, then, to the loss of faith within the Church?*"

Fr. Gabriele furrows his brow and sticks out his chin. He seems very affected.

- *"Indeed,"* he states, *"One day Padre Pio said to me very sorrowfully:*

'**You know, Gabriele? It is Satan who has been introduced into the bosom of the Church and within a very short time will come to rule a false Church.**'"

- '*Oh my God! Some kind of Antichrist! When did he prophesy this to you?*'
  It must have been about 1960, since I was already a priest then.'
- "*Was that why John XXIII had such a panic about publishing the Third Secret of Fatima, so that the people wouldn't think that he was the anti-pope or whatever it was...?*"

A slight but knowing smile curls the lips of Father Amorth.

- "*Did Padre Pio say anything else to you about future catastrophes: earthquakes, floods, wars, epidemics, hunger...? Did he allude to the same plagues prophesied in the Holy Scriptures?*"
- *"Nothing of the sort mattered to him, however terrifying they proved to be, except for the great apostasy within the Church. This was the issue that really tormented him and for which he prayed and offered a great part of his suffering, crucified out of love."*

- *"The Third Secret of Fatima?"*
- **"Exactly."**
- *"Is there any way to avoid something so terrible, Fr. Gabriele?"*
- **"There is hope, but it's useless if it's not accompanied by works. Let us begin by consecrating Russia to the Immaculate Heart of Mary, let us recite the Holy Rosary, let us all do prayer and penance..."** [emphasis added]

Thus ends Steve Skojec's own presentation of certain passages of the new Zavala book on Fatima.

Father Amorth is a witness here to what Padre Pio—whom he first met when he himself was a seventeen-year-old young man—told him directly and personally. Father Amorth states in that same interview that Padre Pio even let him sometimes read his own spiritual diary.

As we reported earlier, Father Amorth had also already stated during his lifetime that he did not believe that the Consecration of Russia has taken place (a statement which was just confirmed by Cardinal Paul Josef Cordes). In December of 2015, Father Amorth had said:

"The Consecration has not yet been made. I was there on March 25 [1984] in St. Peter's Square, I was in the front row, practically within touching distance of the Holy Father. [Pope] John Paul II wanted to consecrate Russia, but his entourage did not, fearing that the Orthodox would be antagonized, and they almost thwarted him.

Therefore, when His Holiness consecrated the world on his knees, he added a sentence not included in the distributed version that instead said to consecrate **especially those nations of which you yourself have asked for their consecration.** *So, indirectly, this included Russia. However, a specific consecration has not yet been made. You can always do it. Indeed, it will certainly be done..."*

As with other spiritual sons of Padre Pio—Dr. Ingo Dollinger and Father Luigi Villa, for example—it seems that Padre Pio is still effectively with us, working through those whom he met and guided while still on earth. It seems to be part of his legacy to help us in these difficult times. Let us then pray to Padre Pio of Pietrelcina and ask for his intercession!

(Article written by Maike Hickson, 23 May 2017)

In an interview done in April, 2020 by the Portuguese periodical **Dies Irae** of Archbishop Viganó, the ex-United-States Nuncio makes the claim that the Vatican authorities have in fact never released the full so-called "Third Secret" of Our Lady of Fatima. Archbishop Viganó further claims that the secret involved a warning involving a grave apostasy: the acceptance by many of a type of secular and "modernist" new creed that would begin in the latter part of the 20th century, cutting the Church off from her unbroken tradition of faith and practice since the time of the Apostles.

Interview with Archbishop Carlo Maria Viganó

Dies Irae:

- *Your Excellency, thank you so much for giving us this interview. The COVID-19 epidemic has, in recent months, affected the lives of millions of people and even caused the deaths of many. In light of this situation, the Church, through the Episcopal Conferences, has decided to close practically all churches and deprive the faithful of access to the Sacraments. On March 27, in front of an empty St. Peter's Square, Pope Francis, acting in a manifestly mediatic way, presided over a hypothetical prayer for humanity. There were many reactions to the way the Pope acted in that moment, one of which tried to associate the solitary presence of Francis with the Message of Fatima, i.e., the third secret. Do you agree?*

Archbishop Viganó:

Allow me first of all to tell you that I am pleased to give this interview for the faithful of Portugal, whom the Blessed Virgin has promised to preserve in the Faith even in these times of great trial. You are a people with a great responsibilitý, because you may soon find yourself having to guard the sacred fire of Religion while other nations refuse to recognize Christ as their King and Mary Most Holy as their Queen. The third part of the message that Our Lady entrusted to the shepherd children of Fatima, so that they could deliver it to the Holy Father, remains secret to this day.

Our Lady asked for it to be revealed in 1960, but John XXIII had a communiqué published on February 8 of that year in which he stated that the Church '*does not wish to take on the responsibility of guaranteeing the truthfulness of the words that the three shepherd children said the Virgin Mary spoke to them.*' With this distancing (of the Vatican) from the message of the Queen of Heaven, a cover-up operation was started, evidently because the content of the message would have revealed the terrible conspiracy against the Church of Christ by its enemies.

Until a few decades ago it would have seemed incredible that we would reach the point that even Our Lady could be silenced, but in recent years we have also witnessed attempts to censor the Gospel itself, which is the Word of Her divine Son.

In 2000, during the pontificate of John Paul II, Cardinal Sodano presented as the Third Secret a version of his own that in several elements appeared clearly incomplete... It is not surprising that the new Secretary of State, Cardinal Bertone, sought to draw attention away to an event in the past (the assassination attempt on John Paul on May 13, 1981) to cause the people of God to believe that the words of the Virgin (in 1917 when she appeared) had nothing to do with the crisis of the

Church (in the decades after 1960) and the marriage of modernists and Freemasonry that was contracted behind the scenes at the Second Vatican Council (1962–1965).

Antonio Socci, who has carefully investigated the Third Secret, unmasked this harmful behavior on the part of Cardinal Bertone. In addition, it was Bertone himself who heavily discredited and censured the Madonnina delle Lacrime (Madonna of Tears) of Civitavecchia, whose message perfectly agrees with what she said at Fatima.

Let us not forget Our Lady's unheeded appeal for the Pope and all the Bishops to consecrate Russia to Her Immaculate Heart, as a condition for the defeat of Communism and atheistic materialism: consecrate not 'the world,' not 'the nation which You want us to consecrate to You,' but 'Russia.' Was it so costly to do that?

Evidently so, for those who do not have a supernatural gaze. It was preferred to walk the path of détente with the Soviet regime, inaugurated by Roncalli (Pope John XXIII, whose baptismal name was Angelo Roncalli) himself, without understanding that without God no peace is possible. Today, with a President of the Russian Confederation who is certainly a Christian, the Virgin's request could be granted, averting further misfortunes for the Church and the world."

(Excerpt of the interview made by the Portuguese Catholic media outlet, **Dies Irae**, April 2020)

Sister Lucia passed away on Sunday, 13 February 2005 at the age of 97 as "Sister Maria Lucia of the Immaculate Heart". The Portuguese visionary died of old age at the Carmelite convent of St. Teresa of Coimbra in central Portugal, at 5:25 pm local time.

When I visited the then Abbot René Laurentin in Evry (France) in 1995, he used to tell me, with his usual slow, well thought-out speech and serene smile, that a sign of a true apparition is this:

*If a message from an apparition site **truly** comes from God, there is nothing that man will ever be able to do to... (*briefly pausing then smiling) *... to impede God's lit candle to be placed ON a bushel for all to see.*

In these grave forewarnings, the Church's highest hierarchy is put in cause, but not just... and to understand the reasons of such a vehement campaign of disobedience (to Heaven), one has only to read the messages of Lady of Good Success, of La Salette, of La Fraudais and of Fatima - in the hidden part of its Third Secret - to understand the reasons for Rome's deafening silence, for the answer is there given by the "Handmaid of the Lord", in plain light, unambiguous, one and the same...

Chapter V

The message of Our Lady of Akita, Japan

(*Our Lady of Akita/Our Lady of all Nations*)

"(…) Each day recite the prayers of the Rosary. With the Rosary, pray for the Pope, the bishops, and priests."

As observed, the Marian apparition case of Akita is *essentially the same* as that of Fatima; hence it is meant to reveal publicly that which was... *hidden under a bushel...* The message of Our Lady of Akita is unquestionably the revelation of the hidden Third Secret of Fatima.

It must be noted that, in addition to the quite remarkable message given by the Blessed Virgin Mary brought forth by the visionary of Akita, Sister Agnes Sasagawa (sister of the Eucharistic Handmaids of the Sacred Heart), the Japanese nun experienced stigmatas and various miraculous physical healings. Notwithstanding, the Marian apparition case of Akita is likewise perceived with other supernatural occurrences such as the statue of the Blessed Virgin Mary (Our Lady of Nations) in the Japanese convent weeping human tears and bleeding human blood on its right hand... All these scientifically unexplainable events added to the "credibility" factor ever so required by the Church investigating authorities, and would lead to the Bishop of Akita's official recognition of this Marian apparition case in 1984, and of Rome's in 1988.

It all began in 1973 in the small Convent of the sisters of the Eucharistic Handmaids of the Sacred Heart in Akita, Japan, with a half-deaf nun named Agnes Sasagawa. The devout religious woman experienced her first encounter with Heaven on a regular day of Adoration. Indeed, as she opened the Tabernacle to prepare her usual time for prayer, a very bright light, to her surprise, came from within the holy Tabernacle and filled the entire chapel of an indescribable soft luminosity. Sister Sasagawa was so overwhelmed, that she threw herself to the floor.

This extraordinary experience occurred on three consecutive days as well as on the Feast Day of Corpus-Christy. When the events took place, Sister Sasagawa asked each time the other Sisters present if they had seen anything out of the ordinary, they all answered no... On yet another occasion, Sister Sasagawa saw in awe a group of angels worship the Holy Eucharist in a circle around the altar. When the little Japanese nun finally reported her remarkable experiences to the Bishop of Akita, who was visiting the convent on said Feast Day, he, without knowing at first what to think of such a claim, phlegmatically advised the good nun to keep this experience private... On 6 June 1973, a Eucharistic prayer written by Bishop Ito was being recited by the nuns in the chapel of Akita, when Sister Sasagawa heard the voice of the Blessed Virgin Mary add the word "truly" to said prayer, emphasizing thus the true physical and spiritual Presence of Our Lord Jesus-Christ in the Holy Sacrament of the Altar:

Most Sacred Heart of Jesus, TRULY present in the Holy Eucharist, I consecrate my body and soul to be entirely one with Thy Heart, being sacrificed at every instant on all the altars of the world and giving praise to the Father pleading for the coming of his Kingdom. Please receive this humble offering of myself. Use me as Thou wilt for the glory of the Father and salvation of souls. Most Holy Mother of God, never let me be separated from Thine Divine Son. Please defend and protect me as Thy special child. Amen.

Later that same day, a bleeding wound appeared, before everyone present, on the Statue of Our Lady of All Nations' right hand in the convent's chapel, and on June 12, the vigil of the Feast Day of the Sacred Heart, some of the convent's nuns, alarmed by the extraordinary sight, reported to their Mother-Superior the drops of blood coming from the statue's right hand. Meanwhile, Sister Sasagawa, who was on that same day ill in the hospital, witnessed the very first apparition of her guardian angel.

In this first remarkable apparition, the angel taught the astonished nun the "Fatima Prayer" (see page 543) to be said after each decade of the rosary... Oddly enough, this prayer was at that time virtually unknown in Japan... On the same occasion, a wound in the form of a cross curiously appeared in the hollow of Sr. Sasagawa's left hand and began to bleed as well... This wound became for the poor little nun unbearable as it began bleeding profusely.

Sister Agnes' distressing pain lowered finally in intensity, and consequently, the good nun decided no longer to complain but rather to offer it up to Our Lord Jesus-Christ. Upon her return to the convent that afternoon, Sister Sasagawa resumed her duties in the convent which was in turmoil due to the extraordinary miracle reported earlier with the bleeding Statue of the Blessed Virgin Mary in their chapel. Later that night, Sister Sasagawa got up (at 3:00 o'clock in the morning.) to change the bandage of her bleeding palm when her angel appeared yet again to her, saying:

Do not fear. Pray with fervor not only because of your sins, but in reparation for those of all men. The world today wounds the most Sacred Heart of Our Lord by its ingratitude and injuries. The wounds of Mary are much deeper and more sorrowful than yours. Let us go pray together in the chapel.

Sister Agnes went to the chapel accompanied by her angel who told her that a wound similar to hers had appeared on the Statue of Our Lady's hand in the chapel, and that this wound was much more painful than hers. The angel then disappeared upon arriving in the chapel. Sister Agnes wanted to see the wound on the statue's hand when suddenly the statue became totally engulfed in a brilliant light. Sister Sasagawa immediately prostrated herself on the floor before the brilliant statue of Our lady of all nations. Sister Sasagawa wrote in her personal journal:

I prostrated myself on the ground and at the same moment a voice of indescribable beauty struck my totally deaf ears.

My dear daughter, my novice, you have obeyed me well in leaving everything to follow me. Is the infirmity of your ears painful? Your deafness will be healed, be certain of this. Persevere! This will be your final trial. Does the wound of your hand cause you to suffer? Pray in reparation for the sins of mankind. Each person in this community is my irreplaceable daughter.
Do you say well the prayer of the Handmaids of the Eucharist? Then, let us pray it together: Most Sacred Heart of Jesus, truly present in the Holy

Eucharist, I consecrate my body and soul to be entirely one with Your Heart, being sacrificed at every instant on all the altars of the world and giving praise to the Father pleading for the coming of His Kingdom. Please receive this humble offering of myself. Use me as You will for the glory of the Father and the salvation of souls.

Most holy Mother of God, never let me be separated from Your Divine Son. Please defend and protect me as Your Special Child. Amen.

Pray very much for the Pope, Bishops, and Priests.

Since your Baptism, you have always prayed faithfully for them. Continue to pray very much... very much. Tell your superior all that has passed today and obey him in everything that he will tell you. He has asked that you pray with fervor.

(The Blessed Virgin Mary, 12 June 1973)

Twelve days later, on 24 June, Sister Sasagawa reported once again to Bishop Ito that which had happened. He listened carefully and most respectfully, and after a deep silence, he counseled her to continue being humble and to pray. On 14 June, the pain in Sr. Agnes' hand became more than she could bare... She went to the chapel to be in solitude when the angel appeared to her and said:

Your suffering will end today. Carefully engrave in the depth of your heart the thought of the blood of Mary. The bloodshed by Mary has a profound meaning. This precious blood was shed to ask your conversion, to ask for peace, in reparation for the ingratitude and the outrages toward the Lord. As with the devotion toward the Sacred Heart, apply yourself to the devotion to the Most Precious Blood. Pray in reparation for all men. Say to your superior that the blood is shed today for the last time. Your pain also ends today. Tell him then what has happened today. He will understand all immediately. And you, observe his directions.

(14 June 1973)

Once the angel disappeared, her unbearable pain in her hand stopped at once... Sometime thereafter, upon the Bishop's next visit, on June 28, Sister Sasagawa asked to speak with Bishop Ito alone. After listening to the nun, Bishop Ito gave her a list of questions to ask the Blessed Virgin Mary upon their next meeting. These questions were:

1) Does the Lord wish the existence of our institute?
2) Is its present form suitable?
3) Is a group of contemplatives necessary in a secular institute?

On 3 August, Sister was in the chapel saying the rosary when the angel again appeared. He said the rosary with her, then he said to Sister:

You *have something to ask? Go ahead, you have no need to be troubled.*

315

Sister had not even gotten the first question started when she heard from the statue of the Blessed Virgin Mary a beautiful voice:

My daughter, My novice, so you love the Lord? If you love the Lord, listen to what I have to say to you. It is very important that you will convey it to your superior. Many men in this world afflict the Lord. I desire souls to console Him, to soften the anger of the Heavenly Father. I wish, with my Son, for souls to repair by their suffering and their poverty, for the sinners and ingrates.

In order that the world might know His anger, the Heavenly Father is preparing to inflict a great chastisement on all mankind. With my Son I have intervened so many times to appease the wrath of the Father. I have prevented the coming of calamities by offering Him the sufferings of the Son on the Cross, His Precious Blood, and beloved souls who console Him forming a cohort of victim souls. Prayer, penance, and courageous sacrifices can soften the Father's anger. I desire this also from your community... that it loves poverty, that it sanctifies itself and prays in reparation for the ingratitude and outrages of so many men.

Recite the prayer of the Handmaids of the Eucharist with the awareness of its meaning; put it into practice; offer in reparation whatever God may send for sins. Let each one endeavor, according to his capacity and position, to offer himself entirely to the Lord.

Even in a secular institute, prayer is necessary. Already souls who wish to pray are on their way to being gathered together. Without attaching too much attention to form, be faithful and fervent in prayer to console the Master.
Is what you think in your heart true? Are you truly decided to become the rejected stone? My novice, you who wish to belong without reserve to the Lord, to become the spouse worthy of the Spouse make your vows knowing that you must be fastened to the Cross with three nails. These three nails are poverty, chastity, and obedience. Of the three, obedience is the foundation. In total abandon, let yourself be led by your superior. He will know how to understand you and to direct you.

(The Blessed Virgin Mary, 3 August 1973)

About a month later, Sister Sasagawa received the following message from the Blessed Virgin Mary:

My daughter, if you love Our Lord, listen to me. Many people in the world grieve Our Lord. I ask for souls who will console Him, and who will make reparation. The Heavenly Father is preparing a great punishment for the world. Many times I have tried with my Son to soften the anger of the Father. I presented to Him many atoning souls who make reparation by prayers and sacrifices. That is what I ask of you. Honor poverty. Live poorly. You must keep your vows, which are like three nails to nail you to the Cross—the nails of poverty, chastity, and obedience.

(The Blessed Virgin Mary, September 1973)

This flowing of blood is significant. It will be shed for the conversion of men and in reparation for sins. To the devotion to the Sacred Heart add the devotion to the Precious Blood.

On 23 September 1973, the statue of Our Lady of all Nations began to sweat from the face to the feet; furthermore, tears began to flow down the beautiful statue's face. Also, a very pleasant fragrance was smelled within the chapel. This happened many times in the presence of others, including of the visiting Bishop's. His Excellency Bishop Ito was ever so touched by this remarkable experience that he ordered the tears produced from the statue to be immediately gathered and sent to the Faculty of Forensic Medicine at the University of Akita, for them to be analyzed.

The technical and scientific tests were performed under the direction of Professor Sagisaka, M.D., a non-Christian specialist in forensics, and proved, to the astonishment of the good Japanese scientist, to be indeed human tears…

On 13 October 1973 (56th anniversary of the last apparition of Fatima), the Blessed Virgin Mary appeared to Sister Sasagawa, but somewhat grave and solemn, giving her a message of the most serious gravity:

- **My dear daughter, listen well to what I have to say to you. You will inform your superior.** After a short silence, the Blessed Virgin Mary continued:
  As I previously told you, if men do not repent and better themselves, the Father will inflict a terrible punishment on all humanity. It will be a punishment greater than the deluge, such as one that has never been seen before… Fire will fall from the sky and will wipe out a great part of humanity, the good as well as the bad, sparing neither priests nor faithful. The survivors will find themselves so desolate that they will envy the dead. The only arms which will remain for you will be the Rosary and the Sign left by My Son. Each day recite the prayers of the Rosary. With the Rosary, pray for the Pope, the bishops and priests.
  The work of the devil will infiltrate even into the Church in such a way that one will see cardinals opposing cardinals, bishops against bishops. The priests who venerate me will be scorned and opposed by their confreres… Churches and altars will be sacked; the Church will be full of those who accept compromises and the demon will press many priests and consecrated souls to leave the service of the Lord.
  The devil will be especially implacable against souls consecrated to God. The thought of the loss of so many souls is the cause of my sadness… If sins increase in number and gravity, there will be no longer pardon for them.
  With courage, speak to your superior. He will know how to encourage each one of you to pray and to accomplish works of reparation.

Sister Sasagawa asked:

Marian apparitions in Akita, Japan

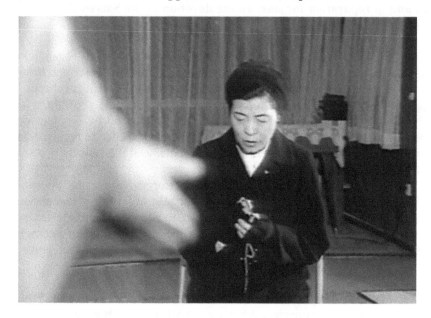

Sister Sasagawa (Stigmatist and visionary of Akita)

Catholic Church of Akita, Japan

Cardinal Ratzinger (Prefect of the Doctrine of the Faith)

His Excellency, Monsignor Ito, Bishop of Akita

Former Cardinal Ratzinger, who conferred face-to-face with Bishop Ito in Rome concerning the Akita apparitions, told Howard Dee, the former Philippines Ambassador to the Vatican, that the Message of Fatima and the Message of Akita are *"essentially the same."* In that case, one would expect to find in the Fatima message *"the same subjects covered"* as the Akita message of 13 October 1973, the very anniversary of the last apparition of Fatima and of the Miracle of the Sun.

Bishop Ito in prayer with the sisters of the Convent of Akita

Sister Sasagawa in 2015

- *Who is my superior?*
- **It is Bishop Ito who directs your community.**

And the Virgin Mary smiled and then said:

- **You have still something to ask? Today is the last time that I will speak to you in a living voice. From now on you will obey the one sent to you and your superior. Pray very much the prayers of the Rosary. I alone am still able to save you from the calamities which approach... Those who place their confidence in me will be saved!**

(The Blessed Virgin Mary, 13 October 1973)

The one of whom Our Lady spoke when she said," **From now on you will obey the one sent to you and your superior**", was the Rev. Father Teiji Yasuda, who was assigned and sent to Akita on 10 March by Bishop Ito. Fr. Yasuda began as a devotional gardener on the property of the convent, a garden which was devoted to Mary; however, his principal task was that of advising and guiding Sister Sasagawa.

The statue of Our Lady of All Nations continued to weep, but on 15 March, the fragrance perfuming the chapel curiously ceased...

On May 1974, the angel appeared again to Sister Agnes and gave her the following message:

Your ears will be opened in August or in October. You will hear. You will be healed. But that will last only for a moment because the Lord still wishes this offering and you will become deaf again. In seeing that your ears are restored again, the hearts of those who still doubt will melt and they will believe. Have confidence and pray with good intentions. Report what I have told you to him who directs you. But speak of it to no one else until it takes place.

(18 May 1974)

Four months later, the angel appeared again to Sister Agnes and said:

You spoke this morning concerning the dream, didn't you? Do not be disturbed. Today or tomorrow begin a novena, one of your choice, and then two more. During the time of these three novenas made before the Lord Truly Present in the Eucharist, your ears will be opened during the Adoration and you will hear. The first thing that you will hear will be the chant of the 'Ave Maria' which you are accustomed to singing. Then you will hear the sound of the bell ringing for the Benediction of the Most Blessed Sacrament.

After the Benediction you will calmly ask the one who directs you to have the Canticle of Thanksgiving sung. Then it will be known that your

ears hear again. At that moment your body also will be healed and the Lord will be glorified.

When he learns this, your superior will be filled with courage; his heart will be consoled and he will bear witness. However, the more you offer with good intentions, the more there will be difficulties and obstacles. To overcome these exterior obstacles pray with more confidence in interior unity. You will be protected, be sure.

Your ears will hear only for a certain time. They will not yet be totally cured. You will become deaf again. The Lord still wishes this offering... Report what I have told you to he who directs you.

(21 September 1974)

The angel's announcement came to pass exactly as he predicted...

Weeks went by and soon became months, and months, years... On 4 January 1975, the statue of Our Lady of all Nations began weeping again. It was recorded that the statue of the Blessed Virgin Mary wept—until 15 September 1981—a total of one hundred and one times. What's more, every scientific examination proved the collected tears to be unquestionably... human tears... The blood, the sweat and the tears produced by the statue of the Blessed Virgin Mary were all sent as well to the Faculty of Forensic Medicine at the University of Akita where Professor Sagisaka, M.D. proceeded as before an exhaustive scientific examination with all rigorous methods to test all three gathered fluids.

The results were absolute and incontrovertible, and as before utterly astonishing! The blood recovered from the wooden statue was human blood and was of type B. The sweat and the tears were human sweat and tears, and were of type AB...

The angel appeared to Sister Agnes on the last day the statue of the Blessed Virgin Mary wept, and said:

There is meaning to the figure one hundred one. This signifies that sin came into the world by a woman and it is also by a woman that salvation came into the world. The zero between the two signifies the eternal God who is from all eternity until eternity. The first "one" represents Eve and the last "one" the Virgin Mary.

(15 September 1981)

On 6 March 1975, as the angel predicted it was from this day forward that Sister Agnes began to have a loss of hearing in both ears and soon thereafter became completely deaf yet again... However, on 30 May 1982, Sister Agnes' deafness was at last completely and permanently healed.

In his pastoral letter, Bishop Ito stated that it would have been difficult to believe in a message from Our Lady that is ever so horrifying, unless there were overwhelming proof that this message came indeed from Her. But he pointed out very rightfully that the terrible chastisement of which Our Lady spoke of is clearly conditional:

If men do not repent and do not better themselves.

The Bishop added that Our Lady's message is a serious warning, while at the same time one perceives in it the maternal love of a mother. In Her message warning the world of the annihilation of a great part of humanity, the Blessed Virgin Mary stated:

The thought of the loss of numerous souls makes me sad.

Formal Inquiry, Commission, and Final and Formal Church Approval

Bishop Ito finally consulted with the Congregation for the Doctrine of the Faith in 1975. In 1976, Bishop Ito created a formal inquiry-commission which declared that:

... it was not in a position to prove the supernatural events taking place in the convent of Akita...

In 1978, the Congregation for the Doctrine of the Faith published norms for examining "the presumed apparitions of Akita". Following the 1978 Congregation for the Doctrine of the Faith's norms, Bishop Ito requested in 1979 the Congregation for the Doctrine of the Faith's formal intervention to create another inquiry-commission to re-examine all the accumulated facts at hand.

In 1981, after two years of examination, investigation and studies of the events in Akita, the Congregation for the Doctrine of the Faith declared itself *"unfavorable to the events"* and informed Bishop Ito that it would not initiate any further examination... But, according to the Japanese Bishop, the 1981 Congregation for the Doctrine of the Faith's response contained some significant *"misunderstandings"*; hence, Bishop Ito meticulously assembled all the theological and scientific evidence gathered in the convent of Akita since 1975 until 1982.

After a full and complete re-examination of the dossier carefully prepared by bishop Ito, Cardinal Ratzinger, Prefect of the Dycasterium of the Doctrine of the Faith in the Vatican, met in Rome with the Bishop of Akita in 1983. After meeting with Cardinal Ratzinger and entrusting him with the precious dossier, Bishop Ito was asked to return the following day to discuss with him the Marian apparition case more in depth. The events of the next day were truly remarkable as we can see in the renown elocutionist Vassula Ryden's[20] testimony to a French magazine herein below.

---

[20] **Vassula Ryden (maiden name: Vassiliki Claudia Pendakis)** was born on 18 January 1942 into a Greek family in Heliopolis, on the outskirts of Cairo, Egypt. She emigrated to Europe with her family at the age of 15. Vassula is a member of the Greek Orthodox Church. In November 1966, Vassula married a Lutheran man in the city of Lausanne, Switzerland, at a Greek Orthodox Church. In November 1980, she

Vassula Ryden' Testimony (10 November 1995)

I was invited with other people on the 26 of November 1992 for an international Marian convention... (brief pause) international Marian convention. There were there Father René Laurentin, and Father Michael O'Corrall[21]... heu... and other priests as well. There was Cardinal Vidal (Filipino Cardinal and Archbishop of Cebu 1985–2010) *as well, and he (Bishop Ito, Bishop of Akita, Japan) wanted to tell us about the messages of Akita and Sister Agnes, and of course he said that... you know... he said something that really surprised us (smiling) that was that he... when he went to Rome, to bring the God would unexpectedly reveal Himself to her in 1985, while she was living with her family in the capital city of Dhaka in Bangladesh. God called her through locutions and charged her with the mission of delivering His Message, which He named **True Life in God**.*

Vassula Ryden has been studied in depth and sponsored by World renown Mariologian Monsignor René Laurentin who likewise wrote many articles and studies on her and on her heavenly experiences. message of Akita for investigation, he encountered Cardinal Ratzinger, and he talked to him about Sister Agnes and the messages, and Cardinal Ratzinger said to leave them with him and he would read them to see what he can do... And they... you know, Bishop Ito thought that he will send an investigation like normal. He always sends an investigation to the sites of the apparitions.

The next day, when he goes there, he said that he surprised him... because Cardinal Ratzinger said to him:

- **"We shall not send an investigation there, nor consultants."**

*And he (Bishop Ito) said: "**Why?**"*

*And Cardinal Ratzinger said: "**Because the message of Akita is the Third Secret of Fatima, so I don't have to investigate...**"*

That's what he said... You know, when we heard this of course we said: "Wow!" You know... "That is the Secret of Fatima?" And you know... I did not hear it... We didn't hear it from another source, like you know "Bishop Ito said so and so" because I wouldn't have believed, you know... But I heard it from the

---

was divorced in Sweden. In June 1981, she married her current husband, Per Rydén, a Swedish Lutheran, at the registry office. On 31 October 1990, she regularized her union in the Greek Orthodox Church in Lausanne.

[21] **Fr. Michael O'Corrall** is of Irish nationality. He is a member of the Congregation of the Holy Spirit. For many years he is a professor and well-known mariologist. He is the author of several books. **Theotokos (Mother of God)** is one of his better known books, and the book about Medjugorje, **Facts, Documents and Theology. Is Medjugorje Approved?**

mouth of Bishop Ito, and so did the others that there will be no investigation because it's not necessary. It is almost word for word the Third Secret of Fatima.

A year after his meeting with Cardinal Ratzinger, Bishop Ito formally declared the events of Akita as being of supernatural origin and worthy of belief, and issued a formal statement on 22 April 1984, declaring that he did not find *"any elements which are contrary to the Catholic faith or morals"* in the Marian apparition case of the convent of Akita. Bishop Ito furthermore declared with full Episcopal Authority that he:

- **Recognized** "the supernatural character of a series of mysterious events concerning the statue" in the convent.
- **Authorized** "the veneration of the Holy Mother of Akita," within the Diocese of Niigata, "while awaiting" a "definitive judgment on this matter" pronounced by the Holy See.
- **Distinguished** that the events were a private revelation and not necessary for salvation like public revelation.

In August 1988, the Union of Catholic Asian News (U.C.A.N.) reported that Mutsuo Fukushima of the Kyodo News Service wrote that he accompanied Bishop Ito to a June 1988 meeting with Cardinal Ratzinger. U.C.A.N. reported that his Eminence Cardinal Ratzinger had in turn formally approved the veracity of the messages of the Blessed Mother Mary at Akita. It was furthermore reported that Fukushima wrote that Cardinal Ratzinger told Bishop Ito that he did not object in any manner to Bishop Ito's Pastoral Letter, and added that:

… the Congregation of the Doctrine of the Faith assured in June 1988 that Bishop Ito had acted properly.

(Note: In 2012, for the first time, the previously Latin only Marian Apparition approval rules were published by the Vatican in English, confirming the formal delegation to local bishops the power to decree one of the following three conclusion (of alleged apparition cases):

1) The local bishop can determine the apparition to be true and worthy of belief.
2) The local bishop can state the apparition to be untrue, leaving the possibility for an appeal.
3) The local bishop can state that at the moment he hasn't reached a conclusion, requesting assistance from a higher authority.

A Message Received by Sister Sasagawa on the Eve of the Amazonian Synod (October 2019)

Sister Sasagawa, who was 88 years old in 2019 and remained ordered to silence and out of public sight by her then local bishop in Akita, witnessed for the first time in 38 years, on October of 2019, the returned apparition of her angel who came with a most surprising message... What follows is what was delivered to the radio channel WQPH (89.3 FM) (recently bought-over by EWTN) in the United States from Sister "M..." who echoed Sister Sasagawa's testimony.

Sister Sasagawa (October 2019)

On Sunday, October 6, at 3:30am in Akita, the same angel appeared before me as he did some 30 years ago. The angel first told me something private... The good thing to convey is:

- *'Cover in ashes! And please, pray the Penitential Rosary every day. You* (Sister Sasagawa), *become like a child, and everyday please give (make) sacrifice.'*

Sister "M...":

- *May I tell everyone about this?*

Sister Sasagawa:

- *Aye. Also, "Please pray that I be able to be like a child and give sacrifice".*

This latest message (first one since 1981) was received on the opening day of the most controversial **Pan-American Amazonian Synod in Rome (6 October 2019)** under the presidency of Pope Francis. Could this be a coincidence? It would not be very objective not to think so. One thing is certain, the reference of the ritual of ashes made by Sister Sasagawa's angel does not leave any room for interpretation for such reference refers to an act of penance and humility as demonstrated in the Book of Jonah:

The word of Yahweh was addressed to Jonah a second time. 'Up!' he said, 'Go to Nineveh, the great city, and preach to it as I shall tell you.' Jonah set out and went to Nineveh in obedience to the word of Yahweh. Now Nineveh was a city great beyond compare; to cross it took three days. Jonah began by going a day's journey into the city and then proclaimed, 'Only forty days more and Nineveh will be overthrown.'

And the people of Nineveh believed in God; they proclaimed a fast and put on sackcloth, from the greatest to the least. When the news reached the king of Nineveh, he rose from his throne, took off his robe, put on sackcloth and sat down in ashes.

He then had it proclaimed throughout Nineveh, by decree of the king and his nobles, as follows: 'No person or animal, herd or flock, may eat anything; they may not graze, they may not drink any water. All must put on sackcloth and call on God with all their might; and let everyone renounce his evil ways and violent behavior. Who knows? Perhaps God will change his mind and relent and renounce his burning wrath, so that we shall not perish.' God saw their efforts to renounce their evil ways. And God relented about the disaster which he had threatened to bring on them, and did not bring it.

(Jonah, Chapter 3:1–10)

The message given to Sister Sasagawa on the exact opening day of the Amazonian Synod architected by Pope Francis and by the hand-picked cardinals and bishops who assisted therein likewise foretells a very grave admonition, a warning of sorts, for such request of penance, as we have seen in the story of Nineveh, was to prevent unmentionable consequences to the crimes committed against God.

Despite of the utterly unexpected decision of Pope Francis not to permit the strongly sponsored requested abolition of Priest celibacy and of women ordination in the Amazon forests, the Pan-American synod has seen nonetheless sordid examples of paganism and idolatry on Vatican grounds under the benevolent smile of Pope Francis... Consequently, the question raised is: how are we to interpret this latest message given to the visionary of Akita who echoed yet again the terrifying Third Secret of Fatima on 13 October 1973?

Today, in 2022, as it was in Fatima since 1953, the policy of the new bishop of Akita sponsors complete silence about the message received from the Blessed Virgin Mary, as Sister Sasagawa has received the express instructions from her diocese to remain silent and not to grant any interviews to reporters, writers or individuals, precisely as Sister Lucia Dos Santos was before her... Why?

Is the Church having History repeat itself as in Fatima? Unquestionably! But again for what reason? Since this recognized and Church-approved Marian apparition case's prophetic message and warning is the same as that given to the three little shepherds of Fatima one hundred years ago, one can observe a bit more of the same from the Catholic Church on this latest call from Heaven, that is to say secrecy, concealment and suppression.

Regardless, and despite all the bad will and entrenched efforts to keep "**under the bushel**" the Virgin Mary's repetitive call and forewarning, one thing remains certain, the Roman Catholic Church is and always will be Jesus-Christ's Church, and, despite man's errors and deviations, the faithful must maintain their focus on Mary's message – which is a pressing echo of her Son Jesus' teachings – just as Peter did when he walked upon the waters. Mary's call is Christ's Hand saving mankind from sinking to his perdition under the waves of doubt...

Chapter VI

Apparitions of Our Lady of Good Success

(*Our Lady of Good Success*)

Prepare your soul so that, increasingly purified, it might enter into the fullness of the joy of Our Lord. Oh! If mortals, and in particular religious souls, could know what Heaven is and what it is to possess God! How differently they would live! Nor would they spare themselves any sacrifice in order to possess Him!

(2 February 1634)

Since the early nineteenth century, the world has gone through a series of wars, butcheries and persecutions of all sorts throughout the world. Every continent of the world has seen massive and bloody wars since the early 1800s. The United States itself, in the New World, was not exempted from a cruel fratricide civil-war which torn the newly established U.S. republic in two.

The South-American countries, which recently became independent from the Spanish crown were quickly influenced and massively armed by the French, the Germans and the English powers, ensuing thus rivalries which quickly led to costly wars which helped generate massive capitals for the European nations half a world away. And there was Europe... From the still smoking ashes of a fallen Napoleonic Empire, the main European powers began to re-arm arsenals of the likes were never seen before; likewise, the ambitions of the heirs of the past began to express the extension of their aspirations through the expansion of colonial empires within the weaker continents of the world.

The Roman Catholic Church was powerful, influential and trying as well as it could to maintain an international scene as peaceful as possible; however... as the 19th century saw the first industrial revolutions, the Church was beginning to notice more and more an underhanded intelligentsia working behind the scenes, investing enormous capitals in the armament industries, placing political lobbies within every major international power government in the world, forming secret societies more and more involved in the political, financial, religious and international aspects of society.

This newly discovered global movement had taken a noticeable momentum in England in the early 18th century which soon thereafter followed in France and in the new world. Freemasonry was born. These secret societies lit the starting sparkles that put fire into the powder cake that became later the French Revolution and the republics that followed suit.

Freemasonry derived from an old middle-age Masonic group that originated from the famous "Illuminati" (derived *from the word Lumen—the enlightened ones*). These organizations were principally anti-Catholic and anti-monarchist as the Catholic and Orthodox crowns of Europe represented, together with the Roman Catholic Church, a major obstacle to a philosophy that lied in the shadows of Society's upper-elites.

Famous Freemason Albert Pike (29 December 1809–2 April 1891) was an American author, poet, orator, jurist and prominent senior officer of the Confederate States Army who commanded the District of Indian Territory in the Trans-Mississippi Theater of the American Civil War. Albert Pike, who was indeed a historical Masonic figure, was a 33rd degree Freemason Luciferian Occultist Grand Master and creator of the Southern Jurisdiction of the Masonic Scottish Rite Order.

The renowned American Luciferian Occultist wrote in 1871 a letter to a likewise well-known European Freemason named Giuseppe Mazzini, an Italian politician, journalist and activist who began to make of name for himself on both sides of the Atlantic for having formed many secret societies in France and Italy. Albert Pike's letter purported to outline the illuminati plan for three world wars that were to come and which had been planned and foreseen by the American freemasons. The letter to Mazzini was on display in the British Museum Library in London until 1977, before being "*inexplicably*" removed from public view...

Extracts from the Letter Pike Wrote to Mazzini

The First World War must be brought about in order to permit the Illuminati to overthrow the power of the Czars in Russia and of making that country a fortress of atheistic Communism. The divergences caused by the "agentur" (*agents*) of the Illuminati between the British and Germanic Empires will be used to foment this war. At the end of the war, Communism will be built and used in order to destroy the other governments and in order to weaken religions.

The Second World War must be fomented by taking advantage of the differences between the Fascists and the political Zionists. This war must be brought about so that Nazism is destroyed and that the political Zionism be strong enough to institute a sovereign state of Israel in Palestine. During the Second World War, International Communism must become strong enough in order to balance Christendom, which would be then restrained and held in check until the time when we would need it for the final social cataclysm.

The Third World War must be fomented by taking advantage of the differences caused by the "agentur" of the "Illuminati" between the political Zionists and the leaders of Islamic World. The war must be conducted in such a way that Islam (*the Muslim Arabic World*) and political Zionism (*the State of Israel*) mutually destroy each other. Meanwhile the other nations, once more divided on this issue, will be constrained to fight to the point of complete physical, moral, spiritual and economical exhaustion...

We shall unleash the Nihilists and the atheists, and we shall provoke a formidable social cataclysm which in all its horror will show clearly to the nations the effect of absolute atheism, origin of savagery and of the bloodiest turmoil. Then everywhere, the citizens, obliged to defend themselves against the world minority of revolutionaries, will exterminate those destroyers of civilization, and the multitude, disillusioned with Christianity, whose deistic spirits will, from that moment, be without compass or direction, and will be anxious for an ideal but without knowing where to render its adoration.

It will receive the true light through the universal manifestation of the pure doctrine of Lucifer, brought finally out in the public view. This manifestation will result from the general reactionary movement which will follow the destruction of Christianity and atheism, both conquered and exterminated at the same time.

This information became widely known throughout the corridors and offices of the Vatican, and soon thereafter came the warnings of La Salette, a subject of popular conversation. Conversely, it appeared that the apparition to Mélanie Calvat et to Maximin Giraud was not the first forewarning of the Blessed Virgin Mary given about the dangers of Freemasonry... Notwithstanding, what is the

Roman Catholic Church's position on Freemasonry? The Church has formally imposed the penalty of excommunication on Catholics who become Freemasons.

The penalty of excommunication for joining Masonic Lodges was explicitly issued in the 1917 code of canon law (canon 2335), and it is contained in the 1983 code (canon 1374). Regardless, due to the revised code of canon law not being explicit on this particular point, some drew the mistaken conclusion that the Church's prohibition of Freemasonry had been dropped...

Nothing could be further from the truth as, shortly before the 1983 code was promulgated, the Sacred Congregation for the Doctrine of the Faith issued a statement indicating that the penalty of excommunication for joining Masonic Lodges was and still is today in force. This statement was dated 26 November 1983 and may be found in "Origins" 13/27 (Nov. 15, 1983), 450.

Our Lady of Good Success

The apparitions of Our Lady of Good Success began in the 16th century, in 1594 in the city of Quito, Ecuador, to a Conceptionist nun who would later become Venerable Mother Mariana de Jesús Torres. The apparitions she received after a careful and methodical Church investigation would later be formally recognized and approved by her local bishop and by the Roman Catholic Church.

As further confirmation of her heavenly and supernatural experiences, in 1906, during the remodeling of the Convent, her three-century old tomb was opened and Mariana de Jesus' body was discovered whole and perfectly incorrupt, complete with her habit and the articles of penance that had been placed in the tomb with her. Likewise, an exquisite aroma of lilies emanated from her whole body.

The Beginning

In 1563, Mariana was born as the daughter of Don Diego and Doña Maria Torres Berriochoa, noble Spaniards and fervent Catholics who, at baptism, named their daughter Mariana Francisca.

Mariana was always raised with a profound Catholic background and noble upbringing. On receiving her first Communion at age nine, so intense was her joy of receiving at last the true Presence of Jesus-Christ, that she fell into a deep ecstasy. She saw Our Lord Jesus as a young boy placing a beautiful ring on her finger, claiming her for Himself, as the Blessed Virgin Mary and Saint Joseph witnessed the event of this "engagement".

In this same vision, the Blessed Virgin showed Mariana that she was called to her Order of the Immaculate Conception (*Saint Beatrix da Silva, a Portuguese lady of noble lineage, had just founded this order. She adopted the rule of Saint Francis of Assisi, and a blue-and-white habit honoring the Immaculate Conception*).

One day, as nine-year-old Mariana was receiving Holy Communion at Mass, Our Lord again appeared to her, inviting her to leave her father's house to embrace His Cross in Ecuador with her aunt. Burning with love and enthusiasm for the new mission entrusted to her, the little girl felt ready. Her parents knew of their daughter's innocence and incapability to lie and were at once convinced of God's manifested will to their young daughter.

Brokenhearted, but resigned, Mariana's parents placed their daughter in her holy aunt Maria's care (Maria Taboada), named Mother-Superior of the convent in Quito, who promised Don Diego and Doña Maria to be Mariana's new mother, and thus to take care of Mariana as her own daughter.

No sooner had the Spanish ship in destination to South America left port, that a cataclysmic tempest overtook their vessel... The Atlantic storm was so fierce and violent that the frightened sailors thought all was lost and were preparing for the worst... Suddenly, young Mariana saw in the raging waters a gigantic, seven-headed snake (dragon) attempting to destroy the ship. At the sight of this horrible vision, Mariana fainted.

Meanwhile, Mother Maria prayed asking that if Our Lord willed that the religious foundation in Quito be accomplished, that He grants a miracle and calms the storm. As soon as Mother Maria said this prayer, Mariana opened her eyes and the light of day overcame the darkness of the weather, but young Mariana heard at once a monstrous voice:

I will not allow this foundation to come about; I will not allow its progress; I will not allow it to endure to the end of time; I will persecute it!

Mariana recovered her calm and addressed her aunt:

Mother Maria, I don't know where I have been, Mother, but I saw a serpent bigger than the sea, twisting and contorting. Then I saw a lady of incomparable beauty, clothed with the sun and crowned with stars holding a babe in her arms. On the lady's breast I saw a monstrance with the Blessed Sacrament. In one of her hands she held a golden cross with a lance point. Anchoring the lance on the Blessed Sacrament and in the infant's hand, she struck at the serpent's head with such force that it split it under. At that moment, the serpent bellowed out his threats about not allowing the founding of the Order of the Immaculate Conception.

Capturing the full significance of this vision, Mother Maria later had a medal cast depicting this scene. To this day, the nuns of the Immaculate Conception of Quito wear this medal over their habits.

Mariana and her aunt successfully crossed the Atlantic, and arrived at last in Quito on 30 December 1576, where they were received by the foundation's nuns with great joy.

Young Mariana would become years later the prioress after her aunt, and would experience a series of truly extraordinary and astonishing occurrences and manifestations that would lead her convent to a mission for her contemporary era, but also for future generations to come... Indeed, Mother Mariana, as she would later be known, would experience the trauma of stigmata, visions, apparitions and even physical struggles against the devil... But one of her most remarkable tasks were to convey the messages and admonitions she received from the Blessed Virgin Mary for the Church and faithful of the 20th century!

On a day of Adoration, in 1582, when Mariana was praying before the Holy Eucharist, she unexpectedly saw the entire church, except for the church's main altar, immersed in a smoke-filled darkness. Without warning, the tabernacle door swung open and Our Crucified Lord came forth, nailed to a life sized cross. The Blessed Virgin Mary, and Saints John the Evangelist and Mary Magdalene stood by, as on Calvary. Our Lord was agonizing. Mariana then heard a voice:

This punishment is for the twentieth century.

Then she saw three swords hanging over Our Lord's head. On each of the swords was written:

"I shall punish heresy"
"I shall punish blasphemy"
"I shall punish impurity"

The Blessed Virgin then addressed Mariana:

- **"My daughter, do you wish to sacrifice yourself for this people?"**
- *"I am ready,"* responded the young nun.

At these words, the three swords plunged into Mariana's heart and she fell dead...

Noting Sister Mariana's absence from communal prayer, her aunt, Mother Maria, and the nuns searched for her. When they found her body in the lower choir dead, they grievingly carried her to her cell and laid her to rest... The community's doctor, Don Sancho, pronounced her dead and there was nothing to be done except to give her proper burial. Outside, the people of Quito clamored at the convent doors to see the body of their beloved "Santa hermanita" (holy little sister), for Sister Mariana was well known in Quito, having helped many with her counsels, penances, prayers and even miracles.

Meanwhile, Sister Mariana did appear before the Divine Judge. Finding no fault in her, Our Lord Jesus-Christ said to her:

Come, beloved of my Father, and receive the crown that We have prepared for you from the beginning of the world.

This said, Our Lord Jesus-Christ was listening quietly to the many supplications of Mariana's mourners on earth... Our Lord then presented to Sister Mariana two crowns, one of glory and the other of lilies intertwined with thorns... She understood that were she to choose the second, she would return to earth. Mariana, hesitant for a moment, asked Our Lord Jesus-Christ to choose for her.

- "No," answered Our Lord. **"When I took you for my spouse I tested your will, and now I wish to do the same."**

The Blessed Virgin Mary spoke:

- **My daughter, I left the glories of Heaven and returned to earth to protect my children. I want you to imitate me in this, for your life is necessary for my Order of the Immaculate Conception.**

Naturally, Mariana agreed at once and returned to earth. Great was the surprise of the convent when they saw the young little nun's cheeks take their usual lively pink color and her lips smile again!

On the night of 17 September 1588, as Sister Mariana was in the convent's chapel in deep prayer, she began to feel severe pain and realized she received the holy wounds of Our Lord Jesus in her hands, feet and side... Shortly thereafter, Sister Mariana fell severely ill and entered an excruciating trial, at the end of which she again expired... Yet, the following morning, as the nuns in mourning filed into the high choir to recite the Office, to their great shock, they found her alive again, praying! Like her Divine Spouse, Whom she sought to copy in everything, she had been resurrected on Easter morning and once again returned to life to continue suffering for souls and for the world...

In 1589, despite being only 36 years old, Mariana was elected Mother Superior as the health of her aunt, Mother Maria, was beginning to fail... Mariana fulfilled her duties as Mother Superior of the convent with admirable kindness, wisdom and charity, but always under the counsel and guidance of her loving aunt who experiences as well visions and revelations.

Both Mother Mariana and her aunt received heavenly insights about the future of their convent. They both knew each nun who would profess in their community, and those in the future who would be souls of great virtue and merit. Unavoidably, they foresaw ungrateful and disobedient ones as well... The holy souls would divert in the future great calamities from Ecuador and would maintain the faith burning even during the calamitous twentieth century.

The Devil plotted to destroy the Ecuadorian convent from within. Both holy women were also shown that soon, incited by God's enemy, some disobedient nuns who wanted a less stringent rule than the Franciscan statutes, and consequently would separate their community from the direction of the Franciscan Friars... Since the order of the Immaculate Conception was a branch of the Franciscan Order, this separation caused the faithful nuns most grievous suffering.

The Death of Mariana's aunt, Mother Maria Taboada, in 1594, caused her niece and the little nun community an inconsolable sorrow... The little community became grief-stricken at the loss of their beloved foundress; despite it all, from Heaven she continued to guide her monastery as she had promised in her last words before entering her agony. Indeed, Mother Maria frequently spoke with her niece in visions and apparitions after her death when the latter sought her guidance and counsel.

Around this time, Mother Mariana suffered cruelly with all the cares of her community. They lacked proper financial support, and the added cross of the threatening separation from the Franciscans was a real martyrdom. In the early morning of 2 February 1594, Mother Mariana was praying in the high choir.

Prostrated with her forehead on the ground, she implored help for her community and mercy for the sinful world. She then heard a sweet voice calling her name. Rising, she saw a lovely woman in a pool of bright light. On her left arm she held the Child Jesus and on her right a crosier of gold adorned with sparkling precious stones:

-   *"Who art thou, beautiful lady?"* she asked, *"and what dost thou wish? Dost thou not know that I am but a poor nun, filled with love for God, but suffering and tried to the utmost?"*

The lady answered:

I am Mary of Good Success, the Queen of Heaven and Earth. Precisely because you are a religious full of love for God and for His Mother who now speaks to you, I have come from Heaven to sooth your burdened heart.

Then the Mother of God showed her how her prayers and penances pleased God. She explained that she held the golden crosier in her right hand because she wished to govern the convent herself, and that the devil would do all in his power to destroy the convent by means of some ungrateful daughters who are living there.

He will not attain his goal, because I am the Queen of Victories and the Mother of Good Success. Under this invocation I wish, in the centuries to come, to perform miracles for the preservation of this, my convent, and its inhabitants.
Until the end of the world I will have holy daughters, heroic souls... who, suffering persecutions and slanders from within their own community, will be much loved by God and His Mother... Their lives of prayer, penance, and sacrifice will be extremely necessary in all times. After having spent their lives unknown to all, they will be called to Heaven to occupy an exalted throne of glory.

Then the Blessed Virgin placed the Infant Jesus in Mother Mariana's arms. Clasping Him tightly to her heart, Mother Mariana felt the strength to suffer all for Him and for humankind. The Blessed Virgin Mary appeared several times more to Mother Mariana under the title of the Mother of Good Success. During some of these apparitions she prophesied many things but most particularly about the twentieth century.

One day, during a difficult period of isolation (in her cell), as Mother Mariana prayed, she witnessed again the apparition of a lady of incomparable majesty and beauty surrounded by a splendid royal light. Once more, Our Lady of Good Success appeared with her Son Jesus and the golden crosier. This time, among many other things, the Mother of Good Success said:

In the nineteenth century, a truly Christian president will govern Ecuador. He will be a man of character to whom God Our Lord will grant the palm of martyrdom on this same central square where my convent stands. He will consecrate the Republic of Ecuador to the Sacred Heart of my most Holy Son, and this consecration will sustain the Catholic Faith in the years to come, which will be ominous for the Church.

During these years, in which Masonry, that cursed sect, will take over the government, there will be a cruel persecution against religious communities. They will also violently attack this convent, which is particularly mine. To those wretched men this monastery will seem finished, but unbeknown to them, I live and God lives to raise in their very midst powerful defenders of this work. We will also place insurmountable difficulties in their paths, and the triumph shall be ours.

Note: These predictions were fulfilled. Gabriel Garcia Moreno (1821–75) was a man of unshakable courage and ardent love for the Church and the Papacy. As president of Ecuador, he led the republic in the paths of Faith and righteousness, accomplishing tremendous educational and economic reform. Shortly after his reelection, he shouldered a huge wooden cross during a Holy Week procession and led the cortege through the streets of Quito.

Shortly thereafter, the Masonic lodges of Peru sent an assassin to kill him. He was brutally murdered on 6 August 1875, as he returned to the presidential palace after Mass and Holy Communion. He fell in the square on which stands the convent of the Immaculate Conception, just as Our Lady had predicted... While dying in a pool of blood from multiple machete wounds, he managed to dip his finger into his own blood and write on the pavement:

Dios no muere. (*God does not die.*)

During this apparition, Our Lady Good Success asked Mother Mariana to have a statue of her made exactly as Mother Mariana saw her. She wished this statue to be placed in the prioress' seat in the high choir so that, from there, she might rule effectively over her convent. She wished a crosier to be placed in her right hand as a sign of her authority as superior, along with the keys of the monastery so she might defend it in the centuries to come.

Mother Mariana was puzzled over how to obtain the Heavenly Lady's exact measurements... Noticing her confusion, Our Lady had her remove the cord from her waist, one end of which she gently took and held it at her forehead while Mother Mariana touched the other end to Our Lady's foot. The cord, too short for such a measurement, stretched to the perfect length.

On 21 January 1610, Our Lady of Good Success appeared again to mother Mariana, now accompanied by the three archangels Michael, Gabriel and Raphael, to request yet again that her statue be made. To that effect, the Blessed Virgin Mary even indicated the artist she wished to work on the assigned project: Don Francisco del Castillo, a God-fearing man and a consummate sculptor, who with his wife and children, scrupulously ruled his life with the Ten Commandments.

Again the holy nun asked to take the heavenly Lady's measurements. Again, the Blessed Mother of Jesus graciously took one end of the cord and placed it to her forehead while Mother Mariana touched the other end of the miraculously extended cord to her foot.

Early on the morning of 2 February 1610, Our Lady appeared again to Mother Mariana and repeated her command to have a statue made. Then she added:

Tell the Bishop that it is My will and the will of My Most Holy Son that your name be hidden at all costs, for it is not fitting for anyone at the present time to know the details or origin of how this Statue came to be made. For this knowledge will only become known to the general public in the 20th century.

During that epoch the Church will find herself attacked by terrible hordes of the Masonic sect, and this poor Ecuadorian land will be agonizing because of the corruption of customs, unbridled luxury, the impious press, and secular education. The vices of impurity, blasphemy, and sacrilege will dominate in this time of depraved desolation, and that one who should speak out will be silent...

Word of Our Lady's request profoundly moved the bishop, but he reprimanded Mother Mariana for not having conveyed it to him sooner. When Francisco del Castillo was contacted, he could scarcely contain his surprise, joy and gratitude at having been named by the Mother of God for this holy project. He refused payment, and only asked that his family and descendants always remain in the prayers of the religious community.

In January 1611, when the statue was nearly done and lacking only the final touches of paint and varnish, Don Francisco del Castillo left on a trip to procure the finest possible materials. On the morning of January 16, before Castillo's return, as the sisters approached the high choir to pray the morning Office, they heard a beautiful melody. On entering the choir they beheld the statue of Our Lady of Good Success, bathed in celestial light, while angelic voices sang the **Salve Sancta Parens.**

They saw that the statue had been exquisitely finished and that its face emitted rays of the brightest light! Francisco del Castillo, arriving and staring in awe at the exquisite statue, fell to his knees saying:

Mothers, what do I see? This precious statue is not the work of my hands. I do not know how to describe what I feel in my heart. This was made by angelic hands!

In fact, the outer layer of the statue lay on the ground. The bishop, kneeling before it, likewise acknowledged the prodigy as large tears welled in his eyes. He attested that the image had been modified and enriched by other than human hands. Afterwards, calling Mother Mariana, who had just been re-elected abbess once again, he asked her to come into the confessional. He knew that she must know something of what had occurred. Mother Mariana revealed indeed that a great light had filled the church and the choir while she prayed. She had beheld the Most Holy Trinity and Mary Most Holy, accompanied by the nine choirs of angels who praised and offered reverence to her.

The three archangels Saints Michael, Gabriel and Raphael each knelt before Mary Most Holy, saying in turn:

Hail Mary, daughter of God the Father
Hail Mary, Mother of God the Son
Hail Mary, most chaste Spouse of the Holy Ghost

Then Saint Francis appeared with his sacred wounds shining like suns. Approaching the unfinished statue and taking his belt from around his waist, he tied it around the statue's waist, placing his beloved convent of the Immaculate Conception in her hands and asking her to be its defender, teacher and mother in the difficult times to come. Meanwhile, the statue shined like the sun. At last, the Blessed Virgin, approached and entered it as the rays of the sun penetrate a transparent crystal.

At that moment, the statue sang the "Magnificat". This happened at 3:00 in the morning. Mother Mariana also saw her aunt, Mother Maria Taboada who was also present. At this, Mother Mariana returned to her senses. Looking at the statue, she saw it radiant and in utter splendor!

On 2 February 1634, as Mother Mariana finished a prayer before the Holy Tabernacle, she saw the sanctuary light extinguish itself, leaving the chapel completely dark... Then the Blessed Virgin Mary appeared before her and revealed to her that Our Lord had heard her prayers and would end her earthly exile in less than a year:

Prepare your soul so that, increasingly purified, it might enter into the fullness of the joy of Our Lord. Oh! If mortals, and in particular religious souls, could know what Heaven is and what it is to possess God! How differently they would live! Nor would they spare themselves any sacrifice in order to possess Him!

The Blessed Virgin Mary then explained to the Ecuadorian nun the 5 meanings of the Tabernacle light that had been extinguished before Mother Mariana's eyes:

- **The first significance is that at the end of the 19th century and into the 20th century, various heresies will be propagated in this land, then a free Republic. As these heresies spread and dominate, the precious light of Faith will be extinguished in souls by the almost total corruption of customs (morals). During this period, there will be great physical and moral calamities, both public and private.**
  The small number of souls who, hidden, will preserve the treasure of the Faith and the virtues will suffer an unspeakably cruel and prolonged martyrdom.
  Many of them will succumb to death from the violence of their sufferings, and those who sacrifice themselves for Church and Country will be counted as martyrs. In order to free men from bondage to these heresies, those whom the merciful love of My Most Holy Son will destine for that restoration will need great strength of will, constancy, valor and much confidence in God.
  To test this faith and confidence of the just, there will be occasions when everything will seem to be lost and paralyzed. This, then, will be the happy beginning of the complete restoration."
- **The second meaning is that My Convent, being greatly reduced in size, will be submerged in a fathomless ocean of indescribable bitterness, and will seem to be drowning in these diverse waters of**

tribulations. Many authentic vocations will perish. Injustice would enter even in this Convent, disguised under the name of false charity, wreaking havoc in souls. And faithful souls, weeping in secret and imploring that such dire times be shortened, would suffer a continuous and slow martyrdom.

- The third reason the lamp was extinguished is because of the spirit of impurity that will saturate the atmosphere in those times. Like a filthy ocean, it will run through the streets, squares and public places with an astonishing liberty. There will be almost no virgin souls in the world... The delicate flower of virginity would be threatened by complete annihilation. However, there will always be some good souls in cloisters where it might take root, grow and live like a shield to deflect Divine Wrath. Without virginity, it would be necessary for the fire from Heaven to fall upon these lands to purify them.

- The fourth reason for the lamp being quenched is that the Masonic sects, having infiltrated all the social classes, will subtly introduce its teaching into domestic ambiences in order to corrupt the children, and the Devil would glory in dining upon the exquisite delicacy of the hearts of children. During these unfortunate times, evil will assault childhood innocence. In this way, vocations to the priesthood will be lost, which will be a true calamity.

Against them, the impious will rage a cruel war, letting fall on them vituperations, calumnies and vexations in order to impede the fulfillment of their ministry. But they, like firm columns, will remain unswerving and will confront everything with the spirit of humility and sacrifice with which they will be vested, by virtue of the infinite merits of My Most Holy Son, Who will love them in the innermost fibers of His Most Holy and Tender Heart.

The secular clergy will be far removed from its ideal, because the priests will become careless in their sacred duties. Lacking the Divine compass, they will stray from the road traced by God for the priestly ministry and they will become attached to wealth and riches, which they will unduly strive to obtain. How the Church will suffer on that occasion—the dark night of the lack of a Prelate and Father to watch over them with paternal love, gentleness, strength, discernment and prudence. Many priests will lose their spirit, placing their souls in great danger.

Therefore, pray insistently without tiring and weep with bitter tears in the secrecy of your heart. Implore our Celestial Father that, for the love of the Eucharistic Heart of My Most Holy Son and His Precious Blood shed with such generosity He might take pity on His ministers and bring to an end those ominous times, and send to the Church the Prelate who will restore the spirit of His priests. My Most Holy Son and I will love this favored Son with a love of predilection, and We will gift Him with a rare capacity, humility of heart, docility to Divine inspiration, the strength to defend the rights of the Church, and a tender and compassionate heart, so that, like another Christ, He will assist the great and small, without despising the more unfortunate souls who ask Him for light and counsel in their doubts and hardships.

Into His hands the scales of the Sanctuary will be placed, so that everything is weighed with due measure and God will be glorified. The lukewarmness of all the souls consecrated to God in the priestly and religious state will delay the coming of this Prelate and Father. This, then, will be the cause of the cursed Devil taking possession of this land, where he will achieve his victories by means of a foreign and faithless people, so numerous that, like a black cloud, it will obscure the pure heavens of the then Republic consecrated to the Sacred Heart of My Divine Son.

With these people, all the vices will enter, which will attract in their turn every type of chastisement, such as plagues, famines, internal fighting and external disputes with other nations, and apostasy, the cause of the perdition of so many souls so dear to Jesus Christ and to Me. In order to dissipate this black cloud which prevents the Church from enjoying the clear day of liberty, there will be a formidable and frightful war, which will see the bloodshed of countrymen and foreigners, of secular and regular priests, and of religious.

That night will be most horrible, for, humanly speaking, evil will seem to triumph. This, then, will mark the arrival of My hour, when I, in a marvelous way will dethrone the proud and cursed Satan, trampling him under My feet and fettering him in the infernal abyss. Thus the Church and Country will finally be free of his cruel tyranny.

- The fifth reason that the lamp was extinguished is due to the laxity and the negligence of those who possess great wealth, who will indifferently stand by and watch the Church being oppressed, virtue being persecuted, and the triumph of the Devil, without piously employing their riches for the destruction of this evil and the restoration of the Faith. And it is also due to the indifference of the people in allowing the Name of God to be gradually extinguished and in adhering to the spirit of evil, freely delivering themselves over to vices and passions.

Alas! My chosen daughter! If it were given to you to live in that tenebrous era, you would die of sorrow to see all that I have revealed to you here take place. But My Most Holy Son and I have such a great love for this land, that We desire even now the application of your sacrifices and prayers to shorten the duration of such a terrible catastrophe!

Overwhelmed by the magnitude of the evils she saw and the countless souls that would be condemned during these times, Mother Mariana fell unconscious. There the Sisters found her, as if dead, except for the violent beating of her heart. All of the convent's doctor's efforts to restore her to consciousness proved useless. In fact, the sisters were told that, humanly speaking, her life should have ended from the shock she had received.

The Sisters surrounded her, knelt and beseeched Heaven to leave them their great treasure, the last of the Founding Mothers, "the mainstay of observance, the column of the house." Two days later, Mother Mariana opened her eyes, encouraged her Sisters to continue to follow the Rule, and consoled by assuring them that she would remain with them a little longer.

On 8 December 1634, Mother Mariana received yet a new apparition from the archangels, Gabriel, Michael, and Raphael escorting the Queen of Heaven. The Archangel Gabriel was carrying a Ciborium filled with hosts. The Blessed Virgin Mary then revealed to her further prophetic events that were to take place over 200 years in the future for a future Pope named Pius IX:

His pontifical infallibility will be declared a dogma of the Faith by the same Pope chosen to proclaim the dogma of the Mystery of My Immaculate Conception (Pope Pius IX). He will be imprisoned in the Vatican by the unjust usurpation of the Pontifical States through the iniquity, envy and avarice of an earthly monarchy.

In the nineteenth century, there will be a truly Catholic president, a man of character whom God Our Lord will give the palm of martyrdom on the square adjoining this convent. He will consecrate the Republic to the Sacred Heart of My Most Holy Son, and this consecration will sustain the Catholic Religion in the years that will follow, which will be ill-fated ones for the Church.

At the end of the 19th Century and especially in the 20th Century, Satan would reign almost completely by the means of the Masonic sect. This battle will reach its most acute stage because of various unfaithful religious, who, under the appearance of virtue and bad-spirited zeal, would turn upon Religion, which nourished them at her breast. During this time, insomuch as this poor country will lack the Christian spirit, the Sacrament of Extreme Unction will be little esteemed.

Many people will die without receiving it—either because of the negligence of their families or their false sentimentality that tries to protect the sick from seeing the gravity of their situations, or because they will rebel against the spirit of the Catholic Church, impelled by the malice of the devil. Thus many souls will be deprived of innumerable graces, consolations and the strength they need to make that great leap from time to eternity... As for the Sacrament of Matrimony, which symbolizes the union of Christ with His Church, it will be attacked and profaned in the fullest sense of the word.

Masonry, which will then be in power, will enact iniquitous laws with the objective of doing away with this Sacrament, making it easy for everyone to live in sin, encouraging the procreation of illegitimate children born without the blessing of the Church. The Christian spirit will rapidly decay, extinguishing the precious light of Faith until it reaches the point that there will be an almost total and general corruption of customs. The effects of secular education will increase, which will be one reason for the lack of priestly and religious vocations...

The Sacred Sacrament of Holy Orders will be ridiculed, oppressed and despised... The devil will try to persecute the Ministers of the Lord in every possible way and he will labor with cruel and subtle astuteness to deviate them from the spirit of their vocation, corrupting many of them. These corrupted priests, who will scandalize the Christian people, will incite the hatred of the bad Christians and the enemies of the Roman, Catholic and Apostolic Church to fall upon all priests. This apparent triumph of Satan will bring enormous sufferings to the good Pastors of the Church...

Moreover, in these unhappy times, there will be unbridled luxury which, acting thus to snare the rest into sin, will conquer innumerable frivolous souls who will be lost. Innocence will almost no longer be found in children, nor modesty in women. In this supreme moment of need of the Church, those who should speak will fall silent.

But know, beloved daughter, that when your name is made known in the 20th century, there will be many who will not believe, claiming that this devotion is not pleasing to God... A simple humble faith in the truth of My apparitions to you, My predilected child, will be reserved for humble and fervent souls docile to the inspirations of grace, for Our Heavenly Father communicates His secrets to the simple of heart, and not to those whose hearts are inflated with pride, pretending to know what they do not, or self-satisfied with empty knowledge.

During this time, the secular Clergy will leave much to be desired because priests will become careless in their sacred duties. Lacking the divine compass, they will stray from the road traced by God for the priestly ministry, and they will become attached to wealth and riches, which they will unduly strive to obtain. How the Church will suffer during this dark night! Lacking a Prelate and Father to guide them with paternal love, gentleness, strength, wisdom and prudence, many priests will lose their spirit, placing their souls in great danger. This will mark the arrival of My hour.

Therefore, clamor insistently without tiring and weep with bitter tears in the privacy of your heart, imploring our Celestial Father that, for love of the Eucharistic Heart of my Most Holy Son and His Precious Blood shed with such generosity and the profound bitterness and sufferings of His cruel Passion and Death, He might take pity on His ministers and bring to an end those Ominous times, sending to this Church the Prelate who will restore the spirit of its priests.

The Blessed Virgin Mary added that all seven Sacraments would come under attack in different ways:

It will be difficult to receive the Sacrament of Baptism and also that of Confirmation... The devil will make a great effort to destroy the Sacrament of Confession by means of people in positions of authority.

There will be an unspeakable profanation of the Holy Eucharist in our time. The enemies of Jesus Christ, instigated by the devil, will steal consecrated Hosts from the churches so that they may profane the

Eucharistic species. My Most Holy Son will see Himself cast upon the ground and trampled upon by filthy feet.

People will not esteem the Sacrament of Holy Unction and many will die without receiving it.

Our Lady predicted that, because of this:

... many souls will be deprived of innumerable graces, consolations and the strength they need to make that great leap from time to eternity.

The Blessed Virgin Mary added:

In the 20th century, this devotion (to Our Lady of Good Success) **will work prodigies in the spiritual as well as temporal spheres, because it is the Will of God to reserve this invocation and knowledge of your life for that century, when the corruption of customs will be almost general and the precious light of Faith all but extinguished...**

(The Blessed Virgin Mary, 8 December 1634)

The number of faithful, we are told, will be small and their faith will be sorely tested. However, the Mother of God promises that when all seems lost, she will intervene and crush Satan under her feet. There will be a great restoration and Jesus-Christ will reign through Mary.

Finally, the time to say goodbye to her daughters had come, Mother Mariana prepared her aggrieved daughters for her final voyage to eternity. She was to go to her Lord at 3 pm on 16 January 1635. She was 72 years old. At approximately 1:00 in the afternoon of that day, she asked the Mother Abbess to summon the community. When all the nuns arrived, she read aloud her magnificent testament, which began by affirming that she died a faithful daughter of the Holy, Roman, Catholic and Apostolic Church.

Then, with a voice vibrant with emotion but firm with the strength of faith and sincerity, she echoed her Master's words:

It is necessary that I go but I will not leave you orphans. I go to my Father and your Father, to my God and your God, and the Divine Consoler will descend to comfort you.

After receiving Holy Viaticum, she calmly closed her eyes and ceased breathing.

The revelations of Our Lady of Good Success were first approved by the Catholic Church in the early 17th century shortly after the statue bearing this title was sculpted at the command of the Blessed Virgin herself. The Bishop of Quito at the time, his Excellency Bishop Salvador de Ribera, went so far as to issue official documents attesting that the statue was miraculously completed and transformed by St. Francis of Assisi and by the archangels Michael, Gabriel and Raphael. Since then, the devotion has continued to enjoy the approval and support of the Church.

(Note: The principal source of the Story of Our Lady of Good Success herein written is principally taken from excerpts taken from the Article written by Andrea Phillips—in the May/June 2011 edition of the "Crusade Magazine".)

Chapter VII

Apparitions of the Blessed Virgin Mary in Garabandal, Spain

(Our Lady of Garabandal)

"If you beg forgiveness with sincerity of soul, He will forgive you I, your Mother, through the intercession of St. Michael the Archangel, want to tell you to amend your lives. You are now receiving the last warnings. I love you very much and do not want your condemnation. Ask sincerely and we will grant your requests. You should make more sacrifices. Think of the Passion of Jesus."

(Message of the Blessed Virgin Mary delivered by St. Michael, 18 June 1965)

Spain has, since 1939, lived in relative peace, managing to keep away from any major geopolitical conflicts since the Spanish civil war which was won ultimately by General Franco who remained in power until his death in 1975.

Before passing away, el "Generalisimo" restored the Spanish Monarchy by placing the heir to the Spanish Crown Juan-Carlos I de Bourbon on the Spanish throne. It was he, after Franco's death, who led Spain outside dictatorship and into a transition to a democratic regime; however, before this took place, a great event was about to bless Spain in a most remarkable manner...

The little village of Garabandal is a small hamlet of some 80 humble dwellings located in the Cantabrian Mountains of northern Spain, in the Santander province, near the Picos de Europa Mountains. The village's full name is San Sebastian de Garabandal. It is located 600 meters above sea level, some 57 miles from the capital of the province. The small village in the mountains was marked between the years 1961 and 1965 by extraordinary apparitions of the Blessed Virgin Mary through over 3,000 public apparitions to four girls between the age of 11 and 12 years of age: Conchita Gonzáles, Mari Cruz Gonzáles, Jacinta González and Mari Loli Mazón.

The first apparition the four little girls experienced was on the evening of 18 June 1961. Hearing a loud noise like thunder on a flat emerald green plain, the girls saw appear suddenly before them the bright figure of the Archangel Michael.

The Archangel looked intensely at the four children while remaining silent, and quickly disappeared... Pale and visibly shaken, the four girls ran back to their village church in search of heavenly refuge. Over the next twelve days, the angel appeared to them various times thereafter in the same place. Little by little, the four girls gained confidence and gradually felt a certain kindness, warmth and trust in this heavenly visitor who came merely to prepare them for what was yet to come, and on 1 July, St. Michael appeared yet again, but this time spoke to them for the very first time, announcing that on the following day, Sunday 2 July, the Blessed Virgin Mary would appear to them as Our Lady of Mount Carmel.

The girls returned running to their village and reported to their families the Archangel's announcement... The news spread quickly like a wildfire throughout the village and region.

2 July, being a Sunday, the town was quite crowded. There were people from all social stations, even a great deal from out of town, among whom doctors and priests. At 6:00 in the evening the girls, followed by a large crowd, went to the place where the Angel had appeared to them in anticipation of the eve's announcements, and to the surprise of the crowd, the four children immediately entered into ecstasy... Our Lady appeared to them accompanied by two angels, one being St. Michael the Archangel, the other was unknown to them.

The girls described the vision as follows:

She was dressed in a white robe with a blue mantle and a crown of golden stars. Her hands were slender. There was a brown scapular on her right arm, except when she carried the Child Jesus in her arms. Her hair, deep nut-brown, was parted in the center. Her face is long, with a fine nose. Her mouth is very pretty with lips a bit thin. She looks like a girl of eighteen. She is rather tall. There is no voice like hers. No woman is just like her, either in the voice or the face or anything else. Our Lady Manifested herself as Our Lady of Mt. Carmel.

(2 July 1961)

From Conchita's diary:

We had not yet arrived at the scene of the apparitions when the Blessed Virgin appeared with an angel on each side. One of the two angels who accompanied her was Saint Michael. The other I didn't recognize. He was dressed exactly like Saint Michael. They looked like twins. Beside the angel, who stood at the Blessed Virgin's right and at the same height as she, was a large eye which seemed to be the eye of God.

That day we talked a lot with the Blessed Virgin, as she did with us. We told her everything. We told her that we went out to the fields, that we were tanned from the sun, that we put the hay in stacks, etc. And she laughed as we told her all these things.

It was the first apparition of Our Lady of Garabandal. The first of many apparitions. Garabandal was going to be converted into a place touched by the presence of Our Heavenly Mother. The apparitions were many, and many were also the graces and heavenly gifts granted through Our Lady's intercession.

After the first apparition, many more followed. In the course of 1961 and 1962, the Blessed Virgin Mary appeared several times each week with the four girls not always together nor always at the same hour of the day. The Blessed Virgin Mary likewise often appeared at night and early in the morning,... *at the same time when Our Lord is most offended by the sins of men...* Nonetheless, the girls arose every morning at the usual early time to work in the fields, carrying bundles of grass or wood, or tending the cattle and sheep without ever showing signs of fatigue.

As the Blessed Virgin Mary continued to appear to the four girls, more and more extraordinary events began to take place, which created awe if not always shock... Indeed, often when the Blessed Virgin Mary appeared to the four young seers, the four girls were seen raising immediately their glance towards the heavens with splendid smiles. Likewise, many were the times when, while in ecstasy, the children began running at great speeds in very rocky terrain—never taking their glance off the heavens—while holding each other's arms (many young and athletic men were simply unable to keep-up with their pace), or walking quickly backwards, always while looking up, never falling nor hurting themselves, with a smile that never left their faces.

Their ecstatic state never let them look where they were stepping, running or jumping, while, remarkably enough, never falling or mis-stepping on a rock, hole or obstacle.... Likewise, before apparitions, the four girls were given large numbers rosaries, sacramentals and religious objects whose owners the children had no way of always knowing; this however never stopped the four little girls

348

from bringing back said objects to their rightful owners (while never taking their attention from their guiding vision high above them)!

This was done on countless occasions, never mistaking the rightful owners of said sacramentals! More remarkably yet was observing them, while in ecstasy, unknotting without the least sign of a struggle massive balls of hopelessly-mingled rosaries, only to return them unharmed to their respective owners after the Blessed Virgin Mary had kissed them. Most extraordinary were the observed cases of levitation, and the instances when they appeared heavy as boulders—witnessed by men who, on occasions, in groups of four or five were not able to lift any of the little girls in ecstasy.

On the other hand, each seer was able to lift any of the others during the apparitions (to help each other kiss the Blessed Virgin Mary) as if they were but mere feathers… Naturally, as in other apparition sites, when the children were conversing with heavenly interlocutors, no light-flash, no prickle, no burning flame, no man-made test or interference were ever able to interrupt the ecstatic exchange… In other words, the extraordinary!

In October of 1961, the Blessed Virgin Mary revealed a message which was meant to be delivered to the world (see page 354 - original message written in Spanish and signed by the visionaries):

Many sacrifices must be made… Much penance must be done… You must make many visits to the Blessed Sacrament, but first of all you must be very good. If you do not, a chastisement will befall you. Already the Cup is filling, and if you do not change, a great chastisement will come upon you…

(The Blessed Virgin Mary to all four girls on 18 October 1961)

Letter of Padre Pio to the Visionaries of Garabandal

On 3 March 1962, Padre Pio wrote a letter, in Italian, to the four visionaries and sent it to San Sebastian de Garabandal. Said letter was translated by Félix López, a seminarian from Bilbao who was present when it was delivered. In said letter, Padre Pio wrote:

Dear children,

At nine o'clock this morning the Holy Virgin told me to say to you:

O Blessed young girls of San Sebastian de Garabandal, I promise you that I will be with you until the end of the centuries, and you will be with me during the end of the world and later united with me in the glory of paradise.

Attached to this letter is a copy of the Holy Rosary of Fatima, which the Blessed Virgin ordered me to send you. The Blessed Virgin has dictated this Rosary, and She desires it to be made known for the salvation of sinners and to preserve humanity from the worst punishments that the good God is threatening it with.

My recommendation is this: pray and encourage others to pray, because the world is on the way to perdition.

They do not believe you or our conversations with the White Lady, but they will believe when it is too late.

ROSARY OF THE VIRGEN OF FATIMA

1) *In this first mystery we see how the Holy Virgin chose Fatima as her favorite city to spread her messages.*

2) *In this second mystery it is contemplated how the Holy Virgin chose the Cova de Iria for her visions.*

3) *In this third mystery we see how the Holy Virgin chose the three little shepherds for their celestial conversations and to entrust the great secret to them.*

4) *In this fourth mystery we see how the secret of Fatima is the greatest secret of all that she has revealed.*

5) *In this fifth mystery we can see how the visions of the Blessed Virgin continues to be present in all parts of the world.*

The Virgin has promised special graces to all who pray this rosary.

(Padre Pio's Letter, 3 March 1962)

When Conchita showed the letter to the Virgin Mary in her next apparition, the Mother of Christ responded by telling her that it was indeed Padre Pio who sent the letter. Conchita never knew who Padre Pio was, but a little later, a seminarian explained that Padre Pio was a most famous and saintly Capuchin Friar from San Giovanni Rotondo, in Italy (see page 354).

In February of 1975, in an interview for the magazine **Needles,** currently **Garabandal Journal,** Conchita talked about her reaction to this letter:

I was taken aback by what it said, and since it came unsigned, I kept it in my pocket until the next apparition. When our Blessed Mother appeared, I showed her the letter and asked her who it was from. Our Blessed Mother answered that it came from Padre Pio. I did not know at the time who Padre Pio was, and it did not occur to me to inquire further.

After the apparition, we were discussing the letter. Then a seminarian who was there (Félix López) explained to me who Padre Pio was and where he lived. I wrote to him telling him that if he ever visited my country, I would very much like to see him. He answered me with a short letter that said:

Do you think I can climb in and out of chimneys?

At 12 years of age, I had no idea what a monastery could be.

In February of 1966, Conchita traveled to Rome due to an invitation she received from Cardinal Ottaviani of the Congregation for the Doctrine of the

Faith. The young woman set out with her mother Aniceta, Father Luis J. Luna (now the parish priest of Garabandal who had substituted Father Valentín the previous summer), and Princess Cecilia de Borbón-Parma, a member of the Carlist royal family and principal organizer of the seer's journey to Italy.

On this trip, one of the contacts of the small Spanish group was Dr. Enrico Medi, friend and personal doctor of Pope Paul VI. Dr. Medi suggested taking advantage of their trip to Rome to visit San Giovanni Rotondo and thus meet Padre Pio.

Conchita was overjoyed at this idea, since she vividly remembered the message that the Capuchin had transmitted to them on behalf of the Blessed Virgin Mary:

I promise you that you will be united with me in the glory of Paradise.

Conchita herself tells the story:

We arrived around nine o'clock at night and we were told that we could not see Padre Pio until the following morning at his 5:00 a.m. Mass. Before Mass, Father Luna and Professor Medi went to the sacristy. The professor told me afterwards what had happened there. He said that Father Luna had told Padre Pio that the Spanish Princess was there to see him (Cecilia de Borbón-Parma). Padre Pio then told Father Luna:

- *"I don't feel well and won't be able to see her until later on today."*

Professor Medi then said:

- *"There is another person who also wishes to see you. Conchita wishes to speak with you."*
- **"Conchita from Garabandal? Come at eight o'clock this morning."**

Upon arrival, Conchita and her mother were led to a small room, finding Padre Pio in a cell with only a bed, a chair and a small table...Conchita remembered that she had the crucifix kissed by Our Lady and told Padre Pio when she was introduced to him:

- *"This is the cross kissed by the Blessed Virgin. Would you like to kiss it?"*

Padre Pio then took the little cross of Christ and placed it on the palm of his left hand, over the stigmata. He then took Conchita's hand which he placed over the crucifix... He then blessed her hand and the cross while speaking her. The young woman was 16 years old, and between her excitement and nerves, she couldn't recall what the saint stigmatist had told her... Nevertheless, there are ample facts to demonstrate the benevolence and love with which the Capuchin viewed the phenomena of Garabandal, something that he will demonstrate on various occasions.

In fact, there are several testimonies from individuals who have been sent to Garabandal by the stigmatized monk of Gargano. Among these is Joachim Boufflet, doctor and philosophy professor at the University of the Sorbonne in Paris and consultant to the Congregation for the Causes of Saints in Rome.

Indeed, on the afternoon of 23 August 1968, after having gone to confession with Padre Pio in the cloister of the convent of San Giovanni Rotondo, he spoke for a few minutes with him. At the end of the confession, Padre Pio told him:

- ***Pray to the Madonna. Consecrate yourself to the Virgin of Mt. Carmel who appeared in Garabandal.***

Joachim Boufflet was confused, but Padre Pio insisted:

- ***Consecrate yourself to the Virgin of Mt. Carmel who appeared in Garabandal.***

Finally, the Frenchman asked him:

- *The apparitions of Garabandal? Then, they are true?*

To which the Capuchin responded emphatically:

- ***Of course they are true.***

Other saints have demonstrated their interest in the Garabandal phenomena – to name but one: Rev. Mother Theresa of Calcutta who became godmother of Conchita's children. But the manner in which Padre Pio involved himself if quite unique. Conchita cites his name in her diary, indicating that she was revealed by the Blessed Virgin Mary, that he will see the miracle from wherever he may be. That is why when the Capuchin monk died on 23 September 1968, Conchita was quite perplexed as to why the prophecy had not come true.

Providence, however was to ease her apprehensions. Indeed, the young Spanish woman received a telegram from Lourdes. The telegram asked her to go to the famous French apparition site to receive a letter that Padre Pio had left for her. Fr. Combe, a French parish priest from Chazay d'Azergues, in the diocese of Lyon, and a great promoter of the cause of Garabandal was in the little Spanish village that day. He and his collaborator, B. L. Ellos, offered to take Conchita and Conchita's mother, Aniceta, in their car and set out that night for Lourdes. She accepted and thanked the Heavens for setting circumstances for her to respond to the invitation in Lourdes.

On the morning of 17 October, Conchita received in the French pilgrimage site from the Rev. Father Bernardino Cennamo, OFM Cap, an Italian Capuchin, a short written message from Padre Pio, a large section of the veil that had covered Padre Pio's face after his death, and one of Padre Pio's gloves. Father Cennamo explained to the young Spanish seer that Father Pellegrino, a priest who took care of Padre Pio in his last years, had transcribed a note for her that had been dictated by the Saint. Father Cennamo then acknowledged that he did not believe in Garabandal for a very long time, but shared with Conchita that when Padre Pio asked him to give her the veil that covered his face after his death, he changed his views.

At Lourdes, on that day, the veil and the letter were delivered to Conchita. But something else interested her more. And so she immediately asked again Father Cennamo:

- *Why did the Virgin tell me that Padre Pio would see the miracle and he has died?*

To which the Capuchin responded:

- *He saw the miracle before he died! He told me himself!*

After receiving the famous veil in Lourdes, Conchita recounted:

I had the veil in front of me, as I was writing later that evening. When suddenly the whole room became filled with fragrance, the perfume so strong I started to cry.

The only other person who had been granted to see the great miracle before he died was Rev. Padre Luis Andreu, a skeptical priest who came to Garabandal to see for himself "the fraud"... but while observing the four visionaries in ecstasy at the pines outside the little village, the good Spanish priest suddenly cried out: *MIRACLE! MIRACLE! MIRACLE! MIRACLE!*

On the drive home with friends that night, Padre Luis Andreu said to his travelling companions:

I feel myself truly full of joy and happiness. What a gift the VIRGIN has given me. How fortunate to have a Mother like her in Heaven! I can't have the least doubt about the truth of their visions.

After saying this, Father Luis Andreu made a slight coughing sound, lowered his head to his chest and passed away. (Testimony of Rafael Fontaneda)

The Night of Screams

In the following months, pilgrims came from all across Spain, and sometimes from very distant countries to see the four little messengers of the Blessed Virgin Mary, including scientists and priests who came to observe and sometime to disprove what was, however, ever so clear a reality to a multitude of faithful... On 19 June 1962, the Blessed Virgin Mary reappeared to Loli and Jacinta with a message for the whole world:

You are not waiting for the chastisement, because you are disregarding my first message by the way you live. It will come because the world has not

care Fanciulle

alle ore nove di questa mattina la Santa Vergine Maria mi ha parlato di voi o care fanciulle, delle vostre visioni e mi ha detto di dirvi:

"o Benedette fanciulle di San Sebastian de garabandal, io vi prometto che sarò voi fino alla fine dei secoli, e voi sarete con me fino alla fine del mondo, e poi unite/a me nel gaudio del paradiso."

Allegato alla presente vi rimetto la copia del S° Rosario di Fatima, che la Santa Vergine mi ha ordinato di spedirvi. Questo rosario è stato dalla Santa Vergine dettato e vuole che sia propagandato per la salvazione dei peccatori e la preservazione dell'umanità dei maggiori castighi, che il buon Dio sta minacciando.

Una sola è la raccomandazione: pregate e fate pregare perché il mondi è sulla via della perdizione.

Non credono in voi e nei vostri colloqui con la bianca Signora ma ci crederanno quando sarà troppo tardi.

3 Marzo 1962

Padre Pio's letter to the visionaries of Garabandal

Hay que hacer muchos sacrificios mucha pe intención y hay que visitar mucho al Santísimo pero antes tenemos que ser muy buenos y si no lo hacemos nos vendrá un castigo. Ya se esta llenando la Copa y sino cambiamos nos vendrá un castigo muy grande.

Conchita González
María Dolores Mazón
Jacinta González González
Maria Cruz González

Message of Our Lady received by the four visionaries of Garabandal on 18 October 1961 (see page 349)

Visionaries of Garabandal (Spain)

Conchita Gonzalez, Mari Loli Mazon, Jacinta Gonzalez, and Mari Cruz Gonzalez

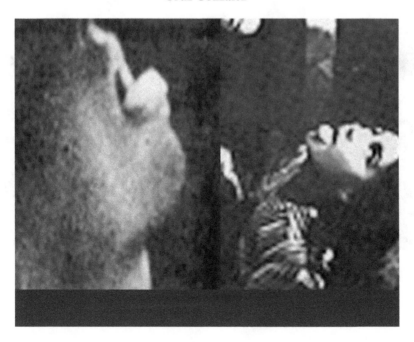

Conchita receiving Holy Communion from Saint Michael the Archangel

355

In one picture (left), one visionary cannot be lifted from the ground. In the other (right), a visionary is light as a feather and is lifted without any difficulty by another seer.

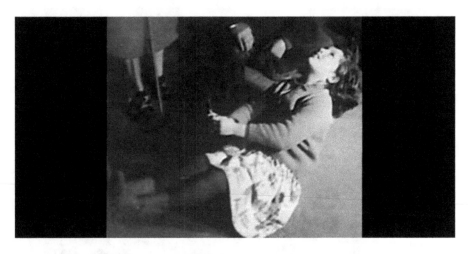

Mari Loli Mazon in ecstasy in stage one of levitation

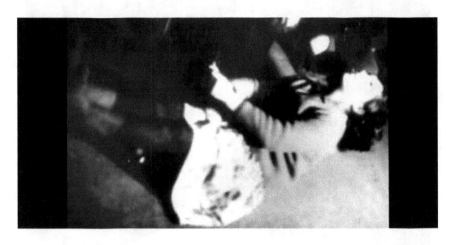

Mari Loli Mazon in ecstasy in stage two of levitation

Nights of the screams: The children (seers) being shown the Chastisements…
(See Page 353)

Conchita Gonzalez (seer from Garabandal) 1980, interview with the BBC
(see page 376)

Conchita Gonzalez (seer from Garabandal) in 2020

changed. Prepare yourselves. Confess, for the chastisement will come soon if the world does not change.

(The Blessed Virgin Mary to Loli and Jacinta, 19 June 1962)

It appeared that the Mother of Christ was pressing to echo a message that was not catching the adequate attention; hence, two nights later, before countless witnesses, the four young visionaries witnessed together, in sheer terror, most profound and yet frightful visions, later to be known in the annals of Garabandal history as "the night of screams"…

Conchita's testimony:

In spite of continuing to see the Virgin, we saw a great multitude of people who were suffering intensely and screaming in terror. The Blessed Virgin explained to us that this great tribulation, which was not even the Chastisement, would come because a time would arrive when the Church would appear to be on the point of perishing. It would pass through a terrible trial. We asked the Virgin what this great trial was called, and she told us it was Communism. Then she showed us how the great Chastisement for all mankind would come, and explained that it would come directly from God.

*At a certain moment, not a single motor or machine would function (*supernatural, natural, or man-made electromagnetic strike?*); a terrible heat wave will strike the earth and men will begin to feel a great thirst… In desperation they will seek water, but this will evaporate from the heat. Then almost everyone will despair and they will seek to kill one another. But they will lose their strength and fall to the ground. Then it will be understood that it is God alone Who has permitted this.*

Then we saw a crowd in the midst of flames. The people ran to hurl themselves into the lakes and seas. But the water seemed to boil, and instead of putting out the flames, it seemed to enkindle them even more. ***It was so horrible that I asked the Blessed Virgin to take all the young children with her before all this happened. But the Virgin told us that by the time it came, they would all be adults.***

(21 June 1962: The Night of the Screams)

To complement this vision, the Blessed Virgin Mary gave a message for the whole world two days later, on 23 June 1962:

The world continues the same… That it has not changed at all. Few will see God… They are so few that it causes the Virgin much Sorrow. What a pity that it does not change. The Virgin told us that the Chastisement is coming, seeing that the world is not changing. The cup is filling up. How sad the Virgin was, although she didn't let us see it because She loves us so much and she suffers alone. She is so good!

Be good, everyone, so that the Virgin be happy! She told us that We who are good should pray for those who are bad. Let us pray to God for the world, for those who do not know Him. Be good... be very good, everyone!

(Maria Dolores Mazon and Jacinta Gonzalez, 23 June 1962)

That we do not expect the Chastisement; that without expecting it, it will come; since the world has not changed, and she has already told us twice; and we do not pay attention to her since the world is getting worse, and it should change very much, and it has not changed at all. Prepare yourself. Confess, because the Chastisement will come soon and the world continues to be the same... I tell you this: the world continues the same. How unfortunate that it does not change! Soon will come a very great Chastisement if it does not change.

(Maria Dolores Mazon and Jacinta Gonzalez, 23 June 1962)

Above the village is a steep hill on which stands a cluster of nine pine trees.

"One day," said the girls, *"an angel with a golden chalice appeared to us at 'The Pines'. He told us to recite the Confiteor and then he gave us Holy Communion."*

Due to the lack of priests, the little village of Garabandal shared a priest with the neighboring town of Cosio; hence, sometimes it became difficult for the four girls to receive Holy Communion as they were prescribed to do so by the Angel and the Blessed Virgin Mary. Hence, the Angel came from time to time to give Communion to the four girls who immediately fell on their knees opening their mouths to receive Our Lord... Often, it was possible to film some of these extraordinary Communions, using cameras with very bright light. The movements of the lips and tongues of the girls gave the exact hint of the event that was taking place.

On 2 May 1962, the Angel told Conchita that God would perform a miracle so that all people would believe: they would see the Sacred Host on her tongue at the moment of Holy Communion. For this granted miracle, the Angel explained, Conchita would have to announce this event fifteen days in advance, and so she did faithfully as instructed...

On 18 July 1962, the town was crowded with visitors. At midnight Conchita, who had remained in her home, which was continually surrounded by visitors, entered into ecstasy in her usual manner and went out into the street. At a short distance from her house she fell down ever so hard on her knees before the crowd. Lanterns were focused on her. After a brief moment, in the midst of a deep silence interrupted by countless camera flashes and endless clicking, Conchita put out her tongue upon which nothing was resting.

Seconds thereafter, a white host appeared out of thin air on her tongue and remained there for a few minutes for everyone to see! Awws, gasps, and loud exclamations could be heard amongst the populace that witnessed the Miracle! A businessman from Barcelona, Don Alejandro Damians, standing less than three feet from the girl, secured some very good moving pictures.

In the film, there appeared 79 pictures of the extraordinary scene. This same witness wrote sometime thereafter a report which he submitted to the Bishop of Santander, together with a copy of the film. The number of witnesses on this occasion was massive... Don Benjamin Gomez, a farmer from Potes, wrote:

I was standing at less than an arm's length from the girl. I saw very well that her tongue was completely clean and had nothing on it. The girl did not move. Suddenly there appeared on it the Sacred Host. It was white, shining and resplendent. It reminded me of a snow flake when the sun strikes it with its brilliant rays. The girl's face was beautifully transformed into heavenly ecstasy. Her face was angelic I can certify that she was there motionless, moving neither hands nor tongue.

In this motionless position she received the Sacred Host. We had enough time to contemplate this marvelous phenomenon without any undue haste, and we were many who've seen this! **I was an unbeliever until that day.** *I am not such a Catholic as to be subject to any hallucination or imagination. I had not concerned myself about God until then except to offend Him. I went to confession in April but previous to that time I had not gone to confession for twenty-three years.*

(Don Benjamin Gomez' testimony translated from Spanish into English)

When the Blessed Virgin Mary asked for priests to come and witness the events in Garabandal, the little seers sadly responded by saying that the bishop of Santander prohibited priests to come... The Blessed Virgin Mary then replied:

"If the bishop said for priests not to come, then let his decision be obeyed."

This sentence is indeed capital as it underlines the Blessed Virgin Mary's teaching of the importance of bishops and priests, and of maintaining obedience towards the Catholic Church...

On another instance, the Blessed Virgin Mary showed yet again special consideration to the priests who came to the village. Indeed, the little seers were told by Our Lady:

"A priest is more important than an angel. If you were to meet a priest and an angel at the same time, you are to greet the priest first."

The Warning, the Miracle, and the Punishment

The Warning

The warning ("el Aviso") will come directly from God and will be visible to the whole world and from any place where anyone may happen to be. It will be like the revelation of our sins and it will be seen and felt by everyone, believers and unbelievers alike irrespective of whatever religion he may belong to. It will be seen and felt in all parts of the world and by every person. It will happen in the sky, no one can prevent it from happening. We are told that the faithful will prefer to be dead rather than to pass through this Warning... Conchita adds:

It will not kill us. It will be a "correction" of our conscience. It will cause great fear and will make us reflect within ourselves on the consequences of our own personal sins. It will be like a warning of the punishment to come... In this way the world will be offered a means of purification to prepare itself for the extraordinary grace of the Great Miracle.

Jacinta was told by Our Blessed Mother that the warning would come **when conditions will be at their worst...**

Mother María de la Nieves García, Superior of the school in Burgos where Conchita studied in 1966 and 1967 stated:

... During the apparitions, the Virgin told Conchita that before the future events occur, a Synod will take place, and important Synod. Then Conchita told the story to her aunt.

*The aunt asked her: **Do you mean a Council**? Because that was the time of Second Vatican Council.*

Conchita told her aunt: 'No, the Virgin didn't say Council. She said Synod, and I think Synod is a small council.'

*It is impossible for a 12-year-old girl without any knowledge and culture to talk about Synod that didn't exist and we didn't know at that time, and in addition she defined the Synod as a **small council**.*

I have heard this from Father Rafinel, and he heard it from Father Pesquera who wrote some of the first books about Garabandal apparitions.

He discussed that with Professor Lacques Serre who works at Paris-Sorbonne University and he decided that Synod as a pre-Warning.

Professor wrote him many letters in which he also described that as a "pre-Warning".

(Mother María de la Nieves García, Superior of the school in Burgos, 1995)

A synod on Synodality is scheduled to take place in Rome on October 2022, a synod described by Pope Francis as:

A *key for the future. Synodality is what the Lord awaits from the Church of the third millennium.*

The year 2022 will likewise be the year seeing the conclusion of the most controversial two-year German Episcopal synod {see page 513} aimed at reforming the German Catholic Church...

362

Let us note that the children of Garabandal were also told that the Warning would take place after… *something very much like a schism takes place within the Church…*

The Miracle

Despite this most extraordinary event, a greater miracle yet was announced and promised… Conchita explained:

About the miracle, Our Lady only told me that I cannot say the date until 8 days before… A great miracle in Garabandal will take place so that all may believe the apparitions and be obedient to the message. As to the punishment, we deserve it for the sins of the world are great; the miracle must also be a great one, for the world needs it. It will occur on a Thursday on the feast day of a saint devoted to the Eucharist, at 8:30 in the evening, and will last for about one quarter of an hour.

It will also coincide with a great event in the Church. The sick who come to Garabandal on that day will be cured, unbelievers will be converted. There will remain a permanent sign at "The Pines" as a proof of Our Lady's tremendous love for all her children. The sign that will remain will be able to be seen, photographed and televised but it will not be able to be touched. It will appear clearly that it is something not of this world, but of God.

Conchita transmitted the date of the event to come to Pope Paul VI, his confessor and to Cardinal Ottaviani who was at the time the Prefect of the Dycasterium of Holy Orders (today the Congregation of the Doctrine of the Faith).

Conchita further added:

With the present means of communication and travel, 8 days are sufficient for people around the world to gather. The day of the miracle may be the last opportunity given us by God, and may be also Our Lady's last effort to save the world from the punishment already threatened. The Blessed Mother will not allow me to reveal the nature of the miracle although I already know it… But before the miracle takes place, Our Mother has said that all mankind will receive a warning from Heaven first…

The date of the Miracle was not revealed to the visionaries, however Mari-Loli does know the year and stated:

The Miracle will happen within one year after the Warning…

Since we are told the announced "Miracle" will occur on a Thursday on the feast day of a saint devoted to the Eucharist, we may consider the earliest dates of said event to be on 12 May 2022, Feast Day of St. Pancracio, or St. Hermenegild's feast day on Thursday, 13 April 2023. Other years that fall under the description of the prophecy are: 2024, 2027, 2028, 2030, 2032, 2034 and 2035...

The Chastisement

Conchita later wrote about the world chastisement (*"el Castigo"*) that had been announced by the Blessed Mother of God:

I cannot reveal what kind of punishment it is except that it will be a result of the direct intervention of God, which makes it more terrible and fearful than anything we can imagine. It will be less painful for innocent babies to die a natural death than for those babies to die because of the punishment. All Catholics should go to confession before the punishment and the others should repent of their sins. When I saw it (the punishment), I felt a great fear even though at the same time I was seeing Our Blessed Mother. The punishment, if it comes, will come after the Miracle...

When our Mother spoke to us, her face had a look of great sorrow... We have never seen her look so serious. When she said the words 'The cup is already filling', she spoke in a very low voice...

On 1 January 1965, Conchita had an apparition of Our Lady who informed her that on 18 June, the fourth anniversary of her apparitions in Garabandal, she would be giving another message for the world; hence, six months before the actual date, Conchita revealed the Blessed Virgin Mary's announcement publicly. As expected, the statement spread ever so quickly throughout the region and even throughout Europe and the United States, and on 18 June 1965, thousands of people came to the village of Garabandal. American, French, English, Italian, German and Polish pilgrims, scientists and journalists came to the little village of Garabandal.

French pilgrims and journalists were the largest group gathered. TV cameras from France, Italy and Spain were likewise present. The tiny Spanish village of Garabandal had been invaded by fleets of cars and buses from which disembarked hordes of people from all across the world.

On the appointed hour, Conchita finally left her house and started walking, amongst a multitude of followers, on the road leading to the place of the Pines called the "Cuadro". Once arrived, she knelt and fell in ecstasy which lasted approximately 16 minutes.

Saint Michael the Archangel appeared to Conchita and announced that he was sent to deliver the Blessed Virgin Mary's message to the world (which was made public the following morning):

Since my message of October the 18 has not been complied with nor has been made known to the world, I tell you that this is my last message. Previously, the cup was filling up. Now it is overflowing. Many Cardinals, many Bishops and many Priests are on the road to perdition and are taking many souls with them. The Holy Eucharist is being given less importance

(honor). You should turn away God's Wrath from you with your efforts at amendments.

If you beg forgiveness with sincerity of soul, He will forgive you I, your Mother, through the intercession of St. Michael the Archangel, want to tell you to amend your lives. You are now receiving the last warnings. I love you very much and do not want your condemnation. Ask sincerely and we will grant your requests. You should make more sacrifices. Think of the Passion of Jesus.

(Message of the Blessed Virgin Mary delivered by St. Michael, 18 June 1965)

Conchita finally added:

Our Blessed mother has told us this is her last message... Because of this, she wants all her children to listen to her plea before the Warning and the Miracle. For these reasons we should propagate this urgent message as widely as possible.

The Last apparition...

On Saturday, 13 November 1965 Conchita had her last apparition of Our Lady in Garabandal. She gives the details in a letter whose English translation goes as such:

One day in church Our Lady told me in a locution that I would see her on Saturday, November 13, at the pines; it would be a special apparition to kiss the religious objects so that I could give them away afterwards. I was anxious for this day to arrive so that I could see again the Blessed Virgin and the Child Jesus who have implanted in my life the seed of God's happiness. It was raining but it did not matter to me. I went up to the Pines carrying with me the many rosaries which people have given to me to distribute them.

As I was going up I was talking to myself, being sorry for my defects, desiring not to fall into them again, for it gave me much worry to appear before the Mother of God without wiping them out. When I arrived at the pines, I began to take the rosaries out and heard a sweet voice, that of the Virgin, which you always distinguish among others, calling me by my name. I answered her 'what?' At that very moment I saw Her with the Child in her arms. She was dressed as usual and smiling. I told her:

- *"I have come to bring you the rosaries so that you can kiss them."*
- **"Yes, I can see."**

I had been chewing gum, but as I was seeing Her I did not chew it; I placed the gum on a tooth. She must have noticed for She said:

- **"Conchita, why don't you get rid of the chewing gum and offer it up as a sacrifice for the glory of my Son?"**

A bit ashamed of myself, I took it out and threw it to the ground. She said to me afterwards:

- **"Do you remember what I told you on your saint's day—that you would suffer much on earth? Now I repeat it to you. Have confidence in Us."**
- *"How unworthy I am, O our Mother, of so many graces received through you, and now you have come to me to help me carry the little cross I have."*
- **"Conchita, I am not coming only for you but I am coming for all my children, with a desire to get them closer to Our Hearts.**
  ***Give them** to me (*the rosaries*) so that I can kiss all you are carrying with you."*

And I gave her everything. I was bringing with me also a small crucifix which I gave her to kiss. She kissed it and said:

- **"Put it in the hands of the Child Jesus."'**

And I did, and He said nothing. I said:

- *"This cross I intend to take with me when I go to the convent."*

But He did not reply... After kissing everything, She commented:

- **"My son, through this kiss, will work wonders. Distribute them to the others..."**
- *"Of course. I will do so."*

After all this, she requested that I tell her all the petitions I received from other people. She said:

- **"Conchita, tell me things about my children. I have all of them under my cloak."**
- *"It is too small! And there is no room for all of us!"*

She smiled at my comment, and then she said:

- **"Do you know, Conchita, why I did not come myself on June 18, to deliver the message for the world? Because it hurt me to give it to you myself. But I must give it to you for your own good, and if you heed it, for the glory of God. I love you very much and I desire your salvation and your reunion here in Heaven with the Father, the Son and the Holy Spirit. We can count on you, Conchita, can we not?"**
- *"'If I could be always seeing you, yes; but otherwise I can't because I am very bad!'"*
- **"You do all you can. We shall help you, and we shall help our daughters Loli, Jacinta and Maricruz as well.**

This is the last time you see me here, but I shall always be with all my children.
Conchita, why don't you go often visit my Son in the Most Blessed Sacrament? Why do you let yourself be carried away by laziness and not go to visit Him Who is waiting for you day and night?"

As I have written above, it was raining hard. Our Lady and the Child did not get wet. I was not aware it was raining while seeing them, but when I stopped seeing them I was soaked. I also told her:

- *"Oh how happy I am when I see you. Why don't you take me with you right now?"*
- **"Remember what I told you on your Saint's day. When you go before God you must show Him your hands filled with good works done by you for your brothers and for the glory of God; now your hands are empty..."**

That's all... I spent a happy moment with my mother from Heaven, my best friend, and with the Child Jesus. I have stopped seeing them but not feeling them close. Again they have sown in my soul great peace, joy and a desire to conquer my defects so that I will be able to love, with all my strength, the hearts of Jesus and Mary who love us so much.

The Blessed Virgin Mary told me that Jesus does not want to send the punishment in order to distress us but in order to help us and reproach us because we pay no attention to Him. And the warning will be sent in order to purify us for the miracle in which he will show us His great love, and in order that we may fulfill the message.

The miracle is going to take place so that we will fulfill the message and also to confirm these apparitions. However, if we fulfill the message, it doesn't matter if we don't believe in the apparitions.

(Blessed Virgin Mary to Conchita Gonzàlez, 13 November 1965)

Interview of Monsignor Bishop del Val Gallo by The Vigil Special Issue (1992)

Q. Where were you born and raised?
A. Something *happened in the family and due to those circumstances, I was born in Burgos, but when I was fifteen days old, I was taken to Santander, and I always lived there after that.*

Q. What made you decide to be a priest?
A. *When I was four years old, the pastor of my church asked me if I wanted to become a priest I said "yes" in a way that a small child would answer. But then, when I was nine years old, an aunt, who was my father's sister and was a nun in the order of The Daughters of Charity died in the order of sanctity*

because there had been a big epidemic of a very contagious disease among the children and (in spite of it) she was taking care of the sick.

She was told to be very careful because she could become contaminated and die, but she said, "My whole life has been consecrated to God by serving the poor and I'm not going to stop now when they need me the most and that is what I will continue to do." She eventually got sick from the epidemic that was going around and died. This was being discussed and talked about in my home when I was nine years old and it made such an impression on me.

This heroic action that the sister of my father did as a Daughter of Charity made me think, "Could I myself do this if I were a priest?" That's when I made my decision; I wanted to be a priest. I was nine years old. Then when I was twelve years old, I entered the Pontifical University of Comillas until I became a priest in 1944.

Q. How old were you when you were ordained... by whom and where?

A. *I was ordained by Archbishop Parrado of Granada when I was 28 years old. He died many years ago. I was ordained in the church of the Political University of Comillas.*

Q. When did you first go to Garabandal and why?

A. *I went eight days after the first apparition. I went there because Bishop Doroteo Femandez called me, he was actually the Apostolic Administrator. Since I was a priest that he trusted, he wanted me to go there as an observer and to report back to him my impressions of everything that I had seen. So I went there about eight days after the first apparition because the Bishop told me to go.*

Q. Who was the bishop of the diocese at that time?

A. *Bishop Doroteo Fernandez.*

Q. How many times did you visit the village during the years of the reported apparitions?

A. *I went only another two times after that by order of the same bishop.*

Q. Did you witness any of the four girls in ecstasy? If so, please describe what you saw and heard. What were your impressions?

A. *Yes. Yes, I saw them. Yes, I saw them in ecstasy. That is what they were calling a psychological trance. I believe it was a trance but not as deep as one's first impression because they were going in and out of ecstasy. I said that I believed that it was a trance and this is what astonished the people and made them believe it was supernatural. My impressions were that of a spectator. We'll see. We'll see what happens because with this type of thing cannot be rushed.*

Q. When were you assigned to the Santander diocese? Was this your first diocese as bishop?

A. *I was given the diocese on December 4, 1971, and I came here on January 16, 1972. This was the first and the last diocese that I have had as a resident bishop. I was here for twenty years. Before that I was in Jerez de la Frontera in the area of Cadiz which belonged to the diocese of Sevilla, I was put* *in charge of that region of Cadiz by the Cardinal of Sevilla carrying on there like any other bishop which today is its own diocese.*

Q. Since the beginning of the reported apparitions, how may bishops preceded you?

A. *Many. There were many if we consider that some were bishops and some were Apostolic Administrators because during those years, there was a lot of movement in the diocese of Santander. There was Doroteo Fernandez, Eugenio Beitia, Vicente Puchol, Enrique de Cabo, acting bishop but was titular vicarate, and then came Jose Maria Cirarda then when he was taking care of the diocese of Bilbao as auxiliary bishop and Apostolic Administrator, another bishop came called Rafael Torrija de la Fuente, and then I came in 1972.*

Q. Isn't it true that of all those bishops, you are the only one who actually witnessed the girls in ecstasy?

A. *I think so. I think I am the only one. I heard say that Conchita had had some ecstasies in front of Bishop Puchol but I am not sure. Yes, I think that I was the only one who saw the ecstasies.*

Q. Did you ever imagine that God would place you in such a unique situation?

A. *I have always tried to be in the hands of God. I always try regardless of whether it is a difficult situation or a joyful one, and this one (that is Garabandal) is both hard and joyful at the same time.*

Q. When did you remove all the restrictions that the previous bishops imposed on the priests and why?

A. *I don't remember clearly the exact date. It was done step by step. I told the pastor to start removing the restrictions, and then it was just announced publicly. But I don't remember the exact date. I think it was about six years before I retired which was last year in September.*

Q. Have the Garabandal apparitions ever been condemned by the church?

A. *No. The previous bishops did not admit that the apparitions were supernatural but to condemn them, no, that word had never been used.*

Q. When did you re-open the study of the apparitions and who did the study, how was it conducted and when was it concluded?

A. *It was finished in April of 1991 during a reunion we held in Madrid, but it was not opened on a specific date. It was opened six years earlier, taking notes of the circumstances here and there. In the beginning, we were going little by little so it took about six or seven years before the study was concluded. Until then I had gone by what the other bishops had done. They had said no. But then it seemed to me that I should personally do something myself.*

I needed to do a personal investigation because the responsibility demands this of oneself; so I had to do something about it and because I thought it was something serious that had happened in Garabandal. It seemed to me that because it was so serious, I had to find out for myself exactly what happened in Garabandal.

Q. What has become of the results?

A. *The results were brought to the Holy See, to the Sacred Congregation for the Doctrine of the Faith. That is where you have to take things like this. They were given to Cardinal Ratzinger.*

Q. Were the Garabandal Messages found to be theologically correct and in accordance to the teachings of the Catholic Church?

A. *I think yes. Theologically correct, yes. But one of the details bothers me like the one: Many bishops and cardinals are walking the path of perdition; it seems to me to be a bit severe... The Messages do not say anything that is against the doctrine of the church.*

Q. When and why did you retire?

A. *I retired because of my age. The church requires all the bishops in the world—and we are more than 4,000—when we reach the age of 75 to write a letter to the pope telling him of the date when you are 75 years old so that the Holy Father can start looking for a replacement. So that's what I did. My 75th birthday was June 13 of last year (1991) so I retired on September 29.*

Q. Do you have any special plans for the future?

A. *Yes. My first plan is to pray more than before because now I have more time, and so that is one of my first plans, to dedicate much more time to prayer. My second plan is to help the under-privileged and my third plan is, well I used to write before becoming a bishop and then after I became a bishop, I didn't do it anymore because there wasn't any time to do that. If you want to be a good bishop there is no time to write because you have too much work. So, that's what I plan to do now.*

At the time I was bishop, I didn't do it because if you write books, you aren't going to do your job well. I used to think that someday when I retire, I will become a writer again. So I am writing a book which will take at least another year and a half before it is finished. But for now, I am thinking that the title can be. The Christian in the Year 2000. It will be a book about today's culture in Europe and how this culture influences our Christian life and how this culture as Christians has to respond to God and to the service of man.

Q. As "Mother of the Redeemer" and "Mother of the Church", what kind of an effect do you believe Our Blessed Mother will have on the life of humanity?

A. *In response to this question, the first thing that comes to my mind is Cardinal Wyszynsky from Poland. You know that he was a cardinal there during the times of the most difficult conditions. With imperial communism the church was so oppressed with so much persecution, there was no freedom. Yet in his worst moment, Cardinal Wyszynsky entrusted his flock to the Blessed Mother, Our Lady of Czestochowa.*

In that extreme moment, the cardinal in his faith found his refuge in the Blessed Mother because she is the One who is going to save The Faith. In this question, I am able to identify with Cardinal Wyszynsky since I think like he did, that is The Blessed Mother is the One who will save The Faith.

I am grateful for your visit, it has been very meaningful.

A final question was asked of Bishop del Val:

Q. Do you believe that The Messages are the most important part of Garabandal?

A. *For sure I consider the messages important! Because they are important! In the area where it is similar to Lourdes and Fatima, it is important for us Christians to live what the Messages of the Blessed Mother are saying, if we consider that she could have said this... but, I'm not saying that she did since this would be admitting that the apparitions are true, and I cannot do that because the church has not said so yet... The church is the onethat has the last word.*

Bishop del Val Gallo in The Vigil Special Issue 1992
By Maria Saraco, editor and publisher of "The Vigil"

Interview with Conchita Gonzalez
Bishop Garmendia (27 August 1981)

Bishop: Does the general public have doubts about the apparitions?

Conchita: *The Virgin told us that before the Miracle, many people will stop believing.*

Bishop: So you believe in the Virgin blindly and you always refer us to what she told you. There's another subject I'd like to bring up, Conchita, and that is Holy Communion. I understand that the Virgin told you girls that if there were priests present the Angel would not give you Communion; that the Angel would only give Communion when there were no priests present. However, I understand that on the day of the Miracle of the (Visible) Communion there were some thirty priests in Garabandal. Can you clarify this?

Conchita: *The Virgin never told us that the Angel would not come if there were priests in the village. It is the Angel who did not come when there were priests in the village. Only that day, the Angel came even though there were priests in the village. I can't explain why.*

Bishop: So, the Virgin did not categorically tell you the Angel will give you Communion only when there are no priests in the village, did she?

Conchita: *No. Because whatever the Virgin says happens just as she says it.(...)*

Bishop: As for the present Bishop of Santander, is he going to have a special sign before the Miracle? Will it be something that happens in nature or something in general?

Conchita: *The Virgin said that she was going to send proof to the Bishop of Santander so that he will allow priests to go to Garabandal.*

Bishop: What kind of proof?

Conchita: *She didn't say. This sign of the truth of the apparitions will be something private for whomever is the Bishop of Santander at the time of the Miracle.*

Bishop: So, it will be for the one who is Bishop at the time of the Miracle?

Conchita: *Yes, he will receive a sign.*

Bishop: So the Bishop will receive a sign and he will know that Garabandal is true. This is clear now. You know, Conchita, that we are attracted to Garabandal because we love the Virgin. We know she utilizes humble people and means like at Lourdes and Fatima and other apparitions. It has been said that the Virgin told you the Miracle will be on a Thursday. Is this true?

Conchita: *Yes. The Virgin said it will be on a Thursday, and she also gave the day, month and year.*

Bishop: Are you sure? Did you check it on the calendar?

Conchita: *No, I didn't have to, because she told me Thursday, the day, month and year.*

Bishop: I am so glad to hear this. I had been told that you knew it was to be a Thursday, and began to guess at the dates. But the Virgin told you the exact date, the exact month and the exact year. No one need have any doubts now. If everything in life were so perfectly clear there would be no problems. I heard you were in Rome.

Conchita: *Cardinal Ottaviani sent me a letter through Princess Cecilia de Bourbon-Parma and I went to Rome with my mother.*

Bishop: I don't want to press you, but what happened?

Conchita: *They interviewed me for two hours and told me that it would be better to keep secret all that was said. I don't remember now all the questions they asked me, but I remember it was for two hours.*

Bishop: Can you tell us your impressions of Rome? I imagine a girl from Garabandal, a remote mountain village, would have a lot to say about Rome, right?

Conchita: *No, not really. I went there because they called me. They asked me questions and I answered them; that was all. After seeing the Virgin I find it difficult to be impressed by Rome. (...)*

Bishop: ... Are there any other relationships between Rome, the Holy Father and the Miracle that you would like to talk about?

Conchita: *Yes. The Virgin told us something related to the Holy Father, and it was that before the Miracle there would be only three more Popes.*

Bishop: I want this to be very clear to all who hear this tape. Conchita was very precise. The Virgin told you that before the Miracle...?

Conchita: *At the time, Pope John XXIII was living. The Virgin said, "Three more Popes are left; there will be only three more Popes." She was then speaking about the end of the times.*

Bishop: So the Virgin spoke to you about the end of the times?
Conchita: *Yes.*

Bishop: So after John XXIII came Paul VI, John Paul I, and then John Paul II. So look out, the noose is tightening! It's the Virgin who is speaking.

Conchita: *The Virgin was talking about the end of the times. She also spoke to us about France. I don't know if you remember but it was being said that a world war would break out in 1962. At the time everyone was afraid including me. Then the Virgin appeared and addressing our concern said: "**Don't be afraid, there will not be another world war.**"*

Bishop: So she said there would not be another world war. There have been local conflagrations, and much has been said about a coming world war. The situation is very tense, but a world war would be the end of nations.

Conchita: *I don't remember any more. I would like to add, however, with reference to Rome, that some priests or people are putting too much pressure on the Church to approve Garabandal. I believe it would be better that this be left in the hands of God. Let them speak about and spread the Message of the Virgin, but leave the rest in the hands of God.*

Bishop: You caution against rushing things and speculating. You prefer that all be left in the hands of God. You have complete confidence in Him.

Conchita: *Yes. Before, when I was so concerned about whether Rome would believe me or not, the Lord Himself told me: "**Don't worry about being believed, especially in Rome. I will do everything.**" I would like to tell this to all those who want the Bishop and Rome to hurry ahead in this matter.*

Bishop: People are always looking for new things. I agree with you; let God and the Blessed Virgin handle it in their own way. You aren't searching for great things, you are simply living a Christian life just as the Blessed Virgin said to.

Conchita: *Yes, every day, and waiting for the Miracle.*

Bishop: Each day you live it.
Conchita: *Yes.*

Bishop: That is what the Gospels and Our Lady say; to live the Christian life every day. This is what you mean, right?
Conchita: *Yes. Live every moment of the day with true faith and devotion.*

(Interview with Conchita conducted by Monsignor Francisco Garmendia, Auxiliary Bishop of New York (1981), **Garabandal Journal,** March-April 2004)

Bishop Juan Antonio del Val Gallo, who was Bishop of Santander between 1971–91, initially was a Garabandal skeptic. But in 1981, the good bishop changed opinion and became a staunched supporter. His successor, however, did not believe in the apparitions… Notwithstanding, Archbishop Carlos Osoro Sierra of Oviedo has ushered in a new spirit towards Garabandal among the Spanish hierarchy, saying he respects the apparitions and has known of "authentic conversions".

Regarding the prophecy of the papacy and the next three popes after John XXIII, I would like to point out that Pope Benedict XVI is the third Pope after John XXIII since John Paul I lived only 33 days and did not reign long enough to reign and leave a significant print behind him… Indeed, on 3 June 1963, as the bells of Garabandal began ringing, Conchita Gonzalez' mother, taken by surprised, wondered out loud before her daughter for the reason of the village church bells ringing. Conchita answered that the bells announced the death of Pope John XIII, and further added that after him three more popes were to come before the end of times… Conchita then corrected herself and stated:

Well, four more popes really, for one will live such a short time that he will not count. (John Paul I)

This clearly confirms that the end of times is to begin under Benedict XVI's lifetime… Benedict XVI, as of this date (2022), has not passed away and although Pope Emeritus, he still makes from time to time public announcement and controversial books. (See **From the Depths of Our Hearts: Priesthood, Celibacy and the Crisis of the Catholic Church.**) Hence, he remains the "third Pope" prophesied in Garabandal.

Conchita goes to Rome:

In February of 1966, Conchita went to Rome at the request of Cardinal Ottaviani, who was then Prefect of the Holy Office. She went with her mother and stayed in the Eternal City some ten days. She was received and interviewed very graciously at the Holy Office by Cardinal Ottaviani and others. Then, she herself asked to see the Holy Father. She was given an appointment, but this was later cancelled… However, the Holy Father sent an envoy to Conchita. He told her that the Pope gave her his blessing and with it the Church's as well. Finally, on the following day, the Holy Father actually received Conchita and repeated verbally what he had said to her the preceding day through his emissary.

Controversies vs. Confirmations of Authenticity

The main two controversies that have struck the apparitions of Garabandal since the late 1960s reside in that in a private message given to Conchita, the Blessed Virgin Mary pre-warned the young seer that the day will come when she and the other girls would come to deny publicly the authenticity of their experience due to horrible doubts that would trouble their minds... This said, the Holy Virgin Mary promised that they would retract their denial and would persevere in the mission that they have been assigned...This indeed took place exactly as the Blessed Virgin Mary announced it to Conchita, but soon enough, in the midst of her denial she and the other girls realized that their experiences have been authentic and immediately thereafter announced – against all pressures, money offers and threats – that their visions and revelations were indeed true and authentic...

The second major controversy resided in that a blind Italian American pilgrim, named Joseph Lomangino, who became famous soon after his visiting and meeting with Padre Pio in San Giovanni Rotondo, and with Conchita Gonzalez in Garabandal, had been promised by the Blessed Virgin Mary to recover his sight on the day of the "Miracle" on the Hill of the Pines:

My Dear Joseph,

Just two lines to tell you the message which the Blessed Virgin gave me for you today at the pines... she told me that the voice you heard was hers and that you shall see on the day of the Miracle. She also told me that the House of Charity you will establish in New York will bring great glory to God.

(Letter from Conchita Gonzalez to Joseph Lomangino, 19 March 1964)

On 18 June 2014, Joseph "Joey" Lomangino, 53 years, to the day, after the first heavenly apparition to the four young girls in Garabandal, Spain (18 June 1961) passed away of a heart attack in his home at 10:30 am, lovingly surrounded by his family... After the first initial appearance of St Michael the Archangel on this date, the Blessed Virgin Mary appeared on numerous occasions thereafter to the children until the final public message on 18 June 1965. And for this reason, 18 June is the primary feast day of the events of Garabandal, since it marks the date of the first apparition to the children in 1961, and also that of the last public message of the Blessed Virgin Mary on that same date in 1965.

Now that Joey Lomangino has passed from this life, many have found themselves in a state of profound doubt and confusion... Indeed, how could a prophecy... a promise issued by the Mother of Christ result to be unfulfilled? And at first appearance, the author of this book confesses to have been one of those who... wondered... but reading carefully the prediction of what the Lady in the vision said to Conchita—*Joey would see on the day of the Miracle*—well, one has to recognize that there could be other interpretations and possibilities than the most obvious and apparent one.

Indeed, the Blessed Virgin Mary did *not* say to Conchita: "*Tell my son Joseph to make preparations to be present on the day of the Miracle on the Hill of the Pines, for on that day and in that place he will recover his sight.*" The actual message to Joey was: "*... you shall see on the very day of the Miracle.*" Couldn't this statement imply that, even from Heaven, Joey would be able to see the "Miracle" announced through the visionaries? Or perhaps even as Saint Padre Pio did... at the moment of death itself?

The Blessed Virgin Mary did say that many will stop believing in Garabandal before the "Miracle". I, for one, would rather follow the famous French mathematician and philosopher Pascal's example and make the same wager[22] and thus be one of the faithful rather than the doubters, for after all, the message given to the four Spanish girls is the same as that of La Fraudais, La Salette, Fatima and Akita. Furthermore, too many signs have already been given, and testimonies have been echoed. Furthermore, could Saint Padre Pio have been mistaken when he stated that the apparitions of Garabandal were authentic? Could he have been led into error by the Blessed Virgin Mary when she appeared to him and asked him to send the girls of Garabandal the letter he sent them in 1962? I, for one, think not.

B.B.C. Interview of Conchita Gonzalez – done in English (1980)

(Here the interview is reproduced faithfully; hence, taking under consideration that English is not Conchita's native tongue, we ask the reader's indulgence for the reproduced exchange.)

Conchita: *When we see the Blessed Mother, she has so much light... We don't see nothing around us... We don't feel where we're at. Then all the time we look up to her.*

Question: **And... She spoke to you?**
Conchita: *Yes, she spoke to us. To me when I see her I feel it's like something you see for so long and then she talks to us right away. She says: 'Hi Conchita' and she says—*(interrupted)

Question: **She says 'Hi Conchita'?**
Conchita: *Yes, in Spanish, you know: 'Hola Conchita', and she talks to all the girls, and then we talk about everything happened to us from the time we see her last. We tell her everything we do in the family.*

---

[22] **Pascal's** wager is an argument in philosophy presented by the 17th century French philosopher, mathematician and physicist, Blaise **Pascal** (1623–62). It underlines the validity in betting that God exists rather than not, for everything would be to gain if He does, and nothing to lose if He doesn't.

Question: **Were you frightened?**
Conchita: *No. I tell you, it's like we see a girlfriend we don't see for so long. It's like... It's like my mother I don't see for so long. I feel like I know her from before.*

The Blessed Mother gave us the message on July 4 (short incomprehensible passage). I am going to say in Spanish because I cannot say in English:

'Hay que hacer muchos sacrificios, mucha penitencia, visitad el Santísimo con frequencia, pero antes tienen que llevar vidas buenas. Ya se esta llenando la Copa. Si no cambiamos, tendremos un castigo muy grande.'

Translation: 'You must make many sacrifices, much penance; visit the Holy Sacrament frequently, but before you must lead good lives. The Cup is already filling-up, and if we do not change a very great chastisement will come upon us.'
This is the message...

About the Warning:

Conchita: *From all over the world, You can't be any place. You can feel "el Aviso" (the Warning). It will be direct from God. No man can give an "explicación", no human way you can explain, you know, the "Aviso", and you're going to feel inside you, and you're going to see with your eyes, but it won't hurt you.*

Question: **It isn't going to hurt you?**
Conchita: *No. Like, to me it's like twin stars... What do you call? Crash, like twin stars in the sky that make a lot of noise, a lot of light but they don't fall down... You know. They don't hit us but we are going to see. In that moment, we are going to see our conscience. You are going to see everything wrong you did.*

Question: **You're going to see everything wrong that you're doing?**
Conchita: *Yes. Everything good you didn't do.*

Question: **Everything right you're not doing?**
Conchita: *Yes.*

About the Miracle:

Conchita: *The Miracle she is going to send to us... the purpose of it is to let us know the message she tells us that which she wants it to be done. She wants to save us, and she thinks that with the Miracle we are going to change our lives.*

Question: **So, it is to tell people that the message is true.**
Conchita: *Yes. All the message.*

Question: **What can you tell us about the big Miracle?**
Conchita: *Well, the only thing I can tell is that it's going to be in my village the Miracle, It's going to be something happening in my village.*

377

Question: **In Garabandal?**
Conchita: *Yes. Everybody is there, around the village, can see it. The people sick there are going to be cured. The Blessed Mother said: 'Los enfermos sanarán.'* (the sick will be healed). *The sinners are going to be converted, and then after that there will be a sign in the pines.*

Question: **There's going to be a sign where?**
Conchita: *In the pines. Yes in the pine-trees. We see the Blessed Mother in the pine-trees a lot of the times. There is going to be one sign there, and she tells us that the sign will be there forever. Like for example, It's going to be something like "los rayos del sol"* (the sun rays)... *Something we can see, from God that will be there forever.*

Question: **Do you know what sort of sign?**
Conchita: *I know the sign but I don't know how to explain it. I know you can see it, you can take pictures but you can't touch you can't... 'palpar'* (feel it)...

Question: **Feel it...**
Conchita: *(nodding) Feel it...*

Question: **It's like a bright light...**
Conchita: *Yes, something like that, and it's going to be there forever.*

Question: **That sign will stay there?**
Conchita: *Yes, forever.*

Question: **And this big Miracle, do you know when it's going to happen?**
Conchita: *Yes. I know the year when it's going to happen; I know the date, but the Blessed Mother said tell eight days before.*

About the (temporary) doubts:

Conchita: *Then I talked to my bishop. I remember I talked to my bishop a lot of hours explaining the whole thing, and I tell the bishop I don't see the Blessed Mother. You know inside it's like I don't know what happened... The only thing is that I don't know who tell me the message. I tell him I fell... 'las llamadas'* (the calls). *I can't explain that... If the Miracle... somebody did tell me about the Miracle. He told me 'Don't worry, You must confess' I confessed to him and he gave me the absolution.*

Question: **Absolution?**
Conchita: *Yes. Then after that the bishop said to me: 'it's better you don't talk no more about the apparitions'.*

Question: **Did you go on doubting, or did you start believing again?**
Conchita: *Then I remembered when the people coming to my village they asked me about the apparitions, and I said: 'I don't believe'. Then it felt like I talked against the Blessed Mother and I don't feel right inside...*

378

Question: **You don't feel right?**
Conchita: *When I tell the people the whole story, I feel I am fooling these people... Because of that I had to leave the village. I couldn't stay there no more...*

Question: **You had to leave the village because of all the people wanting to talk to you?**
Conchita: *Yes. I don't know what to say to the people.*

Question: **You didn't know what to say to them?**
Conchita: *Yes. I say everything is true, I feel like I am folling them... But when I say it's not true, I feel I am talking against the Blessed Mother...*

Question: **So, you thought you were fooling them when you said it was true, but that you were offending the Blessed Mother...** (interrupted)
Conchita: *Yes, when I said it's not true—*

Question: **If it's not true, so you left the village...**
Conchita: *Yes, then I left the village, you know to come to America to work, and I don't know anybody in this country for a lot of months, and where I am working nobody knows who I am.*

Question: **So, you came here anonymously...**
Conchita: *And then, I started remembering a lot of things... I never forgot the Blessed Mother's image in my mind. You know when I saw her... I started remembering the Blessed Mother again. And I still remember her voice. I remembered the angel. And I can never explain how started the apparition.*

Question: **You couldn't explain the apparition?**
Conchita: *I can't explain the apparition. And I know I see the Blessed Mother. I see her. You know... and I talk to her and I see the angel.*

Question: **So you went back to believing it was true?**
Conchita: *Yes, I see her.*

Question: **And how many months was it that—**(interrupted)
Conchita: *A lot! More than one year...*

Question: **More than one year?**
Conchita: *Oh yes. Something like that.*

Question: **For more than one year, you thought your apparitions were a dream?**
Conchita: *Yes... I can't explain...*

Question: **But what do you think now?**
Conchita: *Now, the Blessed Mother, yes and the angel, and I hear her voice. I wait for the Miracle.*

Question: **So now, you believe your visions were true.**
Conchita: *Yes, but I am going to tell you something. If the Miracle doesn't come I won't believe it's true then.*

Question: **If the Miracle doesn't come, you'll think there is nothing true then?**
Conchita: *Yes... Yes... But the Blessed Mother every time she says something, it happens.*

Question: **So, you know the date for the Miracle...**
Conchita: *Yes...*

Question: **... eight days before it**—(interrupted)
Conchita: *I am going to tell everybody.*

Question: **... You'll tell everybody...**
Conchita: *Yes...*

Question: **... If the Miracle doesn't come...**
Conchita: (brief silence...) *I hope this doesn't happen... (*laughing*)*

Question: **But today, you believe it will come.**
Conchita: *Yes, I believe very strongly it's coming. But I know I can't tell when. (I am not allowed yet.)*

Question: **And you believe that your visions of the Blessed Virgin Mary were true.**
Conchita: *I believe I see the Blessed Mother and I believe I see the angel. But then if the Pope is coming and says 'No you don't see the Blessed Mother, it is not the Blessed Mother' I say... you know, I see the lady, beautiful lady. Yes she is beautiful, and the angel looks like an angel...*

Question: **You know, don't you, that many people have delusions. They imagine they see things... Do you sometimes worry that you might have had a delusion?**
Conchita: *I don't worry about that. Before I worried about that. But then we had doctors. They do all kinds of ... They were studying us...*

Question: **They studied you.**
Conchita: *They studied... Yes... And they said we are normal... (Smiling)*

Question: **They said you are normal** (smiling as well).
Conchita: *Yes.* (smiling)

Question: **Did you think that maybe you were sick in the head?**
Conchita: *If they say that we are sick in the head, then I like being sick like that.* (smiling)... *I like being sick like that* (smiling).

Question: **You like to be sick if you see visions like that.**
Conchita: *Sure.* (smiling)

About the future:

Question: **When you are looking at your little children, and you look ahead to the future, are you frightened for them?**
Conchita: (Answering immediately) *Yes! I do. A lot of times I tell God: 'Take my children to Heaven.' I will miss them but I think they will suffer (here on earth).*

Question: **You think they are going to suffer?**
Conchita: *Yes* (looking sad)...

Question: **Why?**
Conchita: *But... I believe after the Miracle all they say we are going to change our lives, but I think we lost a notion of sin, you know... There is sin no more. We got too spoiled, we don't do sacrifice.*

Question: **We lost the sense of sin?**
Conchita: *Yes. It's very hard to start all over again and teach the children... Like I see the way they are teaching the children now, there is no sin no more.*

Question: **No sin?**
Conchita: *Yes. Like I believe we are going to get the punishment.*

Question: **You do? You think the punishment is going to come?**
Conchita: *Yes. And if the punishment come, it will be here in the time of my children...*

Question: **It's going to get your children?**
Conchita: *Yes.* (appearing worried)

Question: **In your children's life time?**
Conchita: *Yes.* (appearing worried and sad...)

Question: **And that worries you.**
Conchita: *Sure it worries me... Yes...* (appearing sad...)

Question: **Can you help them to be safe?**
Conchita: *The only thing I can do, the best thing we can do is... you know... teach the babies to love God and the Blessed Mother, and to have faith in Jesus...*

Question: **And what now do you want for the rest of your life?**
Conchita: *Love God and do His Will.* (smiling)

(Interview with Conchita conducted by the B.B.C., 1980)

<u>Confirmations of Authenticity:</u>

Naturally, the witnessing given by the Rev. Father P. Bernardino Cennamo, Italian Capuchin and friend of Padre Pio, testifying of the Italian Saint having seen the "Miracle" before dying is in itself only but the second testimony of someone having seen the "Miracle", for let us remember Rev. Padre Luis Andreu, initially a skeptic, who was granted the blessing to bear witness of the "Miracle" before he suddenly passed away.

Likewise, the famous 1962 letter written by Padre Pio to the visionaries, and the photo along with the many witnesses of the great miraculous Communion appearing out of nothingness demonstrates... the unexplainable... Furthermore, the message in Garabandal follows, substantiates and complements the message of Fatima.

The innocence, the respect and obedience which the seers of the little Spanish village demonstrates towards the Catholic Church and its hierarchy, along with the fruits produced by the message given by our Lady in Garabandal offer testimony of massive devotion and conversions in Spain and abroad, and thus give further accents of authenticity to this Marisan apparition case which, in no way, contradicts but supports and confirms the Catholic Dogma of the Faith.

The Position of the Roman Catholic Church

As of 2022, there has been no official statement issued from either Rome or Santander, regarding the Church's formal stand on the events of Garabandal. The Church wisely and prudently withholds her opinion until all that has been prophesied takes place. It is rare for apparitions to be strongly endorsed by Rome. Garabandal is no exception.

The local Spanish Bishops have been predictably skeptical. This temperance is commendable as it would be rash to lend apostolic approval to an incomplete apparition case. Indeed, for this apparition to be recognized and approved, the announced Warning, Miracle, and the Sign left at the Pines are necessary for a formal Episcopal recognition. Regarding the theological content of the Messages, in His "Official Note" of 8 July 1965, Bishop Eugenio Beitia of Santander wrote:

We point out, however, that we have not found anything deserving of ecclesiastical censorship or condemnation either in the doctrine or in the spiritual recommendations that have been publicized as having been addressed to the faithful, for these contain an exhortation to prayer and sacrifice, to Eucharistic devotion, to veneration of Our Lady in traditional praiseworthy ways, and to holy fear of God offended by our sins. They simply repeat the common doctrine of the Church in these matters.

Conclusion

In retrospective, one cannot help but notice that the 3,000+ apparitions of the Blessed Virgin Mary and principal messages given to Conchita, Mari Cruz,

Jacinta and Mari Loli in Garabandal from 1961 to 1965 were taking place during the entire course of the Second Vatican Council (1962–1965), and unquestionably appeared to be a continuation of the apparitions of Fatima which ended in 1917 with the specific instructions given to the high Church-Hierarchy to reveal the three secrets to the world in 1960, instructions which, as we know, have been consciously ignored with a deafening silence...

Nevertheless, Heaven appears to have sent the Blessed Virgin Mary one year after the appointed time to echo yet again Our Lady of Fatima's message to reassess Heaven's urgent call and warnings... And yet, as the Second Vatican Council was but concluded with the victory of John XXIII's reforms against Pius XII's conservatism, the last public message given in Garabandal by the Blessed Virgin Mary (in 1965) stated:

(...) Many Cardinals, many Bishops and many Priests are on the road to perdition and are taking many souls with them. The Holy Eucharist is being given less importance.

Although short, the last message brought forth by the Blessed Virgin Mary – in the time when "Vatican II" was taking place – was indeed quite clear. Indeed, alarmingly, clear evidences concerning the Holy Eucharist and Its desacralisation could be observed since the closing of "Vatican II", an instance being Its being received by the faithful no longer on one's knees and directly in the mouth, but standing up and in one's "unconsecrated" hands (thus increasing the chance of accidently dropping It, substituting It, or having It stolen)... Likewise, the new measures instituted by the Second Vatican Council permitted the reformation of the Catholic Liturgy so as to mimic the Protestant rites; how, therefore, can one wonder why the Blessed Virgin Mary stated in Garabandal ever so sadly:

"The Holy Eucharist is being given less importance..."

Ninety-seven years (to the day) before the first apparition of Our Lady of Fatima, 13 May 1917, Blessed Anne-Catherine Emmerich wrote:

Last night, from 11:00 to 3:00, I had a most wondrous vision of two churches and two Popes, and a variety of things, ancient and modern... I saw the fatal consequences of this counterfeit church; I saw it increase; I saw heretics of all kinds flocking to the city. I saw the ever-increasing tepidity of the clergy, the circle of darkness ever widening. And now the vision became more extended. I saw in all places Catholics oppressed, annoyed, restricted, and deprived of liberty.

Churches were closed, and great misery prevailed everywhere with war and bloodshed. I saw rude, ignorant people offering violent resistance, but this state of things lasted not long. Again I saw in vision St. Peter's undermined according to a plan devised by the secret sect (freemasonry) while, at the same time, it was damaged by storms; but it was delivered at the moment of greatest distress. Again I saw the Blessed Virgin extending her mantle over it."

(Blessed Anne-Catherine Emmerich, 13 May 1820)

Among the strangest things that I saw, were long processions of bishops. Their thoughts and utterances were made known to me through images issuing from their mouths. Their faults towards religion were shown by external deformities. A few had only a body with a dark cloud of fog instead of a head. Others had only a head, their bodies and hearts were like thick vapors. Some were lame; others were paralytics; others were asleep or staggering...

I saw what I believe to be nearly all the bishops of the world, but only a small number were perfectly sound. I also saw the holy Father, God-fearing and prayful. Nothing left to be desired in his appearance, but he was weakened by old age and by much suffering. His head was lolling from side to side, and it dropped onto his chest as if he were falling asleep. He often fainted and seemed to be dying. But when he was praying, he was often comforted by apparitions from Heaven.

Then his head was erect, but as soon as it dropped again onto his chest, I saw a number of people looking quickly right and left, that is in the direction of the world. Then I saw that everything that pertained to Protestantism was gradually gaining the upper hand, and the Catholic religion fell into complete decadence... Most priests were by the glittering but false knowledge of young school-teachers, and they all contributed to the work of destruction.

In those days, Faith will fall very low, and it will be preserved in some places only, in a few cottages and in a few families which God has protected from disasters and wars.

(Blessed Anne-Catherine Emmerich, 1 June 1821)

These messages, these testimonies will be difficult for a great many faithful to accept, particularly for those who have embraced a policy of endless compromises and concessions for the sake of peace and conciliation with our Protestant brothers, but these extraordinary manifestations, messages and invitations for conversions from the Blessed Virgin Mary call mankind to a start now its own **Journey to Damas**" so as to see the true "Light of the World", and to evangelize the One and only One Truth instituted upon the Church founded by Jesus-Christ Himself upon Peter, which translate in the infallible Dogma of the Faith, the Roman Catholic and Apostolic Church's Sacraments and in the holy Gospels, all of which reveal Jesus-Christ as the only Son of God and as the "Light of the World":

Ego sum lux Mundis.

Chapter VIII

Apparitions of the Blessed Virgin Mary in Medjugorje

(Gospa - *Our Lady of Peace*)

"One day Satan appeared before the throne of God and asked permission to submit the Church to a period of trial. God gave him permission to try the Church for one century. This century is under the power of the Devil, but when the secrets confided to you come to pass, his power will be destroyed. Even now he is beginning to lose his power and has become aggressive. He is destroying marriages, creating division among priests and is responsible for obsessions and murder. You must protect yourselves against these things through fasting and prayer, especially community prayer. Carry blessed objects with you. Put them in your house, and restore the use of holy water."

(1982)

"Pray, pray! It is necessary to believe firmly, to go to confession regularly, and, likewise, to receive Holy Communion. 'It is the only salvation'."

(10 February 1982)

The apparition case of Medjugorje is, with the one of La Fraudais, undoubtedly the longest running series of apparition in the History of Marian apparition sites; what's more, Medjugorje's messages are "complementary" to those already discussed in this book in that the messages of Heaven to the six children of Medjugorje are enhancing principally the need of the world's urgent conversion through holy Communion, prayer, fasting and Confession, a work which is called *"a work of peace"* very much like the messages of La Fraudais which were called by Our Lord and by the Blessed Virgin Mary *"the work of the Cross"* which went on for over 68 year..

La Fraudais, unlike Medjugorje, did not withhold any secrets through Marie-Julie Jahenny. All its prophecies and forewarnings have been openly revealed for time long after the French stigmatist's passing away; however, our Lady of Medjugorje has entrusted ten secrets to four of its six messengers, ten secrets which are to be revealed to the world ten days before they are to take place... This, in contrast to La Fraudais, announces an alarmingly close time-table well within the life-span of the messengers of Medjugorje.[23]

Bosnia-Herzegovina has become an independent state on March 1, 1992 after 47 years of harsh and repressive Yugoslavian Communist dictatorship. Indeed, after the end of World War II, the Communist party—which was principally supported financially and militarily by the U.S.S.R—managed the union of the modern regions of Slovenia, Croatia, SAP Vojvodina, Bosnia and Herzegovina, Serbia, Montenegro, SAP Kosovo and SR Macedonia with an iron rod, oppressing the freedom of the press, freedom of speech and freedom of religion. Bosnia-Herzegovina and Croatia were no exception.

It could even be said that Bosnia-Herzegovina and Croatia were treated in a somewhat different manner as the other regions for their open collaboration with the German Wehrmacht during the occupying years of 1941–1945... This led, in turn to a population that, despite the suppression of nationalism, was growing more and more patriotic and turned towards a sense of regional identity.

Despite flagrant evidence of collaboration between the Catholic authorities in Croatia and the German occupiers during the war, the Yugoslavian Communist regime allowed the Catholic Church to practice its cult after the liberation of Europe in all its regions, while restraining as well as it could seminaries to teach, train and form new priests into a still practicing local population... Notwithstanding, it was on 24 June 1981 (*ten years before the formal independence of Bosnia-Herzegovina*) that the apparitions of Medjugorje (*which means in Croatian: between mountains*) began.

Indeed, in June of 1981, the "Gospa" (Blessed Virgin Mary) appeared to six children in a small farming village in the mountains of Bosnia-Herzegovina (populated by a large population of Croatians) with an urgent call to conversion for the world, stating that what she began in her apparitions in Fatima she would

---

[23] The same could be said of the secrets entrusted by the Blessed Virgin Mary to Conchita Gonzalez of Garabandal.

fulfill in Medjugorje. Since that first apparition until the day these lines are being written, the Blessed Virgin Mary is still appearing daily to three of the six visionaries.

Her messages are of love, faith and hope, and further give loving guidance on the path to man's conversion, but most of all the Blessed Virgin Mary has given messages which regard the state of the world and where it is heading. Notwithstanding, many of her messages deal as well with grave events in today's political and moral society. These secrets are to be revealed to the world ten days before they are to take place. These secrets concern times of Grace, a major chastisement for the world and... the Church...

The six visionaries of Medjugorje have been subjected for many years to batteries of theological examinations and scientific investigations. In the past 39 years, French American, Italian and English researches, theologians and scientists have dedicate time and considerable means to scrutinize and probe both visionaries and messages. Meanwhile, in this 21st century, as the world awaits for the Church to issue its judgement, Medjugorje has grown to be, with Fatima and Lourdes, one of the most visited Marian shrine in the world.

On the afternoon of 24 June 1981, on the Feast Day of Saint John the Baptist (*Heaven's messenger proclaiming the Kingdom of Heaven*) two girls, Ivanka Ivanković age 15, and Mirjana Dragićević age 16, were walking towards a hill called Crnica hill talking about every-day teenage girl events. After sitting down for a while, at the top of the hill, Ivanka saw suddenly a bright silhouette of a woman in a long grey dress holding a baby in her arms. Ivanka then suddenly stood up and, staring at the very top of the hill, said to Mirjana:

"It is the Gospa! (Our Lady)"

Mirjana did not look towards the top of the hill but instead simply answered Ivanka in a cynical tone:

"Yes... I am sure... As if Gospa hadn't anything better to do..."

Embarrassed because they had been out smoking secretly, Mirjana got up and left... Curiously, having arrived at the village, she felt a very odd but very strong "call"... an overwhelming urge to return to the hill. She turned immediately and started walking rapidly back to the hill... Once back with Ivanka, her friend told her:

"Look now, please."

Mirjana then saw the apparition of the Blessed Mother holding Baby Jesus in her arms... Although she was overwhelmed with emotions, Mirjana ran away in fear. A few hours later (6 pm), Ivanka and Mirjana returned to the Crnica hill but this time with Vicka Ivanković. As the Blessed Virgin became visible once more, Vicka, frightened, returned to the village running, leaving her two friends behind.

On her way back she ended up meeting with Ivan Ivanković. She told him what was happening and thus they both returned to join Ivanka and Mirjana. Once arrived, both Ivan and Vicka saw their friends on their knees before the apparition of the Blessed Virgin Mary. In turn, they knelt as well and observed quietly the magnificent sight before them. This is how they described what they saw:

There was an incredible light. The Blessed Mother held Baby Jesus in her arms, covering and uncovering Him as she called on to us with her hand. It was overwhelming!

When the young people were asked how did they know this was the Blessed Virgin Mary, Mirjana answered:

My whole being knew without a doubt that this lady of unexplainable beauty was the Mother of God. That is why I had such fear…

Ivanka, Mirjana, Ivan, and Vicka returned at last to their village after the Blessed Mother of God and the Child Jesus disappeared. The following day, they all fell an unexplainable feeling of being called yet again at the hill; hence Mirjana, Ivanka, Ivan and Vicka returned accompanied by Jakov Colo, and Milka Pavlović, and by some curious villagers who were following from behind… Those same followers witnessed the children run up the stony hill with unnatural speed and agility.

The children later explained that they felt as if floating all their way to the top of the hill about two meters away from the Blessed Virgin Mary. Once the hill reached, the six children crashed on their knees on the sharp and hardened rock. Jakov even knelt on a rock and a bush of thorns without even feeling any pain… The children saw appear before them the Lady in grey, smiling, dressed in a shiny silver-gray dress with a white veil covering her black hair. She had loving blue eyes and was crowned by twelve stars. She then addressed all six children:

- **Praised be Jesus!**

Ivanka responded:

- *"Where is my mother?"* (Her mother had died two months previously.)
- **She is happy. She is with me.**

The visionaries:

- *"Will you return tomorrow?"*

The lovely Lady in grey answered with a nod of her head.

Mirjana continued:

- *"No one will believe us. They will say that we are crazy. Give us a sign!"*

The Lady in grey responded only with a smile, and then she said:

- **Goodbye, my angels. Go in the peace of God.**

(22 June 1981)

The children crossed themselves and returned to their village weeping with emotion. The apparition lasted 16 minutes. It did not take very long before the entire village found out about the six children's experience. And already a line was being drawn between those who believed and those who didn't. The news spread so quickly, that the neighboring villages and towns heard as well of the apparitions of the Gospa in Medjugorje…

Hundreds, and hundreds of people decided to come the following day and see for themselves… Hence, the following day, the six children returned to the Crnica hill but this time accompanied by massive crowd consisting of 2,000 to 3,000 people. Once there, a brilliant light flashed three times before Our Lady appeared… All present witnessed this remarkable occurrence. Vicka got a bottle of holy water reserved for the awaited vision of the Lady in Grey.

Once the apparition revealed itself, Vicka sprinkled the apparition with holy water and said:

- *"If you are the Gospa, stay with us, if not, go away."*

The apparition only smiled.

Ivanka:

- *"Why have you come here? What do you desire?"*
- **I have come because there are many true believers here. I wish to be with you to convert and reconcile the whole world.**
- *"Did my mother say anything?"*
- **Obey your grandmother and help her because she is old.**

Mirjana:

- *"How is my grandfather?"* (He had recently died.)
- **He is well.**

The seers, on a request from the crowd:

- *"Give us a sign which will prove your presence."*
- **Blessed are those who have not seen and who believe.**
- *"Who are you?"*
- **I am the Most Blessed Virgin Mary.**
- *"Why are you appearing to us? We are not better than others."*
- **I do not necessarily choose the best.**
- *"Will you come back?"*

- **Yes, to the same place as yesterday.**

(23 June 1981)

On returning to the village after the apparition, Maria saw the Blessed Virgin Mary, in tears, near a cross with rainbow colors:

- **Peace, Peace, Peace! Be reconciled! Only Peace. Make your peace with God and among yourselves. For that, it is necessary to believe, to pray, to fast, and to go to confession.**

(**Note:** Ten years later, on 26 June 1991, the Balkan War began and engulfed all the Balkans, completely redrawing the map of Yugoslavia.)

Two months later, as the children continued to receive daily apparition of the "Gospa", on Sunday, 23 August 1981, she appeared again and said to them:

"Praised be Jesus! I have been with Ivica until now. (Ivica: This diminutive refers sometimes to Ivan, sometimes to Ivanka. Here, the context does not permit one to be more specific.)

Pray, my angels, for this people.
My children, I give you strength. I will give you some of it always.
When you need me, call me."

(The Blessed Virgin Mary, 23 August 1981)

In her diary, for the date of 25 August 1981, Vicka wrote:

Yesterday, Monday the 24th at 10:45, Mirjana and I were at Ivan's house. We heard an uproar and we went out running. Outside, everybody was looking at the cross on Krizevac. At the spot of the cross, Mirjana, Jakov, Ivan and I saw the Blessed Virgin, and the people saw something like her statue which began then to disappear, and the cross appeared again. Furthermore, over the entire sky, everyone could see written in letters of gold the word: 'MIR' (PEACE).

Two days later, a little after the Virgin prayed for peace, a large inscription appeared on top of Krizevac. The word "MIR" (Peace in Croatian). The inscription was seen by the pastor and many persons of the village. There is written testimony by those who saw the inscription. The seers affirmed that the Blessed Virgin Mary promised that there would still be many other signs as forerunners at Medjugorje, and in other parts of the world, before a great sign is given.

In other messages, the Blessed Virgin Mary covered in short simple sentences great subjects and affinities involving the local and international scene.

Apparition of the Blessed Virgin Mary in October 1981

Regarding the conflict between the Franciscans and the Bishop of Mostar in Herzegovina:

- **There is going to be a solution. We must have patience and pray.**
- *"What will become of Poland?"*
- **There will be great conflicts but in the end, the just will take over.**

With respect to Russia:

It is the people where God will be most glorified. The West has made civilization progress, but without God, as if they were their own creators.

Apparition of the Blessed Virgin Mary on 21 July 1982

Response conveyed by Father T. Vlasic on Purgatory:

There are many souls in Purgatory. There are also persons who have been consecrated to God: some priests, some religious. Pray for their intentions, at least seven Our Father's, Hail Mary's and Glory Be's and the Creed. I recommend it to you. There is a large number of souls who have been in Purgatory for a long time because no one prays for them.

A response to a question on fasting:

The best fast is on bread and water. Through fasting and prayer, one can stop wars, one can suspend the laws of nature. Charity cannot replace fasting. Those who are not able to fast can sometime replace it with prayer, charity and a confession; but everyone, except the sick, must fast.

Apparition of the Blessed Virgin Mary on 24 July 1982

Answer to some questions which were asked regarding the moment of death:

We go to Heaven in full conscience: that which we have now. At the moment of death, we are conscious of the separation of the body and the soul. It is false to teach people that we are re-born many times and that we pass to different bodies. One is born only once. The body, drawn from the earth, decomposes after death. It never comes back to life again. Man receives a transfigured body. Whoever has done very much evil during his life can go straight to Heaven if he confesses, if he is sorry for what he has done, and received Communion at the end of his life.

Apparition of the Blessed Virgin Mary on July 25, 1982

A response to questions asked regarding Hell:

Today many people go to Hell. God permits his children to suffer in Hell due to the fact that they have committed grave unpardonable sins. Those who are in Hell, no longer have a chance to know a better lot.

Response to questions regarding cures:

For the cure of the sick, it is important to say the following prayers: the Creed, seven Our Father's, Hail Mary's and Glory Be's, and to fast on bread and water. It is good to impose one's hands on the sick and to pray. It is good to anoint the sick with holy oil. All priests do not have the gift of healing. In order to revive this gift, the priest must pray with perseverance and believe firmly.

Apparition of the Blessed Virgin Mary on 6 August 1982 (Feast of the Transfiguration)

A response to questions which were asked concerning Confession:

One must invite people to go to Confession each month, especially the first Saturday. Here I have not spoken about it yet. I have invited people to frequent Confession. I will give you yet some concrete messages for our time. Be patient because the time has not yet come. Do what I have told you. They are numerous people who do not observe it. Monthly Confession will be a remedy for the Church in the West. One must convey this message to the West.

That night the Gospa gave a sign to a group of young people who prayed with Ivan Dragicevic: two luminary signs descended on Krizevac and the church. This phenomenon was observed by Father Tomislav Vlasic near the church.

On 25 May 1983, the Blessed Virgin has repeated her desire that a prayer group, totally abandoned to Jesus, be formed, and on 16 June, she dictated the rules for this group:

1. Renounce all passions and inordinate desires. Avoid television, particularly evil programs, excessive sports, the unreasonable enjoyment of food and drink, alcohol, tobacco, etc.
2. Abandon yourselves to God without any restrictions.
3. Definitely eliminate all anguish. Whoever abandons himself to God does not have room in his heart for anguish. Difficulties will persist, but they will serve for spiritual growth and will render glory to God.
4. Love your enemies. Banish from your heart, hatred, bitterness, preconceived judgments. Pray for your enemies and call the Divine blessing over them.
5. Fast twice a week on bread and water. Reunite the group at least once a week.
6. Devote at least three hours to prayer daily, of which at least, half an hour in the morning and half an hour in the evening. Holy Mass and the prayer of the Rosary are included in this time of prayer. Set

aside moments of prayer in the course of the day, and each time that circumstances permit it, receive Holy Communion. Pray with great meditation. Do not look at your watch all the time, but allow yourself to be led by the grace of God.

Do not concern yourself too much with the things of this world, but entrust all that in prayer to Our Heavenly Father. If one is very preoccupied, he will not be able to pray well because internal serenity is lacking. God will contribute to lead to a successful end, the things of here below, if one strives to do his utmost in working on his own.

7. Those who attend school or go to work must pray half an hour in the morning and in the evening, and, if possible, participate in the Eucharist. It is necessary to extend the spirit of prayer to daily work.

8. Be prudent because the Devil tempts all those who have made a resolution to consecrate themselves to God, most particularly, those people. He will suggest to them that they are praying very much, they are fasting too much, that they must be like other young people and go in search of pleasures. Have them not listen to him, nor obey him. It is to the voice of the Blessed Virgin that they should pay attention. When they will be strengthened in their faith, the Devil will no longer be able to seduce them.

9. Pray very much for the Bishop and for those who are responsible for the church. No less than half of their prayers and sacrifices must be devoted to this intention.

I have come to tell the world that God is truth; He exists.

True happiness and the fullness of life are in Him. I have come here as Queen of Peace to tell the world that peace is necessary for the salvation of the world. In God, one finds true joy from which true peace if derived."

(The Gospa, 16 June 1983)

Pray and fast. I wish that you deepen and continue your life in prayer. Every morning say the prayer of consecration to the Heart of Mary. Do it in the family. Recite each morning the Angelus, five Our Father's, Hail Mary's, and Glory Be's in honor of the Holy Passion and a sixth one for our Holy Father, the Pope. Then say the Creed and the prayer to the Holy Spirit. And, if it is possible, it would be well to pray a rosary.

(27 January 1984)

Pope Francis' public skepticism...

On the 100th anniversary of the first apparition of Fatima, 13 May 2017, Pope Francis was asked his opinion on the contemporary apparitions of Medjugorje, to which the Argentinean Pope answered:

The first apparitions... which were to children... the report more or less says that these need to continue being studied, but as for the 'presumed' current apparitions, the report has its doubts... I am personally more suspicious... I prefer the Madonna as a Mother, our Mother, and not a woman who's the head of an office, who every day sends a message at a certain hour. This is not the Mother of Jesus. And these presumed apparitions don't have a lot of value.

Pope Francis clarified that this is but his "personal opinion", but he further added:

The Madonna does not function by saying, 'Come tomorrow at this time, and I will give a message to those people.'

Odd remarks for a learned man of history... Most curious comments indeed... If Pope Francis were right, how would he explain Our Lady's request to the visionaries of Lourdes, Tilly and Fatima—among others—to come back on such or such date(s) to receive yet other messages?

Notwithstanding, Saint John Paul II, stated one year after his assassination attempt:

Can the Mother, who desires everyone's salvation, keep silence on what undermines the very basis of their salvation? No, she cannot!

So, while the message of Our Lady of Fatima is a motherly one, it is also strong and decisive. It sounds severe. It sounds like John the Baptist speaking on the banks of the Jordan. It invites to repentance. It gives a warning. It calls to prayer. It recommends the Rosary.

The message is addressed to every human being. The love of the Savior's Mother reaches every place touched by the work of salvation. Her care extends to every individual of our time and to all the societies, nations and peoples. Societies menaced by apostasy, threatened by moral degradation. The collapse of morality involves the collapse of societies.

(Saint John Paul II, 13 May 1982)

Many more controversies arose out of Medjugorje. On a particular instance involving a Roman Catholic priest, confused because of the miraculous cure granted to an Orthodox child, the Blessed Virgin Mary specifically addressed him through her visionaries:

Tell this priest, tell everyone, that it is you who are divided on earth. The Muslims and the Orthodox, for the same reason as Catholics, are equal before my Son and me. You are all my children. Certainly, all religions are not equal, but all men are equal before God, as St. Paul says. It does not suffice to belong to the Catholic Church to be saved, but it is necessary to respect the commandments of God in following one's conscience.

Those who are not Catholics, are no less creatures made in the image of God, and destined to rejoin someday the House of the Father. Salvation is available to everyone, without exception. Only those who refuse God

deliberately, are condemned. To him, who has been given little, little will be asked. To whomever has been given much, very much will be required. It is God alone, in His infinite Justice, Who determines the degree of responsibility and Who pronounces judgment.

I do not have the right to impose on anyone, what they should do. You have reason, and a will. You should, after having prayed, reflect and decide. Receive the peace of my Son. Live it, and spread it. Permit Jesus to perform great works in you. The door of your heart, the lock is rusted. Permit Him to open it. May it be open through your prayer, your fasting, your conversion. Pray slowly, and meditate while saying the prayers of the rosary. Take a quarter of an hour to recite: Five Our Father's, Hail Mary's, and Glory Be's.

I love you so much. And if you love me, you will be able to feel it. I bless you in the name of the Most Holy Trinity, and in my name. Remain in peace.

(The Blessed Virgin Mary, Blais, 1986)

As the years went by, Ivanka, Mirjana, and Jakov have been revealed all ten secrets but do not see any longer the Blessed Mother of God on a daily basis... Vicka, Ivan and Milka have, up to date, received nine secrets and receive daily apparitions of the Blessed Virgin Mary. Of all the seers, Mirjana was the first one to receive all ten secrets, and it was to her that our lady entrusted the responsibility to reveal publicly the secrets at the appointed time. She knows the exact dates and places where the secrets are due to take place; however, when Mirjana received all ten secrets, she was not confident that she would be able to remember all the dates and details of each secret.

Consequently, our Lady gave her a physical parchment withholding all ten secrets... This parchment, we are told, is made of a material not found here on earth. Finally, Our Lady asked Mirjana to choose a priest to reveal said secrets to the world. The young woman chose Fr. Petar Ljubicic who immediately accepted this responsibility. Ten days before the occurrence of each secret, Father Petar will gather the parchment but will be able to read only the first secret.

During the ten days, he and Mirjana are to spend the first seven days in fasting and prayer, and three days before the event takes place, Fr. Petar is to announce it publicly to the world. At the appointed time, he will be able to read and announce the second secret, and then the third and fourth and so on... Moreover, Mirjana added that, however shocking or distressful the secrets might be, Fr. Petar will not have the right to withhold any detail of the secrets at hand:

He has to fulfill his mission according to God's Will.

Mirjana added (in her own words):

Daily apparitions I had up until Christmas of 1982. That is when I received the tenth secret, and Our Lady asked me to choose a priest to whom I would tell the secrets. I chose Father Petar Ljubicic.

I am supposed to tell him ten days in advance what will happen and where. For seven days we are supposed to spend (our days) in prayer and fasting, and three days ahead of time he is supposed to reveal it to the world. He doesn't have the right to choose whether to say or not to say... He accepted this mission and he has to fulfill that according to God's Will. But Our Lady always repeats; do not talk about the secrets. You better pray. Because the one who feels Our Lady as a Mother and God as a Father, that person has no fear of anything.

Our Lady says that only those who have not yet felt the love of God, they have fear... But we as people, we always talk about the future—what, when, where will things happen. But I always repeat the same thing, who among us present here, can say with certainty that we will be alive tomorrow? Therefore, Our Lady has been teaching us that we must be ready at this very moment to come before God. What will be in the future is God's Will and our task is to be ready for that.[1]

Interview of Fr. Petar Ljubicic in 2008

Q: **Fr. Petar, your future is connected to Medjugorje. Can you explain a little bit about that?**

Fr. Petar: Maybe you are talking about one of the visionaries that has chosen me to reveal the secrets. Is that what you are asking?

Q: Correct—yes.

Fr. Petar: That is Mirjana—she is a visionary. We don't know when that will take place. She received from our Lady ten secrets. She has also received a parchment that is not from this world, but something our Lady gave her and on it are the ten secrets. They are written right there. When the time comes for the secrets to be released, rather the first secret, ten days before, she will give me this parchment.

I will then be able to read the first secret and then, along with her, I will fast for seven days and pray. Then I would be able to reveal to the world what will take place: where, how, and how long. That is before every secret.

The first two secrets are warnings; especially they are for the people of Medjugorje because Our Lady first appeared there. When that takes place, the first two secrets, then it will be clear to everyone that our Lady was truly there. The third secret will be an indestructible sign that will take place on the Mountain of Apparitions, in the place where Our Lady first appeared. That sign will be a great joy for all those who have believed that She is there all along. And it will be a last call to those who have not converted, and did not hear her messages. But it is not wise to wait for that sign.

This is a moment of conversion. This is a time for prayer. This is the time for our spiritual cleansing. This is the time to decide to live for God, for Jesus Christ. Therefore, we call this time, a time of grace. That is what I can say about the secrets. Therefore we need to take advantage of this time in order to be ready to meet Our Lady with her secrets. That is my duty to tell people, that they should not be surprised over anything.

Q: Fr. Petar, have you thought about how you will release the first secret? How will that happen?

Fr. Petar: I will first tell my closest and intimate friends. They would be ready and pray, and, of course, through the internet, television, and radio now-a-days and satellite. I believe that that would be the easiest duty. For me, it is most important that people would be ready. This is the desire of our Lady and of her Divine Son.

What you should ask yourself is, "Am I ready?" And that is what is important. When He will come, will He find us worthy and ready? We will be called blessed then. If we are not ready right now, we have little time to do it. But we should not permit to be caught by surprise. And then, on that given moment, we would not know what to do...

Q: What do you feel about the secrets as far as your responsibility is concerned? Do you feel that weight on you?

Fr. Petar: No, I am not really having any weight on me as far as that goes. I know that there is a whole army of people that are praying for me. I just can't wait until that will take place. And my point is because of that, many people as possible will be converted. I am always ready for any sacrifice that the Lord would send my way.

Q: How soon do you feel this will come in your heart? Do you have any feelings in your heart as to when the first secret will come?

Fr. Petar: I do have a sense and a feeling that this may come very, very soon, but I really don't want to speculate or tell dates about it. You can look at the world today and you will see how urgent it is for us to convert and turn to God...

On 4 September 1985, Fr. Petar Ljubicic issued the following statement:

Mirjana, who was among the first to have the apparitions, has told us that for her, the daily apparitions ceased at Christmas, 1982. At that time, she was promised that she would have apparitions on her birthday, March 18. As she testifies, she has in fact since then had an apparition on her birthday; that is, she has seen the Virgin Mary just as she used to do when she had daily apparitions.

Mirjana also says that for some time now she has been hearing an internal voice—the same voice that she used to hear during her daily apparitions. She claims that Our Lady is speaking to her, especially about the secrets... She heard this 'inner voice' on the 1 and on the 15 of June, on the 19 and on the 27 of July, and on the 15 and 27 of August (1985).

Sometime previously, Mirjana had told me that I would be the priest to whom she would entrust the secrets; her confidant, that is. After hearing the inner voice on June 1 she told me definitely that she would confide the secrets to me. She told me that ten days before the occurrence of the secret she would give me a paper similar to a parchment. Three days before the event I am to make the secret in question known to the public. When the event takes place, I will give the paper back to Mirjana and wait for the next secret. I add to this report two messages that Mirjana has passed on to me.

On 18 March 1985, during her apparition:

They too are my children (this refers to those who are far away from God), **and I grieve for them, because they do not know what awaits them, if they do not turn back to God... Mirjana, pray for them.**

(18 March 1985)

On 15 August 1985, the inner voice:

My angel, pray for the unbelievers. They will tear their hair; brother will plead with brother, and they will curse their past godless lives, and repent but it will be too late. Now is the time for conversion. Now is the time to do what I have been calling for these four years. Pray for them.

(15 August 1985)

Mirjana emphasizes that the time will be at hand when the first secret will be revealed. That is why she urges vigilance and prayer in the name of Our Lady.

Three Warnings Before a Visible Sign

Before a visible sign is given to the world, there will be three preceding warnings in the form of three terrestrial events. After the three admonitions, the visible sign will appear on the site of the apparitions in Medjugorje for all the world to see. The sign will be given as a testimony to the apparitions and in order to call people back to faith.

The First Secret

Our Lady showed Mirjana the first secret—*the earth was desolate.*

The Blessed Virgin Mary and Mirjana prayed for the weak, the unfortunate, and the forsaken. After the prayer, the Gospa blessed Mirjana. Then she showed her, as in a film, the realization of the first secret. The earth was desolate... It was the upheaval of a region.

- *"Why so soon?"* Mirjana asked.
- **"In the world, there are so many sins. What can I do, if you do not help me. Remember, that I love you."**
- *"How can God have such a hard Heart?"*
- **"God does not have a hard Heart. Look around you and see what men do, then you will no longer say that God has a hard Heart. How many people come to church, to the house of God, with respect, a strong faith, and love of God? Very few! Here you have a time of grace and conversion. It is necessary to use it well."**

To Mirjana:

- "Pray very much for Father Petar, to whom I send a special blessing. I am a mother, that is why I come. You must not fear for I am there."

(25 October 1985)

The Second Secret

The second secret involves the inhabitants of the village of Medjugorje...

The Third Secret

The third secret, we are told, involves a visible and lasting sign that will miraculously appear somewhere on the hill of the first apparition. It will be permanent, indestructible and beautiful (*like the one announced in Garabandal?*) and will remain on the apparition hill until the end of the world, and it will be a confirmation of her presence amongst us; it is something that cannot be made by human hands. The sign will be indestructible, and beautiful, something that has never before been on the earth, and those who do not believe in God will not be able to say it is of human origin.

The Remaining Secrets

Mirjana and Vicka added that: *... half of the seventh secret has been cancelled because of the prayers and fasting of the people responding to Our Lady's call; however, the event will unfold... Our response can lower the severity of the event to come, but it will occur and cannot be averted..."*

However, frightened by the eighth secret, Mirjana prayed to the Blessed Virgin to preserve humanity from this calamity:

I have prayed; the punishment has been softened. Repeated prayers and fasting reduce punishments from God, but it is not possible to avoid entirely the chastisement. Go on to the streets of the city, count those who glorify God and those who offend Him. God can no longer endure that.

(6 November 1982)

The ninth and tenth secrets are very grave... They involve chastisements for the sins of the world. Punishment, we are told, is inevitable... The punishment can be diminished by prayer and penance, but it cannot be eliminated.

"You have forgotten that through prayer and fasting you can avert wars and suspend the laws of nature."

The Gospa revealed to her six messengers that there will be a period of grace and conversion. Once the visible sign appears, those... *"who are still alive"*... will have little time for conversion. For that reason, the Blessed Virgin invites us to urgent conversion and reconciliation.

To Mirjana, after she had received the tenth secret:

Now you will have to turn to God in faith like any other person. I will appear to you on the day of your birthday and when you will experience difficulties in life. Mirjana, I have chosen you, I have confided in you everything that is essential. I have also shown you many terrible things. You must now bear it all with courage. Think of Me, and think of the tears I must shed for that. You must remain courageous. You have quickly grasped the messages. You must also understand now that I have to go away. Be courageous.

(The Gospa, 25 December 1982)

The Gospa invites us constantly to prayer, to fasting, to conversion... She confirms her promises. Questioned with respect to the time of the sign: Which day? Which month? Which year?

Ivan simply answered: *"It is forecast."*

(5 January 1983)

Ivanka had a vision at home, which lasted about an hour: The Blessed Virgin was more beautiful than ever and was accompanied by two angels:

She asked me what I wished. I prayed to her to let me see my mother. The Blessed Virgin smiled and approved with a nod.

Ivanka's mother appeared. She was smiling. Our Lady told Ivanka to stand up. Her mother embraced her, and said:

"My child, I am so proud of you."

She embraced her again and disappeared. Our Lady then said to Ivanka:

- **My dear child, today is our last meeting, do not be sad. I will return to see you at each anniversary of the first apparition (June 25), beginning next year. Dear child, do not think that you have done anything bad, and that this would be the reason why I am not returning near to you. No, it is not that. With all your heart you have accepted the plans which my Son and I formulated, and you have accomplished everything.**
  No one in the world has had the grace which you, your brothers and sisters have received. Be happy because I am your Mother and I

love you from the bottom of my heart. Ivanka, thank you for the response to the call of my Son, thank you for persevering and remaining always with Him as long as He will ask you. Dear child, tell all your friends that my Son and I are always with them when they call on us. What I have told you during these years on the secrets, do not speak to anyone about them.

Ivanka:

- *"Dear Gospa, may I embrace you?"*

The blessed Virgin gave an affirmative sign with her head. Ivanka then embraced the Blessed Virgin Mary. Ivanka asked the Gospa to bless her. She did so with a smile and added:

"Go in the peace of God."

Then she left slowly with the two angels.

(7 May 1985)

Jakov Colo had daily apparitions from 25 June 1981 to 12 September 1998. On that day, Our Lady told him:

Dear child! I am your mother and I love you unconditionally. From today, I will not be appearing to you every day, but only on Christmas, the birthday of my Son. Do not be sad, because as a mother, I will always be with you and like every true mother, I will never leave you. And you, continue further to follow the way of my Son, the way of peace and love and try to persevere in the mission that I have confided to you.
Be an example of that man who has known God and God's love. Let people always see in you an example of how God acts on people and how God acts through them. I bless you with my motherly blessing and I thank you for having responded to my call.

(12 September 1998)

Entrusting to him the tenth secret, Our Lady told him that for the rest of his life he would have one yearly apparition, on Christmas Day.

When the Blessed Virgin Mary appeared to Mirjana, she greeted her and said:

"Praised be Jesus."

Then she spoke of unbelievers:

They are my children. I suffer because of them. They do not know what awaits them. You must pray more for them.

402

The visionaries—Mirjana Dragicevic-Soldo, Ivanka Ivankovic-Elez, and Jakov Colo—have received all ten secrets, and our Lady appears to them once per year, and will do so for the rest of their lives. For Ivanka, who received her tenth secret on 7 May 1985, it is on the anniversary date of the apparitions, 25 June. For Jakov, who received his tenth secret on 12 September 1998, it is on Christmas day. For Mirjana, who received her tenth secret on Christmas 1982, it is on 18 March. In addition, Our Lady told Mirjana that she would experience extraordinary apparitions as well.

In addition to this basic message, Mirjana related on occasions an apparition she had in 1982 which clearly describes the times we are living and the direct conflict between Good and evil. She spoke of an apparition in which Satan appeared to her. Satan asked Mirjana to renounce the Blessed Virgin Mary and thus to follow him. That way she could be happy in love and in life. He said that following the Virgin Mary would only lead to suffering... Mirjana rejected him, and the Blessed Virgin Mary arrived immediately thereafter and Satan disappeared. The Blessed Virgin Mary then gave Mirjana the following message:

Excuse me for this, but you must realize that Satan exists. One day he appeared before the throne of God and asked permission to submit the Church to a period of trial. God gave him permission to try the Church for one century. This century is under the power of the Devil, but when the secrets confided to you come to pass, his power will be destroyed. Even now he is beginning to lose his power and has become aggressive. He is destroying marriages, creating division among priests and is responsible for obsessions and murder. You must protect yourselves against these things through fasting and prayer, especially community prayer. Carry blessed objects with you. Put them in your house, and restore the use of holy water.

The message of our Lady of Medjugorje echoes the essential teachings of the Gospels. It orbits around fasting, prayer and reconciliation (Confession). The message has been delivered for the past 39 years by way of long, repetitive teachings, which, as his holiness Pope John Paul II used to say, is the founding dialogue of every loving mother with her children.

The Holy Eucharist

Our Lady calls man, as a principal means of salvation, to Sunday Mass, and when possible, to daily Mass. The six visionaries all confirmed having seen many times the Blessed Virgin Mary crying when speaking of the Eucharist and the Mass:

You do not celebrate the Eucharist as you should. If you would know what grace and what gifts you receive, you would prepare yourselves for it each day for an hour at least.

(1985)

Marija said that if she had to choose between the Eucharist and the apparition, she would choose the Eucharist.

The Blessed Virgin Mary asked that the prayer to the Holy Spirit always be said before Mass. Our Lady wants to see the Holy Mass as "the highest form of prayer" and "the center of our lives" (according to Marija). Vicka also says that the Blessed Mother sees the Mass as:

... the most important and the most holy moment in our lives. We have to be prepared and pure to receive Jesus with a great respect. Mass should be the center of our lives.

Our Lady is crying because people do not have enough respect toward the Eucharist. The Mother of God wants us to realize the extreme beauty of the mystery of the Mass. She has said:

There are many of you who have sensed the beauty of the Holy Mass... Jesus gives you His graces in Mass.

(3 April 1986)

Let the Holy Mass be your life.

(25 April 1988)

This message takes a special meaning considering that according to the latest polls in the United States (*PEW Research Center*), a mere third of U.S. Catholics believe in the Holy Sacrament of the Altar being the true Body and Blood, Soul and Divinity of Our Lord Jesus-Christ!

Mass is the greatest prayer of God. You will never be able to understand its greatness. That is why you must be perfect and humble at Mass, and you should prepare yourselves for it.

Dear children, I am continuously among you because, with my endless love, I desire to show you the door of Heaven. I desire to tell you how it is opened: through goodness, mercy, love and peace—through my Son; therefore, my children, do not waste time on vanities. Only knowledge of the love of my Son can save you. Through that salvific love and the Holy Spirit He chose me; and I, together with Him, am choosing you to be apostles of His Love and Will.

My children, great is the responsibility upon you. I desire that by your example, you help sinners regain their sight, enrich their poor souls and bring them back into my embrace. Therefore, pray, pray, fast and confess regularly. If receiving my Son in the Eucharist is the center of your life then do not be afraid, you can do everything. I am with you. Every day I pray for the shepherds, and I expect the same of you. Because, my children, without their guidance and strengthening through their blessing, you cannot do it.

Thank you.

(2 June 2012)

Most weekly Mass-goers believe in transubstantiation; most other Catholics do not

% of U.S. Catholics who …

	NET Believe bread and wine become body, blood of Christ	Know church teaching on transubstantiation	Don't know teaching/ unsure about teaching	NET Believe bread and wine are symbols	Know church teaching on transubstantiation	Don't know teaching/ unsure about teaching
	%	%	%	%	%	%
Attend Mass weekly or more	63	58	5	37	14	23
Monthly/yearly	25	23	1	75	25	50
Seldom/never	13	10	2	87	25	62
Men	32	30	3	67	24	44
Women	29	27	3	70	20	50
White	34	32	2	65	25	40
Hispanic	24	21	4	76	19	57
Under age 40	26	23	3	74	27	47
40-59	27	26	2	72	22	50
60 or older	38	35	3	61	18	43
High school or less	26	22	3	74	15	59
Some college	31	27	4	69	19	50
College graduate	37	36	1	62	33	30

Note: Those who declined to answer not shown. Whites include only non-Hispanics. Hispanics can be of any race.
Source: Survey conducted Feb. 4-19, 2019, among U.S. adults.

PEW RESEARCH CENTER

Dear Children! Today also I invite you to prayer, now as never before when my plan has begun to be realized. Satan is strong and wants to sweep away my plans of peace and joy and make you think that my Son is not strong in His decisions. Therefore, I call all of you, dear children, to pray and fast still more firmly. I invite you to self-renunciation for nine days so that, with your help, everything that I desire to realize through the secrets I began in Fatima, may be fulfilled.

I call you, dear children, to now grasp the importance of my coming and the seriousness of the situation. I want to save all souls and present them to God. Therefore, let us pray that everything I have begun be fully realized. Thank you for having responded to my call.

(25 August 1991)

Prayer

Prayer is the center of Our Lady's message in Medjugorje.

Today also I am calling you to prayer. You know, dear children, that God grants special graces in prayer... I call you, dear children, to prayer with the heart.

(25 April 1987)

Without unceasing prayer, you cannot experience the beauty and greatness of the grace which God is offering you.

(25 February 1989)

Our Lady's recommended prayers:

In the beginning, following an old Croatian tradition, Our Lady asked for the daily praying of: The Creed, followed by Seven Our Fathers, Hail Mary's, and Glory Be's.

Later, Our Lady recommended praying the Rosary. First Our Lady asked us to pray five decades, then ten, and finally Our Lady wishes us to pray daily, together or individually, the entire 15 Mysteries of the Rosary (Joyful, Sorrowful, and Glorious Mysteries).

The Blessed Virgin Mary added:

May prayer reign in the whole world.

(25 August 1989)

You know that I love you and am coming here out of love, so I could show you the path of peace and salvation for your souls. I want you to listen to me and not permit Satan to seduce you. Dear children, Satan is strong enough! Therefore, I ask you to dedicate your prayers so that those who are under his influence may be saved. Give witness by your life, sacrifice your lives for the salvation of the world...

Therefore, little children, do not be afraid. If you pray, Satan cannot injure you, not even a little, because you are God's children and He is watching over you. Pray, and let the Rosary always be in your hands as a sign to Satan that you belong to me.

(25 February 1989)

Fasting

In the Old Testament and in the New Testament, there are many examples of fasting. Our Lord Jesus-Christ and His disciples fasted frequently. Certain devils *can be cast out in no other way except by prayer and fasting*, said Jesus. (Mark 9:29). Fasting is essential in order to achieve freedom from addiction of pleasures, self-indulgence, passionate desires and all in all sin. Through fasting, we are told, one is better able to listen to God and to perceive Him more clearly; hence, the Blessed Virgin Mary recommends fasting twice a week:

"Fast strictly on Wednesdays and Fridays."

(14 August 1984)

The Holy Mother of Christ asks the world to accept this difficult message **"... with a firm will."** She asks us to **"Persevere in... fasting."**

(25 June 1982)

The best fast is on bread and water. Through fasting and prayer one can stop wars, one can suspend the natural laws of nature. Works of charity cannot replace fasting... Everyone except the sick, has to fast.

(21 July 1982)

To Mirjana in Sarajevo:

My dear children! I came to you in order to lead you to purity of soul, and then to God. How did you receive me? At the beginning you were fearful, suspicious of the children I had chosen. Later on, the majority received me in their heart. They began to put into practice, my maternal recommendation. Unfortunately, that did not last a long time... Whatever be the place where I appear, and with me also my Son, Satan also comes. You permitted him to subdue you without realizing that you were being led by him.

It is up to you to realize that your behavior is not permitted by God, but that you immediately stifle the thought. Do not give in dear children. Wipe away from my face, the tears which I shed on seeing you act in this manner. Look around you. Take the time to come to God in the Church. Come into your Father's house. Take the time to meet for family prayer, in order to obtain the grace from God.

Remember your deceased; make them happy by offering the Mass. Do not look with scorn on the poor man who is begging a morsel of bread. Do not send him away from your abundant table. Help him and God will help you. It could very well happen that the blessing he leaves you as a sign of gratitude will be fulfilled for you. God may listen to him.

You have forgotten all of that, my children. Satan has influenced you in that. Do not give in. Pray with me! Do not deceive yourselves in thinking, I am good, but my brother, who lives next to me is not good. You will be mistaken. I love you because I am your mother, and I warn you. There are the secrets my children. One does not know what they are; when they learn, it will be too late. Return to prayer! Nothing is more necessary. I would like it if the Lord would have permitted me to show you just a little about the secrets, but, He already gives you enough graces.

Think! What do you offer to Him in return. When was the last time you gave up something for the Lord? I will not blame you further, but once again I call you to prayer, fasting, and to penance.

If you wish to obtain a grace from the Lord by fasting, then let no one know that you are fasting. If you wish to obtain the grace of God through a gift to the poor, let no one know it, except you and the Lord. Listen to me, my children! Meditate on my message in prayer.

(The Blessed Virgin Mary, 28 January 1987)

Daily Reading of the Bible

Usually, Our Lady comes to the visionaries happy and joyful, but on one occasion, while talking about the Bible, the Blessed Virgin Mary was crying. Our Lady said:

You have forgotten the Bible…

The Bible is a book different from any other book on earth. Vatican II says that all the canonical books of the Bible are: "… *written under the inspiration of the Holy Spirit, they have God as their author.*"

(Dogmatic Constitution on Devine Revelation)

The Blessed Virgin Mary asks us to separate the Bible from the other human books; hence, we are asked to place the Bible in a visible place in our homes.

Dear children, today I call you to read the Bible every day in your homes and let it be in a visible place so as always to encourage you to read it and pray.

(The Blessed Virgin Mary, 18 October 1984)

Every family must pray family prayers and read the Bible.

(The Blessed Virgin Mary, 14 February 1985)

Confession

Our Lady asks for monthly confession. From the very first days of the apparitions:

Make your peace with God and among yourselves. For that, it is necessary to believe, to pray, to fast, and to go to confession.

(The Blessed Virgin Mary, 26 June 1981)

Pray, pray! It is necessary to believe firmly, to go to confession regularly, and, likewise, to receive Holy Communion. It is the only salvation.

(The Blessed Virgin Mary, 10 February 1982)

Whoever has done very much evil during his life can go straight to Heaven if he confesses, is sorry for what he has done, and receives Communion at the end of his life.

(24 July 1982)

The Western Church, the Blessed Virgin Mary said in La Fraudais and in Medjugorje, has disregarded confession and its importance. The Gospa added:

Monthly confession will be a remedy for the Church in the West. One must convey this message to the West.

(6 August 1982)

One who comes to Medjugorje is always impressed by the great number of people waiting for confession, and the number of priests hearing confession in and outside the Church of St. James.

Naturally, confession should not be a habit that would allow one *to make sinning easy*. Vicka has the custom to say to every pilgrims group that visits her:

Confession is something that has to make a new human being out of you. Our Lady does not want you to think that confession will free you from sin and allow you to continue the same life after that. No, confession is a call to transformation. You must become a new person!

The Blessed Virgin Mary was quite clear on this holy Sacrament:

Do not go to confession through habit, to remain the same after that. No, it is not good. Confession should give an impulse to your faith. It should stimulate you and bring you closer to Jesus. If confession does not mean anything for you, really, you will be converted with great difficulty.

(7 November 1983)

Heaven

All six of the Medjugorje seers have seen Heaven. They all expressed their astonishment and stated that if we knew what awaits us in Heaven, there would be no difficulties nor trials that wouldn't be worth eternal life in Heaven.

Two of the Medjugorje visionaries, Vicka and Jakov, were physically taken to Heaven, Purgatory, and hell. The other visionaries were merely shown visions thereof. Our Lady told the visionaries that many people do not believe that

Visionaries during an ecstasy in the Church of St. James (Medjugorje)

Ivanka's brain Readings being studied through an encephalogram during an ecstasy

Visionaries on Apparition Hill (Medjugorje)

Mgr. René Laurentin (foremost defender of Medjugorje) / Mgr. Laurentin with Vicka Ivanković in her home.

Visionaries Maria Pavlovic and Ivan Dragicevic being studied with an encephalogram by French scientists of the University of Montpellier

Heaven, Purgatory or hell truly exist; hence, the Blessed Virgin Mary wishes the visionaries to be witnesses of their existence through their experiences.

Vicka:

In describing Heaven in an interview with Fr. Livio for Radio Maria, Vicka explained that she and Jakov went to Heaven. When they arrived, there was a great big wooden door. Vicka said that at first, the door was closed, but when they arrived the Blessed Virgin Mary opened it, allowing them to enter into Heaven. St. Peter was standing at the door's right hand.

Vicka:
- *I immediately understood that it was him. With a key, rather small, with the beard a little sturdy, with hair.*

Fr. Bubalo:
- Please, Vicka, describe Heaven.
- *it can't be described. That is something beyond description. It is filled with some sort of beautiful light…people flowers… angels… All is filled with some indescribable joy. Your heart stands still when you look at it.*

The following is taken from another interview with Vicka:

- **Question:** Vicka, tell us about Heaven.
- Vicka: *Heaven is a vast space, and it has a brilliant light which does not leave it. It is a life which we do not know here on earth. We saw people dressed in gray, pink, and yellow robes. They were walking, praying, and singing. Small angels were flying above them. The Blessed Mother showed us how happy these people are.*

- **Question:** How could you tell they were happy?
- Vicka: *You can see it on their faces. But it is impossible to describe with words the great happiness I saw in Heaven… In Paradise, when the Blessed Mother passed, everybody responded to Her, and She to them. There was a recognition between them… They were standing there communicating with Her, like in a tunnel, only it wasn't exactly like a tunnel, but a tunnel is the closest comparison. People were praying, they were singing, they were looking… People in Heaven know the absolute fullness of a created being.*

- **Question:** How long were you there?
- Vicka: *Maybe twenty minutes.*

- **Question:** … Did the people talk to you?
- Vicka: *It was very unusual. They were speaking, but I could not understand them… The people were in small groups. I was with Jakov and the Blessed Mother. We spoke to each other, but there was no*

communication with anyone else. About the people there, the Blessed Mother only said to us:
'You see how people who are in Heaven are happy?'

Mirjana

Mirjana didn't physically go to Heaven, but saw Heaven during an apparition. The following is her description of what she saw:

- Mirjana: *I saw Heaven as if it were a movie. The first thing I noticed was the faces of the people there; they were radiating a type of inner light which showed how immensely happy they were.*

- **Question:** Is Heaven an actual place?
- Mirjana: *Yes. The trees, the meadows, the sky are totally different from anything we know on the earth. And the light is much more brilliant. Heaven is beautiful beyond any possible comparison with anything I know of on earth.*

- **Question:** Did the people you saw have bodies?
- Mirjana: *Yes.*

- **Question:** What ages were they?
- Mirjana: *They were different from what we are like now. Perhaps they were all around 30 years of age... They were walking in a beautiful park. They have everything. They need or want nothing. They are totally full... They were dressed in the types of clothing that Jesus wore.*

Mirjana was asked why the Blessed Virgin Mary showed her Heaven:

Mirjana: *She told me many people on earth today do not believe Heaven exists. She said God has chosen us six visionaries to be instruments of His Love and Mercy. I have personally seen Heaven. It exists! I've seen it! Those who stay faithful to God to the end will see Heaven as a reward for their faithfulness.*

Ivanka

- **Question:** Did you see Heaven, hell, and Purgatory, Ivanka?
- Ivanka: *I saw Purgatory and Heaven as a picture. I told the Blessed Mother I did not want to see hell.*

- **Question:** What did Heaven look like?

- Ivanka: *It is a place that is very, very beautiful. Most beautiful... Everyone I saw was filled with a happiness I can't explain—and I can't forget.*

- **Question:** Do you long for that happiness yourself?
- Ivanka: *I know some of that happiness when I am with the Blessed Mother, and when I pray.*

- **Question:** Can you tell us more about Heaven?
- Ivanka: *God made us for Heaven. If you pray, you will know that.*

Marija

- **Question:** Were you taken to Heaven or were you shown a vision of Heaven?
- Marija: *I had a vision of Heaven, but Jakov and Vicka were actually taken there.*

- **Question:** When you saw the vision, were you in the rectory room? Or where?
- Marija: *It was in the house of Jakov... It was like you watch a movie on screen or looking out a window. I saw a vision. I wasn't actually there like the other visionaries... I have never seen such a picture before; no one can even begin to imagine how it looks... the people were around the flowers. They were all the same age. No one in Heaven is older than the age of Christ. People in Heaven were full of joy and all of them are giving thanks for the gifts given to them of God. Every day they realize how much love God has for them... There was a multitude of people.*

Ivan

Heaven is worth any cost! Jesus showed us that, with His death on the Cross. His death was not the end. He rose from the dead, glorified to put an end to death forever for God's children. People in Heaven are happy. They live in the fullness of God.

Jakov

Jakov was the other visionary, along with Vicka, that was physically taken up to Heaven. He was only 11 years old at the time.

- **Question:** *Will you tell us about Heaven.*
- Jakov: *When you get there, then you will see how it is.*

- **Question:** *You have said that the reason the Blessed Mother took you there was to show you what it would be like for those who remain faithful to God. Would you tell us anymore?*
- Jakov: ***If I thought about it too much—I would die of loneliness.***

- **Question:** *Tell us your understanding of Heaven.*
- Jakov: ***I have been there. It is difficult for me to talk about it.***

- **Question:** *Is it difficult to live on earth once you have been in Heaven?*
- Jakov: ***That is an understatement.***

- **Question:** *Jakov, you said that if you thought about Heaven too much, you would die of loneliness. How do you handle the memories of Heaven, hell, and Purgatory?*
- Jakov: ***The Blessed Mother asks us to be careful of the problem of the tyranny of memories.***

- **Question:** *What does that mean?*
- Jakov: ***She asks us to trust God's love to make all things well. She asks us to surrender the past to Her maternal care, and to remember only in the light of God's love.***

Hell and Purgatory

In an interview with Vicka, Fr. Janko Bubalo asked Vicka questions about her experiences.

- **Fr. Bubalo:** *You told me, and I read it in one of your notebooks, that on All Soul's Day, 1981, you, the Seers, and all of you were gathered except Ivan, and the Virgin showed you Heaven. It is recorded that Heaven is inexpressibly beautiful, with a multitude of people and angels. And when you asked the Virgin why she showed you Heaven, it is noted in the journal that she said so that you might see what it would be like for those who remain faithful to God. It is also added that Ivanka saw her deceased mother there, and another woman known to her…*
  … Let me remind you of this too: just four days later, it is noted in that journal that the Virgin suddenly, as though at once, disappeared, and that hell appeared before you. That was observed by you, Jakov, and Marija. It is recorded that it was awful! Like a sea of flame. Within a large group of people.
  It is stated that in the midst of all, a blonde longhaired woman with horns was seen, and that the devils are leaping toward her from all sides. Something like that… Did the Virgin tell you why she showed you that?
- Vicka: ***Yes, yes! She told us that she showed it to us so that we might know what it is like for those who go there.***

- **Fr. Bubalo:** ... *The Virgin took you and Jakov somewhere to show you Heaven and hell... tell me about it now as fully as possible.*
- Vicka: ... *Fifteen days—I don't know exactly—after this vision of hell... I and Jakov went to Citluk for something. We returned about three in the afternoon. We stopped at my house a bit, and then continued on to Jakov's to return him safely to his mother... His mother was out somewhere, and the Virgin appeared to us immediately. She greeted us with 'Praised be Jesus!' and said to us that she would take us to Heaven... We became frightened. Jakov began to cry. He said he wouldn't go since she is his mother's one and only, and that I should go by myself.*
- **Fr. Bubalo:** *And the Virgin?*
- Vicka: *She said nothing. We were still kneeling. She took me by the right hand, and Jakov by the left hand and stood between us, with Her face toward us, and we immediately began to lift upward... straight up through the ceiling. The house disappeared, and we were off... It seemed to me that we went upward...*

Jakov was questioned about his experience with Heaven, Purgatory, and hell in a talk he gave to pilgrims in Medjugorje on 12 October 2007:

- Jakov: ... *when Our Lady took us to Heaven, I was very afraid. I was only eleven and when Our Lady told us that she was going to take us with her, I didn't want to go with her. I was afraid I would die. And I said to our Lady, 'why don't you take Vicka only. Her mother has eight children and I am the only child my mother has.'*

In another interview, Vicka stated:

- Vicka: *The Blessed Mother has shown me Heaven, hell, and Purgatory... Many people today do not believe there is a place or state of life after death of the body. They believe that when we die, life is over. The Blessed Mother says no; on the contrary, we are only passengers on earth. She has come to remind us of the eternal truths of the Gospel.*

- **Question:** *Are Heaven and hell actual places?*
- Vicka: *Yes. I saw them.*

- **Question:** *How?*
- Vicka: *Two ways—I saw with my eyes... And then I visited these places. Jakov and I were taken there by the Blessed Mother.*

Marija was interviewed by a Friend of Medjugorje on 6 November 1986 about her visions of Heaven, Purgatory, and hell. The following is part of the interview:

- **Question:** *When you saw the vision of Heaven, did you see Purgatory at the same time?*
- Marija: *I saw all the visions at the same apparition—Heaven, Purgatory, and hell.*

- **Question:** *Has Our Lady ever revealed to you if a soul in Purgatory can be lost and go to hell?*
- Marija: *No, once they are in Purgatory, they can only go to Heaven.*

- **Question:** *In your opinion, some people that are constantly going from good to bad, bad to good, good to bad, yet love God, will they go to hell?*
- Marija: *I don't know. When a man dies, God gives him special graces and blessings to decide where he should go himself. God gives him a scene, reviewing his whole life, what he has done in his life, and so God gives him graces to decide where he should go, according to his life. He has a free choice.*

- **Question:** *Well, say that you deserve hell but you want to go to Heaven. What happens then because didn't God give you a choice?*
- Marija: *Yes, but God gives you these special graces to understand fully so you will only answer truthfully.*

- **Question:** *So, He gives you so many graces you say, 'God, I don't deserve Heaven, I deserve hell or Purgatory.'—like truth serum?"*
- Marija: *Yes, correct.*

- **Question:** *So, God never sends anyone to hell, they decide it themselves?*
- Marija: *Yes, we are judges to our life.*

- **Question:** *So when it is stated, 'God sends no one to hell, they send themselves,' it means just that?*
- Marija: *Yes, correct.*

- **Question:** *Have you, Marija, ever asked Our Lady if you will go to Heaven, like Jacinta, Francisco, and Lucia of Fatima did? They asked Our Lady, 'Are we to go to Heaven?' and She told them, 'Yes.'*
- Marija: *No, I have never asked her that!*

- **Question:** *Are you scared?*
- Marija: *I would be happy to be behind the gates in Paradise, if only I could be there.*

Marija also adds from another interview:

- Marija: *We choose Heaven, hell, or Purgatory for ourselves. The Blessed Mother explained to me that at death we are the same person we are in life, though we no longer have the use of our body. It returns to the earth. We receive the light at death to see the plan God has had for us from the beginning. We then understand how we have chosen to comply with His Divine plan. In the light of truth, we know where we belong, where we fit, and we choose Heaven, hell, or Purgatory.*

Church Recognition and Formal Approval Process

In 2010, Pope Benedict XVI set up a committee on the study of Medjugorje presided over by Cardinal Camillo Ruini, and composed of bishops, cardinals, theologians, experts in Mariology, anthropologists and psychologists. The commission's work ended on 17 January 2014 with a favorable opinion on the recognition of the supernatural nature of the first Apparitions, which took place between 24 June and 3 July 1981.

Monsignor René Laurentin

The Bishop of Mostar, Mgr. P. Zanic, was in July 1981 quite favorable at the extraordinary events taking place with such young children in Medjugorje; however... gradually, Mgr. P. Zanic adopted a more and more hostile position against the apparitions in the hill of Medjugorje due to an old conflict which resurfaced in the diocese with the local Franciscans, whose order was not directly subject to the Mostar's Episcopal jurisdiction nor of the bishop's authority... Consequently, Mgr. Zanic announced a negative judgment in May 1986; but Rome, for the first time in Church History, refused a Bishop's negative condemnation of an alleged Marian apparition site! Hence, a decision was made by the Dycasterium/Congregation of the Doctrine of the Faith—headed at the time by Cardinal Ratzinger—of refusing Mgr. Zanic's negative judgment, and, consequently, of transferring the judgment authority to the Yugoslavian Episcopal Conference.

Indeed, never such a decision had ever been made as no precedent could be found; consequently, Cardinal Kuharic established, upon receiving instructions from Cardinal Ratzinger, a new commission which began its work in March 1987. On all levels, the newly appointed commission was able to distinguish between the actual facts and the undeniably extraordinary fruits produced by the apparitions' messages of the "Gospa" in Medjugorje. These facts were indeed recognized by everyone involved directly in the investigation.

The Medjugorje apparition case has been, however, victim to a great deal of defamation and calumnies. Falsehoods and untrue rumors, inspired by sheer jealousy and pettiness have spread throughout Catholic communities; nonetheless, the staunched defenders of the apparitions' messages, which include multitudes of experts and investigators, have stood by the six young messengers of the Blessed Virgin Mary.

One of those experts who have defended and supported the apparitions and the visionaries of Medjugorje best and longest was French Abbot René Laurentin[24] whose meticulous and unbiased investigation brought forth theological and scientific results which, I am sorry to say, were utterly rejected by the bishop of Mostar…

Mgr. René Laurentin on the apparition-dossier of Medjugorje (1997):

The position of Medjugorje in the Church is a difficult, disputed subject, an object of confusion and ambiguities that is important to dissipate.
Just between us, Medjugorje does not need any explanation… It is a place of grace where Our Lady has manifested herself through exceptional fruits:

- *Spiritual life*
- *Conversions*
- *Healings*

In 1984–5, when Bishop Zanic announced his negative verdict, I had prepared my conscience for this possibility, and I said to myself candidly something like, "In this case, I will stop writing or speaking publicly about Medjugorje, but like the friends of St. Joan of Arc, burned at the order of a bishop in 1431, I will deepen my knowledge about it and put down the reasons for revising such a judgment."
Respect for authority and obedience, from which we should never deviate, in this area, occasionally allows for slight differences in the free service of the faith. Concerning the word "Church", the last word of the topic that was assigned to me ("the Place of Medjugorje in the Church"), another ambiguity here must be clarified.
Before the Council, for the majority of theologians, the Church was the hierarchy: that is to say the Pope and the bishops. Vatican Council II revised this conception. It restructured the Constitution of the Church inversely: the Church is, first of all, the people of God, among which certain faithful (equal to others before God in faith, hope, charity and in the search for holiness) have authority in the name of Christ, but this authority is in service of the people of God.
That is why the Pope has given himself the title "Servant of the servants of God". Now let us examine the place of Medjugorje "in the Church" according to

---

[24] Abbot (later Monsignor) René Laurentin was a French theologian. Internationally recognized as one of the world's foremost Mariologian authority in the world, and author of 150 books and countless scholarly articles on topics involving Marian apparitions in Lourdes, La Salette, la Rue du Bac (Paris), Medjugorje, visionaries and mystics including Bernadette Soubirous, Thérèse de Lisieux, Catherine Labouré, and Yvonne Aimée de Malestroit; as well as biblical exegesis, and theological articles. During the occurrences of the apparition cases of Betania (Venezuela), San Nicolas (Argentina), Soufanieh (Syria), Kibeho (Rwanda), Father René Laurentin, through his personal and direct theological and scientific investigations, has indeed been instrumental in the Episcopal recognition process of said approved apparition sites.

these two complementary meanings of the word "Church", which signifies an organic reality: the mystical but visible Body of Christ.

At Medjugorje, as in other places, <u>the faithful</u> were the first to recognize the presence of the Virgin Mary in these apparitions. The pastor, Fr. Jozo Zovko, a spiritual man, was first of all critical and demanded verification of the apparitions. He said to the parishioners:

What are you going to do on this hill, when you have the Eucharist in the Church?

He brought them all back to the church for daily mass to where the apparitions were transferred. Quite soon thereafter, he believed (in the authenticity of the children's visions) *and had a personal apparition of the Virgin which confirmed his conviction.*

Among Christians, however, there are opponents on the right and on the left side of the spectrum:

1. *The Progressive Christian prefers the negative critique, psychological and psycho-analytical explanations, systematic doubt and suspicion in the face of extraordinary phenomena.*
2. *The Traditionalist wing or moderate integrist, for example,* Fidelity *in the USA, or the extreme right of the Catholic Counter Reform (which excommunicated the Pope as heretical) were the most fierce adversaries of Medjugorje.*

Pilgrims often ask the visionaries:

- *"What should we do to be able to convince the opponents?"*

Vicka answered:

- *Pray for them and be good. The Lord and the Holy Virgin will do the rest.*

That was already the position of Bernadette Soubirous in Lourdes, who did not involve herself in discussions with opponents who wanted to argue with her, but rather when they insisted, she simply answered:

I am charged to tell you. I am not charged to make you believe.

The situation is more complex on the side of the authorities. The local bishop, Mgr. Zanic, successor of the apostles and the one responsible for discernment in his diocese, was at first favorable during the summer of 1981 (although he does not want to remember it today). But the local conflict with the Franciscans (who make up to 80% of the priests of his diocese) aggravated everything step by step. The time allotted here does not permit me to give the details of this problem. For that, I refer you to my books [25].

When I went to Medjugorje for the first time in Christmas of 1983, I believed that he was still favorable but he disillusioned me. I listened to him and did my best to note his objections, although they seemed to me quite external, partial and weak in comparison to the obvious facts, which got me involved in a difficult venture in respect to his spectator authority.

I went to see him as often as I could. He confirmed to me his radical opposition. At the end of the visit with him, I asked for his blessing. Once he found it difficult (to respond in kind). I insisted, saying:

"If I am a problem for you, give me the blessing for my conversion."

To that he responded with his usual magnanimity:

"Remain Laurentin."

His official position of 30 October 1984 against Medjugorje defamed me on several points in a surprising manner: I was supposed to have been guilty of hiding the truth; I therefore disqualified myself as a theologian; I was supposed to have done this for money; I (supposedly) have earned more than a billion dollars!; I had succumbed to the charm of the visionaries of Medjugorje rather than listening to the bishop; and yet, he had never forbidden me to go to Medjugorje nor asked me to stop writing.

I prepared myself to keep silence after the negative verdict, which he had publicly announced, but when he came to Rome in April 1986 to propose said verdict, Cardinal Ratzinger told him (and Bishop Zanic, a man of clarity and of not easily victim to duplicity):

No, you are going to dissolve your diocesan commission. The verdict is transferred to the Bishops Conference.

This was unexpected, because, according to an old tradition, aggravated by Cardinal Ottaviani, who in 1959 and 1960 made the decisions against Sister Faustina (beatified today) and Mother Yvonne Aimée, etc., the Holy Office generally supported bishops who were unfavorable towards apparitions, and rather restrained favorable judgments. Here then it was reversed. One could ask why. I believe I have the explanation:

---

[25] The main problem between Mgr. Zanic and the Franciscan priests in his diocese had to do with the Franciscan Order being put to light *"on the front row"* in this case, and, not being subject to the Bishop's jurisdiction or authority, the dioceses took a most uncomfortable second role in this case before the public view. The Franciscans maintained their open support to the Medjugorje children, regardless of the local Episcopal stand.

In July 1984, Pope John Paul II, into whose own hands I gave my first book, **Is The Virgin Mary Appearing at Medjugorje**? *(February 1984), had read it in Castelgandolfo and had recommended it to Bishop Pio Belo Ricardo of Los Teques (Venezuela).[26] The following year, he also read* **Scientific & Medical Studies on the Apparitions at Medjugorje**, *which I wrote together with Professor Joyeux from Montpellier.*

Finally, I initiated an international meeting of doctors and theologians at Milan to establish ten scientific and ten theological conclusions concerning Medjugorje. Agreement was easily reached in one day of work, and twenty conclusions were sent to John Paul II by Doctor Luigi Farina, the President of ARPA, where this meeting had taken place. The Pope sent all these documents to Cardinal Ratzinger, Prefect of the Congregation of the Doctrine of the Faith, *who seems to have made this new decision after having conferred with John Paul II. It was an unprecedented decision. It took the bishop's ordinary authority away from him without taking it away completely, since he would still be a member of the Yugoslav Bishops Conference, to which the judgment was transferred. The result was a long journey.*

Cardinal Kuharic, with whom Vicka had an apparition (in his living room in 1983, as he told me) was, it seemed to me, open and discretely favorable. In any case, he desired the bishops to peacefully take the responsibility for this important and fruitful place of pilgrimage instead of stirring up one of those conflicts around apparitions that create discomfort and divisions within the Church, which are detrimental to the faithful, the bishops, and God Himself. But being prudent and respectful of Monsignor Zanic, the local bishop who is responsible before God and the parish of Medjugorje, Cardinal Kuharic rightly maintained a prominent place for him.

Every time a question was addressed to the Bishops Conference, he was always the one to speak first. With his characteristic vigor Bishop Zanic repeated all the objections he had developed, twice publicly:

- *The Official Position on Medjugorje of 30 October 1984, dealt a blow to the further expansion of Medjugorje, since he invited all the bishops of the Episcopal conferences of the world to support his negative position, suggesting that official pilgrimages (he underscored the "official") be not authorized.*

He held a severe sermon on 25 July 1987 against Medjugorje during the confirmation ceremony. He expected to see the parishioners revolt, but they silently listened to him with respect, in spite of the deep hurt they felt in their hearts. They gave proof of their heroic respect and obedience, but the bishop interpreted their reaction differently.

During the dinner that followed, he concluded, "**They don't believe so much anymore today.**" *The Franciscans disabused him (the sermon is published with my critical observations in* **Seven Years of Apparitions**, *pp 72–77). After this*

---

[26] *Bishop Pio Belo Ricardo would approve the apparition site of Betania (Venezuela) in November 1987.*

422

first intervention of the local bishop, the other less informed bishops kept silence or supported him out of solidarity.

The only one who pleaded for Medjugorje was Mgr. Franic, archbishop of Split, an authority in these matters, since he was president of the Yugoslav Bishops Commission for the Doctrine of the Faith. But he retired on 10 September 1988, and was no longer a member of the Bishops Conference thus terrain for Bishop Zanic. Under these circumstances, I never came to know how Cardinal Kuharic was able in November 1990 to succeed through the Bishops Conference in obtaining the recognition of pilgrimage and its practice.

It was done according to the directives and criteria published on 25 February 1978 by Cardinal Eper, (the predecessor of Cardinal Ratzinger at the Congregation of the Faith). In the case of apparitions, if no serious objection presents itself and if the fruits are good, the bishop takes charge of pilgrimage in order to direct the piety of the faithful. After that, he can eventually, without haste and with the necessary caution, recognize the apparitions themselves.

Unfortunately, Bishop Zanic accepted this recognition of pilgrimage (to which he was opposed) only on condition that several negative clauses be introduced. These minor restrictions made the text so obscure that the Cardinal and the Bishops Conference decided not to publish it, and to recognize it in action (as was done in Rome without a declaration for the recognition of Tre Fontane). This is how Bishop Komarica, president of the Yugoslav Bishops Commission for the investigation of Medjugorje, came to Medjugorje to celebrate a mass of pilgrimage. He declared officially:

I came not only in my own name but in the name of all the Yugoslav bishops, including Mgr. Zanic. Other bishops will come...

And other bishops followed indeed, including Mgr. Zanic and his archbishop, the future Cardinal Puljic of Sarajevo. Everything seemed to be going well. But on January 2, 1991 the text, kept secret because of its ambiguity, was published by the Italian News Agency ASCA (on the initiative of Mgr. Zanic, according to the Counter Reform which was very much supporting him) with a radically negative commentary. This obscure text, published under savage conditions, created uncertainty and disarray with pilgrims on an international scale. They referred to Cardinal Kuharic, who replied:

The Church is not in a hurry. We, the bishops, after three years of examination by the Commission, have declared Medjugorje a place of prayer and a Marian sanctuary. This means that WE ARE NOT OPPOSED to people coming on pilgrimage to Medjugorje to venerate the Mother of God there, in conformity with the teaching and faith of the universal Church. As to the supernaturality of the apparitions, we have declared: UP TO THIS MOMENT WE CANNOT AFFIRM IT. WE LEAVE IT FOR LATER... THE CHURCH IS NOT IN A HURRY.

(Declaration printed in Vecernji List, August 1993, Latest News 13, page 41)

Several Croatian bishops spoke in the same way. Overwhelmed with questions on an international level, Cardinal Kuharic took the time needed to arrive at a new version of the text, which was clearer and from which some negative ambivalences were absent. The sense of this maneuver became clearer, in spite of the negative declarations circulated in the press. The Yugoslav bishops had to choose between two classic formulas of possible expressions of judgments since the authenticity of the apparitions were not recognized:

1. Non patet supernaturalitas: The supernatural is not proven
2. Patet non supernaturalitas: The non-supernatural character is proven

The bishops chose, not the second formula which excluded the supernatural, but the first, which had an element of doubt: it was not yet possible to recognize the supernatural character, but without excluding it, as Cardinal Kuharic had clearly stated. It is a pity to see how the press and how certain priests or authorities continually confuse the prudent formula which suspends judgment and the formula which definitely excludes it. This confusion, which is frequent in such cases, has never ceased to revive at Medjugorje.

Another ambiguity: the word supernatural in similar circumstances is generally used in an ambiguous sense and is subject to confusion: it is supposed to mean miraculous, extraordinary, inexplicable, which is a very particular meaning of the word supernatural. The ambiguity is unfortunate because it would seem to deprive the aspects of pilgrimage (fervent masses, innumerable confessions, the Way of the Cross and rosaries) of a supernatural character, as if it were a place of superstition!

Thus certain commentaries have suggested. But the Bishops Conference does not leave in any doubt as to the supernatural character of the Medjugorje liturgies, but only maintains that the proof of an extraordinary intervention by God is not yet established.

Archbishop Franic blamed the prudence of the bishops and thought that this had been partially responsible for the war that took place, to the extent that "they did not recognize the voice of the Mother of God who was offering peace," or that they were "relentlessly opposed". The urgent call of Our Lady was not sufficiently heard, she could not save the situation. I leave to the archbishop the responsibility of his judgment published in Gebetsaktion, not personally having the authority nor the competence for this (Latest News 13, 14 and 15: 1994, 1995, 1996).

During the civil war, which subjected his diocese to destruction and bloodshed, Bishop Zanic had taken refuge in Rome where he spent a long time in obtaining the nomination of a successor who would continue his struggle against the Franciscans and Medjugorje. He was successful.

Mgr. Peric, superior of the Croatian College in Rome, who had been his principal assistant in transmitting his objections and complaints to Congregations in Rome, became the new local bishop, with less firmly entrenched convictions, and less impulsive, therefore more effective than Bishop Zanic. Certainly he maintained an appearance of prudence and never gave any official negative judgment against pilgrimages, in spite of many unfavorable declarations and actions.

*On several occasions he interpreted the judgment of the Bishops Conference in a manner which was in some way radically negative. Beginning in 1995 he had his Vicar General state these radical terms which he, himself expressed later in **Crkva na Kamenu** (his diocesan paper Church On the Rock):*

It is impossible to declare that one is dealing with supernatural apparitions (in Medjugorje). **Since the Declaration of the Bishops Conference 10 April, 1991, there has been a negative judgment from the two bishops of Mostar: the former and the current one** (Bishop Peric spoke here of himself in the third person). **Those who affirm the contrary are telling naive children stories. We stand by the opinion that the Holy Virgin has not appeared in person at Medjugorje.**

He nevertheless added (this limits and contradicts his previous statement):

The Ordinary of Mostar (Bishop Peric himself) **is only saying what the bishops said** (10 April 1991) **and does not believe in the stories about Medjugorje. This is what the Vicar General clearly stated before** (in a recent declaration to the press). **The text of the Declaration itself and the interpretation authorized by Cardinal Kuharic, principal author and signatory of the bishops declaration quoted earlier, sets the clock once again at the right time.**

In this confusion, several bishops from all over the world, not understanding anything (as to the position of the new local bishop of Mostar), wondered if they should discourage the members of their dioceses from going to Medjugorje or not... They wrote to the Congregation of the Doctrine of the Faith and several received a reply which echoed the Bishops Conference official Declaration of April 10, 1991, but in terms so ambiguous that the press interpreted it in a very radically negative sense.

*As a consequence of these publications, many of the faithful had the understanding that: "**If you go to Medjugorje, you are in disobedience.**" Here is the essential part of the answer by Archbishop Tarcisio Bertone, Secretary of the Congregation of the Doctrine of the Faith addressed March 12, 1996 to Mgr. Taverdet, bishop of Langres, in reply to his letter of February 14, 1996. After having quoted the essentials of the Yugoslav Bishops Conference Declaration of April 10, 1991, (see above) he concludes:*

From what has been said, it results that official pilgrimages to Medjugorje, understood as a place of authentic Marian apparitions, should not be organized because they would be in contradiction to what was affirmed by the bishops of ex-Yugoslavia.

Under the influence of the two successive statements of the two local bishops, the reply accumulates all the negative characteristics without underlining the positive element of the document. The talk in the press was: "Rome forbids pilgrimages to Medjugorje..."

The bishop of Rottenburg-Stuttgart echoed the same declaration received from Rome in more negative terms, and they were reproduced by the bishop of Metz. Sister Emmanuel wrote to him pointing out quite rightly:

Cardinal Ratzinger has never forbidden pilgrimages to Medjugorje. He was only recalling a law of the Church, which means that for places of apparitions still under examination official pilgrimages are forbidden, but private pilgrimages are authorized.

(Letter of 8 November 1995)

Given the confusion that arose from these contradictory and more or less abusive interpretations, Dr. Joaquin Navarro-Valls, spokesman for the Holy See and director of the press office, clearly denied the negative interpretation on August 21, 1996:

The Vatican has never said to Catholics, "You cannot go to Medjugorje." On the contrary, it said to the bishops: "Your parishes and dioceses cannot (yet) organize OFFICIAL pilgrimages. But one cannot tell people not to go there, insofar as it has not been proved that the apparitions are false... something that has never been declared. Therefore anyone who wants to, can go there."

(Statement of 21 August 1996 to the Catholic New Service)

Dr. Joaquin Navarro-Valls added:

A Catholic who goes to such a place (of apparitions) in good faith has the right to spiritual assistance. The church never forbids priests to accompany journeys to Medjugorje in Bosnia-Hercegovina, organized by the laity, just as it never forbids them to accompany a group of Catholics to visit the Republic of South Africa. Whoever reads the letter of the Archbishop Bertone could think that from now on it is forbidden for Catholics to go to Medjugorje. That would be an incorrect interpretation, since nothing has changed, nothing new has been said.

The problem is not to organize official pilgrimages (led by a bishop or the pastor of a church) which would seem to constitute a canonical recognition of the events of Medjugorje still under investigation. It is altogether another thing to organize a pilgrimage accompanied by a priest, who is necessary for confessions. It is a pity that the words of Archbishop Bertone were understood in a restrictive sense. Would the Church and the Vatican have said no to Medjugorje? No!

*The director of the press office noted correctly that Archbishop Bertone had echoed the Bishops' Declaration which stated that "**the many faithful who go to Medjugorje require pastoral assistance of the Church**" (therefore, the help of priests with their pilgrimage). Thus pilgrimages to Medjugorje, although* unofficial, require the pastoral assistance of priests for mass, preaching, and confessions.

More than one hundred bishops have gone to Medjugorje in spite of the opposition of the local bishop. This is astonishing enough, given the strict way in which episcopal solidarity is carried out in the Church (something which has greatly damaged my reputation since the personal attacks of Bishop Zanic against me were taken seriously).

But many bishops have noted remarkable, profound and lasting conversions of the people of their dioceses at Medjugorje. Some, who were indifferent, opposed and protesting, have themselves become pillars of the Catholic Church. They went to look, they were convinced and they have witnessed to it, according to the statutory freedom established in the Church in this matter. I have given the names and the testimonies of these bishops in the later volumes of my Latest News.

If so many bishops have gone to Medjugorje, in spite of all the dissuasion which the negative position of the local bishop was creating (and of which some of them were aware), there was another reason behind (this popularity of Medjugorje). Those bishops asked (directly) the advice of John Paul II who answered them positively, for instance to Bishop Hnilica:

If I were not Pope, I would have gone there long ago.

I cannot treat in detail the many testimonies of bishops on the position of the Pope. I will be even more discreet about the fact that, having been invited for breakfast with the Pope to submit an important matter to him, and once I did, the holy Father spent the rest of breakfast asking me questions about Medjugorje. What he most frequently pointed out to was the number of bishops who went there and thus were the "good fruits" which are the basis for the authenticity of an apparition, according to the only criterion given by Christ Himself:

One judges the tree by its fruits
(Mt. 7:16–20; 12:23 and similar)

On 6 April 1995, the Vice President of Croatia, Mr. Radi, representing President Tudjman and Cardinal Kuhari, came to thank the Pope after his visit to Croatia, inviting him to come in September 1995 to celebrate the 17th centenary of the founding of the church of Split. The Pope replied:

I will look into it. But if I can come I would wish to visit Maria Bistrica (the national shrine of Our Lady near Zagreb) and... Medjugorje.

These words were reported in the Croatian newspapers (Latest News 14, p. 44).

According to Sister Emmanuel, he told an English group on 31 May 1995: **Pray that I may go to Medjugorje this year** (Latest News 15). This testimony and others are published in Latest News 14, p. 43–44 and Latest News 15, pp. 43–46.

I do not think that the Pope's desire can be realized, given the opposition of the local bishop, for even if the Pope is theoretically all powerful, he shows maximum respect for the established authorities in the Church according to the principle of subsidiarity that: the higher level must avoid interference with the lower level, while maintaining its freedom to confirm its convictions privately.

In reply to the question: "In which direction is it going?" What to answer?

1. *Medjugorje is no longer under the Yugoslav Bishops Conference presided over by Cardinal Kuhari, who had assumed responsibility for pilgrimages. The Yugoslav Bishops Conference no longer exists and by that fact its Commission no longer exists.*

2. *The local bishop, Mgr. Peri, now belongs to the Bosnia-Hercegovina Bishops Conference, presided over by Cardinal Pulji. He has always been in solidarity with the local bishop who is in opposition without formally stating his position.*

   The new Bosnia-Hercegovina Bishops Conference has only three bishops. One is radically negative (the local bishop), and the other (the Cardinal President) is normally in solidarity. The position of the third one, Mgr. Komarica, the persecuted bishop of Banja Luka, president of the Yugoslav Bishops Commission for the investigation of Medjugorje, remains sibylline. In the Commission over which he presided the experts in favor of Medjugorje did not feel free as some of them confided to Archbishop Frani.

The bishop of Mostar seemed to have said privately to some people who repeated it later:

During the war I will not act against Medjugorje... but the time will undoubtedly come after the war.

What is keeping his negative action muffled is that he is not ignoring the Popes discreet but well-known position. The situation of Medjugorje will remain morally protected as long as John Paul II is alive. What will happen afterwards will depend on the next Pope.

From a human point of view the perspective would therefore seem quite gloomy. But it was even gloomier when Bishop Ani announced his negative judgment at different stages which I cannot relate in detail. Each time the worst has been avoided against every expectation. The grace of Medjugorje continues: up to now the Virgin Mary has discretely shown herself to be the strongest even when things were at their worst...

(Monsignor René Laurentin, 1997)

In January 2014, under the Pontificate of Pope Francis, a new Vatican commission concluded an investigation on the doctrinal and disciplinary aspects of the Medjugorje apparition case and subsequent messages, and submitted a document to the Congregation for the Doctrine of the Faith:

The alleged apparitions began June 24, 1981, when six children in Medjugorje, a town in what is now Bosnia and Herzegovina, began to experience phenomena which they have claimed to be apparitions of the Blessed Virgin Mary.

According to these six "seers," the apparitions contained a message of peace for the world, a call to conversion, prayer and fasting, as well as certain secrets surrounding events to be fulfilled in the future.

These apparitions are said to have continued almost daily since their first occurrence, with three of the original six children—who are now young adults—continuing to receive apparitions every afternoon because not all the "secrets" intended for them have been revealed.

Since their beginning, the alleged apparitions have been a source of both controversy and conversion, with many flocking to the city for pilgrimage and prayer, and some claiming to have experienced miracles at the site, while many others claim the visions are non-credible.

In other words, said Vatican commission concluded yet again with a "status-quo" stand, thus declaring the apparition investigations as being simply… "non-conclusive"…

The passing-away of Monsignor René Laurentin[27] at age 99, on 10 September 2017, came just one month shy of the Fatima 100ᵗʰ Anniversary Jubilee. Knowing that Heaven has reasons and purposes for such a timing of events, it comes as no surprise that one of our Lady of Medjugorje's most recent message states:

… with peace in the soul and in a state of grace, hope exists; this is my Son, God, born of God. His words are the seed of eternal life. Sown in good souls, they bring numerous Fruits…

(Apparition of the Blessed Virgin Mary to Mirjana, 2 September 2017)

Known for his deep commitment to our Lady and her apparitions, Msgr. Laurentin, while firmly faithful to Rome, responded without a second thought a firm "Oui!" to the call of the Blessed Virgin Mary to help propagate her message throughout the world. Monsignor Laurentin was indeed the chief person responsible for saving Medjugorje as the initial commission set up by Bishop Pavao Zanic of Mostar was only one day away from issuing a negative verdict and possible condemnation.

Mgr. Laurentin, despite mounting defamation and unfounded accusations against his own person, faced courageously all personal attacks and went to Rome, indifferent and cold of the unjust and unfounded accusations made against him, to defend the case and honor of these six innocent children. Before the overwhelming evidence brought forth by the valiant French theologian, Rome quickly enough realized the bishop of Mostar unobjective and personal

---

[27] Fr. René Laurentin was born on 19 October 1917, six days after the last apparitions of Fatima.

judgment, and after carefully reviewing the cold facts, reached the conclusion that the negative Episcopal verdict was indeed... biased... The investigative commission now resides in Rome.

Certainly, after over 70 years of service to the Church and over 150 books written on Marian apparition sites and on overall Theology, Monsignor René Laurentin will be remembered for his dedication to the Faith, for his instrumental role in the Episcopal recognition process of Betania (Venezuela), Kibejo (Rwanda), Saint Nicolas (Argentina), Soufanieh (Syria) and of his theological and scientific research and study of the visionaries of Medjugorje. Likewise, he will be recognized as well with the immense gratitude and affection of all those who have known him, and of the faithful and pilgrims all across the world.

Pope Francis visited Bosnia and Herzegovina in June 2015 but, unsurprisingly, declined to stop in Medjugorje during his trip... During his return flight to Rome, he indicated to a battalion of surprised journalists his open skepticism on the investigated Marian apparition site... Pope Francis demonstrated yet another 180 degree reverse position to that of his two predecessors benedict XVI and, Saint Pope John Paull II, the latter of which made no mystery on his personal and favorable opinion on the apparition site in Bosnia-Herzegovina.

While visiting the Vatican with a Croatian youth group to Rome for a papal audience on 22 July 1987, Mirjana first encountered John Paul II. As the Pope walked among the people giving blessings, he put his hand over Mirjana's head and blessed her. After he had done so, an Italian priest informed him who Mirjana was.

Mirjana writes about her meeting with his Pope John Paul II in her autobiography:

After hearing that I was one of the reported visionary of Medjugorje, he stopped, came back and reached out to bless me again. I was frozen. His vivid blue eyes seemed to pierce my soul. Unable to think of any words to say. I bowed my head and felt the warmth of his blessing. When he left again, I turned to the Italian priest and joked, 'He just thought I needed a double blessing.' We both laughed.

Later that afternoon... I was shocked to receive a personal invitation from the Pope. He was requesting that I come to meet with him privately the next morning at Castel Gandolfo...

Mirjana writes of Pope John Paul II's profound affection and how she was moved to tears upon meeting him the following morning. She writes of their struggle to understand each other until they found out they both could speak Italian. She wrote:

We talked about many things – some I can share, some I cannot – and soon I felt at ease in his presence. He spoke with such love that I could have talked with him for hours.

- **"Please ask the pilgrims in Medjugorje to pray for my intentions,"** *he said.*

- *"I will, Holy Father,"* I assured him.
- **"I know all about Medjugorje. I've followed the messages from the beginning. Please, tell me what it's like for you when Our Lady appears."**

The Pope listened intently as I described what I experienced during apparitions. At times, he smiled and gently nodded his head.

- *"And when she departs,"* I concluded, *"I feel so much pain, and all I can think of in that moment is when I will see her again."*

The Pope leaned towards me and said:

- **"Take good care of Medjugorje, Mirjana. Medjugorje is the hope for the entire world."**

The Pope's words seemed like a confirmation of the importance of the apparitions and of my great responsibility as a visionary. I was surprised by the conviction in his voice, and by how his eyes sparkled every time he said the word Medjugorje—not to mention how well he pronounced the name of the village, which had always been so amazingly difficult for outsiders to say.

- *"Holy Father,"* I said, *"I wish you could see all the people who go there and pray."*

The Pope turned his head and gazed towards the east, releasing a pensive sigh.

- **"If I were not the Pope,"** he said, **"I would have gone to Medjugorje a long time ago."**

I will never forget the love that radiated from the Holy Father. What I felt with him is similar to what I feel when I am with Our Lady, and looking into his eyes was just like looking into hers. Later, a priest told me that the Pope had been interested in Medjugorje from the very beginning, because right before our apparitions started, he had been praying for Our Lady to appear again on Earth:

'I cannot do it all alone, Mother,' he prayed. *'In Yugoslavia, Czechoslovakia, Poland and so many other communist countries, people cannot freely practice their faith. I need your help, dear Mother.'*

According to this priest, when the Pope heard that Our Lady had appeared in a tiny village in a communist country, he immediately thought Medjugorje had to be an answer to his prayers."

In a talk Mirjana gave to pilgrims, she told the following story of how John Paul II's desire to come to Medjugorje was fulfilled after his death:

On the Mount of Apparitions, I saw a pair of shoes of the Pope in front of me. After the apparition, the gentleman who brought these shoes (he didn't introduce himself) said:

"It was the Pope's desire for a long time to come to Medjugorje. So I said to him, 'If you do not go, I will take your shoes.' And that is how I brought his shoes, so they may be present during the apparition."

And that is how Saint John Paul II's desire to come to Medjugorje was satisfied.

In 2013, after Pope Benedict XVI's surprising abdication, Pope Francis was elected. Known by some as "the Reformist Pope", Francis explained why he did not want to stop by Medjugorje as he expressed, on his return flight from a visit to the Marian shrine of Fatima (*in May 2017*), his "suspicions" on the authenticity of the apparitions... Indeed, the final document of the Medjugorje commission, he stated—sometimes referred to as the "Ruini report," after the head of the commission, Cardinal Camillo Ruini—called it *"very, very good,"*, but he noted a distinction between the first Marian apparitions at Medjugorje and the later ones...

The Pope continued by stating that the first apparitions, which were to children, the report more or less says, need to continue being studied, but as for "presumed" current apparitions, the report has its doubts...

Incomprehensibly, and despite Pope Francis' evident suspicion and public skepticism to the present apparitions of Medjugorje, the Vatican has formally granted permission on May 2019 for Catholics to organize pilgrimages to Medjugorje, as a site of "alleged Marian apparitions", though the Church has not yet given a formal verdict on the apparitions' authenticity.

The Pope's authorization of pilgrimages to the site is not to be understood as an "authentication" of the alleged apparitions, "which still require an examination by the Church". The provision was made as an acknowledgment of the "abundant fruits of grace" that have come from Medjugorje and to promote those "good fruits." It is also part of the "particular pastoral attention" of Pope Francis to the place.

(Papal spokesman Alessandro Gisotti, May 2019)

Once again...

One judges the tree by its fruits...
(Our Lord Jesus-Christ, Mt. 7:16–20; 12:23)

The announcement of the papal authorization was made on 12 May 2019 by the Vatican's apostolic visitor to the site, Archbishop Henryk Hoser, and Archbishop Luigi Pezzuto, apostolic nuncio to Bosnia and Herzegovina.

Amused, and with a bit of a smile on my face, I still can hear in my mind Mgr. René Laurentin say with his characteristic carefully thought-out slow speech say:

... the Virgin Mary has discretely shown herself to be the strongest again, even when things are at their worst...

On 18 March 2020, during Mirjana's annual apparition—which the Blessed Virgin Mary promised her to have for the rest of her life—The Gospa informed Mirjana that she will no longer appear to her on the second of each month... Might this latest turn of event be the preamble of the beginning of prophecy? Only time will tell...

Chapter IX

Apparitions and Revelations to Popes, Saints, and Mystics

Miraculous painting seen bleeding by French Stigmatist/seer Marie-Julie Jahenny, La Fraudais, France (see page 68)

M any extraordinary revelations and apparitions have taken place in History without requiring a formal Church approval or recognition, particularly when it involved Pontiffs or canonized saints.

Most of these messages confirm and often complement those revelations entrusted to the messengers Heaven has chosen throughout History, particularly since the 19th century all the way to our times. All the souls and God's instruments mentioned in this chapter were all extraordinary good and holy souls, who were profoundly in love with kindness, mercy, Love, but above all with Our Lord Jesus-Christ and with the Most Blessed Virgin Mary.

Pope Leo XIII (1810–1903)

Born Vincenzo Gioacchino Raffaele Luigi Pecci on 2 March 1810, Pope Leo XIII was head of the Roman Catholic and Apostolic Church from 20 February 1878 to his death, 20 July 1903. He was the oldest pope in the history of the church (reigning until the age of 93), and had the third-longest confirmed pontificate, behind that of Pius IX (his immediate predecessor) and Saint John Paul II.

His Holiness Pope Leo XIII was a renowned intellectual, and his attempts to define the position of the Catholic Church vis-à-vis modern and reformist thinking—which already was starting its virulent offensive—defined his papacy... In his famous 1891 encyclical, **Rerum Novarum**, Pope Leo outlined the rights of workers to a fair wage, safe working conditions, and the formation of labor unions, while affirming the rights of property and free enterprise, opposing both socialism and laissez-faire capitalism. He influenced Mariology in the Catholic Church, and strongly promoted both the rosary and the scapular.

Leo XIII issued a record of eleven papal encyclicals on the rosary earning him the title as the **Rosary Pope**. In addition, he approved two new Marian scapulars and was the first pope to fully embrace the concept of the **Blessed Virgin Mary as Mediatrix**. He was the first pope never to have held any control over the Papal States after they had been dissolved in 1870. He was briefly buried in the grottos of Saint Peter's Basilica before his remains were later transferred to the Basilica of Saint John Lateran.

Pope Leo XIII was as well renowned for his experience which involved witnessing a major confrontation between God and Satan.

The Vision of Pope Leo XIII (13 October 1884)

Exactly 33 years to the day prior to the great Miracle of the Sun in Fatima, or to be precise on 13 October 1884, Pope Leo XIII had a remarkable experience. At the closing of a private Vatican Chapel Mass, attended by a few Cardinals and members of the Vatican staff, the elderly Pontiff suddenly stopped at the foot of the altar. He stood there for about ten minutes without making a single movement, as if in a trance—a physical exploit indeed even for a man half his age... His face became ashen white.

Then, after coming to, the holy Pontiff went immediately from the Chapel to his office, where he composed the prayer to St. Michael the Archangel, with instructions for it be said after all Low Masses everywhere in the world. When asked what had happened, he explained how, after Mass, as he was about to leave the foot of the altar, he suddenly heard voices... two voices, one kind and gentle, the other guttural and harsh (very much like Marie-Julie Jahenny's experience in La Fraudais see pages 89-91). The voices seemed to come from near the tabernacle. As Pope Leo XIII listened carefully, he heard the following conversation.

A guttural voice, the voice of Satan in his pride, boasted to Our Lord:

- *I can destroy your Church.*

The gentle voice of Our Lord:

- **You can? Then go ahead and do so.**

Satan:

- *To do so, I need more time and more power.*

Our Lord:

- **How much time? How much power?**

Satan:

- *75 to 100 years, and a greater power over those who will give themselves over to my service.*

Our Lord:

- **You have the time, you will have the power. Do with them what you will.**

One of the first changes to come from Vatican II, was the deletion of the Leonine Prayers after Masses which included the prayer to St. Michael the Archangel... These prayers were unfortunately and inexplicably eliminated by the Vatican in 1964...

Padre Pio (1887–1968)

As it was in the days of Noe, they ate and drank, married and were giving in marriage until the day that Noe entered into the Ark and the flood came and destroyed them all... Even shall it be in the day when the Son of Man shall be revealed.

(Luke 17:26–30)

Francesco Forgione was born to Grazio Mario Forgione and Maria Giuseppa Di Nunzio on 25 May 1887, in Pietrelcina, a town in the province of Benevento, in the Southern Italian region of Campania. His parents were peasant farmers. Francesco later served as an altar server in this same chapel. He had an older brother, Michele, and three younger sisters, Felicita, Pellegrina, and Grazia (who was later to become a Bridgettine nun).

His parents had two other children who died in infancy. Padre Pio stated often that by the time he was five years old, he had already made the decision to dedicate his entire life to God. He worked on the land up to the age of ten, looking after the small flock of sheep the family owned.

According to the diary of Father Agostino da San Marco (who was later his spiritual director in San Marco in Lamis) the young Francesco was afflicted with a number of illnesses. At the age of six, he suffered from severe gastroenteritis. At the age of ten, he caught typhoid fever, but remarkably survived...

As a youth, Francesco reported that he had experienced heavenly visions and ecstasies. In 1897, after he had completed three years at the public school, Francesco was said to have been drawn to the life of a friar after listening to a young Capuchin who was in the countryside seeking donations. When Francesco expressed his desire to his parents, they made a trip to Morcone, a community 21 km (13 miles) north of Pietrelcina, to find out if their son was eligible to enter the Order. The friars there informed them that they were interested in accepting Francesco into their community, but he needed to be better educated.

Francesco's father went to the United States in search of work to pay for private tutoring for his son, to meet the academic requirements to enter the Capuchin Order. It was in this period that Francesco received the sacrament of Confirmation on 27 September 1899. He underwent private tutoring and passed the stipulated academic requirements. On 6 January 1903, at the age of 15, he entered the novitiate of the Capuchin friars at Morcone. On 22 January he took the Franciscan habit and the name of Fra (Friar) Pio, in honor of Pope Pius I, whose relic is preserved in the Santa Anna Chapel in Pietrelcina. He took the simple vows of poverty, chastity, and obedience.

Padre Pio was said to have had the gift of reading souls, the ability to bilocate, among other supernatural phenomena. He was said to communicate with angels and worked favors and healings before they were requested of him. The reports of supernatural phenomena surrounding Padre Pio attracted fame and legend. The Vatican was soon enough debriefed, although initially skeptical...

Based on Padre Pio's correspondence, even early in his priesthood, he experienced less obvious indications of the visible stigmata: bodily marks, pain, and bleeding in locations supposedly corresponding to the crucifixion wounds of Jesus Christ. In a 1911 letter, he wrote to his spiritual advisor Padre Benedetto from San Marco in Lamis, describing something he had been apparently experiencing for a year:

Then last night something happened which I can neither explain nor understand. In the middle of the palms of my hands a red mark appeared, about the size of a penny, accompanied by acute pain in the middle of the red marks. The pain was more pronounced in the middle of the left hand, so much so that I can still feel it. Also under my feet I can feel some pain.

(Excerpt of the letter from Padre Pio to Padre Benedetto, 1911)

Already in a letter dated 21 March 1912, to his spiritual companion and confessor, Father Agostino, Father Pio wrote of his devotion to the mystical body of Christ and the intuition that he, Pio, one day himself would bear the stigmata of Christ. Luzzatto points out that in this letter Father Pio uses unrecognized passages from a book by the stigmatized mystic Gemma Galgani. Later Pio denied knowing or owning the cited book.

Padre Pio was interested in future events as he received numerous revelations concerning other apparition sites (Garabandal, Spain), mystics (Fr. Pel), visionaries and Geo-political events. One of these events involved France. Indeed, he understood very well the role that God had entrusted to that country:

Without the support of David's royal power, the Church will fall into decadence under the spirit of the snake who raises its proud head towards the Head of the Church. The republics have the sorrows to unearth the spirits of serpents who sacrifice God's people by impeding it to rise towards the God of Heaven... It is today Europe's evil!

Padre Pio one day spoke of a Will which is kept secret in the Vatican's archives. That Will was written by the Duchess d'Angoulême [28]which not only revealed the truth behind the mystery of her brother, Louis XVII, but hers as well. Padre Pio stated that France was hiding a power which is going to be revealed to the everyone's astonishment:

The folly of men has been to attempt to kill the royalty (monarchy). The world is paying still this error today. Without the true king promised by God among the descendants of David, the Power of God does not reside any longer in the hearts of the heads of state nor of the ministers.

How great will the misery of the world be before men may understand this truth! The true greatness of France resides in the royal power of David who was in the land of France, in the blood of King Louis XVI and of Marie-Antoinette. However, since King Louis XVI forgave France, she (France) retains the right to David's royalty greatness, that which is love and humility.

---

[28] The Duchess of Angoulême, aka Madame Royale, was the Princess of France, daughter of King Louis XVI and of Marie-Antoinette. It was rumored that her brother, the little Louis XVII was rescued and taken out of his prison, and had a descendance.

Padre Pio's close friend, Padre Agostino, asked him specific questions, such as when he first experienced visions, prophetic revelations, whether he had been granted the stigmata, and whether he felt the pains of the Passion of Christ, namely the crowning of thorns and the scourging. Pio replied that he had been favored with visions since his novitiate period (1903 to 1904). Although he had been granted the stigmata, he had been so terrified by the phenomenon he prayed Jesus-Christ to withdraw them from him. He added however that he did not wish the pain to be removed, only the visible wounds, since he considered them to be an indescribable and almost unbearable humiliation.

On 20 September 1918, while hearing confessions, Pio claimed to have had a reappearance of the physical occurrence of the stigmata. The phenomenon was reported to have continued for 50 years, until the end of his life. The blood flowing from the stigmata purportedly smelled of perfume or flowers. He reported to Agostino that the pain remained and was more acute on specific days and under certain circumstances. He also said that he was suffering the pain of the crown of thorns and the scourging. Padre Pio did not specify further, but stated that he had been suffering from them at least once weekly for some years.

Although Padre Pio would have preferred to suffer in secret, away from public attention, by early 1919, news had begun to spread throughout the region, the country and even abroad of Padre Pio's extraordinary stigmatas. Pio often wore red mittens or black coverings on his hands and feet as he was profoundly embarrassed by the marks and by the blood that exuded therefrom. However, most remarkably, no visible scarring was present at the time of Padre Pio's death.

In a letter dated 22 October 1918 to Padre Benedetto, Padre Pio's superior and spiritual advisor, Padre Pio described the experience of his stigmata:

On the morning of the 20th of last month, in the choir, after I had celebrated Mass I yielded to a drowsiness similar to a sweet sleep. (...) I saw before me a mysterious person similar to the one I had seen on the evening of 5 August. The only difference was that his hands and feet and side were dripping blood. This sight terrified me and what I felt at that moment is indescribable.

I thought I should have died if the Lord had not intervened and strengthened my heart which was about to burst out of my chest. The vision disappeared and I became aware that my hands, feet and side were dripping blood. Imagine the agony I experienced and continue to experience almost every day. The heart wound bleeds continually, especially from Thursday evening until Saturday.

Dear Father, I am dying of pain because of the wounds and the resulting embarrassment I feel deep in my soul. I am afraid I shall bleed to death if the Lord does not hear my heartfelt supplication to relieve me of this condition. Will Jesus, who is so good, grant me this grace? Will he at least free me from the embarrassment caused by these outward signs?

I will raise my voice and will not stop imploring him until in his mercy he takes away, not the wound or the pain, which is impossible since I wish to be inebriated with pain, but these outward signs which cause me such embarrassment and unbearable humiliation... the pain was so intense that I began to feel as if I were dying on the cross.

(Excerpt of the letter from Padre Pio to Padre Benedetto, 22 October 1918)

Once made public, the wounds were studied by a number of physicians, some hired by the Vatican as part of an independent investigation. Some doctors claimed that the wounds were unexplainable and never seem to have become infected. Despite seeming to heal they would then reappear periodically. Dr. Alberto Caserta took x-rays of Pio's hands in 1954 and found no abnormality in the bone structure. Many critics, however, bluntly accused Padre Pio of causing artificially his own stigmata by using carbolic acid to make the wounds. In contrast, a number of Catholic clerics have dismissed charges that carbolic acid was used to fake the stigmata:

The boys had needed injections to fight the Spanish Flu which was raging at that time. Due to a shortage of doctors, Padres Paolino and Pio administered the shots, using carbolic acid as a sterilizing agent.

During his period of spiritual suffering, Padre Pio was often attacked by the devil, both physically and spiritually. The Devil often tried to fool Padre Pio appearing as an "angel of light". Padre Pio reported engaging in physical combat with Satan and his minions, not unlike the incidents described of St. John Vianney's experiences, from which he was said to have sustained extensive bruising.

In all of Padre Pio's remarkable lifetime, he left for future generations yet another gift, a spiritual inheritance of sorts, the echo of a prophetic forewarning which called mankind to prepare itself for the Justice of God…

St. Pio's prophecy of the Three Days of Darkness

Translated copy of a personal letter written by Padre Pio addressed to the Commission of Heroldsbach appointed by the Vatican that testifies of the truth and reality of these revelations on the Three Days of Darkness given by Our Lord:

Keep your windows well covered. Do not look out. Light a blessed candle, which will suffice for many days. Pray the rosary. Read spiritual books. Make acts of Spiritual Communion, also acts of love, which are so pleasing to Us. Pray with outstretched arms, or prostrate on the ground, in order that many souls may be saved. Do not go outside the house. Provide yourself with sufficient food. The powers of nature shall be moved and a rain of fire shall make people tremble with fear. Have courage! I am in the midst of you.

(Our Lord Jesus-Christ, 28 January 1950)

Take care of the animals during these days. I am the Creator and Preserver of all animals as well as man. I shall give you a Few signs

beforehand, at which time you should place more food before them. I will preserve the property of the elect, including the animals, for they shall be in need of sustenance afterwards as well. Let no one go across the yard, even to feed the animals. He who steps outside will perish! Cover your windows carefully. My elect shall not see My wrath. Have confidence in Me, and I will be your protection. Your confidence obliges Me to come to your aid.

The hour of My coming is near! But I will show mercy. A most dreadful punishment will bear witness to the times. My angels, who are to be the executioners of this work, are ready with their pointed swords! They will take special care to annihilate all those who mocked Me and would not believe in My revelations.

Hurricanes of fire will pour forth from the clouds and spread over the entire earth! Storms, bad weather, thunderbolts and earthquakes will cover the earth for two days. An uninterrupted rain of fire will take place! It will begin during a very cold night. All this is to prove that God is the Master of Creation. Those who hope in Me, and believe in my words, have nothing to fear because I will not forsake them, nor those who spread My message. No harm will come to those who are in the state of grace and who seek My mother's protection.

That you may be prepared for these visitations, I will give you the following signs and instructions: The night will be very cold. The wind will roar. After a time, thunderbolts will be heard. Lock all the doors and windows. Talk to no one outside the house. Kneel down before a crucifix, be sorry for your sins, and beg My Mother's protection. Do not look during the earthquake, because the anger of God is holy! Jesus does not want us to behold the anger of God, because God's anger must be contemplated with fear and trembling.

Those who disregard this advice will be killed instantly. The wind will carry with it poisonous gases which will be diffused over the entire earth. Those who suffer and die innocently will be martyrs and they will be with Me in My Kingdom.

Satan will triumph! But after three nights, the earthquake and fire will cease. On the following day the sun will shine again. Angels will descend from Heaven and will spread the spirit of peace over the earth. A feeling of immeasurable gratitude will take possession of those who survive this terrible ordeal—the impending punishment—with which God has visited the earth since creation.

I have chosen souls in other countries too, such as Belgium, Switzerland, Spain, who have received these revelations so that other countries also may be prepared. Pray much during this Holy Year of 1950. Pray the Rosary, but pray it well, so that your prayers may reach Heaven. Soon a more terrible catastrophe shall come upon the entire world, such as never before has been witnessed, a terrible chastisement never before experienced! The war of 1950[29] shall be the introduction to these things.

---

[29] Korean War (1950–3): Communist North Korea, supported by China, invaded non-communist South Korea. UN forces, principally made up of U.S. troops, fought

How unconcerned men are regarding these things which shall so soon come upon them, contrary to all expectations! How indifferent they are in preparing themselves for these unheard of events, through which they will have to pass so shortly! The weight of the Divine balance has reached the earth! The wrath of My Father shall be poured out over the entire world! I am again warning the world through your instrumentality, as I have so often done heretofore.

The sins of men have multiplied beyond measure: Irreverence in Church, sinful pride committed in sham religious activities, lack of true brotherly love, indecency in dress, especially at summer seasons... The world is filled with iniquity. This catastrophe shall come upon the earth like a flash of lightning at which moment the light of the morning sun shall be replaced by black darkness! No one shall leave the house or look out of a window from that moment on. I Myself shall come amidst thunder and lightning. The wicked shall behold My Divine Heart. There shall be great confusion because of this utter darkness in which the entire earth shall be enveloped, and many, many shall die from fear and despair.

Those who shall fight for My cause shall receive grace from My Divine Heart; and the cry: "Who is like unto God!" shall serve as a means of protection to many. However, many shall burn in the open fields like withered grass! The godless shall be annihilated, so that afterwards the just shall be able to stand afresh.

On the day, as soon as complete darkness has set in, no one shall leave the house or look from out of the window. The darkness shall last a day and a night, followed by another day and a night, and another day – but on the night following, the stars will shine again [30] and on the next morning the sun shall rise again, and it will be Springtime!

In the days of darkness, My elect shall not sleep, as did the disciples in the garden of olives. They, shall pray incessantly, and they shall not be disappointed in Me. I shall gather My elect. Hell will believe itself to be in possession of the entire earth, but I shall reclaim it!

Do you, perhaps, think that I would permit My Father to have such terrible chastisements come upon the world, if the world would turn from iniquity to justice? But because of My great love, these afflictions shall be permitted to come upon man. Although many shall curse Me, yet thousands of souls shall be saved through them. No human understanding can fathom the depth of My love!

Pray! Pray! I desire your prayers. My Dear Mother Mary, Saint Joseph, Saint Elizabeth, Saint Conrad, Saint Michael. Saint Peter, the Little Therese, Your Holy Angels, shall be your intercessors. Implore their aid! Be courageous soldiers of Christ! At the return of light, let everyone give thanks to the Holy Trinity for Their protection! The devastation shall be

---

successfully to protect South Korea. The Korean War was the first armed conflict in the global struggle between democracy and communism, called the cold war.

[30] Padre Pio's prophecy on the Three Days of Darkness recoup Marie-Julie Jahenny's: Three days less a night.

very great! But I, Your God, will have purified the earth. I am with you. Have confidence!

(Our Lord Jesus-Christ, 7 February 1950)

Padre Pio died on 23 September 1968 at the age of 81. In his life, the saint bore the stigmata (wounds of Christ). He has been credited with thousands of miraculous healings and intercessions, and is considered by many to be one of the most "prayed to" Saint in History:

I have made a pact with the Lord: when my soul has been purified in the flames of purgatory and deemed worthy to be admitted to the presence of God, I will take my place at the gate to paradise, but I shall not enter until I have seen the last of my spiritual children enter.

Keep close to the Catholic Church at all times, for the Church alone can give you true peace, since she alone possesses Jesus, the true Prince of Peace, in the Blessed Sacrament.

(Saint Padre Pio of Pietrelcina)

Padre Pio was canonized on 16 June 2002, in Saint Peter's Square, Vatican City by his old friend Pope John Paul II. Likewise, Padre Pio's body was found incorrupt and is in Rome in display for the faithful.

Anne-Catherine Emmerich (1774–1824)

Anne-Catherine was born on 8 September 1774 in Flamschen, a farming community at Coesfeld, in the Diocese of Münster, Westphalia, Germany, and died at age 49 in Dülmen, where she had been a nun, to become later bedridden.

Emmerich is notable for her extraordinary accurate visions on the life and passion of Jesus Christ, reputed to be revealed to her by the Blessed Virgin Mary under ecstasy. Anne-Catherine was a Catholic Augustanian, Regular Canoness of Windesheim; likewise, she was a well renowned mystic, Marian visionary, ecstatic and well-studied stigmatist.

Emmerich died on 9 February 1824, and was beatified on 3 October 2004, by Pope John Paul II. However, the Vatican focused on her own personal piety rather than her religious writings. Her documents of postulation towards canonization are handled by the Priestly Fraternity of St. Peter.

Anne-Catherine Emmerich's Prophecies and Visions:

I saw very clearly the errors, the aberrations, and the countless sins of men. I saw the folly and the wickedness of their actions against all the truth and all reason. Priests were amongst them, and I gladly endured my suffering so that they may return to a better mind.

(22 March 1820)

I had another vision of the great tribulation. It seems to me that a concession was demanded from the clergy which could not be granted. I saw many older priests, especially one who wept bitterly. A few younger ones were also weeping, but others, and the lukewarm among them, readily did what was demanded. It was as if people were splitting into two camps.

(12 April 1820)

Last night, from 11:00 to 3:00, I had a most wondrous vision of two churches and two Popes and a variety of things, ancient and modern (Vatican II?)... *I saw the fatal consequences of this counterfeit church; I saw it increase; I saw heretics of all kinds flocking to the city. I saw the ever-increasing tepidity of the clergy, the circle of darkness ever widening. And now the vision became more extended. I saw in all places Catholics oppressed, annoyed, restricted, and deprived of liberty, churches were closed, and great misery prevailed everywhere with war and bloodshed.*

I saw rude, ignorant people offering violent resistance, but this state of things lasted not long. Again I saw in vision St. Peter's undermined according to a plan devised by the secret sect while, at the same time, it was damaged by storms; but it was delivered at the moment of greatest distress. Again I saw the Blessed Virgin extending her mantle over it.

(13 May 1820)

I had a vision of the holy Emperor Henry (Henry V of the Cross?—see Chapter II). *I saw him at night kneeling alone at the foot of the main altar in a great and beautiful church... and I saw the Blessed Virgin coming down all alone. She laid on the Altar a red cloth covered with white linen. She placed a book inlaid with precious stones. She lit the candles and the perpetual lamp... Then came the Savior, Himself, clad in priestly vestments. He was carrying the chalice and the veil.*

Two Angels were serving Him and two more were following. His chasuble was a full and heavy mantle in which red and white could be seen in transparency, and gleaming with jewels... Although there was no altar bell, the cruets were there. The wine was as red as blood, and there was also some water. The Mass was short. The Gospel of St. John was not read at the end.

When the Mass had ended, Mary came up to Henry, and she extended her right hand towards him, saying that it was in recognition of his purity. Then, she urged him not to falter. Thereupon I saw an angel, and he touched the sinew of his hip, like Jacob. He (Henry) was in great pain; and from that day on he walked with a limp...

(12 July 1820)

I see more martyrs, not now but in the future... I saw the secret sect (freemasonry) *relentlessly undermining the Great Church. Near them, I saw a horrible beast coming up from the sea. All over the world, good and devout* people, especially the clergy, were harassed, oppressed and put into prison. I had the feeling that they would become martyrs one day.

When the Church had been for the most part destroyed (by the secret sect), and when only the sanctuary and altar were still standing, I saw the wreckers (of the secret sect) enter the Church with the Beast. There, they met a Woman of noble carriage who seemed to be with child because she walked slowly. At this sight, the enemies were terrorized, and the Beast could not take but another step forward. It projected its neck towards the Woman as if to devour her, but the Woman turned about and bowed down (towards the Altar), her head touching the ground.

Thereupon, I saw the Beast taking to flight towards the sea again, and the enemies were fleeing in the greatest of confusion. Then, I saw in the distance great legions approaching, in the foreground, I saw a man on a white horse. Prisoners were set free and joined them. All the enemies were pursued. Then I saw the Church was being promptly rebuilt, and she was more magnificent than ever before.

(August to October 1820)

I see the Holy Father in great anguish. He lives in a palace other than before, and he admits only a limited number of friends near him. I fear that the Holy Father will suffer many more trials before he dies. I see the false church of darkness is making progress, and I see the dreadful influence it has on people. The Holy Father and the Church are verily in so great a distress that one must implore God day and night.

Last night, I was taken to Rome where the Holy Father, immersed in his sorrow, is still hiding to elude dangerous demands (made upon him). He is very weak, and exhausted by sorrows, cares and prayers. He can now trust but few people. That is mainly why he is hiding. But he still has with him an aged priest who has much simplicity and godliness. He is his friend, and because of his simplicity, they did not think it would be worth removing him.

But this man receives many graces from God. He sees and notices a great many things which he faithfully reports to the Holy Father. It was required of me to inform him, while he was praying, of the traitors and evil-doers who were to be found among the high-ranking servants living close to him, so that he might be made aware of it.

(10 August 1820)

I know not now how I went to Rome last night, but I found myself near the church of St. Mary-Major. Around it I saw crowds of poor, pious souls, in great distress and anxiety on account of the Pope's disappearance and the agitation and alarming reports throughout the city. Led by one common impulse, they had come to invoke the Mother of God. They did not expect to find the church open, they intended only to pray outside. But I was inside, I opened the door and they entered, astounded at the door's opening of itself.

I was standing aloof where they could not see me. There was no service, only the chancel-lamps were burning, and the people knelt in quiet prayer. Then the

445

Mother of God appeared. She said that great tribulations were at hand; that the people must pray earnestly with extended arms, if only for the length of three Our Fathers, for it was thus that her Son had prayed for them upon the Cross; that they should rise at midnight to pray thus; that they should continue to come to her church which they would always find open; and that they should, above all, pray for the extirpation of the dark church.

She (the Holy Mother) said a great many other things that it pains me to relate: She said that if only one priest could offer the bloodless sacrifice as worthily and with the same dispositions as the Apostles, he could avert all the disasters (that are to come). To my knowledge the people in the church did not see the apparition, but they must have been stirred by something supernatural, because as soon as the Holy Virgin had said that they pray God with outstretched arms, they all raised their arms. These were all good and devout people, and they did not know where help and guidance should be sought. There were no traitors and no enemies among them, yet they were afraid of one another. One can judge thereby what the situation was like...

(25 August 1820)

I saw the church of St. Peter. It had been destroyed but for the Sanctuary and the main Altar. St. Michael came down into the church, clad in his suit of armor, and he paused, threatening with his sword a number of unworthy pastors who wanted to enter. That part of the church which had been destroyed was promptly fenced in with light timber so that the Divine Office might be celebrated as it should. Then from all over the world came priests and laymen, and they rebuilt the stone walls, since the wreckers had been unable to move the heavy foundation stones.

(10 September 1820)

I saw deplorable things: they were gambling, drinking, and talking in Church; they were also courting women. All sorts of abominations were perpetrated there. Priests allowed everything and said Mass with much irreverence. I saw that few of them were still godly, and only a few had sound views on things. I also saw Jews standing under the porch of the church. All these things caused me much distress.

(27 September 1820)

The Church is in great danger! We must pray so that the Pope may not leave Rome; countless evils would result if he did. They are now demanding something from him. The Protestant doctrine and that of schismatic Greeks are to spread everywhere. I now see that in this place (Rome) the Catholic Church is being so cleverly undermined, that there hardly remain a hundred or so priests who have not been deceived. They all work for destruction, even the clergy. A great devastation is now near at hand.

(1 October 1820)

When I saw the Church of St. Peter in ruins, and the manner in which so many of the clergy were themselves busy at this work of destruction, none of them wishing to do it openly in front of the others, I was in such distress that I cried out to Jesus with all my might, imploring His Mercy. Then I saw before me the Heavenly Spouse, and He spoke to me for a long time.

He said, among other things, that this translation of the Church from one place to another meant that she would seem to be in complete decline. But she would rise again; even if there remained but one Catholic, the Church would conquer again because she does not rest on human counsels and intelligence. It was also shown to me that there were almost no Christians left on the old acceptation of the Word.

(4 October 1820)

As I was going through Rome with St. Francoise and the other Saint, we saw a great palace engulfed in flames from top to bottom. I was very much afraid that the occupants would be burned to death because no one came forward to put out the fire. As we came nearer, however, the fire abated and we saw the blackened building. We went through a number of magnificent rooms (untouched by the fire), and we finally reached the Pope. He was sitting in the dark and slept in a large arm-chair, He was very ill and weak; he could no longer walk.

The ecclesiastics in the inner circle looked insincere and lacking in zeal; I did not like them... I told the Pope of the bishops who are to be appointed soon. I told him also that he must not leave Rome. If he did so, it would be chaos. He thought that the evil was inevitable and that he should leave in order to save many things beside himself. He was very much inclined to leave Rome, and he was insistently urged to do so... The Pope is still attached to the things of this earth in many ways.

The Church is completely isolated and as if completely deserted. It seems that everyone is running away. Everywhere I see great misery, hatred, treason, rancor, confusion, and an utter blindness. O city! O city! What is threatening thee? The storm is coming! Do be watchful.

(7 October 1820)

I also saw the various regions of the earth. My guide (Jesus) named Europe, and, pointing to a small and sandy region, He uttered these remarkable words: **'Here is Prussia, the enemy.'** Then He showed me another place, to the north, and He said: **'This is Moskva, the land of Moscow, bringing many evils.'**

(1820–21—Exact date unknown)

Among the strangest things that I saw, were long processions of bishops. Their thoughts and utterances were made known to me through images issuing from their mouths. Their faults towards religion were shown by external deformities. A few had only a body with a dark cloud of fog instead of a head. Others had only a head, their bodies and hearts were like thick vapors. Some were lame; others were paralytics; others were asleep or staggering...

I saw what I believe to be nearly all the bishops of the world, but only a small number were perfectly sound. I also saw the holy Father, God-fearing and prayful. Nothing left to be desired in his appearance, but he was weakened by old age and by much suffering. His head was lolling from side to side, and it dropped onto his chest as if he were falling asleep. He often fainted and seemed to be dying. But when he was praying, he was often comforted by apparitions from Heaven.

Then his head was erect, but as soon as it dropped again onto his chest, I saw a number of people looking quickly right and left, that is in the direction of the world. Then I saw that everything that pertained to Protestantism was gradually gaining the upper hand, and the Catholic religion fell into complete decadence... Most priests were by the glittering but false knowledge of young school-teachers, and they all contributed to the work of destruction.

In those days, Faith will fall very low, and it will be preserved in some places only, in a few cottages and in a few families which God has protected from disasters and wars.

(1 June 1821)

I see many excommunicated ecclesiastics who do not seem to be concerned about it, nor even being aware of it... Yet, they are (ipso facto) excommunicated whenever they cooperate to enterprises, enter in associations, and embrace opinions on which an anathema has been cast. It can be seen thereby that God ratifies the decrees, orders and interdictions issued by the Head of the Church, and that He keeps them in force even though men show no concern for them, reject them or laugh them to scorn.

(1820–1—Exact date unknown)

I saw a new Pope who will be very strict. He will estrange from him the cold and lukewarm bishops. He is not a Roman, but he is Italian. He comes from a place which is not very far from Rome, and I think he comes from a devout family of royal blood. But there must still be for a while much fighting and unrest.

(27 January 1822)

"Very evil times are coming," my guide said: "The non-Catholics will mislead many. They will use every possible means to entice them from the Church, and great disturbances will follow."

I had then another vision in which I saw the King's daughter armed for the struggle. Multitudes contributed to this with prayers, good works, all sorts of labors and self-victories which passed from hand to hand up to Heaven where each was wrought, according to its kind, into a piece of armor for the virgin warrior. The perfect adjustment of the various pieces was most remarkable, as also their wonderful signification. She was armed from head to foot. I knew many of those who contributed the armor, and I saw with surprise that whole institutions and great and learned people furnished nothing.

The contribution was made chiefly by the poor and lowly. And now I saw the battle. The enemies' ranks were by far the more numerous; but the little body of the faithful cut down whole rows of them. The armed virgin stood off on a hill. I ran to her, pleading for my country and those other places for which I had to pray. She was armed singularly, but significantly, with helmet, shield, and coat of mail, and the soldiers were like those of our own day. The battle was terrible; only a handful of victorious champions survived!

(22 October 1822)

<u>Note</u>: Might this be a reference to the **Birch-Tree Battle** that is yet to come in the 21st century, described in other prophecies? This battle is prophesied to be taking place somewhere in the region of Westphalia (Germany) with, on one side the French Monarch (Henry V of the Cross), and on the other the Russians and Eastern Europeans... According to various prophecies that go back as far as the 6th century, this battle, despite the overwhelming odds against the French armed forces, will result in King Henry's overwhelming victory and in the collapse and defeat of the Eastern armies...

I saw that many pastors allowed themselves to be taken up with ideas that were dangerous to the Church. They were building a great strange and extravagant Church. Everyone was to be admitted in it in order to be united and have equal rights: Evangelicals, Catholics, sects of every description... Such was to be the new Church... but God had other designs...

(22 April 1823)

Formal Ecclesiastical Approval:

The first volume of the work entitled: "Life of Anne-Catherine Emerick" by Father Schnioger C.S.S.R, presented to us in a manuscript, contains nothing contrary to the teachings of the Catholic Church, either as to Dogma or in morals, and, as it seems conductive to faith and piety, we cheerfully give it the approbation solicited by the author.

Peter Joseph
Bishop of Limburg
Limburg, September 26, 1867

Rev. Father Michel Rodrigue (Present...)

(Priest, exorcist, mystic, founder and general superior of the Apostolic Fraternity of Saint Benedict Joseph Labre—Quebec, Canada)

The Reverend Father Michel Rodrigue became the founder of a new religious order formally approved by the Roman Catholic Church known as the Apostolic Fraternity of St. Benedict Joseph Labre in the dioceses of Amos in Quebec, Canada.

Born in a poor but pious Catholic French-speaking family, Fr. Rodrigue was the youngest of 23 siblings, and began to have a vocation of a religious life at the age of three! Indeed, like Padre Pio, God the Father began to speak to him at that tender age:

God began to speak to me and we began to have regular conversations. I remember sitting under a big tree behind the home on our family's farm and asking God: 'Who made this tree?'

*'**I did,**' God answered. And when He pronounced the word '**I,**' I was suddenly given a vast view of the Earth, the universe, and myself, and I understood that everything was made and held in existence by Him. I thought that everyone talked to God the Father.*

From three to six, the Lord instructed me in the Faith, and gave me a thorough theological education. He also told me, when I was three, that I would be a priest.

As Michael grew up, he began studying psychology and certain areas of theology such as Mariology, pneumatology, the writing of the Church's Fathers, thus graduating with a doctorate of general theology.

Years later, after founding a shelter for homeless youth which offered them a spiritual and psychological care, Michel Rodrigue was at last ordained a diocesan priest at the age of 30. He served as a parish priest for five years in Northern Ontario until his local bishop noted in him talents that could be used in the formation and teaching of future clergy. Fr. Rodrigue then became sometime thereafter a Sulpician priest, teaching theology at the Grand Seminary of Montreal.

On 24 December 2009, a major event had Fr. Rodrigue's life make a major turn... In the middle of the night, the good French Canadian priest was awakened by his bedside by none other than St. Joseph Labre who was shaking his shoulder ever so gently to get his attention. As Fr. Michel awoke, he suddenly heard the voice of God the Father say: "**Stand.**"; hence, Fr. Michel stood. God the Father's Voice went on: "**Go to the computer.**"

Fr. Michel obeyed... "**Listen and write.**" That is when the First Person of the Holy Trinity began to dictate the entire constitution for a new religious order faster than Fr. Michael could type. The overwhelmed but humorous priest had to ask God the Father to slow down... Then God whisked Fr. Michel into a mystical flight in the land in the Diocese of Amos, Quebec where He wanted the monastery of the new order built, and showed him in great detail the monastery's designs.

Fr. Michel was further revealed that he would become the founder of said monastery and would start the new religious order called **Fraternité Apostolique Saint Benoît Joseph Labre** in order to prepare for the future of the Catholic Church. Today, much of the monastery is already built exactly as God the Father desired…

Fr. Michel is gifted with extraordinary intellectual and spiritual gifts such as healing, reading souls, a photographic memory (which appeared to have lessened after illness), prophecy, locutions and visions. He has a very joyful disposition and has laughter come to him easily. Notwithstanding, Fr. Michel knows how to be serious and solemn as well, particularly when prophecies and revelations from God and from the Blessed Virgin Mary are concerned. He is, likewise, a seminary professor, a hospital minister, a parish priest, and most recently the founder and superior general of the fraternity order in French-speaking Quebec.Father Michel stated St Michael has instructed him to tell people to do a **life-long confession in 2019**.

He described prophetic geo-polotical and spiritual events that will happen in graphic detail; events which, Fr. Rodrigue assures us, will be life changing and will take place… very soon…

Fr Michel has been to Heaven and was blessed to be handed the Child Jesus by St. Joseph. When he questioned the fact that he is not worthy, the Immaculate Virgin Mary said to him "**you hold My Son at every Mass, do you not?**"

Fr Michel has seen St. Michael at least three times. He has an amazing testimony and he speaks always with warmth, conviction and truth.

Fr. Rodrigue:

He said we should have a three-month supply of food in your home. He said we must consecrate our home to the Holy Family. He said this will allow your home to be a temporary refuge until the Holy Spirit guides you to a permanent refuge. All you need will be provided at the refuges that you will be guided to if one surrenders to God.

He said a soul must go to confession at least once a month to be prepared.

He said that after the Warning (when we will see Jesus on the Cross in the sky with Rays coming from His Sacred Wound that Blood and Water gushed forth as a font of mercy for us) that every soul will encounter Our Blessed Lord. He said small tongues of fire will land on every soul during this process which will last about 15 minutes. Every soul will see their life sins that have not been confessed. If a soul is currently on its way to Purgatory, Hell or Heaven they will experience this. He also said that after this event mankind will have six weeks of calm before all hell breaks loose on earth… six weeks to get to confession and make a decision. He said priests will Baptize 100s at a time and all people will be shown the truth of Christ's One Holy Catholic Apostolic Church. Priests will spend day and night in the confessional.

Fr. Michel added:

... once the Warning happens, TVs must be thrown out. The media will tell people that this event had to do with the rays and radiation of the sun. That will be a lie!

The one world order will commence immediately and the army for the one world order is already in place waiting orders...

Alarming prophecies...

Fr. Michel added that after the announced six week of free discernment, a nuclear war will happen and seven nuclear missiles will be permitted to strike the United States as a result of man's abominations...; however, many nuclear missiles will be deflected by the Hand of God because America does pray the Divine Mercy Chaplet. That was told to him by the Eternal Father. The devil will try to kill one third of humanity just as one third of the angels were cast out of Heaven to Hell. One third of humanity will die in the chastisements. Two thirds of humanity will die in a three-and-a-half-year process which will commence soon. Prayer will mitigate the severity...

Fr. Michel stated that it was revealed to him that the Antichrist will take his throne within the false church. The pope will flee the Vatican before the Warning (and be killed) and there will be a false pope (false prophet). There will further be a required mark, *a chip*, to buy and sell food and supplies, and those who do not accept it will be hunted like the Jews were hunted by the Waffen SS during the second war... He said if you are captured you will be tortured and martyred if you will not convert to the Antichrist and the one world government... This will all precede the Three Days of Darkness, and Our Blessed Lord's Glorious Return.

Fr. Michel added that Satan will be cast to hell for 1,000 years and then released for one final battle:

I don't share this to create fear but to educate. When the Warning happens and it is close: few people will know what happened. Most people will be in shock and unable to function for some time. Businesses will close. Civil services will cease. People will hibernate in their homes. They will think it is the end of the world. These things will happen. And it will be unimaginable. An apple will mean more to a man than a new car. Money will soon have no value and stores will be empty. These events are much closer than most people realize. The underpinnings are all in place on both sides. Now we wait until God says: now is the time.

This message is intended to allow people a chance to prepare. If a soul does not have a healthy sacramental life and prayer life the Warning will be much more difficult. Just receiving the Eucharist and going to Mass is not enough. A soul must frequent the Sacrament of Confession with a sincere intent to repent.

When this happens Bibles will not be available and the Mass will go underground. Father Michel was clear that the Holy Sacrifice / Eucharist will be desecrated... Now is the time to prepare your soul and your temporal needs. Soon the opportunity will have passed us by...

Prophecies of the two popes and the false ecumenical mass

On 3 January, 2019, Father Rodrigue received a revelation from God which would come to be one of the most important prophecies about the Roman Catholic Church ever received by the good French-Canadian priest:

Fr. Michel Rodrigue:

"There has been since long ago people who have infiltrated the Church whose sole objective is to change the sound Doctrine. An ecumenical mass will be introduced in the Church formulated by different religious chiefs first, then by a committee of bishops, and as a final step this model of mass will be proposed to the Holy Father, Pope Francis in Rome... A document by Pope Francis called 'Magnum Principium' which came into effect on October 1st, of the year 2017, granted authority to national conferences and bishops to include new terms, prayers or modifications in the ritual of the Holy Mass, including the consecration for their countries. Many countries are now caught-up in sins and problems of marriages because there have been many divorces and separations, and they have gone astray from the path of the Lord, and there have been already many deviations regarding this subject. Each bishop interprets in his own way the Church's Doctrine and that is dangerous... If synods in countries have the authority to reform and alter the right of the Mass, be assured that they will bring a bad offer to the Holy Father. If Pope Francis does not sign their proposals, which would mean rejecting what the holy father already gave them as authority to do , then that would generate a schism, and this is something that very soon we will seeing the Church... Rome will only sign the document because they will feel that all of the authority has been given to the bishops to make changes in their own countries. This does not mean that the Pope signed the final document, but he will be around to have it changed and we can only discern when we listen during Mass that 'the words at the Consecration will not be the same'... People do not have to attend those false masses, because 'it would be better to eat a soda cookie than to attend those false masses' where the bread will not be consecrated. This is the first sign of the crisis that is about to come... The Church will go through the same steps of Jesus: Passion, Death and Resurrection. 'The antichrist is already in the Hierarchy of the Church right now!' 'The antichrist is NOT Pope Francis!' The antichrist always wanted to sit on the Chair of Peter. 'Pope Francis will be like Peter the Apostle. He will realize his mistakes. He will try to bring the Church together again under the authority of Christ, but he will no longer be able to do so... 'Pope Francis will die as a martyr, then Pope Emeritus Benedict XVI will appear – who still wears his papal ring. He will try to summon a council to save the Church. I saw him weak and fragile, held on both sides by two Swiss guards. I saw him suddenly fleeing Rome due to the all-around devastation. He is hiding but he will be found afterwards, and I also saw his martyrdom...

Pope Francis does many things with good intentions, but he gives trust, relies-on and gives liberties to bishops who are dangerous. He (will) realize that it (will) need rectifications but it will be too late...

God sends His prophets to communicate to His people what is going to happen, His designs, his purposes, but 'only with prayers and fasting you can change part of this prophecy'. Like the story of Nineveh, where God sends Jonah to warn the people that He would destroy it, but through their prayer God gave compassion and forgave Nineveh.

The Holy Mass, as essence, will never disappear nor the Church because the forces of hell will not prevail against It. We will always find faithful priests and faithful bishops who will protect the true doctrine."

<u>Message received by Fr. Michel Rodrigue while in the chapel at the apparition site of Our Lady of Knock, Ireland, on 11 October 2019</u>:

St. John said:

In the beginning was the Word, and the Word was with God, and the Word was God. He was in the beginning with God… And the Word became flesh and made his dwelling among us… but his own people did not accept him. But to those who did accept him he gave power to become children of God… (John 1). **"Behold, I make all things new," says the Lord!** (Rev 21:5)

Then Our Lady said:

My dear children, I am here with you to warn you of what will soon happen on Earth. Behold here, the presence of My Son on the altar of His sacrifice, prefigured by the lamb that was spoken of by the prophet Isaiah, the lamb of the sacrifice for the salvation of the world, the lamb of the pascal mystery. In the mystery of the Eucharist is also present the Body of the Church: as militant in the journey on Earth, as suffering in the purification of Purgatory, and as glorious in Her saints in Heaven.

The Church is the mystical body of Christ, present on the altar of the Cross through the Body of My Son, Jesus.

As your Mother, I came here with Joseph, the patron of the Church and your patron. He is your defender against the evil works of all who have betrayed Jesus.

The figure of John the evangelist, as an apostle, is also here. He was chosen by my Son, Jesus, at the foot of the Cross to protect me from that day until the day of my Assumption into Heaven. He is here as a representative of all my faithful and consecrated children. He is the antithesis of the one who betrayed Jesus.

Joseph, myself, and my Son, the Lamb of God, Who takes away the sins of the world, are your models as the faithful family of the Eternal Father. Open the teachings of the Holy Tradition of the Church in regard to the transmitted teachings of John, my adoptive apostle. Open his letters and the book of Revelation. Soon you will understand what was written and seen in his vision.

The Church will be sacrificed, as my Son was. My faithful will suffer before entering into the places prepared for you.

The Cross of the lamb will shine soon for the Earth and for every person. They shall see their consciences when they see the Lamb of God on the Cross. It will be the Day of their enlightenment!

My attitude of prayer, standing and looking up, and waiting with my open arms, is for the coming of that Day of Warning for everyone. The attitude of prayer shown by Joseph teaches the Church of what She must understand now: Prayers, Penance, Penance...

The last apostle on Earth represents the hierarchy of the Church in these days of confusion. Only the true teachings that go back to the apostles and have been transmitted through the living Tradition of the Church, as revealed by the Holy Spirit Who is the soul of the Church, Her sanctifier, will protect you from the false prophets and the false teaching of their sin. This teaching belongs to Satan, who has infiltrated the mystical hierarchical Body of my Son on Earth.

I call the apostles of the end times. Arise with humble hearts, with obedient and dedicated lives to my Son, Jesus. Listen to what I said in La Salette and in Akita. The time is coming. Be ready. Confess your sins. Go to the confessional, fast, and pray the Rosary that will save you from the snares of the devil.

Pray to your guardian angels. Come and adore my Son in the Most Holy Sacrament of the Eucharist. Meditate on the words of my Son, the Lamb of God, in the Gospel of John and his book of Revelation.

In the end, I promise you the triumph of my Immaculate Heart.

(Our Lady of Knock, Ireland, on 11 October 2019)

Fr. Michel received yet a second message when praying in the same chapel in Knock, Ireland, on 13 October 2019. This time, it was from Our Lord Jesus-Christ:

I am the Lamb of God. Soon, I will open the seven seals to fulfill the Will of My Father.

Whoever welcomes you, welcomes Me, and welcomes the blessing of My Father.

When you see the Host, you see My Body and My Blood. You see My face that is presented to you as white, shining bread. I am the Bread of Life for everyone. Who will eat this Bread of Life will rise on the last day.

A great darkness is coming now upon the world: a darkness of sin, of misery, of Satan, who will try to disfigure the face of My Body, which is My Church. He will try to disfigure My white face in the Holy Eucharist with an abominable sacrilege.

At that moment, time will be up. A great disaster will engulf the world, as never before. Rome will fall. Satan will never prevail over My just and My faithful remnant.

The sign will be in the sky, and the hand of My Father will vanquish the darkness of Satan, his false prophet, and his slithering acolytes.

The seal will be broken. Prepare yourself for this day. My Mother will protect My just everywhere in the refuges prepared by her Immaculate Heart.

My son, Michel, you will have great responsibilities on your shoulders. Know that the burden will be light, and the joy of My children will be great. 'Happy are those who are called to the supper of the Lamb.' I cherish and protect them. I nourish them. I bless them. They will not fear the pestilence of the enemy.

Your Savior, your friend, Jesus

(Our Lord Jesus-Christ, 13 October 2019)

Message of the Blessed Virgin Mary:

My dear children,

You are gathered to pray for the families of the Apostolic Fraternity of Saint Benedict Joseph Labre and for all the families of the earth.

I offer you the gift of finding peace, healing the wounds and deliverance for yourself and your children from the evil one, by reciting the Rosary in your families. Return to the prayer of the Rosary. This is the weapon I have given you to chain evil and defeat it.

Whenever you meditate on the mysteries of the Rosary, not only have you saved many souls from Hell, but you heal your own and allow the Holy Spirit to cast out the darkness.

I repeat to you with my entire Mother's tenderness, come back to the prayer of the Rosary, which will soothe your hearts and prepare you for the Day of my Son.

I love you,
Your Mother.

(The Blessed Virgin Mary, 10 January 2020)

Message from the Virgin Mary to Fr. Michel Rodrigue

My dear children,

I am the Immaculate Conception, Mary, your Mother.

I must warn you of the time of trial and the time of the minor tribulation that you must pass through before entering into the permanent refuge prepared by my Son and me to save you from the grip of the army of Satan.

The trial will begin with agitation and confusion in the consciences of my children. False doctrines and prophets will try to distract you from my Son Jesus. False prophets will perform great signs under satanic power. This type of sign can only be for a time shorter than three days. With this performance, they will lead many of my children away from the true teachings of the Church. They will also manage, inside of the Church, to avoid the teaching of the Gospel, the true relation with your Redeemer by hiding his Name and making their own type of substitute ministry.

I will be your mother, and like the disciples and the apostles assembled around me after the death of my Son, I will be your refuge to protect you.

I bless you, and I ask Joseph to be with you!

(The Blessed Virgin Mary, 13 February 2020)

The message below is a message from The Eternal Father to Fr. Michel. He has asked that this message be given out immediately to all of God's Children, and especially to those children, who Fr. Michel has spoken to while visiting the United States.

Since Fr. Michel has visited several churches during his visits to the U.S. he wants to follow faithfully the directives given to him by God the Father.

Message of God the Father:

My son,

Listen and write:
I demand that this message be communicated to everyone and everywhere that you have preached in the United States and in Canada.

Remember the night when Padre Pio brought you into Heaven to see the Holy Family. It was a teaching for you and for the people who have heard you. It was also a sign to recall the night when My Beloved Son Jesus was born into the world. Remember how My Evangelist Matthew wrote by the divine inspiration of the Holy Spirit how the star stopped over the place where My Baby Son Jesus was born. It was a sign for the Wise men. Today, it is a sign for you and for all Christians and for all nations.

The Holy Family is a sign for every family, and we should model ourselves after them. I demand that every family, who receives this message, should have a representation of the Holy Family in their home. It can be an Icon or a statue of the Holy Family, or a permanent Manger in the center place of the home. The representation must be blessed and consecrated] by a priest. As the star, followed by the Wise men, stopped over the Manger, the chastiment from the sky will not hit the Christian families devoted and protected by the Holy Family. The fire from the sky is a chastiment for the horrible crime of abortion and the culture of death, the sexual perversion, and the cupidity (lust) regarding the identity of a man and a woman.

My children seek their perverted sins more than Eternal life. The increasing blasphemies and persecution of My just people offend Me. The Arm of My justice will come now. They do not hear My Divine Mercy. I must now let many plagues happen to save the most people that I can from the slavery of Satan.

Send this message to everyone. I have given Saint Joseph, My representative on earth, the authority to protect the Church which is the body of Christ. He will be the protector during the trials of this time. The

Immaculate Heart of My daughter Mary and the Sacred Heart of My Beloved Son Jesus, with the Chaste and Pure Heart of Saint Joseph, will be the shield of your home, your family, and your Refuge during the events to come.

My Words are My blessing over all of you. Whoever will act according to My Will, will be safe. The powerful love of the Holy Family will be manifested to all.
I AM your Father,
These words are Mine!

(Message of God the Father, 30 October 2018)

Father Michel Rodrigue:

On August 15, 2018, I was standing near the entrance of the church, welcoming people who were coming to celebrate the joyful event of the bishop enrobing the Fraternity of St. Joseph Benedict Labre with our new vestments. I was preparing for the celebration with all our members because the bishop had approved everything through the Church. The vestments were the first ones we received for the order. The bishop blessed the vestments, and he gave me the first one. This is the same ceremony in which I heard Our Lady say, 'I call the **apostle of the end times,**' *as the bishop placed the robe on me."*

As people were entering the church, I suddenly received a vision of the war to come... It was a nuclear war, but I didn't understand this at first... I saw so much destruction: fire and bombs and many people dying, some already dead. Every dead body I saw there was burnt, their flesh was burnt. It was really big. Not a little war, I assure you. It was very destructive. And I started to ask prayer for that everywhere. And I know that the war will come from two countries: one is Korea and the other is Iran.

*They will come together to face the United States of America. I felt so troubled by this that I started to cry and had to return to the sacristy. There, two more visions came. I could see people's flesh dripping like water from their bodies. This was so terrifying that I said, '**Lord, please stop this. I have to be** **with my people to welcome them with joy today, and I'm just crying now. I** **cannot...**'*

The Father also said that through prayer the war could be diminished but not avoided. This is what I have from the Lord. The war was supposed to have begun already, but it was postponed through prayer, through the Rosary. This is important because peoples' prayers have been heard.

You must pray for your president, please. Sometimes he acts in ways nobody can understand, but I assure you, you're blessed to have him, so you must pray for him. Because he is so erratic, he is thwarting the plans of the One World Government. They cannot control him. But I saw so many countries. After that, I told that to the bishop. He knows everything I see. I tell him everything. I have nothing to hide.

The war was supposed to have begun already in 2019, but it was postponed through prayer, through the Rosary. This is important because peoples' prayers have been heard. At the beginning of 2019, when I travelled the

United States to give talks in seven churches in Michigan and in New York, so many people came. We prayed to the Virgin Mary to stop the war, the nuclear war, and I advised them about their president.

I said to them:

'You know. This president (Donald Trump) is not a saint,' and they laughed. 'But the One World Government doesn't know what to do with him because one day he dances on one leg. The next day, he dances on the other leg. He unbalances every kind of plan or schedule they have made. This is why this guy is such a menace for them.'

What I can say about President Trump is only what the Father has told me. He said: **'This one, I have chosen him. They cannot control him.'** He didn't say that he's a saint. He never said that. **'They cannot control him. They don't know on which leg he is dancing.'** This is what He said. **'Because of this, they have not been able to achieve their task.'** The Father said that Trump was elected because of his angel who modified the vote. He was chosen because the Lord knows his temperament, his skill, his actions, and his will.

He was chosen to block the One World Government. This is important because if he was not there, I can assure you that the One World Government, which is the work Satan, would have taken place by now... And I know that I can be at rest with what I have said. I have told all this to the bishop. He knows everything I see. I tell him everything. I have nothing to hide.

I told the people in the United States:

'Sometimes Trump acts in ways nobody can understand. But I assure you, you're blessed to have him, so you must pray for him. You must pray now for your president because he will be under a great danger. They will try to kill him.'

They knelt and they all prayed the Rosary. A group of them committed themselves to praying for the President every day, and when I was in a chapel recently, the Lord said to me:

'Michel, I heard the prayers of my people in the United States. There was supposed to be an assassination attempt eight months ago. They didn't have success. He was protected because of the Rosary.'

Later, I received another sign. Again, the Lord asked that we pray for this man because they will try again to kill him. We must pray. We must pray the Rosary. The Father also said that through prayer the war could be diminished but not avoided. This is what I have from the Lord.

Today, Father Michel Rodrigue's locutions and visions are submitted to his local ordinary for approval.

Consecration of the Home Revealed to Rev. Father Michel Rodrigue

Fr. Michel Rodrigue:

Consecrate your homes with exorcised salt and exorcised water. You will have to put the exorcised salt in the water yourselves because I will not be able to put exorcised water in every bottle, you know, so you can do it yourselves, but if you have only one (either exorcised water or exorcised salt) and mix it together, the other will become exorcised too.

So, this is what you do. You make a prayer to God the Eternal Father... I give you the frame of the prayer:

Eternal Father, I consecrate my home to you. By the intercession of the Immaculaye Heart of Mary and the Sacred Heart of Jesus, I give you my home as a refuge for the days to come. It will be your Will for your people if You want Your people to come here. I consecrate this home and with the holy water you spray in the Name of the Father and of the Son and of the Holy Spirit in the Sign of the Cross. Amen

Then you go outside, and you consecrate your land in the same manner. You just change the word "house" or "home" for "land" and then you drop the salt on the ground because, the salt will penetrate in the land.

Fr. Rodrigue further explains that once your home will be consecrated, it will become a small refuge of sorts, first for the owners' family, then for anyone who would ask for sanctuary; however, Fr. Rodrigue is quite clear. If the Will of the Father is for the home's owner(s) to go afterwards to a bigger refuge, he/they will be guided by their guardian angel through a mystical flame which is to guide the faithful to said larger sanctuary.

Remedy for those who have been forced to be vaccinated against the COVID-19 Virus

(Message of the Father to Rev. Fr. Michel Rodrigue for the year 2021)

Fr. Michel Rodrigue:

"I am including the message for the year 2021:

'If people have been forceably vaccinated against COVID 19, drink the exorcised holy water. If you do not have any, take the blessed Miraculous Medal and let it soak in the water by saying this prayer: 'Holy Virgin Mary, bless this water to purify me from the attacks of evil in my body in the Name

of the Father, and of the Son and of the Holy Spirit. Amen' Drink it. You will be protected'".

(Message of the Eternal Father to Rev. Fr. Michel Rodrigue, March 2021)

March 2021 Message from St. Gabriel the Archangel to Fr. Michel Rodrigue regarding December 2021
(Delivered publicly on 29 September, 2021):

Fr. Michel Rodrigue:

On the night of March 17 to 18, 2021, the Angel of the Lord (later I understood that it was Saint Gabriel the Archangel) came around 2:30 in the night to tell me about the Holy and Great discretion of Saint Joseph with the Holy Family and his role at the end of bad times. I say "end of bad times" to express a period different from that of Christ's Glorious Return at the end of time.
This experience which I am going to relate, I call it a dream. Gabriel first presented himself as a splendid radiant light. Gradually I made out the form of a being of light with what looked like wings of light. There emanated from his being a luminosity which brought both joy and very deep peace in God. It was like stepping into a part of the sky looking at it. Then his voice was heard:

"I come to reveal the discretion of Saint Joseph from the time I spoke to him until the day he was to leave the earth. His role as protector and guardian of the Holy Family was one of great serenity and great confidence in God the Eternal Father. To Him as to the Most Holy Virgin Mary was given to be the first in the most holy knowledge of the Mystery of the Trinity of the Father and of the Son and of the Holy Spirit. The free acceptance of taking the Virgin Mary as his bride gave him the joy of an infused knowledge imbued with a living and fatherly relationship with Jesus, his Creator, his King and his Love. This knowledge Joseph received from the love he had for Mary His Bride and from the Will of the Almighty Father. From that moment, Joseph took Mary to his wife's home and actualized the Ministry of his love for Mary and the Child. [Note from Daniel: Joseph was always absolutely celibate. This line does not imply Joseph had another wife before or along with Mary; it only means that Joseph took Mary to *her* home.]

The drama which occurred at the time of the Savior's birth raises the consideration of his great authority which made it possible to preserve the Child-God and his Mother from any omen that could have put the identity of the Child at risk. Thus, the devil and his henchmen could have harmed Jesus and his Mother. His strength and his Love kept the devil and his acolytes at bay. Until the day of the birth of the Child King, even Herod and his entourage knew nothing about it. Yet the Sign was in heaven, the Magi were already walking to meet the Child-God and the shepherds, the smallest of the people, were instructed by the voice of the angels!

At the moment when Herod wanted to kill the Child-God, I warned Joseph in a dream, by the Will of the Eternal Father, to take the Child and his Mother and flee to Egypt. He remained there until the death of the tyrant. Back in Nazareth, the Holy Family remained there during all the years of Jesus' growth. No one suspected who Jesus and his Mother were. Joseph's discretion was perfect so as not to attract the eyes of the Evil One and thus hinder the plan of God our Father. Joseph's putative fatherhood covered the Child and his Mother in such a great way that no one can express or approach. Joseph's paternal tenderness was like the cave of the Rock to protect the Child and his Mother from the untimely moods of this world. This discretion will continue in Silence and prayer, in the daily work and even in the rests so as not to let suspect the existence of the Messiah of God. Joseph's obedience to doing the Will of the Eternal Father with a humble and pure heart made him the most representative male figure on earth at the center of the Holy Family. His Fatherhood and his Masculinity were similar to that desired by God from the beginning of everything. So as Saint Joseph protected the Child and his Mother, he protects the Church in its historical growth. In an even more solemn way in these times of yours.

The present times require the lifting of the veil of God's discretion for Saint Joseph in his role for the Church of Christ. Now is the time to reveal the words of the second letter to the Thessalonians hidden from the beginning of the Church. Indeed the mysterious figure, which holds back or prevents the manifestation of the antichrist and his present domination, must now be unveiled to enable all the righteous to understand the events which are taking place. You must stand ready and keep your lamps on for the manifestation of the Son of Man. Here is the Sacred Text of Saint Paul's second letter to the Thessalonians, chapter 2:

We ask you, brothers, with regard to the coming of our Lord Jesus Christ and our assembling with him, a not to be shaken out of your minds suddenly, or to be alarmed either by a "spirit," or by an oral statement, or by a letter allegedly from us to the effect that the day of the Lord is at hand. Let no one deceive you in any way. For unless the apostasy comes first and the lawless one is revealed, the one doomed to perdition, 4who opposes and exalts himself above every so-called god and object of worship, so as to seat himself in the temple of God, claiming that he is a god— do you not recall that while I was still with you I told you these things? And now you know what is restraining, that he may be revealed in his time. For the mystery of lawlessness is already at work. But the one who restrains is to do so only for the present, until he is removed from the scene. And then the lawless one will be revealed, whom the Lord [Jesus] will kill with the breath of his mouth and render powerless by the manifestation of his coming, the one whose coming springs from the power of Satan in every mighty deed and in signs and wonders that lie, and in every wicked deceit for those who are perishing because they have not accepted the love of truth so that they may be saved. Therefore, God is sending them a deceiving power so that they

462

may believe the lie, that all who have not believed the truth but have approved wrongdoing may be condemned. But we ought to give thanks to God for you always, brothers loved by the Lord, because God chose you as the firstfruits for salvation through sanctification by the Spirit and belief in truth.

Indeed, "the mystery of iniquity is already at work; it suffices that the one who retains it now be discarded. Today, I say it to you: The one who holds it back is Saint Joseph! Through his prayer and his intercession, Saint Joseph assists believers in a spiritual struggle for the defense of the faith of the militant Church. With the prayers of the saints and souls in purgatory, that is to say the Triumphant Church and the Suffering Church, the assistance of Saint Joseph and the Virgin Mary constituting a shield of faith which holds back the antichrist until now.

Hear my words well. The cup of iniquity is overflowing, and soon a time will come for the Church when the persecution of the righteous will take place. It is by the Will of the Father and of the Son and of the Holy Spirit that this year 2021 has been proclaimed by Pope Francis the year of Saint Joseph. A great blessing of protection has been offered to you. During this year you will be forced to make a choice. What presents itself as a vaccine-savior is just an illusion. Soon the mark of the Beast will be imposed on you to buy, to eat or to travel. <u>The year 2021 is a year of discernment for those who want to be faithful to Christ. To all those who wish to follow Christ, Saint Joseph will assist you. But He must withdraw discreetly on December 8.</u>

By that time, and it has already started, all those who reject Christ find themselves entering into a force of delusion that makes them believe a lie. A social and planetary lie organized and prepared by the acolytes of the antichrist. They form a false Church which is indeed the social body of the antichrist. They are the ones who rule by fear, domination, by communist and socialist ideologies. They are manipulating for a false universal brotherhood. They have infiltrated the Church of Christ with a view to disfiguring it and desecrating its sacraments. Everything falls into place. Until December 8, these evil acolytes organize themselves through the media and create a climate of suspicion, fear and denunciation.

They must prepare for the coming of the Unholy by organizing a world order where division and confusion will reign to the detriment of the Truth of the teaching of the Church. Scandals and accusations will hit the Church everywhere. Movements that deny men and women will become the new judges of this social lie. Conflicts will arise in families arguing the need for vaccines and the Mark of the Beast. Conflicts between nations will come to such a point that everything will seem hopeless. Hearts will cool, consciences will be bound and darkened by the sin that has pervaded everywhere.

Even though the antichrist's tares seem to suffocate the righteous and the saints, giving the impression of the death of God and the end of the Catholic Church, all of this is only an appearance. When Saint Joseph retires, the Immaculate Heart of Mary will begin the beginnings of the triumph of her Immaculate Heart for her children and for the Church. The

Church will go through the pains of a purification where the Virgin Mary will accompany her as Mother of sorrows. Some of her children will be martyrs, they will wear the palm of the Victory of Christ on the day of the triumph of the Immaculate Heart of Mary. At the time when the antichrist will appear, the time of the refuges prepared by the Holy Hearts of Jesus and Mary and the very pure heart of Saint Joseph will sound. The Refuges are the work of the three and a half years announced in the Book of Revelation. They are the work of God.

Small herd do not be afraid. Look with the eyes of faith, hope and love. The shelters are under the special protection of Our Lady of Mount Carmel. This is how her Immaculate Heart wanted it. Can you not now see the work of the Holy Family of Jesus, Mary and Joseph? Everything you need to know has been said. Live in confidence to accomplish his Divine Will and repeat this prayer often: Jesus, I trust in you!"

Rev. Father Constant Louis-Marie Pel (1876–1966)

The reverend Father Constant Louis Marie Pel was born in 1878 in Lantenay in the region of Ain, France. He was a mystical priest invisibly stigmatized... He was ordained in 1901, and after having gotten two theological doctorates, he became a seminary Professor... Doctor in theology, seminary professor, founder of a convent for women and of a seminary for men, with a great devotion to the Sacred Heart of Jesus and to the Immaculate Heart of Mary.

He was a personal friend of Charles de Foucault, spiritual Director of Marthe Robin and personal friend of Padre Pio who said of him to some French pilgrims in San Giovanni Rotondo:

Why do you come to see me when you have so great a Saint in France?

Cardinal Maurin used to say to Rev. Father Pel that he was a holy Curé d'Ars but with science added.

Father Pel was present with Father Cennamo—who became later the Superior of San Giovanni Rotondo—during the message given by St. Michael the Archangel to visionary Conchita Gonzalez on 18 June 1965 in Garabandal, Spain (Chapter VII).

During the very last apparition in the little Spanish village of Garabandal, St. Michael the Archangel requested that Father Pel be next to Conchita Gonzalez. No one knows how, but the French priest found himself indeed next to the young Spanish visionary, and, along with two other Frenchmen, Fr. Pel kissed the Crucifix before the apparition. The three Frenchmen were the only ones on that day to beneficiate from that special favor...

Back in France, Fr. Pel would spend nights on his feet in church with his forehead leaning against the Tabernacle, conversing with God in a permanent ecstasy. He died, despite an ironclad health, in a car accident in 1966 (just after Vatican II), but not before a seminarian, one of his spiritual sons, had been able to write down a prophecy Fr. Pel gave, dating from 1945, concerning the chastisement which will strike France and the world:

"My son," said Fr Pel, *"know that with the sins of the world increasing in horror as this age carries on, great punishments from God will come down on the world and no continent will be spared from the Wrath of God. France, being guilty of apostasy and denying its vocation, will be severely chastised. East of a line stretching from Bordeaux in the south-west to Lille in the north-east, everything will be laid to waste and set on fire by peoples invading from the east, and also by great flaming meteorites falling in a rain of fire upon all the earth and upon these regions especially. Revolution, war, epidemics, plagues, chemical poison gases, violent earthquakes and the re-awakening of France's extinct volcanoes will destroy everything...*

France to the west of that line will be less affected... because of the faith rooted in the Vendée and in Brittany... but none of God's worst enemies seeking refuge there from the worldwide cataclysm will be able to find any; wherever they hide, they will be put to death by devils, because the Wrath of the Lord is just and holy. Thick darkness caused by the war, gigantic fires and fragments of burning stars falling for three days and nights will cause the sun to disappear, and only candles blessed on Candle Mass (February 2) will give light in the hands of believers, but the godless will not see this miraculous light because they have darkness in their souls.

In this way, ¾ of mankind will be destroyed, and in some parts of France survivors will have to go 100 km (c. 60 miles) to find another (living) human being. It will reach the point where people have to eat human flesh to survive..."

Several nations will disappear off the face of the world's map. France will become very small, but a small part of it will survive until the end of time. And thus purified, France will again become the "Eldest Daughter of the Church"—renewed—because all the Cains and Judases of humanity will have disappeared in this "Judgment of the Nations." But this is not yet the end of time, which will take place later.

The Mediterranean Sea will disappear totally; the oceans will cast enormous jets of burning steam up to the skies and will deluge the continents in a frightful tidal wave that will annihilate everything in its path. New mountains will erupt out of the earth and the oceans, while the Alps and the Rhine Valley to the north will collapse as they are inundated by the sea. In this way, the map of the world will be totally changed; the earth will undergo great shocks that will prevent it from turning normally on its axis. The seasons will cease to exist for three years, after which the earth will once again produce it plants and vegetation. There will be great famine in the entire world. Paris will be destroyed by the revolution and burned by atomic fire from Russians in Orleans and the region of Provins... In the meantime, Marseille and the French Riviera will collapse and will be immersed under water...

In the future, when you see that this frightful time is near, take leave to Brittany (on the western coast of France) but go to the center, far from the coasts—because they will collapse. This global scourge will begin on a cold winter's night and with a terrifying roar of divine thunder—an unnatural sound filled with demonic screaming—that will be heard by the entire world. It will be the voice of sin that terrified men will hear on that night.

Abbot D. Souffrant (1755–1828)

The Abbot Souffrant was born in 1755. Once ordained he began his priesthood in 1780 as vicar of Maumusson near Ancenis in the diocese of Nantes, Brittany. He braved the turmoil of the French Revolution, during which time he remained firm in his faith before the French blood-thirsty Republicans; hence, the legitimate bishop had made him his vicar general. Abbot Souffrant ran many dangers and later, under the imperial regime and that of the Restoration, he suffered several persecutions.

After the Revolution, he believed that the little ten-year-old Dauphin, son of King Louis XVI and Queen Marie-Antoinette, had survived and had escaped from the Temple prison. The good abbot consequently wrote two letters, one to Napoleon I and the other to King Louis XVIII, reproaching them their 'usurpation' of the French throne; hence he caused a measure of the government's persecutions against him.

The French abbot lived for nearly 50 years in his parish of Maumusson. Despite the offer of a more important parish, he would never leave it and remained there until his death in 1828. It was there that the good pious and gifted Churchman wrote his many prophecies which, to this day, remain most popular and discussed. Unfortunately, copies of his written work have been lost, but copies of his supernatural visions continue to circulate today.

According to a note left in the records of the parish of Maumusson by his successor, Abbé Siché:

In the year 1821, I arrived as vicar to the venerable Monsieur Souffrant, then 66 years old, and with whom I spent six years; how sweet and agreeable his society was! At that time, he often spoke of prophecies, and people came from far away to hear him, and I saw many great people in his house who spent days and nights with him taking notes, the most was to see in Mr. Souffrant two characters in the same man. He spoke of his ministry, he always did it with calm and moderation. It was with prophecies that he was much more animated always appearing deeply convinced of what he was saying; how sorry I was for not listening and copying what he was saying, but, I confess, I could not believe, only (until) the events (occurred) that triumphed over my unbelief.

Abbot D. Souffrant's prophecies:

1. "At the end of the fifth age, where we are, we will no longer believe," says the venerable Holzhauser, "that in the time of Noah they were called foolish, because he was building the ark to save himself from the flood. (**Note**: It will be like the age of Noah when everyone thought him mad for building the Ark, instead of seeing it as a warning sign. Also, could mean people in the latter times will no longer believe those who mocked Noah were 'foolish', i.e., the people of the latter days will be doing the same sins, and are 'worldly wise' in their own eyes, while those who are like Noah will be considered the 'foolish' ones.)
   Do not rejoice over the Restoration because your joy will not be long. You will still see the tricolor flag (French flag: blue, white, and red), and three governments succeed each other before the Great Monarch appears: Orleanism, the Republic, Bonapartism. (**Note**: Half has come to pass, the restoration of the French throne with Charles X did not last long. He was forced into exile. The Orleans then later fought against the Count of Chambord from his rightful throne. The Republic came after. Next, is a Bonapartist restoration. That came as well with the arrival on Napoleon III, but the Republic returned afterwards.)
   The eldest branch of the Bourbons will still leave France, and the movement will be near, when the vicinals will be arranged everywhere and the war against the Turks will be waged. The prophecy also is mostly related to the rise of Napoleon III. The Count of Chambord's throne was usurped again when Napoleon III came to power during the Second Empire and the Count of Chambord was forced to stay out of France.

2. However, it is argued that Henry de Bourbon could have come to the throne but the revelation given to him by the little visionary of La Salette, Maximin Giraud, convinced him not to sit on the throne of France as he knew his cousin Louis XVII survived "the Temple" and had a heir (see page 49).

3. After the fall of Charles X, we shall have a prince of Orleans who will do a lot of harm to religion. Under his reign, we will establish pernicious schools that will do a great deal of harm.

4. In the reign of the usurper, a movement will be attempted in the Vendee, by the Duchess of Berry and her friends, but it will be little and it will have no success... The Duke and Duchess of Angoulême (Daughter of Louis XVI and Marie-Antoinette) remain strangers to this attempt. The usurper will be hunted in his turn, the moment of his fall will be preceded by movements in Italy. It will arrive in a moment of great prosperity; it will usually be said that I am wrong.
   Note: This prophesy came true. The Orleans usurper, Louis-Philip I was forced to abdicate after the outbreak of the French Revolution of 1848. He lived out his life in exile in the United Kingdom. His supporters were known as Orléanists, as opposed to Legitimists who supported the main line of the House of Bourbon. Napoleon III, the next usurper, founded the Second French Empire and was its emperor until the defeat of the

France as seen in the future by Rev. Father Pel

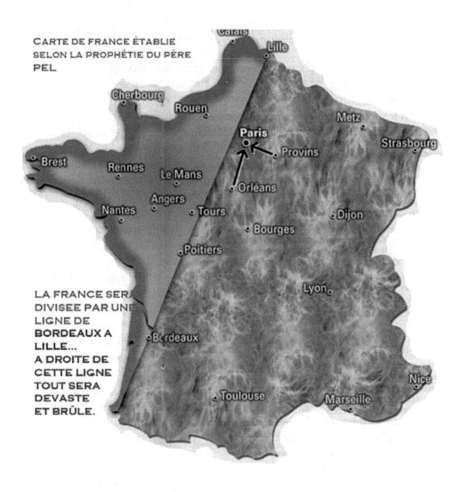

CARTE DE FRANCE ÉTABLIE SELON LA PROPHÉTIE DU PÈRE PEL

LA FRANCE SERA DIVISEE PAR UNE LIGNE DE BORDEAUX A LILLE... A DROITE DE CETTE LIGNE TOUT SERA DEVASTE ET BRÛLE.

"France will be divided by a line from the city of Bordeaux to the city of Lille. To the right of that line everything will be devastated and burnt.

Paris will be destroyed through two nuclear blasts – One coming from Orléans and the othe from outside Coulommiers."
"

(Rev. Father Pel)

France as seen in the future by Father Pel, Abbot Souffrant and Stigmatist and Visionary Marie-Julie Jahenny

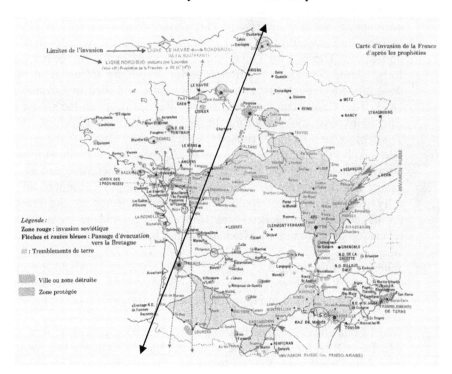

Blue zone: Protected towns and areas (*according to Marie-Julie Jahenny*)
Red zone: Cities and zones destroyed (*according to Marie-Julie Jahenny*)
Blue roads: Evacuation roads to Brittany (*according to Marie-Julie Jahenny*)

Lines of demarcation:

Black: (East from Lille to Bordeaux everything will be burnt) (*as per Rev. Father Pel*)
Blue: (Limit of Russian invasion from le Havre to Bordeaux) (*as per Rev. Father Souffrant*)
Red: (Limit of Russian invasion from Caen to Lourdes) (*as per Marie-Julie Jahenny*)

-----: **France will be cut in two. The foreign invasion will stop east of the line between Caen and Lourdes. (Revelation by Marie-Julie JAHENNY)**

-----: **France will be cut in two enemy's invasion will be between <u>a line in between the cities of le Havre and Bordeaux</u>. (Revelation by Abbot SOUFFRANT)**

French army in the Franco-Prussian War of 1870, and until Napoleon III himself was captured by the Prussian army…

He however, before the war, worked on modernizing the French economy, rebuilding the city of Paris, expanding the French overseas empire, and engaging in the Crimean War and the war for Italian unification. The war for Italian unification must be the 'movements in Italy' Abbé Souffrant predicted. After Napoleon III's defeat and downfall, the French Emperor went into exile and died in England in 1873. The Third Republic commenced after his death as the Count of Chambord never took the throne for the reasons explained in chapter I.

5. The replacement of the "Tricolore" with the white flag with the golden fleurs de lys demanded by the Count of Chambord as a condition for his return to the throne was in fact but a mere pretext orchestrated as an excuse not to take the crown… Indeed, the Count of Chambord knew fully well his proposal would be vehemently rejected by the French Parliament, but his decision was firm and taken on the basis of the revelation given to him by Maximin Giraud from La Salette (see chapter I).

6. When a law is enacted to regulate the practice of hunting, you can expect the Republic to be near. (**Note**: 3 May 1844, a major hunting regulation was passed in France. This happened right before the historic events listed above.)

7. When France is crisscrossed by highways, the usurper will be near his fall. He will be hunted and die in exile. (**Note**: This came true, at the time, Napoleon III was the last to oversee the creation of new highways in France that began under the reign of Napoleon I according to an article dated 1893. Napoleon, furthermore went indeed in exile in London after the fiasco of the Franco-Prussian war.)

8. After him, a Republic will be proclaimed that will give full and complete freedom and will not do much harm to religion.

9. It will not be long, and you will have a Napoleon who will govern you.

10. He will do great harm to religion by his hypocrisy. Under his reign, universal impetus for the construction of very beautiful churches. (**Note**: Here, the prophecies have backtracked. Napoleon III may have helped support the Church, but by reigning under a constitutional monarchy favorable to the ideal of the French Revolution, and sitting on a throne that wasn't his, his reign was illicit and, some argue, that of a hypocrite. About building churches: Napoleon III continues to seek the preservation of numerous medieval buildings in France, which had been left disregarded since the French revolution. With Viollet-le-Duc acting as chief architect, many buildings were saved, including some of the most famous in France: Notre Dame Cathedral, Mont Saint-Michel, Carcassonne, Vézelay Abbey, Pierrefonds, and Roqietaille Castle.)

11. What will be his power? I cannot say it too much, but he will have enough power to coin money.

12. He will be near his fall when we travel with the swiftness of a swallow. He will make a heavy fall. (**Note**: travel with the swiftness of a swallow

obviously means future times when the ability to travel fast will be made possible.)

13. Then a bad republic that persecutes religion will come, and will end up with a catastrophe.

14. A great number of honest people, royalists, priests, and nobles, will be eager, more eager than others, to recognize the Republic, to find it good, to desire its maintenance.

15. There will be several assemblies of deputies: the royalists will put their hopes in these assemblies, but they will not bring them any realization of these hopes.

16. Peace is impossible: we will be afflicted with the greatest evils. Terrible events will happen. These misfortunes that God will send us to do penance, will not be so great if we convert.

17. These evils, and all that the Republic gives birth to, are necessary to purify the area and to bring in the good grain before the arrival of the Great Monarch.

18. The conversion of the bourgeois would serve marvelously to diminish or arrest many evils.

19. The moment of great events will be near when one travels with the greatest speed. I do not know how these trips will be, but I see the vehicles (cars/wagons) go with the speed of the bird.

20. The coming of the Great Monarch will be very near when the number of Legitimists who have remained truly faithful will be so small that, to tell the truth, they will be counted.

21. In these events, the good ones will have nothing to do, because it will be the republicans, the bad guys who will load each other. (**Note**: Possibly means the good people or monarchists on the side of the king will be able to do nothing as the Republicans will have all the power at the time.)

22. The upheavals will be appalling. Religion will be persecuted and its ministers will be forced to hide in many places, at least momentarily, the churches will be closed for a while.

23. Before the arrival of the Great Monarch, there will be great evils, frightful disorders, misfortunes must happen.

24. The blood will flow in torrents to the north and to the south, and I will see it run like rain on a stormy day, and I see the horses having blood to the straps.

25. It is mainly in the cities that blood will flow.

26. In these times and after a new republic (a sixth French republic?) will then be proclaimed, but that will last little, you will see three parties in France, two bad and one good. The first two will do much harm in Paris which will be destroyed, and in the rest of the North and the South of France.

27. These evils and ruins will, above all, ruin the great cities.

28. Paris will be treated with unparalleled rigor, as the center of crime and corruption. Paris will be destroyed in the midst of all these calamities, so destroyed that the plough will pass there.

29. The upheaval will be general in Europe and everywhere republics will be established.
30. The West, which was so roughly treated under the first revolution, will be spared in the events. It is because of this that the West has found favor with God, because of its faith, the misfortunes that may happen in the West will be very small compared to that of other countries. It will suffer only the counter-blow of the great concussions.
(**Note**: The west of France is meant here, Brittany and the Vendée—they suffered much during the French Revolution, but will be spared many of the upheavals in the coming events. This was also foretold to Marie-Julie Jahenny many years later.)
31. The countryside will be spared. (**Note**: possibly also refers to the rural areas of Brittany and the Vendée.)
32. A Bonaparte will cause great sorrows to the Sovereign Pontiff, and will eventually force him to flee. He may go to Russia. (**Note**: May be one of the contenders who will rise up again before the Great Monarch comes. The usurpers will cause trouble.)
33. Cries will be uttered; those who dominate will be those of: "Vive la république!", "Vive Napoleon!", and finally "**Long live the Great Monarch through whom God guards us!**" (**Note**: The evil Republican parties will be strong until finally the monarchists will win out.)
34. Invisible things will happen; thunder, lightning, and earthquakes will have to convert more people than other evils, wars and massacres. There will come a moment when one will believe everything is lost. (**Note**: The chastisements that will shake the earth.)
35. The misfortunes predicted above will be the result of our crimes. If, as God desires, we enter into his views and those of the Church, our ills will be alleviated. (**Note**: Conversions and repentance for sins will lessen the chastisements.)
36. It is when one believes everything lost that everything will be saved; because between the cry: "All is lost!" and the cry: "All is saved!" there will be no interval the time to turn (or flip) a cake.
37. The foreign powers will arm themselves and march against France.
38. The Emperor of Russia will come at the head of a great army to the Rhine. Russia will come to water her horses in the Rhine, but they will not pass it.
39. Then, in this sixth age, God will comfort the Catholic priests and the other faithful by sending the Great Monarch and the Holy Pontiff.
40. At that time, a monk who has peace in his name and in his heart, shall pray; he will have the same mission as Joan of Arc.
41. Driven on all sides, he will come to take refuge in his seminary in the West of France, and (also) the Great King whom God reserves for us, descendant of the king martyr... (**Note**: It appears the holy monk with the same mission of St. Joan of Arc to aid the Monarch claim his throne, will flee to Brittany or to Vendée in a seminary. He will take refuge there, and so will the King. The King is a descendant of a 'king martyr': Louis XVI. The man who was revealed to Marie-Julie Jahenny as the

Great Monarch will be a descendant of King Louis XVI and of Marie-Antoinette, and will be called Henry V of the Cross.)

42. They will have many difficulties with some prelates. (**Note**: Means some church officials will oppose the Great Monarch and his followers. Marie-Julie Jahenny foretold the same thing, only four bishops will support him according to the French stigmatist.)

43. The Great Monarch who will be (of the) Lys, will arrive by the South of France; he will be brought by the Holy Pontiff and the Emperor of Russia, a prince of the North who will be converted. It is especially by the care of the Sovereign Pontiff that this emperor will be determined to be recognized (by) him.

44. The French generals, who will march for the fight, will not fire a single shot; they will lay down their arms as soon as the Great Monarch is presented to them, so surprising will his arrival be, and accompanied by dazzling proofs of his right and his virtue.

45. The Great Monarch is from the elder branch of the Bourbons, and comes from the branch of a cut branch.

46. The great Monarch will appear against all odds, when the friends of the Church and the legitimate rulers are in consternation, and so anguished, that they will be obliged to take the weapons to which God will give the most marvelous and the most brilliant success.

47. Brilliant and manifest signs will make the prince be recognized by everyone and overcome all obstacles. (**Note**: Miracles will point out the Great Monarch chosen by God.)

48. The good republicans, more impressed than the others, will be much more eager to submit to him than the royalists.

49. For the rest, few will resist; the striking signs and calamities will have sufficiently prepared the minds to receive it.

50. The Great Monarch will do such extraordinary things that the most incredulous will be forced to recognize the finger of God.

51. Moreover, it will be the beginning of a new era of peace and triumph for the Church, an era of innumerable conversions.

52. The success that will be the triumph of the Church and the friends of legitimacy will take its main source in the devotion to the Sacred Heart. This devotion, without stopping events, can greatly diminish the extent and intensity of the evils announced. (**Note**: Not only will the Reign of the Sacred Heart begin under the Great Monarch.)

53. A noble of the Loire-Inferior—a Breton general—will be called to take part in the events and he will play an important role for the restoration of the Holy Pontiff and the Great Monarch. He will bring him back.

54. France, pacified first, will restore calm and prosperity to other nations.

55. The Great Monarch will reform everything, make a new code, a new nobility, and all his acts will be so perfect that all the other sovereigns will be submissive to him.

56. With the Emperor of Russia, he will put an end to confusion, usurpation and injustice all over Europe.

57. But above all, both will re-establish the reign of religion and the authority of the Church.

58. They will both have such supremacy over other powers that they will be like the only two monarchs.
59. Of course, the Emperor of Russia will convert to the Catholic faith so brilliantly that he will be regarded as another Constantine.
60. In concert with him, the Great Monarch will exterminate the race of heretics and the ungodly, restore order, and restore to each his good: "reddet cuique suum bonum".
61. There will be, so to speak, only two empires in Europe, the Eastern Empire and the Western Empire.
62. Russia will convert and help France restore peace and tranquility to the world. But above all, they will restore the reign of religion and the authority of the Church.
63. Under the reign of this Great Monarch, all justice will be done. The Catholic religion will flourish throughout the universe, except in Palestine, a country of curse.
64. Full of the spirit of God, he will weigh the merit of each person like gold in the scales and will do him the most scrupulous justice.
65. Those who possess stolen goods will be the first to return them. National assets will be taken away from their buyers.
66. Then he will only take the crown and place it on the head of his direct heir.
67. God, at the same time, will raise up the holy Pontiff, who, supported by the great Monarch (called "Auxilium Dei"), "The Help of God" will exterminate all the heretical sects, all the superstitions of the Gentiles, will spread and shine more than ever the reign of the Catholic Church in all the Universe, except in the infernal region of Palestine, a country of curse where the Antichrist must be born.
68. Under the reign of the Great Monarch, religion will be honored and God glorified as it has not been for centuries; the greatest virtue will be observed around the world and the earth will produce fruit in abundance.
69. After the crisis, despite certain oppositions made by the clergy themselves, everything will end with a general and decisive Council to which the entire universe will submit until the last persecution, that of the Beast, or the Antichrist. (**Note**: There will be one last great council held in which all will be restored, until the coming of the Antichrist.)
70. Then there will be one flock and one shepherd, because all the infidels and all the heretics, but not the Jews, whose mass will be converted after the death of the Beast, will enter the Latin Church, whose triumph will continue until the destruction of the Antichrist.

Jeanne Royer (Sister of the Nativity) (1731–98)

The good sister of Nativity was a sensible soul and profoundly devoted to God, King and country. When the horrid and barbaric revolution in France started to take effect against the French nobility and against the Church, she remained firm in her faith:

On a day when I was praying before the Holy Sacrament, the Lord made me see that the King would be put to death. I begged Him not to allow such a thing. My prayers were too weak...

I see that the century which begins in 1800 shall not yet be the last. The reign of Antichrist is approaching. The thick vapors which I have seen rising from the earth and obscuring the light of the sun are the false maxims of irreligion and license which are confounding all sound principles and spreading everywhere such darkness as to obscure both faith and reason.

One day I heard a voice which said:

The new Constitution will appear to many others than what it really is. They will bless it as a gift from Heaven; whereas, it is in fact sent from hell and permitted by God in His just wrath. It will only be by its effects that people will be led to recognize the Dragon who wanted to destroy all and devour all.

One night I saw a number of ecclesiastics. Their haughtiness and air of severity seemed to demand the respect of all. They forced the faithful to follow them. But God commanded me to oppose them:

They no longer have the right to speak in my name.' *Jesus told me.* **'It is against My wish that they carry out a mandate for which they are no longer worthy.**

I saw a great power rise up against the Church. It plundered, devastated, and threw into confusion and disorder the vine of the Lord, having it trampled underfoot by the people and holding it up to ridicule by all nations. **Having vilified celibacy and oppressed the priesthood**, *it had the effrontery to confiscate the Church's property and to arrogate to itself the powers of the holy Father, whose person and whose laws it held in contempt.*

I had a vision: Before the Father and the Son—both seated—a virgin of incomparable beauty, representing the Church, was kneeling. The Holy Ghost spread His shining wings over the Virgin and the two other persons. The wounds of Our Lord seemed alive. Leaning on the Cross with one hand, He offered to His Father with the other hand the chalice which the Master held in the middle. The Father placed one hand on the up and raised the other to bless the Virgin.

I noticed that the chalice was only half-filled with blood, and I heard these words spoken by the Savior at the moment of presentation: **'I shall not be fully satisfied until I am able to fill it right up to the brim.'** *I understood then that the contents of the chalice represented the blood of the early martyrs, and that this vision had reference to the last persecutions of the Christians, whose blood would fill the chalice, thereby completing the number of martyrs and predestined. For at the end of time, there will be as many martyrs as in the early*

Church, and even more, for the persecutions will be far more violent. Then the Last Judgment will no longer be delayed.

I see in God that a long time before the rise of Antichrist the world will be afflicted with many bloody wars. Peoples will rise against peoples, and nations will rise against nations, sometimes allied, sometimes enemies, in their fight against the same party. Armies will come into frightful collisions and will fill the earth with murder and carnage.

These internal and foreign wars will cause enormous sacrifices, profanations, scandals, and infinite evils, because of the incursions that will be made into the Church.

In addition of it all, I see that the earth will be shaken in different places by frightful earthquakes. I see whole mountains cracking and splitting with a terrible din. Only too happy will one be in one can escape with no more than a fright; but no, I see come out of these gaping mountains whirlwinds of smoke, fire, Sulphur, and tar, which reduce to cinders entire towns. All this and a thousand other disasters must come before the rise of the Man of Sin.

I saw in the light of the Lord that the faith and our holy Religion would become weaker in almost every Christian kingdom. God has permitted that they should be chastised by the wicked in order to awaken them from their apathy. And after the justice of God has been satisfied, He will pour out an abundance of graces on His Church, and He will spread the Faith and restore the discipline of the Church in those countries where it had become tepid and lax.

I saw in God that our Mother, Holy Church, will spread in many countries and will produce her fruits in abundance to compensate for the outrages she will have suffered from the impiety and the persecutions of her enemies.

I saw the poor people, weary of the arduous labors and trials that God sent to them. They shall then be thrilled with a joy that God will infuse in their good hearts. The Church will become by her faith and by her love, more fervent and more flourishing than ever. Our good Mother the Church will witness many amazing things, even on the part of her former persecutors, for they will come forward and throw themselves at her feet, acknowledge her, and implore pardon from God and from here for all the crimes and outrages that they had perpetrated against her. She will no longer regard them as her enemies, but she will instead welcome them as her own children.

Now all the true penitents will flow from all sides to the Church, which will receive them into her bosom. The entire community of the faithful will pour out their hearts in hymns of penance and thanksgiving to the glory of the Lord.

I see in God a great power, led by the Holy Ghost, which will restore order through a second upheaval. I see in God a large assembly of pastors who will uphold the rights of the Church and of her Head. They will restore the former disciplines. I see, in particular, two servants of the Lord who will distinguish themselves in this glorious struggle and who, by the grace of the Holy Ghost, will fill with ardent zeal the hearts of this illustrious assembly.

All the false cults will be abolished; all the abuses of the Revolution will be destroyed and the altars of the true God restored. The former practices will be put into force again, and our religion—at least in some respects—will flourish more than ever.

I see in God that the Church will enjoy a profound peace over a period which seems to me to be of a fairly long duration. This respite will be the longest of all that will occur between the revolutions form now till the General Judgment. The closer we draw to the General Judgment, the shorter will be the revolutions against the Church. The kind of peace that will follow each revolution will be shorter also. This is so because we are approaching the End of Time, and little time will be left for either the elect to do good or for the wicked to do evil.

One day the Lord said to me:

A few years before the coming of my enemy, Satan will raise up false prophets who will announce Antichrist as the true Messiah, and they will try to destroy all our Christian beliefs. And I shall make the children and the old people prophesy. The closer we get to the reign of Antichrist, the more will the darkness of Satan spread over the earth, and the more will his satellites increase their efforts to trap the faithful in their net.

When the reign of Antichrist draws near, a false religion will appear which will deny the unity of God and will oppose the Church. Errors will cause ravages as never before.

One day I found myself in a vast plain alone with God. Jesus appeared to me and from the top of a small hill, showed to me a beautiful sun on the horizon. He said dolefully:

The world is passing away and the time of My second coming draws near. When the sun is about to set, one knows that the day is nearly over and that the night will soon fall. Centuries are like days for me. Look at this sun, see how much it still has to travel, and estimate the time that is left to the world.

I looked intently and it seemed to me that the sun would set in two hours. Jesus said:

Do not forget that these are not millennia, but only centuries, and they are few in number...

But I understood that Jesus reserved to Himself the knowledge of the exact number, and I did not wish to ask Him more. It sufficed me to know that the peace of the Church and the restoration of discipline were to last a reasonably long time.

God has manifested to me the malice of Lucifer and the perverse and diabolical intentions of his henchmen against the Holy Church of Jesus Christ. At the command of their master these wicked men have crossed the world like furies to prepare the way and the place for Antichrist, whose reign is approaching. Through the corrupted breath of their proud spirit they have poisoned the minds of men. Like persons infected with pestilence, they have communicated the evil to each other, and the contagion has become general. The storm began in France, and France shall be the first theater of its ravages after having been its cradle. The Church in Council shall one day strike with anathemas, pull down and destroy the evil principles of that criminal constitution. What a consolation! What a joy for the truly faithful!

One day, Our Lord Jesus-Christ told Sister of the Nativity:

I have chosen since your childhood to stop the multitude of sinners who fall every day into hell... I have communicated to you visions and revelations in order for you to publish them and have them known to My Church. The time is short... What I tell you here, My daughter, will be read and told until the end of centuries.

The General judgment is close at hand, and My Great Day arrives. Alas! So many sorrows accompany it! So many children will perish before being born! So many young (children) of both sexes will be crushed by death in the middle of their journey (to birth)! Children on their mothers' bosoms will perish with their mothers (Abortion). Woe to sinners who will live still in sin without having offered penance!

Woe! Woe! Woe to the last century!

Here is what Our Lord has allowed me to see in His Light. I began to look in the Light of God the century that was about to begin with 1800; I saw through the Light that the Judgment would not be then, and that it wouldn't be the last century; I then considered upon the favor of this same Light the century of 1900, or that of the 2000; but what I saw was that if the judgment came in the century of the 1900, it would only come towards its ending part, and that, if it were to cross the century of the years 2000, the Judgment would intervene within the first two decades; that is what I saw in the Light of God.

Assaults against the Church:

Satan's spirit will inspire, against the Church, leagues of assemblies, of secret societies. The Church will condemn first their sordid doctrine (Freemasonry). Then Satan's supporters will hide in the shadows and will produce volumes of works which will cause a great deal of harm. Everything will be done in silence within an envelope of unbreakable secrecy... It will be like a fire from underneath, without noise and which will be spreading little by little. This will be grave and dangerous for the Holy Church for she will not realize of these fores... Some priests will see the first smokes of the evil fire. They will rise against those who will be noticed has having the preceding signs of lack of devotion and thus separating from the good customs of the Church. These poor followers of those new doctrines will say amongst themselves:

Let us be careful not to be discovered... Let us not reveal what we are about nor what our secret is... In appearance, we must seem submissive like defenseless little children. Let us approach the Sacraments. Let us not debate, but let us act with peace and softness...

When they will see that they have gained a great number of disciples, a number as important as that of a great kingdom, then these thieving wolves will come out of their caverns, dressed with sheep's skins. Oh! The Holy Church will have to suffer ever so much! She will be attacked on all sides by foreigners but also by her own children who, like vipers, will tear apart her entrails and will side with her enemies...

In the beginning, they will hold secret their cursed law. This law will be approved by all their accomplices, but will come out only a few years before the arrival of the antichrist. I see in God that the priests will be surprised of such a change which will come forth without much of an announcing sermon... However, some of the Lord's ministers, more enlightened by the Holy Spirit, will be taken by fear of the incertitude on the outcome of these events...

Oh God! Such distress I see in the Holy Church when she will realize all of a sudden of the progress of these ungodly ones, of the extent of their works and of the number of souls that they will have enrolled in their party! This heresy will spread so far that it will seem to envelop every country and every state. Never has any heresy been more sordid!

Jeanne Royer, the good sister of Nativity, saw that much time will have passed, perhaps half a century or a little more, (sinc) the moment when everything will have begun until the time when the Church will at last realize the dangers that threatens her... In the beginning, this heresy will have a magnificent appearance. It will impose itself by its appearance of kindness and of religiousness... This will be a trap seducing a great number of people:

To better succeed in their endeavors, these sinners will pretend a great respect for the Gospel and Catholicism. They will even publish books of spirituality in order for no one to doubt their holiness. By spirit of curiosity, some people who are weakest in their faith will relieve their curiosity by seeing what this new religion offers. No one has ever seen such lies and deceit under the colors of religion! These proud hypocrites will make beautiful speeches to attract souls that are vain and curious. These lost souls will run to all these novelties, letting themselves be caught in an easier manner than it is for fishes to be caught themselves in a net...

To avoid such sorrows, it will be necessary, with the help of Divine Grace, to attach oneself, in an unbreakable manner, to the Faith. One will have always to remember one's first beliefs (Catholic Faith) in order for the Holy Law of Jesus-Christ to remain, until one's last breath, the support of one's conduct. For the Love of God it is imperative to reject these upcoming extraordinary singularities!

Bernadette Soubirous (Sister Marie-Bernarde) (1844–79)

Everyone knows quite well the extraordinary story of the apparitions of Our Lady of Lourdes, and of the remarkable miraculous pools of water which have healed countless sick and dying men, women and children. It is also well known, that Bernadette Soubirous became a pious and religious nun in the convent of Saint Gilardin in the city of Nevers, where Bernadette Soubirous passed away at the age of 35.

Her body has been found to be incorrupt, and is, to this day, exposed in the young visionary's convent for all pilgrims to come and ask for her intercession. What is less known however, is the fact that the young visionary received from the Blessed Virgin Mary in Lourdes five extraordinary prophetic secrets which were sent in 1879 to his Holiness Pope Leo XIII. A few years later, the holy Pontiff authorized (in 1883) the construction of the magnificent Church of the Rosary to be built above the grotto. Since that time, millions have visited the shrine of Lourdes and countless faithful have been unexplainably physically and spiritually healed.

Pope Leo XIII who followed ever so closely in the footsteps of Pope Pius IX—the Pope who did not proclaim the dogma of the Immaculate Conception, but ruled favorably the apparitions at Lourdes in 1858, giving Ecclesial approbation in 1862—never revealed these secret prophecies sent by young Bernadette Soubirous, nor did his successors... It is somewhat understandable as the contents therein were, at the time somewhat too incredible to accept, and would have had the possible effect of taking away credibility from the apparition site itself; consequently, this document was lost in the course of the years and decades deep in the entrails of the Vatican's underground library.

Notwithstanding, it will be a century later, that a French priest named Father Antoine LaGrande, a researcher on the apparition case of Lourdes, found - deeply covered under a massive pile of folders and books - an old looking iron box without any title sign or sticker upon it... "*Odd...*" He thought, and as he put away the massive pile of documents and books covering the mysterious box, he opened it to find, at his amazement, five pages where were written the five prophecies revealed to Saint Bernadette of Lourdes by the Blessed Virgin Mary!

"It is by the Providence of God that these secrets have been found... and found now, in God's time!" he exclaimed.

The secret prophecies revealed to the young French saint were written in five pages, each revealing a particular prophecy. The first four have already been fulfilled and proven to be unequivocally true. The fifth one... is yet to take place and reveals realities that, although difficult to absorb, sound in our time and age quite realistic.

The First Prophecy of Lourdes

The first Prophecy confirmed that Lourdes would become a renowned center for healing after Bernadette's death, and would see the shrine visited by millions of faithful who come to be physically and spiritually healed.

The Second Prophecy of Lourdes

The second Prophecy dealt about mankind developing, before the 20th century dawned, new technologies among which that of harnessing lighting. There would be important scientific discoveries including "the use of electric energy" and the invention of several types of machines.

The Third Prophecy of Lourdes

The third Prophecy foretold of the terrible evil that would rise in Germany and harm most of Europe... She predicted the rise of an evil dictator in Germany which would cause "something horribly evil". His rule of terror would end in a war in which "nearly all nations will participate".

The Fourth Prophecy of Lourdes

The Blessed Virgin Mary told Bernadette that man will fly in outer space and would walk on the moon around 1970...

The Fifth Prophecy of Lourdes

These are Bernadette Soubirous' exact words written of the fifth page:

Your Holiness, the Virgin has told me that when the 20th century passes away, with it will pass away the Age of Science. A new Age of Faith will dawn around the world. Proof will come at last that it was Our Lord Who created the world and man, and this will be the beginning of the end for the scientists, in whom the people will cease to believe. Millions will return to Christ.

As the numbers of believers swell, the power of the Church will grow as never before. Also causing many to turn their backs on science will be the arrogance of physicians who use their knowledge to create an abomination.

These doctors will find the means to combine the essence of a man and the essence of a beast. The people will know in their hearts that this is wrong, but they will be powerless to stop the spawning of such monsters. In the end they will hunt scientists down as ravening wolves are hunted. On the eve of the year 2000, a final clash between the followers of Mohammed and the Christian nations of the world will take place.

A furious battle will be waged in which 5,650,451 soldiers are killed and a bomb of great power will fall on a city in Persia. But in the fullness of time the sign of the cross will prevail and all of Islam will be forced to convert to Christianity. There will follow a century of peace and joy as all the nations of the earth lay down their swords and shields. Great prosperity will follow as the Lord showers His blessings down upon the faithful. No family on earth will know poverty or hunger. One person in ten will be granted by God the power to heal and they will cast out all sicknesses from those who seek their aid. Many will rejoice at these miracles.

The 21st century will come to be known as the Second Golden Age of Mankind.

Blessed Elena Aiello (Sister Elena Aiello) (1895–1961)

Sister Elena was the founder of the Minim Sisters of the Passion of Our Lord Jesus Christ. Elena Aiello joined the Sisters of the Most Precious Blood but was forced to leave due to her grave health that soon kept her confined to her home where she began experiencing visions of both Jesus Christ and of the Madonna.

Her desire to become a nun was stalled, for her father asked her to delay her entry in the convent until the end of the war (World War I) which was raging in Europe... She agreed and dedicated herself on aiding refugees and countless war victims.

A well renown anecdote involved Elena meeting on one occasion a Freemason named Alessandro and, failing to persuade him to convert and receive the holy sacraments, she insisted and continued to preach at him until, being exasperated to his limit, Alessandro took a bottle and flung it violently at her, striking her on the neck which began bleeding profusely...

Elena held a cloth to it and told him calmly that his soul was in mortal danger and resolutely stated, with her hand and cloth still on her bleeding wound, that she would not leave the room until he called for a priest to convert him. Alessandro became so moved that he told her he'd receive the sacraments on the condition she continue to tend to him which she did for another three months.

In 1920, Elena finally joined the Sisters of the Most Precious Blood—her father directed her to that specific order for an unknown reason—but was later forced to leave that order due to a necrotic shoulder... Elena had her shoulder operated on without anesthetic while holding a small wooden cross and looking at a Marian image, but the inept doctor cut nerves that caused her lockjaw and a vomiting spell for several weeks... hence, Elena could not partake in the vesting, for her superior judged her situation to be so bad that it was decided that she could not participate in said ceremony, thus forcing her departure.

The doctor told her father to sue the order for her ailments (her shoulder now had gangrene setting in) but she convinced him not to do so. Elena also was diagnosed with stomach cancer and couldn't even retain liquefied food which prompted her doctor to deem her condition incurable... She placed her faith in Saint Rita for a cure, which remarkably took place! These conditions were inexplicably healed in 1921. Her intercessor, Saint Rita herself, even appeared to Elena in a dream. Such was the beginning of a supernatural and spiritual life yet to come.

Two years later, Elena began experiencing the stigmata each Good Friday from 1923 until shortly before her death. The first time this happened the Lord appeared in a white garment with the crown of thorns. He then slowly placed it on Elena's head, prompting lots of blood to gush forth. The servant Rosaria was about to leave the house when she heard wailing and was petrified to see Elena covered in blood, believing someone murdered her. Rosaria rushed to get help.

When she returned with Elena's family members, they all saw the blood but saw she was still alive and so ran outside the street to bring a doctor and several priests. Upon arrival, the doctor attempted to halt the bleeding but could not do so for three hours! But at the end, the blood flow stopped, and the Italian woman fell asleep to regain consciousness, perfectly normal...

Years later, Elena also started experiencing visions of the Blessed Mother in 1947; she made predictions of future events following these visions. Elena also experienced visions of Jesus Christ and of various saints such as Saint Francesco di Paola and Saint Thérèse of Lisieux.

On 28 January 1928, she founded on her own a new religious order that she named the Minim Sisters of the Passion of Our Lord Jesus Christ. His holiness Pope Pius XII knew of Elena Aiello's story, and was the one who issued pontifical approval for the order in July 1949.

On 22 April 1940, Our Lord Jesus-Christ appeared to her, and told her to deliver a message to Benito Mussolini to tell him not to join Adolf Hitler during the war that started seven months earlier, for that would bring both terrible defeat and divine punishment upon Italy; this plea was left ignored in the form of a letter she had sent to him on 6 May 1940...

Blessed Sister Elena Aiello is remembered as an Italian stigmatic nun who died in 1961, and was beatified fifty years later by Pope Benedict XVI on 14 September 2011.

Blessed Sister Elena Aiello's Prophecies

People are offending God too much. Were I to show you all the sins committed on a single day, you would surely die of grief. These are grave times. The world is thoroughly upset because it is in a worse condition than at the time of the deluge. Materialism marches on, ever fomenting bloody strife and fratricidal struggles. Clear signs portend that peace is in danger. That scourge, like the shadow of a dark cloud, is now moving across mankind: only my power, as Mother of God, is preventing the outbreak of the storm.

All is hanging on a slender thread. When that thread will snap, Divine Justice shall pounce upon the world and execute its dreadful, purging designs. All the nations shall be punished because of sins, like a muddy river, that are now covering all the earth. The powers of evil are getting ready to strike furiously in every part of the globe.

Tragic events are in store for the future. For quite a while, and in many a way, I have warned the world. The nation's rulers do indeed understand the gravity of these dangers, but they refuse to acknowledge that it is necessary for all people to practice a truly Christian life to counteract that scourge. Oh, what torture I feel in my heart, on beholding mankind so engrossed in all kinds of things and completely ignoring the most important duty of their reconciliation with God.

The time is not far off now when the whole world shall be greatly disturbed. A great deal of blood of just and innocent people as well as saintly priests will be poured out. The Church shall suffer very much and hatred will be at its very peak. Italy shall be humiliated and purged in her blood. She shall suffer very much indeed on account of the multitude of sins committed in this privileged nation, the abode of the Vicar of Christ. You cannot possibly imagine what is going to happen!

A great revolution shall break out and the streets shall be stained with blood. The Pope's sufferings on this occasion may well be compared to the agony that will shorten his pilgrimage on earth. His successor shall pilot the boat during the storm. But the punishment of the wicked shall not be slow. That will be an exceedingly dreadful day. The earth shall quake so violently as to scare all mankind. And so, the wicked shall perish according to the inexorably severity of Divine Justice. If possible, publish this message throughout the world, and admonish all the people to do penance and to return right away to God.

Listen attentively, and reveal to all: 'My Heart is sad for so many sufferings in an impending world in ruin. The justice of Our Father is most offended. Men live in their obstinacy of sin. The wrath of God is near. Soon the world will be afflicted with great calamities, bloody revolutions, frightful hurricanes, and the overflowing of streams and the seas'.

'Cry out until the priests of God lend their ears to my voice, to advise men that the time is near at hand, and if men do not return to God with prayers and penances, the world will be overturned in a new and more terrible war. Arms most deadly will destroy peoples and nations! The dictators of the earth, infernal specimens thereof, will demolish the churches and desecrate the Holy Eucharist, and will destroy things most dear. In this impious war, much will be destroyed of that which has been built by the hands of man'. 'Clouds with lightning flashes of fire in the sky and a tempest of fire shall fall upon the world. This terrible scourge never before seen in the History of Humanity will last seventy hours (Three Days of Darkness)[31].

Godless persons will be crushed and wiped out. Many will be lost because they remain in their obstinacy of sin. Then shall be seen the Power of Light over the power of darkness... 'Be not silent, my daughter, because the hours of darkness, of abandonment, are near. 'I am bending over the world, holding in suspension the justice of God; otherwise these things would already have now come to pass. Prayers and penances are necessary because men must return to God and to My Immaculate Heart—the Mediatrix of men to God, and thus the world will be at least in part saved.

'Cry out these things to all, like the very echo of my voice. Let this be known to all, because it will help save many souls, and prevent much destruction in the Church and in the world.'

(Our Lord and the Blessed Virgin Mary on 16 April 1954)

The Madonna:

The hour of the justice of God is close, and will be terrible! Tremendous scourges are impending over the world, and various nations are struck by epidemics, famines, great earthquakes, terrific hurricanes, with overflowing rivers and seas, which bring ruin and death.

If the people do not recognize in these scourges (of nature) the warnings of Divine Mercy, and do not return to God with truly Christian living, another terrible war will come from the East to the West. Russia with her secret armies will battle America and will overrun Europe. The river Rhine will be overflowing with corpses and blood. Italy, also, will be harassed by a great revolution, and the Pope will suffer terribly.

---

[31] Not unlike Marie-Julie Jahenny and Padre Pio's prophecy on the Three Days of Darkness.

Spread the devotion to my Immaculate Heart, in order that many souls maybe conquered by my love and that many sinners may return to my Maternal Heart. Do not fear, for I will accompany with my maternal protection my faithful ones, and all those who accept my urgent warnings, and they— especially by the recitations of my Rosary—will be saved.

Satan goes furiously through this disordered world, and soon will show all his might. But, because of my Immaculate Heart, the triumph of Light will not delay in its triumph over the power of darkness, and the world, finally, will have tranquility and peace.

(The Blessed Virgin Mary on 22 August 1960)

It is also interesting to note that in addition to associating the eschatological earthquake with the martyrdom of a future Pope, Blessed Sister Elena also appears to have foretold that fire would fall from the sky to consume the earth after a great flood which would see "the overflowing of streams and the seas"— which also confirms a mega-tsunami described in other Marian apparitions' prophesies... Finally, a big war is likewise prophesied. Russia and her secret armies (weapons) will sweep Western Europe and very quickly reach the Rhine and invade Italy.

Blessed Anna-Maria Taigi (1769–1837)

Anna-Maria Giannetti was born in Siena on 29 May 1769 and baptized the following day. Because of financial difficulties, her parents, Louis Giannetti and Mary Masi, moved to Rome when Anna-Maria was six years old. In the Italian capital, Anna-Maria attended the school conducted by the Filippini Sisters for two years. Following her schooling, she worked at various occupations, even that of a maid, to bring financial assistance to her parents.

When still a young girl, she married Domenico Taigi, a pious young man but of difficult and rather coarse character. Disregarding these facts, Anna-Maria was more concerned with his virtue, and for the 49 years of their married life she conducted herself with the greatest kindness and mercy, finding ample opportunity to exercise continually the virtues of patience and charity.

Understanding the profound social and moral values of the Christian marriage and considering it, above all, as one of the highest missions from Heaven, Blessed Anna-Maria transformed her home into a real Christian sanctuary with God in the Center of the home. Docile to her husband in every way, she avoided anything which might initiate a conflict with her husband and thus disturb the family peace. Serious and hardworking, she saw to it that nothing lacked to her family and, in so far as one in her impoverished circumstances could, she was generous to the poor. She bore seven children, three of whom died in childhood.

Two boys and two girls grew to maturity and she provided them with the most accurate and complete religious upbringing. Anna-Maria had one desire only: to love God and to serve Him in everything; she had only one preoccupation: to please God. She was greatly devoted to the Holy Eucharist, to the Most Holy Trinity, to the Infant Jesus, to the Sacred Passion of Our Lord, and had a most tender and profound devotion to Our Lady.

Anna-Maria Taigi was unquestionably one of the greatest mystics of the 19th century; and yet, she achieved her sanctification by living the ordinary life of a wife and a mother in a spirit of Christian mission and always in compliance with God's will. Her daily attendance at Mass, her total surrender to God, her readiness to help anyone in need, and her being an active member of the Third Order of the Most Holy Trinity were, at the same time, the sources and the fruits of her intense spiritual life.

One of her closest friends was Blessed Elizabeth Canori-Mora, who was a wife and mother as well. They helped and supported each other in their marriages and difficulties, and grew together in holiness and sanctity. Blessed Anna Maria entered the Third Order of the Most Holy Trinity on 26 December 1808.

God enriched her with many supernatural gifts. The most unusual of these was the apparition of a luminous globe like a miniature sun, which shone before her eyes and in which, for 47 years, she could see present and future events anywhere in the world as well as the state of grace of individuals, living or dead. Anna-Maria Taigi died 9 June 1837.

In testimony to how an ordinary housewife and mother could become a saint and positively affect society and the lives of those who came in contact with her, the Church declared her "Blessed" in 1920. Her mortal and incorrupt remains lie in the Chapel of the Madonna in the Basilica of San Crisogono in Rome, Italy.

Anna-Maria Taigi's Extraordinary Prophecies

God will send two punishments: one will be in the form of wars, revolutions and other evils; it shall originate on earth. The other will be sent from Heaven. There shall come over the whole earth an intense darkness lasting three days and three nights. Nothing can be seen, and the air will be laden with pestilence which will claim mainly, but not only, the enemies of religion. It will be impossible to use any man-made lighting during this darkness, except blessed candles. He, who out of curiosity, opens his window to look out, or leaves his home, will fall dead on the spot.

During these three days, people should remain in their homes, pray the Rosary and beg God for mercy. On this terrible occasion so many of these wicked men, enemies of His Church, and of their God, shall be killed by this divine scourge, that their corpses around Rome will be as numerous as the fishes, which a recent inundation of the Tiber had carried into the city. All the enemies of the Church, secret as well as known, will perish over the whole earth during that universal darkness, with the exception of some few, whom God will soon after convert. The air shall be infested by demons, who will appear under all sorts of hideous forms.

After the three days of darkness, Saints Peter and Paul, having come down from Heaven, will preach throughout the world and designate a new Pope. A great light will flash from their bodies and settle upon the cardinal, the future pontiff. Then Christianity will spread throughout the world. Whole nations will join the Church shortly before the reign of the Antichrist. These conversions will be amazing.

Those who survive shall have to conduct themselves well. There shall be innumerable conversions of heretics, who will return to the bosom of the Church; all will note the edifying conduct of their lives, as well as that of other Catholics. Russia, England and China will come into the Church.

France will fall into frightful anarchy. The French people shall have a desperate civil war, in which old men themselves will take up arms. The political parties having exhausted their blood and their rage, without being able to arrive at any satisfactory understanding, shall at the last extremity agree by common consent to have recourse to the Holy See. Then the Pope shall send France a special legate, in order that he may examine the state of affairs and the dispositions of the people. In consequence of the information received, His Holiness himself shall nominate a most Christian king for the government of France...

Religion shall be persecuted, and priests massacred Churches shall be closed, but only for a short time. The Holy Father shall be obliged to leave Rome.

Marcelle Lanchon (Sister Marie-France) (1891-1933)

Sister Marie-France was born in Rouen on 31 December 1891. She belonged to the Group named: "Les Enfants de Marie" (The children of Mary) and was one of the first members of the **Pious Union of the Adorators of the Heart of Jesus**, an association founded by a few pious souls, all members of "the Children of Mary", guided by Canon Vaury.

Marcelle Lanchon became Sister Marie-France; she died of tuberculosis on 20 October 1933 at the age of 41...

The Bishop of Versailles, Mgr. Roland-Gosseling, Bishop of Versailles since 1931 until 1952, formally approved the **Pious Union of the Adorators of the Heart of Jesus**. This union was a sort of third order. It was officially authorized and approved on 29 April 1939 by Mgr. Roland-Gosselin which allowed the printing of the picture of Mary, Queen of France. Mgr. Roland-Gosselin approved as well the apparitions to Sister Marie-France, but the Catholic Church Hierarchy did not pronounce itself formally despite the French Bishop of Versailles' formal approval.

On 8 September 1914, we know that on that day, the Blessed Virgin Mary stopped the German advance towards Paris during the famous battle of the Marne (see page 249). On this miraculous day, at 10:00 in the morning, Marcelle Lanchon, who was at the time 23 years old, was praying in the chapel of Notre Dame des Armées (Our Lady of Armies) on four, Impasse des Gendarmes in Versailles.

Suddenly, the Mother of God, surrounded by St. Therese of the Little Flower and of St. Michael the Archangel appeared to the pious young French woman and told her:

If in union with my Son, I love all the nations which He has redeemed with His Blood, see how I particularly cherish your dear country. My Son desires that pictures and statues representing me this way be made, and that I be invoked under the invocation of Queen of France. If this new desire of His Divine Heart is answered favorably, France will become once again most particularly mine; I shall take her under my maternal protection, and my Son will be pleased in granting her abundant graces.

Then, the Blessed Virgin Mary began to pray to her beloved Son:

My Son, forgive her; she loves You still since she never stopped loving me…

(8 September 1914)

On the same day of 8 September 1914, the Blessed Virgin Mary appeared a second time "surrounded by clouds". Her feet seemed to rest on half of a globe; the word **France** was inscribed on the left of the Virgin Mary in a blue cloak adorned with fleurs-de-lys, edged with white ermine and her hands joined. Suddenly, the Virgin Mary opened her coat, discovering a white dress and a blue belt falling in a tricolor scarf.

On 31 December 1914, Marcelle Lanchon attended the salvation of the Blessed Sacrament in the Chapel of Our Lady of the Armies. Suddenly, Our Lord Jesus-Christ appeared to her standing on the high altar, wearing a white tunic and bearing the marks of his Passion. He wore a tricolor stole. On the blue was his Heart surmounted by a cross and surrounded by a crown of thorns. Marcelle saw Saint Joan of Arc on His left and Saint Michael the Archangel on His right.

Jesus says:

I want to see the image of My Heart painted on the flags.

Marcelle made a vow of a victim on 11 June 1915. Four days later, while she was praying in this same chapel, Our Lord Jesus-Christ appeared to her a second time, in a supernatural light, dressed in the same scarf, girded with a golden crown adorned with fleurs de lys and a purple cloak. His feet rested on a terrestrial globe where the word **France** was written in golden letters. His Heart, which he showed with his left hand, crowned with thorns and bleeding, appeared on the white of the stole. On the red was written:

"He wants to reign over France."

Many faithful were present in the chapel at the same time as Marcelle; the ecclesiastical authorities were warned of the facts. But the First World War buried the file and since then nothing was done… On the other hand, very humble, Marcelle wanted the graces she had received to remain ignored. Only her sisters from the Pious Union of Worshipers knew about it. It is thanks to the little journal of the superior, Miss Marie Patron, or Sister Marguerite-Marie, a small newspaper, that the testimony of these apparitions and messages were written at the express request of Canon Vaury.

The Blessed Virgin Mary taught Sister Marie-France the following prayer:

O Mary, conceived without sin, Our good Mother who wanted us to invoke you under the invocation, ever so consoling to our hearts, of Queen of France, look upon your subjects who, prostrated at your feet are ever so sorrowful.
Have mercy on us; be our advocate before your Divine Son, our Beloved King.
We know we have greatly offended Him, even outraged Him; we have despised His Commandments, stepped underfoot the Holy Laws of His Church; but we know as well, O kind Sovereign Queen, that you are all-powerful upon the Heart of this King of Love who He, Himself only asks to forgive. Kindly obtain for us this national and individual peace so much desired by all for the great glory of your dear Son. Amen.

Prophecies

The Canon Vaury wished to be made aware of Sister Marie France's visions in writings, since he was not at the Congregation site in Chesnay. It is thanks indeed to the little diary of the Mother Superior, Sister Marguerite Marie, that we know of the visions and revelations to Sister Marie France:

France will no longer be called France, but New France.
It will be thanks to Brittany that she will not be cursed by God.
They will wonder for a long time why there remained a green leaf on the dead branch of France...
Versailles, which will have as its motto "between Heaven and earth", will see the Virgin Mary enthroned Queen of France, by the King of the Sacred Heart (King Henry V of the Cross).
He will come at the foot of the gates of the castle, and he will give his crown to King Louis XVI and the diadem to Marie Antoinette before the people of France that will be in such bad health that he will have tears in his eyes. This king will be more like a priest than a monarch. He will rebuild his cathedrals with the help of all nations.

Conclusion

*A*fter finishing these nine chapters and dotting the very last line of the last page, I put down my pen on my desk with a long sigh, and closed my eyes pondering of the overall picture that these puzzle-pieces displayed all together... The message that Heaven is and has been sending to mankind for the past one hundred and seventy-five years is truly of the gravest and most serious importance, and only a person blinded by an obstinate denial or by bad faith would fail to see the accent of authenticity in these extraordinary admonitions.

The same message, call and the prophetic warnings through different times, peoples and places, which at the time of their disclosure did not always fit the contemporary geopolitical scene, today are rediscovered as a perfect match to today's world stage, and yet the Church chooses to still remain quiet... Indeed, the prophetic messages of an Islam, that was utterly insignificant in the 19th and early 20th century, has grown today to a one billion and a half faithful religious structure in nations where imams sponsor, from the rims of the pacific ocean to the Atlantic edges of Africa and Europe, an alarming holy war against Israel and against the infidels of the West.

Its virulent and aggressive nature has already engendered armed conflicts and murderous acts of terrorism not merely in the usual third world countries, but in the heart of the United States and throughout Western European countries... Through an unrestrained and massive immigration, Muslim populations have proliferated by the millions throughout a naïve and liberal European continent that has opened blindly its borders for the past 50 years.

Consequently, this sophomoric overture towards Arabic and African populations have caused today an irresolvable problem involving a gradual population-replacement and an alarmingly growing terrorism coming from a part of a people which refuses to assimilate to its hosting countries' laws and cultures. These new so called "Communautarist European societies"—consisting principally of second, third, and even fourth generation Algerians, Moroccans, Tunisians, Libyans, Turks, Pakistanis, Afghans, Syrians, and Sub-Saharans—harbor a profound feeling of resentment towards their European hosting countries, and most particularly towards France due to its religious roots and to its past colonization of their native homelands.

Likewise, Muslim dogma, such as the Sharia, dictates within growing Muslim communities irreconcilable differences with European laicity by-laws. Consequently, today entire European suburbs, municipalities, and districts are today no longer subject to the laws of the hosting nations but of that of a Fundamentalist Islam, and as terrorism progresses whereas the victims are mostly Christians and Jews, the aggressors always perpetrate their crimes under the war-cry of "Allah Akbar!". To take but an example: the country of France, a nation which has suffered the largest loss of victims to Islamic terrorism these past ten years, is the perfect illustration of a European country projecting today a foreign nation within its own borders.

The storm will break over France where I wanted to show the prodigies of My Divine Heart and unveil its secrets. My children, France will be the first to be wounded, torn, persecuted. When I showed this Divine Sun to Blessed Margaret-Mary, I let my lips utter these words: 'The land which saw your birth and which will see your death, will be in dire danger, especially from 80 to 83.[32]'

I let My humble servant understand that the third one will be full of sorrows. There will 'be nothing but apostasies and violations in the Orders of the persons who are consecrated to Me, whether in the priesthood or the religious life.

(Our Lord Jesus-Christ to Marie-Julie Jahenny, June 1882)

Elsewhere, a newly reborn Christian-Orthodox Russia—that doesn't bother compromising with neither Muslim demands of integration, nor with social or cultural Western liberalism—is jealously defending its borders, its national identity and its independence, rearming at an alarming rate (that goes beyond Western expectation), and moving into a most concerning "alliance of convenience" with a wide awaken China whose ambition in the Pacific and Indian oceans holds no longer any limit... Evidently today, a red line has now been drawn.

On one hand, the United States and its conventional allies: the European Union (N.A.T.O), Israel, the kingdoms of the Middle-East, Japan, South Korea Australia/New Zealand; and on the other, Russia, China, North Korea and some Islamic nations (*beginning with Iran, Syria, part of Iraq and others who harbor a profound hatred for the Zionist state of Israel, but who, for the moment, are buying quietly their time*).

Today's world crisis falls perfectly in the script forewarned in the apparitions of the Blessed Virgin Mary to the mystics, saints and visionaries we have exhaustively discussed in this book; however, if we are now to believe in the events foretold by the messengers of the Blessed Virgin Mary, the future that now appears imminent, projects an unthinkable tomorrow... The third Secret of Fatima did announce a third World War before the end of the 20th century; however, Maximin Giraud, in La Salette, did say that the Blessed Mother revealed to him that these prophecies would be realized either before the end of the 20th century or sometimes within the first two decades of the 21st century:

---

[32] The years 80 to 83 are **the only dates given in the Heavenly apparitions** to Marie-Julie Jahenny. Could the years 80 and 83 use Marie-Julie Jahenny's death-year as a point of reference (1941)? If so, this would bring the prophecy between **2021 to 2024.**

Everything I am telling here will happen in the next century, **or at the latest in the years 2000.**

(Excerpt of Maximin Giraud's letter to his Holiness Pope Pius IX, 3 July 1851)

"… *The war was supposed to have begun already in 2019, but it was postponed through prayer, through the Rosary…*"

(Our Lord Jesus-Christ to Rev. Father Michel Rodrigue, 2020)

And we have Jeanne Royer, also known as Sister of the Nativity, who wrote:

One day I found myself in a vast plain alone with God. Jesus appeared to me and from the top of a small hill, showed to me a beautiful sun on the horizon. He said dolefully:

The world is passing away, and the time of My second coming draws near. When the sun is about to set, one knows that the day is nearly over and that the night will soon fall. Centuries are like days for me. Look at this sun, see how much it still has to travel, and estimate the time that is left to the world.

I looked intently and it seemed to me that the sun would set in two hours. Jesus said:

Do not forget that these are not millennia, but only centuries, and they are few in number…

But I understood that Jesus reserved to Himself the knowledge of the exact number, and I did not wish to ask Him more. It sufficed me to know that the peace of the Church and the restoration of discipline were to last a reasonably long time.

Here is what Our Lord has allowed me to see in His Light. I began to look in the Light of God the century that was about to begin with 1800; I saw through the Light that the Judgment would not be then, and that it wouldn't be the last century; I then considered upon the favor of this same Light the century of 1900, or that of the 2000; but what I saw was that if the judgment came in the century of the 1900, it would only come towards its ending part, and that, if it were to cross the century of the years 2000, the Judgment would intervene within the first two decades; that is what I saw in the Light of God.

(Jeanne Royer, Sister of the Nativity)

People are disappointed in that what I have ordered to be announced, for men to convert, has not yet taken place… They will think to be able to affront the elected souls who, because of their actions, I shall have delayed somewhat the terrible events that are yet to come.

If in My Kindness and because of the expiation which have been offered to Me I delay the disaster, I do not eliminate it! This does not depend on the judgment of ignorant men! Must I Myself give accounts to those who do not want to know anything?

(Our Lord Jesus-Christ to Marie-Julie Jahenny, unknown date…)

In all the apparitions of the Blessed Virgin Mary, we are told that history and chastisement can be postponed or averted if man converts and returns to God in time. Indeed, in Medjugorje, one of the principal cornerstones of the Gospa's message is that History and natural events can be changed **through prayer and fasting preferably on Wednesdays and Fridays**.

Notwithstanding, if we are not able to draw a calendar for the prophetic revelations given, we are at least entrusted a clear insight as to the time-frame of these prophecies by "observing the signs of the times" through the series of events that are to follow one another according to Heaven's messages. Indeed, according to the revelations given by the Blessed Virgin Mary these are the events that are to take place.

Announced prophecies of the Blessed Virgin Mary (La Salette, La Fraudais, Tilly, Fatima, Akita, Marcelle Lanchon, Blessed Sister Elena Aiello, Jeanne Royer (Sister of the Nativity), Rev. Fr. Souffrant, Rev. Fr. Pel, Rev. Fr. Rodrigue, St. Padre Pio)

- France will send large numbers of its military force into Arab and eastern countries, leaving France without an important part of its conventional armed forces in its homeland. The French army will struggle abroad and will lose its tactical advantage in various Arab theaters… (This is as well beginning to take place in Syria and Mali).
- Civil unrest will steadily grow into alarmingly violent revolts in France led by workers who find no longer a balance between their daily salary and their survival needs…
- French citizens of immigrant origins will likewise raise protests, revolts and manifestations throughout France, and will bring the country into chaos through countless lootings, destructions, deaths, rapes and burning. Paris is to suffer the largest damage of this upheaval… This is today a reality seen through the pillage in every French public protest that are followed by the violence of the "Black Blocks" and through the burning vandalizing and destruction of Christian cemeteries, churches and Cathedrals in France.
- Geo-political tensions will rise in England, Iran and Israel;
- England will make a difficult decision which will split the United Kingdom into four independent sovereignties (*England, Wales, Scotland, and Northern Ireland?*). Could this prophecy be a future event that is yet to come as a consequence of Brexit?
- A queen will step down (Elizabeth II) and a decision against God's Will shall be reached. A leader of England, or leader(s) of England will be struck by death (Plague, terrorism, accident?).

- Russia will seal an alliance with some Muslim powers in the Middle-East and in Northern Africa.
- The mixing of all rages in France will lead to a national revolution. Paris will be in such a state of blood, fire and destruction, that the National Crisis will force the country's government to flee from France, seeking refuge abroad…; meanwhile, in Italy, a similar civil unrest will take place, bringing back the Communist Party to a position of Power. Rome will likewise see crimes, violence, looting and destruction (the anger caused by Europe's forcing vaccination against the Corona virus is already causing massive and angry protests in Italy and in France);
- The "Warning" or the "Illumination of Conscience" or el "Aviso" will take place throughout the world allowing every single person on earth to see the state of his soul as God sees it. For six weeks and a half, there will be major conversions and confessions throughout the globe.
- Less than seven weeks thereafter, many scientists and politicians will try to explain the phenomena of the "Warning" to major solar activities that caused mass-hallucinations throughout our planet…
- Within a year after the announced global "Warning" "Miracles" will take place leaving undestructible and unmovable signs for all to see (one in Garabandal and another in Medjugorje – *and perhaps in all true Marian apparition sites?*).
- In Rome, Pope Francis, regretting many past errors, will try to restore the Church under Christ's Authority and rectify many past reforms, but he will fail. The Church will go through a sort of "civil war", and Pope Francis will die a martyr… Pope Benedict XVI will then re-appear and try to put the affairs of the Church in order but will fail as well. He will flee Rome due to an all-around unrest and desolation, but will be found. He will die as a martyr as well…
- The seat of Peter will remain empty for a long time, and an antipope will lead the Vatican, and apostasy will spread. Various Episcopal colleges (in Europe) will separate from the Church's Magisterium's authority;
- The revolution in France will take a turn for the worse. As the French government will have left Paris, parts of the French Capital will burn under protesters' fires and disorder, and crimes will reign throughout France. Churches will be sacked, burnt and destroyed. The "mixed-French" (foreign-origin citizens) will put France on its knees through pillage, fire and destruction;
- The Communist party in Italy and in France will come to power and bring shameful anti-social and anti-clerical laws in both countries;
- Various revolutions will likewise gain ground in other Western-European countries;
- A war will start in Europe with Turkey being involved;
- A Nuclear war will start as well with an alliance that will begin between Russia, China, North Korea and Iran against N.A.T.O. the Pacific alliance and Israel.
- Marie-Julie revealed that in times, preceding a war in Europe, the Lord reserved three months of "fatal and terrible" chastisements for France…

- Nuclear attacks will be launched against the United States. Many warheads will be deviated and will not reach their targets; however, **seven nuclear missiles will succeed in reaching their targets in the United States and will cause massive destruction and casualties...** (Nuclear attack from China and/or North Korea?).
- Taking advantage of the chaotic disorder in Western Europe and in the United States, Russia will initiate a lightening invasion of Western Europe, swiftly brushing all of NATO conventional military defenses between its borders and the Northern Sea. Russian forces will reach very quickly the Rhine River where they will pause ever so briefly... Then, they will cross the French border...

  Brief note: For this event to take place, one must assume that if Russia would indeed initiate such a military campaign and reach the Rhine river quickly, it would do so with the condition that its Task Force spearhead's right and left flank be protected and covered on both its flanks, meaning that Scandinavia (Finland, Norway, Sweden and Denmark), Germany and the Benelux countries (Belgium, the Netherlands and Luxemburg), and the Mediterranean Sea would be seized under control. The Mediterranean Sea would have to be secured principally by Muslim/Islamic forces supported by the powerful Russian Navy from the Black Sea. This would mean major naval battles with NATO naval groups. To that effect, Russian hypersonic missile attacks (Flat-Tops killers) would be immediately deployed and launched against American, French, British, Spanish and Italian aircraft carriers, while major air offensives would start at the same time all over the Western European continent. At the same time, it would be logical to assume that the Atlantic Ocean would be temporarily secured through massive submarine activities aiming at blocking the arrival in Europe of U.S. economic and/or military reinforcement...
- After securing the "Blitzkrieg" invasion of Scandinavia, the Baltic states, Poland, Germany, Denmark, Holland, Belgium and Austria, a double offensive will be immediately thereafter launched against England, Italy and France (*no nuclear strike will be exchanged so far...*).
- From the Rhine river, a major Russian task-force will then be launched towards the city of Orléans while a second and somewhat smaller – but still powerful – attack will be thrusted towards Paris and Normandy.
- A major Muslim task force will at the same time disembark in Southern Spain, Southern Italy and on the French Riviera. The battles in Southern France and Southern Spain are announced to be particularly bloody. The battle in Marseille will be particularly horrific...;
- In a matter of 40 days, Paris, Eastern, Northern and Southern France will be completely invaded and ravaged by a Russian/Muslim joined-coalition force... The remnant of the French army, supported by Breton reinforcements will stop at last the Russian main Task Force outside the city of Nantes, and after a bloody battle will push them back. Part of Normandy and Gascony will be invaded, but Brittany and the French Western coast will remain under French control. 'Neither the Eastern

European nor the Muslim armies will ever reach the French Atlantic coast.

- A brief pause will take place while a front in western France will be established and remain for a very short while relatively stable…, until the arrival of the great French Monarch, Henry V of the Cross who will return to France from an eastern country bordering its bounderies (Belgium, Luxemburg, Germany, Switzerland, or Italy?)…
- When the rage of the 'unfaithful' will temporarily pause (in France), a great disease will appear almost suddenly… This chastisement will leave victims as if they were lifeless; they will continue to breathe without being able to speak, with skinless wounds as if severely burnt. This disease will be very contagious and no one will be able to stop it… This will be a punishment of the Lord to bring back many back to the Faith;
- As Paris will be under a very brief Russian occupation (*with Muslim units called to help maintain order and collaboration with French Muslims*), Rome will be invaded and taken by Russian troops which will have its banner float above the Basilica of St. Peter… Some Muslims military units will likewise enter therein. A Pope will be made prisoner in the Vatican itself which will be pillaged and transformed as a jail of sorts. A new Italian collaboration-government will be formed…
- Spain will likewise lose large territories to Muslim armies and Eastern European commando units, and the Spanish King will be forced to flee from Spain for a very short time, only to return victoriously in a war of liberation against the foreign invaders in the Iberian peninsula;
- The Russian occupying force will put in place a "puppet government" in France, with corrupt Frenchmen choosing, in a secret place in Alsace-Lorraine, an illegitimate king chosen from the d'Orleans Family Branch to collaborate with the enemies of France – through a written treaty – and, most likely to gather around Muslim and non-Muslim French citizens;
- Henry of Bourbon (direct descendent of Louis XVI and of Marie-Antoinette) will appear and, with a group of friends and small armed force, will come in France through an eastern nation (*Switzerland? Luxembourg? Belgium? Germany? Italy?*). Armed forces of the illegitimate French king will come to his encounter (*along with a Russian armed force in support?*) but will lose its first combat against Henry's smaller army.
- Henry de Bourbon, called Henry V of the Cross, will join at last the French armed forces from Brittany and take over command, thus beginning his campaign of liberation. At the same time, his cousin the King of Spain will have returned to his homeland to liberate the Spanish peninsula;
- Henry's army will regain quite quickly most of France, pushing back the Russian and Muslim invaders (*and their collaborators*) who will not understand how such a smaller force will be able to overwhelm such a larger coalition one…

- As the Russian army will be forced to withdraw and leave Paris, the city will be hit by the fleeing Russian forces with two nuclear warheads. One will be launched from the area of Orléans while the other from the outskirt of the city of Reims. The French capital will then be pulverized at night and consumed by a violent fire and wind which will cause the earth to swallow a burning city within immeasurable depths…
  "These poor souls! In one darkest night, the Center (Paris) will be bombarded, and the victims will not survive…"
  Paris and its suburbs will be reduced to dust, and its grounds will collapse violently in a deep and dark *"bottomless crater"*… In a populated area of over 8,000,000 inhabitants, **the Blessed Virgin Mary tells us, only 88 people will survive**…; Marseille will likewise cease to exist as it will be completely wiped-out from the map, engulfed through a massive tsunami… Two other French cities will be as well completely destroyed (Bordeaux? Rouen?)…
- **Half of the population of France will be completely annihilated**… Some villages in France will be left without a soul.
- Henry of the Cross, victorious against his enemies, will finally reach the remnants of a destroyed French capital… The French King will find among the few ruins and ashes left of what used to be Paris, the Cathedral of Notre Dame partially standing on the island of "l'île de la Cité"; Henry, however will have to wait for weeks for a Prelate to come to anoint him and crown him King of France…
  Henry of the Cross will be crowned at last in the Cathedral of Notre-Dame ("in the Middle of the Center") by a young bishop of Aachen, who will come with four other French bishops, to crown him in Paris, and later in the Cathedral of the liberated city of Reims(**[31]**) where the French newly crowned monarch will finally be known as Henry V of the Cross, King of France and of Navarre. The Spanish King, in the meantime, will liberate likewise the remaining parts of Spain.
- The illegitimate French king of the House of the d'Orléans family will step down humiliated and ashamed, leaving the Crown of France to King Henry V of the Cross.
  Once France and Spain are freed (the re-conquest of France is to last seven months), both kings will join-up forces and a Franco-Spanish army (made-up of mostly French forces) will move in Northern Italy to free the Pontiff who has been kept prisoner in the Vatican for now two years and a half. This new Pope will be angelic and chosen by God. Notwithstanding, France will come out of the war suffering overwhelming destruction…
- Italy, in the meantime will have suffered a great deal as the Church will have been persecuted and the Christians hunted as the Jews were during the Second World War… Most bloody carnage in Italy will have taken place under a Germano-Turk leader who will come from Iran under the name of **Archel de la Torre.**
- Five months after peace is reestablished in France by King Henry V of the Cross, a revolution like no other will start in Rome… The horrible war in Italy will be long; it will last for more than two years… There

497

will be many admonitions from Heaven during these difficult moments to open the eyes of those (whose hearts) are harder.

Once Rome and the Pope are freed, God's chastisements will take place through the great three days of darkness which will put to an end to all armed conflicts... Major world Earthquakes, massive tsunamis, mountains splits and collapses, rains of fire, meteorites falls, volcanos explosions will reshape the world map in the course of three days of Darkness and will have the earth's axis wobble unevenly for three years thereafter...

- After the announced Three Days of Darkness end, the world will find in itself in utter consternation, agonizing and on its knees... **Three quarters of the global population will have perished...**
- Entire countries will have disappeared... Immense territories will have been burned through a horrid rain of fire (*meteorites?*). The earth will be covered with corpses and will appear as a giant cemetery... **One of the regions of the world less affected by these cataclysmic events will be the region of Brittany([32]) in France.**

The war will immediately cease for lack of combatants and man's will to fight... King Henry V of the Cross' enemies will seek immediate terms for peace and will convert to Catholicism which will be reborn throughout the world under the guiding leadership of an angelic and holy new Pope and under King Henry V.

- (We are told that all three Crisis should last approximately three years...);
- King Henry will set the terms for peace and will return to La Fraudais where he will have a magnificent Cathedral (Basilica) built, and from where he will order other basilicas, convents, monasteries, churches and Cathedrals to be built or re-built throughout France.
- A long era of peace under the guidance of the Pope and of King Henry will begin.

I cannot emphasize this more, this is but a mere speculation on my part, however, if we are to consider the only dates given in La Fraudais to Marie-Julie Jahenny: year 80 to 83 (from the date of Marie-Julie Jahenny's passing-away—1941?), and Garabandal's possible earliest date for the sign on the hill of the Pines, the year 2022 might be of the utmost importance in the prophesies of the Blessed Virgin Mary;

France sending more troops to Arab lands (Syria, Chad, Jordan, etc.), civil unrest increasing throughout France to pre-civil war levels, and, as of late, the first world pandemic virus contagion (Covid-19 and its endless list of variants)... Naturally, this future is not written in stone and the future can still be changed if, as our Lady of Fatima implored us over a century ago, man converts in time; notwithstanding, one thing remains certain, all the signs appear to announce a certain imminence, but all is at the feet of the Cross and in God's hands.

"If people do what I tell you, many souls will be saved. If my requests are granted, Russia will be converted and there will be peace. If not, she will scatter her errors throughout the world, provoking wars and persecution of

the Church. The good will be martyred, the Holy Father will have much to suffer, and various nations will be destroyed... But in the end, my Immaculate Heart will triumph."

(Our Lady of Fatima, 1917)

The hour of the justice of God is close, and will be terrible! Tremendous scourges are impending over the world, and various nations are struck by epidemics, famines, great earthquakes, terrific hurricanes, with overflowing rivers and seas, which bring ruin and death.

If the people do not recognize in these scourges (of nature) the warnings of Divine Mercy, and do not return to God with truly Christian living, another terrible war will come from the East to the West. Russia with her secret armies will battle America and will overrun Europe. The river Rhine will be overflowing with corpses and blood. Italy, also, will be harassed by a great revolution, and the Pope will suffer terribly.

Spread the devotion to my Immaculate Heart, in order that many souls maybe be conquered by my love and that many sinners may return to my Maternal Heart. Do not fear, for I will accompany with my maternal protection my faithful ones, and all those who accept my urgent warnings, and they—especially by the recitations of my Rosary—will be saved. Satan goes furiously through this disordered world, and soon will show all his might. But, because of my Immaculate Heart, the triumph of Light will not delay in its triumph over the power of darkness, and the world, finally, will have tranquility and peace.

(Message of the Blessed Virgin Mary to Sister Aiello on 22 August 1960)

Surely enough, as Monsignor René Laurentin often stated:

One doesn't have to believe in the messages brought forth by the extraordinary apparitions of the Blessed Virgin Mary, even when they are formally approved and recognized as supernatural from their local bishops and from the Vatican itself. We have already everything in the Gospels.

Of course, this statement is undeniably true considering that no new doctrine can be brought to light that is not already revealed in the Gospels and affirmed by the Catholic Dogma of the Faith; nonetheless, The Blessed Virgin Mary hasn't come to add to the teachings of her Son, but to remind them to us and to incite humanity to live them. The Gospel's teachings today are indeed no longer taught nor infused properly, as they are indisputably and utterly rejected by a Society that spouses today a notion of easy compromise, convenience, and immediate self-satisfaction such as free-fornication, abortion[33], pedophilia, euthanasia, homosexuality, recreational drug-use, and the more and more

---

[33] Abortion breaks new records every year, and has become today one of society's preferred method of contraception.

common practice of a paganism that professes anti-Christian doctrines and values.

Consumerism, globalism, egoism are likewise mirages that blind men away from the Faith, while abortion becomes a most effective medium of contraception and of population growth-control, ridding society of the unwanted and of the weakest.

Finally, there are as well the "puppet-masters", those who behind the international, and financial scenes have subscribed, in the shadows of their most exclusive and secret societies, into *the* antichristian ideology with, for sole aim, the pursuit of domination and ultimate power through the control of every major pillar of Western Society: financial, governmental, political, civil, scientific, industrial, and religious.

We have been warned of these "secret societies" as early as the 17th century from, of all places, the city of Quito, Ecuador, from a small convent of nuns whose prioress, Mother Mariana de Jesús Torres, was blessed of the gift of miraculous visions and stigmata (see chapter: VI). The Blessed Virgin Mary's first warnings of Freemasonry for the future people of the 20th century through the Spanish prioress were clear and certainly not subject to any interpretation but one.

Thus, I make it known to you that from the end of the 19th century and from shortly after the middle of the 20th century, in what is today the Colony which will then be the Republic of Ecuador, the passions will erupt and there will be a total corruption of customs, for Satan will reign almost completely by means of the *Masonic sects*. They will focus principally on the children in order to sustain this general corruption. Woe to the children of these times! (...) As for the Sacrament of Matrimony, which symbolizes the union of Christ with His Church, it will be attacked and deeply profaned. *Freemasonry*, which will then be in power, will enact iniquitous laws with the aim of doing away with this Sacrament, making it easy for everyone to live in sin and encouraging the procreation of illegitimate children born without the blessing of the Church.

During that epoch, the Church will find herself attacked by terrible hordes of *the Masonic sect*, and this poor Ecuadorian land will be agonizing because of the corruption of customs, unbridled luxury, the impious press, and secular education.

(...) *the [Masonic] sect*, having infiltrated all the social classes, will be so subtle as to introduce itself into domestic ambiences in order to corrupt the children, and the Devil will glory in dining upon the exquisite delicacy of the hearts of children.

(Messages of the Blessed Virgin Mary to Mother Mariana de Jesús Torres, 21 January 1610, 2 February 1610, 2 February 1634)

These truly fantastic revelations and references—formally approved by the Roman Catholic Church—took place about one century before Freemasonry became ever known... It was indeed, only in the year 1717 that freemasonry was ever introduced into Society when the first four Freemason lodges in London formed the first "Grand Lodge of England"; thenceforth that organization experienced a rapid expansion on the European continent, later to expand in the new world, recruiting members of the elite class of all branches of governments, business and industrial backgrounds... Other visionaries and mystics made as well countless references in their visions or echoed messages on Freemasonry:

(...) Again I saw in vision St. Peter's undermined according to a plan devised by the secret sect while, at the same time, it was damaged by storms; but it was delivered at the moment of greatest distress. Again I saw the Blessed Virgin extending her mantle over it.

(Anne-Catherine Emmerich, 13 May 1820)

Satan's spirit will inspire, against the Church, leagues of assemblies, of secret societies. The Church will condemn first their sordid doctrine. Then Satan's supporters will hide in the shadows and will produce volumes of works which will cause a great deal of harm. Everything will be done in silence within an envelope of unbreakable secrecy... It will be like a fire from underneath, without noise and which will be spreading little by little.

This will be grave and dangerous for the Holy Church for she will not realize of these fores... Some priests will see the first smokes of the evil fire. They will rise against those who will be noticed has having the preceding signs of lack of devotion and thus separating from the good customs of the Church. These poor followers of those new doctrines will say amongst themselves:

Let us be careful not to be discovered... Let us neither reveal what we are about nor what our secret is... In appearance, we must seem submissive like defenseless little children. Let us approach the Sacraments. Let us not debate, but let us act with peace and softness...

When they will see that they have gained a great number of disciples, a number as important as that of a great kingdom, then these thieving wolves will come out of their caverns, dressed with sheep's skins.

(Jeanne Royer, Sister of the Nativity)

I see more martyrs, not now but in the future... I saw the secret sect relentlessly undermining the Great Church. Near them, I saw a horrible beast coming up from the sea. All over the world, good and devout people, especially the clergy, were harassed, oppressed and put into prison. I had the feeling that they would become martyrs one day. When the Church had been for the most part destroyed (by the secret sect), and when only the sanctuary and altar were still standing, I saw the wreckers (of the secret sect) enter the Church with the Beast.

(Anne-Catherine Emmerich, August-October 1820)

All nine chapters in this book bring each a separate a complementary revelation, depicting the events to come in the next few years in France, Europe and the world. Likewise, it reveals hidden truths on the Church: the announced apostasy, the corruption of the Clergy and the infiltration of Freemasonry within its higher hierarchy... Might these prophecies, in their time, have become an embarrassing reality which has engendered the reason for Rome's long silence and utter reluctance to promote these messages to the faithful?

Perhaps, I would even dare to say most likely, however, the message of the Blessed Virgin Mary has been released nonetheless but, alas, to too few faithful... Regardless, when one reflects on the common argument that, despite the Church's corruptions, depravities, miscarriages of morality and good-standing, Heaven's revelations and manifestations on earth are not necessary as *we have the Gospels, and in the Gospels we have everything!*

One cannot help but think at the same time that if Heaven thought it necessary to send again and again a new "Jonah" (*the Most Blessed Virgin Mary*) in different places around the globe, though different messengers in different times of history to call ever so repeatedly Humanity to repent, to convert, to abandon man's evil ways before God's Justice catches up to it, I am forced to ask myself: who might dare to think knowing better than Heaven and thus to say "*There is no need to spread these sensationalistic messages, prophecies and warnings to the masses, nor to pay heed to them! It is an error of judgment to think otherwise*"?

Fortunately for the people of Nineveh, its King made such "an error of judgment" by listening and paying heed to the sensationalistic messages, prophecies and warnings brought forth by Heaven's messenger: Jonah:

The word of Yahweh was addressed to Jonah a second time. 'Up!' he said, 'Go to Nineveh, the great city, and preach to it as I shall tell you.' Jonah set out and went to Nineveh in obedience to the word of Yahweh. Now Nineveh was a city great beyond compare; to cross it took three days. Jonah began by going a day's journey into the city and then proclaimed, 'Only forty days more and Nineveh will be overthrown.'

And the people of Nineveh believed in God; they proclaimed a fast and put on sackcloth, from the greatest to the least. When the news reached the king of Nineveh, he rose from his throne, took off his robe, put on sackcloth and sat down in ashes. He then had it proclaimed throughout Nineveh, by decree of the king and his nobles, as follows: 'No person or animal, herd or flock, may eat anything; they may not graze, they may not drink any water. All must put on sackcloth and call on God with all their might; and let everyone renounce his evil ways and violent behavior.

Who knows? Perhaps God will change his mind and relent and renounce his burning wrath, so that we shall not perish.' God saw their efforts to renounce their evil ways. And God relented about the disaster which he had threatened to bring on them, and did not bring it.

(Jonah, Chapter 3:1–10)

As the preparations for the launching of what was to be formally known as the Second Vatican Council (Vatican II) were well on their way, Pope John XXIII ordered the two envelopes written by Sister Lucia Dos Santos containing the Third Secret of Fatima be brought to him so as to follow suit with our Lady of Fatima's request, and thus have her message conveyed publicly to the world before 1960. On August 17, 1959, Monsignor Philippe (Official of the Holy Office) delivered the two envelopes to the Pope in Castelgandolfo. John XXIII did not open them right away, but instead expressed his wish to read the Third Secret of Fatima with his confessor. A few days later, as he broke the seal of the second envelope (Our Lady's message) and read it silently, to everyone's surprised the Pontiff became suddenly white as a sheet, appearing momentarily alarmed..., then he stated, while quickly folding back the document and nervously placing it back inside its envelope:

This message is not for our time.[34]

Cardinal Ottaviani (Prefect of the Holy Office) read it as well as per instructions of the Holy Father, but on 8 February 1960, a Press Agency Communiqué was sent from the Vatican, stating that the Third Secret of Fatima would not be published, and would not most likely ever be disclosed... The Vatican's communiqué further read:

Although the Church recognizes the Fatima apparitions, She does not desire to take the responsibility of guaranteeing the veracity of the words the three shepherd children said the Virgin Mary had addressed to them.

Despite men's pressing efforts to keep Our Lady's message quiet, God's designs remain unfaltering and steady, while the world today is starting to see before their television sets the unfolding prophecies revealed through Heaven's messengers... The world is at war with itself and with nature (Covid-19). The Catholic Church has been in a steady but alarming decline since the 1960s.

Likewise, Rome, for the sake of attracting larger masses and for the sake of compromise, has evidently allowed within its inner circles a new idealism based on freethinking and self-worship. Often, such reformist ideas openly embrace the Credo of the Protestant Church, particularly that of the Lutheran denomination, which, I regret to say, has severely split the Catholic Church in two. Indeed, some argue that Pope Francis' overture towards other religions and faiths, in contrast with his war-waging against traditional Roman rites, is a dangerous path that steps on basic Catholic principles which have formed, in the past two millennia, the infallible Dogma of the Faith.

A particular message given to Marie-Julie Jahenny in 1904 (13 years before the apparitions of Fatima) exposed the immense sorrow the Church causes Heaven for ignoring, and keeping away Heaven's message from the faithful:

(...) I had the painful sorrow to see placed under seal these last pages which should have been delivered to the world... It's because it involves a great deal of shepherds and the priesthood that they have revolted (against

---

[34] Contradicting Our Lady of Fatima who expressly asked for the third Secret of Fatima to be publicly revealed no later than 1960.

my instructions) and that they folded the last pages of this divine secret... How can you expect for the chastisement not to befall earth?

They go as far as enveloping my last words on the holy mountain and to have them disappear! (They go as far) as making suffer those who devoted themselves for this holy cause with the joy to glorify me in this solemn prediction. It's because these last lines are all about the priesthood, and it was because it was I who pronounced them, who revealed them, that pride was mortified. I show how they serve my Son in the holy Orders, and how they live in all times in their priesthood. How can you expect Heaven to bless them? I do not speak of all shepherds, of all of priesthood, but the number I am exempting is truly small.

They let all the souls wonder (blindly) in utter emptiness. They take care in a very small manner of their salvation. They like rest, good food and good living... My dear victim priests; the true ones are truly few... They love the Holy Tribunal with indifference. They walk up the Altar because they are forced to accomplish this act, but you will see soon their joy for not having to do so any longer; you will see their happiness to be discharged of souls and of their forgiveness. What vain words! What conversations that are ever so unpleasant to Heaven!

What will they (the priests) be on the great day? What will they be in those horrible and unforgettable days! I do not repeat the bad part that you know of my secrets given on the holy mountain.

(The Blessed Virgin Mary to Marie-Julie Jahenny, 4 August 1904)

Apostasy

As these lines are being written, I leave the contemporary examples discussed in this book as testimony to the history of the beginning of "the smoke of apostasy entering the Church". And what greater apostasy than that of Sacrilegious Communions? Indeed, since the election of Pope Francis, it has been widely sponsored – through the Argentinean Pontiff's Post-Synodal Apostoli Exhortation **Amoris Laetitia** – that Holy Communion could be given (illicitly) to remarried couples (without prior annulments of their first marriages) thus ignoring the Sixth and Ninth Commandment)[35], and to non-Catholic subjects married to Catholic faithful (without pre-requiring the sacraments of Baptism nor of First Communion).

In the midst of the confusion caused by Pope Francis' Post-Synodal Apostoli Exhortation **Amoris Laetitia**, a Dubia of Cardinals was formed to ask the Holy Father for greater explanation of what may appear at first glance an utter contradiction with the teachings of Our Lord Jesus-Christ. To date, this Dubia has been ignored by a most deafening silence...

Grave "errors" of the Faith – Amazonian Pan-American Synod of October 2019

---

[35] Sixth Commandement: **Thou shall not commit adultery** * Ninth Commandment; **Thou shall not covet your neighbor's wife.**

In further matters, the well-known and celebrated Cardinal Burke and Bishop Schneider bring to light other dangerous errors which have surfaced from the Vatican in September-October 2019 in the Amazonian Pan-American synod, errors which flirted with heresy and sacrilege, and which present characteristics that dangerously contradict the infallible Catholic Dogma of the Faith... Cardinal Burke and Bishop Schneider wrote that they believed... *their duty to make the faithful aware of six "principal" errors being spread through the "instrumentum laboris"* employed for the October 2019 Amazonian Pan-American synod:

The first error they listed was: **implicit pantheism**—the identification of God with the universe and nature where God and the world are one. This theory is utterly rejected by the Roman Catholic's Dogma of the Faith; consequently, to insist in sponsoring it would be an act of... heresy...

Secondly, Cardinal Burke and Bishop Schneider criticized the notion put forward in the working document that pagan superstitions are *sources of Divine Revelation and alternative pathways for salvation*. This implied Amazon tribes have pagan superstitions that are an *expression of Divine Revelation,* deserving *dialogue and acceptance* by the Church. Citing church documents, Cardinal Burke and Bishop Schneider stated the Magisterium rejects such **relativization** of God's revelation, and instead affirms that there is but one, and only one Single Savior, Jesus Christ, and the Church is His unique Mystical Body and Bride.

Thirdly, Cardinal Burke and Bishop Schneider pointed out the erroneous the theory contained in the document that "aboriginal people have already received divine revelation, and that the Catholic Church in the Amazon should undergo a 'missionary and pastoral conversion.'" The Magisterium rejects such a notion of missionary activity as "merely intercultural enrichment," they argued that enculturation is primarily about "evangelization" that makes the Church a "more effective instrument of mission".

Fourthly, the two prelates criticized the working document for its support of "tailoring Catholic ordained ministries to the ancestral customs of the aboriginal people, granting official ministries to women and ordaining married leaders of the community as second-class priests, deprived of part of their ministerial powers but able to perform shamanic rituals."
"The Magisterium of the Church rejects such practices, and their implicit opinions," Cardinal Burke and Bishop Schneider state, and draw on a number of Church documents supporting religious celibacy and rules of priests' ordination such as Pope Paul VI encyclical **Sacerdotalis Coelibatus** and Pope John Paul II's apostolic letter **Ordiniatio Sacerdotalis** to underline their point.

Fifthly, Cardinal Burke and Bishop Schneider stated that consistent with the document's **"implicit pantheistic views"**, the **instrumentum laboris** "relativizes Christian anthropology" by considering man "a mere link in nature's ecological chain" and "socioeconomic development as an aggression to 'Mother Earth.'" The Magisterium rejects such beliefs that man does not possess "a unique dignity" above "material creation" and the "technological progress is bound up with sin," they strongly affirmed.

Lastly, Cardinal Burke and Bishop Schneider warned against what the working document calls an integral "ecological conversion" which included "the adoption of the collective social model" of aboriginal tribes, where "individual personality and freedom are undermined." The Magisterium, Cardinal Burke and Bishop Schneider reaffirm, "rejects such opinions" and went on to quote from the Compendium of the Social Doctrine of the Church.

Manifestation of Confusion

In conclusion, Cardinal Burke and Bishop Schneider adamantly stated that these "implicit and explicit" errors represent an "alarming manifestation of the confusion, error and division which beset the Church in our day." They added that "no one" can say they were not aware of the "gravity of the situation" and so excuse themselves from "taking appropriate action" for love of Christ and His Church. Given such a threat, they called on "all members" of the Church to "pray and fast" for her members "who risk being scandalized, that is led into confusion, error and division" by the synod text.

Cardinal Burke and Bishop Schneider further wrote that "every Catholic, as a true soldier of Christ" is called to "safeguard and promote the truths of the faith" lest the synod bishops "betray" the synod's mission which is to assist the Pope in the "preservation and growth of faith and morals", recalling that Blessed John Henry Newman—who was canonized during the Pan-American synod—issued two writings in which he "warned against the same theological errors as written in the synod's **"instrumentum laboris"**.

Cardinal Burke and Bishop Schneider closed by calling on the Blessed Virgin Mary and the intercession of missionary saints to the indigenous American people to protect the synod's bishops and the Holy Father *"from the danger of approving doctrinal errors and ambiguities, and of undermining the Apostolic rule of priestly celibacy."*

If these latest disconcerting synod's bases were not enough, various episodes, of the utmost gravity, took place during the course of the synod which involved an explosive but revealing pagan idolatry on Vatican's ground before a benevolently smiling Pope Francis. Indeed, the world-media witnessed live, in the own gardens of the Vatican and within the Basilica of St. Peter, an Amazonian religious priestess presiding over a man wearing a Franciscan tunique and a score of Amazonian Indians giving homage and reverence – *all in adoration with their foreheads on the ground* – to a wooden figure of a pregnant naked Indian woman known as the Amazonian goddess Pachamama[36].

---

[36] **Wikipedia's definition of Pachamama:** Pachamama is *a goddess revered* by the indigenous people of the Andes. She is also known as the earth/time mother. In Inca mythology, Pachamama is a fertility goddess who presides over planting and harvesting, embodies the mountains, and causes earthquakes. She is also an ever-

This non-Catholic cult then started, through its Indian priestess, to pray before Francis:

Pachamama, good mother, be propitious to us! Be propitious to us! Let the seed taste good, that nothing bad happens, that frost should not disturb it, that it produces good food. We ask you: give us everything! Be propitious to us! Be propitious to us![37]

As one could expect, the idolatry of this pagan deity inspired scandal amidst masses of Roman Catholics all across the globe... These rituals which displayed the native Amazonians prostrated on the ground, in adoration before statuettes of the renowned deity called "Pachamama", not only weakened the faith of many Catholics who did not understand how the Church of St. Peter could have fallen so low as to facilitate on its grounds such paganism, but reinforced the firm belief of the various Protestant denominations across the world that such disgraceful display of utter idolatry is further evidence that indeed the Roman Catholic Church is no longer Christ's true Church, thus earning Pope Francis the shameful nickname of... Pachapapa.

Pope Benedict XVI reacts

Pope Emeritus Benedict XVI, who promised to remain silent when he resigned as head of the Roman Catholic Church in 2013, has re-entered the public arena yet again over the controversial subject of priestly celibacy which has been put into question in the Pan Amazonian synod of October 2019. The participants of said synod indeed have been carefully hand-picked by the Vatican, later to be approved by Pope Francis himself to insure a wanted vote-result in favor of an exceptional break of priest celibacy and approval of women ordination in the Amazonian forests of South America.

Unsurprisingly the overwhelming majority of the Synod of Bishops in the Pan-Amazonian Region voted in favor of the pope allowing older, married men to be ordained to fill the severe shortage of priests in South America, but Pope Francis seemed to have been taken completely by surprise when he learned of Pope Emeritus Benedict XVI publicly stating—through the publication of the book **From the Depths of Our Hearts**, co-authored with Guinean Cardinal Robert Sarah—not being able... *to stay silent any longer*... by defending the traditional Roman Catholic position on priest celibacy.

The publication of this extraordinary book has been widely interpreted as a fervent opposition to what many suspect has been Pope Francis' carefully plotted synod to justify a first step to do away with celibacy in religious life. Indeed, the masterful work in **"From the Depths of Our Hearts"** clearly defends the "necessity" of celibacy in the priesthood by exposing the utterly evident conflict

---

present and independent deity who has her own self-sufficient and creative power to sustain life on this earth.

[37] Prayer to Pachamama published in the context of the Amazon Synod by the **Fondazione Missio**, an organ of the Italian Episcopal Conference.

of interest married men might have between their obligations as husbands and fathers with their obligations towards their parish flocks.

The French newspaper **Le Figaro** printed excerpts which clearly underline the message conveyed by the two eminent churchmen before the entire Catholic Church as a witness:

"The priesthood of Jesus Christ causes us to enter into a life that consists of becoming one with Him and renouncing all that belongs only to us."

"For priests, this is the foundation of the necessity of celibacy but also of liturgical prayer, meditation on the Word of God and the renunciation of material goods."

"Since a married man is devoted entirely to his family, and "serving the Lord" requires a similar degree of devotion, it does not seem possible to carry on the two vocations simultaneously, which is why celibacy became a criterion for priestly ministry."

(Excerpts of "**From the Depths of Our Hearts**")

In a joint introduction, the co-authors said they had written *in a spirit of filial obedience, to Pope Francis*. However, they also said the current "crisis" in the church compelled them to speak out.

In one particular passage, Cardinal Sarah, who is well-known for his traditional views in the Church, addresses Pope Francis directly:

I humbly beg Pope Francis to… veto any weakening of the law of priestly celibacy, even limited to one or the other region.

It is urgent and necessary for everyone—bishops, priests, and laypeople— to stop letting themselves be intimidated by the wrong-headed pleas, the theatrical productions, the diabolical lies and the fashionable errors that try to put down priestly celibacy.

Both authors added that the practice helps the Church to *"… (protect) her mystery."*

Massimo Faggioli, a noted historian and theologian at Villanova University, told the **National Catholic Reporter** that Benedict's decision to write the book was a **serious breach**:

It interferes with a synodal process that is still unfolding after the Amazon synod… and threatens to limit the freedom of the one pope.

(Massimo Faggioli, January 2020)

On the other hand, in April 2020, Archbishop Viganó stated, in no uncertain terms, to a Portuguese periodical, **Dies Irae**, his views of the Pan-American Amazonian Synod:

Dies Irae:

- *In the middle of Holy Week and after the Pan-Amazonian Synod, the Pope decided to establish a commission to discuss and study the female diaconate in the Catholic Church. Do you believe that this is meant to pave the way for the ordination of women or is, in other words, an attempt to tamper with the Priesthood established by Our Lord Jesus Christ on Holy Thursday?*

Archbishop Viganó:

- *It is not possible, and will never be possible, for the Sacred Order to be modified in its essence. The attack on the Priesthood has always been at the center of the actions of the heretics and their inspirer, and it is understandable why this is the case: a blow to the Priesthood means the destruction of the Holy Mass and the Most Holy Eucharist and the entire sacramental edifice.*

  Among the sworn enemies of the Sacred Order there were also the modernists, of course, who, from the 19th century on, theorized about a Church without priests, or with priests and priestesses. These delusions, which were foreshadowed by some exponents of Modernism in France, subtly re-emerged at the Council, with an attempt to insinuate a certain equivalence between the ministerial priesthood deriving from Holy Orders and the common priesthood of the faithful deriving from Baptism.

  It is significant that, precisely by playing on this intentional ambiguity, the reformed liturgy (i.e., the new Mass, introduced after the Council) also suffered from the doctrinal error of Lumen Gentiumand ended up reducing the ordained Minister to the (status of a) simple president of an assembly of priests. To the contrary; the priest is an alter Christus, not by popular designation, but by ontological configuration to the High Priest, Jesus Christ, whom he must imitate in the holiness of his life and in his absolute dedication represented also by Celibacy.

  The next step had to necessarily be taken, if not by annulling the Priesthood itself, at least by making it ineffective by extending it to women, who cannot be ordained: exactly what happened in the Protestant and Anglican sects, which today also experience the embarrassing situation of having lesbian female bishops in the so-called Church of England.

  But it is clear that the ecumenical 'pretext'—that is, drawing closer to dissident communities by acquiring even their most recent errors—is based on Satan's hatred for the Priesthood and would inevitably lead the Church of Christ to ruin.

  On the other hand, ecclesiastical Celibacy is also the object of the same attack, because it is distinctive of the Catholic Church and constitutes a precious defense of the Priesthood that Tradition has jealously guarded through the centuries.

The attempt to introduce a form of ordained female ministry within the Church is not recent, despite repeated statements by the Magisterium. John Paul II also unequivocally defined, and with all the canonical requirements of an infallible ex Cathedra declaration, that it is absolutely impossible to question the doctrine on this subject. But just as it was possible to fiddle with (metter mano) the Catechism to declare the death penalty 'not in conformity with the Gospel'—something unheard of and heretical—so today an attempt is being made to create ex novo some form of female diaconate, evidently preparatory to a future introduction of the female priesthood.

The first commission created by Bergoglio years ago gave a negative opinion, confirming what should not even have been the subject of discussion; but if that commission could not obey the wishes of Francis, this does not mean that another commission, whose members, chosen by him, are more 'docile' and relaxed in demolishing another pillar of the Catholic Faith, may not do so.

I do not doubt that Bergoglio has persuasive methods and that he can exert pressure on the theological commission; but I am equally certain that in the unfortunate event that this consultative body were to give a favorable opinion, it would not necessarily require an official declaration by the Pope to see a multiplying of deaconesses in the dioceses of Germany or Holland, with Rome remaining silent.

The method is well known, and on the one hand it makes it possible to strike at the priesthood while on the other it gives a convenient alibi to those within the ecclesiastical structure who can always appeal to the fact that 'the Pope has not allowed anything new.' They did likewise by authorizing the Episcopal Conferences to legislate autonomously about Communion in the hand, which, imposed by abuse, has now become universal practice. It should be said that this will to promote women in the hierarchy betrays the urge (of such movements within the Church) to follow the modern mentality that has taken away the woman's role of mother and wife in order to unhinge the natural family.

Let's keep in mind that this approach to the Church's dogmas confirms an undeniable fact: Bergoglio has adopted the so-called "situation theology", whose theological pillars are accidental facts or subjects: the world, nature, the female figure, young people... This theology does not have God's immutable and eternal truth as its founding center; on the contrary, it starts from the observation of whatever is the current pressing need of these phenomena in order to give answers that are consistent with the expectations of the contemporary world.

Dies Irae:

- *Your Excellency, according to historians of recognized merit, the Second Vatican Council represented a rupture of the Church with Tradition; hence the appearance of currents of thought that want to transform it into a simple humanitarian association that embraces the world and its globalist utopia. How do you see this serious problem?*

Archbishop Viganó:

- *A Church that presents herself as new with respect to the Church of Christ is simply not the Church of Christ... The Mosaic Religion, that is, the 'Church of the ancient law,' willed by God to lead His people until the coming of the Messiah, had its fulfillment in the New Covenant, and was definitively revoked on Calvary by the Sacrifice of Christ: from His rib was born the Church of the New and Eternal Covenant, which replaces the Synagogue. It seems that also the post-conciliar Church, modernist and Masonic, aspires to transform, to overcome the Church of Christ, replacing it with a 'neo-Church,' a deformed and monstrous creature that does not come from God.*
The purpose of this neo-Church is not to bring the Chosen People to recognize the Messiah, as it is for the Synagogue; it is not to convert and save all people before the second coming of Christ, as for the Catholic Church, but to constitute itself as the spiritual arm of the New World Order and an advocate of Universal Religion.
In this sense, the (Second Vatican) Council's revolution first had to demolish the Church's heritage, its millenary Tradition, from which she drew her vitality and authority as the Mystical Body of Christ, then free herself from the exponents of the old Hierarchy, and only recently has this revolution begun to offer itself without pretense for what it intends to be.
What you call utopia is actually a dystopia, because it represents the concretization of Freemasonry's plan and the preparation for the advent of the Antichrist.
I am also convinced that the majority of my brethren, and even more so almost all the priests and faithful, are absolutely unaware of this hellish plan, and that recent events have opened many people's eyes. Their faith will allow Our Lord to gather the pusillus grex (the "little flock") around the true Shepherd before the final confrontation.

Dies Irae:

- *To restore the ancient splendor of the Church, it will be necessary to question many doctrinal aspects of the Council. What points of Vatican II would you question?*

Archbishop Viganó:

- *I believe that there is no lack of eminent personalities who have expressed, better than me, critical viewpoints of the Council. There are those who believe that it would be less complicated and certainly wiser to follow the practice of the Church and the Popes as it applied to the Synod of Pistoia (a diocesan Synod in Pistoia, Italy in 1786, later condemned on 85 points by Pope Pius VI in Rome on August 28, 1794): there was something good in this Synod as well, but the errors it affirmed were considered sufficient to let it fall into oblivion.*

Dies Irae:

-   *Does the present Pontificate represent the culmination of a process that opened with the Second Vatican Council, desired in the so-called 'Pact of the Catacombs' or is it still in an intermediate phase?*

(**Note**: The Pact of the Catacombs is an agreement signed by 42 bishops of the Catholic Church at a meeting following Mass in the Catacombs of Domitilla near Rome on the evening of 16 November 1965, three weeks before the close of the Second Vatican Council. The bishops pledged to live like the poorest of their parishioners and adopt a lifestyle free of attachment to ordinary possessions.)

Archbishop Viganó:

As is the case with every revolution, the heroes of the first hour often end up falling victim to their own system, as Robespierre did. One who yesterday was judged to be the standard-bearer of the Conciliar spirit today appears almost to be a conservative: the examples are before everyone's eyes.

And there are already those who, in the intellectual circles of progressivism (such as the one frequented by a certain Massimo Faggioli, haughty in his first name and ungrammatical in his surname), start spreading here and there some doubts about Bergoglio's real ability to make 'courageous choices'—for example, to abolish Celibacy, to admit women to the Priesthood or to legitimize communicatio in sacris ("Communion in sacred things," that is, the Eucharist) with heretics—almost hoping that he would step aside to elect a Pope even more obedient to those elites who had in the Catacombs and in the St. Gallen Mafia their most unscrupulous and determined followers.

Dies Irae:

-   *Your Excellency, we Catholics today often feel isolated from the Church and almost abandoned by our Pastors. What can Your Excellency say to the hierarchs and the faithful who, despite the confusion and error that are spreading in the Church, try to persevere in this hard battle to maintain the integrity of our Faith?*

Archbishop Viganó:

-   *My words would certainly be inadequate. What I limit myself to doing is repeating the words of Our Lord, the eternal Word of the Father:*

"Behold, I am with you every day, until the consummation of the ages."

We feel isolated, of course: but didn't the Apostles and all Christians feel this way as well? Did not Our Lord even feel abandoned in Gethsemane? These are the times of trial, perhaps of the final trial; we must drink the bitter cup, and even if it is human to implore the Lord to let it pass from us, we must repeat confidently: 'Not my will, but Yours', remembering His comforting words:

"In the world you will have tribulations, but have courage, for I have conquered the world!"

After the trial, no matter how hard and painful, the eternal prize is prepared for us, which no one can take away from us. The Church will shine again with the glory of her Lord after this terrible and prolonged Easter Triduum.
But if prayer is certainly indispensable, we must also not fail to fight the good fight, making ourselves the witnesses to a courageous militancy under the banner of the Cross of Christ.
Let us not find ourselves being pointed out as the handmaiden did with Saint Peter in the high priest's courtyard: 'You too were one of his followers', only to then deny Christ.
Let us not be intimidated! Let us not allow the gag of tolerance to be placed on those who want to proclaim the Truth!
Let us ask the Blessed Virgin Mary that our tongue may proclaim with courage the Kingdom of God and His Justice.
Let the miracle of Lapa be renewed, when Mary Most Holy gave the word to little Joana, born mute.

(**Note:** In Portugal in the late 900s, nuns fleeing the troops of Almançor, the Caliph of Cordoba, hid an image of the Virgin under a boulder, covering a small grotto. Five hundred years later, in 1493, the image was uncovered by a 12-year-old shepherdess named Joana, who found it after squeezing through the narrow crevasse. Joana was born mute, but when her mother tried to cast the image into a fire, she recovered her speech.)

> **May She also give voice to us, Her children,**
> **who for too long have been mute.**
> **Our Lady of Fatima, Queen of Victories, Ora pro nobis.**

(Excerpt of the interview made by **Dies Irae** (Days of Wrath), April 2020)

If this sad example of yet another controversy was not enough, the Vatican, in the midst of the countless financial, sexual, and doctrinal scandals afflicting the Holy See is seeing yet a new threat whose gravity predicts a most devastating dominoes effect if it were indeed to succeed: the beginnings of an openly orchestrated schism by the German Episcopal Conference... Cardinal Reinhard Marx of Munich and Freising, President of the German Bishops' Conference, has gathered early 2019—against Vatican's sponsorship—a following of German Cardinals and bishops, calling for a German synod to completely review the Universal Church's teaching and discipline on a range of sensitive matters including sexual morality (*homosexuality, acceptance of the LGBT, divorce and re-marriage, etc.*), the role of women in offices and ministry, and clerical celibacy.

Indeed, Cardinal Marx first announced the "*binding synodal path*" early 2019. A secondary subject of this upcoming two year-synod is the creation of a new Synodal Assembly in partnership with the Central Committee of German Catholics, a German Magisterium of sorts acting independently and in parallel fashion as to that of the Vatican's... If this German Catholic movement were indeed to accomplish its objective, how long, one wonders, before other European and/or American Episcopal Conferences follow suit?

Marie-Julie Jahenny:

*The crowd roars around the Vicar of Jesus Christ. A meeting of the Fathers of the Church will form councils against the Father of the universe. It will be presented (*a written declaration*), at the hands of the governor, the Holy Father, a piece of paper written and worked on by hands that, many times will hit the Body of Christ (*The Church*). This written piece will include three things*:

- *That the Pope leaves more liberty to the greater part of those over whom he rules with his authority of Pontiff. (*i.e., they will demand that their obligation of obedience to him be relaxed.*)*
- *We have met (*or we have all united*) and we are of the opinion that if the mortal head of the Church makes an appeal to his Roman clergy to reform the Faith to an even stronger degree, (at the same time when) they want to force us to answer, to declare in the face of the powers of the earth that there must be obedience and submission, we declare (that) we want to keep our freedom. We consider ourselves as free to do nothing more in the eyes of the people, that what we are now doing, and (state) that it is we who will do all.*

Marie-Julie Jahenny:

Bitter and agonizing pain awaits the Pope before such insubordination and disobedience to answer the call of his heart. It will not be in person by which he will make the call, but in writing. The voice of the Flame says that the third thing written will thrill the little people of the earth. It will come from the clergy that aspires to a broader freedom: the clergy of France, Italy, Belgium and many other nations that God reveals.

This will get worse before the people can be assured of the sign of God's wrath...

- *The next call will throw consternation into the hearts where the Faith still reigns. (These bishops) want to break the unity between the Holy Father and the priests of the universe, to separate them from the Head*

514

of the Church, so that everyone is free to itself, and without any supervision... A poster will be (publicly) posted and will only mention this disunion and this separation of the apostles of God with the Pope. The people will be invited to lend support and agreement to the ever so guilty authority (rebellious and treacherous bishops) of that time.

(Marie-Julie Jahenny, November 1882)

In June 2019, Pope Francis wrote a letter to the German Episcopal college offering a "Corrective" to their synodal plans. He warned against a "new Pelagianism" and the temptation to "adapt" the Church "to the spirit of the age". Some argued that Pope Francis responded as a pyromaniac fire-fighter who started the fire in the first place with his open reforms expressed through various speeches, gatherings and writings... The Pope's letter was to no avail, for the German bishops were and remain poised to disregard and even defy the universality of the teaching and discipline of the Roman Magisterium, particularly in matters regarding the position of the Church vis-à-vis the LGBT community. However, incomprehensibly, Pope Francis encouraged two years later the German Synod to continue while refusing Cardinal Marx' request for retirement and replacement!

In 2013, the pope on a return-flight to Rome stated when asked his position on homosexuality: "*Who am I to judge?*" Indeed, the Argentinean Pontiff's position on homosexuality became along the years of his pontificate more and more ambiguous... Such ambiguity could be yet again discerned upon the occasion of his requesting Father James Martin, a well-known Jesuit priest, who had written and published a book sponsoring Catholic LGBTs, to deliver a talk at the World Meeting of Families in Ireland on the summer of 2019...

Pope Francis' endless collection of controversies sadly did not end there as Pope Francis judged necessary to add further confusion by issuing a statement in October, 2020 which proved to be one of his yet most divisive and contentious statement yet, shaking the Catholic Church throughout the world, and leading millions of more faithful Catholics to utter perplexity: the calling for the creation of civil union laws for same-sex couples...

- "*What we have to create is a civil union law,*" the pope stated in his interview with filmmaker, Evgeny Afineevsky in a documentary-film released in Rome in October 2020. "*That way, they (homosexuals) are legally covered...*"
- "*They're children of God and have a right to a family...*"
- "*Nobody should be thrown out, or be made miserable because of it...*"

Such comments were not "*Ex-Catedra*" and thus did not alter Catholic doctrine; notwithstanding such declarations undoubtedly represent a remarkable shift for a church that has fought against LGBT legal rights—with past popes calling same-sex unions "*inadmissible and deviant*". To name but Pope Francis' last two predecessors, his Holiness Pope Benedict XVI called homosexuality an "***intrinsic moral evil.***" In 2003, under Pope John Paul II, the church issued a lengthy document laying out the "***problem with homosexual unions.***" The

515

document, issued by the Vatican's doctrinal office, said that "***Legal recognition of homosexual unions or placing them on the same level as marriage would amount to the approval of a deviant behavior.***" Regardless, it is true that Pope Francis has never postulated any official or direct actions to change Church Dogma on homosexuality, but conservatives have still been repeatedly astonished of the Pope's obvious tolerance and acceptance on the subject, thus reproaching him to have been the principal "catalyst" of the German Episcopal schism taking place today. Likewise, the German Synod, presently openly championed by Pope Francis, is now seen as a reason for yet further reforms regarding the position the Church is to have vis-à-vis homosexuals, transgenders and bi-sexuals. Notwithstanding, Rome addressed the German Episcopal Conference and stated:

"Communion with the whole Church and respect for the hierarchy, are vital to any authentic understanding of synodality."

Cardinal Walter Kasper responded, describing explicitly the Pope's effect on the German bishops:

"In Germany, the Pope's letter was much praised, but then put aside and the process continued as previously planned..."

On September 4, 2019, Cardinal Ouellet, Prefect of the Congregation for Bishops and president of the Pontifical Commission for Latin America([39]), wrote to the German bishops, presenting an official assessment of the German plans from the Pontifical Commission for Legislative Texts, which concluded that:

"... the synod's proposed structures were not ecclesiologically valid, and its proposed subject matter cannot be the object of the deliberations or decisions of a particular Church without contravening what is expressed by the Holy Father in his letter."

Cardinal Marx and his followers remain indifferent and see the German synodal plans as the means of reshaping the global Catholic Church. Cardinal Marx further added to the consternation of the Rome's Curia: *"It is the German Church's duty to lead on the path for others to follow on these matters... There is no question of wishing to break the communion with the Universal Church, but to remake it for a more modern Church."*

In the process of writing this book, it has become to me alarmingly clear that the catastrophic events in the Catholic Church we have been warned against since the apparition of our Lady in La Salette, La Fraudais, Fatima, Garabandal and Akita can clearly be seen today, and more so as the months pass by. In the instances discussed, as we have seen hereinabove, one can no longer say: "***One doesn't have to believe in the messages brought forth by the apparitions of the Blessed Virgin Mary, for we have already everything in the Gospels.***", for knowing the Gospels hasn't stopped men like Cardinal Marx and the greater part of the German Conference of Bishops to enhance what appears more and more like a clear apostasy and schism against Rome, or what, Cardinal Burke, Cardinal

Müller and Bishop Schneider call an *"**alarming manifestation of the confusion, error and division which beset the Church in our day**"…*

Reverend Father Thomas G. Weinandy, OFM is an American Roman Catholic priest and a renowned leading scholar in the United States. He is known in Catholic circles as a prolific writer in both academic and popular works, and has observed closely the Pan-American Synod. Here is an excerpt of an article he wrote on the leading Catholic magazine, "**Catholic Thing**", which was echoed on Raymon Arroyo's show, "**The World Over**" on EWTN, on October 10, 2019:

(…) "As has been often noted, Pope Francis and his cohort never engage in theological dialogue, despite their constant claim that such dialogue is necessary. The reason is that they know they cannot win on that front. Thus, they are forced to resort to name-calling, psychological intimidation, and sheer will-to-power.

Now, as many commentators have already pointed out, the German church is more likely to go into schism. The German bishops are proposing a two-year "binding" synod that, if what is proposed is enacted, would introduce beliefs and practices contrary to the universal tradition of the Church.

I believe, however, that such a German schism will not formally happen either, for two reasons. First, many within the German hierarchy know that by becoming schismatic they would lose their Catholic voice and identity. This they cannot afford. They need to be in fellowship with Pope Francis, for he is the very one who has fostered a notion of synodality that they are now attempting to implement. He, therefore, is their ultimate protector.

Second, while Pope Francis may stop them from doing something egregiously contrary to the Church's teaching, he will allow them to do things that are ambiguously contrary, for such ambiguous teaching and pastoral practice would be in accord with Francis' own. It is in this that the Church finds herself in a situation that she never expected.

It's important to bear in mind that the German situation must be viewed within a broader context: the theological ambiguity within Amoris Laetitia; the not so subtle advancing of the homosexual agenda; the "re-foundation" of the (Roman) John Paul II Institute on Marriage and Family, i.e., the undermining of the Church's consistent teaching on moral and sacramental absolutes, especially with regard to the indissolubility of marriage, homosexuality, contraception, and abortion.

Similarly, there is the Abu Dhabi statement, which directly contradicts the will of the Father and so undermines the primacy of Jesus Christ His Son as the definitive Lord and universal Savior.

Moreover, the present Amazon Synod is teeming with participants sympathetic to and supportive of all of the above. One must likewise take into account the many theologically dubious cardinals, bishops, priests, and theologians whom Francis supports and promotes to high ecclesial positions.

With all of this in mind, we perceive a situation, ever-growing in intensity, in which on the one hand, a majority of the world's faithful – clergy and laity alike – are loyal and faithful to the pope, for he is their pontiff, while critical of his pontificate, and, on the other hand, a large contingent of the world's faithful –

clergy and laity alike – enthusiastically support Francis precisely because he allows and fosters their ambiguous teaching and ecclesial practice.

What the Church will end up with, then, 'is a pope who is the pope of the Catholic Church and, simultaneously, the de facto leader, for all practical purposes, of a schismatic church.' Because he is the head of both, the appearance of one church remains, while in fact there are two.

The only phrase that I can find to describe this situation is "internal papal schism," for the pope, even as pope, will effectively be the leader of a segment of the Church that through its doctrine, moral teaching, and ecclesial structure, is for all practical purposes schismatic. This is the real schism that is in our midst and must be faced, but I do not believe Pope Francis is in any way afraid of this schism. As long as he is in control, he will, I fear, welcome it, for he sees the schismatic element as the new "paradigm" for the future Church.

Thus, in fear and trembling, we need to pray that Jesus, as the head of His body, the Church, will deliver us from this trial. Then again, he may want us to endure it, for it may be that only by enduring it can the Church be freed from all the sin and corruption that now lies within her, and be made holy and pure.

On a more hopeful note, I believe it will be the laity who bring about the needed purification. Pope Francis has himself stated that this is the age of the laity. Lay people see themselves as helpless, having no ecclesial power. Yet if the laity raise their voices, they will be heard. (...) "

Excerpt of the article on "Catholic Thing": "Pope Francis and Schism"
By Rev. Fr. Thomas G. Weinandy, OFM Tuesday, October 8, 2019
(EWTN on October 10, 2019)

In February, 2020, when Pope Francis was expected to give his blessing to the "Amazonian celibacy exception", at everyone's surprise he remained quiet and did not sponsor the allowance of married man to be ordained priests nor of women to be made deacons...; notwithstanding, let us not be mistaken; Pope Francis is unquestionably the most reformist Pontiff since John XXIII, and favors, as we have seen in the Pope's writings the relaxing of Catholic traditional Sacraments while sponsoring tolerance, reconciliation and rapprochement with the Protestant Church, paganism and even atheism. Indeed, such Vatican's unjustifiable compromises with atheism cannot be better demonstrated but through the official agreement Rome has negotiated (through Cardinal McCarrick), signed and sealed in secret with the Communist regime of China. This horrendous secret treaty with the Chinese Communist government has ultimately led to the persecution of bishops, priests and faithful, to the bulldozing of many Catholic churches and chapels, and to countless Chinese faithful going underground; furthermore, as stipulated in the terms of said agreement, the Holy See was to designate government-chosen bishops, all of whom – before Pope Francis' lifted their past Church-given excommunication – had been declared out of communion with Rome for heresy, disobedience and violation of celibacy... Notwithstanding, to respect his furtively sealed treaty with the Chinese government, Pope Francis replaced exemplary Chinese bishops, all righteous and faithful men of the Cloth ready to die for their faith, with shameless men, most of whom are married with illegitimate children, disgraceful men who are nothing short of glorified "bishops of operetta", pretenders under the payroll of the Chinese Communist party…

Cardinal Joseph Zen's Interview

Retired Chinese cardinal of Hong-Kong blasts 'disastrous' rapport with Vatican
(CRUX Magazine)

Retired archbishop of Hong Kong Cardinal Joseph Zen gestures during an interview in Hong Kong, Friday, 9 February 2018.

MIAMI—In a new interview, Cardinal Joseph Zen, a former bishop of Hong Kong and a vocal opponent of Pope Francis's approach to China, has called his contacts with the Vatican during his time as a cardinal "disastrous", particularly on the issue of engagement with Beijing.

He also blasted former top Vatican officials, accusing two successive heads of the Congregation for the Evangelization of Peoples, also known as *Propoganda Fidei*, the Vatican's missionary department with responsibility for China, of shoddy, ineffective policies that did "almost nothing" to help Catholics on the ground.

Zen, the bishop emeritus of Hong Kong, who has consistently voiced harsh criticism of the Vatican's secret 2018 agreement with the Chinese government on the appointment of bishops, voiced his frustrations anew in an interview with *New Bloom Magazine*, an online publication following social and political events in Taiwan and the Asia Pacific region.

Referencing the ongoing, and, at times, violent protests that have gripped Hong Kong since June and put in doubt the future of the territory and its status as an autonomous diplomatic territory, Zen said that at the moment, he is "much more" concerned about the Vatican's recent deals with China.

"The whole Church in China—terrible, terrible. Terrible. Terrible," he said, adding that, "Unfortunately, my experience of my contact with the Vatican is simply disastrous," he said.

Zen was named bishop of Hong Kong in 2002. He got his red hat from Benedict XVI in 2006 and retired in 2009. In his retirement, Zen has become the public face of what can arguably be called the "resistance movement" in China and among Catholicism's more conservative camps when it comes to the papacy's approach to China.

Noting that he was appointed cardinal by John Paul II, Zen said that his red hat was not necessarily of the pope's own accord, but was encouraged by the then-head of *Propoganda Fidei*, Slovakian Cardinal Josef Tomko, who oversaw the department from 2001–2007.

At the time, Zen said China had a more open policy toward religion, and church officials had been able to exchange unofficial contact with the government thanks to Tomko's firm, but "open" policy on engagement with the Chinese Communist Party.

"Tomko was a very balanced man. He started from a hard line to defend the Church from persecution… but he was open to reason," Zen said, adding that some compromise was necessary, but most important was "to say the right position of the Church."

"Unfortunately, in the Church there's a law regarding an age limit. So at 75, Tomko had to retire. Then the successor was no good. And the successor of the successor, even worse," Zen said, referring to Italian Cardinal Crescenzo Sepe, Tomko's immediate replacement and the current Archbishop of Naples, and the late Indian Cardinal Ivan Dias, who succeeded Sepe and later died in 2017.

"Sepe was no good," Zen said, explaining that in his view, *Propoganda Fidei* "did almost nothing" on his watch, but rather attempted weakly to continue Tomko's strategy, "but not really in that spirit."

When Dias stepped in, the decision was applauded given his extensive experience serving in so-called "mission territories," both as a bishop and a papal diplomat.

However, Zen criticized Dias's approach to China, saying he was "a disciple" of Cardinal Agostino Casaroli, a former Vatican Secretary of State who was a firm supporter of an *Ostpolitik* approach to dialogue with communist nations.

At the time Dias was in office, the Vatican's current Secretary of State and the author of the Vatican's recent agreement with China on episcopal appointments, Italian Cardinal Pietro Parolin, was working as an official of *Propoganda Fidei* and in that role, was deeply involved in the Holy See's negotiations with China.

As he has in the past, Zen criticized Parolin and his methods, saying "nobody can be sure" of what he wants at a given moment.

"It's a real mystery how a man of the Church, given all his knowledge of China, of the Communists, could do such a thing as he's doing now," Zen said, adding that in his view, "the only explanation is not faith. It's a diplomatic success. Vainglory."

Zen also criticized Francis's approach, arguing that in his view, given the pope's moves on China, "he has low respect for his predecessors."

"He is shutting down everything done by John Paul II and by Pope Benedict," he said, accusing Francis's allies of giving "lip service" when they insisted the pope's moves are in continuity with his predecessors. "But that's an insult," Zen said.

RELATED: Love it or hate it, Francis's China deal has a deep Vatican pedigree

Zen said that in 2010 Dias and Parolin pitched a draft agreement with China to Benedict, but it was never signed. Zen voiced his belief that Benedict XVI "refused" to sign the document, however, he admitted that he has "no evidence" to back this theory up.

Regarding the current agreement, which has been in force since September 2018, Zen said that although he is one of two Chinese cardinals and has been to Rome three times since rumors of the agreement began to circulate in early 2018, he has yet to see it and, like most, does not know the terms.

Despite his opposition to Francis on the China issue, Zen said that personally they enjoy "wonderful relations," noting that he dined with the pope in July.

However, "he doesn't answer my letters. And everything that happened is against what I suggested."

The main topics Zen said he takes issue with are the agreement, the lifting of the excommunication of seven illicitly ordained bishops as part of the deal, and what he said was the subsequent "killing" of the so-called underground church, composed of those who refused to register with the official, government-sanctioned Catholic Patriotic Association (PA) in a bid to stay faithful to Rome.

"You cannot cheat yourself. You cannot cheat the Communists. You are cheating the whole world," he said, because a person registers PA, "you accept to be a member of that church under the leadership of the communist party."

Referring to Francis's remark on a flight back from Madagascar in September, when he said that while he doesn't want a schism he's not afraid of one either, Zen insisted that if he gets the chance, he's going to tell the pope that he is "encouraging a schism. You are legitimizing the schismatic church in China."

In terms of peacefully practicing their faith independently in Communist China, Zen said that because of the Catholic Church's global dynamic, "there's no hope, no hope at all."

By Elise Harris, **CRUX Magazine**, 4 December 2019

Archbishop McCarrick's negotiation in China

It is today widely known that Archbishop McCarrick had a decisive role in the negotiation with the Chinese government for the implementation of a Catholic presence in China. Nevertheless, his appointment as Chief negotiator for the Vatican was a major issue of controversy as a major scandal was echoed through the well-known and respected Archbishop Carlo Maria Viganò, former Nuncio to the United States, who accused publicly Pope Francis to have misrepresented the truth about never having known about the now infamous American Archbishop's well recorded sexual evidences, nor of Pope Benedict XVI's ordering him to egress from public life, as he himself informed him so of these facts personally.

Consequently, Archbishop Viganò vigorously called... *"Pope Francis to resign..."* for matters of exemplarity, naming with the same breath a string of cardinals and archbishops who, he added, knew as well about the McCarrick infamies.

All the examples underlined hereinabove bring to light—without any wish to undermine the holy office of the Supreme Pontiff of the Catholic Church—a series of numerous crisis's which are splitting the Church in various camps. Notwithstanding, these reports might appear to criticize severely not merely the highest Church Hierarchy, but most particularly Pope Francis—who, in April 2020, publicly stated his refusal to be referred, publicly or privately, as **the Vicar of Jesus-Christ** – but in fact they merely wish to underline the present state of affairs within the Catholic Church in comparison with the extraordinarily lucid forewarned messages brought forth since 1846 by the visionaries discussed in this book.

In retrospective and in view of all the discussed bewildering events in Rome, some argue that the Pope's statements and actions these past few years have indeed been most confusing, to say the least, but reporting in a more "diplomatic" fashion the changes that took place in the Vatican since 2013 would be nothing short of a form of dishonesty, and I suppose a way to lessen or camouflage what is simply extremely difficult to justify.

Before what is clearly one of the greatest crisis period in Church History today, one may feel today the temptation to silent indifference, or to a sense of false neutrality, or worse, to indulge in the enticement of leaving a Church which one may consider to be no longer one… And yet, this is where the apparitions of the Blessed Virgin Mary have such a vital importance, as her soft loving voice can be heard in the hearts of disillusioned men, imploring the faithful to remain loyal to the One true Church of her Son Jesus-Christ, to pray for the Pope, and to stay the course despite the hail storm and high sea-swells that are crashing ever so violently against the ship of Christ.

Despite heresy, apostasy, infiltration, and sedition, loyalty to the Pope, and to bishops remains imperative, but when, and only when, their doctrine does not contradict the Roman Catholic and Apostolic Dogma of the Faith. As St. Joan of Arc used to say: "*God first served*"! Hence, we are not to condemn the Pope nor the Catholic hierarchy, even if one is in sheer disagreement with their established new realpolitik, statements and/or practices; the faithful are called by the Blessed Virgin Mary to pray for the Pope, bishops and priests, regardless of errors, sin, and betrayal. We, as Catholics, are not to condemn the Pope, the Clergy, nor to fall under the trap of being tempted in leaving the Catholic Church, for Christ was very clear:

The gates of hell shall not prevail against it.

Bishop Anathesius Schneider, author of the book **Christus Vincit**, stated in a video interview passed on the John Henry Western Show (4 February 2020):

> *We have to pray for our Mother Church even more in these times of her Passion. We have to say to people that our Mother Church is now enduring…* (short pause) *Holy Friday… because the Church is the mystical Body of Christ, and, by divine permission, God permitted that the Church in the past 50–60 years entered a time really… um… her Way of the Cross… the Stations of the Cross, and I think now that we have arrived in this our current time we have arrived to the Calvaria, Golgotha.*
> *Our Mother Church is humiliated as Jesus-Christ was. (It) is… um… in chains as Jesus was, tied… um… and the day those humiliated our Mother the Church and… not so much (by) the enemies of the Church but, incredibly, (by) the Clergy mostly, and even higher Clergy in the Church. This is the mystery in some ways of Judas…*

(Bishop Schneider, on the John Henry Western Show, 4 February 2020)

Bishop Schneider uses here a very strong language as well (*This is the mystery in some ways of Judas…*), a language that hardly leaves any room for interpretation, but clearly shows that whether a man of the Cloth or a layman, one cannot stay silent before heresy and apostasy without risking to subject oneself to a form of silent complicity. Cardinal Müller, ex-Prefect of the Dycasterium of the Doctrine of the Faith, wrote in his **Manifesto of Faith**:

To keep silent about these and the other truths of the Faith, and to teach people accordingly is the greatest deception against which the Catechism vigorously warns. It represents the last trial of the Church and leads man to a religious delusion, "the price of their apostasy" (CCC 675). It is the fraud of Antichrist.

He will deceive those who are lost by all the means of injustice, for they have closed themselves to the love of the truth by which they should be saved.

(2 Thess: 2–10).

In **Rorate Caeli** in 2008, Cardinal Carlo Caffarra of Bologna and President of the Pontifical John Paul II Institute for Studies on Marriage and Family from 1981 to 1995, was asked a question involving the prophecies and messages of the Blessed Virgin Mary on the Devil's attack on the Church and on the family as a whole:

Q. There is a prophecy by Sister Lucia dos Santos, of Fatima, which concerns 'the final battle between the Lord and the kingdom of Satan'. The battlefield is the family. Life and the family. We know that you were given charge by John Paul II to plan and establish the Pontifical Institute for the Studies on Marriage and the Family.
A. Yes, I was. At the start of this work entrusted to me by the Servant of God, John Paul II. I wrote to Sister Lucia of Fatima through her Bishop as I couldn't do so directly. Unexplainably however, since I didn't expect an answer, seeing that I had only asked for prayers, I received a very long letter with her signature—now in the Institute's archives. In it we find written:

"… the final battle between the Lord and the reign of Satan will be about marriage and the family. Don't be afraid, she added, because anyone who operates for the sanctity of marriage and the family will always be contended and opposed in every way, because this is the decisive issue. And then she concluded: however, Our Lady has already crushed its head."

Q. Talking also to John Paul II, you felt too that this was the crux, as it touches the very pillar of creation, the truth of the relationship between man and woman among the generations. If the founding pillar is touched the entire building collapses and we see this now, because we are at this point and we know it. And I'm moved when I read the best biographies of Padre Pio, on how this man was so attentive to the sanctity of marriage and the sanctity of the spouses, even with justifiable rigor on occasion.
A. Does this come as any surprise to those watching the events currently unfolding in the Church? We have referenced various apparitions in the past that

are related to this, beginning with Our Lady of Good Success, in the 17th century:

Thus I make it known to you that from the end of the 19th century and shortly after the middle of the 20th century... the passions will erupt and there will be a total corruption of morals... As for the Sacrament of Matrimony, which symbolizes the union of Christ with His Church, it will be attacked and deeply profaned. Freemasonry, which will then be in power, will enact iniquitous laws with the aim of doing away with this Sacrament, making it easy for everyone to live in sin and encouraging procreation of illegitimate children born without the blessing of the Church... In this supreme moment of need for the Church, the one who should speak will fall silent.

When we reflect on the division among prelates that came as a result to the Amazonian Synod, our Lady of Akita comes to mind:

The work of the Devil will infiltrate even into the Church in such a way that one will see cardinals opposing cardinals, bishops against bishops. The priests who venerate me will be scorned and opposed by their confreres... churches and altars sacked; the Church will be full of those who accept compromises and the demon will press many priests and consecrated souls to leave the service of the Lord.

Q. Catholics are not required to believe in even the most approved and venerated private revelations, but many of us choose to do so. Does this battle relate to the famous discourse Pope Leo XIII was alleged to have heard in a vision between Christ and Satan, which led him to compose the prayer to St. Michael? How long the final battle will last, and what will come after?

A. *It is impossible to know. But the notion that there is at this very moment a battle taking place for the heart of the Church and the souls of the faithful is no longer in dispute.*

(Interview in **Rorate Caeli** of Cardinal Caffarra of Bologna, 2008)

Further comment from Bishop Schneider.

"The Catholic Faith in the voice of the perennial Magisterium, the sense of the faith of the faithful (sensus fidelium) as well as common sense clearly reject any civil union of two persons of the same sex, a union which has the aim that these persons seek sexual pleasure from each other. Even if persons living in such unions should not engage in mutual sexual pleasure—which in reality has been shown to be quite unrealistic—such unions represent a great scandal, a public recognition of sins of fornication against nature and a continuous proximate occasion of sin. Those who advocate same-sex civil unions are therefore also culpable of creating a kind of structure of sin, in this case of the juridical structure of habitual fornication against nature, since homosexual acts belong to sins which cry to heaven, as the Catechism of the Catholic Church says

(see n. 1867). Those who advocate same-sex civil unions are ultimately unjust and even cruel against those persons who are living in these unions, because these persons will be confirmed in mortal sin, they will be solidified in their interior psychological dichotomy, since their reason tells them, that homosexual acts are against reason and against the explicit will of God, the Creator and Redeemer of men.

Every true Catholic, every true Catholic priest, every true Catholic bishop must with deep sorrow and a weeping heart regret and protest against the unheard fact, that Pope Francis, the Roman Pontiff, the successor of the apostle Peter, the Vicar of Christ on earth, uttered in the documentary film "Francesco" that premiered on October 21st 2020 as part of the Rome Film Festival his support for civil same-sex unions. Such support of the pope means support for a structure of sin, for a lifestyle against the sixth Commandment of the Decalogue, which was written with the fingers of God on stone tables on Sinai (see Ex. 31:18) and delivered by the hands of Angels to men (see Gal. 3:19). What God has written with His hand, even a pope cannot erase nor rewrite with his hand or with his tongue. The Pope cannot behave as if he were God or an incarnation of Jesus Christ, modifying these words of the Lord:

"You have heard that it was said, 'You shall not commit adultery.' But I say to you that everyone who looks at a woman with lustful intent has already committed adultery with her in his heart. *"*

(Mt 5:27–28)

And instead of this, say, more or less, the following:

You have heard that it was said, 'You shall not commit adultery', 'if a man lies with a male as with a woman, both of them have committed an abomination' (Lev. 20:13), men who practice homosexuality will not inherit the kingdom of God' (1 Cor. 6:9); 'the practice of homosexuality is contrary to sound doctrine' (1 Tim. 1:10).

But I say to you that for persons who feel same-sex attraction "we have to create a civil union law. That way they are legally covered" every Shepherd of the Church and the Pope above all should always remind others of these serious words of Our Lord:

"Anyone who sets aside one of the least of these commands and teaches others accordingly will be called least in the kingdom of heaven"

(Mt. 5:19).

Every pope has to take very much to heart what the First Vatican Council proclaimed: "The Holy Spirit was not promised to the successors of Peter that by His revelation they might make known new doctrine, but that by His assistance they might inviolably keep and faithfully expound Revelation, the Deposit of

Faith, delivered through the Apostles." (Dogmatic Constitution Pastor aeternus, chap. 4)

The advocating of a legal union so that a lifestyle against the explicit Commandment of God, against human nature and against human reason will be legally covered, is a new doctrine, which "sews cushions under every elbow and makes pillows for the heads of persons" (Ez. 13:18), a new doctrine that "perverts the grace of our God into sexual pleasure" (Jude 4), a doctrine which is evidently against Divine Revelation and the perennial teaching of the Church of all times. Such a doctrine is scheming with sin, and is therefore a most anti-pastoral measure. To promote a juridical lifestyle of sin is against the core of the Gospel itself, since persons in same-sex unions through their sexual acts grievously offend God. Our Lady of Fatima made the maternal appeal to all humanity to stop offending God, who is already too much offended.

The following voice of the Magisterium, is faithfully echoing the voice of Jesus Christ, Our Divine Master, the Eternal Truth, and the voice of the Church and the popes of all times:

- *"Civil law cannot contradict right reason without losing its binding force on conscience." (cf. John Paul II, Encyclical Evangelium vitae, 72)*
- *"Laws in favor of homosexual unions are contrary to right reason because they confer legal guarantees, analogous to those granted to marriage, to unions between persons of the same sex. Given the values at stake in this question, the State could not grant legal standing to such unions without failing in its duty to promote and defend marriage as an institution essential to the common good" (Congregation for the Doctrine of the Faith, Considerations regarding proposals to give legal recognition to unions between homosexual persons, n. 6)*
- *"It might be asked how a law can be contrary to the common good if it does not impose any particular kind of behavior, but simply gives legal recognition to a de facto reality which does not seem to cause injustice to anyone. In this area, one needs first to reflect on the difference between homosexual behavior as a private phenomenon and the same behavior as a relationship in society, foreseen and approved by the law, to the point where it becomes one of the institutions in the legal structure. This second phenomenon is not only more serious, but also assumes a more far-reaching and profound influence, and would result in changes to the entire organization of society, contrary to the common good. Civil laws are structuring principles of man's life in society, for good or for ill. They "play a very important and sometimes decisive role in influencing patterns of thought and behavior". Lifestyles and the underlying presuppositions these express not only externally shape the life of society, but also tend to modify the younger generation's perception and evaluation of forms of behavior. Legal recognition of homosexual unions would obscure certain basic moral values and cause a devaluation of the institution of marriage." (ibid.)*

- *"Sexual relations are human when and insofar as they express and promote the mutual assistance of the sexes in marriage and are open to the transmission of new life." (ibid., n. 7)*
- *"By putting homosexual unions on a legal plane analogous to that of marriage and the family, the State acts arbitrarily and in contradiction with its duties." (ibid., n. 8)*
- *"The denial of the social and legal status of marriage to forms of cohabitation that are not and cannot be marital is not opposed to justice; on the contrary, justice requires it. There are good reasons for holding that such unions are harmful to the proper development of human society, especially if their impact on society were to increase." (ibid.)*
- *"It would be gravely unjust to sacrifice the common good and just laws on the family in order to protect personal goods that can and must be guaranteed in ways that do not harm the body of society" (ibid., n. 9)*
- *There is always "a danger that legislation which would make homosexuality a basis for entitlements could actually encourage a person with a homosexual orientation to declare his homosexuality or even to seek a partner in order to exploit the provisions of the law" (Congregation for the Doctrine of the Faith, Some considerations concerning the response to legislative proposals on the non-discrimination of homosexual persons, July 24, 1992, n. 14)*

All Catholics whether they be lay faithful as little children, as young men and young women, as fathers and mothers of family, or as consecrated persons, as cloistered nuns, as priests and as bishops, are inviolably keeping and "fighting for the faith which was once and for ever delivered to the Saints," (Jude 3), and who are for this reason despised and marginalized at the periphery in the life of the Church of our days, should weep and cry to God that, through the powerful intercession of the Immaculate Heart of Mary, who in Fatima said that people should stop offending God, who is already too offended, Pope Francis may convert and retract formally his approval for the civil same-sex unions, in order to confirm his brethren, as the Lord has commanded him (see Luke 22:32).

All these little ones in the Church (children, young men, young women, fathers and mothers of family, cloistered nuns, priests, bishops) would surely say to Pope Francis: Most Holy Father, for the sake of the salvation of your own immortal soul, for the sake of the souls of all those persons who through your approval of the same-sex unions are by their sexual acts grievously offending God and exposing their souls to the danger to be eternally lost, convert, retract your approval and proclaim with all your predecessors the following unchangeable teaching of the Church:

The Church teaches that respect for homosexual persons cannot lead in any way to approval of homosexual behavior or to legal recognition of homosexual unions." (Congregation for the Doctrine of the Faith, Considerations regarding proposals to give legal recognition to unions between homosexual persons, n. 11)

Legal recognition of homosexual unions or placing them on the same level as marriage would mean not only the approval of deviant behavior, with the consequence of making it a model in present-day society, but would also obscure basic values which belong to the common inheritance of humanity. The Church cannot fail to defend these values, for the good of men and women and for the good of society itself." (ibid., n. 11)

By the incredible approval of same-sex unions through the pope, all the true children of the Church feel like orphans, no more hearing the clear and unambiguous voice of the Pope, who should inviolably keep and faithfully expound Revelation, the Deposit of Faith, delivered through the Apostles.

The true children of the Church of our days might use these words of Psalm 137, saying: We feel as if in exile, by the rivers of Babylon, weeping when remembering Zion, when remembering the luminous and crystal-clear teaching of the popes, of our Holy Mother Church. Yet we unshakably believe in the words of Our Lord, that the gates of hell will not prevail against His Church. The Lord will come, even if He will come late, only in the fourth watch of the night, to calm the storm within the Church, to calm the storm within the papacy of our days, and He will say:

-   **"Take heart; it is I. Do not be afraid. O you of little faith, why did you doubt? And when they got into the boat, the wind ceased."**

(Mt. 14:27;32–33)

Our Lord will say also to Pope Francis:

-   **"For what does it profit a man, if he gains the whole world, and suffers the loss of his own soul? Or what exchange shall a man give for his soul? For the Son of man shall come in the glory of his Father with his angels: and then will he render to every man according to his works."**

(Mt. 16:26–27);

And Our Lord will say in addition to Pope Francis:

-   **"I have prayed that your own faith may not fail; and that once you have converted, you must strengthen your brothers"**

(Luke 22:32)

(October 22, 2020 Athanasius Schneider, Auxiliary Bishop of the Archdiocese of Saint Mary, Astana – https://www.gloriadei.io/same-sex-civil-unions-and-the-catholic-faith/)

The guardians of the Faith within the Catholic Church still remain numerous and loudly outspoken. Such valiant men are the likes of Cardinal Gerhard

Ludwig Müller KGCHS, ex-Prefect of the Congregation of the Doctrine of the Faith, Cardinal Carlo Caffarra of Bologna, Cardinal Viganò, ex-Nuncio to the United States, Cardinal Sarah, Cardinal Raymond Burke, San Francisco Archbishop Salvatore Cordileone, Philadelphia Archbishop Charles Chaput, Archbishop Schneider, Rev. Father Gerald E Murray, JCD and so many others with them. These remarkable Churchmen constitute one of the Church's principal lines of defense.

- **"Do you believe in the infallibility of the Church"?**
- *Yes, yes, my dear Spouse. The Church is infallible. Our Lord said so to*

Saint Peter. Yes I believe in the triumph of the Church.

(Exchange between Our Lord Jesus-Christ and M.J. Jahenny, 24 April 1877)

The revelations of Our Lord Jesus-Christ and of the Blessed Virgin Mary echoed in this book are indeed more necessary than ever today... The Blessed Virgin Mary is not *"a woman who's the head of an office, who every day sends a message at a certain hour for the sake of sending a message"...;* she is in fact a loving mother who, despite her Son's Church ruthless attempts to muffle her, to silence her, to make her calls insignificant, is insistently pleading, and trying to convey an invitation to pray for the Pope and the Clergy, while calling for an ever so urgent conversion. The consequences, if men were to refuse this pressing loving summon, we are told in no uncertain terms, would truly be... unspeakable...

"As I told you, if men do not repent and better themselves, the Father will inflict a terrible punishment on all humanity. It will be a punishment greater than the deluge, such as one that has never been seen before... Fire will fall from the sky and will wipe out a great part of humanity, the good as well as the bad, sparing neither priests nor faithful. The survivors will find themselves so desolate that they will envy the dead. The only arms which will remain for you will be the Rosary and the Sign left by My Son. Each day recite the prayers of the Rosary. With the Rosary, pray for the Pope, the bishops and priests.

The work of the devil will infiltrate even into the Church in such a way that one will see cardinals opposing cardinals, bishops against bishops. The priests who venerate me will be scorned and opposed by their confreres... Churches and altars will be sacked; the Church will be full of those who accept compromises and the demon will press many priests and consecrated souls to leave the service of the Lord.

The devil will be especially implacable against souls consecrated to God. The thought of the loss of so many souls is the cause of my sadness... If sins increase in number and gravity, there will be no longer pardon for them.

With courage, speak to your superior. He will know how to encourage each one of you to pray and to accomplish works of reparation.

(…) … Those who place their confidence in me will be saved*!*

(Our Lady of Akita, 13 October 1973)

God is a God of love and mercy to those who do ask for it, but He is a God of Justice for those who do not… The greatest act of "Mercy" and "Overture" a Christian can have for his fellowman is to open his eyes leading the way to his own salvation with the instruments that Heaven has sent through the Gospels, and the Catholic Holy Sacraments, but as well through the messages of the Blessed Virgin Mary which is a recall of the first two! Her message is this:

"Do everything my Son Jesus tells you."

The Blessed Virgin Mary invites us as well, as in the times of the Crusades, to take the Cross, and arm ourselves with:

- **Holy Mass (weekly if not daily)**—The reception of Holy Communion but never in a state of mortal sin… If subject to mortal sin, one must go to Confession before receiving the *true* Body and Blood, Soul and Divinity of Our Lord Jesus-Christ.
- **The Gospels**—Over and again, the Blessed Mother invites us to read daily the Holy Gospels. Surely the ever so many versions of the Bible make this task somewhat confusing… Which Bible are we to read? The best and longest used in the Holy Roman Catholic and Apostolic Church is the **BIBLE OF JERUSALEM**.
- **Confession**—The Blessed Virgin Mary asks over and over again for her faithful children to go back to this most important Sacrament but with a truly sincere a repentant heart. The Blessed Mother of Christ recommends Fatima's Devotion of the first five Saturdays of five consecutive months (see page 561), but all in all, one is called to Confession once a month.
- **The Holy Rosary**—Christians are called to pray daily the Holy Rosary as a special power has been granted on said prayers. This prayer is constantly referred by the Blessed Virgin Mary as one major means to one's salvation. The meditation of the fifteen mysteries is in itself a reflection on the life of Christ on earth, and on the sacrifices He has taken upon Himself to redeem Humanity.
- **Fasting**—The principle of sacrifices united to prayer is, we are told, a most powerful combination to overcome daily temptations and to remain steady in the faith. The combination of such a practice vary, but the one most put into emphasis is a fasting on bread and water alone, **preferably on Wednesdays and Fridays**. Beginning such a practice is recommended to be gradual, as an immediate practice is considered too disheartening and difficult.
- **The Catholic Church**—Despite the many mistakes, errors and falls of the Church, the Blessed Virgin Mary implores repeatedly with profound emotion and sorrow the faithful to remain unconditionally and

irrevocably loyal to the only Christian Church founded by her Son Jesus-Christ (*upon Peter and his successors*)[38].

The Catholic Church, Mary tells us, despite its attempts to reconcile the faithful with today's culture and Society's pagan trends, will never be destroyed by the enemy of God, for the Church of her Son is and will always remain under His protection and inspired by the Holy Spirit through the Holy Scriptures and the Church seven sacraments:

- Baptism
- Holy Eucharist
- Confirmation
- Confession
- Anointing of the sick
- Marriage
- Ordination

There is even an Eighth Sacrament which hasn't been used in France in over two centuries: the Coronation of Catholic Kings with the Holy Flask of St. Remy.[39]

- **The Most Blessed Virgin Mary**—Finally, the Mother of God offers herself, she said, through her loving intercession, through her motherly recourse and through her apparitions throughout the world, as our last weapon and tool for salvation.

In the words of Sister Lucia dos Santos (visionary of Fatima):

(...) In the plans of the Divine Providence, when God is going to chastise the world He always first exhausts all other remedies. When He sees that the world pays no attention whatsoever, then, as we say in our imperfect way of talking, He presents us the last means of salvation: His Blessed Mother. If we despise and reject this last means, Heaven will no longer pardon us, because we will have committed a sin that the Gospel calls a sin against the Holy Spirit. This sin consists in openly rejecting—with full knowledge and will—the salvation that is put in our hands.

(Letter of Lucia Dos Santos to Rev. Father Fuentes, 1957)

In conclusion, one of the most extraordinary message from Our Lord Jesus-Christ to mankind covers the importance of the Holy Mass and of the Holy Rosary, and of the importance to pray His Blessed Mother for her children of

---

[38] The Roman Catholic Church is indeed the only Christian Church founded by Jesus-Christ. It is an Apostolic Church from St. Peter (the Church's first Pontiff) to Francis. All the other Christian Churches were by founded by mere men.

[39] The Crowning of French Kings with the holy Oil of Saint Remy is indeed recognized by the Church as a holy Sacrament.

predilection, the priests, but this message resumes as well the Third Secret of Fatima and Akita, and forewarns men of the consequences of falling to the seduction and temptation of Satan:

"Men have not listened to the words pronounced by My most holy Mother in Fatima. Woe to those who do not listen now to My Words! Men have not understood the language of war. Many men live in sin, very often in the sin of impurity. Woe to those who seduce the innocent!

You must not be upset with those who do not want to believe, for they know not what they do... But woe to those who laugh, or who allow themselves to judge before informing themselves.

The frequent apparitions of My good Mother are the results of My Mercy. I send her with the strength of the Holy Spirit to forewarn men, and to save that which must be saved... I must let happen (that which must) on the whole world so that many souls be saved which otherwise would have been lost. For all the crosses, for all the sufferings and for all that is still to come that will be worse yet, you must not curse My Father from Heaven, but thank Him. It is the work of My Love. You'll understand it later on... I must come in My Justice because men have not recognized the time of My Grace.

The measure of sin is at its fullest, but to My faithful no harm will come. I shall come to the sinful world in a terrible rumble of thunder on a cold winter night. A very hot wind from the south will precede this storm, and a heavy grail will hit the earth. From massive red-fire clouds, devastating lightening will zigzag, enflaming and reducing everything to ashes... The air will be filled with toxic gases and mortal vapors which, within cyclones, will rip apart the works of daring (pride?), of madness and of the City of Night's will of power (Paris).

Humankind will have to recognize that above it, is a Will that will make its audacious plans collapse like a castle of cards. The Angel Destroyer will destroy forever the lives of those who will have devastated My Kingdom...

You, souls who profane the Name of the Lord, guard yourselves from mocking Me! Guard yourselves from the sin against the Spirit! When the Angel of Death will mow the bad weed with the cutting sword of My Justice, hell will then project itself with anger and tumult against the just and, above all, against the consecrated souls in order to try to destroy them through a frightful terror...

I want to protect you, My faithful ones, and give you the signs which will indicate the beginning of the judgment: When by a cold winter night thunder will rumble so hard as to make mountains shake, then close very quickly all doors and windows (of your house). Your eyes must not profane the terrible events with curious looks... Gather around the Crucifix. Place yourselves under the protection of My most holy Mother. Do not let any doubt take over you involving your safety.

The more trusting you will be, the more impenetrable will the rampart be. I want to surround you with (...). Burn blessed candles and recite the chaplet. Persevere for three days and two nights. The following night, the terror will calm down... After the horror of this long obscurity, with the upcoming rising day, the sun will appear in all its brightness and warmth.

There will be a great devastation... I, your God, shall have purified everything. The survivors must thank the Holy Trinity for Its protection. Magnificent will My Kingdom of Peace be, and My Name will be invoked and blessed from sunrise until sunset.

Pray! Pray! Pray! Convert and do penance! Do not fall asleep as My disciples did in the Garden of Olives, for I am very close. The Anger of the Father against Humankind is very great. If the prayer of the Rosary and the Gift of the Precious Blood weren't so pleasing to the Father, there would already be a misery on earth that has no name... But My Mother intercedes to the Father, to Me and to the Holy Spirit. This is why God lets Himself be moved. Thank then My Mother for the fact that Humankind still lives... Honor her with the respect of a child—I gave you the example—for she is the Mother of Mercy.

Never forget to renew continuously the Gift of the Precious Blood. My Mother begs me unceasingly, and with her, many penitent and expiatory souls. I cannot refuse her anything; it is therefore because of My Mother and because of My elected that these days have been shortened.

Be consoled, you who honor My Precious Blood. Nothing will happen to you.

I shall inspire My Representative to place continuously in honor the Sacrifice of My Precious Blood, and the veneration of My Mother...

Would some of My priests like to be more Pope-like than the Pope himself? They will crucify Me, for they will delay the works of My Mother. Pray a great deal for the favorites of My Heart, the priests. The time will come when My priests will understand all this (...)

(Message of Our Lord Jesus-Christ to Marie-Julie between 1917 and 1938)

These are the truths revealed these past 175 years, and although it might be today *politically correct* to say that God wills various faiths, various realities, various truths, this is yet another error, for if God *tolerates* different faiths, He certainly does not will them, for the Truth is but one.

Indeed, today idolatry is tolerated inside Vatican grounds[40], secret treaties with Communist regimes are signed[41], leading to Christian persecutions, church burnings and bishops and priests arrests... Likewise, new doctrines are published by the highest authorities in Rome[42] openly

contradicting the Faith, causing massive confusion and division amongst millions of faithful around the world; traditional methods of veneration of the Gospels and of the Holy Eucharist – permitted by Vatican II – are today ordered to be banned for a more wide-opened Protestant-like liturgy – which concentrates

---

[40] Pachamama (see page: 506)

[41] Secret treaty signed between the Vatican and the People's Republic of China (Communist China),

[42] "Amoris Laetitia" (19 March 2016)

more on the consideration of man rather than of God. To add insult to injury, conditions on the reception of the Holy Body of Christ is no longer prohibited to non-Catholics but widely distributed to Catholics who are in open defiance with the Church's positions on abortion and euthanasia. Finally, as open rebellions and schisms are flourishing within the Church, Pope Francis – who embraces different faiths and cultures, sponsors same-sex civil union and issue letters of recommendation to LGBT champions[43] – paradoxically did not hesitate to ban the adoration rituals through the Roman Rite of yesteryears by ordering the celebration of the Tridentine Mass[44] in Latin outside Catholic churches, receding thusly Benedict XVI's special permission granted in 2007. This said, we must not fall in the trap of anger, for that is precisely the design of the "fallen one", and if we must not rebel against Rome, we can certainly oppose error and apostasy; we must love our enemies and in this case pray fervently for Pope Francis. God's Mercy extends even now with these last calls which have been echoed repeatedly through Heaven's best Emissary: the Blessed Virgin Mary. Sadly, these calls are hardly ever spoken of in churches, nor therefore answered... Convert! Change your lives, for the messages of the Blessed Virgin Mary is a message of love and, most of all of extraordinary hope and mercy for all men.
God's Mercy is the expression of His ever-lasting love for mankind, even for the worst of sinners, if, and only if he repents and converts sincerely, asking from the depth of his heart forgiveness. After all, wasn't the first man to ever enter Heaven, even before the Blessed Virgin Mary, the very last of us all?

"One of the criminals hanging in crucifixion blasphemed him: "Aren't you the Messiah? Then save yourself and us." But the other one rebuked him: "Have you no fear of God, seeing you under the same sentence? We deserve it, after all. We are only paying the price for what we have done, but this man has done nothing wrong." He then said, "Jesus, remember me when you enter upon your reign." And Jesus replied, "I assure you: this day you will be with me in Paradise."

(Luke 23: 39–43)

---

[43] Father James Martin (promoter of LGBT's)

[44] Francis, 84, issued on July 16, 2021, a "Motu Propio" through *"Traditiones Custodes",* requiring individual bishops to approve celebrations of the old Mass before their being performed. *"Traditiones Custodes"* also calls the Tridentine Mass, requires newly ordained priests to receive explicit permission to celebrate it from their bishops, in consultation with the Vatican. Under the new law, local bishops must also determine if the current groups of faithful attached to the old Mass accept the precepts of Vatican II, which allowed for Mass to be celebrated in the vernacular rather than Latin. These groups of faithful cannot use regular churches; instead, bishops must find alternate locations for them without creating new parishes... Furthermore, Pope Francis stated that bishops will no longer be allowed to authorize the formation of any new pro-Latin Mass groups in their dioceses.

Recommended Prayers

1) Marie-Julie Jahenny then revealed a special prayer to be said to King St. Louis in his honor and for the coming of the Great Catholic Monarch:

-   **Great Saint Louis, King of France**, hero of France, pray for France.
-   Great Saint Louis, King of France, beautiful lily of purity, friend of the Sacred Heart of Jesus, pray for France.
-   **Great Saint Louis, King of France**, who preserved your purity and your beautiful innocence and who never sullied this crown on the throne that Jesus and Mary gave you, grant peace, pray that France humbles itself at the feet of Jesus and Mary and before you.
-   **Great Saint Louis, King of France**, who comes to reconcile Heaven with Earth and to whom Jesus, the God of France, gives His graces, bring peace to France, grant that the Faith will flourish there, pray for France, the Holy Pontiff and the Church.
-   **Great Saint Louis**, you, the friend of the Sacred Heart of Jesus, you, the fervent servant of Mary whom you loved so much and for whom you desired to die on a Saturday, a day that was consecrated to her, pray for us, unhappy children of France.
-   **Great Saint Louis, King of France**, you whom Jesus and Mary have received in their arms and who they then gave a most beautiful crown, pray for France.
-   Great Saint Louis, King of France, France calls you and requests that you bring that beautiful crown that you have never sullied, give it to her like a second crown, pray for France.
-   **Great Saint Louis**, who prays with the Immaculate Mary for the Sovereign Pontiff in the midst of his sufferings, the calumnies, the persecutions, deliver the Sovereign Pontiff.
-   **Great Saint Louis, King of France**, come today with Immaculate Mary, reconcile France and Heaven. We are all present, we pray together. He will come to our aid, to make truthfulness and innocence flourish in the midst of faded France, as Mary has given him the power, pray for France.
-   **Great Saint Louis, King of France**, Jesus and Mary have permitted that you take by the hand the King that will govern and you will give him his crown that you never tarnished. Mary permits you to place this King on the throne, he who will bring peace. Pray for the Sovereign Pontiff who calls upon you for France. We see in you a beautiful hope, we see your blessed hand! Mary will refuse you nothing, you who have loved her so much. Come to our assistance. Come, You also, O Sacred Heart of Jesus, You open it completely that we may hide in It never to come out.
-   All for You, O Sacred Heart, all for You Jesus and Mary, and all for you O good Saint Louis, King of France. Amen.

2) Prayers for France

a) The Virgin Mary has spoken to me a great deal of France. She asked me three prayers for France to recite every day: **1 Magnificat, 1 Ave Maris Stella and 1 Sabat Mater.** *What's more, one must kneel and pray fervently while looking towards Heaven. The Blessed Virgin Mary will deliver her (France) through a king who will save her and govern her a long time. She told me that she is not being asked enough for that king and that we do not pray her fervently enough for her to grant him to us. She names him Henry V, and recommends us to pray a great deal as well St. Michael the Archangel. As for the Sacred Heart, He complained as well on many occasions that Frenchmen do not ask Him for the king...*

b) **(...)The Blessed Virgin Mary has asked as well for France the "*Salve Regina*" (Hail Holy Queen) four to five times prayed a day as an act of contrition, bowing on the ground.**

(Jesus-Christ, 1 June 1877)

3. Special message of the Blessed Virgin Mary concerning the plants to use as remedies:

Oh, my beloved little children, when you use those little flowers and those little plants, pray to me:

**O Holy Queen of Heaven,
Health of the sick, prodigy of power,
Extend your benedictions on this infusion, all powerful Mother.
Show us that you are our Mother by relieving our miseries.**

My little children, when you take this little flower, invoke me:

**O Immaculate Mary! O our Mother! O our Mother!
Look down on us and let your benediction be revealed in our suffering.**

And for those tending the sick:

My dear Child, there is no need to say lengthy prayers. Simply say:

**O Good Mother!
Look at my little work for someone ill or afflicted.
Please bless it.**

4. Prayers to the Cross:

Marie-Julie was taught two particular manners to pray, saluting the Cross:

The "Crux Ave" Prayer (to be prayed in times of fear and Chastisements):

I salute You, I adore You, I embrace You,
O Adorable Cross of my Savior!
Protect us, guard us, save us!
Jesus loved You so much,
Following His Example, I love You.
Your Holy Image calms my fears,
I feel only peace and confidence.

The "Crux Ave" Prayer, Number 2:

O Crux, ave, spes unica!
Et Verbum caro factum est.
O Jesus Vanquisher of Death, save us!
Translation:
'O Cross, hail! Our only hope!
And the Word was made flesh.'

5. Prayer to the Cross of Pardon

O God, Crucified Savior, set me ablaze with love, faith and courage for the salvation of my brothers.

To obtain my assistance (Our Lady of Good Guard) **during your life and death, you will say:**

> **I salute you, beloved Daughter of the Father,
> Lily of Purity, pray for us. (Hail Mary, etc.)**

> **I salute you, Spouse of the Holy Spirit, Violet of
> Humility, pray for us. (Hail Mary…)**

> **I salute you, O Mother of the Word Incarnate,
> Rose of Charity, pray for us, (Hail Mary…)**

6. The "Crux Ave" prayer to be said during the time of evils and great fears:

> **I salute You, I adore You, I embrace You,
> O Adorable Cross of my Savior!
> Protect us, guard us, save us!
> Jesus loved You so much,
> Following His Example, I love You.
> Your Holy Image calms my fears,
> I feel only peace and confidence.**

Promise with this prayer: **"You will feel so many graces, so much strength and love that this big flood will pass by you as something unobserved. It is a grace of My tenderness."**

Our Lord also promised: **"I will bless those who say this prayer at least once a day, I will give them a solemn benediction."** When Marie-Julie passed on the litany Our Lord Jesus-Christ taught her, she asked: *"Lord, will You be willing to remain with us until the end of time?"* (i.e., in the Blessed Sacrament.) He answered. **"This is Love."**

7. The Litany of the Passion (to be prayed before the Holy Sacrament):

- Oh my very dear Jesus, what brought You to suffer for us a mortal agony in the Garden of Olives: It is Love.
- Oh My Adorable Jesus, what brought You to separate Yourself from Your Apostles during this Agony: It is Love.
- Oh My Jesus, what brought You to let the executioners and the Jews torture and bind You: It is Love.
- Oh My Jesus, what brought You to appear before Pilate's tribunal: It is Love.
- Oh My Jesus, what brought You to descend into Herod's obscure prison: It is Love.
- Oh Holy Victim, what brought You to allow the executioners to scourge You without a complaint from You: It is Love.
- Oh Holy Victim, what brought You to separate Yourself from Your Holy Mother in order to suffer insults: It is Love.
- Oh Holy Victim, what brought You to cast a glance at St. Peter when leaving the Praetorium: It is Love.
- Oh Holy Victim, what brought You to fall before Your enemies under the weight: It is Love.
- Oh Holy Victim, what brought You to die for us on a Cross: It is Love.
- Oh Holy Victim, what brought You to give Yourself to our souls in the Most Holy Sacrament: It is Love.
- Oh Holy Victim, what brought You to reside for us in all the Shrines and Tabernacles in the entire world: It is Love.
- Oh Holy Victim, what brought You to tell us: 'Dear Children, do not fear, come close, I sleep, but My Heart watches': It is Love.
- Adorable Sacred Victim, what brought You to let us approach Your Holy Tabernacles, to possess You and dissolve into these delights: It is Love. It is Love.
- Oh Most Holy Victim, what brought You to love us with a Love so Ardent and full of Goodness: It is Love. It is Love.

Our Lord requested this prayer to be said to console Him on Thursday mornings at 9 am before the Blessed Sacrament, and on Fridays in the afternoon.

8. Prayer to Save 1,000 Sinners

Our Lord gave Marie-Julie on 3 September 1925 a very simple way to save 1,000 sinners every time we receive Holy Communion.

Tell them to rest five minutes on My Heart throbbing with love. Think only of Me by this simple word: *Thank you, my Beloved, You live in me and I live in You.* You see the sweetness you will taste and how you will give Me consolation. Ask of Me, in the fifth minute the conversion of a thousand sinners. It will be a great joy for My Divine Father, for Heaven, I ask you the same favor. I will be there, inside you, infinite goodness, the splendor of all beauties. Only five minutes thinking about Me and asking Me at the fifth minute the salvation of souls. My Divine Heart is overflowing with joy at this request of graces and I will also grant it.

9. Promises to the Devotion to the Wound on Our Lord's left Shoulder

During various ecstasies Our Lord disclosed to Marie-Julie that the devotion to His left Shoulder's Wound was a great consolation for Him, and thus granted great promises to those who would practice this devotion.

Our Lord showed to Marie-Julie this open Wound and revealed to her its depth:

"The Pain is incomprehensible in the hearts of My children. How this devotion pleases and consoles Me, how often have the prayers of these Wounds risen to My Heart and have torn (open) the (way of) salvation for souls entrusted to Hell."

(17 May 1878)

Promises collected during the ecstasies of Marie-Julie, for souls who propagate and are faithful to this devotion:

1. **"I will bless all the souls who propagate this devotion: I grant them abundant graces."** (29 March 1878)
2. **"O souls who love Me, who propagate this devotion, I take you under My protection, I keep you under the mantle of My affection."** (29 March 1878)
3. **"I will dispel the darkness that will come to their heart."** (28 December 1877)
4. **"I will console them in their pains." "I will come in the midst of their greatest afflictions, to enlighten, to comfort them."** (8 February 1878) (28 December 1877, 8 February and 12 April 1878)
5. **"I will come to bless them in their undertakings."** (29 March 1878)
6. **"I will give them a tender love for the Cross. I will come to assist them at the time of death, with this cross and I will introduce them into My Heavenly Kingdom."** (12 April 1878)

7. "I will sweeten their agony." (28 December 1877). "I will come at the hour of death. I will console them in their passage." (8 February 1878). "Especially at the hour of death, I will come to give them a sweet moment of calm and tranquility. I will tell them: 'O good holy soul, who has spread this devotion (knowing) that I had so much at heart that it be made known, come to receive the reward of your labors, the fruit of blessing.'" (29 March 1878)

8. "I will shelter them, I will assist them, I will console all the souls that seek to propagate this Sacred Wound. At the time of death, I will console the souls that have compensated Me by their devotion and compassion to the Wound so deep and painful. I will come to strengthen them in their final fears. I will come and prepare their passage: Thank you, you who have compensated Me for My pains." (17 May 1878)

9. "See," Jesus said, pointing to His Sacred Wound with extreme tenderness, "all My children who have recognized this Wound, who have venerated it, have prayed to it, will have on the Last Day a great and generous reward. I do not simply show it, I pronounce it. My Word is Divine." (17 May 1878)

10. Prayer to Our Lady of La Salette

In 1937, Rome deigned to favor the Reconciliation of sinners, by granting 500 days of indulgences to the recitation of the Recollection, and of '300 days to the invocation':

Our Lady of La Salette, Reconciler of Sinners, pray without ceasing for us who have recourse to you.

11. Spiritual Communion

This prayer is to be prayed when Holy Communion is/will not be available, and is to invoke the Holy Spirit to accept a Spiritual:

My Jesus,
I believe that You
are truly present in the Most Holy Sacrament.
I love You above all things,
and I desire to receive You into my soul.
Since I cannot at this moment
receive You sacramentally,
come at least spiritually into my heart. I embrace You as if You were already there and unite myself wholly to You. Never permit me to be separated from You.

12. <u>Prayers to be prayed for the souls in Purgatory (Medjugorje)</u>

There are many souls in Purgatory. There are also persons who have been consecrated to God: some priests, some religious. Pray for their intentions, at least seven Our Father's, Hail Mary's and Glory Be's and the Creed. I recommend it to you. There is a large number of souls who have been in Purgatory for a long time because no one prays for them.

I. Rosary recommended by the Virgin Mary

1. Sign of the Cross

2. Invocation of the Holy Spirit (optional)

"Come ô Holy Spirit, fill the hearts of thy faithful and enkindle in them the fire of your love. Send your Spirit and they will be renewed, and you will renew the face of the earth.

Let us pray.

O God, who has instructed the hearts of the faithful through the Light of the Holy Spirit, grant us in the same spirit to be truly wise and to rejoice in His consolation;

Through Christ our Lord, Amen."

3. Prayer of St. Michael the Archangel (optional):

"St. Michael the Archangel, defend us in the day of Battle; be our safeguard against the wickedness and snares of the Devil. May God rebuke him, we humbly pray, and do thou, O Prince of the Heavenly Host, by the power of God, cast into Hell, Satan and all the other evil spirits, who prowl through the world, seeking the ruin of souls.
Amen."

4. Creed:

"I believe in God the Father the All-Mighty, Creator of Heaven and earth, I believe in Jesus-Christ, His Only Son, our Lord, who was conceived by the power of the Holy Spirit, was born of the Virgin Mary, suffered under Pontius Pilate, was crucified, died and was buried. He descended into Hell, but on the third day He rose from the dead. He ascended into Heaven and He is seated at the right hand of the All-Mighty Father. From there He will come back to judge the living and the dead. I believe in the Holy Spirit, in the Catholic Church, in the Communion of Saints, in the forgiveness of sins, in the resurrection of the Body and in the Eternal Life.
Amen."

5 One "Our Father"

"Our Father, Who art in Heaven hallowed be Thy Name. Thy Kingdom come; Thy Will be done on earth as it is in Heaven. Give us this day our daily bread, and forgive us our trespasses as we forgive those who trespass against us, and lead us not into temptation, but deliver us from evil. Amen."

6 Three "Hail Mary's"

"Hail Mary, full of grace, the Lord is with Thee. Blessed are Thou amongst women, and blessed is the Fruit of thy womb, Jesus. Holy Mary, Mother of God **and our Mother**, pray for us, now and at the hour of our death. Amen."

7 One "Glory be to the Father"

"Glory be to the Father, and to the Son and to the Holy Spirit, as it was in the beginning is now, and ever shall be, now and forever. Amen."

The Five Joyful Mysteries

The first joyous mystery:

The Annunciation:

I. **One** "Our father"
"Our Father, Who art in Heaven hallowed be Thy Name. Thy Kingdom come; Thy Will be done on earth as it is in Heaven. Give us this day our daily bread, and forgive us our trespasses as we forgive those who trespass against us, and lead us not into temptation, but deliver us from evil.
Amen."

II. **Ten** "Hail Mary's."
"Hail Mary, full of grace, the Lord is with Thee. Blessed are Thou amongst women, and blessed is the Fruit of thy womb, Jesus. Holy Mary, Mother of God **and our Mother**, pray for us, now and at the hour of our death.
Amen."

III. **One** "Glory be to the Father:"
"Glory be to the Father, and to the Son and to the Holy Spirit, as it was in the beginning is now, and ever shall be, now and forever.
Amen."

IV. Prayer of Fatima:
"O my Jesus, forgive us our sins. Save us from the fires of Hell and lead all souls to Heaven, especially those who are most in need of your Mercy.
Amen."

V. Additional prayer (Optional):
"O Mary conceived without sin, pray for us who have recourse to thee.
Amen." (Devotion to Our Lady of the Miraculous Medal)

The Second Joyful Mystery:

The Visitation:

One "Our father":

"Our Father, Who art in Heaven hallowed be Thy Name. Thy Kingdom come; Thy Will be done on earth as it is in Heaven. Give us this day our daily bread, and forgive us our trespasses as we forgive those who trespass against us, and lead us not into temptation, but deliver us from evil.

Amen."

Ten "Hail Mary's":

"Hail Mary, full of grace, the Lord is with Thee. Blessed are Thou amongst women, and blessed is the Fruit of thy womb, Jesus. Holy Mary, Mother of God **and our Mother**, pray for us, now and at the hour of our death.

Amen."

One "Glory be to the Father":

"Glory be to the Father, and to the Son and to the Holy Spirit, as it was in the beginning is now, and ever shall be, now and forever.

Amen."

Prayer of Fatima:

"O my Jesus, forgive us our sins. Save us from the fires of Hell and lead all souls to Heaven, especially those who are most in need of your Mercy.

Amen."

Additional prayer (Optional):

"O Mary conceived without sin, pray for us who have recourse to thee. Amen." (devotion to Our Lady of the Miraculous Medal).

The Third Joyful Mystery:

The Nativity

One "Our father":

"Our Father, Who art in Heaven hallowed be Thy Name. Thy Kingdom come; Thy Will be done on earth as it is in Heaven. Give us this day our daily bread, and forgive us our trespasses as we forgive those who trespass against us, and lead us not into temptation, but deliver us from evil.

Amen."

Ten "Hail Mary's":

"Hail Mary, full of grace, the Lord is with Thee. Blessed are Thou amongst women, and blessed is the Fruit of thy womb, Jesus. Holy Mary, Mother of God **and our Mother**, pray for us, now and at the hour of our death.

Amen."

One "Glory be to the Father":

"Glory be to the Father, and to the Son and to the Holy Spirit, as it was in the beginning is now, and ever shall be, now and forever.

Amen."

Prayer of Fatima:
"O my Jesus, forgive us our sins. Save us from the fires of Hell and lead all souls to Heaven, especially those who are most in need of your Mercy.
Amen."

Additional prayer (Optional):
"O Mary conceived without sin, pray for us who have recourse to thee.
Amen." (devotion to Our Lady of the Miraculous Medal).

The Fourth Joyful Mystery:

The Presentation:

One "Our father":
"Our Father, Who art in Heaven hallowed be Thy Name. Thy Kingdom come; Thy Will be done on earth as it is in Heaven. Give us this day our daily bread, and forgive us our trespasses as we forgive those who trespass against us, and lead us not into temptation, but deliver us from evil.
Amen."

Ten "Hail Mary's":
"Hail Mary, full of grace, the Lord is with Thee. Blessed are Thou amongst women, and blessed is the Fruit of thy womb, Jesus. Holy Mary, Mother of God **and our Mother**, pray for us, now and at the hour of our death.
Amen."

One "Glory be to the Father":
"Glory be to the Father, and to the Son and to the Holy Spirit, as it was in the beginning is now, and ever shall be, now and forever.
Amen."

Prayer of Fatima:
"O my Jesus, forgive us our sins. Save us from the fires of Hell and lead all souls to Heaven, especially those who are most in need of your Mercy.
Amen."

Additional prayer (Optional):
"O Mary conceived without sin, pray for us who have recourse to thee.
Amen." (devotion to Our Lady of the Miraculous Medal).

The Fifth Joyful Mystery:

The Finding of the Child Jesus in the Temple:

One "Our father":
"Our Father, Who art in Heaven hallowed be Thy Name. Thy Kingdom come; Thy Will be done on earth as it is in Heaven. Give us this day our daily

bread, and forgive us our trespasses as we forgive those who trespass against us, and lead us not into temptation, but deliver us from evil.
Amen."

Ten "Hail Mary's":
"Hail Mary, full of grace, the Lord is with Thee. Blessed are Thou amongst women, and blessed is the Fruit of thy womb, Jesus. Holy Mary, Mother of God **and our Mother**, pray for us, now and at the hour of our death.
Amen."

One "Glory be to the Father":
"Glory be to the Father, and to the Son and to the Holy Spirit, as it was in the beginning is now, and ever shall be, now and forever.
Amen."

Prayer of Fatima:
"O my Jesus, forgive us our sins. Save us from the fires of Hell and lead all souls to Heaven, especially those who are most in need of your Mercy.
Amen."

Additional prayer (Optional):
"O Mary conceived without sin, pray for us who have recourse to thee.
Amen." (devotion to Our Lady of the Miraculous Medal).

The Five Sorrowful Mysteries

The Agony in the Garden
The prayers are to be prayed following exactly the same steps *I* to *V* *(page 543)*

The Scourging on the Pillar:
The prayers are to be prayed following exactly the same steps *I* to *V* *(page 543)*

The Crowning of Thorns
The prayers are to be prayed following exactly the same steps *I* to *V* *(page 543)*

The Way of the Cross
The prayers are to be prayed following exactly the same steps *I* to *V* *(page 543)*

The Crucifixion
The prayers are to be prayed following exactly the same steps *I* to *V* *(page 543)*

The Five Glorious Mysteries

The Resurrection
The prayers are to be prayed following exactly the same steps *I* to *V* *(page 543)*

The Ascension
The prayers are to be prayed following exactly the same steps *I* to *V* *(page 543)*

The Descent of the Holy Spirit
The prayers are to be prayed following exactly the same steps *I* to *V* *(page 543)*

The Assumption (*)
The prayers are to be prayed following exactly the same steps *I* to *V* *(page 543)*

The Crowning of the Virgin Mary (*)
The prayers are to be prayed following exactly the same steps *I* to *V* *(page 543)*

(*): The Blessed Virgin Mary has requested the fourth and the fifth Glorious Mystery to be prayed in Latin.

Prayers of the Rosary in Latin

"Our Father—Pater"

"Pater Noster, qui es in caelis: sanctificètur nomen tuum; adveniat regnum tuum; fiat voluntas tua, sicut in caelo, et in terra. Panem nostrum cotidiànum da nobis hodie; et dimitte nobis, dèbita nostra, sicut et nos dimittimus debitoribus nostris; et ne nos inducas in tentationem; sed libera nos a malo. Amen."

"Hail Mary—Ave Maria"

"**Ave Maria,** gratia plena, Dominus tecum: benedicta tu in mulieribus et benedictus fructus ventris tui Jesus. Sancta Maria, Mater Dei (et Mater nostra), ora pro nobis peccatoribus, nunc et in hora mortis nostrae. Amen."

"Glory be to the Father—Gloria"

"**Gloria** Patri et Filio et Spiritui Sancto sicut erat in principio et nunc et semper et in saecula saeculorum. Amen."

One "Our Father", one "Hail Mary", and one "Glory be to the Father":
After the last "Glory be to the Father" (in Latin) of the fifth Glorious Mystery, the Blessed Virgin Mary has requested an "Our Father," one "Hail

Mary" and one "Glory be" for the intentions of the Pope, to obtain the indulgences of the Holy Rosary and for the souls in Purgatory.

The "Hail Holy Queen" (Salve Regina):
"Hail Holy Queen, Mother of Mercy: our life, our sweetness and our hope. To Thee do we cry, poor banished children of Eve, to Thee do we send up our sights, mourning and weeping in this valley of tears. Turn then, Most Gracious Advocate, Thine eyes of Mercy towards us, and after this our exile show unto us the Blessed Fruit of thy womb Jesus. O Clement! O Loving! O Sweet Virgin Mary! pray for us O Holy Mother of God,

That we may be worthy of the promises of Christ.
Amen."

Consecration to the Immaculate Heart of Mary (Optional):
"Queen of the Holy Rosary and Gentle Mother of men, we consecrate ourselves to you and to your Immaculate Heart, and we entrust unto you our community, our family, our country and all of humankind. Accept our consecration, O beloved Mother, and use us as ever you desire to accomplish your designs on earth. O Immaculate Heart of Mary, teach us how to have the Heart of Jesus reign and triumph within and around us as It has reigned and triumphed in you.
Amen."

Prayer of the Angel of Peace (Optional):
"O Most Holy Trinity, Father, Son and Holy Spirit, I adore Thee profoundly and I offer Thee the Most Precious Body and Blood, Soul and Divinity of Our Lord Jesus-Christ, present in all the Tabernacles of the whole world in amendment for the outrages, sacrileges and indifference with which He is Himself offended, and by the infinite merits of the Sacred Heart of Jesus and of the Immaculate Heart of Mary, I pray for the conversion of poor sinners.
Amen."

The Magnificat (Optional):
"My soul magnifies the Lord, and my spirit rejoices in God my Savior; because he has regarded the lowliness of his handmaid; for, behold, henceforth all generations shall call me blessed; because he who is mighty has done great things for me, and holy is his name; and his mercy is from generation to generation on those who fear him. He has shown might with his arm, he has scattered the proud in the conceit of their heart. He has put down the mighty from their thrones, and has exalted the lowly. He has filled the hungry with good things, and the rich he has sent away empty. He has given help to Israël, his servant, mindful of his mercy—even as he spoke to our fathers—to Abraham and to his posterity forever."

Prayer of St. Michael the Archangel:
"St. Michael the Archangel, defend us in the day of Battle; be our safeguard against the wickedness and snares of the Devil. May God rebuke him, we

humbly pray, and do thou, O Prince of the Heavenly Host, by the power of God, cast into Hell, Satan and all the other evil spirits, who prowl through the world, seeking the ruin of souls.

Amen."

II. Rosary of the Virgin of Fatima

This Rosary praying layout was given by the Blessed Virgin Mary to Saint Padre Pio for the Children seers of Garabandal, Spain, 3 March 1962 (see Chapter VII).

1) In this first mystery, we see how **the Holy Virgin chose Fatima as her favorite city to spread her messages**.

2) In this second mystery, it is contemplated how **the Holy Virgin chose the Cova de Iria for her visions**.

3) In this third mystery, we see how **the Holy Virgin chose the three little shepherds for their celestial conversations and to entrust the great secret to them**.

4) In this fourth mystery, we see how **the secret of Fatima is the greatest secret of all that she has revealed**.

5) In this fifth mystery, we can see how the visions of **the Blessed Virgin continues to be present in all parts of the world**.

The Virgin has promised special graces to all who pray this rosary.

III. The Fifteen Promises of the Virgin Mary to Christians who Recite the Holy Rosary

1. Whoever shall faithfully serve me by the recitation of the rosary, shall receive signal graces.
2. I promise my special protection and the greatest graces to all those who shall recite the rosary.
3. The rosary will be a powerful armor against Hell; it will destroy vice, decrease sin and defeat heresies.
4. It will cause virtue and good works to flourish; it will obtain for souls the abundant mercy of God; it will withdraw the hearts of men from the love of the world and its vanities, and will lift them to the desire of eternal things. Oh, that souls would sanctify themselves by this means.
5. The soul which recommends itself to me by the recitation of the rosary, shall not perish.
6. Whoever shall recite the rosary devoutly, applying himself to the consideration of its sacred mysteries shall never be conquered by misfortune. God will not chastise him in His Justice, he will not perish by an un-provided death; if he be just, he will remain in the grace of God, and become worthy of eternal life.
7. Whoever will have a true devotion for the Rosary will not die without the sacraments of the Church.
8. Those who are faithful to recite the rosary will have during their life and at the moment of death the light of God and the plenitude of His Graces; at the moment of death they will participate in the merits of the saints in Paradise.
9. I shall deliver from Purgatory those who have been devoted to the Rosary.
10. The faithful children of the rosary will merit a high degree of glory in Heaven.
11. You will obtain all you ask of me by the recitation of the Rosary.
12. All those who propagate the Holy Rosary shall be aided by me in their necessities.
13. I have obtained from my Divine Son that all the advocates of the rosary will have for intercessors the entire Celestial Court during their life and at the hour of death.
14. All who recite the Rosary are my sons, and brothers of my only Son Jesus Christ.
15. The devotion of my Rosary is a great sign of predestination.

IV. Chaplet of St. Michael

I. This chaplet begins with the following prayer (on the medal):

O God, come to my assistance.
O Lord, make haste to help me.
Glory be to the Father, etc.

II. One "Our Father" and three "Hail Mary's" are to be prayed after each of the following nine salutations in honor of the nine choirs of Angels.

1

By the intercession of St. Michael and the Celestial Choir of Seraphim, may the Lord make us worthy to burn with the fire of perfect charity. Amen.

2

By the intercession of St. Michael and the Celestial choir of Cherubim, may the Lord vouchsafe to grant us the grace to leave the ways of wickedness to run in the paths of Christian perfection. Amen.

3

By the intercession of St. Michael the Archangel and the Celestial Choir of Thrones, may the Lord infuse into our hearts a true and sincere spirit of humility. Amen.

4

By the intercession of St. Michael and the Celestial Choir of Dominions, may the Lord give the grace to govern our senses and subdue our unruly passions. Amen.

5

By the intercession of St. Michael and the Celestial Choir of Powers, may the Lord vouchsafe to protect our souls against the snares and temptations of the Devil. Amen.

6

By the intercession of St. Michael and the Celestial Choir of Virtues, may the Lord preserve us from evil and suffer us not to fall into temptation. Amen.

7

By the intercession of St. Michael and the Celestial Choir of Principalities, may God fill our souls with a true spirit of obedience. Amen.

8

By the intercession of St. Michael and the Celestial Choir, may the Lord give us perseverance in faith and in all good works, in order that we gain the glory of Paradise. Amen.

By the intercession of St. Michael and the Celestial Choir of Angels, may the Lord grant us to be protected by them in this mortal life and conducted hereafter to eternal glory. Amen.

Once the chaplet is concluded, say one "Our Father" in honor of each of the following angel:

St. Michael the Archangel, St. Gabriel the Archangel, St. Raphael the Archangel, our Guardian Angel.

The chaplet is concluded with the following prayers:

"O glorious Prince of the Heavenly Hosts, guardian of souls, vanquisher of rebel spirits, servant in the house of the Divine King, and our admirable conductor, thou who dost shine with excellence and superhuman virtue, vouchsafe to deliver us from all evil, who turn to thee with confidence, and enable us by thy gracious protection to serve God more and more faithfully every day.

V. Pray for us, O glorious St. Michael, Prince of the Church of Jesus Christ.
R. *That we may be made worthy of His promises.*
Almighty and Everlasting God, who by a prodigy of goodness and merciful desire for the salvation of all men, hast appointed the most glorious Archangel St. Michael, Prince of Thy Church, make us worthy, we beseech Thee, to be delivered from all our enemies that none of them may harass us at the hour of death, but that we may be conducted by him into the August presence of Thy Divine Majesty. This we beg through the merits of Jesus Christ our Lord. Amen."

V. Chaplet of the Divine Mercy

1. Sign of the Cross

2. One "Our Father

3. One "Hail Mary"

4. One Apostles' Creed

5. On the "Our Father" beads, the following prayer is recited:
   Eternal Father, I offer Thee the Body and Blood, Soul and Divinity of Thy Most Beloved Son and our Lord and Savior Jesus Christ, in atonement for our sins and the sins of the whole world.

6. On the "Hail Mary" beads, the following prayer is recited:
   For the sake of His sorrowful Passion have mercy on us and on the whole world.

7. In between each decade, the following prayer is recited:
   O Blood and Water which spurt out from the Sacred Heart of Jesus as a never ending source of mercy for us, we pray to you.

8. After the fifth decade is achieved, the following prayer is prayed three times:

   "O Holy God, Holy Mighty One, Holy Immortal One, have mercy on us and on the whole world."

9. The chaplet is concluded with the sign of the Cross.

VI. Conjuration of the Holy Angels

God All Mighty and Eternal, One in three persons! Before conjugating the Saints, your angels, your servants, and before calling them to our aid, we bow before you and we adore you Father, Son and Holy Spirit.

Be blessed and praised for all eternity. May all the angels and all men who you have created adore you, love you, serve you, Holy God, Holy Mighty One, Holy Immortal One!

And you Mary, Queen of angels, Mediatrix of all graces, All Powerful in your prayer, receive with kindness the prayer which we are addressing to your servants, and have it arrive before the Throne of the All Mighty so that we may receive grace, salvation and assistance.

Amen.

Angels, great saints, God sends you to protect us and aid us! We invoke you in the Name of God, One in Three Persons,

Fly to our aid!

We invoke you in the Name of the Precious Blood of Our Lord Jesus Christ,

Fly to our aid!

We invoke you in the All Mighty Name of Jesus,

Fly to our aid!

We invoke you by all the wounds of Our Lord Jesus Christ,

Fly to our aid!

We invoke you by all the tortures suffered by Our Lord Jesus Christ,

Fly to our aid!

We invoke you by the Holy Word of God,

Fly to our aid!

We invoke you by the Sacred Heart of Our Lord Jesus Christ,

Fly to our aid!

We invoke you in the Name of the Love of God for us poor ones,

Fly to our aid!

We invoke you in the Name God's Mercy for us poor ones,

Fly to our aid!

We invoke you in the Name of Mary, Queen of Heaven and Earth,

Fly to our aid!

We invoke you in the Name of Mary, your Queen and Sovereign,

Fly to our aid!

We invoke you in the Name of Mary, Mother of God and Mother of men,

Fly to our aid!

We invoke you by your own exultation,

Fly to our aid!

We invoke you by your own fidelity,

Fly to our aid!

We invoke you by your combative force for the Kingdom of God,

Fly to our aid!

We invoke you, cover us with your shields!

We invoke you, protect us with your swords!

We invoke you, illuminate us with your light!

We invoke you, harbor us under Mary's mantle!

We invoke you, shut us in the Heart of Mary!

We invoke you, entrust us in Mary's hand!

We invoke you, show us the way to the door of life: the opened Heart of our Lord!

We invoke you, lead us safely to the House of the Celestial Father!

All the choirs of the blessed spirits,

Fly to our aid!

Angels of life,

Fly to our aid!

Angels of strength of God's Word's,

Fly to our aid!

Angels of charity,

Fly to our aid!

Angels assigned to us by God as our companions,

Fly to our aid!

Fly to our aid, we invoke you! For we have received in heritage the Blood of Our Lord and King.

Fly to our aid, we invoke you! For we have received in heritage the Heart of Our Lord and King.

Fly to our aid, we invoke you! For we have received in heritage the Immaculate Heart of Mary, the Most Pure Virgin and your Queen.

Fly to our aid, we invoke you!

Saint Michael the Archangel, you are the Prince of the Celestial Armies, the vanquisher of the Infernal Dragon. You have received from God the strength to annihilate, through the means of humility, the pride of the power of darkness. We invoke you, place in us an authentic humility of heart, an unshakable fidelity so as always to accomplish the Will of God, our strength in the suffering and in the need. Help us to subsist before the Tribunal of God.

Saint Gabriel the Archangel, you are the Angel of Incarnation, the faithful messenger of God. Open our ears to perceive the smallest signs and calls of the Loving Heart of Our Lord. Remain always before our attention, we beg you, so that we may learn, follow and obey the Word of God and so that we may accomplish God's Will. Make us vigilant in the Lord's hope so that He may not find us asleep when He will arrive!

Saint Raphael the Archangel, you are the messenger of God's Love! We beg you, mark our hearts with an ardent love for God and do not allow this wound ever to heal in order to remain upon the path of love in daily life, and in order to vanquish any and all obstacle through the strength of this love.

Help us, great and holy brothers, servants, as we are, before God! Protect us against ourselves, against our own cowardice and lukewarmth, our selfishness and greed, our envy and lack of trust, our self-sufficiency and our comfort, against our desire to be appreciated! Free us from the ties of sin and from any attachments to the world! Untie the blindfold which we, ourselves, have placed upon our eyes so as not to see the misery which surrounds us and to see ourselves without discomfort but rather with compassion.

Nail in our hearts the bolt of God's Holy Apprehension so as never to cease looking for Him with passion, contrition and love!

Look in us for the Blood of Our Lord which was poured for us! Look in us for the tears of your Queen poured for our cause! Look in us for the destroyed, discolored, deteriorated image of God, image which was taken and which God has wanted to create us out of love!

Help us to recognize, to adore, to love and to serve God! Help us in the fight against the powers of darkness which surround us and which distress us with deceits; help us so that none of us be lost and so that one happy day we may gather in eternal happiness!

Amen.

VII. The Stations of the Cross

i.   **The 1st Station of the Cross:**
Jesus is condemned to death.

ii.   **The 2nd Station of the Cross:**
Jesus bears His Cross.

iii.   **The 3rd Station of the Cross:**
Jesus falls for the first time.

iv.   **The 4th Station of the Cross:**
Jesus meets his mother.

v.   **The 5th Station of the Cross:**
Jesus is helped by Simon.

vi.   **The 6th Station of the Cross:**
Veronica wipes the face of Jesus.

vii.   **The 7th Station of the Cross:**
Jesus falls a second time.

viii.   **The 8th Station of the Cross:**
Jesus speaks to the women of Jerusalem.

ix.   **The 9th Station of the Cross:**
Jesus falls for the third time.

x.   **The 10th Station of the Cross:**
Jesus is stripped of His garments.

xi.   **The 11th Station of the Cross:**
Jesus is nailed to the Cross.

xii.   **The 12th Station of the Cross:**
Jesus dies on the Cross.

xiii.   **The 13th Station of the Cross:**
Jesus is taken from the Cross.

xiv.   **The 14th Station of the Cross:**
Jesus is laid in the tomb.

JESUS RESURRECTS FROM THE DEAD...

VIII. Promises to Brother Estanislao (1903–27) of Our Lord Jesus Christ for All those who Have a Devotion to the Practice of the Way of the Cross (Via Crucis)

1. I shall grant everything that is asked of Me with Faith, when making the Way of the Cross.
2. I promise Eternal Life to those who pray from time to time the Way of the Cross.
3. I shall follow them everywhere in life and I shall help them, especially at the hour of death.
4. Even if they have more sins than blades of grass in the fields, and grains of sand in the sea, all of them will be erased by the Way of the Cross. (*Note: This promise does not eliminate the obligation to confess all mortal sins before receiving Communion.*)
5. Those who pray the Way of the Cross often, will have a special glory in Heaven.
6. I shall deliver them from Purgatory; indeed, if they go there at all, the first Tuesday or Friday after their death they shall be delivered.
7. I shall bless them at each Way of the Cross, and my Blessing will follow them everywhere on earth and, after their death, in Heaven for all Eternity.
8. At the hour of death I shall not permit the devil to tempt them; I shall lift all power from him in order that they will repose tranquilly in my Arms.
9. If they pray it with love, I shall make of each one of them a living Ciborium in which it will please me to pour my Grace.
10. I shall fix my Eyes on those who pray the Way of the Cross often; my Hand will always be open to protect them.
11. As I am nailed to the Cross, so also Shall I always be with those who honor Me in making the Way of the Cross frequently.
12. They will never be able to separate themselves from Me, for I shall give them the grace never again to commit a mortal sin.
13. At the hour of death I shall console them with my Presence and we shall go together to Heaven. Death will be sweet to all those who have honored Me during their lives by praying the Way of the Cross.
14. My Soul will be a protective shield for them, and will always help them, whenever they have recourse.

IX. Prayer of St. Gertrude the Great

Our Lord dictated the following prayer to St. Gertrude the Great to release one thousand (1,000) Souls from Purgatory each times it is said.

"Eternal Father, I offer Thee the Most Precious Blood of Thy Divine Son, Jesus, in union with the masses said throughout the world today, for all the holy souls in Purgatory, for sinners everywhere, for sinners in the universal church, those in my own home and within my family. Amen."

St. Gertrude's life was the mystic life of the Cloister—a Benedictine nun. She meditated on the Passion of Christ, which many times brought a flood of tears to her eyes. She did many penances and Our Lord appeared to her frequently. She had a tender love for the Blessed Virgin and was very devoted to the suffering souls in Purgatory. She died in 1334. Her feast day is 16 November.

X. Fatima's First Five Saturdays Devotion

"I promise to assist at the hour of death with the graces necessary for salvation all those who, in order to make reparation to me, on the First Saturday of five successive months, go to confession, receive Holy Communion, say five decades of the Rosary, and keep me company for a quarter of an hour, meditating on the fifteen mysteries of the Rosary."

The elements of this devotion, therefore, consist in the following four points, all of which must be offered in reparation to the Immaculate Heart of Mary. **One should make this intention before carrying out Our Lady's requests.** A renewal of the actual intention at the time is best; however, if such an intention is made now, it will fulfill the requirements if, for instance, the actual intention is forgotten at the time of confession.

- **Confession:** This confession can be made before the First Saturday or afterward, provided that Holy Communion be received in the state of grace. In 1926, Christ in a vision explained to Lucia that this confession could be made a week before or even more, and that it should be offered in reparation.

- **Holy Communion**: Before receiving Holy Communion, it is likewise necessary to offer it in reparation to Our Lady. Our Lord told Lucia in 1930, **"This Communion will be accepted on the following Sunday for just reasons, if my priests allow it so."** So if work or school, sickness, or another just reason prevents the Communion on a First Saturday, with this permission it may be received the following Sunday. If Communion is transferred, any or all of the other acts of the devotion may also be performed on Sunday.

- **Rosary**: The Rosary is a vocal prayer said while meditating upon the mysteries of Our Lord's life and Passion and Our Lady's life. To comply with the request of our Blessed Mother, it must be offered in reparation and said properly while meditating.

- **15-minute meditation:** Also offered in reparation, the meditation may embrace one or more mysteries; it may include all, taken together or separately. This meditation should be the richest of any meditation, because Our Lady promised to be present when she said "… those who keep me company…"

To those who faithfully follow Our Lady's requests for the Five First Saturdays, she has made a wonderful **promise** which she, as Mediatrix of All Graces, will fulfill:

"I promise to assist at the hour of death with the graces necessary for salvation."

XI. Prayer for the Souls in Purgatory

"There are many souls in Purgatory. There are also persons who have been consecrated to God: some priests, some religious. Pray for their intentions, at least seven Our Father's, Hail Mary's and Glory Be's and the Creed. I recommend it to you. There is a large number of souls who have been in Purgatory for a long time because no one prays for them."

(Our Lady of Peace, Medjugorje, 21 July 1982)

XII. Prayer Requested by the Blessed Virgin Mary

"Pray and fast. I wish that you deepen and continue your life in prayer. Every morning say the prayer of consecration to the Heart of Mary. Do it in the family. Recite each morning the Angelus, five Our Father's, Hail Mary's, and Glory Be's in honor of the holy Passion and a sixth one for our Holy Father, the Pope. Then say the Creed and the prayer to the Holy Spirit. And, if it is possible, it would be well to pray a rosary."

(Our Lady of Peace, Medjugorje, 27 January 1984)

XIII. Prayer — Devotion to the Holy Wound of Our Lord Jesus-Christ Shoulder — Saint Bernard De Clairvaux

Our Lord Jesus-Christ revealed one day to Saint Bernard of Clairveaux (1090–1153):

I had, while wearing the Cross, a profound wound, three fingers deep, exposing three bones on My Shoulders. This wound which is not known by men has caused Me more sorrow and pain than all the others. But reveal It to the faithful Christians, and know that any grace that will be asked of Me in virtue of this Wound will be granted.

And to all who, out of love for It, will honor Me every day with three "Our Father's", three "Hail Mary's", and three "Glory Be's", I will forgive their venial sins and I shall no longer remember their mortal ones; they will not expire out of an unforeseen death; at the hour of their death, they will be visited by the Blessed Virgin Mary and they will obtain yet again the Grace and Mercy.

This devotion, accepted by His holiness Pope Eugene III is as well part of the "apocryphes indulgence prayers":

O most beloved Lord, sweet Lamb of God, I (... name...), poor sinner, adore and venerate the most holy Wound you received on your shoulder carrying in Calvary the very heavy Cross which exposed three holy bones, causing such an immense pain.

O Jesus, I beg of you, in virtue of the merits of said wound, to have pity on me by granting me the grace of (...) which I ask imploringly while asking you to forgive me all my mortal or venial sins, assisting me at the hour of my death, and leading me into Your happy Kingdom. Amen.

XIV. The Sacred Heart: Safeguard of the Body, of the Soul, and of the Homes

Marie-Julie Jahenny added:

Let us wear this picture on us; let us put it on our houses; **let us stick the Sacred Heart Safeguards on the doors and on the windows of our homes.** *After that, can we not hope that the inscription* **"Stop! (or Cease!) The Heart of Jesus is here! (or the heart of Jesus is with me!),** *together with our own profound prayers, will preserve us from our enemies inside and out?*

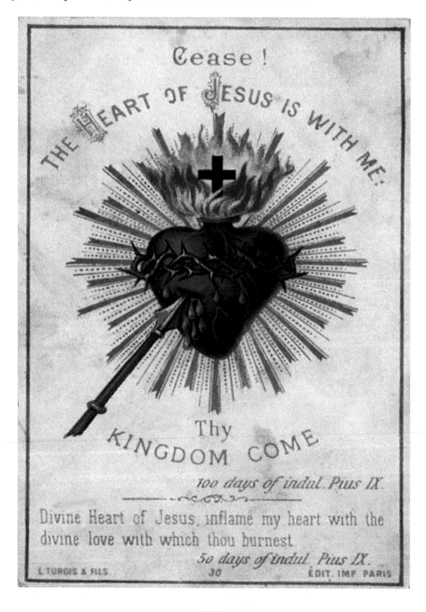

Notes

All the sacramentals, candles, and healing herbs and discussed in pages 193 to 211 can be ordered in the United States to:

Mrs. Kathleen LONEY

E-mail: kathleenlloney@gmail.com

All our thanks to Mrs. Lonely for her kind assistance and efficiency in propagating the devotions to Marie-Julie Jahenny's holy sacraments. Mrs. Lonely is a charming lady and is devoted to helping distributing, often at cost, sacramentals and the healing herbs recommended by the Blessed Virgin Mary to Marie-Julie Jahenny.

Bibliography

- Marquis de la Franquerie, Marie-Julie Jahenny the Breton Stigmatist, self-published, 1977.
- Doctor Imbert-Gourbeyre, La Stigmatization—l'extase divine et les miracles de Lourdes—réponse aux libres penseurs, 2 vol. Editions Bellet, Clermont-Ferrand 1895.
- Pierre Robehdel, Marie-Julie Jahenny, la Stigmatisée de Blain 1850–1941—Broché, 1978.
- P. Roberdel (2000) Les Prophécies de La Fraudais, Broché.
- Isabelle Szczebura, Marie-Julie Jahenny prophétise, Sté Tirage, 2000.
- Jacqueline Bruno, Quelques souvenirs sur Marie-Julie, La Stigmatisee de Blain, Edition du-Courrier de Saint Nazaire, 1941.
- Abbot René Laurentin et Michel Corteville, Découverte du Secret de La Salette / The Great News of the Shepherds of La Salette, Broché, 2002.
- Rev. Father P. Liaud, Les Fleurs mystiques de la sainte montagne de La Salette, ou les Enseignements de l'apparition de N. D. de La Salette, par le Reliure inconnue, 1897.
- Abbot Roger Rebut, Je ne peux plus sursoir, Sté Tirage, 2019.
- Laurent Morlier, Vrai ou Faux le Troisème Secret de Fatima, Editions D.F.T., 2003.
- Antonio Socci (2000) *The Fourth Secret of Fatima*, Broché.
- José-Maria Zavala (2017) *El Sécreto Mejor Guardado de Fátima*, Broché.
- Sister Lucia Dos Santos (2005) *Calls from the Message of Fatima*, International Edition.
- Teiji Yasuda (1999) *Akita: The Tears and Message of Mary*, 101 Foundation, Incorporated.
- John M. Haffert (1989) *The Meaning of Akita*, Foundation.
- Marian Therese Horvat (1999) *Our Lady of Good Success: Prophecies for Our Times*, Tradition In Action, Inc.
- Rev. Father Manuel (2013) *Brief History of Our Lady of Good Success and Novena*, Society of St. Pius X.
- Francisco Sanchez-Ventura (1966) *Las Apariciones de Garabandal*, San Miguel Publishing Comp.
- Ed Kelly (2017) *A Walk to Garabandal: A Journey of Happiness and Hope*, CreateSpace Independent Publishing Platform.
- Abbot René Laurentin and Ljudevit Rupčić (1984) Is the Virgin Mary appearing in Medjugorje?: an urgent message for the world given in a Marxist country, Word among us Press.
- Abbot René Laurentin and Professor Joyeux (1988) Scientific & Medical Studies on the Apparitions at Medjugorje, Veritas.

- Mirjana Soldo (2018) *My Heart will Triumph*, Catholic Shop.
- Finbar O'Leary (2017) *Vicka... Her Story*. Dufour Editions, Incorporated.
- Xavier Reyes Ayral (1998) *Un Message d'Amour*, Resiac.
- Pope Pius XII, Apostolic Letter "Sacro Vergente Anno", 7 July 1952, In Brother Michael of the Holy Trinity: The whole truth about Fatima, Volume III, Prt I, Ch. VII.
- Pope Francis, Amoris Laetitia, Post-Synodal Apostoli Exhortation, Libreria Editrice Vaticana, 2016.
- Pope Emeritus Benedict XVI (Author), Robert Cardinal Sarah (Author) (2019) *From the Depths of Our Hearts: Priesthood, Celibacy and the Crisis of the Catholic Church*, Ignatius.
- Gombault-F, Les Apparitions de Tilly-Sur-Seulles: Etude Scientifique Et Theologique: Reponse A M. Gaston Mery, Hachette, 2013.
- Bishop Anathesius Schneider (2019) *Christus Vincit*, Angelico Press.
- Cardinal Joseph Zen (2019) *For LOVE OF MY PEOPLE I WILL NOT KEEP SILENT*, Ignatius Press.
- Christine Watkins (2019) *THE WARNING, Testimonies and prophecies of the Illumination of Conscience*, Queen of Peace Media.

Internet websites:

www.marie-julie-jahenny.fr

https://www.garabandal.it/en/documentation/interviews-and-testimonies/p-pio

http://jeanneshouseafire.blogspot.com/2013/11/blessed-anne-catherine-emmerich.html

https://www.medjugorjehotelspa.com/en/history-of-medjugorje-the-first-apparitions/

https://medjugorje.org/concordance/framconc.htm

https://gadelali.wordpress.com/2011/03/13/our-lady-of-akita/

https://sspx.org/en/news-events/news/private-heavenly-apparitions-sister-lucia-fatima-1925–1952

http://nova.evangelisation.free.fr/apparitions_mariales.htm

https://w2.vatican.va/content/dam/francesco/pdf/apost_exhortations/documents/papa-francesco_esortazione-ap_20160319_amoris-laetitia_en.pdf

https://www.eugeneshannon.net/ventura/Ventura%20Book%20.pdf

WQPH (89.3FM) in the United States (http://wqphradio.org/2019/10/27/a-new-message-from-sister-agnes-of-our-lady-of-akita/)

https://onepeterfive.com/chief-exorcist-father-amorth-padre-pio-knew-the-third-secret/

http://wqphradio.org/2019/10/27/a-new-message-from-sister-agnes-of-our-lady-of-akita

(https://medjugorjecouncil.ie/fr-rene-laurentin-medjugorje-1997/)

"www. Lifesitenews.com—Five Cardinals and two bishops speak about the end of times"

https://video.search.yahoo.com/yhs/search?fr=yhs-itm-001&hsimp=yhs-001&hspart=itm&p=Vassula%2C+Akita+and+the+Third+Secret+of+Fatima#id=2&vid=9e560ea73bc0c52c900f05b742541644&action=click

(https://w2.vatican.va/content/dam/francesco/pdf/apost_exhortations/documents/papa-francesco_esortazione-ap_20160319_amoris-laetitia_en.pdf)

https://whatisgarabandal.blogspot.com/2014/09/a-synod-before-warning-update.html

https://www.youtube.com/watch?v=e7EcHeiueMg&t=823s

https://www.youtube.com/watch?v=cwHZbsr1YFA&t=2s

https://www.youtube.com/watch?v=9nRfzTkR2B4&t=18s

https://www.youtube.com/watch?v=cwHZbsr1YFA&t=17s

https://www.youtube.com/watch?v=V6nhFWVYzvM

https://www.youtube.com/watch?v=0BfNC1Is5pY

https://www.youtube.com/watch?v=mewMBbbvRNI&t=55s

https://www.youtube.com/watch?v=ux5KEaZF7KA&t=2831s

https://www.countdowntothekingdom.com

http://wqphradio.org/2019/09/21/fr-michel-rodrigue-apostle-of-the-last-times-part1/ Fr. Michel Rodrigue

https://www.countdowntothekingdom.com Quotations from Fr. Michel Rodrigue

http://mrcabitibi.qc.ca/services/evaluation-municipale Amos, Quebec

https://www.planetdeadly.com/human/incredible-nuclear-explosion-photos

Fraternité Apostolique Saint Benoît-Joseph Labre New Apostolic Fraternity of St. Benedict-Joseph Labre vestments

https://www.hearingreview.com/inside-hearing/legislation/president-trump-signs-otc-hearing-aid-legislation-law
https://dsdoconnor.com/2021/09/27/new-prophecy-from-father-michel/

Printed in the USA
CPSIA information can be obtained
at www.ICGtesting.com
LVHW010628210923
758644LV00006B/40

9 781649 790989